World Civilizations

World Civilizations

VOLUME II
From the Sixteenth Century
to the Contemporary Age

F. ROY WILLIS

University of California, Davis

D. C. HEATH AND COMPANY
Lexington, Massachusetts   Toronto

Maps and plans prepared by Richard D. Pusey.

Published simultaneously in Canada.

Printed in the United States of America.

International Standard Book Number: 0-669-04688-4

Library of Congress Catalog Card Number: 81-83370

PREFACE

The author of a history of world civilizations owes his readers a justification—or at least an explanation—for his temerity in attempting to encompass the whole sweep of human achievement throughout the world since ancient times. My own intellectual commitment to the concept of a course in world civilizations goes back to 1960–1964, when I had the privilege and challenge of teaching the course in world history pioneered at the University of Washington in Seattle. At the same time, my choice of the history of Western Europe since the Second World War as my period of research specialization was confirming for me the necessity of placing a dwarfed Europe in the broader context of world history. My full emotional commitment to the study of world civilizations came in the summer of 1966, when, setting off for a year of research in Rome, I decided to take the long route from California to Europe. That exciting summer, I saw the Zen rock gardens of Kyoto, watched dawn break over the Wat Arun temple in Bangkok, and explored the fantastic series of Mogul tombs that lead from the mausoleum of the emperor Humayun on the edge of Delhi to the final culmination of Moslem architecture, the Taj Mahal in Agra. It was heady stuff, as the English travel writers used to say, and led me to make many more visits over the following years to the great urban centers outside Europe. For an inveterate traveler, the study of world civilizations must inevitably become the ultimate objective.

This book is an expansion to world scale of my original survey of Western history, *Western Civilization: An Urban Perspective.* In the preface to the second edition of that book, I explained the rationale for the decision to organize the material around the study of great cities. My aim was to avoid the feeling of superficiality and perhaps of boredom that the reader feels when every detail of the past is presented in a totally balanced, meticulously calculated sequence. Too often, I suggested, "the study of Western civilization was like an infinitely long train ride with no stopovers allowed, a kind of Orient Express in which Paris, Vienna, and Istanbul were viewed as little more than names on railroad stations. In a way, this book was to be an invitation to the student to stop and explore the intricacies of the great cities that might otherwise have flashed by largely unobserved. Better yet, as historians we could visit the city as it was at the time of its greatness."

In expanding the text, in order to maintain the proportion of Western to non-Western history frequently adopted in courses in world civilization, I decided to use as a model Chapter 16, in which the expansion of Europe in the fifteenth and sixteenth centuries is viewed through the Lisbon of Manuel the Fortunate, the Tenochtitlán of Montezuma, and the Madrid of Philip the Prudent. Thus, within the non-Western chapters, we pause on several occasions to provide a detailed look at the civilization of a great city at its height—for example, to describe Chinese civilization through study of the seventh-century Ch'ang-an of the T'ang emperor T'ai-tsung, and Indian reaction to British rule in the nineteenth century through consideration of the Calcutta of the Tagore family. In this way, it becomes possible to use not only traditional political and literary materials but the vast quantity of new historical research, based on the techniques of other social sciences, that is throwing light on classes, ethnic groups, social institutions, and even ways of thought hitherto unexplored.

I would like to acknowledge with gratitude my debt to the many colleagues whose suggestions have helped me greatly in the preparation of this book. The chapters on Western civilization, which comprised the third edition of *Western Civilization: An Urban Perspective*, were reviewed in whole or in part by Patricia Branca, Carnegie-Mellon University; Allen D. Breck, University of Denver; Ronald E. Coons, University of Connecticut; Robert Davis, Chaffey College; George Drake, The Colorado College; Richard W. Hull, New York University; Eugene E. Kuzirian, University of Texas at El Paso; Marvin Lunenfeld, State University College, Fredonia; Bruce T. Moran, University of Nevada; David Parker, Vanderbilt University; Jan Rogainis, Clemson University; Edward Ruestow, University of Colorado; Jane Slaughter, University of New Mexico; and George Y. Windell, University of New Orleans. The non-Western chapters (primarily 2, 6, 9, 17, 25, and 31) have benefited from the suggestions of Stephen Baier, Boston University; Milton Meyer, California State University, Los Angeles; V. Dixon Morris, University of Hawaii at Manoa; Neil Rabitoy, California State University, Los Angeles; and my colleagues at the University of California, Davis: Cynthia L. Brantley, Earl H. Kinmonth, Kwang-Ching Liu, Don C. Price, and Rollie E. Poppino. It is hardly necessary to say that, although I have been greatly helped by the scholars mentioned, all errors are mine and all idiosyncrasy is deliberate.

F. Roy Willis

CHINESE TRANSLITERATION

The traditional system of transliteration of Chinese words, known as Wade-Giles after the two English scholars who invented it, is used in this book because it is the system utilized in almost all the works to which the student is referred in the Suggested Reading at the end of each chapter. However, since it is becoming increasingly common for contemporary writers to use the system of transliteration known as Pinyin, which was developed by the People's Republic of China, it is important for students to be familiar with Pinyin as well as Wade-Giles spellings. The two forms are given below for the most important names mentioned in this book. In the few instances where it is customary to use a familiar English version of a Chinese name (e.g., Peking) instead of Wade-Giles, those forms are given in parentheses.

DYNASTIES		CITIES		PEOPLE	
Wade-Giles	*Pinyin*	*Wade-Giles*	*Pinyin*	*Wade-Giles*	*Pinyin*
Hsia	Xia	Cheng-chou	Zhengzhou	Lao-tzu	Laozi
Shang	Shang	Sian	Xi'an	Shih Huang-ti	Shi Huangdi
Chou	Zhou	Ch'ang-an	Chang'an	Wen-ti	Wendi
Ch'in	Qin	Loyang	Luoyang	Yang-ti	Yangdi
Han	Han	(Nanking)	Nanjing	T'ai-tsung	Taizong
Chin	Jin	(Kaifeng)	Kaifeng	Hsüan-tsung	Xuanzong
Sui	Sui	(Hangchow)	Hangzhou	Hung-wu	Hongwu
T'ang	Tang	(Soochow)	Suzhou	Sun Yat-sen	Sun Zhongshan
Sung	Song	(Peking)	Beijing	Chiang Kai-shek	Jiang Jieshi
Yüan	Yuan	Shanghai	Shanghai	Mao Tse-tung	Mao Zedong
Ming	Ming	(Canton)	Guangzhou	Chou En-lai	Zhou Enlai
Ch'ing	Qing			Chiang Ch'ing	Jiang Qing
				Teng Hsiao-p'ing	Deng Xiaoping
				Lin Piao	Lin Biao

CONTENTS

MAPS AND PLANS

CHRONICLE OF EVENTS

Major cities are capitalized.

1500–1700

1500

Europe	Near East and Africa	India and Southeast Asia	East Asia	Americas and Pacific
Manuel, Portugal, 1495–1521 (LISBON).	Destruction of Swahili city-states.		Ming dynasty, China, 1368–1644 (PEKING).	Aztecs in Mexico, (TENOCHTITLÁN).
Henry VIII, England, 1509–1547.	Safavid dynasty, Persia, 1502–1736.		d. Shen Chou, 1509.	Cortés conquers Mexico, 1519–1522 (MEXICO CITY).
Protestant Reformation begins.	Suleiman the Magnificent, Turkey, 1520–1566 (CONSTANTINOPLE).	Portuguese take GOA, 1510.		Magellan circumnavigates globe, 1519–1522.
d. Leonardo da Vinci, 1519.		Babur forms Mogul Empire, 1526.		Pizarro defeats Incas, 1530.
Charles V, Holy Roman Emperor, 1519–1556.		Akbar, Mogul emperor, 1556–1605 (FATEHPUR SIKRI).	Portuguese reach Japan, 1543.	
Philip II, Spain, 1556–1598 (MADRID).			St. Francis Xavier in Japan, 1549.	
French Wars of Religion, 1562–1598.				
Shakespeare, 1564–1616.		Moslems take VIJAYANAGAR, 1568.	Azuchi-Momoyama period, Japan, 1568–1598.	Spanish take Philippines, 1564 (MANILA).
d. Michelangelo, 1564.			Wan-li, emperor, China, 1573–1620.	
Revolt of Netherlands begins, 1568.	Idris Alooma, Kanem-Bornu, 1571–1603 (N'GAZARGAMU).		d. Nobunaga, 1582.	Raleigh's attempts to colonize Virginia, 1585, 1587.
Battle of Lepanto, 1571.	Shah Abbas, Persia, 1587–1629 (ISFAHAN).			
Murder William of Orange, 1584.	Moroccans defeat Songhai, 1591.		Japanese invasion of Korea, 1592.	
Defeat of Spanish Armada, 1588.			d. Hideyoshi, 1598.	

Americas	East Asia	South Asia	Near East / Africa	Europe
Settlement of JAMESTOWN, Virginia, 1607. Foundation of QUEBEC, 1608.	Tokugawa Ieyasu becomes shogun, Japan, 1603 (EDO/TOKYO). Creation of castle-cities, Japan. Japan becomes a closed country.	English East India Company founded, 1600. Jahangir, Mogul emperor, 1605–1627 (LAHORE).	Murad IV, Ottoman emperor, 1623–1640. Dutch settlements in West Africa, 1637–1642.	Baroque style created. d. Elizabeth I, England, 1603. Rembrandt, 1606–1669.
Pilgrim Fathers land PLYMOUTH, 1620. Foundation of NEW AMSTERDAM (NEW YORK), 1624.		Dutch take Indonesia, 1610 (BATAVIA).		Plan of the Three Canals (AMSTERDAM), 1610.
Foundation of MONTREAL, 1642. Dutch discover New Zealand, 1642.	Manchu dynasty, China, 1644–1911 (PEKING). Japanese novel developed by Ihara Saukaku, 1642–1693, and Chikaimatsu Monzaemon, 1653–1725. K'ang-hsi, emperor, China, 1661–1722.	Shah Jahan, Mogul emperor, 1627–1658; building of Taj Mahal, 1631–1653 (AGRA); foundation of SHAHJAHANABAD (OLD DELHI), 1638. Aurangzeb, Mogul emperor, 1658–1707.	Dutch settle CAPETOWN, 1652.	d. Lope de Vega, 1625. Vermeer, 1632–1675. Frederick William I, elector, Prussia, 1640–1688. English Civil Wars, 1642–1648. Louis XIV, France, 1643–1715 (VERSAILLES). Treaty of Westphalia, 1648.
French claim Louisiana, 1682.		British found CALCUTTA, 1690.	Portuguese defeat Kongo, 1665. English Royal Africa Company founded, 1672. Rise of Dahomey.	Turks besiege VIENNA, 1683. Newton's Principles, 1687. Glorious Revolution, England, 1688. Peter I, Russia, 1689–1725 (SAINT PETERSBURG).

	Europe	Near East and Africa	India and Southeast Asia	East Asia	Americas and Pacific
1700	Great Northern War, 1700–1721. War of Spanish Succession, 1702–1713. Rococo style developed.	Decline of Ottoman Empire begins. Rise of Ashanti Empire.	d. Aurangzeb, Mogul emperor, 1707; expansion of British power begins.	Urban expansion in Japan (OSAKA, EDO).	Treaty of Utrecht, 1713; British right to trade with Spanish America.
				Tokugawa Yoshimune, shogun, Japan, 1716–1745. Woodcuts of Suzuki Harunobu, 1725–1770.	
	Kay's flying shuttle, 1733. John Wesley begins Methodist movement, 1738. Frederick II, Prussia, 1740–1786 (BERLIN). First volume of French *Encyclopédie*, 1751. Mozart, 1756–1791. Voltaire's *Candide*, 1759. George III, England, 1760–1820.	Nadir Shah, Persia, 1736–1747. Expansion of African slave trade.	Nadir Shah sacks DELHI, 1739.	Ch'ien-lung, emperor, China, 1736–1795; Summer Palace constructed (PEKING).	Seven Years' War, 1756–1763; British take French Canada.
			Battle of Plassey, 1757; British control Bengal.	European trade permitted in Canton, 1759.	
	Watt patents steam engine, 1769. Beethoven, 1770–1827. First Partition of Poland, 1772. Adam Smith's *Wealth of Nations*, 1776. d. Rousseau, 1778.	Russo-Turkish wars begin, 1768.	Regulating Act, 1773; Bengal Governor-General rules British India.	Manchu dynasty in decline.	Voyages of Captain Cook, 1768–1779. Bougainville in Tahiti, 1768. American War of Independence, 1776–1783.

Europe	Africa / Middle East	Asia	East Asia	Americas / Oceania
d. Diderot, 1784. Mozart's *Don Giovanni*, 1787. French Revolution begins, 1789. Leopold II, Austria, 1790–1792. Francis II, Austria, 1792–1835. Revolutionary wars begin, 1792. Execution Louis XVI, 1793. Reign of Terror, 1793–1794. Napoleon's victories in Italy, 1796–1797. d. Catherine the Great, Russia, 1796. Napoleon seizes power, 1799.	Russo-Turkish war, 1787–1792. Selim III, Ottoman emperor, 1789–1807. British seize CAPETOWN, 1795. Freed slaves settle in Sierra Leone, 1797. Napoleon in Egypt, 1798. Battle Aboukir Bay, 1798. U.S. war with Barbary Corsairs, 1800–1815.	Rama I, Siam, 1782–1809 (BANGKOK). Impeachment Warren Hastings, 1787. Dwarkanath Tagore, 1794–1846. British take Ceylon, 1796. Arthur Wellesley, governor-general, India, 1797–1805. d. Tipu, sultan, Mysore, 1799. Dutch government takes administration of Indonesia, 1799.	Chinese expedition against Vietnam, 1788–1789. Lord Macartney, embassy to China, 1793. China bans import of opium, 1796. White Lotus Rebellion, China, 1796–1804.	Foundation of SYDNEY, Australia, 1788. Adoption of U.S. Constitution, 1789. Washington, president, U.S.A., 1789–1797. Foundation of WASHINGTON, D.C., 1790. Revolt of Toussaint L'Ouverture, Haiti, 1791. Formation of Upper and Lower Canada, 1791. John Adams, president, U.S.A., 1797–1801.

Europe	Near East and Africa	India and Southeast Asia	East Asia	Americas and Pacific
Napoleon becomes emperor, France, 1804. Metternich, Chancellor, Austria, 1809–1848. Napoleon invades Russia, 1812. Congress of Vienna, 1814–1815. Battle of Waterloo, 1815.	Sayyid Said, sultan, Zanzibar, 1806–1856. British abolish slave trade, 1807. British ceded CAPETOWN, 1815. Shaka, King, Zulu, 1818–1828. Russo-Turkish war, 1828–1829. IBADAN founded, 1829.	Ram Mohun Roy, 1772–1833. British defeat Marathas, 1818. British take SINGAPORE, 1819. First Burma War, 1824–1826.	Chia-ch'ing, emperor, China, 1796–1820. Tao-kuang, emperor, China, 1821–1850.	Louisiana Purchase, 1803. U.S.A. declares war on Britain, 1812. Revolutions throughout Latin America. End of Manila-Acapulco trade, 1815. Brazil independent, 1822. Bolivar defeats Spanish, 1825. Pomare, queen, Tahiti, 1827–1877.
d. Beethoven, 1827. Rocket railroad locomotive, 1829. Belgium independent, 1831. Dickens's *Pickwick Papers*, 1836. Victoria, Britain, 1837–1901. *Communist Manifesto*, 1848. Continentwide revolutions, 1848. Francis Joseph, Austria, 1848–1916.	Slavery illegal in British colonies, 1833. Liberia independent, 1847. al-Hajj, Tokolor emperor, 1848–1864. LIBREVILLE, Gabon, founded, 1849.	Culture System in Dutch East Indies, 1830. British annex Sind, 1843. British annex Punjab, 1849.	Opium War, 1839–1842. British ceded HONG KONG, 1842. Taiping rebellion, China, 1850–1864.	British annex New Zealand, 1840. Pedro II, Brazil, 1840–1865. U.S.-Mexican war, 1846–1848.

1800

Australian Gold Rush, 1851. d. Kamehameha III, Hawaii, 1854.	Lincoln, president, U.S.A., 1861–1865; American Civil War. Abolition slavery, U.S.A., 1865. Creation of Dominion of Canada, 1867. Expansion of BUENOS AIRES, 1860s.		Slavery abolished, Brazil, 1888. Liliuokalani, queen, Hawaii, 1891–1893. Spanish-American War, 1898.
Hsien-feng, emperor, China, 1851–1861. Perry forces opening of Japan, 1853–1854.	Dowager empress Tz'u-hsi controls Chinese government, 1861–1908.	Meiji restoration, Japan, 1868; abolition of Tokugawa shogunate.	Japan given constitution, 1889. Sino-Japanese War, 1894–1895. Boxer uprising, 1900–1901.
Second Burma War, 1852.	End of Mogul Empire, 1857. Indian mutiny, 1857–1858. French seize SAIGON, 1859. Rabindranath Tagore, 1861–1941.	Rama V, Siam, 1868–1910. Victoria named empress of India, 1876.	Third Burma War, 1885. Curzon, viceroy, India, 1899–1905.
Crimean War, 1853–1856. Mutesa I, Buganda, 1854–1883. Faidherbe develops Senegal, 1854–1865 (DAKAR). Boers make Great Trek, 1855.		Scramble for Africa begins. Gold Coast colony established, 1874. Russo-Turkish War, 1876–1878. British protectorate, Egypt, 1882. Congo Free State, 1884–1908. Conference of Berlin on Africa, 1884–1885. French defeat Dahomey, 1894. British defeat Ashanti, 1896. Boer War, 1899–1902.	
Great Exhibition, 1851 (LONDON). Napoleon III, France, 1852–1870.	Emancipation of serfs, Russia, 1861. Bismarck becomes chancellor, Prussia, 1862. Austro-Prussian War, 1866. Dual Monarchy of Austria-Hungary formed, 1867.	Franco-Prussian War, 1870–1871. d. Dickens, 1870. Proclamation of German Empire, 1871.	Igor Stravinsky, 1882–1971. Impressionist painters, France. William II, emperor, Germany, 1888–1918. Dreyfus affair, France, 1894–1906. Nicholas II, Russia, 1894–1917. Victoria's Diamond Jubilee, 1897.

1900–Present

	Europe	Near East and Africa	India and Southeast Asia	East Asia	Americas and Pacific
1900	d. Victoria, queen, Britain, 1901. Einstein's special theory of relativity, 1905. Bosnian crisis, 1908. Atonal music developed.	Moroccan crisis, 1905–1906.	Curzon, viceroy, 1899–1905.	Boxer uprising, 1900–1901. Russo-Japanese war, 1904–1905. d. Dowager empress Tz'u-hsi, China, 1908. Japan annexes Korea, 1910.	Commonwealth of Australia, 1901. U.S. takes Panama Canal Zone, 1903.
	Balkan wars, 1912–1913. Serajevo crisis, 1914.	French annex Morocco, 1912.	Indian capital moved from CALCUTTA to NEW DELHI, 1912. Nobel prize to Tagore, 1913.	China becomes a republic, 1912.	Mexican revolution, 1912. U.S. intervention in Nicaragua, 1912.
		FIRST WORLD WAR, 1914–1918			
	Communist revolution, Russia, 1917. Weimar Republic, Germany, 1918–1933. d. Proust, 1922.	British and French mandates in Near East, 1919. Development oil deposits in Near East.	First satyagraha campaign, 1921–1922.	d. Yüan Shih-kai, 1916. Chinese Communist party formed, 1921. Earthquake, TOKYO, 1923. d. Sun Yat-sen, 1925. Chiang heads Kuomintang, 1925. Hirohito becomes emperor, Japan, 1926.	Obregón, president, Mexico, 1920–1924. Mackenzie King chosen prime minister, Canada, 1921.
	d. Lenin, 1924; supremacy of Stalin, Russia. General strike, Britain, 1926. First Five-Year Plan, Russia, 1929. Great Depression, 1929–1933.	Ibn Saud, Saudi Arabia, 1925–1953. Transjordan independent, 1927. Iraq independent, 1930.	Gandhi's salt march, 1930.		Vargas, president, Brazil, 1930–1945, 1951–1954.

SECOND WORLD WAR, 1939–1945

1940

Europe

Hitler becomes chancellor, Germany, 1933.
Popular Front, France, 1936.
Spanish Civil War, 1936–1939.
Germany annexes Austria, 1938.

Russo-Finnish war, 1939–1940.
Fall of France, 1940.
German invasion of Russia, 1941.
D-day, Allied landings in France, 1944.
Labour government, Britain, 1945–1951.

Formation of NATO, 1949.
West and East German states created, 1949.
d. Stalin, 1953.
Khrushchev ascendancy, Russia, 1955–1964.

Common Market, 1958.
De Gaulle returns to power, France, 1958.

Middle East / Africa

Italy invades Ethiopia, 1935–1936.

Jinnah heads Moslem League, 1934.

Independence Syria, Lebanon, 1946.

Creation of Israel, 1948.

Independence Morocco, Tunisia, 1956.
Nasser, president, Egypt, 1956–1970.
Franco-British Suez invasion, 1956.
French sub-Saharan colonies in Africa independent, 1958–1960.

Asia / Far East

Japan seizes Manchuria, 1931.
Long March, China, 1934.
Sino-Japanese war, 1937–1945.

Japanese empire, Southeast Asia, 1941–1945.

Independence India, Pakistan, 1947.
Nehru, prime minister India, 1947–1964.

Gandhi murdered, 1948.
Indonesia independent, 1949.
French leave Indochina, 1954.

U.S. occupation, Japan, 1945–1951.
Civil War, China, 1946–1949.

Mao Tse-tung's rule in China, 1949–1976.
Korean War, 1950–1954.

Great Leap Forward, China, 1958.

Americas

Roosevelt, president, U.S.A., 1933–1945.
Cárdenas, president, Mexico, 1934–1940.
Commonwealth of Philippines, 1935.

U.S.A. enters world war, 1941.
Philippines independent, 1946.
Juan Perón, president, Argentina, 1946–1955, 1973–1974.

López Mateos, president, Mexico, 1958–1964.
Castro takes power in Cuba, 1959.

1960	Europe	Near East and Africa	India and Southeast Asia	East Asia	Americas and Pacific
	BERLIN Wall, 1961.			Russo-Chinese conflict begins, 1960.	BRASÍLIA inaugurated, 1960. Alliance for Progress, 1961. Cuban missile crisis, 1962. Military takes power in Brazil, 1964.
		Algeria independent, 1962. Kenya independent, 1963.	Formation of Malaysia, 1963. Indira Gandhi, prime minister, India, 1966–1977, 1980–.	Cultural Revolution, China, 1966–1969. Japanese economic boom.	
	Soviet invasion of Czechoslovakia, 1968. Riots in PARIS, France, 1968.	Arab-Israeli war, 1967.			
	Resignation de Gaulle, president, France, 1969.	Sadat, president, Egypt, 1970–1981.	Resignation Ayub Khan, president, Pakistan, 1969. Ali Bhutto, prime minister, Pakistan, 1971–1977. U.S. withdraws from South Vietnam, 1973.	d. Lin Piao, 1971. Tanaka, premier, Japan, 1972–1974.	
	Britain, Denmark, Ireland join Common Market, 1973.	Yom Kippur war, 1973.			Overthrow of Allende, president, Chile, 1973. U.S. president Nixon resigns, 1974. Army takes power, Argentina, 1976.
	OPEC boosts oil prices, 1974. Increased terrorism, Italy, Germany, Spain. Helsinki security conference, 1975.	Portuguese ousted from Angola, Mozambique, 1975–1976.	North Vietnam conquers South Vietnam, 1975.	d. Chou En-lai, 1976. Modernization program, China, 1976–.	
		d. Kenyatta, 1978. Iranian revolution, 1979. End of white rule, Zimbabwe (Rhodesia), 1980.	Refugee flight from Indochina. Soviet invasion of Afghanistan, 1979.	Suzuki, premier, Japan, 1980–.	Overthrow of Somoza, president, Nicaragua, 1979. Reagan, president, U.S.A., 1981–. Civil war in El Salvador, 1981–.
	Mitterrand, president, France, 1981–. Martial law, Poland, 1981.				

INTRODUCTION:
CIVILIZATION AND THE CITY

Cities have been a major driving force in the development of civilization. Humanity's highest achievements, Sophocles proclaimed in his play *Antigone*, are "language, and wind-swift thought, and city-dwelling habits." The city, from the time of its earliest appearance some ten thousand years ago, has focused and magnified human energies in the task of mastering the environment, enriched our understanding by providing a multiplicity of human contacts, and provided the stimulus to the highest creativity in all forms of science and art. It has at the same time been responsible for many of the darkest features of civilization—the spoliation of the environment; the coercion of vast numbers of individuals by governments, armies, and economic exploiters; the exclusion of vast segments of the population from intellectual and social advancement; and perhaps even the glorification of war.

In recent years, the process of urbanization has been explored with considerable success by a wide range of social scientists, including the urban geographer, the political scientist, the sociologist, the social anthropologist, the economist, and the historian. Their findings have thrown much light on such basic concerns as the impact of population growth, the spatial patterns of city development, the occupational structure of cities at varying stages of development, class relationships, family structure and mores, the functioning of political systems, and relationship to environment. All of this is enormously helpful to historians of civilization. But historians must always remember the one task that distinguishes them from the other social scientists: to respect the uniqueness of each period of civilization.

This book seeks to meet that challenge by focusing on the achievements of the world's great cities. Over half of the book is devoted to studies of twenty cities at the height of their creativity. Several questions have been asked about each city. To analyze the city's economic and social structure, we ask first the most basic question, *How did the city produce its wealth?* The city was a provider of services—religious, governmental, legal, military, and commercial. It was a manufacturer of goods, by artisans in the preindustrial age and by factory workers after the industrial revolution of the eighteenth century. And often it was an exploiter, using military force to acquire the economic wealth of others.

Second, we ask, *What social relationships developed inside this economic system?* We shall be interested in the distribution of wealth, the status accorded to birth or profession, the relationship between classes, the extent of mobility within the social structure, and the distinctive ways of life developed within each stratum of society.

Third, we turn to the political superstructure to ask, *How did the citizens conceive the relationship of the individual to the state in theory and carry it out in practice?* Underlying all political systems is a theory or theories of government, though these assumptions are not always explicitly formulated. In times of dissatisfaction with an established political system, theorists construct new formulas based on their own conception of human nature and the ideal form of state; and as we shall see, these theories are occasionally put into practice, usually as the result of revolution. Political theory will therefore accompany the analysis of the distribution of power within the city and, since most of these cities are also capitals, within the state.

Fourth, we consider, *How did the city spend its wealth?* The consumption habits of different social classes have been subject to a vast amount of detailed research, and it is increasingly possible to recreate the way of life of the less privileged classes as well as that of the elite. Public expenditure as well as private must be assessed, especially that used for the beautification of the city or the improvement of its amenities; but we must also consider the waste of a city's resources, from military adventuring to the ravaging of the natural surroundings.

Fifth, we examine the city's intellectual life, asking, *To what goals was the intellectual activity of its citizens directed?* In cities as multifaceted as these, we must emphasize the most salient features of each city's contribution to the intellectual advance of civilization, such as the contribution of Athens to philosophy and drama, of Rome to law, of Ch'ang-an to painting and poetry. But in each case the contribution of the environment of the city must be explained: why Paris was a magnet for Europe's theologians in the thirteenth century and for artists and writers in the late nineteenth century; why the Heian court in Kyoto gave birth to the psychological novel; why Berlin could be transformed in months from the center of military science to an incubator of avant-garde artistic talent and then in an even shorter time back to its military preoccupations.

Finally, we ask, *How did the cultural and scientific achievements of the city reflect the citizens' conception of human nature, of God, and of beauty?* Much of this creation was the possession of an elite, but that is hardly a reason for excluding it from a history of civilization. Hence, we shall consider what the Parthenon tells us of the Greek concept of beauty, how a Botticelli Venus reveals the Florentine conception of the divine, how Newton's laws of motion justify a naturally ordered universe, how the Forbidden City of Peking illustrates the Confucian concept of an ordered society.

City and countryside, however, cannot and should not be isolated from each other. As late as 1800, only three percent of the world's population lived in cities of more than 5,000 people; and even in 1950, only thirty percent did so. Throughout the development of civilization, most people have lived on the land; and the city has always depended on the countryside for food and raw materials. We are therefore concerned throughout the book with the life of the rural population as well as the urban, with agrarian technology and the nature of bulk transportation of agricultural products, with the social structure of the countryside and its impact upon the city, and with the needs, values, and aspirations of the inhabitants of the countryside. We must consider the farms of the Roman *campagna* as well as Rome, the decaying aristocratic estates as well as prerevolutionary Paris, the rice paddies of the Yangtze Valley as well as the factories of Shanghai.

This book is undisguisedly enthusiastic about cities, with a few notable exceptions. I only wish that one could show the same admiration for urban creations that Wordsworth did for London, one bright morning at the beginning of the last century:

> *Earth has not anything to show more fair:*
> *Dull would he be of soul who could pass by*
> *A sight so touching in its majesty:*
> *This city now doth, like a garment, wear*
> *The beauty of the morning; silent, bare,*
> *Ships, towers, domes, theatres, and temples lie*
> *Open unto the fields, and to the sky;*
> *All bright and glittering in the smokeless air.*
> *Never did sun more beautifully steep*
> *In his first splendor, valley, rock, or hill;*
> *Ne'er saw I, never felt, a calm so deep!*
> *The river glideth at his own sweet will:*
> *Dear God! the very houses seem asleep;*
> *And all that mighty heart is lying still!*[1]

[1] "Composed upon Westminster Bridge, September 3, 1802."

World Civilizations

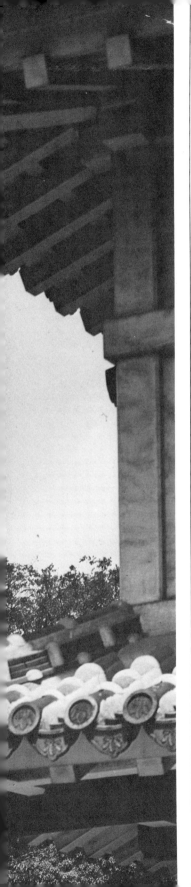

17

THE EARLY MODERN AGE IN THE NON-WESTERN WORLD

The great European voyages of discovery that began in the fifteenth century demonstrated the superiority of the West in maritime technology; but they were stimulated by the desire to gain access to civilizations whose material and intellectual achievements in many ways outstripped those of the European powers. The reports sent back by ambassadors, merchants, and explorers glowed with admiration and amazement at the elegance of life, the standard of material comfort, and the artistic sophistication of the civilizations to which they had penetrated.

Only one of these non-Western civilizations, the pre-Columbian civilization of Central and South America, succumbed immediately to European power. Three great Moslem empires—the Ottoman Empire, the Safavid Empire of Persia, and the Mogul Empire in India—achieved new heights of power and economic achievement between the fifteenth and seventeenth centuries. In the mosques and palaces of their great capitals of Constantinople, Isfahan, Delhi, and Agra, Islamic architecture reached its culminating glory.

In China, after the humiliation of a century of Mongol rule under the Yüan dynasty, national pride had been restored in the fourteenth century by the Ming emperors, who were able for the next three centuries to maintain a remarkably stable society devoted to traditional Chinese values. Much of the Forbidden City, their palace in Peking, remains as one illustration of the Ming achievement. Moreover, the Manchus, the non-Chinese dynasty that overthrew the Ming in the mid-seventeenth century, set out to defend the same traditional Chinese institutions and, at least until the eighteenth century, felt able to treat contacts with the Europeans as a minor, and easily dispensable, convenience.

White Heron Castle, Himeji, Japan   (Consulate General of Japan)

The Japanese, once they had restored internal order at the end of the sixteenth century, decided to avoid outside contacts almost entirely. Shoguns of the Tokugawa family, governing from a new administrative capital at Edo (Tokyo), made Japan a "closed country" in which, with almost no stimulus from outside trade or intellectual contacts, social stability and economic progress were achieved simultaneously.

Finally, most of the states of sub-Saharan Africa adjusted to European trading demands, even to the extent of becoming partners in the slave trade; and, although Kongo and the Swahili city-states were ruined by Portuguese interference, others, such as Benin and Sokoto, became richer and more powerful. In the early modern age the cities of sub-Saharan Africa—Ife, Benin, Kakaya, and Kano among many—remained flourishing centers of indigenous African or of Moslem culture.

THE HEIGHT OF THE OTTOMAN EMPIRE

The conquest of Constantinople in 1453 by the Ottoman Turks under the command of the young sultan Mohammed II (reigned 1451–1481) was the prelude to the greatest century of territorial expansion, economic prosperity, and cultural advance in the history of the Turks. Perhaps because there was a ruthless battle among the sons of each sultan to determine which of them would succeed their father, the victors in the power struggles of the next hundred years proved to be efficient if cruel rulers. Bayezit II (reigned 1481–1512) consolidated Ottoman power by his handling of the empire's economic and social problems. Selim I (reigned 1512–1520) resumed the military expansion of the empire into southeastern Europe, Russia, and the Near East. Finally, Suleiman the Magnificent (reigned 1520–1566), as he was known in Europe, not only engaged in constant wars that took the Ottoman forces to within striking distance of Vienna, but also reorganized the governmental and judicial system (winning from his subjects the title of Suleiman the Lawgiver) and encouraged a cultural flowering in Constantinople that again gave the great city the fascination it had exercised a thousand years earlier under the emperor Justinian.

The Ottoman Wars of Conquest

In the fifteenth and sixteenth centuries the Ottoman armed forces were among the most formidable in the world. The main body of the army was the feudal cavalry composed of the holders of fiefs (*timars*), which were usually conquered territories that had been subdivided among the military aristocrats and the soldiers they were required to support and equip. They were normally commanded by special agents of the sultan—officially slaves of the ruler—who were Moslem converts recruited at first from prisoners or from purchased slaves and later from a draft on Christian children from the Balkan possessions. A similar system of recruitment was employed to expand the sultan's household into a standing army of *janissaries* ("new

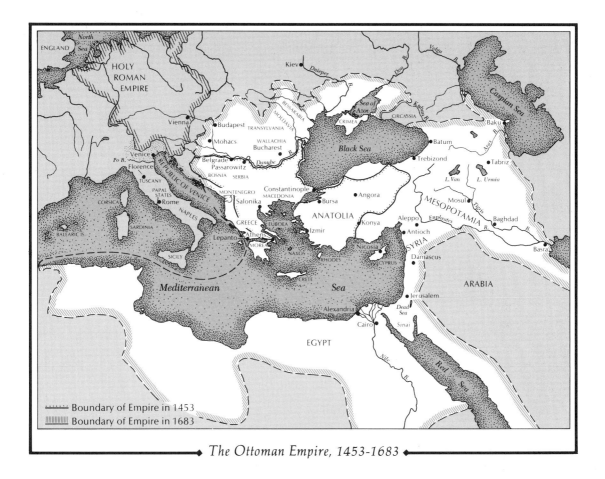

The Ottoman Empire, 1453-1683

····· Boundary of Empire in 1453
▓▓▓▓▓ Boundary of Empire in 1683

troops"), who acted as the infantry in time of war and as urban garrisons and security guards in peacetime. In addition, there were more specialized troops such as the artillery corps, who handled the guns and cannon that gave the Ottoman armies great effectiveness in siege warfare. The navy, modeled in organization and technology on the fleets of Venice and Genoa, included a number of large galleys with crews of 600 sailors and soldiers. By the sixteenth century Ottoman ships had been able to secure the eastern Mediterranean despite the loss of the sea battle of Lepanto in 1571 to the Spanish fleet. Turkish naval power was predominant in the Black Sea and even for a time in the Red Sea and at the mouth of the Persian Gulf.

After the capture of Constantinople, Mohammed II led his armies into the Balkans, where he conquered the Serbians. He completed his annexation of Greece with the taking of Athens and the Peloponnesus by 1460, took control of the area of present-day Rumania, and extended his power to the north coast of the Black Sea by bringing the Tatar khanate to recognize Ottoman overlordship. Selim I ("the Grim") was faced with a challenge to the Sunni Moslem faith (see Chapter 9) favored by the Ottomans, posed by the takeover of neighboring Persia by the Shi'ite leader Ismail Safavi, who was crowned shah in 1502. Selim struck viciously at a rebellion of Shi'ites within his own empire in Anatolia, and took northern Mesopotamia and Kurdistan after defeating Ismail at the battle of Chaldiran (1514). His most important campaigns, however, took him south into Syria and Egypt, which had been made part of the empire by 1517. Selim himself then took the title of caliph, thereby claiming for his dynasty the spiritual leadership of the Moslem world. The leaders of the Bedouin tribes of Arabia proclaimed their loyalty, and Selim took control of the holy cities of Mecca and Medina without need of a military campaign.

Suleiman was fortunate both in the strength of the empire he inherited from Selim and in the weakness of many of his foreign rivals. Selim had secured control over the central and local government officials by use of the janissaries, whom he had expanded to a corps of 35,000, to coerce them. The lands conquered by Selim had brought vast new revenues, as well as the prestige of leadership of the Moslem world. Territorial annexations in the Balkans and the Near East had given the victorious Ottoman armies ideal strategic positions from which to advance into central Europe and against Persia. The strengthened navy gave him the power not only to seize more Christian islands in the Mediterranean but also to attack his principal enemy, the emperor Charles V, by sea as well as by land. Charles, moreover, was constantly distracted from meeting the Turkish danger by other problems within his vast empire—a revolt of the cities in Spain, the advance of the Protestants in Germany, quarrels with the pope, and the unremitting enmity of France. No other European power presented a serious threat to the Turks. In the East the military power of Safavid Persia was in temporary decline, and the Turks had won a valuable ally in their campaigns against Persia in the Uzbeks of Bokhara. Suleiman himself, moreover, was a fine and inexhaustible general, who campaigned personally for ten years of his reign.

After a long siege of the island of Rhodes, a fortress-city administered and defended by the Knights of Saint John, Suleiman took possession of this last Christian outpost in the eastern Mediterranean in 1522. His own principal goal was to take the kingdom of Hungary, whose fertile plains would give him control over the middle reaches of the Danube. In 1526 he defeated a much inferior Hungarian force at Mohacs and slaughtered thousands of the Hungarian nobility and their king. From Hungary in 1529 he mounted the first Turkish siege of Vienna and succeeded in penetrating the outer suburbs before withdrawing with the onset of winter. With Hungary safe from Habsburg attack, he shifted his armies to the east, where, in alliance with the Uzbeks, they again invaded Persia. In this way he established a pattern of avoiding a two-front war in any one year.

In all, Suleiman mounted three invasions of Persia, during which the Safavids were compelled to flee from their principal cities. Unable to ab-

Sultan Suleiman I (reigned 520–566)

Europeans called Suleiman "the Magnificent" because of the splendor of his court in Constantinople, but his own subjects preferred to call him "the Lawgiver" after his transformation of the empire's legal codes. (The Metropolitan Museum of Art, Harris Brisbane Dick Fund, 1925)

Battle of Lepanto (1570)
Turkish advances in the Mediterranean were halted when a largely Spanish fleet destroyed over 150 Ottoman galleys in a battle off the Greek coast. More than 10,000 Christian galley slaves were liberated. (The National Maritime Museum, London)

sorb the whole of Persia, however, he had to be satisfied with the annexation of lower Mesopotamia and the eastern coast of the Black Sea. The Turkish navy remained active in the Mediterranean and the Red Sea throughout his reign. In the western Mediterranean Suleiman was able to enlist the pirate fleets of Tunis, Algiers, and Tripoli—the so-called Barbary corsairs—in attacks on Spanish shipping. He even appointed the most skillful of the corsairs, Hayruddin Barbarossa, as commander of his navy. To end Portuguese pretensions to control the trade routes of the Indian Ocean, the Ottoman Red Sea fleet was sent to capture Aden and Yemen and thus to safeguard the Asian trade of Egypt, which the Portuguese had blocked.

Suleiman's later campaigns were less successful than his earlier ones, and the many battles along the Hungarian frontier and in Persia proved very costly. After Suleiman's death in 1566, there were only a few more territorial acquisitions—the islands of Cyprus and Crete, an additional strip of Hungarian territory, uncertain control over the western provinces of Persia. The definitive check of the last Ottoman siege of Vienna in 1683 marked the beginning of Ottoman military decline, which permitted the piecemeal dismemberment of the empire over the following two and a half centuries.

Political and Economic Structure

At the time of its greatest efficiency, under Suleiman, the Ottoman government was both in theory and in reality an absolute monarchy. The sultan-caliph was theoretically head of both the religion and the state. In fact, his religious powers were strictly prescribed by Islamic law (*sheriat*) and were supervised by the leading Islamic cleric called the chief preserver of the sheriat. Moreover, the Moslem clerics (*ulema*) were assigned important civil functions such as education through the mosque schools and justice through the Islamic courts. They were also the principal intellectuals and were responsible for much of the empire's literary creation. For this reason the Islamic clerics were officially known as the Learned Institution. The political structure was divided between the Palace Institution (the sultan's household in the Topkapi palace in Constantinople) and the Scribal Institution, which comprised the main departments of government.

The physical structure of the palace, a vast series of courts, mosques, villas, and pleasure gardens occupying the site of the earlier Byzantine palace, corresponded to the three principal functions of the sultan's household. The furthest, most secluded section was the harem, where the sultan's mother, wives, concubines, and children were guarded by eunuchs. The Inner Service occupied the adjacent courts, where a vast array of officials, from pages and valets to sword bearers and treasury officers, carried out the day-to-day administration of the court itself. The Outer Service in the large outer courtyard handled some of the services linking the sultan to the world beyond the palace walls, such as public works, grain supply, and reception of ambassadors. The main work of government was, however, carried out by the Scribal Institution, whose leading members were housed in a building that came to be known as the Sublime Porte (although a more accurate translation would have been "high gate"). As a result, just as foreign governments were said to maintain relations with Whitehall in London, so they dealt with the Sublime Porte in Constantinople in all their relations with the Ottoman government. The chief minister of the sultan was the grand vizier who acted with the aid of the imperial council (*divan*). Under these officials was a hierarchical bureaucratic system stretching throughout the provinces of the empire. The Palace Institution, the Scribal Institution, the Learned Institution, and the Military Institution (feudal army, janissaries, and navy) were together known as the ruling class. The rest of the population were the subject class, or *raya*—the sultan's "protected flock." Children of the rayas could be accepted into the ruling class, especially as the result of recruitment and conversion to the Moslem religion of the clever Christian children required to staff the palace and the imperial administration as well as the corps of janissaries. Non-Moslems in general were permitted to retain their own religions and institutions, except where these conflicted with Moslem practices or imperial law. The patriarch of Constantinople, for example, was permitted to remain head of the Orthodox churches throughout the empire. Jews were regarded as similarly placed under the authority of the grand rabbi of Constantinople. In the sixteenth century conditions for

Jews were so favorable that many refugees came to the Ottoman Empire to escape persecution in Spain and in northern and central Europe.

The effectiveness of so centralized a government depended to a large extent on the ability of the rulers, who after Suleiman were almost without exception weak, indolent, or depraved. When the habit of establishing control of the throne by the murder of all rival claimants, including one's brothers, was replaced in the seventeenth century by designation of the eldest male child as heir, the virtual imprisonment of the heir within the palace turned many into drunkards or even lunatics. Power passed to the leading clerics of the ulema and to the grand viziers, but they were subject to frequent interference by the janissaries. From the top, corruption spread throughout the system. No office could be obtained without payment of large bribes, which the officeholder then recovered by squeezing more and more from the subject population.

As long as the economic system functioned well, these grievances could be tolerated; and throughout the reign of Suleiman the empire was prosperous. The principal purpose of many of the wars of conquest had been the acquisition of such rich agricultural lands as those of Hungary, which could be parceled out in feudal fiefs to the victorious armies. The taxes on the peasantry provided the main source of revenue for both the state and the feudal lords. Trade, however, also flourished within the vast empire, with Constantinople again exercising a role as commercial entrepôt and manufacturing center in its own right. Customs duties provided further income. The Ottoman Empire under Suleiman was regarded with some justification as richer by far than any European state.

By the end of the sixteenth century, however, the Ottoman economy was in difficulties. Population was increasing faster than the food supply. The influx of precious metals from the Americas into Europe also provoked inflation within the Ottoman Empire and led to demands within the army for higher pay, which culminated in a mutiny of the janissaries. In the seventeenth and eighteenth centuries the artisans in the cities found themselves unable to compete with the cheaper products of northern Europe; and the Turkish economy was shifted toward export of raw materials and precious metals and import of mass-produced metallurgical and textile products. The Ottoman cities became home to a dispossessed population, swelled by landless peasants from the countryside. However, political and economic decline was slow and was delayed by occasional measures of reform. The Ottoman state, although forced progressively to give up the outer provinces of the empires, was able to survive as the "Sick Man of Europe" until World War I.

The Reconstruction of Constantinople

Immediately after conquering Constantinople in 1453, Mohammed II had set out to make the city once again the economic and cultural center of a great empire. Fearing that the Turkish army would pillage their city, many of Constantinople's remaining Christian inhabitants had fled, reducing the population from about 60,000 during the siege to only 10,000. Mohammed pursued the ideal of a city of mixed religion and race, welcoming not only Moslems from throughout his empire and from other Moslem countries, but also Jews, Slavs, Armenians, and Greeks. Peasants from the Balkans were compelled to settle near the city in order to grow the crops and tend the animals needed to feed the growing population. Venetians and Genoese were given special trading privileges. The city's public works were quickly reconstructed, especially the aqueducts, sewers, bridges, and roads. A vast covered market was constructed, which became the center of the city's commerce. Religious foundations were encouraged to build mosques, schools, and hospitals; as the city's Moslem population grew, more and more of the Byzantine churches were converted into mosques. The sultan himself built two palaces, the more grandiose being the Topkapi. On the ruins of the Church of the Holy Apostles, he constructed the Fatih mosque, where, following the example of the Byzantine emperors, the sultans were to be buried. By the time of his death the city's population had reached 100,000.

Suleiman was fortunate in having the services of perhaps the greatest of all Islamic architects, Sinan (1489?–1578?) when he turned to beautifying Constantinople. Sinan's greatest achievement in the capital was the mosque and mausoleum of Suleiman, whose soaring dome dominates the

The Mosque of Suleiman, Constantinople

The rebuilding of Constantinople in the early sixteenth century was directed by the court architect Sinan, who designed this great mosque as the mausoleum for Suleiman the Magnificent. In this photograph taken in about 1900, the Bosphorus is dominated by the vast dome of the mosque. (Popperfoto)

central rocky spine of the city and may even rival Hagia Sofia itself in beauty and technical mastery. In Constantinople and throughout the empire, Suleiman continued to build not only mosques and religious schools but also castles, bazaars, inns, bathhouses, fountains, and roads. In addition to his interest in architecture, he showed great enthusiasm for poetry, which he often wrote himself, and he presided over poetry competitions in Constantinople. In many ways his reign resembled that of Justinian, who also was famous for reforming the courts and reissuing the law codes and for sponsoring theological research and the writing of imperial history.

As Ottoman decline progressed in the eighteenth and nineteenth centuries, Constantinople, and especially Topkapi palace, known as the Grand Seraglio, came to symbolize all the weaknesses of the empire—its corruption, cruelty, inefficiency, and inability to change. When the sultan was overthrown by reformers under the leadership of Kemal Atatürk in 1922, one of the first acts of the new government was to transfer the capital of the Turkish state from Constantinople to Ankara in central Anatolia.

SAFAVID PERSIA

The revival of the military power and economic strength of Persia under the Safavid dynasty (1502–1736) challenged the Ottoman Empire on its eastern borders, a challenge that was made more threatening by the Safavid championship of the Shi'ite branch of Islam against the Sunni faith of the Ottomans. In 1502 Ismail Safavid crowned himself shah in the capital city of Tabriz and further displayed the military prowess of the devoted tribesmen of Turkish origin he commanded by capturing Baghdad and by defeating the Uzbeks on his northern border. Even though Ismail was defeated when the Ottoman armies came to the aid of their Uzbek allies, the Ottoman janissaries refused to penetrate further into Persia. Ismail was able to strike back from within Ottoman borders by instigating an uprising of Shi'ites in Anatolia itself. By the time of his death in 1524, the Persian state had thus revived the threat to the great empire governed from Constantinople that the Sassanid Empire of Persia had earlier exercised against Justinian.

Ismail's successor, Tahmasp (reigned 1524–1576), was able to coordinate operations with the European powers, especially with Charles V when the latter was desperately seeking to defend Vienna from the Turks. Thus, although Persia was invaded on several occasions by the Ottoman armies, Tahmasp was able to maintain a luxurious and cultivated court life at a new capital city of Qazvin. Here he even offered refuge to Humayun, the Mogul emperor of India, who for a time proclaimed his own adherence to the Shi'ite faith.

The most powerful of the Safavid rulers was Shah Abbas the Great (reigned 1587–1629), who, though ruthless and cruel when state policy required it, was also a brilliant statesman and general. At first he had to buy peace from the Ottomans by ceding territory on his northern borders. With the aid of an English general, however, he reconstructed his forces, purchased modern artillery, and equipped his infantry with muskets. After first defeating the Uzbeks, he launched his forces against the Ottoman occupants of western Persia, who were finally ejected in 1612 after thirteen years of fighting. Abbas further increased his ties with England by granting the East India Company the right to trade with Persia and to maintain a factory at his new capital city of Isfahan. With English naval aid he drove the Portuguese from their settlement at Hormuz on the mouth of the Persian Gulf, thus breaking their stranglehold on the sea routes by which Persian silk could be shipped. He also welcomed the Dutch East India Company to open a factory in the capital, although in a less advantageous position than the British.

Shah Abbas of Persia and Emperor Jahangir of India
Although the two rulers never met, this allegorical Indian painting depicts them united in the halo of the light of the Islamic religion. The peaceful lion on which Jahangir stands has, however, edged the sheep of Abbas into the Mediterranean. (Courtesy of the Freer Gallery of Art, Smithsonian Institution, Washington, D.C.)

The Shah's Square, Isfahan
The Maidan-i-Shah, or Shah's Square, laid out by Shah Abbas in the early seventeenth century, can be seen through the minarets of the Shah's Mosque. To the right is the smaller Lutfullah Mosque and in the distance the entrance gate of the bazaar. (© Paolo Koch/Rapho/ Photo Researchers, Inc.)

In spite of the constant wars with the Ottomans and Uzbeks, Abbas was able to encourage an economic boom throughout the country, primarily through a program of public works that included the building of bridges and roads, the opening of new agricultural land, and the construction of a port at Bandar Abbas where the British and Dutch maintained trading stations. His most ambitious project, however, was to convert the city of Isfahan into one of the world's most beautiful capitals. He envisaged a city full of gardens, for which ample space was available within the twenty-mile-long walls. Rather than reconstruct the center of the old town, he built a new center a mile to the south, focused on his royal palace and on a small, beautifully tiled mosque facing it. Beyond the two buildings he laid out one of the finest squares ever built, the Maidan-i-Shah, 1,674 feet long by 540 feet wide. At the north end was a massive gateway that led into the royal bazaar; the south end of the Maidan was taken up entirely by a vast new Mosque of the Shah, every inch of which was covered with brightly colored tile mosaics or painted tiles. To provide his city with a more worthy entrance, he laid out a superb two-mile-long promenade called the Chahar-Bagh ("four gardens"), which crossed the Isfahan River on a bridge supported by thirty-three arches. Down the center of the street, which a French writer later compared to the Champs Elysées of Paris, ran a stream bordered by alleys of trees and by splashing fountains. In this beautiful city all the traditional Persian arts and crafts—painting, ceramics, carpets, tile, metalwork—again flourished, providing the principal inspiration for the culture of the more powerful Moslem empire to the south—the Mogul Empire of India.

THE MOGUL EMPIRE IN INDIA

Moslem invaders had penetrated India in four waves during the Middle Ages, each time succeeding in taking possession of a larger area of the peninsula (see Chapter 9). The fourth invasion, led by Babur, the ruler of a small principality in what is now Soviet Turkestan, created the Mogul Empire, under which for two centuries Moslem civilization reached heights comparable in quality and creativity to those being achieved during the Renaissance and Baroque periods in Europe. The showplaces of this culture were the twin capitals of Delhi and Agra.

The Establishment of the Mogul Empire

Babur, the first Mogul emperor (reigned 1526–1530), was a man of many gifts—a fine military commander, a superb athlete and archer, a designer of gardens, a connoisseur of poetry and painting, and a lover of great cities. When, late in life, he wrote his perceptive autobiography, it was the cities that inspired his greatest admiration. His original goal had been to recreate the empire of his Mongol ancestor Timur, and one of his first expeditions had captured Timur's capital of Samarkand. This Moslem city, which had flourished on the great trading route across central Asia that linked China to Europe, with its buildings dating back to the Ummayad and Abbasid dynasties, inflamed Babur's imagination. "Samarkand is a wonderfully elegant city," he wrote, surrounded with meadows and carefully planned gardens. Great mosques and colleges, tombs, baths, observatories, and immensely long walls reminded him of the magnificence that had existed less than a hundred years earlier. In India, however, he was sharply disappointed:

Hindustan is a country that has few pleasures to recommend it. The people are not handsome. They have no idea of the charms of friendly society, of frankly mixing together, or of familiar intercourse. They have no genius, no comprehension of mind, no politeness of manner, no kindness or fellow-feeling, no ingenuity or mechanical invention in planning or executing their handicraft works, no skill or knowledge in design or architecture . . . they have no aqueducts or canals in their gardens or palaces. In their buildings they study neither elegance nor climate, appearance nor regularity. . . . The chief excellency of Hindustan is, that it is a large country, and has abundance of gold and silver.[1]

In the four years between his defeat of the sultan of Delhi at the battle of Panipat in 1526 and his death in a gunpowder explosion, Babur was principally occupied in extending his control down the Ganges Valley. His own contribution to improving the amenities of his new empire was his pleasure garden, with palace and baths, built on the banks of the river Jumna at Agra.

Babur's son Humayun (reigned 1530–1556), who inherited his father's literary but not his military genius, was driven out of India by insurgent Afghan princes and recaptured the empire only after fifteen years of exile.

Babur, the First Mogul Emperor of India
Shortly after his conquest of northern India, Babur created a delightful pleasure garden on the banks of the Jumna River at Agra, where he could find refuge from the heat of the Indian plains. (British Library)

The Uleg-Beg Mosque, Samarkand (1420)
The mosques erected in Samarkand in the fourteenth and fifteenth centuries by Tamerlane and his successors were the inspiration for the first Mogul buildings in India. (Russell A. Thompson/Taurus Photos)

Babur, 1526–1530	Agra: Foundation of Fort, Persian Gardens
Humayun, 1530–1556	Delhi: Tomb
Akbar, 1556–1605	Fatehpur Sikri: New capital city Agra: Palace Sikandra: Tomb
Jahangir, 1605–1627	Lahore: Palace, Tomb, and Shalimar Gardens Agra: Tomb of Itimat-ud-Daulah (emperor's father-in-law)
Shah Jahan, 1627–1658	Agra: Taj Mahal, Palace Delhi: Red Fort and Palace, Jama Masjid (Great Mosque)
Aurangzeb, 1658–1707	Aurangabad: Tomb of Rabia Daurani (empress) Lahore: Great Mosque

Note: The last Mogul emperor was deposed by the British in 1857.

Delhi, however, had prospered during his absence as a result of the construction of the Grand Trunk Road, which linked it to the northwest with the Indus Valley and to the southeast with Bengal at the mouth of the Ganges. Humayun died of a fall on the polished marble floor of his library only one year after his return, and he is mainly remembered for the magnificent mausoleum erected for him on the edge of Delhi by his widow, Hamida Begum. Built of red sandstone and decorated with inlay of black, white, and yellow marble, the mausoleum is surmounted by a soaring dome and set amid gardens, fountains, and reflecting pools. It formed the pattern of opulence and elegance that was to culminate a century later in the Taj Mahal.

Akbar the Great Emperor

Humayun's son Akbar (reigned 1556–1605) was only thirteen on his father's death, but an able and loyal regent governed on his behalf until he took power personally at the age of eighteen. A contemporary of Elizabeth I of England and Philip II of Spain, he became one of India's most farsighted and long-lived rulers, whose achievements are often compared to those of the Mauryan emperor Asoka. Akbar's conquests brought the boundaries of his empire to the edge of the Deccan in the south and to Kabul in Afghanistan in the north. Within the empire he solved the problem of the rebellious Hindu princes known as the *Rajputs*, who controlled the area immediately to the west of Delhi and Agra, by defeating them individually and

[1] *Memoirs of Zehir-Ed-Din Muhammed Baber, Emperor of Hindustan*, translated by John Leyden and William Erskine (London: Longman, Rees, Orme, Brown, and Green, 1826), p. 333.

then striking alliances with them. He himself married Rajput princesses and enlisted Rajput soldiers and administrators in his army and government.

Akbar's most lasting achievements were the creation of an imperial bureaucracy and the establishment of an effective system of revenue collecting that would later be adopted by the British. Akbar divided his administrative officials into thirty-three ranks, subdivided according to the number of cavalry each official was expected to bring to the emperor's service for military emergencies. The highest officials commanded between five and ten thousand, the lowest ten. Although the majority of the officials were Moslems born outside India, Akbar enlisted in his service the most intelligent of the Hindus, who composed about fifteen percent of his administrators. Within the twelve provinces into which he divided his empire, the cities were run by their own municipal governments; the countryside was supervised by local military commanders and the revenue collectors. By establishing the imperial taxes as one-third of the harvest, or one-third of the harvest's cash value, Akbar lessened the burden on the peasantry. He even ordered that at times when the harvest failed the taxes

Akbar on Campaign in Northern India
To enable his fighting elephants to cross the Jumna River, Akbar constructed a bridge of boats. His campaigns subjected all the rebellious Hindu princes of Rajasthan who threatened the security of Delhi and Agra. [*The Victoria and Albert Museum, London (Crown Copyright)*]

should be reduced. Akbar's system of bureaucracy and taxation was perhaps the principal reason for the longevity of the Mogul Empire.

Above all, Akbar attempted to reconcile the different religions of India, especially the Hindus and Moslems. He ended the discriminatory tax on non-Moslems and stopped the destruction of Hindu temples. Although he ordered complete religious toleration, he did attempt to stop those Hindu customs he found reprehensible, such as the marriage of children and the burning of widows on their dead husbands' funeral pyres. Akbar's tolerance was attributable to the fact that he kept an open mind on religious matters and delighted in the discussion of theology with experts from different faiths. He met on Thursdays in a special hall of worship in the palace with Moslems, Brahmans, Jains, and Zoroastrians, and eventually with a group of Jesuits for whom he had sent to the Portuguese colony of Goa. One of these Jesuits, Father Monserrate, has left an insightful commentary on the months the priests spent at Akbar's court, where they felt they had almost succeeded in converting Akbar to Catholicism. Instead, Akbar produced his own religion, called the Divine Faith, which mingled Moslem, Hindu, and Jain beliefs. It was adopted only by a few of his courtiers, and it disappeared after his death.

Jahangir and Nur Jahan

Akbar's successors, although they continued to expand the empire, proved less competent as statesmen. His son Jahangir (reigned 1605–1627) was addicted to opium and alcohol and shifted unstably between callous repression and enlightened reform. Real power fell into the hands of his wife, Nur Jahan, a woman of great beauty and strong will. She not only engaged in the palace diversions of horseback riding and tiger shooting, but also undertook the duties her husband neglected, issuing coinage, countersigning decrees, and aiding the poor. The emperor himself wrote, "Nur Jahan was wise enough to conduct the business of state, while he [the emperor] only wanted a bottle of wine and a piece of meat to make merry."

In the northern town of Lahore, which they preferred to Delhi or Agra, the imperial couple patronized many painters, calligraphers, musicians, and poets. Jahangir himself belied his reputation for indolence by composing his own *Memoirs*, which, like those of Babur, abound in lyrical descriptions of birds and flowers and especially of the lake valleys of Kashmir, where, "in the soul-enchanting spring the hills and plains are filled with blossoms, the gates, the walls, the courts, the roofs, are lighted up by the torches of the banquet-adorning tulips." As for his father's mausoleum at Sikandra, near Agra—the principal monument remaining from Akbar's reign—Jahangir recounts how he had to have it rebuilt to meet his standards. "By degrees, a lofty building was erected, and a very bright garden arranged around the building of the shrine, and a large and lofty gateway with minarets of white stone was built. On the whole, they told me the cost of this lofty edifice was 1,500,000 rupees."[2]

[2] *Memoirs of Jahangir,* translated by Alexander Rogers (London: Royal Asiatic Society, 1909), vol. I, p. 152.

Facade of the Tomb of Akbar, Sikandra
Akbar's tomb on the edge of Agra was built by his son Jahangir in 1613. The entrance to the tomb is decorated with intricate, inlaid patterns of brightly colored stone and is inscribed with the ninety-nine names that describe the glory of Allah.   (Fritz Henle/Photo Researchers, Inc.)

Shah Jahan

Shah Jahan (reigned 1627–1658) brought Mogul cultural life to its climax by his patronage and plunged the empire into economic ruin through his extravagance. His military campaigns in the Deccan, though mostly successful, were very costly, as were his massive building programs. To finance them, he was compelled to increase taxation on the peasantry in spite of widespread famine. Abandoning Akbar's policy of religious toleration, he renewed the ban on the building of Hindu temples and pulled down a number of Christian and Hindu buildings.

Aurangzeb

Wearying of his father's exactions and seeking immediate power himself, Shah Jahan's third son, Aurangzeb (reigned 1658–1717), imprisoned his father in the Agra palace and had himself proclaimed emperor. His resultant demands for revenue overburdened the economy and led to widespread peasant revolts. Aurangzeb aggravated the disaffection by embarking on persecution of Hindus, whose temples he again began to destroy. He also reimposed the taxes on non-Moslems. Furthermore, he prompted the conversion of the followers of an offshoot of Hinduism called Sikhs into a military brotherhood deeply committed to struggle against the Moslems. The

Sikh religion had been formed in the early sixteenth century by a mystic named Nanak, who was known as the first *guru* or teacher. Attempting to combine Hinduism and the Moslem faith, Nanak taught monotheism, the fundamental similarity of all religions, and the value of meditation. He also refused to recognize the caste system. Although the sect was at first completely peaceful, persecution led them to arm; when Aurangzeb had their ninth guru killed, they became a military brotherhood. They adopted a number of rules that Sikhs still follow, including wearing the turban and never cutting the beard or hair, and they partook of communal meals and a kind of baptism. From their holy city of Amritsar, the Sikhs succeeded by the late eighteenth century in gaining control of most of the Punjab.

Nevertheless, Aurangzeb proved to be a brilliant administrator, unhampered in his attention to government by the charm of the harem or the counsels of moderation. He brought the Mogul Empire to its largest extent, exceeding even the size of the empire of Asoka. Yet for the last twenty-six years of his life he campaigned for the conquest of the south, squandering human life for ephemeral victories. It has been estimated that one hundred thousand people were killed each year in Aurangzeb's warfare in the Deccan. His successors as emperor lacked even the justification of military success and administrative efficiency for their economic exactions. Just as the Europeans were probing for weakness from their coastal trading posts, the Mogul Empire entered an irreparable decline (see Chapter 25).

THE DELHI AND AGRA OF SHAH JAHAN

Location and Growth

The capital of the Mogul Empire moved with the emperor, the personal source of all government and all justice. During the frequent campaigns the government was run from elaborate tent-cities; and it is possible that the beautiful marble canopies of the palaces and mosques of Delhi and Agra are derived from the temporary awnings beneath which the emperor dispensed justice while encamped with his armies. However, the building of capital cities—and often their almost equally rapid abandonment—was already established as a habit of the early Moslem rulers in India. This passion for creating vast cities, resplendent with mosques and palaces within massive stone walls, was carried to such an extreme by the Mogul emperors that it played an important part in bringing their empire to the edge of bankruptcy. Jahangir's favorite city was Lahore, which he greatly expanded. Akbar founded a totally new capital called Fatehpur Sikri, near Agra, around the tomb of a holy man he revered, but abandoned it after only fourteen years. Most of the Mogul emperors, however, divided their time between the two great capitals, Delhi and Agra.

These two cities are located on the river Jumna, a tributary of the Ganges; Delhi lies about one hundred and twenty miles north of Agra. Delhi controlled the great invasion routes from the northwest that had brought so many conquerors, including the Moguls themselves, from central Asia. Agra faced south, blocking the way to attacking armies of the nearby Rajput princes or of the Hindu powers farther south. Both cities were on fords, and both enjoyed access to the Bay of Bengal by way of the thousand-mile-long waterway of the Jumna-Ganges valley. Delhi, by far the more ancient city, had expanded greatly under the Turkish sultans in the thirteenth and fourteenth centuries. Agra was a small Hindu town of little importance until Babur laid out his pleasure garden there on the left bank of the river. However, he did not have time to turn it into another Samarkand; it was Akbar who became the first important Mogul city builder. While the mausoleum of Akbar's father Humayun was being completed in Delhi by his widow, Akbar began to transform Agra by erecting an enormous citadel, the Fort, on the river bank. His son Jahangir later wrote, with his usual attention to cost, that it was "a fort of cut red stone, the like of which those who have travelled over the world cannot point out. It was completed in the space of fifteen or sixteen years. It had four gates and two sally-ports, and its cost was 35 lakhs of rupees." Akbar had in fact followed the pattern of such Arab palaces as the Alhambra of Granada of establishing within impregnable defense walls an elegant palace, complete with mosque, bath, audience hall, and harem. His example was followed by the later Mogul builders.

Akbar also established a pattern of court life that was to be preserved by his successors. In the morning, after rising to the sound of musical instruments, he engaged in religious meditation. Then he gave audience to a crowd of his poorer subjects gathered in the palace courtyard. After blessing the sick and receiving petitions, he met the greater nobles and officials in his audience hall. His only meal, eaten at noon, was vegetarian and was followed by rest during the heat of the day. In the late afternoon he inspected the troops and the household horses and elephants or visited the arms factory. In the early evening recreation consisted of animal fights, polo, or backgammon. Finally, there was entertainment by musicians or poets or participation in the theological discussions that fascinated Akbar. The palace had to be adapted to this combination of government and justice, indoor and outdoor entertainment, and imperial residence.

During the reign of Jahangir, who was far less of a builder than a lover of literature and painting, the painting of miniatures and the art of calligraphy reached their height. As in architecture, Persian influence was strong and was linked to a long Hindu tradition of illustrating scenes from poems like the *Ramayana*. Akbar himself greatly admired Hindu painters and employed them in the imperial studios, which were commissioned to produce portraits of the emperor and his family as well as an illustrated life of Akbar called the *Akbarnama*. Jahangir himself, who claimed to be so well informed about painting that he could name the painter of any portrait shown him, became interested in the European paintings shown him by the Jesuits. His son, Shah Jahan, continued this patronage of art, but on a much-reduced scale. He was, however, to become one of the most ambitious and talented patrons of architecture of all time.

The Buildings of Shah Jahan

Shah Jahan *(The Metropolitan Museum of Art, Gift of Alexander Smith Cochran, 1913)*

Shah Jahan's first major undertaking was also to be his most famous. He had ruled only three years when his wife, Mumtaz Mahal, died. During nineteen years of marriage they had had fourteen children. Heartbroken, the emperor ordered the construction of the world's most beautiful tomb, the Taj Mahal. Its construction took twenty-two years (1631–1653) and employed over twenty thousand workers. Architects, masons, stone carvers, and mosaic workers were brought from all over India and central Asia. Precious stones were acquired from as far away as Tibet, Ceylon, and China. The purest of white marble was mined at Markrana, two hundred and fifty miles away.

The tomb, which stands on a vast platform of sandstone and marble overlooking the river Jumna, is reached through a narrow opening set in a tall sandstone gateway that provides a dramatic view of the temple beyond. Reflected in long pools and set in a lush garden, the Persian dome of the tomb itself, seen in a frame of four soaring minarets, seems to float, especially when viewed by moonlight across the river's waters. The beautifully inlaid tomb of the emperor's wife is inscribed with the simple Persian verse: "The illustrious sepulcher of Arjuman Banu Begum, called Mumtaz Mahal. God is everlasting, God is sufficient. He knoweth what is concealed and what is manifest. He is merciful and compassionate. Nearer unto Him are those who say: Our Lord is God." Shah Jahan had originally intended to build for himself a companion tomb in black marble on the opposite

◆ The Delhi and Agra of Shah Jahan ◆

Period Surveyed	Mogul Empire, especially the reign of Emperor Shah Jahan (1627–1658)
Population	Delhi: 2 million Agra: 600,000
Area	Delhi: Shahjahanabad, 2 square miles; metropolitan area, 50 square miles Agra, 2–3 square miles (?)
Form of Government	Absolute emperor. Administration of empire through provincial governors. Main revenue from land tax, based on annual values of crops.
Political Leaders	Emperor Shah Jahan; Prince Aurangzeb (future emperor)
Economic Base	Imperial revenues, especially land tax. Commerce in luxury goods for court, textiles, foodstuffs. Artisan manufacturing (weapons; jewelry; clothing; artwork in ivory, marble, teak)
Intellectual Life	Painting, calligraphy, poetry, history
Principal Buildings	Delhi: new imperial capital of Shahjahanabad; Red Fort; Jama Masjid (Great Mosque) Agra: Fort; Taj Mahal
Public Entertainment	Animal fights, archery, boxing and wrestling, magic shows, acrobatics
Religion	Hindu, Moslem, Sikh

Mumtaz Mahal

On the death in childbirth of his second wife, Mumtaz Mahal ("Exalted of the Palace"), the Mogul emperor Shah Jahan vowed that her tomb, the Taj Mahal, be the most beautiful building ever constructed. (Courtesy of the Free Library of Philadelphia)

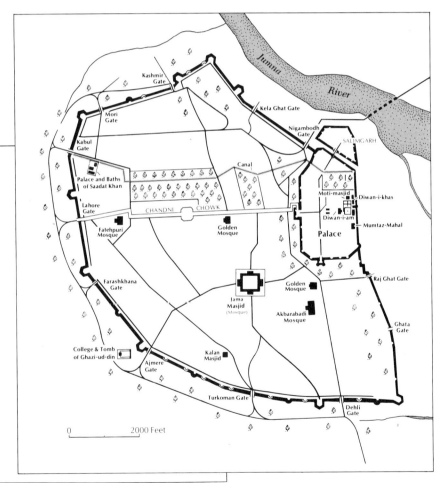

THE DELHI AND AGRA OF SHAH JAHAN

The Taj Mahal, Agra
Constructed in white marble and inlaid with designs in jasper, lapis lazuli, and car- nelian, the domed mau- soleum contains the graves of Mumtaz Mahal and her husband, the Mogul emperor Shah Jahan. Twenty thou- sand workers labored for eighteen years (1630–1648) to complete the tomb. (Courtesy of the Information Service of India)

bank of the river. After his imprisonment by his son, however, he was buried next to his wife beneath the dome of the Taj Mahal.

Shah Jahan continued to build in Agra throughout his reign, concen- trating on the beautification in his own favored inlaid marble of the fort begun by Akbar. Had he not also built the Taj Mahal, he would be remem- bered for the exquisite little mosque called the Moti Masjid, or Pearl Mosque, as well as for the palace in which he could sit looking across a bend in the river to the dome of the Taj Mahal. In 1638, however, he sud- denly decided to build another capital city at Delhi, named Shahjahana- bad after himself and now called Old Delhi. A wall five and a half miles long, with seven gates, surrounded his new city. Within the wall Shah Ja- han constructed one of the finest mosques in India, the Jama Masjid. Fi- nally he built the imperial citadel called the Red Fort, separated from Shahjahanabad by its own red sandstone wall. The Red Fort became the center of Mogul government. Here thousands of people lived and worked; and European visitors wrote back glowing descriptions of the extravagance of the great receptions in Diwani-i-am, the Hall of Public Audience, and of the restrained elegance of the small audience hall to which only the most

The Jama Masjid ("Great Mosque"), Delhi
Shah Jahan built the mosque, the largest in India, at the center of his new capital city of Shahjahanabad in Delhi. The use of striped bands of red or black stone as decoration on the white marble onion-domes was an innovation in Mogul architecture. (F. Roy Willis)

privileged were invited. The ceiling was of solid silver, the famous Peacock Throne encrusted with jewels. On the wall was inscribed the verse:

If there be paradise on earth,
It is here! It is here! It is here!

These were the last of the great Indian buildings, whether Hindu, Buddhist, or Moslem. Later Mogul emperors built tombs and palaces, but both the wealth and the taste were failing. The British, penetrating India in the eighteenth century, found a great civilization that was entering its decadence.

THE PEKING OF THE MING

Europeans' admiration for the physical splendors of the Mogul Empire in India was matched by the astonishment of visitors to the great cities of China during the Ming dynasty (1368–1644). For almost three hundred years this native dynasty enforced internal peace, often by means of extreme cruelty justified by a partial return to Legalist philosophy, which since the Han dynasty had always been an element of "imperial Confucianism," as distinguished from the more idealistic Confucianism of many scholars. Under the Ming the centralization of government was enhanced. The rule of the scholar-administrators continued, and the gentry (a term used by Western historians to describe officials out of office, as well as local degree holders who enjoyed prestige in their own districts and were often also landlords) remained important as an intermediary between the government and the people. The general attitude of scholars and gentry was conservative as a result of their study of the Confucian writings of the Chu Hsi school that they mastered for their examinations and of their vested interest in maintaining their bureaucratic connections and in ensuring the continuance of a stable kinship-centered society. The economy remained strong, although little technological progress was made. The population rose from between 60 and 75 million in 1400 to 150 million in 1644. The achievements of the earlier dynasties in poetry, painting, and architecture were revived, although imitation rather than originality was the rule.

Such a society, "governed by philosophers," as the Jesuit Matteo Ricci commented, with its bustling cities, its ornate temples and harmonious gardens, and its total conviction of its own superiority, fascinated the European rulers both as a source of wealth and as a cultural treasure trove. The dream of reaching China was the principal force driving the early European sea captains to take the extraordinary risks of crossing the Atlantic or rounding the southern cape of Africa.

The Emperor Hung-wu

The despotism of the Ming dynasty was created by the first emperor, Hung-wu (reigned 1368–1398). To destroy the memory of the Yüan dy-

◆ *The Peking of the Ming* ◆

Period Surveyed	Ming Dynasty (1368–1644), especially during the reign of Yung-lo (1403–1424)
Population	c. 400,000
Area	12.25 square miles
Form of Government	Absolute Emperor. Administrative bureaucracy chosen by competitive examination on Confucian classics and political problems. Central administration by Six Ministries, Board of Censors. Local government through provinces, prefectures, subprefectures, and counties.
Political Leaders	Emperor Hung-wu (1368–1398); Emperor Yung-lo (1403–1424); Chang Chü-cheng (Grand Secretary, 1573–1582)
Economic Base	Imperial court and bureaucracy; tax receipts; national and international commerce; artisans (pottery, silk, metalwork, woodwork)
Intellectual Life	Traditional scholarship (*Yung-lo Encyclopedia*); philosophy (Wang Yang-ming); painting (Shen Chou; Tung Ch'i-ch'ang); novel
Principal Buildings	Forbidden City; Temple of Agriculture; Temple of Heaven; Ming Tombs
Public Entertainment	Music concerts; plays; opera; hunting; country excursions; street entertainment; wine parlors
Religion	Confucian; Taoist; Buddhist

nasty, Hung-wu razed the Yüan palace at Peking and moved the government to Nanking in the lower Yangtze Valley. Suspicious that his premier had been plotting against him, he abolished the office and executed thirty thousand people connected with the ousted official. To ensure fear of the monarch among the higher officers, he had them beaten with bamboo poles by the eunuchs who served in his palace, and even executed some suspected of criticizing him. Garrisons were spread throughout the country to ensure obedience and tax payments, and households were strictly classified according to the kinds of labor service they had to provide. However, Hung-wu was able to stabilize tax rates, promote irrigation works, and widen educational opportunity. It was hardly surprising that his exactions, which fell most heavily on the landlords and peasants of the rich Yangtze

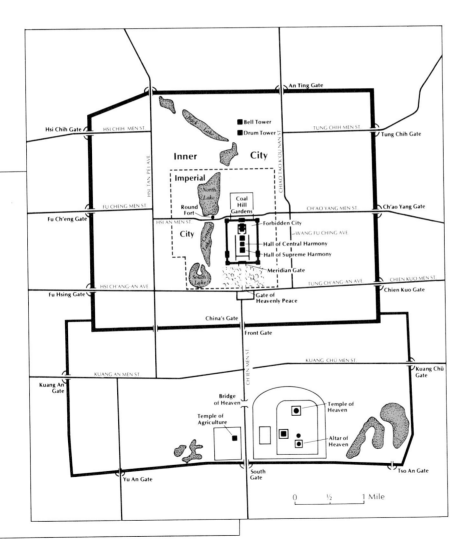

Valley, should have roused anger directed at the ruler in Nanking. For this reason and in order to defend the northern frontiers, the emperor Yung-lo (reigned 1403–1424) moved the capital back to Peking in 1421.

Hung-wu also succeeded in making the neighboring states, such as Korea, Vietnam, and Siam (Thailand), become vassals, with the duty of paying tribute in money, military aid, and ritual self-abasement. This tribute system, which allowed the neighboring autonomous kingdoms to trade with China provided they acknowledged China's symbolic suzerainty, notably by having their envoys perform the *kowtow* ("three kneelings and nine prostrations") at the Chinese court, can be traced to the Han dynasty. It was based on a Sinocentric view of foreign relations, and especially of Chinese relations with the countries of East and Southeast Asia, that remained dominant among China's rulers until the nineteenth century and made it difficult for them to understand the nature of the threat that technologically advanced nations would pose. Indeed, the Chinese found it difficult to regard foreigners as other than barbarians or to take their national pretensions seriously. They believed that foreign rulers

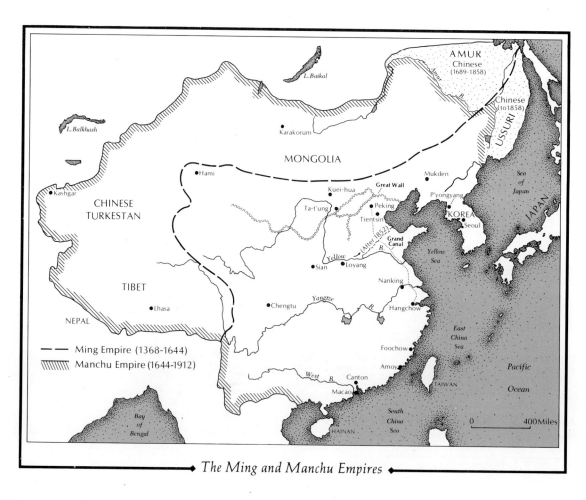

→ *The Ming and Manchu Empires* ←

would wish to recognize the universal suzerainty of the Chinese monarch, the Son of Heaven, and would desire to pay tribute to the Middle Kingdom. Tribute was to them merely the recognition of this superior position of China. In return the Chinese ruler would show paternal interest in the tributary state, offer it military aid against outside danger, and occasionally preach a lesson in good behavior. The outer world would thus gain the benefits of an orderly, Confucian style of society, expressed in a hierarchy of superior and inferior states designated by China, similar at the international level to the form of hierarchy imposed within Chinese society. During the Sung, because of China's military weakness, the Chinese emperors had reluctantly bought temporary peace by sending tribute missions to the northern kingdoms created by the nomadic peoples. The Ming now reasserted the universal suzerainty of the Son of Heaven and enforced elaborate rituals recognizing that suzerainty.

In many ways Korea was the archetypal vassal state. Although its people were of Altaic descent and unrelated to the Chinese, throughout its history it was deeply and often willingly under the influence of its vast neighbor. Emperor Wu-ti of the Han dynasty had conquered a Sinicized northern Korean state called Choson in 109–108 B. C., and China had then been able to exercise suzerainty over the whole peninsula for four centuries from its military capital at Pyongyang. In the fourth century, however, three purely Korean kingdoms emerged and threw off Chinese authority; but Chinese cultural influence remained strong. Buddhism and Confucianism were introduced from China, and the states themselves emulated Chinese governmental practices. With the reestablishment of strong government in China under the Sui and T'ang dynasties in the late sixth and early seventh century, the Chinese attempted to reincorporate Korea in their empire. However, driven back in a number of military campaigns and faced with the unification of the major part of Korea under the kingdom of Silla, the T'ang finally agreed that Silla should remain autonomous as a tributary state. For the next two centuries the state of Silla, which controlled two-thirds of the Korean peninsula, was a model vassal. It sent annual embassies to pay tribute, copied Chinese governmental institutions, and became deeply permeated with Chinese Buddhist thought. The overthrow of Silla and the formation under a new dynasty of a Korean state named Koryo further reinforced Chinese influence. The new capital at Kaesong was modeled on Ch'ang-an. Governmental institutions copied those of the T'ang, and a civil service examination was set up to test would-be bureaucrats in the Confucian classics. Tribute continued to be paid the Sung during the thirteenth century, although the Koreans found it necessary to pay tribute also to the Liao, who had taken northern China in the mid-tenth century.

The Koryo dynasty remained in power as a tributary of the Mongol rulers of China through the thirteenth and fourteenth centuries, although the Mongols annexed the northern third of the peninsula. The dynasty was overthrown in 1392, however, by a general named Yi Song-gye, who

Korea as a
Tributary State

seized the capital. The Yi dynasty, which he founded and which lasted until 1910, recognized the suzerainty of the Ming and for five centuries proved to be its most loyal vassal. The tribute missions, soon increased to three a year, became a primary influence for the reinforcement of Chinese political and cultural influence.

Yung-lo's Building of Peking

Yung-lo, the fourth son of Hung-wu, was as energetic and as stern as his father. His buildings in the northern capital established the physical setting for the lofty despotism that governed China for the rest of the Ming dynasty and for the whole of the succeeding dynasty, the Manchu, or Ch'ing (1644–1912). Yung-lo began the rebuilding of Peking in 1404 and completed it in 1421. It was designed like a series of Chinese boxes, one walled city inside another. At the core was the imperial palace, or Forbidden City, surrounded by a red brick wall and by a moat about two miles long. Around the Forbidden City was the Imperial City, itself surrounded by a wall fourteen miles long. The Forbidden City lay at the end of a wide north-south street, carefully laid out by the cosmologists so that the emperor, the Son of Heaven, would sit enthroned at what they regarded as the axis of the universe, where "earth and sky meet, where the four seasons merge, where the wind and rain are gathered in, and where *yin* and *yang* are in harmony."

The architects of the Forbidden City constructed one of the most exciting architectural progressions ever made. Passing through the vast Meridian Gate, one entered an inner court crossed by the meandering Golden Water River, and then moved through the Supreme Imperial Gate into the largest courtyard of the palace. The drama of this huge inner space was

A Courtyard of the Forbidden City, Peking
The Forbidden City, the Chinese imperial palace, was a complex of halls, gardens, and courtyards covering 250 acres in the center of Peking. Its basic plan was charted by the emperor Yung-lo, who began its construction in 1404. (© Gwendolyn Stewart, 1981)

Hall of Prayer for Good Harvests, Temple of Heaven, Peking
Each spring the emperor made a ceremonial visit to the temple to pray for a bountiful harvest in the coming months. The original fifteenth-century building was reconstructed after a fire in 1889. (© *Gwendolyn Stewart, 1981*)

achieved by the play of roof lines of golden tile, with upswinging eaves decorated with mythical ceramic animals and with golden dragons symbolizing the power and wisdom of the emperor. Dominating the view rose the marble platform and the red-columned Hall of Supreme Harmony, in which the emperor held audience. Beyond this lay two other halls, the first used by the emperor in preparing for his ceremonial appearance, the second for restricted receptions for non-Chinese envoys and scholars who had passed the highest examinations. Beyond these lay yet more halls, used by the Ming monarchs as their residences and given the delightful names of Palace of Heavenly Purity; Hall of Vigorous Fertility (used, curiously enough, for storing imperial seals); and Palace of Earthly Tranquillity. In the far northwestern corner, next to the Palace of Established Happiness and the Palace of Vigorous Old Age, was the aptly named Punishment Palace.

To the south of the city, in an area later walled in during the sixteenth century, Yung-lo sited two of the most important temples. At the Temple of Agriculture the emperor each year dug the first furrow of the season and made the sacrifices necessary for rain. At the Temple of Heaven the emperor came every spring to report to heaven on the happenings of the past year and, later, to sacrifice in the three-tiered, circular Hall of Prayer for Good Harvests, which no ordinary citizen was ever allowed to enter. The reconstructed temple remains one of the most beautiful monuments of Peking. Copying the example of the Chou and T'ang emperors at Ch'ang-an, Yung-lo also decided to build for his dynasty a great mausoleum twenty miles north of the city, where thirteen Ming emperors were eventually buried in elaborate rooms beneath earthen mounds, surrounded by vast quantities of jewelry, pottery, bronzes, gold, and silver.

Cultural Achievements Under the Ming Emperors

In Peking, Yung-lo continued the imperial patronage of letters and art. His largest project was the compilation of the *Yung-lo Encyclopedia*, which kept two thousand scholars busy for three years writing down or summarizing every significant piece of work in every field of Chinese scholarship for the past three thousand years. It comprised eleven thousand volumes. The passion for collecting facts continued throughout the Ming period and led to the writing in the sixteenth century of a famous medical encyclopedia and in the seventeenth century to a huge technological compilation. Original thought tended to be stifled, however; only rarely did one of the Ming scholars, such as the Neo-Confucian philosopher Wang Yang-ming (1472–1528), produce work of lasting importance. Wang's intuitive approach to Confucianism, emphasizing *hsin* ("mind-and-heart"), an intuitive knowledge of self achieved by meditation, rather than Chu Hsi's *li* ("principle"), encouraged more unconventional ideas and behavior. Although still within the confines of Confucian ethical precepts, this approach added richness to Chinese thought and literature during the sixteenth and seventeenth centuries.

The mainstream of Ming culture, as well as that of the succeeding Ch'ing dynasty, continued to be heavily conventional. The monarchy's formulation of the syllabi for the examinations was crucial. Since one passed the examinations largely by rote learning, it was unwise to be too adventurous in ideas. The emphasis on convention is also seen in painting under Yung-lo and the later Ming rulers. The Ming ordered leading painters to their court, gave them titles, and commissioned work from them; but they also imposed their own tastes, especially since some emperors were painters themselves. Hence pictures of birds and trees and fairly conservative landscapes were the main paintings produced. Nonetheless, a certain individuality broke through the prescribed patterns. Shen Chou (1427–1509), who avoided becoming an official and lived in his native city of Soochow, produced original landscapes, with a fine economy of brush strokes, that were clear, firm, and deceptively simple. The best known of the later Ming painters was, however, Tung Ch'i-ch'ang (1555–1636), who managed to combine conventional, elaborate landscapes with charm and the unexacting pleasure of observing nature.

The Overseas Expeditions, 1405–1433

One reason for the conservatism that affected every part of Chinese life was that, soon after Yung-lo's death, China turned in on itself, deliberately spurning the influences of the outer world. Yung-lo and his immediate successors had sent out seven great maritime expeditions led by a Moslem eunuch from Yunnan named Cheng Ho, to force Southeast Asia and, if possible, Indonesia, southern India, and even eastern Africa to become vassals of the emperor and send tribute missions. On the first voyage Cheng Ho's fleet of sixty-two ships, each of which carried five hundred men, reached southern India. Later voyages took him to the Persian Gulf and Aden, and other Chinese ships traded along the eastern coast of Africa. The Chinese thus had proved that in both navigation and shipbuilding, especially with their charts, compasses, and watertight compartments, they were well ahead of the Europeans, who were not to cross the Indian Ocean for another century. Moreover, the Chinese had shown that they were adept at long-distance trade, exchanging their silk, pottery, and tea for a vast array of goods like timber, spices, precious metals, copper, and rice. They had also begun the practice, to be followed by the European powers later, of policing the waters where their ships sailed, especially the northern seas, where Japanese pirates had begun to raid as far as the Chinese ports themselves.

After Cheng Ho's seventh expedition in 1431–1433, the Chinese suddenly abandoned these voyages, which they never resumed. Undoubtedly they had proved very expensive at a time when the building of Peking and the defense of the northern frontier against the reviving Mongols demanded very large resources. The psychological motivation was even more significant, however. The Ming rulers had decided to revive the traditional Chinese disapproval of commerce and of the merchant class, basing their political system on the bureaucracy and the gentry and their taxes on agriculture. Dredging of the Grand Canal, built by Kublai Khan to link Peking with the Yangtze Valley, even enabled the Ming emperors to abandon the

Scholar and Crane Returning Home, by Shen Chou
The painter Shen Chou was also a famous calligrapher who decorated his deceptively simple landscapes with poems of his own composition. He is considered the founder of the so-called Wu school of painters, who worked in or near the city of Soochow during the Ming period. [Nelson Gallery, Atkins Museum, Kansas City, Missouri (Nelson Fund)]

coastal shipping that had been used under the Yüan for transport of the tax-grain. Encouraging this land-based approach was a growing antiforeign emotion in China that had begun during the rule of the Mongols and was encouraged by the Ming rulers and by the Neo-Confucian scholars. Nonetheless, the early Ming naval expeditions had lasting effects in that they paved the way for overseas voyages of private merchant vessels from the China coast and for the migration of Chinese traders and laborers to many Southeast Asian lands. Today Chinese communities in Southeast Asia number in the millions.

The Decline of the Ming Dynasty

The Ming dynasty produced no further rulers with the vigor of Hung-wu or Yung-lo. Many came to the throne as children and never asserted personal power. The emperor who ruled the longest, Wan-li (reigned 1573–1620), preferred never to leave the Forbidden City except for an occasional venture into the city in a closed carriage. He spent enormous sums on extravagant entertainments and presents for his relatives and favorites and, when he was only twenty-six, ordered the construction for himself of the most grandiose of the Ming tombs. In the absence of imperial guidance, the palace eunuchs frequently took power, establishing a sinister type of secret police. Political struggles on the accession of a new emperor were often solved only by the execution of the political losers, although these struggles also gave the scholar-administrators an opportunity to try to regain power.

Meanwhile, both army and navy were in decline, as was the orderly fiscal system of the early Ming. A war to defeat two Japanese invasions of Korea at the end of the sixteenth century, though eventually successful, proved very costly in both lives and money; and increased taxes, coming at a time of agricultural troubles in the northwest, led to renewed rebellions. In 1644 Peking was seized by a rebel band led by an ex-postal official turned bandit, and the last Ming emperor hanged himself on a hill in the palace grounds. The rebel leader was not able to make himself emperor, as previous rebels had done, because the Ming general guarding the strategic pass across the Great Wall to Manchuria allied with the powerful Manchu state there. Manchu forces, aided by the general, took Peking; and the Manchu ruler, a five-year-old child advised by a regent, was proclaimed emperor of China.

THE EARLY MANCHU RULERS, 1644–1800

Creation of the Manchu State

The Manchu state created to the north of the Chinese border in the late sixteenth and early seventeenth centuries was already deeply influenced by Chinese culture. Chinese soldiers and administrators had been employed alongside the Manchu, and the rulers had deliberately chosen to follow the Chinese pattern of government and the Confucian teachings that formed its rationale. When they took possession of China, they intended to reinvigorate traditional Chinese society rather than to

Examination Cells (c. 1900) *Under the Ming and Manchu dynasties, degree candidates took examinations lasting several days in special cells constructed by the thousands in the provincial capitals. About five percent of those successful were permitted to proceed to the highest examination, administered only in Peking. (Library of Congress)*

impose alien notions of government. Their one preoccupation was to maintain the separation of the Manchus, who made up no more than two percent of the population, from the Chinese. They required that all state documents be written in Manchu as well as Chinese, banned intermarriage, and forbade Chinese to settle beyond a ditch planted with willows, known as the Willow Palisade, in their Manchurian homeland. Manchu women were forbidden to follow the Chinese practice of foot binding; however, Chinese men were compelled, as a symbol of inferiority, to braid their hair in a Manchu pigtail and to shave their foreheads. In Peking itself almost all Chinese were compelled to live in the southern part of the city within their own walls; the Manchus arrogated the Forbidden and the Imperial Cities to themselves. There the revenues of the Manchu imperial household were accumulated separately from the state finances, providing a source of patronage to the privileged Manchus.

With this separation institutionalized, the Manchu rulers attempted to win the cooperation of their Chinese subjects. The examination system was quickly reinstated; and the scholars were won over with prestigious appointments, including the task of writing a sympathetic official history of the overthrown Ming dynasty. Top administrative positions were shared equally between Chinese and Manchus, and lower positions were almost entirely in Chinese hands at the provincial and local level; most governors and almost all lower administrators were Chinese. Traditional scholarship was encouraged and even expanded; one five-thousand-volume encyclopedia was printed. Painting was especially favored, and some of the Manchu emperors were excellent Chinese calligraphers.

Manchu control over the military organization was ensured by the establishment of "banner garrisons" under Manchu generals. This entire force totaled no more than 350,000, but the garrisons were stationed in strategic places around Peking, on the northern borders, along the Grand Canal, and in some of the principal cities. In addition, a Chinese army used essentially as a police force, totaling six hundred thousand men and called the Green Standard Army, was responsible for maintaining order in localities within each province and especially for putting down bandits. For almost a century and a half the Manchu banner forces, which included Chinese and Mongols whom they had recruited, were undefeated. Following the capture of Peking in 1644, they pressed on into southern China, which was finally subjugated in 1681; and the island of Taiwan was conquered in 1683 with the help of Dutch ships. The Manchus also dealt with the threat from the resurgent Mongolian tribes and, in a long series of exhausting campaigns led at times by the emperors personally, brought both Inner and Outer Mongolia under control, as a territory under Manchu "residents," by the end of the seventeenth century. Tibet was made a protectorate during the first half of the eighteenth century, although the leader of the Tibetan Buddhists, the Dalai Lama, was recognized as the spiritual as well as the temporal ruler of the country.

Emperor K'ang-hsi

The early Manchu monarchs, like so many of the founding rulers of new Chinese dynasties, restored good government and encouraged economic prosperity. The most successful and the longest lived of these emperors were K'ang-hsi (reigned 1661–1722) and Ch'ien-lung (reigned 1736–1795). K'ang-hsi, who had completed the reconquest of the south, made six long tours there to inspect for himself the condition of the inland waterways, to meet with local officials, and to persuade the Chinese population of his own devotion to the Confucian classics. In Peking he built up the palace library and appointed numerous scholars to produce works of history and lexicography. To some extent he was also open to the new ideas that could be obtained from the West. He was particularly interested in talking with the Jesuit missionaries who, since the time of Matteo Ricci in 1601, had been allowed to reside in Peking. K'ang-hsi displayed his tolerance in his famous edict of 1692:

We have seriously considered this question of the Europeans. . . . They do not excite disturbances in the provinces, they do no harm to anyone . . . and their doctrine has nothing in common with that of the false sects of the empire, nor has it any tendency to excite sedition.

Since, then, we do not hinder either the Lamas of Tartary or the bonzes [Buddhist monks] of China from building temples . . . much less can we forbid these Europeans, who teach only good ways, from having also their churches and preaching their religion publicly in them.[3]

When, however, the pope later denounced Chinese ancestor worship, K'ang-hsi reacted by imposing sharp restrictions on Catholic missionaries.

[3]Nigel Cameron, *Barbarians and Mandarins, Thirteen Centuries of Western Travellers in China* (Chicago: The University of Chicago Press, 1976), pp. 248–249.

Ch'ien-lung set out to emulate his grandfather K'ang-hsi in every way, even down to the length of his reign: he abdicated after ruling for sixty years. He fought campaigns in central Asia, Burma, and Vietnam; made six tours of the southern provinces; patronized scholars; and wrote poetry himself. He banned Catholic proselytism but continued to allow the Jesuits to serve as imperial astronomers, employing the new science of Europe to set an accurate Chinese lunar calendar that was of great value to the farmers. Ch'ien-lung even permitted the European priests to design for him a new summer palace in baroque style (although with a Chinese roofline), similar to the many copies of Versailles being built in eighteenth-century Europe.

In spite of the cost of Ch'ien-lung's wars, Chinese prosperity was perhaps greater during his reign than ever before. Certainly the population increased at exceptional speed, from about 150 million in 1644 to about 300 million in 1800. At the basis of this demographic explosion was an agricultural revolution that involved the opening up of large mountainous areas of southern China; further improvement of the strains of rice; and the introduction of New World crops such as sweet potatoes, maize, and peanuts. In the last years of Ch'ien-lung's reign, however, there were already signs of the crisis that was to seize China in the nineteenth century—insufficient food for the growing population, military disorganization and feebleness, and government corruption made worse by Manchu callousness in selling offices and giving local officials short tenure. China's weakness was in fact so far advanced that the famous comments of the emperor Ch'ien-lung to the British ambassador sent to him in 1793 by King George III were already outdated:

The virtue and prestige of the Celestial Dynasty having spread far and wide, the kings of the myriad nations come by land and sea with all sorts of precious things. Consequently, there is nothing we lack, as your principal envoy and others have themselves observed. We have never set much store on strange or ingenious objects, nor do we need any more of your country's manufactures. . . .[4]

JAPANESE UNITY RESTORED: ODA NOBUNAGA, TOYOTOMI HIDEYOSHI, AND TOKUGAWA IEYASU

The chaotic fighting between rival provincial overlords known in Japanese history as the Age of Warring States (1467–1568) was brought to an end by the victories and subsequent reorganization of the country by three great military leaders: Oda Nobunaga (1534–1582), Toyotomi Hideyoshi (1536–1598), and Tokugawa Ieyasu (1542–1616). Although of the three only Ieyasu took the title of shogun (in 1603), all three had virtually dictatorial power, although acting in the name of the emperor. To-

[4]Cited in Teng Ssu-yü and John K. Fairbank, *China's Response to the West* (Cambridge, Mass.: Harvard University Press, 1954), p. 19.

gether they created a system of highly efficient, centralized government, based on administration through the local lords or *daimyo*, which gave Japan internal peace and effective, albeit repressive, government until the mid-nineteenth century. For this reason they are often compared with the so-called New Monarchs of Europe in the late fifteenth and early sixteenth centuries, who also ended generations of internal warfare by creating effective governmental machinery that would last for several centuries. The essential difference, however, was that in Europe the New Monarchs destroyed the political power of the feudal class, whereas in Japan the power of the feudal lords was harnessed and perpetuated.

Oda Nobunaga

Nobunaga was a minor lord from estates to the east of Kyoto who had drilled his local peasants into a reliable fighting force that was able to defeat one of the principal lords of Japan. Rebuilding his army with battalions carrying long spears and with brigades armed with the matchlock muskets introduced by the Portuguese in 1543, he captured Kyoto in 1568 and soon expanded his control over most of the island of Honshu, driving especially at the fortified Buddhist monasteries that were his greatest enemies. To strike fear in his potential opponents, Nobunaga massacred thousands of monks, women, and children at the headquarters of the Tendei sect on Mount Hiei overlooking Kyoto. At another Buddhist stronghold he built a wall around the monastery and burned twenty thousand people to death. Not surprisingly, many of his former opponents made terms with him; and he then permitted them to administer under his command. Although he was to overthrow him only five years later, he constructed for the shogun a fortress in Kyoto. For this task he conscripted twenty-five thousand workers, who were compelled to tear down Buddhist statues and use them in the castle's stonework. Nobunaga, sitting on a tiger-skin robe, supervised the building. He constructed for himself at Azuchi on Lake Biwa an even larger castle, which controlled the main road to the east. Using Azuchi as his governmental center, he reorganized the administration, standardized the currency, patronized the merchant class, and welcomed the Jesuits as an antidote to the hated Buddhist military orders. His work was still incomplete, however, when he was murdered by one of his own generals.

Toyotomi Hideyoshi

Nobunaga's principal supporter, a brilliant general of peasant birth named Hideyoshi, immediately took power, making his authority clear by surrounding the temple at Nobunaga's funeral with his own troops. He proved at least as fine a military campaigner as Nobunaga, and he was a better administrator. To ensure his own wealth and power, he took possession of the richest agricultural lands around Kyoto and built himself two castles, one at Momoyama overlooking Kyoto and another, even grander, at Osaka. (The rule of Hideyoshi is often called the Momoyama period). His most important general and eventual successor, Tokugawa Ieyasu, was isolated in the north of Honshu by the grant of vast estates around present-day Tokyo. Other vassals were given estates in areas where they were strangers.

After completing the conquest of the rebellious lords on the islands of Kyushu and Shikoku and getting Tokugawa Ieyasu to recognize his overlordship, Hideyoshi maintained control over the principal aristocrats by holding their wives and children as hostages in his court. A detailed land survey gave him accurate information for purposes of tax assessment. The possibility of local uprisings was eliminated by confiscating the weapons, and especially swords, owned by the peasantry. The class structure was frozen by laws forbidding individuals to change their occupations. Samurai, for example, were not permitted to engage in agriculture or trade. As an outlet for the military ardor of the warrior class, Hideyoshi sent an army of 160,000 soldiers to conquer Korea, which had refused to join him in an attempt to conquer China or even to permit his soldiers free passage across the country. His army ravaged much of Korea, provoking the Ming dynasty to send forces that compelled the Japanese to open prolonged negotiations. A second invasion force sent by Hideyoshi in 1597 was withdrawn precipitately after his death in 1598, and Japan gained almost nothing from its Korean military adventure.

Deciding that the Catholic missionaries, who may have converted as many as 300,000 Japanese, had become a danger, Hideyoshi ordered them banished. When the ban was evaded, he gave them warning by the crucifixion of twenty-six missionaries and their converts in 1597. Even this demonstration was ineffective, however, and within fifteen years the number of converts had doubled.

Hideyoshi nevertheless is remembered as more humane than Nobunaga, with a love of pageantry, good living, and exuberantly colored art, although according to one Jesuit he had "one weakness, namely a passionate delight in killing." His great castle at Osaka was the monument to his taste. Designed to withstand artillery attack, it was surrounded by eight miles of impregnable walls, within which winding streets offered further barriers to attacking troops. But the main tower-residence, rising seven stories high in a riot of swooping rooflines, impressed visitors by the lavishness of its proportions and its decorations. Even the locks and hinges in Hideyoshi's apartments were of gold, and he personally would point out to visitors: "This room which you see here is full of gold, this one of silver; this other compartment is full of bales of silk and damask, that one with robes, while these rooms contain costly swords and weapons."[5] All the inner walls were decorated with wood carvings of flowers, animals, and birds; and movable panels and screens were decorated with brightly colored paintings. Other lords followed Hideyoshi's lead, so that the principal buildings remaining from this period are the elegant keeps of such castles as the White Heron Castle at Himeji.

[5] Cited in Michael Cooper, ed., *They Came to Japan: An Anthology of European Reports on Japan, 1543–1640* (Berkeley and Los Angeles: University of California Press, 1965), pp. 136–137.

Toyotomi Hideyoshi (1536–1598)
Hideyoshi was a soldier of peasant stock who gained control of the government of Japan by his military skills. The long samurai sword by his side reminded the lords called to appear before him of his prowess in combat. (Hokuku Shrine, Osaka, Japan)

Ieyasu and the Foundation of the Tokugawa Shogunate

Tokugawa Ieyasu was already fifty-six when Hideyoshi died and had fought for both Nobunaga and Hideyoshi. Although he was a regent for Hideyoshi's infant child Hideyori, he led his armies against the other leading daimyo and compelled the emperor to name him shogun in 1603. At first content to leave Hideyori confined in Osaka castle, he finally attacked the castle and forced Hideyori, the last potential obstacle to his own family's power, to commit suicide. The Tokugawa were then able to retain predominance until 1868.

Although Ieyasu built a new palace in Kyoto on the site Nobunaga had chosen, from which he could maintain liaison with the imperial court, he felt that it was unwise for the military government to remain so close to the scheming courtiers. He decided to govern Japan from his castle at Edo (Tokyo), where he had made his headquarters in 1590. Thus, although Kyoto remained the imperial capital, Japan was in fact governed from Edo. Ieyasu again reshuffled the fiefs, ensuring that his own traditional supporters would own the rich, strategic central estates, whereas newer adherents, known as the outer daimyo, were located in remote areas where they could do little damage.

All daimyo, however, were compelled to spend half their time in Edo and to leave their wives and children as hostages when they returned to their estates. In this way a centralized government system was created by placing strictly defined duties on a hierarchy of lords whose position derived from their family's previous relation to the Tokugawa. Although strictly supervised, the daimyo were responsible for local government and justice, as well as for providing military forces to the shogun when called on. Members of the samurai class, deprived of their normal occupation as

Garden of Sambo-in Temple, Kyoto
Hideyoshi set the style for the elaborate gardens of the following century when in 1598 he ordered the reconstruction of the ruined Buddhist temple of Sambo-in and brought eight hundred carefully chosen rocks from all parts of Japan to place among its lakes and waterfalls. (Consulate General of Japan)

warriors by the enforcement of internal peace, and forbidden to work the land, grouped at the daimyo's headquarters, where they could retain their rigid code and their skills as swordsmen.

The Tokugawa family assigned the members of the imperial court clearly defined ceremonial and religious duties and supplied them with the income necessary to maintain their palaces. This period produced the two most charming residences and gardens of the imperial family, both built into the hillsides around Kyoto—the restful simplicity of the Katsura palace, whose grounds were designed by Japan's greatest garden planner, Kobori Enshu (1579–1647), and the Shugakuin palace, designed by the emperor himself.

Ieyasu was commemorated in his shrine built at Nikko in the mountains north of Tokyo, where the extravagantly carved gateways and soaring pagoda come closest to resembling the baroque creations of contemporary Europe. Just before his death the shogun was planning his own deification; the shrine is dedicated to him as the "East-Illuminating Incarnation of Bodhisattva."

The comparative contributions of the three military rulers to the reestablishment of Japanese prosperity—force, guile, and patience—were summarized in a favorite Japanese story. When a cuckoo fails to sing, Nobunaga declares, "I'll kill the cuckoo if it won't sing." Hideyoshi remarks, "I shall invite it to sing." Ieyasu sits down, "I'll wait until the cuckoo does sing." By their complementary talents, they had reunified Japan.

JAPAN UNDER THE TOKUGAWA SHOGUNATE

Perhaps the most startling decision of the Tokugawa shogunate founded by Ieyasu was to enforce the almost total isolation of the islands, which was to last until the mid-nineteenth century. While the West advanced through the great intellectual and technological changes of the Renaissance, the Enlightenment, and the industrial revolution, Japan turned in on itself. Falling behind technologically within their rigidly stabilized society, the Japanese nevertheless maintained a prosperous economy, booming cities, and a fecund intellectual and cultural life that became increasingly differentiated from that of the rest of the world.

The Closed Country

Japan had always prized its contacts with China and, at least for its religious message, with India. When the first Europeans reached Japan in the mid-sixteenth century, the Japanese were prepared to learn from them as well. A Portuguese ship landed in Kyushu in 1543 and was soon followed by other ships bringing silks from China and Jesuit missionaries from Goa in India, among whom in 1549 was Saint Francis Xavier. Both traders and missionaries found the Japanese honorable, eager for trade and religious and technical knowledge, and grateful for their presence. Winning the support and occasionally the conversion of some of the coastal daimyo—especially the ruler of the little seaport of Nagasaki, which became the center

Arrival in Japan of a Portuguese Trading Ship, (Sixteenth Century)

The arrival of the first Portuguese ships, with their cargoes of Chinese silks, guns, and unfamiliar plants, caused great excitement in Japan. The strange foreigners were frequently depicted on Namban-byobu, or "screens of the Southern Barbarians." (Asian Art Museum of San Francisco, the Avery Brundage Collection)

of Portuguese trade—the Portuguese eventually were received by Nobunaga, Hideyoshi, and Ieyasu.

Nobunaga welcomed the Christians as allies in his attack on the militant Buddhist sects and for their knowledge of firearms and ammunition. Hideyoshi also tolerated the missionaries at first, although by the 1590s he had decided that their influence, especially that of the Spanish Franciscans, was undermining his power. Despite persecution the Christians remained influential; and Ieyasu and his son determined to drive out the Catholic missionaries and force their Japanese converts to renounce Catholicism. This program was soon extended to a full-scale policy of isolation from all foreign influences. All Europeans were expelled, except for the Dutch, who were allowed to bring one shipload of goods annually to a tiny island in Nagasaki harbor. Trade with China and Korea was severely restricted. No Japanese was permitted to travel abroad, and those living abroad were forbidden to return, under pain of death. No oceangoing ships were to be constructed. Even Western ideas were kept out of the country by means of a ban on the import of European books. The success of this program is proved by the fact that the Japanese government was able to abandon the use of firearms and to restore the sword as the principal weapon and, consequently, the samurai as the principal warrior.

Social Stability and Economic Prosperity

Successfully isolated from disruptive foreign influences, the shoguns set out to prevent political or social change. The vested interests of the samurai class, who were officially recognized as part of the highest military—and hence social—group, formed the cement of the social system. The samurai were separated from the rest of society by dress and by the privilege of carrying a long and a short sword, but they were often employed as government bureaucrats rather than as warriors. By compelling the daimyo to maintain residences in Edo (Tokyo) and on their estates, the shogun ensured that the great lords would be constantly in financial difficulties, while under the supervision of the central authorities. At the same time, since they were expected to carry out all local government, including expensive public works, the daimyo found it difficult to convert their local authority into independent political power. The remaining classes—peasants, artisans, and merchants—were also expected to remain strictly within their own group.

For the peasant, increased agricultural production—a result of greater specialization, improved seeds and technology, and adoption of commercial crops like cotton—slowly provided a higher standard of living. The principal source of change in the society was the advance of internal trade and the growth of cities. Internal peace enabled goods to flow more freely, either by the coastal shipping that was still permitted or along the great highways, such as the famous Tokaido Road between Edo and Kyoto. The annual journeys of the daimyo between their home estates and Edo were often vast expeditions of hundreds of people who required lodging, food, and supplies.

The greatest stimulus to economic development was the founding of castle-cities in the last two decades of the sixteenth and the first two decades of the seventeenth century. Beginning with the creation of Azuchi castle by Nobunaga, every daimyo felt compelled to build himself a massive fortress intended not merely for defense, but also as a new administrative center. The samurai were forced to leave their own villages, where their country houses were burned down, and to reside around the fortress under the supervision of the daimyo. Since the samurai were not permitted to engage in trade, a merchant class also congregated in the growing city at the base of the castle to supply the needs of the daimyo's household and administration and those of the transplanted samurai. These castle-cities were almost always new creations in undeveloped countryside, chosen for their strategic location commanding avenues of communication and for their central position among the open farmland of the daimyo's domains (han). Earlier cities, which had been formed around religious communities or around harbors engaged in oceanic trade, went into decline; many of their merchants simply transferred their activities to the castle-cities, where they found both a growing market for their goods and the protection of the daimyo. As a result, this forty-year period of castle-city growth was perhaps one of the most rapid periods of urbanization in world history. The network of castle-cities formed the urban structure of modern Japan. Kyoto, Nagasaki, Yokohama, Kobe, and the cities of Hokkaido are the only important cities in contemporary Japan that were not founded as castle-cities.

The Castle-Cities

Increase in the Urban Population

The population of the cities grew throughout the Tokugawa period. By 1700 Kyoto and Osaka each had a population of 300,000, and Edo already had reached 1 million. By that time ten percent of Japan's population lived in cities of 10,000 inhabitants or more. Until about 1680 Kyoto retained its primacy as the cultural and even the economic center of the country. Then Osaka, the booming center of commerce and banking, predominated, to be slowly overtaken by Edo. It was hardly surprising that many peasants attempted to move into the cities, although the Tokugawa government was never able to enforce on them the conduct recommended by one of its political philosophers:

Peasants and their wives may drink neither tea nor sake and are forbidden to smoke. . . . The peasants are people without spirit. They must not feed rice to their wives or children during the harvest season, but must put it aside as seed grain. They must eat millet, vegetables, and other coarse foods in place of rice. . . . The husband must work in the fields, and the wife must weave. Both must work at night making straw ropes or baskets with great care. . . . They must wear only garments of cotton or hemp, never silk. . . . They are forbidden to play games.[6]

Many samurai also moved into the cities, as did artisans, students from the schools on the feudal estates, and youngsters, usually women, who found work in the entertainment districts. The cities also provided opportunities for those of creative ability in writing, painting, music, or acting. The merchant families dominated both the economic and the cultural life of the cities. Many of these merchants were *nouveaux riches* like the newly established capitalists of contemporary Paris. Others had moved to the cities after making their fortunes in the provinces, like the rich Mitsui family, originally brewers of sake in Omi, who branched out in Edo into banking and commerce. Merchants like these could become extremely wealthy, especially since taxation was light and the main cities were under the direct protection of the shogun.

How to make (and lose) money was one of the main themes in the work of two of Japan's favorite writers, the novelist Ihara Saikaku (1642–1693) and Chikamatsu Monzaemon (1653–1725). In one of Saikaku's stories a group of young men are sent to a miser to learn how to become rich. After they have all become hungry and are expecting dinner, the miser remarks: "Well, now, you have kindly talked with me from early evening, and it is high time refreshments were served. But not to provide refreshments is one way of becoming a millionaire. The noise of the mortar which you heard when you first arrived was the pounding of starch for the covers of the account book."[7]

[6]Cited in Louis Frédéric, *Japan: Art and Civilization* (London: Thames and Hudson, 1971), p. 409.
[7]Cited in R. H. P. Mason and J. G. Caiger, *A History of Japan* (New York: Free Press, 1973), p. 193.

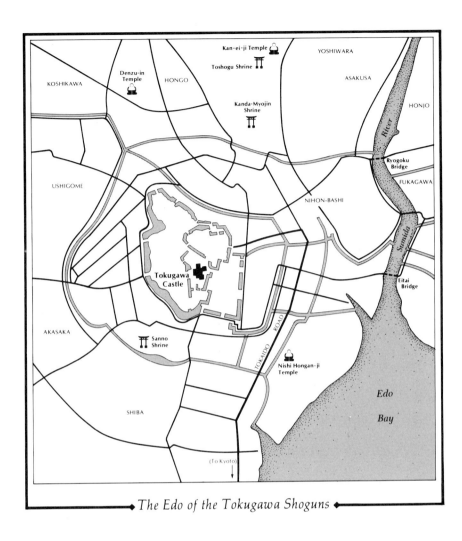

The Edo of the Tokugawa Shoguns

Edo—unlike Nara and Kyoto, which had been deliberately copied from the Chinese capital of Ch'ang-an—was virtually unplanned.* The city grew up around a small castle built in the fifteenth century but transformed by Tokugawa Ieyasu at the beginning of the sixteenth century. As the principal residence of the shogun after 1603, the palace was expanded and beautified, surrounded by a lovely park, and cut off from the rest of the city by a moat. The palace was capable of sheltering eighty thousand soldiers. Around the castle the daimyo began to construct mansions in which they could spend the required months of residence; some of these were sur-

*Edo was renamed Tokyo ("eastern capital") in 1868, when the imperial court moved there from Kyoto.

The Expansion of Edo

rounded by beautiful gardens, such as the Koraku-en (1625), which still survives. Smaller homes were built near them for lesser lords receiving a stipend from the shogun.

The merchant quarter of the city began at the most important bridge, the Nihon-bashi (Japan Bridge), which was built at almost exactly the same time as Henry IV's Pont Neuf in Paris and served much the same function of linking the palace to the middle-class districts. Nihon-bashi was, however, the terminus of the Tokaido Road and four other major highways, and it came to serve the function of the umbilicus stone in ancient Rome—the point from which all distances in the country were calculated. Houses around the river and its many marshy tributaries were usually one-story and, to cut down the risk of fire, roofed in wooden tiles rather than straw. Visitors from Europe found the streets "so clean that you might well think that nobody ever walks along them." Each street was reserved for the members of a different profession, such as carpenters, cobblers, blacksmiths, and tailors. A whole section of town specialized in a particular foodstuff. Fresh fish was always available from the fish market, where both saltwater and freshwater fish were kept in tubs. Fruit and vegetables were sold in yet another district. Inns were, rather inconveniently, also grouped together; and horses for hire were on their own street. In the east of the city were the dockyards, where the coastal shipping brought in most of the needed provisions, which could then be transported to almost any part of the city on the small canals. Nearby was an area occupied by the very poorest class, who, almost like the outcastes of India, were regarded as impure and required to do the lowest work in leather tanneries or slaughterhouses. A complete entertainment district with restaurants and brothels, called Yoshiwara, was officially tolerated.

The first shoguns also provided for the foundation of Buddhist monasteries, usually on the little hills near the city; and gradually more temples were constructed in the city itself. Although many became wealthy and the centers of secular as well as religious education, their buildings never rivaled the shrines of Kyoto. Very few have survived Tokyo's many fires and earthquakes.

Kano Painting and Kabuki Theater

The early shoguns were patrons of painting and set up a school of art near the palace at the Kaji-bashi Gate. Here Tan-yu and his disciples practiced a Chinese style of painting known as the Kano school after the Kano family who had created it during the Ashikaga period in Kyoto. Since these painters specialized in colorful painting of sliding doors and walls, they were also employed in decoration of the shogun's palace. This somewhat rarefied art, which made little effort to break with its Chinese originals, was popular with the court aristocracy. However, in a far more robust and entertaining form of art, the portrayal of the life of the city streets and palaces of entertainment in what was known as *ukiyo-e* ("pictures of the floating world") was more widely popular. These entertaining pictures, fre-

Cooling Off at Ryogoku Bridge, by Okamura Masanobu

In the many series of woodblock prints known as pictures of the floating world (ukiyo-e), Japanese artists depicted such subjects as the geisha houses of the entertainment quarter of Edo (Tokyo). (Honolulu Academy of Arts, Honolulu, Hawaii)

quently reproduced by the colored block printing developed in Edo in the seventeenth century, provide an insight into the daily life of Edo, with its theaters, taverns, geisha houses, and markets. The style reached great artistic heights in the eighteenth and early nineteenth centuries, especially in the series called *bijin* ("beautiful women") of Suzuki Harunobu (1725–1770) and the well-known series of scenes along the Tokaido Road ("The Fifty-Three Stages of the Tokaido") of Ando Hiroshige (1797–1858).

A similar divergence appeared in theater. The court, in both Kyoto and Edo, continued to favor the No drama. Most city dwellers, however, flocked to puppet shows called *bunraku* and to a new form of theater, created in Kyoto at the beginning of the seventeenth century, called *kabuki*. By the 1670s three kabuki theaters were operating in the Negi-machi district beyond the Nihon-bashi Bridge, often to the scandal of the authorities, who had already felt compelled in 1629 to forbid women to act, thus creating a tradition that has lasted to this day of having men take the female roles. Kabuki plays could be either historical dramas or contemporary romances; but they were always spectacular, employing gorgeous costumes, a large orchestra, a chorus to chant the narrative, and actors who were idolized like matinee stars. The favorite kabuki play of all time has been *Chushin-gura*, the true story of the forty-seven samurai who in 1703 avenged their former lord and then uncomplainingly committed suicide on the orders of the government.

The Decline of the Shogunate

The rise and decline of the Tokugawa shogunate is sometimes compared with the evolution of a Chinese dynasty. The first three shoguns were strong, efficient rulers who succeeded in creating a governmental system that could operate for a time regardless of the ability of future shoguns. Throughout the entire seventeenth century Japan remained peaceful and prosperous. During the eighteenth century, however, signs of weakness appeared. A number of natural calamities struck, including an eruption of Mount Fuji and a number of earthquakes, typhoons, and fires. As a result the peasantry suffered from the threat of starvation, with at least twenty-two serious famines occurring between 1690 and 1840. Decline in the tax income of the shogunate reduced its effectiveness, although there were occasional efforts under such shoguns as Yoshimune (ruled 1716–1745) to restore the vigor of the old system. Thus, although Japan's isolation allowed the feudalistic nature of the Tokugawa system to survive, it was slowly decaying from within, as the many rural and even occasional city disturbances gave evidence. Its own insecurity was further shown by its need to rely on a nationwide system of spies that fostered a sense of distrust and mutual fear among the population—without, however, being especially effective in strengthening the shoguns.

By the first half of the nineteenth century, the justification for the continuance of the system of government of the Tokugawa shogunate had been undermined. Its emphasis on an unchanging agrarian economy was at variance with the reality of the growing strength of the urban merchant class and even of a profit-minded stratum of wealthy peasants in the countryside. Awareness of the technological and military superiority of the Western powers had come from acquaintance with the Dutch traders at Nagasaki. This superiority was demonstrated even more effectively by Western encroachments on China. Meanwhile, the very classes on which the shoguns had based their rule, most notably the daimyo and the samurai, were in great economic difficulties, not least because of the frequent debasements of the currency to which the shoguns had resorted as short-term solutions to their own financial problems. Nevertheless, the system might well have continued to function, however inefficiently, had not the Japanese been driven to reexamine the value of the shogunate when it proved incapable of maintaining national autonomy in the face of American and Western European intervention in the 1850s and 1860s.

EUROPEAN INFLUENCE IN SUB-SAHARAN AFRICA, 1400–1800

The many achievements of the native states of sub-Saharan Africa—whether savanna empires like the Songhai, forest empires like Benin, or trading city-states like the Swahili—are proof that into the sixteenth century and later the people of Africa had maintained an indigenous civilization of great variety and subtlety. The entry of five European powers—Portugal, Spain, England, France, and the Netherlands—between the fifteenth and eighteenth centuries began the process of undermining African independence that was to be completed in the late nineteenth century with the annexation by European states of almost every part of the continent.

The Portuguese were at first welcomed as they stopped at the Atlantic ports of Africa in the fifteenth century. The local rulers not only were curious to know more about Europe, but also saw specific benefits for themselves in opening up relations with the Portuguese. The Europeans in fact made a major contribution to Africa by bringing new foodstuffs, including tomatoes, pineapple, peanuts, corn (maize), and manioc (cassava). They also brought manufactured goods and guns. Moreover, although the first Portuguese captured and enslaved whatever Africans they could from the beaches, what was regarded as a mutually beneficial trade pattern was soon worked out between them and the local rulers. The Portuguese were permitted to establish fortified trading posts, beginning with their settlement at Arguin Island and with their fort at Elmina in present-day Ghana; and they were supplied by the rulers of the coastal states with gold, cotton textiles, ivory, and slaves.

At first the Portuguese took only a few thousand slaves a year, sending them to Portugal itself or to their Atlantic islands. With the opening of the Americas, however, and especially with the decimation of the native population of the Caribbean, and of Central and South America by European diseases and overwork, African slaves were wanted in vastly greater numbers, especially for the plantations of lowland tropical America. Spain legalized the sale of Africans in its American colonies in 1510, and from then on the trade boomed. The king of Kongo, who had so admired the Portuguese that he had renamed his capital São Salvador, complained in 1526 that because of the slavers "our country is being completely depopulated." With the entry of the Dutch, the English, and the French into the slave trade from the late sixteenth and early seventeenth centuries on, the numbers of slaves demanded and the horrors of the "middle passage" to America increased. It has been estimated recently that between eleven and thirteen million Africans were sold into slavery between the fifteenth and nineteenth centuries, and many more died during capture or waiting in the factories for the arrival of the slavers.

Oddly, there seems little proof that depopulation occurred, except in isolated cases like the kingdom of Kongo. Other results were certain and iniquitous, however. In order to supply the Europeans, the African rulers embarked on constant wars on their neighbors, since they preferred to sell prisoners of war rather than their own subjects. In order to make war, they required more guns, and, to buy guns, needed more slaves to sell. Moreover, many of the Africans sold into slavery were the most able-bodied and the most skilled in tropical agriculture and metalworking—precisely the people most needed by the African states themselves. By taking large numbers of older children and young adults, the slavers also unbalanced the demography of African society, leaving behind young children and the elderly and increasing the proportion of the population dependent on the labor of others. Concentration on this trade in human beings stunted the African economies, which, as we have seen, possessed trading skills, advanced manufactures in metal and textiles, and the urban organizing network essential for a rapid advance into a modern economic system similar to that created in Europe in the late Middle Ages.

French Slave Ship, 1772
French participation in the slave trade grew rapidly in the eighteenth century, bringing vast profits to the merchants of Nantes and Bordeaux. The slaves were chained in specially constructed holds deep in the ship. (Cliché Ville de Nantes—Musées du Chateau des Ducs de Bretagne)

The deleterious effects of the European penetration were at first local-ized. The first notable blow to the African economy was the Portuguese de-struction of many of the Swahili trading cities at the beginning of the six-teenth century; and, when the Arabs from Oman finally drove out the Portuguese from the Swahili cities in the late seventeenth century, they re-mained to exploit the slight economic resurgence that followed. Although the Portuguese were driven from the interior of southern Africa, where they had attempted to penetrate the valley of the Zambezi, they clung to Mozambique. They and the Omani Arabs on the Swahili coast began to de-velop the slave trade in East Africa in the eighteenth century and were soon joined by French and British traders as well. Arab-controlled Zanzibar had become the center of the East African slave trade by the 1800s. Portu-gal also brought about the fall of its one-time admirer, the kingdom of Kongo. In 1556 it supported a destructive war for independence by Ngola (called Angola by the Portuguese), one of Kongo's vassal states. It then em-barked on uncontrolled raiding for slaves throughout Ngola and finally sent its troops and mercenaries to destroy the governments of the Kongo in 1665 and of Ngola in 1671.

The inland states of the northern savanna, notably the Songhai Empire and Kanem-Bornu, suffered first from the disruption of the trans-Sahara trade network, as the Portuguese and then the Dutch opened up the Atlan-tic sea routes to Europe and to the East. Songhai, as we have seen, was con-quered by a Moroccan army in 1591; but no contacts were formed with the Moroccan centers of Fez and Marrakesh; and the once-great cities of Timbuctu, Jenne, and Gao began to decline. They became the prey of no-mads like the Tuareg of the Sahara Desert, against whom they had once stood as defensive barriers. Along the West African coast, however, a num-ber of states grew strong with European arms and the profits of European trade.

The first to expand were Oyo and Benin, which had received the Por-tuguese in the fifteenth and sixteenth centuries and proved to be more than their equals in trading skills. (Benin, secure behind its mangrove swamps, was even able to prosper without participating on a large scale in the slave trade.) After the founding in 1672 of the Royal Africa Company, English ships began to trade on a large scale with the small city-states that controlled the many mouths of the Niger River at its delta, especially in the eighteenth century with the slave center of Bonny. Here the retainers of local leaders would depart in canoes large enough for a hundred and twenty people, to the sound of drums, horns, and gongs, and would return six days later with between fifteen hundred and two thousand slaves, whom they sold to the slavers the same evening for iron bars, cotton rolls, and cowrie shells. The price was thirteen bars of iron for a male slave and ten for a female.

As the English stepped up their demand for slaves, in order to supply Spanish America in accordance with the Treaty of Utrecht in 1713, the state of Dahomey fought its way into a large share of the slave trade.

Figurehead from Kingdom of Oyo, West Africa
The facial markings indicate that the person depicted was of the lineage of the Alafin, or king, of Oyo, the most powerful kingdom of the Yo-ruba peoples. Only Yoruba kings were permitted to wear this type of patterned, beaded garment and head-dress. (Lowie Museum of Anthropology, University of California, Berkeley)

Dahomey fascinated the Europeans by enrolling its women in the army in all-female regiments like the mythical Amazon warriors, as well as by its authoritarian system of slave plantations, secret police, and state control of the economy. Even more powerful among the new states was the Ashanti Empire in the area of contemporary Ghana. The strong Ashanti army took taxes from all trade passing across their territory and gained an important hold on the supply of gold to the European traders, especially the Dutch, who had taken over the trading fort of Elmina from the Portuguese. The Ashanti capital of Kumasi became an impressive city by 1800, with broad streets, comfortable houses, many markets, and Moslem colleges of learning. Dahomey and the Ashanti Empire both remained strong into the late nineteenth century. The French defeated Dahomey in 1893; the British conquered Ashanti in 1896 and made it part of the Gold Coast colony in 1901.

The European destruction of native African civilizations was thus a long process, extending over five centuries and aided by African collaboration. Moreover, it was never complete. African traditions of art and architecture, poetry and music, religion and society survived, to be fostered again when independence finally was restored in the mid-twentieth century.

SUGGESTED READING

Detailed and reliable surveys of the history of the Ottoman Empire in the early modern period include Stanford J. Shaw, *History of the Ottoman Empire and Modern Turkey*, vol. 1, *Empire of the Gazis: The Rise and Decline of the Ottoman Empire, 1280–1808* (1976) and M. A. Cook, *A History of the Ottoman Empire to 1730* (1976). Much information on the economic situation of the Ottoman empire will be found in Fernand Braudel's *The Mediterranean and the Mediterranean World in the Time of Philip II* (1972). On Ottoman society, see Halil Inalcik, *The Ottoman Empire: The Classical Age, 1300–1600* (1973). Mohammed II's attempt to repopulate Constantinople is analyzed in Inalcik's article, "The Policy of Mohammed II Toward the Greek Population of Istanbul and the Byzantine Buildings of the City," *Dumbarton Oaks Papers*, no. 23 (1970), pp. 213–249. On the life of Suleiman the Magnificent, the only reliable studies in English are Inalcik's "The Heyday and Decline of the Ottoman Empire," *Cambridge History of Islam*, vol. 1 (1970), pp. 324–353, and V. J. Parry, "The Ottoman Empire, 1520–1566," *New Cambridge Modern History*, vol. 2 (1958), pp. 510–533.

Constantinople under Suleiman and later is described in Raphaela Lewis, *Everyday Life in Ottoman Turkey* (1971) and in Bernard Lewis, *Istanbul and the Civilization of the Ottoman Empire* (1963). Further details may be found in two books in French: Robert Mantran, *La Vie quotidienne à Constantinople au temps de Soliman le Magnifique et ses successeurs* (1965) and, also by Mantran, *Istanbul dans la seconde moitié du XVIIe siècle* (1962).

Safavid Persia can be explored in the rather old-fashioned work, Percy M. Sykes, *A History of Persia*, 2 vols. (1930). On the buildings of Shah Abbas, see Laurence Lockhart, "Shah Abbas's Isfahan," in Arnold Toynbee, ed., *Cities of Destiny* (1967), pp. 210–225, and the brief account in Lockhart's *Persian Cities* (1960), pp. 18–30, which also discusses the two previous capitals, Qazvin and Tabriz.

Percival Spear, *India: A Modern History* (1972) provides a short introduction to the Mogul emperors; H. G. Rawlinson, *India: A Short Cultural History* (1952) and Bamber Gascoigne, *The Great Moghuls* (1971) are more graphic in the use of contemporary witnesses. V. A. Smith, *Akbar the Great Mogol* (1958) is pleasant reading, but its research is somewhat outdated; more recent scholarship is presented in J. M. Shalat, *Akbar* (1964).

The autobiographies of Babur and Jahangir remain fascinating. See *Memoirs of Zehir-ed-Din Muhammed Baber* (1826), translated by John Leyden and William Erskine, and *The Tuzuk-I-Jahangiri or Memoirs of Jahangir* (1909), translated by Alexander Rogers and Henry Beveridge. A beautifully illustrated introduction to Delhi, Agra, and Fatehpur Sikri is given by Gavin Hambly in *Cities of Mogul India* (1968), and Martin Hürlimann mingles photographs of contemporary and historic India in *Delhi; Agra; Fatehpur Sikri* (1965). Contemporary visitors to the Mogul capitals have left fascinating memoirs, including *The Commentary of Father Monserrate, S.J.: On His Journey to the Court of Akbar* (1922), translated by J. S. Hoyland, and François Bernier, *Travels in the Mogul Empire (1656–1668)* (1934), translated by Archibald Constable. Bernier includes a long study of Delhi and Agra, which he compares to the Paris of Louis XIV. Standard studies of Mogul culture include S. C. Welch, *The Art of Mughul India* (1963) and Percy Brown, *Indian Painting Under the Mughals* (1924). Some of the older guidebooks provide a glimpse of an India that still had much in common with the country of Shah Jahan. These include E. B. Havell, *A Handbook to Agra and the Taj* (1904); Frederick Cooper, *The Handbook for Delhi* (1865); and Colonel Sir Gordon Hearn, *The Seven Cities of Delhi* (1928). A survey of social customs including *purdah*—the veiling of women that the Hindus adopted from the Moslems—is given in D. N. Chopra, *Life and Letters Under the Mughals* (1976).

Perhaps the best introduction to Ming China is offered by the sixteenth-century Jesuit Matteo Ricci in the translation by Louis J. Gallagher, *China in the Sixteenth Century: The Journals of Matthew Ricci, 1583–1610* (1953). Testimony of other European visitors is presented in the fine study by G. Francis Hudson, *Europe and China; A Study of Their Relations from the Earliest Times to 1800* (1961) and in Donald Lach, *China in the Eyes of Europe: The Sixteenth Century* (1968). More specialized studies of the form of government include two books by Charles O. Hucker, *The Traditional Chinese State in Ming Times (1368–1644)* (1961) and *The Censorial System of Ming China* (1966). The failure of Chinese sea power is evident in So Kwan-wai, *Japanese Piracy in Ming China During the Sixteenth Century* (1975). The troubled life of a scholar-poet illustrates the disorder at the beginning of the Ming period in Frederick W. Mote, *The Poet Kao Ch'i (1336–1374)* (1962). The painting and architecture are analyzed in detail in Laurence Sickman and Alexander Soper, *The Art and Architecture of China* (1956).

The two most important of the Manchu (Ch'ing) emperors are placed within the perspective of Confucian concepts of political power in Jonathan D. Spence, *Emperor of China: Self-Portrait of K'ang-hsi* (1974) and Harold L. Kahn, *Monarchy in the Emperor's Eyes: Image and Reality in the Ch'ien-lung Reign* (1971). On the Manchu military system and government, see Franz Michael, *The Origin* of *Manchu Rule in China* (1942). The impact of economic growth on population is documented in Ho Ping-ti, *Studies on the Population of China, 1368–1953* (1959). Frederic Wakeman, Jr., *The Fall of Imperial China* (1975) is a readable general work on the entire Manchu dynasty.

For Peking, see two excellent surveys: Roderick MacFarquhar and the Editors of the Newsweek Book Division, *The Forbidden City* (1972) and Lin Yutang, *Imperial Peking: Seven Centuries of China* (1961). See also the two architectural studies by Osvald Siren, *The Walls and Gates of Peking* (1924) and *The Imperial Palaces of Peking* (1926).

The impressions of the European travelers who visited Japan before the imposition of the "closed country" policy are usefully grouped by Michael Cooper in *They Came to Japan: An Anthology of European Reports on Japan, 1543–1640* (1965). These can be compared with the reports of one of the few Europeans allowed to visit after isolation was declared, in Engelbert Kaempfer, *The History of Japan* (1906), especially vol. III, which was originally written at the end of the seventeenth century.

A. L. Sadler, *The Maker of Modern Japan: The Life of Tokugawa Ieyasu* (1937) is a somewhat old-fashioned description of the founding of the Tokugawa shogunate. It should be supplemented by the more detailed analyses of Conrad D. Totman, *Politics in the Tokugawa Bakufu, 1600–1843* (1967) and Peter Duus, *Feudalism in Japan* (1969). For the world of the peasant, see Thomas C. Smith, *The Agrarian Origins of Modern Japan* (1959) and, for more intimate details, C. J. Dunn, *Everyday Life in Traditional Japan* (1969), which also gives good coverage to urban life in Edo (Tokyo). Religious evolution is analyzed in Joseph M. Kitagawa, *Religion in Japanese History* (1966). The high degree of literacy is explained by R. P. Dore, *Education in Tokugawa Japan* (1965).

The rapid urban growth at the beginning of Tokugawa period is analyzed in John W. Hall, "The Castle Town and Japan's Modern Urbanization," in John W. Hall and Marius B. Jansen, eds., *Studies in the Institutional History of Early Modern Japan* (1968). The theory that Japanese population growth stagnated after 1700 is challenged by Susan B. Hanley and Kozo Yamamura, *Economic and Demographic Change in Pre-Industrial Japan* (1977). David John Lu, *Sources of Japanese History* (1974) provides many documents concerning urbanization and social policy.

To sample the delightful and somewhat scandalous tales of Ihara Saikaku, try *The Japanese Family Storehouse or the Millionaire's Gospel Modernized* (1959), translated by G. W. Sargent, or *The Life of an Amorous Woman* (1963), translated by Ivan Morris. For the principal playwright of Tokugawa Japan, see Donald Keene's translation of the *Major Plays of Chikamatsu* (1961). The most convenient introduction to the painting of the period is Robert Treat Paine and Alexander Soper, *The Art and Architecture of Japan* (1955). The rise of kabuki theater is described in Earle Ernst, *The Kabuki Theater* (1959) and Aubrey S. Halford and Giovanna M. Halford, *The Kabuki Handbook* (1965). Donald Keene, *World Within Walls: Japanese Literature of the Pre-Modern Era, 1600–1867* (1976) is a fine survey of writing in the Edo period.

The buildings of Kyoto during the Tokugawa period are discussed in detail in R.A.B. Ponsonby-Fane, *Kyoto: The Old Capital of Japan (794–1869)* (1956) and Gouverneur Mosher, *Kyoto: A Contemplative Guide* (1964). For Edo, the one comprehensive history is in French: Noël Nouet, *Histoire de Tokyo* (1961). However, the biography by Leon M. Zolbrod, *Takizawa Bakin* (1967), describes much of the Edo that the novelist Takizawa Bakin knew in the late eighteenth and early nineteenth centuries.

The impact of the European powers on Africa during the Early Modern period can be followed in Philip Curtin et al., *African History* (1979). The Portuguese destruction of the kingdom of the Kongo is graphically described in Jan Vansine, *Kingdoms of the Savanna* (1966). Michael Crowder's fine studies of West Africa include *West Africa Under Colonial Rule* (1968); *West African Resistance* (1971); and *The Story of Nigeria*, 4th ed. (1978). Philip D. Curtin's statistical study, *The African Slave Trade: A Census* (1969), led to the downward revision of estimates of the numbers of slaves transported. Their sufferings are recalled in their own words in Philip D. Curtin, ed., *Africa Remembered: Narratives by West Africans from the Era of the Slave Trade* (1967).

18

THE AMSTERDAM
OF REMBRANDT

In this flourishing republic, this city second to none, men of every nation and every sect live together in the utmost harmony; and all they bother to find out, before trusting their goods to anyone, is whether he is rich or poor and whether he is honest or a fraud.—Baruch Spinoza

In 1610 the city fathers of Amsterdam approved the Plan of the Three Canals, one of the most ambitious and most beautiful projects of urban planning ever undertaken. The city was to expand from 450 to 1,800 acres, to accommodate a population growing rapidly from an influx of refugees from Spanish rule, of intellectuals and Jews enjoying freedom from persecution, and of workers and merchants seeking profit from the city's economic boom. The population, fifty thousand in 1610, had doubled since the beginning of the Dutch revolt against the Spanish in 1567; it doubled again in the next ten years; and by 1660, it was two hundred thousand. The genius of the team of men who provided for this growth—the director of city works and the city's master mason, carpenter, and sculptor—was to combine aesthetic appeal, sanitation, and economic function. Three enormous semicircular canals were dug by laborers

(Left Page) Houses Along the Prinsengracht Canal, Amsterdam (*Louis Goldman/Photo Researchers, Inc.*); (Inset) Self-Portrait, by Rembrandt (*Bildarchiv d. Ost. Nationalbibliothek*)

around the old city. Radial canals made access easy between the new waterways and the rivers and canals of the central core. Building lots were created by driving wooden piles through the soft mud until they became firmly embedded in the hard sand below. Wide roadways were left in front of the houses and planted with lime trees. At points where vistas linked, space was provided for four great churches, known respectively as the North, South, East, and West churches. The whole impression was one of a complex panorama of color, presented with controlled dignity rather than with the exotic exuberance of the Venetian canals. The rippling greens of the canal waters reflected bright red tiles, buff brick, green doors, white-framed windows, and blue slate stoops, providing a favorite subject for the city's well-patronized artists. Moreover, the city required that sanitation should be provided in every house, and it inspected drains and sewers. (Visitors still complained that the burghers threw their refuse into the canals, "which causes ill Scents and Fumes which is a nasty thing.") The canals enabled the business people to use their homes as warehouses, since the goods could be brought by small boat and lifted into the upper floors of the house by means of the block and tackle that jutted out from the gable. For greater volume, specialized warehouses were built along the canals, with easy access to the port at the river mouth; and in Amsterdam even the warehouses had charm. "Among the large towns," wrote a French visitor, "Amsterdam is the most beautiful I have seen."

◆ *The Amsterdam of Rembrandt* ◆

Period Surveyed	Lifetime of Rembrandt (1606–1669)
Population	50,000 (1610); 100,000 (1620); 200,000 (1660)
Area	0.7 square mile (1610); 2.81 square miles (1630)
Form of Government	Federal government (Stadholder; States General representing seven United Provinces); oligarchic city government (sheriff, burgomasters, aldermen, councillors, known collectively as regents)
Economic Base	Merchant marine; principal commodity trader in Europe; overseas trading companies (East India Company; West India Company); financial services (Exchange Bank; Lending Bank; Stock Exchange); local foodstuffs
Intellectual Life	Painting (Rembrandt; Vermeer; Ruisdael; Cuyp; Steen); poetry (Vondel); philosophy (Spinoza); mathematics (Descartes)
Principal Buildings	Burgher homes on the Three Canals; North, South, East, and West churches; City Hall
Public Entertainment	Parades and dinners of civic guards; dances; banquets; skating
Religion	Calvinism; toleration of other religions, including Judaism

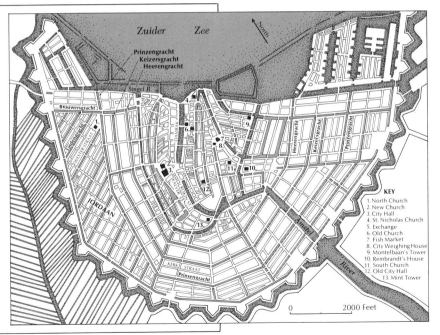

The West Church, by Jan van der Heiden (1637–1712)
Rembrandt was buried in this Calvinist church on the Prinsengracht. (Bildarchiv d. Ost. Nationalbibliothek)

KEY
1. North Church
2. New Church
3. City Hall
4. St. Nicholas Church
5. Exchange
6. Old Church
7. Fish Market
8. City Weighing House
9. Montelbaan's Tower
10. Rembrandt's House
11. South Church
12. Old City Hall
13. Mint Tower

Zuider Zee

Prinzengracht
Keizersgracht
Heerengracht

Singel R.

Brouwersgracht

North

JORDAAN

KERK STRAAT
Prinsengracht

Amstel River

0   2000 Feet

The Dutch, however, had created not only a unique city but also a unique way of life. They had accepted Calvinism and fought for eighty years to be free of Spanish Catholicism, without turning Amsterdam into another Geneva. Their religious toleration gave the world both a moral lesson and an example of the economic benefits of freedom of conscience. With no natural resources other than agriculture, they had made Amsterdam the world's greatest trade center and an important manufacturer. They had even turned constant war into a source of profit. Breaking into the colonial struggle a century later than the Portuguese and the Spanish, they had outstripped the former and equaled the latter. The Spanish treasure fleets were soon neglecting Lisbon and Seville and sailing on to the Netherlands. Its sober middle classes had turned their home life, perhaps more than even the Florentines, into a work of art; and their painters had responded by creating great works of art from the scenes of that life. "The name of Amsterdam became so famous," one contemporary reported, "that many people in distant countries believed it to be not a city but an entire country, and desired to form alliances with it."

THE REVOLT OF THE NETHERLANDS

**The Netherlands
Under Charles V**

The successful revolt of the seven northern provinces of the Netherlands against Spain made Amsterdam the predominant commercial center of northern Europe. When Charles V had inherited the Netherlands as part of his Burgundian territories, they consisted of seventeen provinces roughly equivalent to the present-day Netherlands, Belgium, and Luxembourg. Their wealthiest cities were the textile towns of Flanders, like Ghent and Bruges, and the banking and trading metropolis of Antwerp. Amsterdam, by contrast, was smaller even than the other towns of the province of Holland, like Haarlem and Alkmaar. Its port, where the river Ij flowed into the huge inland sea of the Zuider Zee, had been created artificially on marshland. Expansion seemed uneconomical, and the location was inconvenient for both North Sea trade and overland commerce with Germany. The assembly, or States, of the province of Holland summed up their difficulties clearly in a petition to the emperor in 1548:

It is noticeably true that the province of Holland is a very small country, small in length and even smaller in breadth, and almost enclosed by the sea on three sides. It must be protected from the sea by reclamation works, which involve a heavy yearly expenditure for dykes, sluices, mill-races, windmills and polders. Moreover, the said province of Holland contains many dunes, bogs, and lakes which grow daily more extensive, as well as other barren districts, unfit for crops or pasture. . . . Consequently, the main business of the country must needs be in shipping and related trades, from which a great many people earn their living, like merchants, skippers, masters, pilots, sailors, shipwrights, and all those connected therewith. [1]

[1] Cited in C. R. Boxer, *The Dutch Seaborne Empire, 1600–1800* (New York: Knopf, 1965), p. 5.

This seaborne trade was largely with the Hanseatic cities of the Baltic, in beer, grain, timber, and especially herring; there was also trade in textiles and wine with western Europe. But the revolt known as the Eighty Years' War (1566–1648) stimulated an economic boom in Amsterdam for two reasons. The Spanish armies of the duke of Alva and his successors destroyed its rivals in the southern Netherlands, especially Antwerp, which was sacked in 1585; and political independence of the northern provinces alone gave Amsterdam the position of capital city, in all but name, of a country of two million people. (Amsterdam became the constitutional capital of the country in 1814, although most government offices remained in The Hague.)

The Netherlands had developed strong economic ties with Spain during the reign of Charles V. Two-thirds of the Netherlands' exports were sent to Spain, a ready market for finished cloth, metalwork and arms, cereals, and naval stores. In return the Spanish sent two-thirds of their wool exports to the Netherlands, as well as large amounts of their tropical products like spices and sugar. The Spanish had allowed the Netherlands' cities to gain greater profit than the cities of Spain itself from the trade of their empire. Charles had even used moderation in his repression of Protestantism. Lutheranism had penetrated the southern Netherlands somewhat, and Calvinism considerably more when missionary work was undertaken in the French-speaking provinces from Geneva and Strasburg. Charles had, however, attempted to squeeze huge tax revenues from the Netherlands as part of his continual desperate search for money to finance his huge empire and to mount his military attacks on the Protestants in Germany. He had been compelled to reconstruct the fortress of Bruges to hold down a tax revolt. There was thus already in the Netherlands deep distrust of Spanish rule that Philip II was to exacerbate further by his unwise measures of exploitation and political and religious repression. Philip's greatest mistake was to attempt simultaneously to reduce the political powers of the aristocracy, to overtax the merchant class, and to repress Protestantism. In doing so, he stimulated three revolts at once.

In 1559 Philip appointed his half-sister Margaret of Parma, an illegitimate daughter of Charles V, as regent of the Netherlands. Margaret, who had married Ottavio Farnese, duke of Parma, in 1538 and was the mother of the renowned general Alessandro Farnese, proved to be a wise and conciliatory ruler. She was hampered, however, in her attempts to work with the Netherlands nobility by the advisers Philip had appointed to the council of state, especially Cardinal Granvelle, whom Philip had entrusted with the religious repression. Margaret at first sided with the high nobility of the Netherlands, led by the counts Egmont and Horne, and by William the Silent, prince of Orange, who opened the first phase of the revolt by attempting to stop the religious persecution of the Inquisition. Although he was a Catholic, William spoke out in 1564 in favor of toleration. "However strongly I am attached to the Catholic faith," he told the council of state, "I cannot approve the princes' attempting to rule the consciences of their

The Opening of the Revolt

Margaret of Parma (1522–1586)
Margaret was appointed regent of the Netherlands in 1559 by her half-brother, Emperor Philip II. Her policy was at first conciliatory, but she later provoked violent opposition by her use of mercenary troops and her executions of rebel leaders. (Giraudon)

subjects and wanting to rob them of the liberty of faith." Although Margaret succeeded in having Cardinal Granvelle removed, a spontaneous Calvinist uprising began in 1566 in the textile towns of Flanders and spread rapidly northward. In the "Calvinist Fury," the city mobs sacked Catholic churches, destroyed paintings and statues, and turned many churches into Calvinist meetinghouses. The revolt, however, remained localized in the southern Netherlands, and when the iconoclastic fever reached Amsterdam, the merchant oligarchy took tough measures immediately to stop its excesses. Nevertheless, Margaret lost patience and called in German mercenary troops; in 1567 she ordered mass executions of the rebels. Philip himself was determined on even tougher measures, and he forced the revolt into a second, more desperate phase by sending the tough, stupid duke of Alva to the Netherlands with a large Spanish army to extirpate Protestantism, break the nobility, and centralize in Brussels the rule of the seventeen provinces. Margaret, who had warned Philip against excessive harshness, found she could not work with Alva and resigned as regent.

Failure of Spanish Repression

Alva's legal instrument for dealing with rebels, both political and religious, was the Council of Troubles, nicknamed the Council of Blood, a commission of seven members with absolute powers of inquiry and punishment. The council arrested over twelve thousand people during its six years of activity, striking indiscriminately at Netherlanders of every class and religion and thus uniting the population in a common hatred of Spain. The counts Egmont and Horne were captured by trickery and executed. Alva then created a third opposition to his rule, in addition to the nobility and the Calvinists, by imposing enormously heavy taxation on the merchant class. "A great deal remains to be done," he wrote to the king in 1568:

The towns must be punished for their rebelliousness with the loss of their privileges; a goodly sum must be squeezed out of private persons; a permanent tax obtained from the States of the country. It would therefore be unsuitable to proclaim a pardon at this juncture. Everyone must be made to live in constant fear of the roof braking down over his head. Thus will the towns comply with what will be ordained for them, private persons will offer high ransoms, and the States will not dare to refuse what is proposed to them in the King's name.[2]

[2]Cited in Pieter Geyl, *The Revolt of the Netherlands, 1555–1609* (London: Williams and Norgate, 1932), pp. 102–103.

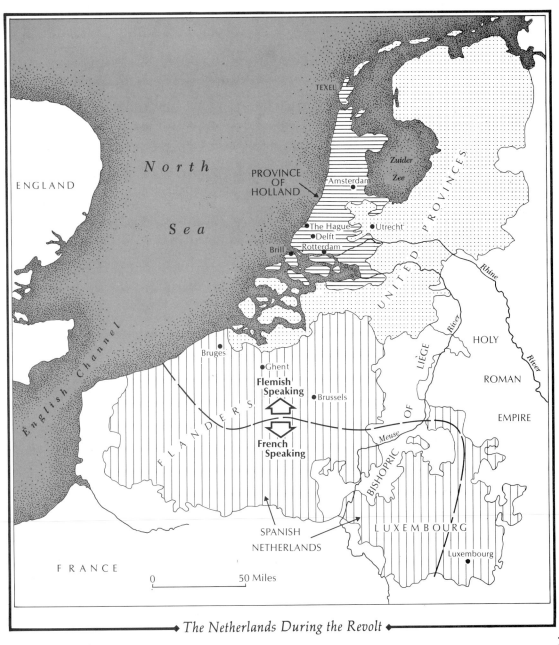

◆ *The Netherlands During the Revolt* ◆

In the southern Netherlands Alva succeeded in breaking the opposition to Spanish rule, and he moved the council to Amsterdam, which was soon known as Moorddam, or Murderdam. The city government collaborated wholeheartedly in attacking the lesser merchants, since this self-perpetuating oligarchy had concluded that its own power was dependent on maintaining Spanish rule. Amsterdam, however, was isolated in rebel territory. While Alva's army was ravaging the southern cities, many of the lower nobility and the merchant class had taken to the sea, joining with others who were little more than pirates, to harass the fleets coming from Spain. In 1572 these Sea-Beggars (a name they took from a derisive remark by one of Margaret's advisers about the Netherlands nobility) seized the port of Brill commanding the mouth of the lower Rhine and in a few weeks were in control of all the provinces of Holland and Friesland except Amsterdam. This territorial conquest, supplied from the sea and protected from the Spanish armies in the south by the great rivers, estuaries, and network of dikes, was never lost. It was a natural fortress; and the Sea-Beggars at once gave it political cohesion by recognizing their allegiance to William of Orange, the patient, courageous statesman whose charismatic leadership fused the various motives for rebellion into a movement for national independence.

The northern towns had accepted the Sea-Beggars without much enthusiasm, as little more than an alternative to the Inquisition and the

The Old Town Hall of Amsterdam, by Pieter Saenredam (1597–1665)
This intimate hall, which burned down in 1651, was replaced by a gigantic neoclassical building more fitting the pretensions of the city's merchant-oligarchy.   (Courtesy of the Rijksmuseum, Amsterdam)

Spanish sales tax. Meanwhile, Calvinist minorities engaged in a conquest of the city governments from within. The city government of Amsterdam withstood the pressure until 1578, although the city was surrounded by the rebels, the Zuider Zee blockaded, and foodstuffs dwindling. Then in May the workers and shopkeepers of the city swarmed into the central market street, the Dam, in a violent demonstration against the city council and were joined by the citizen militia companies, those well-to-do burgher civic guards presented in Rembrandt's famous painting *The Night-Watch*. In the Alteration, as this municipal revolution was called, the city council and the leading churchmen were rounded up, put aboard two ships, and set ashore on a distant dike. Exiled merchants poured back into the town, with large numbers of Calvinist refugees from the southern Netherlands. A new city government of moderate Catholics and Calvinists rapidly restored the city's economic life, and within seven years prosperity was so great that the first expansion beyond the old ramparts was undertaken. For a time it even appeared as though the whole of the Netherlands would be united under William of Orange. Alva, for lack of money, had been unable to put together an army that could defeat the North, and he had fled from Amsterdam by night to avoid his personal creditors. His successor, Don John, saw his own troops mutiny for lack of pay, and he himself died of typhus. For a brief period, both northern and southern Netherlands joined in the Union of Brussels, but the South soon withdrew. The southern nobility supported Spain against the mercantile oligarchies of the northern cities. Catholics in the South felt themselves threatened by the bellicose attitude of the Calvinists. Finally, in 1578, Philip II sent in a first-class general and statesman, Alessandro Farnese, duke of Parma and son of the former regent Margaret. Parma drew on Spanish troops from the loyal southern provinces and fought his way north, reducing the great Flemish cities one by one. Again, however, he was unable to break the river line north of Antwerp, even though Philip had engineered the assassination of William of Orange in 1584. With the help of a tiny army from England, the Dutch doggedly drove back every Spanish attempt to cross the Rhine.

During the next twenty years, Philip strained his resources. To stop English sailors from pillaging the Spanish fleets and ports in the American colonies, to end English support of the Dutch rebels, and to restore Catholicism in England, he sent an armada of one hundred and thirty ships from Lisbon to meet Parma's army in Flanders and attack London. Arriving a year later than originally planned as a result of a raid by Sir Francis Drake on Cadiz harbor, the Spanish ships were too ungainly to maneuver in reply to English attack. After moving slowly up the Channel in nine days of ineffectual skirmishes, they withdrew to the harbor of Calais. Drake, however, forced them out to sea again by sending fireships among them and picked a number of them off individually when they panicked. A tempest forced the rest to flee around the north of the British Isles. Only half limped back to Spain.

The Failure of the Spanish Armada (1588)

For the Dutch, the defeat of the armada provided a much needed respite; but the battles along the Rhine soon resumed. Under the leadership of a son of William of Orange, the Dutch won a few local victories. The truce of 1609 recognized that a standoff had been reached. The independence of the seven northern provinces, or the Dutch republic, which had been claimed originally in 1581, was officially accepted by Spain; and after a renewal of fighting in 1621–1648, this recognition was again affirmed. For Amsterdam, however, prosperity had preceded peace by a quarter of a century. By 1609 the capitalism of Amsterdam was already a source of amazement and irritation to its rivals. Amsterdam, wrote a Frenchman, was "swollen with people, chock-full of goods, and filled with gold and silver." It was a surprising record after forty years of war.

AMSTERDAM BECOMES THE HUB OF EUROPEAN COMMERCE

In the sixteenth century, Antwerp had been the center of European banking and international commerce. It was sacked, however, by unpaid and mutinous Spanish soldiers in 1576 and six thousand of its citizens killed; and it was occupied by the duke of Parma in 1585 after a fourteen-month siege. With Dutch ships blockading the mouth of the Scheldt River and cutting off Antwerp's remaining trade, Amsterdam was able before the end of the war to take over its commercial and financial role, and it sustained this preeminence for almost a hundred fifty years. "Here is Antwerp itself changed into Amsterdam," one refugee rejoiced. Rivals were determined to unearth the reasons for this metamorphosis. Dutch "riches and multitude of shipping is the envy of the present and may be the wonder of all future generations," wrote an English merchant in the mid-seventeenth century, "and yet the means whereby they have advanced themselves are sufficiently obvious and in a great measure imitable by most other nations, but most easily by us of this Kingdom of England."[3]

Economic Basis of Amsterdam's Prosperity

Many of the factors that aided Amsterdam's rise could have been turned to advantage by other great seaports. The refugees from Antwerp, with their capital and commercial skills, scattered to every port of northern and southern Europe from Danzig to Livorno, although a majority of them did settle in Amsterdam. Several of these cities could have competed for the desperately sought role of kingpin in the highly developed network of European trade. Great profits could be made by shipping companies able to buy up the surplus grain of Poland and the eastern European plains in order to supply lands where famine threatened, notably southern Europe in the last decade of the sixteenth century and parts of western Europe

[3]Cited in Charles Wilson, *The Dutch Republic and the Civilisation of the Seventeenth Century* (London: Weidenfeld and Nicolson, 1968), p. 33.

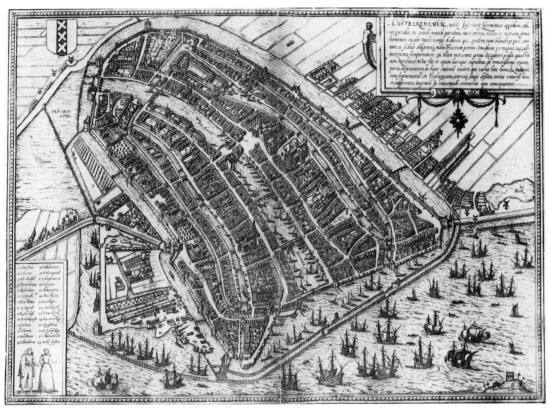

Panorama of Amsterdam, 1575

On the eve of its expansion in the Plan of the Three Canals, Amsterdam was protected by the sweep of the river Singel. Smaller ships could follow the Damrak into the center of the city. (Bildarchiv d. Ost. Nationalbibliothek)

through much of the seventeenth. The failure of Spain and Portugal to develop the industries that could supply export goods to their own empires left extraordinary opportunities for other countries to supply the textiles, metalwork, armaments, furniture, rope, tar, and timber that would be exchanged for the bullion of the Americas. The decline of Spanish strength in the last years of Philip II and especially the weakness of the Portuguese during the union with Spain (1580–1640) left not only the treasure fleets but even parts of the colonial empire open to foreign seizure. The vast expansion of European shipping offered a great opportunity for the country that could gain a semimonopoly on the naval supplies, especially wood and tar, which as a result of the great deforestation of western Europe completed in the sixteenth century had to be obtained from Scandinavia. Even greater profits could be obtained by the sale or lease of fully equipped ships. It was, however, Amsterdam more than any other port of Europe that was ready to capitalize on these lucrative opportunities.

Amsterdam's first advantage was its superb merchant marine. Visitors spoke of a forest of masts along the city waterfront and were impressed that most of the ships were owned by Amsterdam merchants. Many had been built for the North Sea fisheries, which had boomed suddenly when the herring shoals had inexplicably moved from the Baltic into the North

Panorama of Amsterdam in the Seventeenth Century
(Bildarchiv d. Ost. Nationalbibliothek)

Sea in the sixteenth century. Herring, smoked or pickled, had become one of Holland's most important exports, as well as a principal food item for its own cities; and warships were sent out to defend the herring fleets as they ranged along the coasts of England and Scotland. Other ships specialized in carrying bulky goods, especially for the Baltic trade in cereals, timber, and copper and iron. In the 1590s the Dutch invented an extremely important type of freight carrier, the flyboat, or fluit, which revolutionized the carrying trade. It was little more than a low-draught barge, manned by a few sailors and almost unarmed, that could be built quickly and cheaply and used for transport of goods. The flyboats made it possible for the Dutch to undercut all their rivals in freight rates, although some asserted that inhumanly low wages paid the crews were also a factor. With the beginning of interloping voyages to the Indies at the end of the sixteenth century, the Dutch also turned out larger ships that could make the long transoceanic voyages. By the mid-seventeenth century, they owned half the merchant ships in Europe.

Second, the Amsterdam merchants were prepared and able to trade in almost every commodity in world commerce. The Amsterdam price lists, published weekly, became the reference prices for all parts of Europe. All commercial services were offered, including skilled classification of merchandise, credit facilities, insurance, brokerage, and rational legal treat-

ment of commercial disputes. Goods traded through Amsterdam were handled with exemplary efficiency. Ships could be unloaded and filled again with purchases in a matter of days. But the variety of goods available was the greatest inducement to foreigners to buy in Amsterdam. It was Europe's biggest seller of wheat, naval supplies, armaments, and fish. It controlled most of the metal exported from Sweden and of the wool from Spanish sheep, much of the salt from Denmark, and even a good share of the unfinished woolen cloth from England. Many of the goods brought into Amsterdam were raw materials or semifinished goods that could be turned, at a large profit, into finished goods for export. In Amsterdam and neighboring cities like Delft and Leiden, small manufacturing companies were created. In Amsterdam itself, unfinished cloth was dyed and dressed, beer brewed, glass blown, armaments cast, tobacco cut, paper manufactured, books printed, jewels shaped, and leather dressed. Even the agricultural produce of the rich wet fields around Amsterdam and the newly reclaimed land, or polders, fed the Amsterdam trade. The high-quality butter and cheese of the Dutch were exported, while low-quality butter and cheese were imported to feed the farmers who had produced the finer dairy products. But the greatest temptation, to which the Dutch succumbed in 1594 with the foundation of the Company of Far Lands, was to break the spice monopoly of the Portuguese and Spanish.

The Overseas Trading Companies of Amsterdam

The first fleet sent out by the new company used charts drawn up by Jan van Linschoten, a Dutchman who had spent several years in Goa in the service of the Portuguese archbishop there. Linschoten's book *Itinerario*, with its detailed instructions for sailing to America and India, was significant in bringing both the Dutch and the English to open up the East Indies. The little Dutch fleet of four ships made its way as far as Java and the Moluccas and brought back a moderately profitable cargo of pepper and mace. Thus with direct access to the spice lands made possible and the enormous difficulties of Portugal in maintaining its monopoly made obvious, large numbers of ships were sent by companies in Amsterdam and the other Dutch ports. A few tried the route around South America but most sailed without trouble around Africa to the islands of Indonesia. Once again, Dutch commercial skills triumphed. They brought suitable goods for trade, such as armor, glassware, and toys; they traded honestly; they made no attempt to proselytize. They did, however, compete with each other; and in 1602, they were pressured by the States General into forming one monopoly company, the United Netherlands Chartered East India Com-

The Geographer, by Jan Vermeer (1632–1675)
Vermeer often emphasized the play of light on his subjects by showing them through a dark doorway, between opened curtains, or at a window. He set almost all his scenes in his own house in Delft. (Stadelsches Kunstinstitut Frankfurt, a.m.)

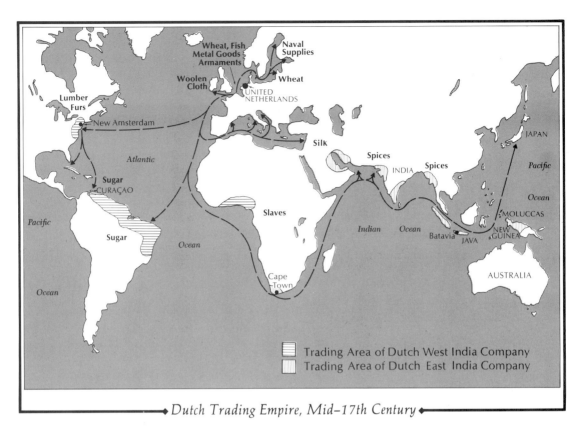

Labels on map: Wheat, Fish Metal Goods Armaments; Naval Supplies; Woolen Cloth; Wheat; UNITED NETHERLANDS; Lumber Furs; New Amsterdam; Atlantic; Sugar CURAÇAO; Silk; Spices; INDIA; Spices; JAPAN; Pacific; Ocean; Pacific; Slaves; Sugar; Ocean; Indian Ocean; MOLUCCAS; Batavia; JAVA; NEW GUINEA; Cape Town; AUSTRALIA; Ocean

Trading Area of Dutch West India Company
Trading Area of Dutch East India Company

pany. It was given sole rights to Dutch trade between the Cape of Good Hope and the Straits of Magellan, and it could make war and peace, build forts, capture foreign vessels, and coin money. Amsterdam, which subscribed half of the original capital, was dominant in the company, and its main offices and warehouses, which are still standing, were built in the city. The East India Company was soon sending annually a fleet to the spice islands, bringing back spices, silks, and cottons. Its members quickly made treaties with native princes, and territorial claims, first on the Moluccas and then on the Indonesian archipelago. In Batavia on Java, they built their administrative and military capital and used it to set up a trading empire among Asian states, from which they could also draw profit. They drove the Portuguese out of Malaya and Ceylon and massacred the last few English merchants in Amboina in the Moluccas, founded a trading post at Nagasaki to which the Japanese entrusted a monopoly of their export trade, and planted a settlement on the Cape of Good Hope as a supply center for their fleets traveling to the Far East. To the European goods available in their warehouses they had thus added pepper, cinnamon, nutmeg, cotton, silks, porcelain, tea, and coffee.

Nineteen years after the foundation of the East India Company, bellicose Calvinist elements founded the West India Company, to attack the trade, possessions, and ships of the Spanish in the western hemisphere. Its most spectacular achievement was the capture of the whole Spanish treasure fleet in 1628, as it lay at harbor in Cuba. It established a superb base for trading and marauding by taking the rocky island of Curaçao in the Caribbean, held the sugar producing provinces of Brazil for several years, and sold slaves from west Africa in the Spanish colonies. Following Henry Hudson's exploration of the river subsequently named for him, the company attempted to found a colony of the New Netherlands, establishing both a settlement called New Amsterdam on the tip of Manhattan Island and a trading post up the river at the site of present-day Albany. Only a few thousand emigrated, however, and the colony was seized by the English without trouble in 1664. New Amsterdam was renamed New York, and descendants of the original settlers like the Rensselaers and the Roosevelts quickly adapted to the new regime. The West India Company was soon torn with dissensions between the Amsterdam merchants and the other Dutch traders, especially as many of its ventures lost money. It was eventually declared bankrupt.

Nevertheless, the two companies had won for the Netherlands an immense trading empire. The great Amsterdam poet Joost van der Vondel summed up their achievement with customary honesty. "For love of gain the wide world's harbors we explore," he commented.[4]

Amsterdam as Financial Center

Amsterdam's third advantage was the availability of large quantities of capital together with the means for its investment. The Amsterdam middle classes had been accumulating wealth all through the sixteenth century from the Baltic trade in grain and naval supplies; and to this was added the large patrimonies brought into the city by the refugees who moved there from the textile towns of Flanders and from Antwerp during the war with Spain. The Jews who were expelled from Spain and Portugal brought some capital, but they were more significant for the wealth they created in the Brazilian sugar trade and, later in the century, by trading in shares. The English poet Andrew Marvell scorned this close identification of religious toleration and money making:

> Hence Amsterdam—Turk, Christian, Pagan, Jew,
> Stable of sects and mint of schism grew:
> That bank of conscience where not one so strange
> Opinion but finds credit and exchange.[5]

The imperial trade conducted by the East and West Indian companies enriched many investors, notably their own boards of directors; many of the rich homes along the new canals were owned by the famous Heeren ("Gentlemen") XVII and Heeren XIX, the seventeen directors of the East

---

[4]Cited in Boxer, *Dutch Seaborne Empire*, p. 113.
[5]Cited in Wilson, *Dutch Republic*, p. 27.

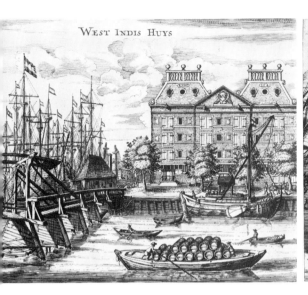

WEST INDIS HUYS

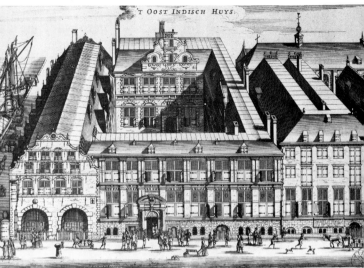

'T OOST INDISCH HUYS

India Company and the nineteen directors of the West India Company. Others profited from war. According to one Amsterdam burgomaster, "It is known to all the world that whereas it is generally the nature of war to ruin the land and people, these countries [the Netherlands] on the contrary have been noticeably improved thereby." Amsterdam merchants supplied the armies of the dukes of Alva and Parma and later the armies of Louis XIV during the wars against the Dutch. They supplied ships for both sides in the war between Denmark and Sweden. They fed both Roundheads and Cavaliers in the English civil war. By the end of the century, Amsterdam was the foremost supplier of all forms of military supplies; like Milan a century earlier, it had several stores that could equip an army of five thousand men. Finally, Amsterdam was also the center where the savings of hundreds of thousands of poorer people were invested. Land in the coastal provinces of Holland and Zeeland was scarce and expensive and thus not a normal investment. Agricultural investment frequently had to be done by buying into companies attempting to drain the polders, which required a large-scale technological enterprise. Greater merchants were also able to draw on the savings of their less well-to-do relatives when outfitting ships for the East India trade.

To make wealth readily available for productive investment, the city of Amsterdam founded and continued to supervise the most efficient and reliable bank in northern Europe, the Amsterdam Exchange Bank. Money poured in from as far away as Russia and Turkey, as the continent's rich sought security for their fortunes. The bank's reputation, wrote an English nobleman, was "another invitation for People to come, and lodge that part of their Money they could transport, and knew no means of securing at home. Nor did [only] those people lodge Moneys here, who came over into the Country; but many more, who never left their own; Though they

The West and East India Houses, Amsterdam
The handsome dark-red-brick West India House (left), built in 1641, was first used as a warehouse and slaughterhouse, and as a meeting place for the company directors. The original warehouses and offices of the East India Company (right) were quite modest in size; but as the company's wealth grew in the seventeenth century, it erected on the harborfront an enormous warehouse and arsenal. (Courtesy of the Rijksmuseum, Amsterdam)

provided for a retreat, or against a storm, and though no place so secure as this, nor from when they might so easily draw their Money into any parts of the World."[6] Shortly afterward, the city founded the Amsterdam Lending Bank, which offered loans to its best customers at three percent and soon succeeded in driving out the Italian moneylenders. Finally, there was the Amsterdam Stock Exchange, or Beurs, which was the center for trading in commodities. In its colonnaded courtyard, merchants from all over the world conducted the most concentrated trading in Europe. The Beurs, wrote Vondel,

> *Received the burghers' life breath*
> *From old and new side of the town*
> *All foreign blood that afternoons collected here*
> *Flowed in a single auricle*
> *Fed by many veins*
> *Giving life to the blood of the city.*[7]

The city of Amsterdam, in short, was a superbly organized creator of wealth. It had the highest per capita income in Europe. Its wealth, however, was far from being divided equally per capita.

SOCIAL STRUCTURE OF REMBRANDT'S AMSTERDAM

The Grauw (The Rabble)

At the base of Amsterdam's society, as in all the large cities of seventeenth-century Europe, was the class that the Dutch called the *grauw*, the dregs or rabble, whose miserable poverty comes alive in the etchings of Rembrandt. They varied from the old reduced to beggary to the unskilled day laborers who found occasional, badly paid work in the dockyards or warehouses. The reputed riches of Amsterdam and the ease of migration to the Netherlands brought into the slums large numbers of unfortunates from neighboring countries; and the Amsterdam upper classes lived in contempt and sometimes in fear of the temper of this mob. The grauw had turned on the Catholics before the revolt. After independence, members of the mob had lynched captains for losing sea battles and city fathers for supposed malfeasance. One of the wealthy burghers referred to them as "the sottish ill-natured rabble, who ever hate and are ready to impeach the aristocratic rulers of their republic." They were a stratum almost totally alienated from the well-being of Dutch society. They could be aided by charity; the city of Amsterdam made a weekly distribution of money to the poor. Large numbers of orphanages, almshouses,

[6]Cited in Violet Barbour, *Capitalism in Amsterdam in the Seventeenth Century* (Baltimore: Johns Hopkins University Press, 1950), p. 46.
[7]Cited in John J. Murray, *Amsterdam in the Age of Rembrandt* (Norman: University of Oklahoma Press, 1967), p. 60.

The Giving of Alms, by Rembrandt (1606–1669)
Help for the poor was largely left to private individuals, who either gave directly to beggars calling at their doors or, if wealthier, established almshouses in the poorer districts, where old people received free board and lodging. (Courtesy of the Rijksmuseum, Amsterdam)

and hospitals were founded by private individuals for the poor. But the most effective remedy was force. The poor were kept unarmed, while the wealthy joined in militia companies whose ostensible purpose was civil defense but who could be relied on to support the city government in the event of a mob uprising. Judicial punishment was harsh and fast. Criminals were branded with hot irons. Torture, the pillory, and executions by burning were common. A gallows stood at every entrance gate to the city. Prisons were rarely used; mutilation was cheaper. As a result, the grauw was usually submissive, if not entirely docile.

The Kleine Man (The Little Man)

The artisans and manual laborers of Amsterdam were known collectively as the *kleine man.* Most were members of guilds or worked for guild members. A distinction was made between craft guilds, such as the furriers' guild, and the guilds of the manual laborers, such as the beer carriers' or the herring packers' guilds. In spite of the large population, it was remarkable that only a small number of people actually gained membership in a guild. At the end of the seventeenth century, the furriers' guild had only thirty-six members. Even the cobblers' had only six hundred fifty-eight. But the number of professions was very large. There were, for example, spoon makers, shoelace makers, shuttle makers, drum makers, comb makers, and clasp makers, all of whom have left their names to some tiny

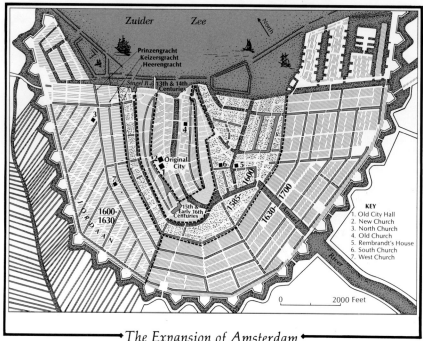

→ *The Expansion of Amsterdam* ←

alley in the city. Most guild members ran small establishments of six to ten workers. In the plan for the city's enlargement, the artisans were squeezed into an area called the Jordaan just beyond the three new canals. The land was left lower than the main city, without the fill or the same pilings. Streets followed the diagonal lines of the old fields and were no more than eighteen feet wide, divided by tiny canals. The width of a block was only one hundred twenty feet, a size that could have fitted into many of the gardens on the more princely canals. Profits were made quickly as houses were built for the Flemings, Poles, Huguenots, Jews, and the poorer native Amsterdamers. But the quarter developed a character of its own, a genuine class solidarity. Everyone called the other "aunt" and "uncle." Artists loved the familiarity of the society and the quaintness of the streets and chapels. Rembrandt, de Hoogh, and Hobbema all lived there for a while. And the streets were laced with almshouses, as the merchants gave recognition to the labor that nourished their enterprise. It was perhaps this sense of a common way of life, of genuine camaraderie, that took the sting out of social discontent in seventeenth-century Amsterdam.

The Middle and Upper Classes

Directly above the kleine man who lived in the Jordaan came the professional class, Calvinist ministers, lawyers, teachers, company bureaucrats, and members of the wealthier guilds. Immediately above them in social status were the landed nobility, who were a class apart in a society where commercial wealth was the highest recommendation. They maintained town houses whenever possible, occasionally intermarried with the wealthiest burghers, and took service with the state. But they could not adopt any of the pretensions of the French or English aristocrats: "Those that govern themselves with prudence and moderation and make themselves familiar with their inferiors are highly respected and popular, while those that are still and haughty are generally hated and despised," an English visitor noted.

The summit of Amsterdam society was a small group of enormously wealthy merchants. They included the Heeren of the big companies, wholesale merchants, large-scale manufacturers, and shipyard owners. They had been the leaders in the struggle against Spain; and from the truce of 1609 they had held tight control not only of the city government of Amsterdam but of the States General itself. These were the families who built the great houses that lined the three new canals—the Herengracht ("Gentlemen's canal"), Keizersgracht ("Emperor's canal"), and Prinzengracht ("Princes' canal"). At 123 Keizersgracht, for example, lived Louis de Geer, whose rapid acquisition of enormous wealth was due to his winning control of a large part of Sweden's armaments industry. De Geer's family had moved to Amsterdam from the Belgian mining town of Liège and had set up a munitions trade in 1615. Three years later, in company with some

Portrait of a Lady of Rank, by Gerard Dou (1603–1675)
Dou studied painting as an apprentice in the studio of Rembrandt. He became one of the most popular painters in the Netherlands, noted for his closely observed portraits of the Dutch middle classes. (The Norton Simon Foundation)

other Amsterdam merchants, he made himself responsible for repayment of a large loan owed by the Swedish king to the States General, and in return he was given mining concessions in Sweden. He virtually created the munitions industry in Sweden and then branched out into timber, naval supplies, and the retail trade. His weapons were used by the Scottish covenanters, the English royalists, the Venetian mercenaries, the Turks, the Russians, the Portuguese, and the Dutch themselves. De Geer divided his time between Sweden and Amsterdam, where in 1634 he bought the House with the Heads, an elaborate example of Dutch Renaissance building, so-called because six Roman busts are affixed to the facade. It is colorful, picturesque, and playful, with a kind of Roman triumphal arch topping a foursquare functional home. This indeed was typical of the early seventeenth-century building in Amsterdam. The burgher homes made little contribution to the advance of architecture; external decoration was the main variant in the style. In the second half of the century, a severely correct classicism was introduced, beginning with the palatial city hall and spreading to the more majestic mansions, such as the Trippenhuis built in 1660 for de Geer's nephews.

Canal House, Amsterdam
Dutch housebuilders achieved variety in simple facades by use of patterns in red brick and white stone and by ornamentation of the upper gables. (Consulate General of the Netherlands)

What impressed foreigners about these wealthy burghers was the simple dignity of their way of life, at least at the beginning of the century. The Calvinist Church discouraged ostentation; and the well-to-do were thus careful to appear in public in dark, simple clothes, mostly black with an occasional touch of violet. On special occasions the men wore a ruff of stiffened lacework around the neck, while the women were able to enliven their appearance with a colored bodice and cloak. In the home all furnishings were of sturdy quality, ostentatious only in their solidity. The average room had but three main pieces of furniture—a table, chair, and wardrobe. Floors were of tile or marble slabs, arranged in alternating colors; ceilings were of dark wooden beams; staircases so narrow and steep as to give one vertigo. Cleanliness was almost a fetish. Foreigners complained that Amsterdam women often failed to cook properly to avoid dirtying their sparkling pans. By the middle of the century, however, wealth had begun to erode the pristine simplicity of this way of life. According to the English consul in Amsterdam,

The old severe and frugal way of living is now almost quite out of date in Holland; there is very little to be seen of that sober modesty in apparel, diet, and habitations as formerly. Instead of convenient dwellings, the Hollanders now build stately palaces, have their delightful gardens, and houses of pleasure, keep coaches, wagons and sleighs, have very rich furniture for their horses, with trappings adorned with silver bells. . . . Yea, so much is the humor of the women altered, and of their children also, that no apparel can now serve them but the best and richest that France and other countries afford; and their sons are so much addicted to play that many families in Amsterdam are quite ruined by it.[8]

Expensive clothes of silk and velvet, elaborate sashes and swords, and feathered hats aped the styles of the French court. "The grave and sober people [of Holland]," Sir William Temple noted, "are very sensible of the great alteration that now is in this country."

Sensitivity to the change in manners was increased by the changes in the well-to-do class's attitude to government. At the time of the revolt against Spain, the great merchants' theory of government had been quite simply the right and duty of the wealthy to rule as an oligarchy. Amsterdam was governed by a sheriff, four burgomasters, nine aldermen, and thirty-six city councillors, known collectively as the regents. A small number of families held permanent control of the regents' positions in Amsterdam. Amsterdam dominated the provincial assembly for Holland; and Holland, which contributed more to the federal budget than the other six provinces combined, controlled the States General. The essential characteristic of this merchant oligarchy was its determination to place economic progress ahead of religious uniformity. The regents of Amsterdam regarded intolerant Calvinism as a threat to the city's prosperity, and they fought contin-

[8]Boxer, *Dutch Seaborne Empire*, p. 38.

The Marriage Contract, by Jan Steen (c. 1626–1679)
Steen transferred the Old Testament story of the marriage of Tobias and Sara to a setting in contemporary Holland. (The Fine Arts Museums of San Francisco, Gift of De Young Museum Society)

ually against the medieval restraints that the Calvinist Church attempted to place on economic enterprise. It was partly a matter of class feeling, since the preachers of the Calvinist Church came mostly from the lower middle class. But the regents were mainly concerned with preventing the creation of a theocracy like Calvin's in Geneva. Conflict between the regents and the extreme Calvinists came to a crisis in 1618–1619. The more liberal Calvinists, called Arminians after a theological professor named Arminius who held only mild views on predestination, were defeated in the national synod by the dogmatic, persecuting Calvinists, and the regent who had supported them was executed in Amsterdam on trumped up charges. But apparently triumphant within the Church, these extremists found that they could do little to make the ruling class of Amsterdam accept their rule in any sphere other than the theological. Catholics were persecuted in theory but not in practice and most continued to worship in private chapels built into the upper floors of the larger Catholic homes. Even church attendance was not required of Calvinists themselves, and attempts by the preachers to ban the theater, dancing, and drinking parties were completely unsuccessful. The most the regents would do was don the appearance of Calvinist godliness. It is thus not correct to say, as has been frequently asserted since the publication in 1904 of Max Weber's *The Protestant Ethic and the Spirit of Capitalism*, that Amsterdam was a perfect proof that Calvinism encouraged the virtues basic to capitalist economic expansion. Amsterdam was not a city where extreme Calvinists controlled political and economic life.

The other challenge to the regents' oligarchy came from the House of Orange. The official position of William the Silent and his descendants was stadholder of one or more provinces and commander-in-chief of the armed forces. Their strength lay in family popularity with the poorer classes and in the support of the Calvinist preachers. Their eventual goal was to be recognized as kings. At times the stadholders intervened directly against the regents of Amsterdam and appeared triumphant. After the victory over the Arminians, the stadholder Maurice (1584–1625) was able to force the regents to accept most of his wishes, including the formation of the West India Company. But after Maurice's death in 1625, the regents of Amsterdam refused to support his successor Frederick Henry (1625–1647) in his plans to reconquer Antwerp, which they had no desire to see revived as a rival to Amsterdam. By extending the financial aid and naval resources of the city only to those stadholders they approved, the regents were able to reestablish their influence over his policy. In the war between Denmark and Sweden, the munitions kings de Geer and the Tripps and their friends were able to force intervention on the side of Sweden in spite of the stadholder's desire to help Denmark; and in 1648 they brought an end to the long war with Spain, against the wishes of the stadholder. The new stadholder, Prince William II (1647–1650), laid siege to Amsterdam, which prepared to defend itself by cutting the dikes and calling out the garrison, but it gave in to avoid the economic damage of a civil war. William II, however, died of smallpox on the eve of his triumph, and no new stadholder was appointed for twenty-two years. Only when French invasion threatened did the country turn again to the House of Orange for leadership, appointing William III stadholder in 1672. By then the character of regent government itself had changed.

The most noticeable sign of the decline of the quality of regent government was in its nepotism and outright corruption. The regents filled all governmental and many commercial offices with their relatives and friends. Bribery became common at the lower ranks of the bureaucracy; and at the higher levels political control was used to make diplomatic decisions, such as the intervention in the Dano-Swedish War, for the purpose of serving the interests of individual companies owned by members of the regent class. But a more important transformation was a shift in the regents' economic interests from commerce into real estate and securities. From the middle of the century, the regents lived off their investments and as a result showed less understanding of the needs of overseas commerce. A cleavage developed between them and the wealthy merchants, the class from which they themselves had originally come, with a resultant weakening of the city's prosperity and of its power. The decline in the quality of regent government was thus one factor among many that marked the middle of the seventeenth century as the beginning of Dutch decline.

REMBRANDT AND THE GOLDEN AGE OF DUTCH PAINTING

The decline is perhaps most obvious in Dutch painting, because there was hardly a single great painting produced in Holland between the death of Rembrandt in 1669 and the appearance of Vincent van Gogh two centuries later. Dutch painting achieved a brief, superlative triumph of a duration almost exactly equivalent to the period of merchant oligarchy in Amsterdam.

The Roots of Dutch Art

The character of Dutch painting was strongly influenced by the society to which it catered. It was Protestant in the negative sense that the painters were not asked, and were often forbidden, to paint great religious tableaux like those of the Italian Renaissance. All paintings had been removed from the Dutch churches, and the Calvinist ministers were not commissioning any new ones. Corporate commissions were given by the militia guilds, or *schutterij*, by the merchant guilds and professional guilds like those of the surgeons, and by the governing boards of orphanages and almshouses. Calvinist morality prevented the political leaders from being portrayed as burgomasters or city councillors, and thus the group portraits were always in their economic or social roles. Wealthy merchants commissioned portraits of themselves and their families; four of Rembrandt's finest paintings were portraits of the Tripp family. Finally, artists painted, for future sale in art dealers' shops or in open-air fairs and street stalls, everyday scenes that people of all classes from the wealthy even down to the peasantry liked to hang in their homes like additional pieces of furniture. The subject matter was severely restricted, and artists usually specialized in a particular subject: landscapes, seascapes, and skyscapes; interiors of homes; gardens and backyards; city streets and squares; church interiors; still lifes; and, in at least one instance, cows. These genre paintings had to be small enough to hang in the restricted wall space of a Dutch home and, at the same time, wide enough in appeal to represent an investment that could be converted into cash without difficulty. The Naturalist style was one method of achieving this.

In each of these specialized painting subjects, one or two artists became preeminent, because they achieved so individual a quality to their work that simple scenes were transformed in their hands. In landscape painting, especially of gnarled trees blowing wild on days of cloudy sunshine, it was Jacob van Ruisdael. In portraits, conceived with a masterfully implemented air of gay and casual abandon, it was Frans Hals. In cows, it was Aelbert Cuyp. In the painting of interiors, the master was Jan Vermeer, who was second only to Rembrandt in his understanding and love of light. Vermeer's pictures are all deceptively simple—a cook pouring milk into a brown bowl from a porcelain jug, a girl reading a letter, a young lady at a spinet. In all, the technique seems to be the same. There is a window, often invisible, in one corner of the room, which lights up one or two figures in fairly mundane clothes doing some simple action in a barely decorated room. But the light has become the most important object in the picture. It sparkles in folds in a silk dress, flickers through creases in a wall map, vibrates in pearls in a necklace, or picks out the studs in the side of a chair. His paintings have the quality achieved in only the greatest art, of heightening our appreciation of the reality round us.

The realism of Dutch painting had several roots. It was a continuance of an uninterrupted tradition of accurate, detailed observation that began in Flanders in the fifteenth century with the van Eycks. But a great advance in the technical skills of science in seventeenth-century Holland

The Concert, by Jan Vermeer
(Isabella Stewart Gardner Museum, Boston)

was also put to work by the artist. To aid navigation the Dutch invented the telescope at the beginning of the seventeenth century. They developed great skill in making and polishing lenses, and Amsterdam entomologist Leeuwenhoek used them in the microscope to investigate such structures as blood corpuscles and, of special interest to painters, drops of water. They turned naturally to the study of light. While the painters were exploring every possible method for conveying the different character of light in clouds, sunlit rooms, rich fabrics, or human features, a great Dutch scientist suggested that light traveled in waves. Around the same time, the University of Leiden became one of Europe's centers of medical research that made great advances in the study of anatomy. If the advantage of this knowledge to artists was not obvious, it was made so by the startling paintings of anatomical dissections that many undertook. The most famous of

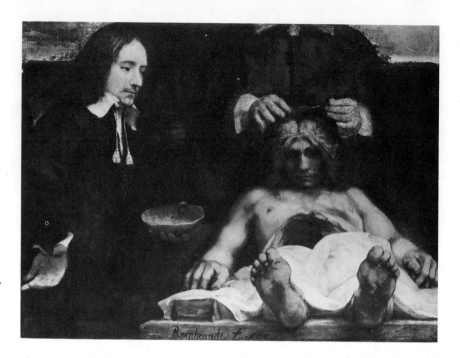

Detail from The Anatomy Lesson of Dr. Deyman, by Rembrandt
(Courtesy of the Rijksmuseum, Amsterdam)

all was Rembrandt's *The Anatomy Lesson of Dr. Deyman;* and his heart-breaking etching *The Descent from the Cross* is truer to death than any of the idealized views of a firm-limbed Christ being lowered to the ground after his crucifixion.

The Young Rembrandt

Rembrandt was both the greatest and the most individual of the Dutch painters; and his life is tied, more closely than that of any of the other painters mentioned, to Amsterdam. He settled permanently in the city in 1631 at the age of twenty-five, already equipped with the skills that brought him rapid popularity among the wealthier patrons: a mastery of the depiction of light, an ability to bring motion to group scenes, and a psychological penetration in portraiture. He bought into an art dealer's partnership and was at once introduced to the fashionable society of the three canals. Within months he had completed portraits of two rich merchants who were acquaintances of his art dealer. By 1639 he was wealthy enough to buy a large house and to have married Saskia, the daughter of one of the regents of the neighboring province, who became one of his favorite models. During the 1630s and 1640s Rembrandt rose to be the most popular painter in Amsterdam, showered with commissions by such families as the Tripps and by the merchant and militia guilds. Rembrandt thoroughly enjoyed Amsterdam's years of prosperity, made and spent a great deal of money, collected art himself, and until Saskia's death in 1642 filled their home with such exotic imports of the East India Company as Indonesian pottery, Japanese armor, and Arab swords.

During these early years Amsterdam's patrician society accepted with admiration the changes that he made in conventional portraits, the darkness behind the head that fills with light the longer one looks, the organized disarray of the figures in a group portrait, or the introduction of a moment of drama, as when Dr. Deyman slices open the scalp of the corpse he is dissecting. A myth is still spread that many of the militia members portrayed in Rembrandt's most famous group painting, *The Night-Watch*, were furious that his determination to create a dramatic scene had led to their subordination in the background and that they refused to pay him. Rembrandt was paid in full, however, and the painting was hung in a place of honor in the militia's guild hall. *The Night-Watch* marked Rembrandt's mastery of the baroque style in art (see Chapter 19). In particular, Rembrandt had used to the full the technique of *chiaroscuro*, the contrasting

Saskia Van Ulenborch, by Rembrandt
Rembrandt married Saskia, the daughter of a burgomaster, in 1634. She brought him a large dowry that, during the period of his greatest popularity as an artist, enabled him to indulge his taste for collecting art and exotic objects from the East. Rembrandt's happiness was broken by her death in 1642 after the birth of their son Titus. (Courtesy of the Trustees of the National Gallery, London)

The Night-Watch, by Rembrandt
(Courtesy the Rijksmuseum, Amsterdam)

of light and dark developed in Italy in the sixteenth century. The figures are in surging movement through space, as the captain and his lieutenant move forward leading the congested mass of their civic guards outward toward the onlooker. Flags, drums, spears, halberds, and rifles create a sense of confused activity in the darkness. And the economy of color, lavished only on the red sash of the captain, the yellow uniform of the lieutenant, the dress of the little girl, and the pink velvet of the guard on the left, makes those few colors all the more dramatic. (The name *Night-Watch* is however a misnomer: when the painting was cleaned recently, the militia were found to be on a day-watch!)

The same baroque qualities of movement in space, contrast of light and shade, and dramatic coloring were present in the large number of religious paintings Rembrandt carried out during these years. At the time he was the only important painter in Amsterdam still interested in illustrating the Bible; but many of his paintings were sold without difficulty. His great series of paintings of the passion of Christ was commissioned by the prince of Orange for his palace in The Hague. Rembrandt was also proving that similar effects could be achieved in etching, by drawing with a needle on a wax-coated plate on which nitric acid was poured to produce a printing plate. Biblical scenes abounded; but he also produced sad little prints of crippled beggars, blind fiddlers, and lepers, the human debris of the great city. Thus at the height of Rembrandt's fame, his central interest in deep human experience was already evident. Up to this point the taste of Amsterdam was able to grow with him.

From the 1640s Rembrandt and the patrons of Amsterdam drifted slowly apart in their conception of art. Some wealthy merchants continued to patronize him to the end, and he never lost his reputation entirely. But he was not called on for any more lucrative group paintings until 1661; his painting for the city hall was rejected; and he was unable to sell more than a few of his religious subjects. The society of Amsterdam at midcentury was becoming more elegant, ostentatious, and superficial in its tastes. Even the painters of interiors found that bare rooms with simply dressed burghers had to be replaced with overelaborate decorations and Frenchified clothing. Rembrandt on the other hand was plunging deeper inside himself in his search for an art that would lay bare the depths of humanity. He was heartbroken at the death of Saskia, probably from tuberculosis. Commissions fell off, debts accumulated, and he was eventually declared bankrupt and forced to sell his house and art collection. His mistress Hendrickje was

The Tragedy of Rembrandt's Late Years

The Three Crosses, by Rembrandt
As personal tragedies struck in his later life, Rembrandt turned with ever deeper penetration to the depiction of Biblical events. His etching of the crucifixion, made in 1653, displays his unrivaled ability to use subdued lighting to magnify the drama of a scene. (National Gallery of Art, Washington, Horace Gallatin Collection)

REMBRANDT AND THE GOLDEN AGE OF DUTCH PAINTING

Portrait of Hendrickje Stoffels, by Rembrandt

The death in 1663 of Hendrickje, with whom Rembrandt had lived for more than twenty years and with whom he had had a daughter, Cornelia, was one of the deepest blows the artist suffered in his tragic later life. (Courtesy of the Consulate General of the Netherlands)

called before the Calvinist authorities for living with him; but she continued to stay with him until her death, also from tuberculosis, in 1663. His only son, Titus, died a year before Rembrandt himself. With tragedy piling up on him, Rembrandt's art became quieter, more subdued, and even more penetrating. In his self-portraits one can trace, above all, the passage of a deeply independent man through the despair of suffering, which tightens the skin around the mouth and fills the eyes with sadness, to a reconciliation with old age that returns the glimmer of a smile to the face of a man in his last months of life.

FROM THE AGE OF GOLD TO THE AGE OF PERIWIGS

Amsterdam's Economic Decline

In Dutch history the eighteenth century is often referred to contemptuously as the Periwig age, when the once independent burghers copied French manners and modeled their society on the country that had driven them into decline. By then economic disaster had affected much of the Netherlands. "Most of their principal towns are sadly decayed," wrote James Boswell in 1764, "and instead of finding every mortal employed you meet with multitudes of poor creatures who are starving in

Self-Portraits, by Rembrandt: Youth, Middle Age, Old Age

Rembrandt painted many self-portraits, tracing his own journey from the exuberance of his early days in Amsterdam through personal tragedy to his final reconciliation with life's burdens. (above left, left: Bildarchiv d. Ost. Nationalbibliothek; above right: The Fine Arts Museums of San Francisco, Roscoe and Margaret Oakes Foundation)

idleness."[9] Amsterdam alone retained its prosperity. Lovely new homes in restrained classical style were built along the three canals. The same number of ships docked along the Ij as in the mid-seventeenth century, and Amsterdam capitalists were pouring money into the purchase of government securities in all their neighboring countries. But the wealth no longer had a secure basis in commercial innovation, industrial productivity, and an expanding population. There was almost no change in the population of the Netherlands as a whole, nor of Amsterdam itself, between 1660 and 1800, while the populations of France and England were booming. Throughout most of the eighteenth century, the total number of houses in Amsterdam remained the same. Its industry declined in size, and many of its shipyards were idle for lack of orders. Its herring fleet was down to a quarter of its peak size. Its armaments makers were no longer supplying every army in Europe. Amsterdam was living precariously on the heritage of its golden age.

The reasons for the end of Amsterdam's economic expansion, and thus for its decline relative to such mushrooming cities as London and Paris, were partly the fault of the Dutch themselves. At its height Amsterdam had laid far greater emphasis on overseas commerce than on industry. Money made in small-scale industry was invested in commerce; and the profits of commerce moved in the late seventeenth century into investments in land or securities. The movement of accumulated wealth worked against the coming of a large-scale industrial revolution. Moreover, the Dutch had permitted many of their skilled workers to be lured away by higher wages to other countries like Prussia and England, and may even have driven many out by their enormously high level of indirect taxation on everyday necessities. A Dutch worker paid three times as much in taxes as an English worker. The burden of taxes, and indeed the general impoverishment of the country, were due in part to wars in which the Dutch had engaged for profit. Their struggles with the Portuguese, their intervention in the Dano-Swedish war, their continual skirmishing with native dynasties and with European rivals in the Far East, their provision of convoys for their fleets in European waters to ensure "freedom of seas," were enormously costly.

It was primarily, however, the advance of their rivals that destroyed Amsterdam's economic supremacy. The Dutch in the role of middleman had always been resented, while their concentration on finishing for resale raw materials or unfinished goods produced elsewhere left them vulnerable when other nations took over their own manufacturing. Dutch freight declined when Britain and France built merchant navies in the eighteenth century and achieved new shipbuilding techniques in advance of the Dutch. The fisheries were invaded by large numbers of English, Scottish, Scandinavian, and Belgian ships, which sold their catch at home or chose a new market for it in Hamburg. Dutch industry proved unable to compete

[9]James Boswell, *Boswell in Holland* (London: W. Heinemann, 1952), p. 288.

with the luxury industries being founded in France with the financial support and control of the state; and it could not compete in price or quality with the mass production that began in England, especially in the textile industry, at the end of the eighteenth century. Even in agriculture the Dutch began to fall behind the English, who adapted new productive techniques of capitalistic farming, the so-called agricultural revolution, in the eighteenth century.

This increased competition would not have been so damaging if it had not been accompanied by acceptance by the English and French governments, and indeed by the Dutch themselves, of the economic theory called mercantilism. No one great theorist laid down the tenets to be followed, as Adam Smith was to do in the eighteenth century for free trade; and governments made only piecemeal efforts to apply the mercantilist views. Nevertheless, the opposition of England and France to the Dutch had an important theoretical basis. The mercantilist held that bullion—gold and silver—constituted national wealth. To accumulate wealth beyond what could be dug from its own mines, a country had to export more than it imported, so that the difference would be paid in bullion. In short, a country had to strive for a favorable balance of trade. Moreover, the mercantilist felt that the amount of trade possible in the world was limited and that a country could increase the amount of its trade only at the expense of another country. "What matters this or that reason?" an English general commented shortly before England attacked the Dutch. "What we want is more of the trade the Dutch now have." Colonies and trade empires were necessary for supplying raw materials or trade goods that the home country could not produce, and they were to be kept as captive markets. Interlopers had to be kept out by force from a colonial, or commercial, monopoly overseas. The state was to intervene in the national economy to maintain quality production, to found new industries, and thus to make possible greater exports; and the power of the state could be used to force open other countries' trade monopolies or to acquire colonies, by war if necessary.

Mercantilism

The Dutch were happy to follow mercantilism when it suited their purposes. They used force to keep control of the spice trade of Indonesia and the Moluccas, and they won international agreement that lasted from 1648 to 1863 that the mouth of the Scheldt be kept closed, to prevent the revival of Antwerp as a rival to Amsterdam. But they lacked the strong central government necessary for state direction of industrial production, and also the desire for one. Moreover, it became clear during their three wars with England (1652–1654, 1665–1667, and 1672–1674) and their war with France (1672–1678) that they would be the principal victims of the English and French conversion to mercantilism. English shipbuilding was stimulated by the government policy of requiring that imports be carried in English ships or ships of the exporting country. Tariffs in England and France were used to keep out Dutch goods, while subsidies were lavished on newly founded industries. In spite of the Dutch feat of sailing into the mouth of the Thames to destroy the British fleet in 1667, the Anglo-Dutch wars inflicted great damage on the Dutch economy. The invasion by the French king Louis XIV in 1672 was stopped only by breaking the dikes and flooding the vast area from the Zuider Zee to the Rhine. War, while not destroying the prosperity of Amsterdam, had become a primary factor in sapping its expansive energies and diverting its resources to unproductive ends.

Amsterdam's hegemony had been brief, but it had left a number of valuable lessons to civilization: that toleration not only adds to the happiness of the greatest number but is good business as well; that a great city can be created in a small country of poor natural resources by skillful provision of commercial and manufacturing services that larger, better endowed countries fail to supply; that a large city can quadruple in size in twenty years and become more beautiful in the process; and that restrained quality can be as great a virtue of civilization as exuberant magnificence.

SUGGESTED READING

Violet Barbour's *Capitalism in Amsterdam in the Seventeenth Century* (1950) is a short but incisive introduction to the city's economic life, and John J. Murray, *Amsterdam in the Age of Rembrandt* (1967) is a pleasant survey of its cultural growth. A superb short analysis of all aspects of Dutch civilization in its golden age, especially good on the Dutch influence abroad, is Charles Wilson, *The Dutch Republic and the Civilisation of the Seventeenth Century* (1968). For evocative essays by the great historian J. Huizinga, see his *Dutch Civilization in the Seventeenth Century and Other Essays* (1968).

C. V. Wedgwood provides a good introduction to the war with Spain in her biography *William the Silent* (1944). Primary sources are gathered in E. H. Kossman, ed., *Texts Concerning the Revolt of the Netherlands* (1974). The English contribution to the revolt is assessed in C. Wilson, *Queen Elizabeth and the Revolt of the Netherlands* (1974). Much fuller accounts are given in Pieter Geyl, *The Netherlands in the Seventeenth Century* (1961–1964) and in his two fine studies, *The Revolt of the Netherlands (1555–1609)* (1932) and *The Netherlands Divided (1609–1648)* (1936).

C. R. Boxer's *The Dutch Seaborne Empire, 1600–1800* (1965) is up to date, amply illustrated from contemporary sources, and full of information on Amsterdam as both an economic and a social unit. On Dutch agriculture, see J. deVries, *The Dutch Rural Economy in the Golden Age, 1500–1700* (1974). J. A. van Houtte, *An Economic History of the Low Countries, 800–1800* (1977) describes the cereal trade of Amsterdam in the seventeenth century and explains the economic decline of the Netherlands in the eighteenth. An interesting comparison of the social structure of Amsterdam and Venice is made by Peter Burke, *Venice and Amsterdam: A Study of Seventeenth Century Elites* (1974).

English visitors and diplomatic representatives wrote many accounts of the Netherlands, of which the best are Sir William Temple's *Observations Upon the*

United Provinces of the Netherlands (1676) and W. Carr, *An Accurate Description of the United Provinces* (1691). The English poet Andrew Marvell wrote a splendidly vindictive poem called "Character of Holland," which comments freely on Amsterdam and which should be set beside the appreciative French view, Jean Parival, *Les Délices de la Hollande* (1662). The daily life of Amsterdam is revived with many contemporary references by Paul Zumthor in *Daily Life in Rembrandt's Holland* (1962).

As for Rembrandt himself, Joseph-Emile Müller, *Rembrandt* (1967) sticks closely to an analysis of artistic growth, while R. H. Fuchs, *Rembrandt in Amsterdam* (1968) discusses the painter's relationships with the city, especially its art patrons, theater, medicine, and religious communities. There are beautiful illustrations and a reliable text in Robert Wallace, *The World of Rembrandt 1606–1669* (1968), and authoritative treatment of Rembrandt and other Dutch painters, especially of the Rembrandt school, in Jakob Roenberg, Seymour Slive, and E. H. Ter Kuile, *Dutch Art and Architecture 1600 to 1800* (1966). Deric Regin ascribes the artistic patronage of the Dutch burghers to the pride in their city that followed the winning of independence in *Traders, Artists, Burghers: A Cultural History of Amsterdam in the 17th Century* (1977).

The influence of the unique geographical environment of the Netherlands is discussed in two excellent studies, Gerald L. Burke, *The Making of Dutch Towns: A Study in Urban Development from the Tenth to the Seventeenth Centuries* (1960) and Audrey M. Lambert, *The Making of the Dutch Landscape: An Historical Geography of the Netherlands* (1971).

19

THE BAROQUE CITY
AND ITS RULERS

I n every period when civilization has achieved a kind of homogeneity, the city is the most revealing physical expression of the social and political realities of the age, or, to put it more bluntly, of the character and taste of the ruling classes. This was never truer than in the baroque city of the seventeenth and early eighteenth centuries.

The baroque city was created either by remodeling and expanding existing cities, especially capital cities, on an enormous scale, or by creating totally new cities of equally magnificent proportions. Pope Sixtus V (1585–1590) completed the dome of Saint Peter's, the centerpiece of his city, and cut long avenues through the medieval and Renaissance fabric of Rome, linking in shimmering vistas great piazzas dominated by ancient Egyptian obelisks. At the Square of the Four Fountains, where the pope's architect ingeniously constructed a church the exact size of one of the piers of Saint Peter's, two long avenues crossed. One linked the monumental entrance gate to the city, which had been designed by Michelangelo, with the papal palace of the Quirinale. The other joined the ancient basilica of Santa Maria Maggiore with Santa Trinità dei Monti, from which the view extended over the whole of ancient Rome. The popes had become stage designers, and Rome was their theater. In Paris the Bourbon kings, masters of a bureaucrat-designed absolutism, brought the shape of the city under the same discipline they were enforcing on society at large. The riverfront became a display of grandiose facades raised by royal decree, especially where the squat courtyard of the Louvre Palace was expanded in long pedimented galleries to link it with the tall pavilions of the Tuileries Palace and the controlled vistas of the regimented gardens beyond. Great squares with inner gardens were built to provide apartments for the nobles—at first playful

Library, Wiblingen Monastery, Germany *(Courtesy of the German Information Center)*

Aerial View of St. Peter's Cathedral, Rome

After the completion of Michelangelo's dome in 1590, the nave of the cathedral was lengthened; and in 1656 Bernini began the great baroque colonnade around the entrance square. (Georg Gerster/Photo Researchers, Inc.)

and jovial in red brick with yellow plastered motifs, as suited the taste of the popular king Henry IV, later grey and somber in massive limestone, reflecting the growing self-esteem of Louis XIII and Louis XIV. Where the river Neva emptied into the rain-drenched marshes of the Gulf of Finland, the autocrat of Russia, Tsar Peter I (reigned 1689–1725), laid the foundation stone for the new imperial capital of Saint Petersburg, which soon became a pastel panorama of palaces, schools, ministries, triumphal arches, monumental avenues, and geometric gardens. Even in London, amid the congeries of a medieval city rebuilt in all its confusion after the Great Fire of 1666, Christopher Wren raised the vast dome of Saint Paul's Cathedral. Frustrated in his desire to impose an orderly plan on the city as a whole, he brought to the more amenable task of building suburban palaces the baroque ideals of orderly vistas and splendid facades.

The baroque city was the direct expression of the will of powerful monarchs or of privileged upper classes, who had succeeded in establishing their predominance in the power struggles of the sixteenth and seventeenth centuries. During this time the politics of almost all the European states was concerned with a dialogue between the monarchy and the landed nobility and wealthiest bourgeoisie, who constituted the upper classes, a dialogue from which the majority of Europe's inhabitants were excluded. As a result of this dialogue, which ran the gamut from genuine debate over principles to all-out civil war, three major forms of monarchical government emerged. In Russia the system of monarchical rule—strengthened by Tsar Peter I—was autocracy, the most extreme form of absolute monarchy, in which virtually no constraints on the actions of the ruler could be imposed by the Church, the legal system, or constitutional bodies representing even the most influential of his subjects. The perfect urban expression of this form of monarchy was Peter's Saint Petersburg. In France the second form of monarchy, absolutism, found its ideal form in King Louis XIV (reigned 1643–1715). In this type of state, the monarchy was able to weaken almost irreparably the medieval institutions, both constitutional and legal, that had existed to prevent the unfettered exercise of its power, although the king continued to recognize the controls over his own actions exerted by the law of God, by traditional limitations on the functions of government, and by his need to compromise with the most powerful and wealthy nobles and bourgeois. In Paris and in Louis XIV's palace-city of Versailles nearby, we can observe both the strength and the limitations of absolutism. In England the upper classes gained political predominance against would-be absolute monarchs and created a type of limited monarchy—or oligarchy—that functioned for their own benefit. The ideals of this oligarchy were reflected in the limited reconstruction of London after the Great Fire of 1666.

Yet we must be careful to avoid exaggerating the variations that exist within this urban culture and among these forms of government. The baroque style was the result of a fusion. It combined wild emotional exuberance with disciplined order, particularly with mathematical regulation of space. It joined the desire for order and the desire for freedom, the unrestricted imagination of the artist with the orderly experimental mind of the scientist, the sensuous religiosity of the South with the puritanical abnegation of the North. And the governments of the baroque age differ in degree more than in kind. France was not completely enslaved and England was not completely free. We are about to explore variations within a surprisingly unified culture, not unrelated societies.

In this chapter we shall first examine the functions served by the baroque city and the style of city building developed to satisfy those functions. We shall then consider the three types of government developed in Russia, France, and England—autocracy, absolutism, and oligarchy—and in each case we shall see how the type of government influenced the form of city created.

FUNCTIONS OF THE BAROQUE CITY

The Renaissance had merely modified the medieval city, changing the character of a few streets or squares and adding a few great palaces or churches to quarters that remained essentially medieval in character. Great new cities, like those of Filarete, were conceived on paper, but they were never completely built. But in the seventeenth and early eighteenth centuries, old cities were transformed and vast new cities completed; and the function of the new city and the style in which it was built were in perfect harmony.

The Palace

The most important function of the new city was to be the residence of the ruler and that small group of the upper classes that formed the court. It therefore required a palace or palaces and a large number of palatial houses

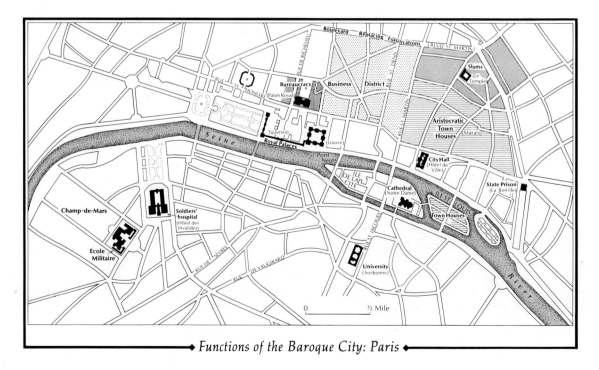

→ *Functions of the Baroque City: Paris* ←

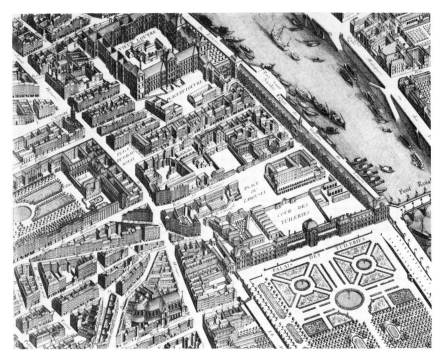

The Louvre Palace, Paris
The long facade facing the river Seine was constructed in the sixteenth century by Catherine de Médicis and Henry IV to link the old courtyard of the Louvre Palace with a new Tuileries Palace that was destroyed in 1871. (Courtesy of French Embassy Press and Information Division)

in fairly close proximity. The palace served a kind of psychological function, impressing on the masses their inferiority by the contrast of their own homes with that of the sovereign and emphasizing by physical separation their remoteness from political decision making. The most obvious separation occurred when kings moved just outside their capital cities to palaces built as towns in themselves, as the French king Louis XIV did at Versailles or the Austrian empress Maria Theresa did at Schönbrunn. In these cases the common people of the city had to walk ten or twenty miles to glimpse even the outside of their sovereign's residence. But even where the palace was built as the central building of a city, as was more often the case, the architect used every trick he possessed to emphasize its separation from the rest of the city. The east facade of the Louvre Palace in Paris, added by Louis XIV, has a ground floor so plain and forbidding that few would be attracted to approach it. Were one tempted to go nearer, especially at the smaller palaces of the tiny German states or the houselike palace of the Danish kings, a permanent military detachment acted as a discouragement, or long rows of serrated grillwork provided a physical barrier. Louis XIV's chief minister Colbert summed up the purpose of palace building neatly: "In the absence of impressive acts of war, nothing marks the greatness of mind of princes better than the buildings that compel the people to look on them with awe, and all posterity judges them by the superb palaces they have built during their lifetime."[1]

[1] E. A. Gutkind, *Urban Development in Western Europe*, vol. 5, *France and Belgium* (New York: Free Press, 1970), p. 115.

The palace was the setting wherein an extremely complicated ceremonial was acted out. Every aspect of the ruler's day was exploited to provide time-consuming tasks for the court nobility, who were in many cases almost entirely excluded from the real exercise of political power. Louis XIV was the model copied by almost every monarch of Europe. At his levée, or getting-up, for example, he expected all the courtiers to assemble outside his bedroom. The most privileged were admitted first to see him presented with holy water and to ask him favors. Then all were brought in to see him put on his clothes and to note who was specially favored with the task of handing him his shirt. They stayed long enough to see him shaved, take a glass of wine and water, and say prayers. Finally, they trailed after him to daily mass. Such meaningless ceremonies enabled the king to exploit the vanity and ambition of his nobility, keep them in sight and thus unable to plot sedition, and sap their finances in ostentatious expenditure. This artificial court life existed even in the smallest courts, like that of Nassau, which controlled a principality of only a few thousand inhabitants; and it was enforced on the most recalcitrant nobility. Peter compelled nobles to look like Frenchmen by shaving them himself! (It should not be forgotten, however, that hardheaded economic calculations justified the decoration of the palace with the finest products of the country's handicraft and industry. Participants, both native and foreign, in the palace ceremonial were being subtly pressured to purchase for themselves similar examples of the country's glassware, tapestry, silver, and armor.)

Staircase of Schloss Augustburg, Brühl, Germany
Baroque architects, among them Balthasar Neumann (1687–1753), achieved the height of theatricality in their treatment of monumental staircases, in which complex geometrical patterns were combined with colorful stucco designs and ceiling paintings. (Courtesy of the German Information Center)

The Bureaucracy

The palace also accommodated the bureaucrats who actually exercised the power of government; and if the palace became insufficiently large for the growing horde of middle-class administrators required by the centralizing monarchs, special government ministries were erected nearby. The world-wide affairs of the Catholic Church were run from the Vatican palace, which expanded to include more than a thousand rooms, twenty courtyards, and eighty staircases. Government ministries in Versailles were concentrated around the entrance to the palace courtyard, where three vast avenues met in an arrowhead. Here, in carefully proportioned buildings, were the mansions for Messieurs des Bâtiments (buildings); Messieurs des Receveurs Généraux (tax collectors); and so on. Peter the Great decided to copy the bureaucratic pattern of Stockholm; thus in the original design for Saint Petersburg, he assigned a frontage of the central Basil Island in the Neva River to twelve identical government ministries. The idea of a governmental section of town, devoted solely to office buildings, was born with the baroque city. Only too frequently monotony was the architect's inspiration as well as the character of the bureaucrat's life.

Townhouses of the Aristocracy

The presence of the court required large numbers of houses for the aristocracy, built on a splendid enough scale for them to entertain each other. Peter insisted that every Russian noble build himself a house in Saint Petersburg and forbade the use of stone for building anywhere else in Russia until his city was completed. French nobles demanded a townhouse separated from its neighbors by high walls, with an inner court surrounded by stables and offices, and frequently a broad garden behind the house. One of the most sumptuous examples of real estate speculation occurred in Paris when a group of engineers, in return for building a bridge, was given the right to drain the two little islands upstream from the Ile de la Cité and to sell off the resultant building lots. In a short time, the Ile Saint Louis became the favored quarter for nobles and lawyers, whose mansions rimmed the island and provided ever-changing views of the river and its traffic. In London, where aristocratic life was considerably less formal, most of the well-to-do lived in terrace houses; but from the seventeenth century on, homes were built in squares. Not only did a square have the advantage of creating open space, which was turned eventually into a park of lawns and trees, but it established the class homogeneity of those who lived on it by making its houses roughly the same in price, a triumphant distinction not even achieved on the Amsterdam canals.

The Army's Demands on the City

The army accompanied the monarch into the city and was indeed the insurance of his power. "The name citadel is given to a particular part of a town, fortified on both the town and the country sides, and it is principally intended for the quartering of soldiers to keep the inhabitants of the town loyal in their duty," wrote one French theorist. The army required a fortified building or area as a center of operations in times of rebellion, and as a position from which it could retake the city, a place that would symbolize to the citizens the power of the monarch. The slender spire of the Peter and Paul Cathedral marked for Saint Petersburg the fortress island where Russia's tsars held their political prisoners. In London and Paris, medieval fortresses, the Tower and the Bastille, remained the principal royal garrisons; but vast numbers of barracks buildings were also put up. This was even truer in Berlin, where soldiers composed almost one-quarter of the population.

The soldiers required parade grounds, which were created in the center of the town. The Champ-de-Mars, where the Eiffel Tower now stands, was the main parade ground in Paris. The English horse guards drilled on the wide sandy grounds behind Whitehall. Even in a city like Boston, Massachusetts, one of the principal uses of the common was for drilling the militia. To see soldiers on parade was one of the most popular free entertainments for city crowds; and when James Joyce, at the end of his novel *Ulysses*, has Molly Bloom meditate on the regiments she has known, he is appealing to emotions that have been three centuries in the making:

I love to see a regiment pass in review the first time I saw the Spanish cavalry at La Roque it was lovely after looking across the bay from Algeciras all the lights of the rock like fireflies or those sham battles on the 15 acres the Black Watch with their kilts in time at the march past the 10th hussars the prince of Wales own or the Lancers O the lancers theyre grand or the Dublins that won Tugela.[2]

[2]James Joyce, *Ulysses* (New York: Random House, 1966), p. 749.

Molly felt something of the fascination of the French aristocrat Saint-Simon when he watched the mock battle rehearsed for Louis XIV on the plain outside Compiègne:

A wonderful sight—the vast army, cavalry, and infantry deployed, and the game of attacking and defending the city. But what struck me most, and remains as clear in my mind today after forty years, was the King on that rampart in supreme command over the whole army and that vast mass of myrmidons around him crowded on the rampart and spread out across the plain.[3]

The army also wanted triumphant avenues, long broad streets up which it could march in victory or simply in routine celebrations. These streets also served the purpose of breaking up the rebellious lower-class quarters of the city into isolated islands that could be subdued individually, while the intersections of the new avenues, marked by a circle, or *rond point*, were ideal points for placing artillery in times of insurrection.

The longer and more accurate range of cannons constricted the city enormously because new fortifications of a more complex and land-consuming size had to be constructed. The medieval wall was almost useless by the beginning of the seventeenth century, and military engineers were creating ever more ingenious patterns of masonry and earthworks to blunt the bombardment of artillery. But the new walls were so large that once constructed they could hardly ever be moved outward to accommodate increased populations. Space had to be made inside the city by giving up the gardens and orchards that had sweetened most medieval cities, by building upward to an average six stories and sometimes to ten, and especially by crushing the poor into ever more constricted quarters. Fortunately for Paris, Louis XIV decided that France was to be defended at its frontiers, where his engineer Vauban was constructing the most impregnable fortress cities in Europe. He allowed Paris to become an open city, turning the ramparts into boulevards and the city gates into triumphal arches; and when a wall was constructed at the end of the eighteenth century around a Paris that had doubled in area, its purpose was not defense but to facilitate the collection of city import taxes. London, too, managed without a new city wall; but most capitals did not. Berlin, Copenhagen, Amsterdam, Vienna, Munich, Rome, were all restricted by their walls, the one advantage for the future being the easy conversion of the ramparts and their line of fire, or esplanade, into a green belt around the old city. The famous ring of boulevards in Vienna is the product of such a conversion.

New Fortifications

The economic function of the city, even of those primarily administrative capitals, remained important. The need for a central machinery for handling the business transactions of the commercial revolution was met by

Needs of Business

[3]Duc de Saint-Simon, *Louis XIV at Versailles*, trans. Desmond Flower (London: Cassell, 1954), p. 50.

Hotel des Invalides, Paris
This military hospital was founded by Louis XIV to house seven thousand disabled soldiers. The emperor Napoleon I was buried beneath the great dome. (Hirmer Fotoarchiv)

the stock exchange and the banks. Wren made a new Royal Exchange, not Saint Paul's Cathedral, the focal point of his plan for the rebuilding of London. Peter gave the tip of Basil Island to the Bourse (stock exchange), which was rebuilt several times to give it the dominant position in the city's river facade. The location of the stock exchange, the great banks, and the overseas trading companies near to each other led to the specialization of one area of the city in commercial transactions. In London it was the City, the area that lay between Saint Paul's Cathedral and the Tower of London, that developed the extraordinary mixture of specialized stores, stock traders, bankers, artisans, guildsmen, news reporters, shipping companies, and lawyers that delighted such observers of humanity as Dr. Johnson in the eighteenth century and Charles Dickens in the nineteenth.

Immediately below the City lay the docks, the other requirement of all the great commercial centers. Here again there was a great similarity in Europe's major cities. The same forest of masts could be seen in the Pool of London, in the Sea of Straw of Lisbon, or at the Elbe River docks in Hamburg. Even the inland cities were dependent on water transport, and crowded docks were to be found on the Seine in Paris, the Moskva in Moscow, the Danube in Vienna and Budapest, and the Main in Frankfurt. For all the large cities, one primary function of this shipping was to supply food and raw materials for its artisan classes, supplies usually brought from distant areas. The social peace of the city was dependent on the regular maintenance of this supply. When the Seine froze in 1788, preventing the arrival of food barges, it added directly to the misery of the lower classes that erupted in revolution the next year.

Church Building in the City

Finally, the requirements of religion had to be met, although churches rarely were the most important buildings constructed. At one extreme were churches deliberately conceived as the physical expression of great religious movements. The church of the Gesú in Rome was the triumphant assertion by the Jesuit order of the ambition of the Catholic Reformation. The four churches named after the points of the compass in Amsterdam represented a Calvinism that had won independence from Spain's repression. Saint Paul's in London is the most urbane expression of the ecumenical character of the Anglican Church. But frequently the churches served other purposes. The splendid domed church of the Invalides in Paris is, as its name suggests, attached to a military hospital, while the great Austrian and South German monasteries in which baroque architecture achieved its most fanciful forms seem more calculated to provide a wide range of aesthetic and worldly pleasures to the monks rather than to satisfy the code of Saint Benedict.

Thus the urban planners had to provide for the requirements of a royal court and aristocracy, a well-to-do commercial bourgeoisie, a large military class, and, to a minor degree, the churches. They presupposed the existence of a large laboring class, but they rarely made provision for it.

THE STYLE OF THE BAROQUE CITY

The style of the baroque city builder exactly suited the functions of the baroque city, and many of those who disapprove of the style are in reality disapproving of the function; for example, nineteenth-century Protestants disapproved of the sensual appeal of Rome's Catholic Reformation churches. We must begin by removing the confusion of nomenclature. The word *baroque* originally meant "odd-shaped," but it came to be applied to the architecture of Italy from the mid-sixteenth century on because that architecture too was characterized by unusual, extravagant shapes. This style was predominant in Italy throughout the seventeenth and much of the eighteenth centuries, and it passed from there to Spain and Portugal and to the Catholic states of Germany and Austria. The main characteristics of the style in architecture were movement and tension, theatricality, and emotionalism. Movement and tension were attained by use of undulating curves, sculptured figures, and vast, wildly colorful wall and ceiling paintings. Theatricality was created by constant employment of optical illusions and by the combination of richly colored marbles, precious stones, stucco, and shining metals with statuary of unrestrained voluptuousness. Emotionalism was achieved through direct representation in exaggerated form of the sufferings of the saints or of the kindliness of the Virgin or simply by the appeal to the senses through color or form. Baroque eventually came to mean a series of specific tricks in architecture, sculpture, and painting. Facades were composed of two convex and one concave curve. Altars were designed like theater stages. Statues swarmed over walls and ceilings instead of sitting in well-defined niches. Ground plans were composed of ovals rather than squares or circles. Ceiling paintings gave the illusion of an opening to the sky.

Meaning of Baroque

Relationship of Baroque Style to Northern Classicism

It is often said that northern Europe rejected the baroque because its artists and patrons were repelled by these features of its style. Inigo Jones, the English king's architect at the beginning of the seventeenth century, wrote scornfully of the style of Rome: "Ye outward ornaments oft to be sollid, proporsionable according to the rulles, masculine and unaffected.... All thes composed ornaments the which Proceed out of ye aboundance of dessigners and wear brought in by Michill Angelo and his followers in my oppignon do not well in solid Architecture."[4] The answer of these northerners, in England, France, and the Netherlands in particular, was to revert to what they considered pure classicism, by which they meant continuance of the style of the High Renaissance. This implied correct use of the orders of capitals, solid balance rather than movement in facades, simplicity and sobriety of interior decoration, and restraint in the use of color. What is important, however, is that the artists and architects of the North never achieved this classical ideal partly because they never entirely rejected characteristics of baroque style and partly because they shared the intellectual ideals of the baroque age. For this reason it is justifiable to speak of the baroque city in both southern and northern Europe. Whether the motifs were those of Roman baroque or French classicism, the cities were baroque creations. Let us look more closely at what they had in common.

[4]Cited in Nikolaus Pevsner, *An Outline of European Architecture* (Harmondsworth, England: Penguin, 1964), p. 309.

(Near Right) The Baldacchino, St. Peter's Cathedral, Rome, by Giovanni Lorenzo Bernini (1598–1680)
Bernini's baldacchino, or canopy, over the high altar and tomb of St. Peter was erected in 1624–1633. Its twisted bronze columns and huge scrolls supporting a ball and cross were fashioned of metal taken from the Pantheon. (Peter Menzel)

(Far Right) The Ecstasy of St. Theresa, Cornaro Chapel, Santa Maria della Vittoria, Rome, by Bernini
Bernini designed the chapel as a theatrical setting for his statue of the angel penetrating the heart of the Spanish mystic St. Theresa with the arrow that brings about her union with Christ. The saint seems to float in golden light as beams of sunlight shine from a hidden opening onto shafts of gilded metal. (Editorial Photocolor Archives/Alinari)

Royal Naval College, Greenwich
Designed by Christopher Wren (1632–1723) originally as a home for pensioned sailors, the college combines strict adherence to classical detail in the decorative aspects of its buildings with a baroque freedom in the treatment of the twin towers. (Courtesy of the British Tourist Authority)

One should first note that the baroque artists and architects of Italy were admirers of geometry and mathematics, a taste they inherited from the Renaissance that was greatly magnified by the scientific progress of the century. The city planners were fascinated by geometrical patterns, and they loved to work out abstractly all the variations possible in the planning of the city. In the simplest form, they worshipped the straight line, the search for the infinite, and from this they hit on the notion of the endless vista down a street of identical houses. They loved the intersections of straight lines, which could be opened out into traffic circles embellished with fountains or statues, or where vistas could be dramatically terminated with some impressive building. They elaborated squares, oblongs, ovals, and stars, all of which were eventually tried in actual city building. This mathematical basis for the city was just as appealing in the North as in the South because the functions it served were the same. Everywhere the pedestrian was displaced along with the curved medieval streets, and the well-to-do in their carriages enjoyed the long avenues that on foot were both tiresome and tiring. The London squares, the half-star of the new city of Karlsruhe, even the canals of Amsterdam, carried on this baroque absorption with the geometrical ordering of space. The three avenues that converge at the entrance to the chateau of Versailles and those that meet in the Piazza del Popolo in Rome are virtually identical.

The desire for the infinite showed itself in many other ways in South and North. Mirrors became a favorite interior decoration, the most grandiose use of them being in the Hall of Mirrors in Versailles, the most important room in the whole kingdom of France. The ceiling painting was adopted in the North with almost no change of style, as when Louis XIV masquerading as Apollo floated over the heads of his courtiers in the acres of canvases painted for Versailles by the court painter Le Brun. Expansive

Principal Features of the Baroque Style

formal gardens sought to merge the artificial and the natural, preferably at the infinite horizon. The great palaces, whether at Munich, Hampton Court, or Versailles, made use of artificial canals to lead the eye out through receding forest to the far skyline.

Above all, it was in espousing baroque emotionalism that the artists and architects satisfied the desires of their patrons. Sheer size was emotionally impressive. The garden front of Versailles is six hundred yards long. It took the brass roof from the Pantheon to construct the huge twisted columns of Bernini's shrine over the high altar of Saint Peter's. The exuberance of Italy reached the North in such devices as the use of fountains and the decoration of parks or streets with writhing or soaring statues of pagan gods. Also, in the planning of interior space, the key was the use of the oval—for floor plans, ceiling paintings, and even niches in facades. The result of using ovals instead of squares or circles was a charming, vibrant elegance that the seventeenth- and eighteenth-century courtiers thought ideally suited their way of life. These patterns produced what is often called spatial polyphony, a weaving of several important lines of archi-

Fountain of the Rivers, Rome

Bernini modeled his statues after ancient Roman river gods in creating a center-piece for Rome's oval Piazza Navona. (Photo Researchers, Inc.)

Plan for Washington, D.C., by Charles L'Enfant (1754–1825)
L'Enfant's plan of 1791, conceived before the Supreme Court had gained significant power, envisaged two centers of political power, the White House and the Capitol, from which avenues would radiate diagonally to break through the gridiron pattern of the streets. His plan was not fully implemented until 1901. (Courtesy of French Embassy Press and Information Division)

tectural emphasis into an intricate pattern. Christopher Wren was the great master of this art in England; and he used it fully when, after the Great Fire, he was given the task of drawing up new plans for fifty-one city churches. His ingenuity reached its greatest height in the church towers he created, an amazing variety of them within a simple form achieved by playing with geometric patterns. And this same quality can be felt in all the baroque cities, even when the most determined attempt has been made to use pure classical forms. The Paris and Versailles of Louis XIV, the London of Wren, the Saint Petersburg of Peter the Great, the Washington, D.C., of the French city planner L'Enfant, the Rome of Bernini, all are unmistakably the products of the same age.

AUTOCRACY IN RUSSIA

After examining the features of function and style that gave every baroque city a certain family resemblance, we turn now to the rich variations that existed within the pattern. In Russia, France, and England, we shall follow the rise of three different types of monarchical rule and the consequent variation in the form of urbanism adopted in Saint Petersburg, Paris and Versailles, and London.

The most extreme example of absolute monarchy occurred in Russia. The first Russian state, governed from Kiev from the ninth to the mid-thirteenth century, had been at least as advanced as contemporary states in

Origins of the Russian State

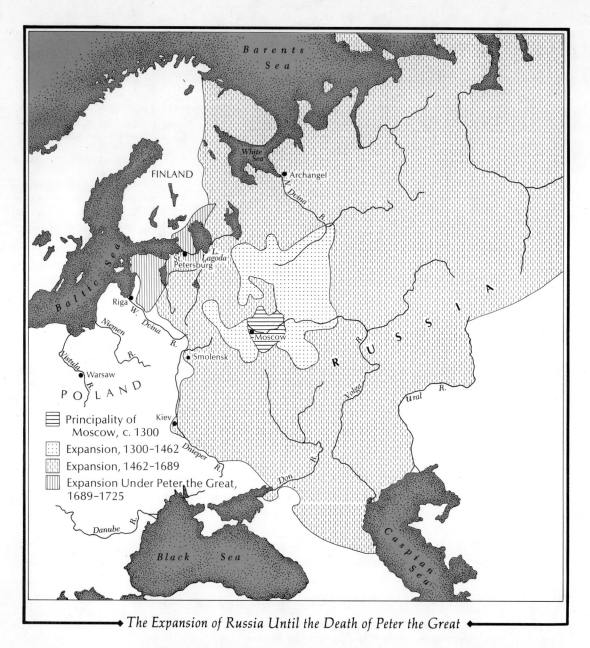

♦ *The Expansion of Russia Until the Death of Peter the Great* ♦

Map legend:

- ▤ Principality of Moscow, c. 1300
- ▦ Expansion, 1300–1462
- ▥ Expansion, 1462–1689
- ▥ Expansion Under Peter the Great, 1689–1725

western Europe. It had given the Russians a common language written in the Cyrillic alphabet and a common religion, the Greek Orthodox faith it had accepted from Byzantium. While a powerful noble class of boyars clustered around the prince, the majority of the peasantry were probably free; and flourishing trade with Byzantium and to a lesser degree with the West supported a numerous merchant class in such cities as Pskov and Novgorod. This promising evolution was interrupted by the invasion of the Mongol tribes of Tartars led by Genghis Khan and his nephew Batu Khan who, after conquering most of Asia, swept into southern Russia and destroyed Kiev in 1240. The Tartars exercised overlordship in Russia for the next two hundred years, effectively cutting off Russia from its contacts with the West and destroying its commercial ties except those through Novgorod. After the savagery of the initial conquest, the Tartars were satisfied to exact tribute in money and military recruits; but they left behind a tradition of autocratic government that was inherited by the native rulers they used as their intermediaries, especially the princes of Moscow. The city of Moscow was a relatively new creation, begun on the frontiers of settlement in the twelfth century. By the fifteenth century its rulers had annexed so many surrounding territories that they possessed the most important principality under the Tartar ruler. By 1480 they were strong enough to deny the Tartars their tribute and to confine them to three Khanates in the extreme south of Russia. The prince of Moscow, Ivan III (reigned 1462–1505), took the Byzantine emperor's title of *autocrat* after the fall of Constantinople in 1453, married the niece of the last East Roman emperor, and supported the claim that Moscow had inherited the religious preeminence of Constantinople and was thus the Third Rome. At the same time he declared that Moscow had inherited the lands of the former Kievan state, which had extended to Lithuania and Poland; and in a series of wars, he seized from the Lithuanian prince huge territories extending westward as far as Smolensk.

Ivan III, the Great, was the true founder of Russian absolutism. Like the Tartars, he acted as though he were unimpeded in his exercise of power by the control of law. He controlled a state church that recognized him as its supreme authority. And he conceived of the landed nobles as a service aristocracy, who were to receive their privileges only to the extent that they served the state. To achieve this goal, he founded a class called *pomietchiks*, who were given lands for their lifetime in return for service to the tsar and in particular for their support against the hereditary aristocracy. He also began the custom, to be greatly expanded later, of tying the peasant to the land so that he could not avoid working for the landlord or paying taxes to the state. The symbol of this new monarchy in eastern Europe, an area considered by most western Europeans as the extreme of barbarism, was the magnificent Kremlin, built for Ivan by architects brought in from Italy. The original fortress of Moscow had been built in the twelfth century on the junction of two rivers, in the triangular form favored for most Russian cities, and it had been extended a few times, usually in wood. But in 1485–1495 Ivan's Italian architects constructed the huge Kremlin walls that still exist, one and a half miles in length, sixty feet high, and fifteen feet thick, using deep red brick and breaking the regular crenelation of the wall with riotously decorated watch and gate towers. They created inside, contrasting with the horizontal lines and rich color of the walls, a fantasy of cathedrals, not one vast church but six, brilliantly white

Moscow Under Ivan III, 1462–1505

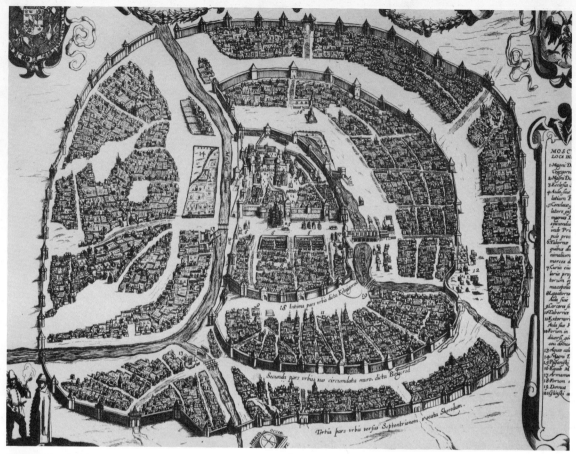

Moscow in the Sixteenth Century

The inner fortress of the Kremlin is dominated by the belltower of Ivan the Great. Just outside the wall rise the bulbous domes of St. Basil's cathedral.

and topped with a breathtaking array of onion-shaped domes whose gold leaf could be seen shining from miles away. And next to the cathedrals they built a palace for the metropolitan of Moscow, the head of the Russian Church, and a splendid palace for the tsar. In a period of twenty years they created one of the most beautiful complexes of buildings in the world, comparable in its harmony to the Periclean temples on the Acropolis.

The grandeur of this creation of Ivan III belied the real strength of Russian absolutism, however. The immense size of Russia, constantly being increased by conquest and eastward colonization, defied any efforts at strict control, while encouraging the constant movement of peasants in search of better lands. The landed aristocrats resisted the tsar's attempts to control them so vigorously that Tsar Ivan IV, the Terrible (reigned 1534–1584), determined to use violence to break them. He resettled many Moscow aristocrats on the frontiers and gave their lands to the new service nobility. Thousands of the old boyars were executed, while a regime of terror, called the *oprichnina*, or "separate kingdom," was loosed against the nobles. The oprichniks were the first grim secret police of Russia, blackclad sadists on black horses with a dog's head on their saddle who struck indiscriminately throughout central Russia. The reaction came during the reign of Ivan's idiot son, Russia's "Time of Troubles," when the nobles attempted to run the country as an oligarchy, the peasantry rose in agonized rebellion, and the Poles struck as far as Moscow itself. The compromise settlement in 1613, by which an undistinguished nobleman called Michael Romanov became tsar, did not restore in practice an absolutism that had never been challenged in theory. The legal enserfment of the peasantry in 1649 strengthened the control of the nobles. The patriarch of Moscow even claimed theoretical supremacy over the tsar. Taxation of the peasants brought in inadequate revenue for maintaining an efficient military force, yet it drove them into constant rebellions. Finally, a reaction against foreigners following the Polish invasion led to the isolation of foreign merchants and technicians in ghettos in the big Russian cities, so that the pernicious modernizing influences of the West could not destroy the old ways of Muscovy.

The reign of Peter the Great is a watershed in Russian history because he achieved efficient autocracy by linking it to the enforced modernization of the political, economic, and social structure of Russia. Peter grew up in the foreign quarter of Moscow, exiled from the Kremlin by the regent; and he learned there a fascination with the technical achievements of the West, contempt for the determined resistance to progress of the Muscovite aristocracy, a distaste for the ambitions of the Orthodox clergy, and distrust of the intrigues of the palace guard, or *streltsi*. His admiration for Western technology was confirmed during his first visit to western Europe in 1697–1698. The many early defeats in the Great Northern War (1700–1721) with Sweden convinced him of the superiority of the Swedish army and navy and also of the Swedish civil service. Traditional Moscow became for him the great obstacle to a modernized Russia.

Aims of Peter the Great, 1689–1725

At first he attempted to change the ways of Moscow, compelling the nobles to wear Western dress, to shave their long beards, and to work in the government ministries. But in 1703 he captured the mouth of the Neva River, which enters the Gulf of Finland, a window on the West where he at once began to construct the new capital of Saint Petersburg. To build his city he reopened the dialogue with the Russian nobility. The peasantry was to be more firmly tied to the land; and the landowners were to discover a new way of life in the service of the state. They were to be educated in Western knowledge, in the guards regiments, the Naval Academy, the artillery, and the engineering schools. They were to be given a chance to rise through a table of ranks, by their service to the state in the military or civil service. And in Saint Petersburg, under the watchful eye of the tsar himself, they were to enjoy the amenities of European social life, whose economic requirements would be met by the forcible transfer of the merchant colony from Archangel.

The Creation of Saint Petersburg

Everything in Saint Petersburg, however, indicated the autocratic character of its founder. The site was sloppy marshland, where dysentery killed ten thousand of his first conscripted city builders. The nobility had to be compelled to leave the cold but salubrious climate of Moscow for the eternal drizzle of the Baltic coast. They were ordered to build homes whose size was assigned them by the police after an inspection of their homes in Moscow. Tradesmen were moved into segregated streets, such as the Street of the Cannonmakers, the Street of the Armorers, and so on. The government ministries were grouped in identical pavilions on the central island, which Peter had hoped to turn into a new Amsterdam. The navy was given the island of Kronstadt, out in the river. The army had its barracks on the island of Saint Peter and Saint Paul and later its parade grounds, as in Paris, on the Champ-de-Mars. During the next hundred years, Peter's successors shifted their model of urbanism from Amsterdam to Rome and Paris. On the south bank of the river, great baroque perspectives were opened up: the three avenues converging on the new Winter Palace, now the Hermitage Museum; the long facades of the imperial and aristocratic palaces along the river front, which remind the present-day viewer of Paris; gigantic squares and gardens; and everywhere the unifying force of color in the light yellow stucco that decorated all the buildings. Saint Petersburg was an artificial creation, the will of one man. It forced Russia headlong into the technology of the West, especially the military technology. But it split Russia between the autocracy and the part of the upper classes and bourgeoisie that had accepted western European ways, and the vast majority of the population, which remained untouched by them, except to provide the human and financial resources to pay for the modernization.

The Winter Palace, Leningrad
The vast Winter Palace, with 1,050 rooms, was designed in 1764 by Bartholomeo Rastrelli, the son of an Italian sculptor brought to St. Petersburg by Peter I. It now houses the rich art collections of the Hermitage gallery. (Klaus D. Francke/ Peter Arnold, Inc.)

ABSOLUTISM IN FRANCE

T he absolutism of Louis XIV in France was the model for the majority of European states in the seventeenth and early eighteenth centuries. To create it, Louis did not have to work at such breakneck speed as Peter, because the foundations of French absolutism had been securely laid during the previous two centuries. At the end of the fifteenth century, Louis XI had left the monarchy a standing army, a large income from regular taxation, the undisputed right to legislate and to judge, the power to make war or peace, and the right to nominate bishops and abbots. Louis's successors for the next half-century, in spite of such wasteful wars in Italy as those waged by Francis I (reigned 1515–1547), ran France as a supreme example of the "new" monarchy. This evolution was interrupted, although temporarily, by the Wars of Religion (1562–1598). The wars were only partly an attempt by the more fanatical of France's fourteen million Catholics to wipe out Calvinism, which was the religion professed by about one million of the country's most enterprising commercial and professional classes. The French kings attacked the Calvinists because they regarded their fortified cities and their superbly organized network of congregations as a threat to the absolute powers of the monarchy, especially in the outlying provinces. Three great factions of the nobility fought each other, and incidentally laid much of France waste, to gain control of the throne. The queen mother, Catherine de Médicis, controlled the policy of her three ineffective sons, Francis II, Charles IX, and Henry III, who reigned successively from 1559 to 1589. She considered the measures to which she sank, including the murder of three thousand Calvinists in

Catherine de Médicis (1519–1589), Sixteenth-Century French Portrait
Catherine, the great-granddaughter of Lorenzo the Magnificent, controlled the government of France for the last thirty years of her life, during the reigns of her three sons. She actively participated in planning the massacre of French Huguenots on St. Bartholomew's Day, 1572. (H. Roger–Viollet)

Paris on Saint Bartholomew's Day in 1572, as necessary for the protection of her family. The surprising result of the wars was, however, to strengthen the monarchy.

Henry IV and the Restoration of Order, 1589-1610

The victor in the wars, the Bourbon faction's leader Henry of Navarre, who became king on the assassination of Henry III in 1589, was a cynical, tough, and charming character, whose qualities were precisely what the monarchy required to end the chaos of the wars. He displayed his cynicism by three times converting from Calvinism to Catholicism—as a boy at court, at the Saint Bartholomew's massacre, and four years after becoming king. Then, as a Catholic, he granted religious toleration to the Calvinists by the Edict of Nantes (1598), turning them in one stroke of the pen into the most loyal and productive segment of his population. He used force for ten years after his accession to crush the extreme Catholics and bring an end to Spanish intervention in France. And finally, by sheer charm—or rather by being himself the ideal Renaissance courtier, a combination of scholar, soldier, and lover—he created for himself the image of being the *vert galant*, the "green gallant." This reputation of royal popularity was to serve the monarchy well in later years, although recent scholars have argued that during his reign Henry actually enjoyed far less popularity than was attributed to him by royalist propagandists.

The wars, moreover, had strengthened the monarchy in relation to any opposition. The nobility had killed off each other. The chaos had severely weakened the middle classes, forcing many Calvinists to emigrate and hampering the development of industry and commerce. The commercial classes in France, unlike those in England and Holland, were not in a position to make a claim for a share in political power, but rather they sought the king as their sole guarantor against a return to feudal confusion. This attitude was expressed in a new political philosophy by a group called the *Politiques*, who held that royal sovereignty was the only guarantee of peace and internal order. Their great writer Jean Bodin (c. 1530–1596), in his influential *Six Books on the Republic*, argued that a true state exists only when it has a sovereign who exercises "supreme power over citizens and subjects, unrestrained by law"; that a king governs by the will of God and is responsible only to God; and that the king is the sole maker of law, including, if he wishes, laws giving toleration to Calvinists. The wars, in short, had given the French monarchy a well-reasoned justification of its own pretensions to absolute power.

Henry IV and the Renovation of Paris

Perhaps most important of all, Henry made Paris a true capital city once more. Under Catherine de Médicis, Paris had been in a state of more or less open rebellion against the monarchy, a city divided into isolated social groups alien to each other, tormented by disease and starvation, and ignored by an extravagant court. It had finally welcomed Henry in 1594, after he had become a Catholic for the third time. (He supposedly remarked, "Paris is worth a mass"!) Henry in turn repaid Paris by beginning the process of making it a city worthy of the monarchy's new pretensions. First came work of restoration, including the clearing of the garbage-piled streets, repair of ruined buildings, restoration of the water supply, and rebuilding of the bridges. Then came the revival of commerce, aided by the policies of Henry's able financial minister Sully, whose frugality restored the reliability of government bonds and whose mercantilism encouraged the foundation of new industries in Paris. Last came the shaping of the city according to royal standards of taste, a practice that was to continue for almost three centuries and was to be responsible for the present-day appearance of the city. "I would be very pleased," the king wrote Sully about a street being built on the Left Bank, "if you would see to it that those who are beginning to build in the aforesaid street make the facades of their houses all of the same [architectural] order, for it would be a fine ornament to see this street with a uniform facade from the end of the bridge." The tip of the Ile de la Cité set the standards for new urban groupings—a charming combination of grey stone bridge, uniform red brick houses with yellow stone facing, and tall slate roofs. In its triangular form and bold play of perspective, which led the eye to a strategically placed statue of Henry on horseback, it was already heralding the baroque city. Delighted with this first effort at urban planning, Henry created the first residential square, the Place des Vosges at the eastern, aristocratic edge of Paris; and he indicated the precise social character of the individual houses by selling off one side himself to chosen families who had been ennobled for legal and bureaucratic service.

Henry's assassination in 1610 flung France back into chaos, as his wife struggled unsuccessfully to prevent the nobility from ignoring the nine-year-old king Louis XIII (reigned 1610–1643). The state treasury was shared out among them, and the provinces became virtually independent of the crown. To end this state of administrative anarchy, Cardinal Richelieu, the brilliant, secular-minded churchman who ran the government on Louis's behalf from 1624 to 1642, made use of the one class of bureaucrats he felt to be completely trustworthy, the traveling commissioners. These officials, renamed *intendants*, were assigned to specific provinces and given greatly expanded duties in running the taxation, law courts, and police. They remained the primary instrument of royal absolutism until the revolution of 1789. Under Richelieu royal government was centralized round the person of the chief minister, who worked through his own appointees on the royal council and in the main government ministries in Paris and through the provincial intendants. Even the buildings of Paris showed this new emphasis: just to the north of the Louvre, Richelieu constructed for himself the Palais Cardinal (now the Palais Royal), a large palace with a long rectangular and completely private garden. Around the Richelieu Quarter, all his top bureaucrats sought to build themselves homes in the same formal style as their patron's, the solid, luxurious buildings themselves a proof of the wealth that could come to the middle classes who served the crown faithfully.

The Rule of Cardinals Richelieu and Mazarin

Louis XIII, by Peter Paul Rubens (1577–1648) and Anne of Austria, by Peter Paul Rubens

Rubens, the greatest baroque painter of Flanders, used sumptuous costumes and elegant backgrounds to create auras of opulence around his royal sitters. (The Norton Simon Foundation)

Richelieu's successor as chief minister, Cardinal Mazarin, was a clever, persuasive Italian who made himself the lover, and perhaps the husband, of Anne of Austria, the widow of Louis XIII. He attempted to run France on behalf of Louis's five-year-old son Louis XIV by relying entirely on the system created by Richelieu. He was challenged, however, by the Paris uprising known as the Fronde, which almost upset all the progress toward absolutism that the monarchy had made in the previous half-century.

The Fronde (1648–1652), so-called after the mud-throwing of Paris children, was an unplanned explosion of anger by all the classes in France who felt they had grievances against the monarchy. It began when a decade of poor harvests drove the peasantry into violent attacks on the tax collectors and the wealthy Parisians who were trying to buy up their lands cheap. It reached Paris when the Parlement, which represented the rich lawyers and claimed the right to register all royal edicts before they became law, demanded both reform of the corruption caused by sale of government offices and reduction in the powers of the intendants. When the monarchy granted the Parlement's demands, the great nobles in turn took over. Paris was occupied by noble armies, while in the rest of France private forces of aristocrats plundered and burned. Mazarin fled the country. The Paris mob terrified the king, who was then thirteen, pouring into his bedroom in the palace and forcing him to flee—perhaps the formative experience of his life, since it left him with such distrust for Parisians that only a complete move of the government to Versailles could assuage it. Royal armies eventually defeated the remaining noble armies, and both Louis XIV and Mazarin were able to return to Paris.

The real results of the Fronde were not evident until the death of Mazarin in 1661 left Louis free to run France his own way by becoming his own first minister. The utter chaos of the religious wars and of the Fronde had proven the need for strong monarchical rule; it remained to be seen what use a conscientious despot would make of his powers. The situation had never been more favorable for an international display of the French monarchy's powers. All France's rivals were in decline or disorder. England had just emerged from civil wars. The Dutch were severely weakened by naval wars with England and land wars with Spain. Spain itself could no longer raise the great armies and navies whose cost had buried Philip II in bankruptcy. The Thirty Years' War had left Germany in economic shambles. Poland was in the hands of an anarchical nobility. Austria was distracted by a new attack of the Turks, who in 1683 were to besiege Vienna itself. France, by contrast, was the strongest and wealthiest state in Europe. It had a large population, 18 million as compared with England's 5 million. Its agriculture was the most varied and prosperous in Europe, even though France had occasional times of famine. Richelieu had given it a strong navy and a renovated infantry that scored a landmark victory over the Spanish at Rocroi in 1643. Above all, in spite of its continual social conflicts, France had a genuine national patriotism that expressed itself in veneration of the monarch.

Louis XIV, by Hyacinthe Rigaud (1659–1743)
Rigaud became the favorite court painter of Louis XIV after 1688. To emphasize the high social rank of his sitters, he depicted them in velvets, silks, and furs, and used brilliant colors and intricate swirling designs. (Giraudon)

Entrance to the Hall of Mirrors, Palace of Versailles; Louis XIV's Passage of the Rhine, by Antoine Coysevox (1640–1720)

The Hall of Mirrors (left), the principal room in the palace, was used for royal receptions and festivals. It is eighty-two yards long. Seventeen large mirrors reflect the light from windows in the opposite wall that open onto the park. The triumphs of Louis XIV (right) in his early wars provided subject matter of a suitably sycophantic kind for the fifty sculptors and painters who decorated the ceremonial rooms of Versailles.
(H. Roger-Viollet; Editorial Photocolor Archives/ Alinari)

Louis believed sincerely that it was his duty to France and to God to profit from these advantages. He intended to be the Sun King of France. From his birth, when the mint issued a coin inscribed with the sign of the zodiac and the inscription "Thus Rises the Sun of France," he was associated like Caesar and the pharaohs with the sun. He made constant, propagandistic use of this identification in all the festivals, wall paintings, and even fireworks displays that enlivened life at Versailles. Like the majority of Europeans of his day, he held that only through an absolute monarchy could order be guaranteed and the energies of the nation harnessed for the common benefit. In the memoirs he wrote for his son, he described the misery of peoples governed by popular assemblies and limited monarchies:

The more you grant it [the popular assembly], the more it demands; the more you caress it, the more it scorns you; and what it once has in its possession is retained by so many hands that it cannot be torn away without extreme violence. Out of so many persons who compose these great bodies, it is always the least sensible who assume the greatest license. Once you defer to them they claim the right forever to control your plans according to their fancy, and the continual necessity of defending yourself against their assaults alone produces many more cares for you than all the other interests of your crown, so that a prince who wants to bequeath lasting tranquility to his people and his dignity completely intact to his successors cannot be too careful to suppress this tumultuous temerity.

But I am dwelling too long on a reflection that seems useless for you, or that can at most serve you only to recognize the misery of our neighbors, since it is patent that you will reign in a state where you will find no authority that is not honored to derive its origin and its status from you, no body that dares to depart from expressions of respect, no corporation that does not see its principal greatness in the good of your service and its sole security in its humble submission.[5]

He proposed to set the example of hard work and conscientious attention to all duties, no matter how trivial. As a child he had been taught to hate the do-nothing kings of the Merovingian period, especially Louis the Idle; and his own characteristic sobriety, backed by a splendid physique, enabled him to combine long hours of administration with punctilious observance of the even more fatiguing round of court ritual. He was the only person at Versailles who was never bored, and he accepted discomfort as a matter of principle. Told that some of the fireplaces at Versailles would stop smoking if the chimneys were made taller, he replied that the smoke would be endured because the chimneys had to remain invisible from the gardens. Food was brought several hundred yards and was cold when he ate it; wine froze in the glass. The king remained stoically indifferent. The essential factor was to maintain the majesty of kingship regardless of personal hardship. In this work Louis believed he was answerable to God, who had appointed him, and only to God. This theory of the divine right of kings sustained him with a sense of self-righteousness, when it became evident even to his leading general that his wars were leading France into ruin. To the courtier Saint-Simon, Louis's conception of government seemed at the end to be the product of his personal failings, "his blindness, his pride in doing everything himself, his jealousy of experienced ministers and generals, his vanity in choosing only such leaders as could not be expected to earn credit for successes."

Military Aggression and Glory

Throughout his reign, Louis's main preoccupation was to achieve *la gloire*, military glory for France and the monarchy. The interior of Versailles is filled with florid portrayals of Louis's victories in his early wars; but in each case there is a material justification, such as the capture of a strategic fortress or the surrender of a rich city. In his first war, the War of Devolution (1667–1668), Louis sought glory by straightening the southward bulge in his border with the Spanish Netherlands, from which, he was told, an invader could reach Paris in four days. His second war, with the Dutch (1672–1678), was partly inspired by the mercantilist desire to destroy the commercial supremacy of the Netherlands, partly by the religious determination to wipe out one of the strongholds of Calvinism, and partly by continuing territorial ambitions on the Spanish possessions on his eastern frontier. For two years his armies were totally successful; but in 1674 the

[5]Louis XIV, *Mémoires for the Instruction of the Dauphin*, trans. Paul Sonnino (New York: Free Press, 1970), pp. 130–131.

Dutch pierced the dikes to create a flooded barrier between the Rhine and Zuider Zee, and they used the time they had gained to put together a coalition of European powers fearful of France's ruthless use of force in support of its growing ambition. To stop Louis's attempt at European hegemony, the Dutch were joined by the English, the Spanish, and the Austrians, and several German states. The French were held to a stalemate; and peace was finally bought at the expense of the Spanish, by giving Louis a little more territory from the Spanish Netherlands and the valuable French-speaking province of Franche-Comté, which blocked the invasion route from Germany through the Belfort Gap.

Once peace was restored, legal chicanery gave France a pretext for seizing important cities in Alsace, including the important bridge town of Strassburg; and in 1688 Louis's forces crossed the Rhine to subjugate the little German state of the Palatine, where they destroyed the elector's palace in Heidelberg. This action precipitated Europe into almost three decades of continuous war, in which France made no further territorial gains. In his third war, the War of the League of Augsburg (1689–1697), Louis faced again the powers that had foiled his attack on the Netherlands, and again he was brought to a standstill.

In 1700 he played for the greatest prize of his reign. He would risk war with the rest of Europe to enable his second grandson to inherit the whole Spanish empire that the dying Spanish king had bequeathed to him rather than to the other claimant, the second grandson of the Austrian emperor. In the War of the Spanish Succession (1702–1713), the French armies were defeated again and again, in Italy by the forces of Savoy and Austria and in Germany and the Spanish Netherlands by the English under the duke of Marlborough. With a national debt of three billion livres, the peasantry starving, and Paris on the verge of revolt, Louis agreed to the Treaty of Utrecht of 1713, by which Austria was to take most of the European possessions of Spain, including Milan and the Spanish Netherlands. Britain was to take Gibraltar and the island of Minorca and have a monopoly on the supply of slaves to the Spanish empire. Louis's grandson was to retain Spain and its overseas empire, but the thrones of Spain and France were never to be united. The establishment of the younger Bourbon line on the Spanish throne proved of almost no value to France during the next hundred years. The one worthwhile result of twenty-eight years of war was to establish a defensible frontier from the Channel to Switzerland.

Strengths and Weaknesses of the French Economy

In economic policy as in foreign policy, Louis's absolutism produced beneficial results only through the early 1680s. Under the direction of his parsimonious finance minister Colbert, tax collection was made more efficient and more just. Internal barriers to trade were reduced. Roads and canals were constructed, including the Languedoc Canal that linked the Mediterranean and the Atlantic. New industries, such as silk and glassmaking, were established. Overseas trading companies were founded. But mercantilism led Colbert into some drastic errors, such as a high tariff on Dutch

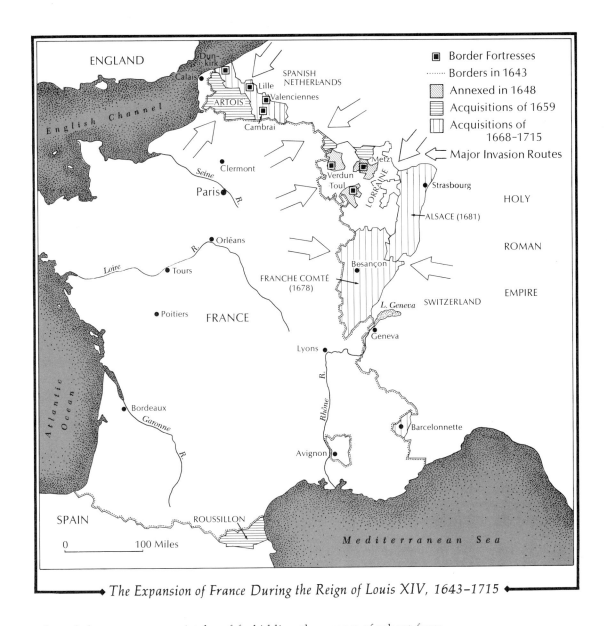

The Expansion of France During the Reign of Louis XIV, 1643–1715

trade and the even worse mistake of forbidding the export of wheat from France; and it led him to accept war as a necessary adjunct to commercial expansion. The wars, however, led to Colbert's own eclipse in the king's favor and to the rise of Louvois, the war minister, who though efficient as an army organizer only encouraged the king's provocation of the anti-French coalition.

Colbert also could do nothing to make the king value the economic contribution that the French Huguenots were making. During Colbert's lifetime, Louis attempted to convert Huguenots by billeting troops with them; and in 1685, two years after Colbert's death, Louis revoked the Edict of Nantes. To gain religious uniformity, which he felt was essential to royal absolutism, he drove out of France one hundred thousand Protestants, who included many of France's finest artisans and business leaders, nine thousand sailors, six hundred army officers, and twelve thousand soldiers. In Europe the persecution of the Huguenots aroused enormous indignation. In France itself many thought it a shameful error. According to Saint-Simon:

The revocation of the Edict of Nantes, decided upon without the least excuse or any need, and the many proscriptions as well as declarations that followed it constituted a terrible plot which depopulated one-quarter of the kingdom, destroyed its commerce, enfeebled all parties, caused widespread pillage and condoned the dragonnades, allowed tortures and torments in which many innocent persons of both sexes died by thousands, ruined a numerous people, tore families to pieces, set relatives against one another in a fight for food and property, caused our manufacturers to move abroad, where they flourished and brought wealth to other States at our expense and enabled new and flourishing towns to be built, and gave them the spectacle of so remarkable a people being proscribed, stripped of their possessions, exiled, made to wander over the face of the earth without being guilty of any crime, seeking shelter from their own country. [6]

The Centralization of Culture

Only in the arts did Louis's centralization of French life around himself produce an almost unblemished success. It is the achievements of the writers, sculptors, painters, architects, and musicians of his reign that won it the lasting reputation of being France's golden age.

The preparation for this new age of French literature had been made in Paris during the first half of the seventeenth century. Already in 1637, Pierre Corneille (1606–1684) had created a great romantic hero in *Le Cid*, his play about the eleventh-century Spanish military commander, and had continued to delight Parisian theatergoers with a series of dramas set in ancient Rome. But the majority of the literate Parisians were indulging in the far less exacting pages of the sentimental novel. The first to take the public by storm was *Astrée* by Honoré d'Urfé, set in the French central mountains in the fifth century A. D., where shepherds and shepherdesses engage in highly stylized conversations about unrequited love. It is also an early feminist novel: the government of the community is in the hands of women, and the heroine d'Astrée is a model for the learned women, the so-called *femmes savantes*, of the latter part of the century. Some of France's most popular women writers entered this tradition. The best known was Mademoiselle de Scudéry (1607–1701), who made herself wealthy with a series of novels including *Illustrious Women* and *The Great Cyrus* and who later, through her salon, extended patronage to new and struggling writers. She was thus able to carry through into the reign of Louis XIV the role of hostess that had been created by the most famous lit-

[6]Cited in Maurice Ashley, *Louis XIV and the Greatness of France* (London: Hodder and Stoughton, 1964), p. 93.

erary patronesses of the century, Marquise Catherine de Rambouillet and her daughter Julie. The word *précieux* ("precious") was first applied to the Rambouillet salon without any pejorative sense, but the Scudéry salon was so excessive in its demands for literary and personal refinement that it became the subject of biting satirical attacks in the 1650s by some of France's leading male writers. The vigor of the denunciation of the "precious" women was partly due to their reviving the argument of the relative superiority of men and women, a subject that provoked an enormous volume of literature throughout the seventeenth century. Marie de Gournay (1565–1645), in *Equality of Men and Women*, argued that society rather than nature had made men and women different and that changes in education and marriage customs would end the inequitable stereotyped roles assigned to them. However, since such changes were not merely changes in the relationship of men and women but simultaneously changes in the nature of social classes, the opposition resisted the emergence of women into public debate. The precious women, it was felt, were better off staying home, where, Nicolas Boileau pointed out in his satire "Against Women," they could curb and bridle their menfolk.[7] When King Louis XIV's mistress Madame de Maintenon founded a famous school for girls at Saint-Cyr in 1686, it was not, however, to teach girls a new role in society but to strengthen them in their traditional domestic role.

The centralization within the court, by Louis XIV and Colbert, of the process of patronage and the establishment of artistic standards went further to diminish the influence of the Parisian salons. From the 1660s all painters were brought into an Academy of Painting and scientists into an Academy of Sciences. Intellectual life was dominated by the French Academy, which had been founded by Richelieu. Colbert's admiration for Rome and his desire to make Paris a new Rome were evident everywhere—in the Louvre facade, in the antique subjects favored by the painters, in the triumphal arches at the city gates. But when Louis XIV began the expansion of the chateau of Versailles, both the focus and the style changed. Versailles itself became the training ground for the new architects, interior designers, sculptors, and painters. The new generation of artists was to be trained under the three great masters who were creating Versailles: Le Vau in architecture, Le Brun in painting, and Le Nôtre in landscape gardening. From Versailles, too, came the patronage of France's greatest comic playwright Molière (1622–1673) and tragic playwright Racine (1639–1699). Molière was an incisive but humane satirist, who made the court rock with laughter at the foibles of the excessively religious, in *Tartuffe*; of the social climber, in *Le Bourgeois Gentilhomme*; and of learned women, in *Les Femmes Savantes*. And he could achieve the point at which the greatest comedy probes so deeply that it becomes tragedy, as in the scene from *L'Avare (The Miser)* in which the old miser becomes almost demented at the loss of his money:

Françoise d'Aubigné, Marquise de Maintenon, by Pierre Mignard (1612–1695)
Governess of Louis XIV's children and later his mistress, Madame de Maintenon married the king in 1684. Although brought up a Calvinist, she became a devout Catholic and attempted to enforce stricter morality on the palace nobility. She retained a deep interest in the education of girls and founded a school for the daughters of poor nobles. (Giraudon)

[7]Carolyn C. Lougee, *Le Paradis des Femmes: Women, Salons, and Social Stratification in Seventeenth-Century France* (Princeton: Princeton University Press, 1976), p. 61.

Thief! Thief! Murderer! Killer! Justice, just heaven! I am lost, I am killed! Some one has cut my throat, some one has stolen my money! Who can it be? What has happened to him? Where is he hiding? What can I do to find him? Where shall I run? Where shall I not run? . . . My mind is troubled, and I don't know where I am, who I am, and what I am doing. Alas! my poor money, my poor money, my dear friend, they have taken you away from me! And, since you have been taken away, I have lost my support, my consolation, my job; everything is finished for me, and I have nothing more to do in the world! Without you it is impossible to live. It is over, I am finished, I am dying, I am dead, I am buried. Is there no one who wants to bring me back to life by giving me back my money?[8]

Racine, by contrast, was a superb poet who was able to build the classical Alexandrine verse, with its strictly prescribed rhythms, into an almost musical form of evocation of deep psychological insights. In *Phaedra*, for example, Phaedra, the wife of Theseus, is almost mad for the love of her stepson Hippolytus and attempts to reveal her passion to him:

> *Ah, yes. For Theseus*
> *I languish and I long, not as the Shades*
> *Have seen him, of a thousand different forms*
> *The fickle lover, and of Pluto's bride*
> *The would-be ravishers, but faithful, proud*
> *E'en to a slight disdain, with youthful charms*
> *Attracting every heart, as gods are painted,*
> *Or like yourself. He had your mien, your eyes,*
> *Spoke and could blush like you, when to the isle*
> *Of Crete, my childhood's home, he cross'd the waves,*
> *Worthy to win the love of Minos' daughters.*
> *What were you doing then? Why did he gather*
> *The flower of Greece and leave Hippolytus?*[9]

It was writers like Racine who made it possible for a mediocre man like Louis XIV to appear to be a Sun King.

OLIGARCHY IN ENGLAND

The third type of monarchical rule, limited monarchy, was created in England in the seventeenth century. Building on the powers and the wealth they had achieved under the Tudors, the English propertied classes, both the landed gentry of the countryside and the merchant class of the cities, rejected the attempts of the Stuart kings to form an absolute monarchy on the French pattern. In its place they created a partnership, not of king and people but of king and well-to-do.

[8] Molière, *L'Avare*, act 4, sc. 7. Author's translation.
[9] Racine, *Phaedra*, trans. R. Boswell (New York: Colonial, 1900).

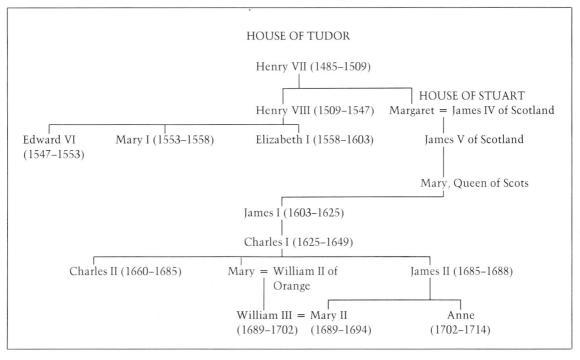

HOUSE OF TUDOR

Henry VII (1485–1509)

HOUSE OF STUART

Henry VIII (1509–1547)   Margaret = James IV of Scotland

Edward VI   Mary I (1553–1558)   Elizabeth I (1558–1603)   James V of Scotland
(1547–1553)

Mary, Queen of Scots

James I (1603–1625)

Charles I (1625–1649)

Charles II (1660–1685)   Mary = William II of   James II (1685–1688)
                                 Orange

William III = Mary II   Anne
(1689–1702) (1689–1694)   (1702–1714)

The classes who succeeded in limiting the monarchy had, almost without exception, grown wealthy under the Tudors. By the reign of Henry VIII, the old feudal nobility had almost disappeared and been replaced by new lords named by the Tudors from the rising class of gentry. The confiscation of the lands of the monasteries and the sale of crown lands had enabled many city merchants, government officials, and lawyers to become landed gentlemen; and they farmed their newly acquired lands with an eye to profit as well as social status. Some great families, intimately trusted by the Tudors, acquired huge portions of the land of the monasteries and thereby laid the basis for their later demand for political power. Money was also being made in what some writers have called the first industrial revolution. Rapid advances were made in coal mining and in the use of coal as an industrial fuel; in metalworking, especially of brass, iron, and lead; in production of unfinished cloth; and in glassmaking. But the really dramatic rise to fortune was made by merchants in overseas commerce. Under Elizabeth great trading companies were founded to open up trade with countries like Russia or with the East Indies. English ships were sent to find a northwest passage to China and ended by exploring the northeast coast of North America. Other sailors plundered the Spanish possessions and treasure fleets in the Americas and supplied African slaves to the Spanish colonies. Some companies, like the Virginia company founded in

Rise of the Tudor Gentry

1606, saw the settlement of English colonists in overseas plantations as a source of profitable investment; and the establishment of export crops, like tobacco in Virginia and sugar cane in the West Indian islands, helped the companies turn a belated but large profit for their stockholders. Thus, by the end of the sixteenth century, there were a substantial number of landholders, industrialists, and merchants who felt economically independent of the crown and who were prepared to demand greater influence in government when the policies of the crown were unsatisfactory to them.

The Age of Elizabeth

As long as the threat from Spain remained, Elizabeth had little opposition from Parliament, to which she turned repeatedly for money for defense and administration. Indeed, the national struggle that culminated in the defeat of the armada, combined with a widespread sense of economic prosperity and power, produced a great feeling of national solidarity that, by some inexplicable alchemy, encouraged the genius of William Shakespeare (1564–1616). The culture of the Elizabethan age was just what a sturdy, exuberant, self-confident, and assertive people wanted—madrigals to sing, love poems to recite, gory tragedies to shudder at, bawdy comedies to rollick over, picturesque manors to be comfortable in. Without Shakespeare it would have been little more than a charming and somewhat adolescent creation. But in Shakespeare, with his mastery of psychology, his superb sense of the stage, and above all his unparalleled poetry, drama reached its highest achievement. The language of Shakespeare (and the contemporary translation of the Bible into English, the King James version) bestowed on English speech a rhythm, a subtlety, and an emotional significance that have never been lost. This language, taught to successive generations of schoolchildren in England while students on the other side of the Channel were acquiring the sharp clarity of the logic of Descartes, played its role in the dangerous mutual incomprehension between the English and French peoples that underlay their willingness to fight each other throughout most of the seventeenth and eighteenth centuries. What could be more provocative of national pride than the beautiful lines Shakespeare put in the mouth of John of Gaunt in his play *Richard II:*

> *This royal throne of kings, this sceptered isle,*
> *This earth of majesty, this seat of Mars,*
> *This other Eden, demi-paradise,*
> *This fortress built by nature for herself*
> *Against infection and the hand of war,*
> *This happy breed of men, this little world,*
> *This precious stone set in the silver sea,*
> *Which serves it in the office of a wall,*
> *Or as a moat defensive to a house*
> *Against the envy of less happier lands—*
> *This blessed plot, this earth, this realm, this England.*[10]

[10]William Shakespeare, *Richard II*, act 2, sc. 1.

Queen Elizabeth I, by Nicholas Hilliard (1537–1619)

Elizabeth was thirty-nine when painted by Hilliard, the son of a goldsmith and jeweler, who was famous for his depiction of the intricate detail of jewelry and clothing. (Courtesy of the Frick Art Reference Library)

At the very time that Shakespeare was writing these lines, Elizabeth had been compelled to appear personally in Parliament to urge the granting of the revenues she asked, because the sense of national urgency aroused by the Spanish armada had subsided. Elizabeth could only appeal to the memory of great deeds done together and to their common pride in England: "I know that I have the body of a weak and feeble woman," she told the prostrate parliamentarians, "but I have the heart of a king, and of a king of England too." Thus, by sheer force of personality, she kept the absolutism of her father vital until her death.

Her successor King James I (reigned 1603–1625) was incapable of understanding the secret of Tudor absolutism, that it was a partnership for mutual convenience of king and well-to-do classes. He believed in the divine right of kings, wrote a book explaining the theory, and lectured on it frequently to Parliament. "That which concerns the mystery of the King's power," he said, "is not lawful to be disputed; for that is to wade into the weakness of Princes, and to take away the mystical reverence that belongs

Constitutional Struggle Under the Early Stuarts

unto them that sit in the throne of God." Unlike the French kings, however, the English monarchs did not possess a standing army, the right to tax, or a docile bureaucracy. They required parliamentary consent to raise troops and money other than their traditional revenues from customs and their own lands; and they were dependent on the gentry to carry out the administration in the local districts. Both James I and his son Charles I (reigned 1625–1649) attempted to remedy this weakness, which was particularly apparent as the inflation of the price revolution ate into their customary sources of revenues. Between 1603 and 1640 almost all the possessing classes of England united against James I and Charles I, because their methods of increasing revenue were regarded as constitutional innovations. This is the clearest theme in the English constitutional struggles of the seventeenth century. James I and Charles I attempted to raise revenues that would be independent of parliamentary control by reviving feudal dues, taking forced loans, and levying payments that were taxes in all but name. They attempted to circumvent the regular administration by founding new bureacratic councils to be the instruments of their absolutism. In 1640–1642 both the House of Lords and the House of Commons joined to sweep away these pretensions to royal absolutism. The king's chief minister was executed, and laws were passed to ensure that Parliament would meet at least every three years and would control any extraordinary expenditures.

The Puritan Opposition

The constitutional issue was, however, deeply involved with the problem of Puritanism. The English Calvinists, or Puritans, had made many converts among the landed gentry of the east of England, in the University of Cambridge, and in the merchant class of London. The Stuart kings, like Louis XIV, sought religious uniformity and not only refused the Puritan demands for change in the Church of England but actively persecuted them. Some fled to Holland and to the settlement of Massachusetts; but most stayed behind to oppose the king in England. During the eleven years when Charles I governed without Parliament (1629–1640), he permitted his archbishop of Canterbury to restore extreme ceremonial within the Church and to enforce the use of the Anglican prayer book on the Calvinist Church in Scotland. The Scots reacted by going to war with England in 1638–1639, and their invasion forced Charles I to call Parliament to ask it for money. But the Puritans in Parliament, once they had helped destroy the king's attempt to create a constitutional absolutism, demanded in 1641 that the position of bishop be abolished and that the Church of England be remodeled on Calvinist lines. As a result of this controversy, the king found supporters among those who had opposed his absolutist pretensions but could not tolerate the radical religious changes proposed. In 1642 the king attempted to arrest the radical leaders in Parliament and, failing to find them, was forced to leave London to gather his supporters near the loyal city of Oxford. By August both the king and Parliament were gathering armies for a trial of strength.

King Charles I at His Trial, by Edward Bower

Charles was tried by a special high court of justice on grounds that he had committed treason by levying war against Parliament. He refused to plead innocent or guilty but was condemned and executed in 1649. (Reproduced by permission of her Majesty, Queen Elizabeth, the Queen Mother)

The English Civil Wars (1642–1648)

Historians are divided as to the motives that drove individuals to choose between king and Parliament. They do agree on the geographical division. The great landowners and their laborers in the north and west supported the king in opposition to the yeomen and lesser gentry and the majority of the merchant class of the big cities in the east and south. The majority of convinced Calvinists supported Parliament, while loyal Anglicans supported the king. And here again was a class basis to the decision, since the Calvinist support was among the lesser gentry and the merchants. Recent investigations into the attitudes of English women to the civil war have suggested that many of the smaller extremist sects, such as the Independents and the Brownists, appealed greatly to women because of their willingness to treat them as equals with men, and that these strongly antiroyalist sects were composed in many cases mostly of women. On the other hand, vociferous and often violent demonstrations by women in London, petitions to Parliament by women, and innumerable examples of individual pressure within families, show that great numbers of women were opposed to the war itself, for the human and economic suffering it caused. Their despair over the consequences of the war led them to speak out, as women, thus achieving a kind of political voice that was denied to them in peacetime. It has also been argued that women's demands to be allowed to follow a religion different from their husbands' challenged the patriarchal nature of the family, as taught by both Anglicans and Calvinists. There is, however, little evidence that a desire for greater equality with men led women to side with the Puritans in the war.

The ultimate problem of interpretation is whether the civil war was a class war. There is no doubt that among extreme Puritans it was. The Diggers were a small group who believed in communal ownership of property; the Levellers demanded universal manhood suffrage and were willing to resort to violence to destroy either royalist or parliamentary despotism. But it is difficult to prove that among the majority of the supporters of both king and Parliament, economic determinism, that is, class sympathy or materialistic motives, dictated the direction of loyalty. People chose which side to fight for primarily in terms of religious or political loyalty. Many who approved of greater powers for Parliament simply could not bring themselves to fight against the annointed king; many who disapproved of Parliament's pretensions followed their Puritan faith in opposing the king. Members of the same family often joined different sides, a fact that proves to many historians the inadequacy of an economic analysis of the struggle.

In the first phase of the civil wars (1642–1646), the Parliamentarians, or Roundheads, succeeded in defeating the undisciplined armies of the king. In the Puritan country squire Oliver Cromwell, they found a great general, whose New Model Army, composed mostly of Puritan farmers, was a tough, fanatical force that destroyed the king's main forces at the Battle of Naseby (1645) and soon after captured the king himself. Success, however, brought about the dissolution of the parliamentary side, and for the next fourteen years, it tried in vain to produce a viable alternative to royal government. In 1646–1648 Calvinist extremism in Parliament won Charles many supporters from among the parliamentary side; and Cromwell had to go to war again to defeat the new coalition of Scots, Anglicans, and disillusioned Parliamentarians that Charles had succeeded in putting together. "We will cut off his head with the crown upon it," Cromwell announced; and in 1649 he did.

England became a Puritan republic, or commonwealth. Cromwell purged the Parliament to make it representative of the extreme Presbyterians, but finding them impractical fanatics, he felt compelled in 1653 to take over the state himself. "There was nothing in the minds of these men but overturn," he commented. But Cromwell himself as Lord Protector was even less able to put together a viable government, having as his only support the power of his army. He could not solve the dilemma of combining rule of the godly, as Calvin proposed, and rule of the whole people, which he sincerely sought. He fought the Dutch at sea, at enormous expense to his own middle-class supporters, and he faced the continual burden of financing his fifty-thousand-man army. These financial exactions destroyed much of his support. The requirements of the godly, which involved as great a proscription of pleasure as in Calvin's Geneva, became increasingly irksome. After Cromwell's death moderate leaders in the army itself decided to restore the monarchy as the only way to avoid chaos. Charles II,

Oliver Cromwell, by Peter Lely (1618–1680)

Cromwell's military skill and organizing genius played a large part in the defeat of the royalist armies in the civil war. He proved less adept at creating a workable constitutional government to replace the monarchy; and in 1653–1658 as lord protector, he kept power largely in his own hands.

The following legend appears on the map:

Controlled by Parliament, 1642

Controlled by Charles I, 1642

★ Battles

Map labels: Edinburgh, SCOTLAND, Durham, *North Sea*, Battle of Marston Moor 1644 ★, Hull, *Irish Sea*, Nottingham, WALES, Battle of Naseby ★ 1645, Naseby, EASTERN, Cambridge, Battle of Edgehill 1642 ★, ASSOCIATION, Oxford, London, Newbury ★, Battle of Newbury 1642, 1644, Dover, Southampton, *English Channel*, FRANCE, CORNWALL, 0 — 100 Miles

◆ *The English Civil Wars* ◆

son of the executed king, was called back to England and the throne, on the explicit condition that the powers of the monarchy would be those defined in the constitutional settlement of 1640–1641.

The Restoration period (Charles II, reigned 1660–1685; James II, reigned 1685–1688) was the height of England's baroque age. In reaction to the drabness of the Puritan revolution, the revived aristocracy led by its new

The Restoration, 1660–1688

St. Paul's Cathedral, London, by Christopher Wren (1632–1723)

Wren used strictly classical forms, including a triumphal arch, for the nave of St. Paul's Cathedral but introduced baroque curves in the towers of the west front. (Courtesy of the British Tourist Authority)

pleasure-loving king engaged in all the sensual and emotional excesses, in life and in art. The theater was filled with convoluted tales of amorous intrigue, many of which were being acted out in reality in the court circles. All the foppery of Louis XIV's Versailles was introduced to aristocratic living—the wigs, the ribbons, the high-heeled shoes, the powder and lorgnettes, and the formalized politeness. But for all the artificiality, there were real achievements in Restoration culture. It produced England's finest composer, Henry Purcell, whose opera *Dido and Aeneas* ranks with the best of the Italian operas of the period; England's greatest architect, Christopher Wren; and some passable poets, including Andrew Marvell. In 1667 the great Puritan poet John Milton published the finest of all baroque poems, alien in spirit to the court of Charles II but with a real affinity for the style of the Catholic Reformation in Rome with its swirling heavens filled with saints and angels, fallen and otherwise. In Milton are joined the color and drama of Bernini and the deep diapasons and complex harmonies of Bach, the perfect mingling of the arts that is so typical of the baroque ideal. Here is a baroque painting in words, the fall of Satan from the opening of *Paradise Lost:*

> *. . . Him the Almighty Power*
> *Hurled headlong flaming from th' ethereal sky*
> *With hideous ruin and combustion down*
> *To bottomless perdition, there to dwell*
> *In adamantine chains and penal fire*
> *Who durst defy th' Omnipotent to arms.*

James II, the rather stupid and excessively conscientious brother of Charles II, was unable to live within the framework of government set up in 1660, and he succeeded in uniting both Anglican and Puritan against him by attempting to restore Catholicism, by keeping a standing army, and by accepting French subsidies in place of taxes granted by Parliament. In 1688 the leading aristocrats in England invited the stadholder of Holland, William of Orange, who had married James's Protestant daughter Mary, to invade England and hold the throne jointly with his wife. In the Glorious or Bloodless Revolution, James was sent into exile—that is, he was allowed to escape after he had been captured, to avoid any bloodshed—and Parliament restored once again the constitutional situation of 1641. But this time the circumstances were different. It was taking for itself the role of nominating the king of England, ending by that act any pretense future kings might have to govern by divine right.

This constitutional development has its urban counterpart in the physical development of London, whose contrast with Paris is itself graphic evidence of the divergence between the two monarchies. In 1619 the classicist architect Inigo Jones began the creation of a vast palace complex in Whitehall, which would eventually have run along the Thames north of Parliament as the Louvre ran along the Seine. Work was interrupted by Charles's quarrel with Parliament over funds. It was taken up again at the end of the first fighting in the civil war and broken off with the execution of Charles I in front of the barely begun palace. A new start continued for a brief while until Charles II sought to avoid reliance on Parliament for his funds. The land intended for the palace was bought for private homes by members of the nobility. London was to be denied also the baroque town plan that Wren drew up for it after the fire of 1666 destroyed most of the western part of the city. An absolute monarch might have enforced the plan, giving London its river terraces, its boulevards, and its monumental vistas. Private owners refused to pool their property, however, and rebuilt on the plots laid out in the Middle Ages. No power existed to subordinate private capitalism to public planning.

Physical Evolution of London

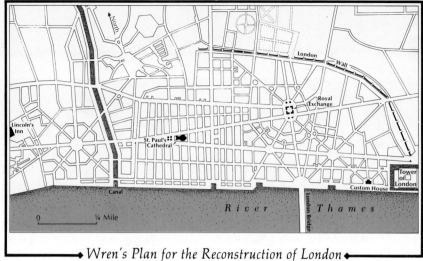

◆ *Wren's Plan for the Reconstruction of London* ◆

Yet there was a compromise with the demands of the baroque city planner. The king was not reduced to a position of *primus inter pares* ("first among equals") like the stadholder of the Netherlands, whose palaces were only glorified townhouses. His importance could be asserted on the edge of the city by rebuilding palaces like Hampton Court in the style of Versailles, and even in the parkland he owned in the center of town where avenues, as in Saint James's Park, could be laid out in geometrical patterns like Le Nôtre's. But the well-to-do dominated most of the city, and their baroque was the domesticity of the city square, created not by royalty but by real estate speculators. The only requirement of the city government was that new buildings should be in brick. Thus in a century when the population of London grew from two to five hundred thousand, the predominant feature of the city was the street or square, lined with three- to four-story houses of undeniable comfort, which had cozily compromised with the demands of the baroque just as their inhabitants had equally satisfactorily compromised with the absolutist demands of their monarchy.

SUGGESTED READING

Perhaps the best way to understand the baroque city is to begin with a specific city that was thoroughly remodeled according to baroque principles. Paris is a good example, seen through Orest Ranum, *Paris in the Age of Absolutism* (1968) or Léon Bernard, *The Emerging City* (1970). But one must turn again to Pierre Lavedan's *Histoire de l'urbanisme* (1941), vol. 2, or to Lewis Mumford's *The City in History* (1966) for a general survey of the principles underlying city building throughout Europe and its colonies.

The baroque style is described in Victor L. Tapie, *The Age of Grandeur: Baroque Art and Architecture* (1960), while the achievements of individual countries can be admired in Judith Hook, *The Baroque Age in England* (1976); H. Gerson and E. H. Huile, *Art and Architecture in Belgium, 1600 to 1800* (1960); Rudolf Wittkower, *Art and Architecture in Italy, 1600–1750* (1958); and Anthony Blunt, *Art and Architecture in France, 1500–1700* (1953). For music, see Manfred F. Bufkozer, *Music in the Baroque Era* (1947).

There are several good surveys of the politics of the baroque age, among them Henry Kamen, *The Iron Century: Social Change in Europe, 1550–1660* (1971), which employs economic quantification and is especially good on the recession of the first half of the seventeenth century; Carl J. Friedrich, *The Age of the Baroque, 1610–1660* (1952); Frederick L. Nussbaum, *The Triumph of Science and Reason, 1660–1685* (1953); John B. Wolf, *The Emergence of the Great Powers, 1685–1715* (1951); and Carl J. Friedrich and C. Blitzer, *The Age of Power* (1957).

For the social background, on which much important research has been carried out recently, one might begin with the pioneering work of Pierre Goubert, *Beauvais et le Beauvaisis de 1600 à 1730* (1958), which can be compared with Emmanuel Leroy Ladurie's study of southern France, *The Peasants of Languedoc* (1977). Robert Mandrou, *Introduction to Modern France, 1500–1640* (1975) attempts a sketch of the mental conception of the world around them held by the average French people during the period of transition from the Middle Ages to the reign of Louis XIV. The relationship of economic to social change in England is analyzed in B. A. Holderness, *Pre-industrial England: Economy and Society, 1500–1750* (1976).

Richard T. Vann, "Toward a New Lifestyle: Women in Preindustrial Capitalism," in Renate Bridenthal and Claudia Koonz, eds., *Becoming Visible: Women in European History* (1977), discusses the changes in patterns of life for women in the early modern age caused by the fact that they began to outlive men, by the growing separation of employment from the home, and by the recognition of motherhood as a career. Natalie Zemon Davies, "Ghosts, Kin, and Progeny: Some Features of Family Life in Early Modern France," *Daedalus*, 106 (Spring 1977), pp. 87–114, shows how family structures changed under the impact of urbanization. On family life in England, rather different methodological approaches are taken by Lawrence Stone, *The Family, Sex, and Marriage in England, 1500–1800* (1977) and Peter Laslett, *Family Life and Illicit Love in Earlier Generations* (1977), while Roger Thompson makes a not wholly convincing case that women were better off in colonial America than in England in *Women in Stuart England and America: A Comparative Study* (1974). Carolyn Lougee discusses the social reasons for the blast of criticism of "learned women" in seventeenth-century France in *Le Paradis des Femmes: Women, Salons, and Social Stratification in Seventeenth-Century France* (1976), while the literature of seventeenth-century feminism is recounted in enormous detail by Ian Maclean, *Woman Triumphant: Feminism in French Literature, 1610–1652* (1977).

The character of Moscow during the long struggles of the tsars to reaffirm their power during the conflict with the Tartars and after the overthrow of the Tartar yoke is evident in John Fennell, *The Emergence of Moscow, 1304–1359* and in the biographies of the great tsars, such as Harold Lamb, *The March of Muscovy* (1948) and J. L. I. Fennell, *Ivan the Great of Moscow* (1962). The battles for the throne are best covered in one of the general surveys, of which Nicholas A. Riasanovsky, *History of Russia* (1963) is among the best. C. Bickford O'Brien, *Rus-*

sia *Under Two Tsars, 1682–1689* (1952) prepares us for Peter, whose move to Saint Petersburg is explained in B. H. Sumner, *Peter the Great and the Emergence of Russia* (1951) and Harold Lamb, *The City and the Tsar: Peter the Great and the Move to the West, 1648–1762* (1948). For further biographical details, see M. S. Anderson, *Peter the Great* (1978) and L. Jay Oliva, *Russia in the Era of Peter the Great* (1969). The condition of the peasantry is the key to understanding Russian social history in Jerome Blum, *Lord and Peasant in Russia* (1961). James H. Billington, *The Icon and the Axe* (1966) is a stimulating interpretation of the whole of Russian cultural history. A sweeping overview is provided in Marc Raeff, *Imperial Russia, 1682–1825: The Coming of Age of Modern Russia* (1970).

On the creation of absolutism by the immediate predecessors of Louis XIV, see Roland Mousnier's *The Assassination of Henry IV* (1972), whose title misleadingly conceals the book's broad treatment of the reign, V-L. Tapie, *Richelieu and Louis XIII* (1967), and A. D. Lubinskaya, *French Absolutism: The Crucial Phase, 1620–1629* (1968). The day-to-day absolutism of Louis XIV, with its minute regulation of noble life in Versailles, is described by Saint-Simon, *Louis XIV at Versailles* (1963), translated by Desmond Flower, which is a good selection from his diaries. The whole life of France comes alive in W. H. Lewis, *The Splendid Century* (1953). For the Grand Monarque himself, good biographies include John B. Wolf, *Louis XIV* (1968) and Maurice Ashley's brief *Louis XIV and the Greatness of France* (1946). Pierre Goubert's *Louis XIV and Twenty Million Frenchmen* (1970) describes public policy against an economic background, while his *Ancien Regime, 1600–1750* (1974) extends his study in time and space. Theodore K. Rabb, *The Struggle for Stability in Early Modern Europe* (1975) is a comprehensive survey of the political stress that brought about the creation of the new forms of state in the seventeenth century. The impact of the absolutist government of France upon the countryside is seen in Roland Mousnier's comparative analysis, *Peasant Uprisings in Seventeenth-Century France, Russia, and China* (1970).

David Maland, *Culture and Society in Seventeenth Century France* (1970) and J. Lough, *An Introduction to Seventeenth Century France* (1954) show the relationship of literature to society. Robert M. Isherwood, *Music in the Service of the King: France in the Seventeenth Century* (1973) is a learned study of the musicians of Louis XIV's court. On the palace of Versailles, see P. de Nolhac, *Versailles et la Cour de France: L'Art de Versailles* (1930). The highlights of the literature of the age can be sampled in Corneille, *Le Cid*, Molière, *L'Avare*, and Racine, *Phèdre*. The most important novel is Madame de Lafayette's *Princess of Clèves*, the best letters, those of Madame de Sévigné (*Letters*, many editions).

Tudor English history abounds in fine biographies, perhaps because the people themselves were so excitingly expressive. J. J. Scarisbrick, *Henry VIII* (1968) and J. E. Neale, *Queen Elizabeth I* (1952) are superb. G. R. Elton explains the constitutional development under the Tudors in *England Under the Tudors* (1960), and A. L. Rowse makes *The Elizabethan Age* (1950–1955) one of the more colorful periods of history.

For the social background to the English constitutional struggles of the seventeenth century, one should turn to Lawrence Stone, *The Crisis of the Aristocracy, 1558–1641* (1965) and his *Causes of the English Revolution, 1529–1642* (1972), or to H. R. Trevor-Roper, *The Gentry, 1540–1640* (1953). Christopher Hill, *The Century of Revolution, 1603–1714* (1961) is a reliable survey, while his *World Turned Upside Down: Radical Ideas During the English Revolution* (1972) reveals the astonishing variety of radical movements that surfaced briefly in the 1640s and

1650s. After C. V. Wedgwood's biography *Oliver Cromwell* (1956) and her excellent studies of the revolutionary years, *The King's Peace, 1637–1641* (1955) and *The King's War, 1641–1647* (1959), one should consult Michael L. Walzer, *The Revolution of the Saints* (1965) for an explanation of the social origins of Puritan politics.

The participation of English women in the sects is seen as of ephemeral importance by K. V. Thomas, "Women and the Civil War Sects," *Past and Present* (April 1958), pp. 40–62. Their political role in petitioning Parliament is illustrated with rich contemporary quotations (e.g., "Things have come to a fine pass if women come to teach Parliament how to make laws") in Patricia Higgins, "The Reactions of Women, with special reference to women petitioners," in Brian Manning, ed., *Politics, Religion and the English Civil War* (1973), pp. 179–222.

Finally, for a far-ranging, difficult, and stimulating attempt to make sense of economic and political developments on a worldwide scale in the early modern age, try Immanuel Wallerstein, *The Modern World-System: Capitalist Agriculture and the Origins of the European World-Economy in the Sixteenth Century* (1974).

20

THE PARIS OF THE PHILOSOPHES

If Julian [the Roman emperor, who was born in Paris in A. D. 331] could now revisit the capital of France, he might converse with men of science and genius capable of understanding and instructing a disciple of the Greeks; he might excuse the graceful follies of a nation whose martial spirit has never been enervated by the indulgence of luxury; and he must applaud the perfection of that inestimable art which softens and refines and embellishes the intercourse of social life—Edward Gibbon, Memoirs

Paris was the cultural center of eighteenth-century Europe. It exercised a unifying influence on the society and intellect of the continent that was felt from Lisbon to Saint Petersburg and from Edinburgh to Palermo. Its taste and ideas were spread by a million admirers who came to love Paris as much as or more than their native lands. Called back to Naples, Abbot Galiani lamented: "Yes, Paris is my homeland. . . . They are exiling me in vain, I shall be back. . . . Ah, my dear Paris! Ah! how I miss you!" English visitors were similarly impressed. "London is good for the English," commented the actor David Garrick, "but Paris is good for everyone." And the Russian aristocrat Karamsin, visiting Paris on the eve of the Revolution, expressed the fulfilled enthusiasm of a literate admirer:

So here it is, here is this city which during the course of so many centuries was the model of all Europe, the source of taste, of man-

(Left Page) The Swing, by Jean-Honoré Fragonard (1732–1806) *(Reproduced by permission of the Trustees of the Wallace Collection, London)*; (Inset) Denis Diderot, by L. M. Van Loo *(Cliché des Musées Nationaux-Paris)*

ners, whose name is pronounced with respect by the learned and the ignorant, by philosophers and artisans, by artists and peasants, in Europe and in Asia, in America and in Africa, whose name has been known to me as long as my own, about which I have read so many things in novels, have learned so many things from travellers, have dreamed and thought so many things. . . . Here it is! I am going to see it! I am going to live there! Ah! my friends, this moment has been one of the most charming of my journey! I have never approached any town with feelings so lively, with such curiosity, with such impatience![1]

But Paris was also the capital of France in a far more practical sense; it had begun, in Montesquieu's words, "to swallow the provinces." All French life—intellectual, artistic, economic, bureaucratic, judicial, social— was centralized in Paris. Paris, which at the time of Saint Louis had served a largely beneficial function in unifying the disparate provinces, in providing order and law, and in stimulating the artistic genius of France, was be-

[1]Pierre Gaxotte, *Paris au XVIIIe siècle* (Grenoble: B. Arthaud, 1968), p. 9. Author's translation.

◆ The Paris of the Philosophes ◆

Period Surveyed	From the death of Louis XIV (1715) to the beginning of the French Revolution (1789)
Population	560,000 (1730); 650,000 (1789)
Area	4.5 square miles (1715); 15.5 square miles (1789)
Form of Government	Absolute monarchy; reviving power of *parlements* (traditional law courts in Paris and provinces); administration through intendants
Political Leaders	King Louis XV (reigned 1715–1774); Duke of Orléans (Regent, 1715–1723); Cardinal Fleury (Chief Minister, 1726–1743); King Louis XVI (reigned 1774–1792); Turgot; Necker; Calonne
Economic Base	Royal bureaucracy; provincial income of resident nobility, clergy, and bourgeois; profits from tax-farming and overseas trade; manufacture of luxury goods; textiles; artisan crafts; construction industry
Intellectual Life	Philosophy and political theory (Montesquieu, Voltaire, Diderot, d'Alembert, Rousseau); novels (Voltaire, Rousseau, Abbot Prévost); economics (Quesnay); science (Fontenelle, Buffon, Lavoisier); painting (Watteau, Boucher, Fragonard, Chardin); decorative arts (Boulle, Huet, Meissonier); drama (Marivaux, Beaumarchais); architecture (Gabriel, Soufflot)
Principal Buildings	Place Louix XV (Place de la Concorde); Elysée Palace; St. Sulpice; Ste. Geneviève; several theaters; Wall of the Farmers-General
Religion	Catholic (but Church under attack from philosophes); deism

ginning to sap the vitality of the rest of the French state. The rivalry between Paris and the provinces of France that was to run through the rest of French history was already apparent. The English agricultural expert Arthur Young was told by the townsfolk of Nancy on the day after the storming of the Bastille, the state prison in Paris: "We are a provincial town, we must wait to see what is done at Paris; but everything is to be feared from the people [there] because bread is so dear, they are half starved, and are consequently ready for commotion."[2] Thus, excessive centralization ensured that violent change in Paris would produce vast repercussions throughout the country, to a far greater extent than would have been true in any other country of Europe. In delineating the role of Paris in the eighteenth century, we shall therefore consider three of its many roles: its position as the cultural arbiter of Europe, its function in the centralized society of France, and its character as the incubator of revolution.

[2] Arthur Young, *Travels in France During the Years 1787, 1788, and 1789* (Garden City, N.Y.: Doubleday Anchor, 1969), p. 148.

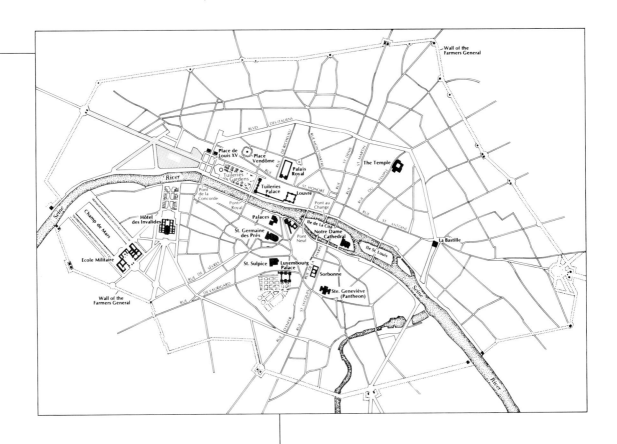

THE CULTURAL CENTER OF EUROPE

**Subordinate
Relationship of
Versailles to Paris**

In the reign of Louis XIV, Versailles rather than Paris had been the center of French culture, and thus to a large extent, of European culture. But with the unlamented death of the Sun King in 1715, *La Cour* ("The Court") and *La Ville* ("The City"), as Versailles and Paris were called, changed in relative importance. Louis-Sébastien Mercier, the author of *Tableau of Paris*, which is one of the most revealing commentaries on Parisian society in the eighteenth century, noted the end of Versailles' dominance:

The word "Court" no longer deceives us as it did in the days of Louis XIV. We do not accept the dominant opinion of the Court, which can no longer make or unmake reputations of any kind, nor do we murmur with ridiculous humility as of yore, "The Court has decided" this or that. The verdict of the Court is merely quashed, and we just say: "They don't know anything about it at Versailles; they have no ideas on the subject; they could not have any; they have, in short, no conception about the matter at all." The Court itself, as all can see, dare not pronounce any favorable verdict on a book, a play, or some other new masterpiece, nor on any event of remarkable or extraordinary nature without first awaiting the sentence of the capital. [3]

The importance of Paris had first been reasserted by the regent, Philip of Orléans, when he moved the five-year-old king, Louis XV, into the Tuileries Palace and himself took over Richelieu's old home across the street in the Palais Royal. The court never recovered from the attack on its empty ceremonial led by the debauched but able regent; and when, in 1722, Louis XV returned to Versailles he was not accompanied by all the

[3]Louis Ducros, *French Society in the Eighteenth Century*, trans. W. de Geijer (London: G. Bell, 1926), pp. 97–98.

Gersaint's Sign, by Antoine Watteau (1684–1721)
Five years after the death of Louis XIV, the art dealer Gersaint has found no purchasers for the king's portrait, which is being put in storage. The shimmering fabrics of ladies browsing in a picture gallery were used by Watteau to create an atmosphere of studied elegance. (Staatliche Schlösser und Gärten, Berlin)

great nobility and high administrators. Even the foreign ambassadors lived in Paris and paid only occasional visits to Versailles. The old Capetian palace on the Ile de la Cité remained the seat of the most important law courts. Among government ministries, only those for foreign affairs, war, and the navy were in Versailles; the rest were scattered in Paris, mostly across the Right Bank. All the great state cultural and scientific organizations were in Paris. To Louis XV this neglect of Versailles was immaterial, since he was seeking a privacy that had never appealed to his great-grandfather. To Marie Antoinette, the Austrian wife of Louis XVI, Paris was appealing in its frivolity, and she escaped there when she could to revel in its masked balls or its evenings of opera. Louis XVI himself preferred the distraction of his hobby as an amateur locksmith to the tedium of court life. Without a Sun King, Versailles could not hope to rival the attractive power of Paris.

Paris as Patron of the Intellect

What most distinguished Paris was a form of society in which the well-to-do, whether noble or bourgeois, met on terms of relative equality and interacted with the leaders of intellectual and artistic life. The centralization of French life in Paris had led to a concentration of most of the country's talent and, to some degree, that of the continent. Of all the great writers of the century, scarcely one was a native Parisian. Among the writers, Montesquieu was from Bordeaux, Diderot from Champagne, Rousseau from Geneva. The very names of the artists betray their non-Parisian origins. The painter Watteau was Flemish; the furniture maker Oppenord from a Dutch family; Meissonier, the master of rococo decoration, from Provence, though born in Italy. Yet Paris attracted them all because in the first place it offered the patronage that was lacking in Versailles and the provinces. Louis XV and Louis XVI were far from being the extravagant patrons of architecture and art that the Sun King had been. Louis XV did little more at Versailles than erect the delightful cube of the Petit Trianon Palace. Marie Antoinette's principal effort at building was the erection of the Little Hamlet, a make-believe farm with little cottages and dairy stalls where she and her courtiers could retire to an unspoiled and carefully cleaned setting. But there was little here to employ the artists of France, who found their patrons among the financiers, the tax farmers, the industrialists, and occasionally the nobility of the capital. Typical among this new class of patrons was Antoine Crozat, who made a fortune as the banker for the Paris clergy and from the monopoly of the Louisiana trade. Crozat built a fine country mansion near Paris and a splendid town house in Paris, where Watteau lodged while he was painting the four panels of *The Seasons.* In Paris, too, could be found the wider patronage of the general public, the organized market for art that was beginning to enable the artist to dispense with the favors of an individual patron.

Paris thus became the chief art market in Europe in the eighteenth century, with highly institutionalized methods of sale. Members of the Academy displayed their paintings for sale every two years in the Louvre. Artists who were not members of the Academy displayed their paintings in the open air on the Place Dauphine. Lavishly illustrated catalogs were sent all over Europe so that foreign patrons could send their orders or auction bids to their representatives in Paris. In this way Paris filled the palaces and mansions of Europe not only with its paintings but also with that cornucopia of lesser arts that was the finest creation of the rococo style— the inlaid furniture of Boulle, the tapestry wall panels of Huet, the clocks of Meissonier, the hand-painted porcelain from Sèvres, and snuffboxes, silver spoons, chandeliers, and candlesticks by the thousand. So great was the market in Paris in the latter part of the century that foreign artists began to flock in to share in it and thereby contribute to its fame. Even foreign playwrights found it worthwhile to come to Paris to present their works, as the Italian comedy writer Goldoni testified in his *Memoirs.* He accumulated a modest fortune and furthermore found Paris to be a city that fascinated and nearly overwhelmed him:

Paris is a world of itself: everything is on a large scale, the good and bad both in abundance. Whether you go to theaters, promenades, or places of pleasure, you find every corner full. Even the churches are crowded. In a town of eight hundred thousand souls there must necessarily be more of both good and bad people than anywhere else; and it rests with ourselves to make our choice. . . . Every day I felt myself more and more confused in the ranks, the classes, the manners of living, and the different modes of thinking. I no longer knew what I was, what I wished for, or what I was becoming. I was quite absorbed in the vortex. [4]

What Goldoni had found, however, was a common experience among the sensitive who gave themselves up to the challenge of Paris; the city acted as a hothouse for the intellect, stimulating the growth of one's abilities and rewarding one's achievement. Even the most cynical were compelled to recognize this characteristic. Jean-Jacques Rousseau, who spent

[4]Carlo Goldoni, *Memoirs,* trans. John Black (Boston: Osgood, 1877), pp. 352–353.

much of his career denouncing the evil effects on natural man of the artificial restraints of society, declared that "the spirit which pervades society in Paris develops clear thinking and broadens the mind as much as possible. If you have even a spark of genius, go and spend a year in Paris. Soon you will be all that you can ever be, or else you will never be anything at all." Mercier, after wandering through the teeming crowds in the colonnades of the Palais Royal, where talk rattled as vibrantly as in the stoa of Athens, was struck by the difference from his native province:

I am not so absurdly prejudiced as to suppose that there is no good talk outside the capital; or that the clear sun of the arts shines only on Parisians, while the provinces are illumined only by occasional wandering stars. . . . All the same, the mind of man, pressed like a grape by the teeming interests of the city all about him, gives here a more abundant yield. Ideas come more easily to birth, and are themselves more fruitful here; they must be strong enough to withstand the buffetings of criticism, and remain firm in contact with the thousand different and changing individualities which crowd the townsman's life; characters in Paris are more sharply distinct than in the provinces, and some more eccentric. There is a kind of peaceful quality in the life of the smaller towns, where day follows day smoothly as a river flows; but the capital is a storm-tossed sea, eternally troubled by contrary winds. [5]

Moreover, Paris in the seventeenth century had succeeded in developing an institution, the *salon*, that focused all the city's intellectual stimulation. The great hostesses of the age of Louis XIV, like Mademoiselle de Scudéry, had survived the attack upon their "preciosity" led by Molière and others; and in the eighteenth century their successors had made the institution less personally idiosyncratic, even if less immediately exciting. Perhaps one hundred hostesses conducted salons on regular days of the week—gatherings at which dinner was usually served, cards occasionally played, but conversation predominated. The character of the guests and the conversation was dictated by the hostess; and certain salons came to be recognized as conferring on their habitués membership in the highest rank of the social and intellectual elite of the capital. In these salons was the ideal mixture of leading intellectuals, open-minded nobles, and clever, elegant women.

The Parisian Salons

During the Regency, the serious-minded Marquise de Lambert brought together in her drawing room in part of Mazarin's old palace such authors as Montesquieu, Marivaux, and Fontenelle; works ready for publication were read aloud and criticized; and for a time acceptance in her salon was almost a prerequisite for acceptance into the Académie Française. On her death, her place was taken by a far livelier and more entertaining woman, Alexandrine de Tencin, an unfrocked nun, the unmarried mother of the great philosopher d'Alembert, a financial speculator, and a well-paid spy. It

[5] Louis-Sébastien Mercier, *The Waiting City: Paris, 1782–88*, trans. Helen Simpson (London: Harrap, 1933), p. 275.

An Evening Reception in Madame Geoffrin's Salon
On Wednesdays Madame Geoffrin invited a group of nobles and intellectuals to her salon. The authors she patronized would read aloud to her guests from the latest books and plays, which they would then discuss.
(H. Roger-Viollet)

was at Tencin's salon that some of the ablest foreign visitors to Paris, such as Lord Bolingbroke and Lord Chesterfield from England, were introduced to France's writers, like the Abbot Prévost, author of *Manon Lescaut*, or Tencin's favorite, Montesquieu, whose best book, *The Spirit of the Laws*, she rescued from oblivion by giving away at her expense most of the first edition. But by far the most important was that of Madame Geoffrin, who gathered around her (on Mondays) the finest painters, including Boucher and Chardin, and also (on Wednesdays) the leaders of the French Enlightenment, Diderot, d'Alembert, and Marmontel, at the very time they were preparing the most important statement of their opinions, the *Encyclopédie*; and she contributed almost half the cost of that twenty-eight-volume work.

Distinguished foreigners gained easy access to the Paris salons. "I well remember seeing all Europe standing three deep around her chair," wrote one of Mme Geoffrin's admirers. Back home they sought constant news of the intellectual excitement of Paris, exchanging long letters with their hostesses, buying up the books that the Paris presses were pouring out, and begging France's intellectuals and artists to join them in their exile from Paris. Frederick the Great of Prussia, who despised the German language and spoke French almost exclusively, admired Voltaire inordinately, exchanged letters with him for forty-two years, and even brought him to Potsdam for a tormented three-year stay. Catherine the Great of Russia offered to publish the *Encyclopédie* in Russia to avoid the French censors, bought Diderot's library and paid him a salary to keep it for her, and finally brought him to Saint Petersburg for a five-month stay that merely convinced her of the impracticality of his ideas. The leading French intellectuals found themselves in similar demand in Stockholm, Warsaw, Leipzig, and Florence; and even England, the one country that contested the dominance of the French language as the principal vehicle for the intercourse of human minds, fêted Voltaire and Rousseau on their prolonged visits.

Thus with very few exceptions, Europe recognized the cultural preeminence of Paris and admired the extraordinary instrument for the sharpening of the human mind that had been created by the society of that city. But what precisely was the content of this culture that had been brought to such an exciting peak? And, perhaps more important, what were the effects inside and outside France of the admiration of this culture?

THE AGE OF ROCOCO

For the first time since Paris had become one of the principal shapers of European civilization in the thirteenth century, its cultural impact was not primarily visual. Paris remained a center of the visual arts and itself a superb embodiment of them; but in comparison with its earlier achievements in both Gothic and baroque, its artistic contribution was charming but minor. The city itself expanded greatly with the erection of whole new districts for the aristocracy and wealthier middle classes on the western edge of town; and here French architects created ever more elegant variations on the basic ground plan of the aristocratic townhouse. In particular, they recognized the greater intimacy of social life and especially the function of the living room, or *salon*, by developing a style of sparkling, graceful interior decoration known as *rococo*.

The Rococo Style in Paris

The rococo style was an outgrowth of the baroque, accepting the emotional fantasies of baroque but rejecting its fascination with geometric patterns and its search for magnificence. Its main characteristics were the forms of decoration called *rocaille* (rock) and *coquille* (shell), which were elaborated in infinite variations for almost every type of artistic object, whether gun barrel, wall panel, doorknob, or saltshaker. There was thus a unity to an eighteenth-century room that was missing in any earlier period; and the artists recognized their task of producing that unity by mastering every form of decorative art themselves. Meissonier designed houses, tapestry, cutlery, plates, caskets, and chairs with equal skill.

The French painter who epitomized this achievement was Antoine Watteau (1684–1721), a tubercular genius whose brief career laid down the goals of French painting for the next century. Watteau specialized in movement, the meeting of delicate curves; but he broke with the baroque style of painters like Rubens by suffusing his paintings with a soft languor and an atmosphere of hazy sensuality. His work was exquisitely delicate, with its masterly presentation of the play of light on silks or taffeta, on

Drawing Room from the Hotel St. James, Place Vendôme, Paris (1776)
The unity of style of this room of the Louis XVI period is achieved by a return from rococo to a more classical use of straight lines, rectangles, and Roman floral motifs. (The Fine Arts Museums of San Francisco)

Madame de Pompadour, by François Boucher (1703–1770)
Pompadour, the mistress and advisor of Louis XV, was influential in the choice of government ministers and in foreign policy decisions. Of the many artists she employed to decorate her palaces, Boucher was her favorite. (Cliché des Musées Nationaux-Paris)

bouffant hair, or twirling fans. He perfected the *fête galante*, the picture of a group of courtiers idling away the late afternoon in a shadowy glade of some indeterminate forest, pictures of gentle and emotional recollection of the passing of moments of perfect, and undistinguished, contentment. His most famous painting, *The Embarkation for Cythera* (1717), displaying a group of nobles preparing to leave the mythical island of love where Venus emerged from the sea, became the model for France's favorite painters until the Revolution. Under the spell of Watteau came such paintings as *The Swing* of Jean-Honoré Fragonard (1732–1806) and the many portraits of Louis XV's mistress Madame de Pompadour by François Boucher (1703–1770), works as charming and as deliberately devoid of emotional stress as a Louis XV wall panel.

On the outer face of Paris, these rococo fripperies left little impression. The architects of the major monuments returned to a sound, if less grandiose, resumption of seventeenth-century taste. To this return, Paris owed the marvelous dome of the Church of Sainte Geneviève, designed by Soufflot in 1755 and turned during the Revolution into a Pantheon "for the ashes of the great men of the period of French liberty"; and one of the finest squares in the world, the Place de la Concorde, begun by Gabriel the same year.

The Rococo Style in Spain, Austria, and South Germany

Outside Paris, however, the rococo style was adopted with great enthusiasm and skill. In Spain and Portugal there had been a long tradition of enriching the outside and inside of buildings with complicated patterns of ornament in stone, gilded wood, stucco, and tile, derived in large measure from Moslem buildings like the Alhambra. In the late medieval churches of Spanish towns like Valladolid and Salamanca, whole facades were covered with intertwining lacework of stone, displaying figures of saints and royal and heraldic emblems in a fantastically creative display. The style was transformed without difficulty into the swirling design of the famous Trasparente (1732) in Toledo Cathedral, where the architect knocked out the ceiling of a Gothic vault to create an illusion of angels, bathed in golden sunlight, floating through swirling clouds to reach a celestial celebration of the communion. The style passed to the Spanish colonies in Central and South America, to reach California in the gilt altarpieces of the missions founded in the eighteenth century by the Franciscan friars.

In Austria and South Germany the style achieved its greatest architectural glory, in buildings as subtle in their use of spatial counterpoint as the great fugues that Johann Sebastian Bach was writing contemporaneously in musical counterpoint. The patrons who built these vast new churches, monasteries, and palaces were the rulers of the independent German states, like the elector of Saxony or the bishop of Würzburg, the abbots of the wealthy monasteries, and the Austrian royal family and nobility. Their architects were native-born Germans and Austrians who had, however, grasped the best that Italian baroque and French rococo had to offer and who were prepared to develop their own unique variation of style.

St. Stephen's Monastery, Salamanca, Spain (Sixteenth and Seventeenth Centuries)
Whereas the richly decorated facades of fifteenth-century churches in Valladolid, Spain, were still Gothic in style, those built in Salamanca in the following two centuries were inspired by the Italian Renaissance. The style of facades like St. Stephen's is called plateresque, the implication being that they were so finely carved, they appeared to be the work of a platero, or silvermith. (© Peter Menzel)

They accepted the value of complex spatial planning and the use of the oval in the ground plan, the interplay of convex and concave curves in outer facades and inner galleries, and the writhing columns like Bernini's at Saint Peter's. But they subdued the emotional thrust of the style's theatricality, muting the colors to pastel shades of pink and blue, mingling whites and gold in all the complexity of rocaille decoration.

Entering the stairwell of the episcopal palace of Würzburg, glancing up at the undulating facade and bulbous towers of the monastery of Melk

The Pilgrimage Church of Vierzehnheiligen, near Bamberg
The spatial complexity of Balthasar Neumann's Church of the Fourteen Saints is achieved by a ground plan of linked ovals and circles that replace the rectangular nave and aisles of the customary basilican church. (Bildarchiv Foto Marburg)

above the Danube, and especially passing into the sparkling interior of the pilgrimage church of Vierzehnheiligen near Bamberg, one realizes at once that the great success of such German rococo architects as Balthasar Neumann (1687–1753) was to achieve in the molding of space what the French artists had succeeded in doing only in decoration. Here rococo had become a great architectural style. It is impossible even to list the main achievements of this style, without which central Europe would have been infinitely more barren. Of the multitude of buildings that drained off the wealth of the countryside of Germany and Austria, one must at least mention Frederick's palace of Sans Souci at Potsdam, where he entertained Voltaire; the exuberant pavilions of the Zwinger Palace in Dresden, whose startling succession of curving facades served little more purpose than an art gallery and an orangery; the splendid monasteries that lined the Danube, from Melk to Klosterneuburg on the edge of Vienna; and the vast palaces that the Habsburg emperors built in the capitals of their separate possessions, such as Schönbrunn outside Vienna. Here were the real mas-

The Zwinger Palace, Dresden, Germany, by Mathäus Daniel Pöppelmann (1662–1736)
Designed as a picture gallery and "orangery" where orange trees could be raised behind glass in the cool German climate, the Zwinger Palace was used by the elector of Saxony for tournaments and court pageants. This rococo masterpiece has been restored since the firebombing of Dresden in 1945. (Courtesy of the German Information Center)

terpieces of a style that originated in France but found the weight of tradition too great at home for it to pass from decorative and minor arts into architecture.

THE FRENCH ENLIGHTENMENT

It was in "philosophy" rather than art that eighteenth-century Paris dominated Europe, philosophy in the sense of the broadest possible intellectual activity—in political theory, economics, natural science, philosophy, jurisprudence, even technology. France's thinkers, the philosophes, believed that they had made their century the *siècle des lumières*, or the century of enlightenment; and until the unhappy shock of the Revolution they found few to disagree with them.

The intellectual achievements of the French Enlightenment came rapidly in the sixty years between the death of Louis XIV and the beginning of the American Revolution. In the first place France's intellectuals had thoroughly absorbed both the substance and the significance of the scientific advances represented by the work of Isaac Newton and the psychological and political theories of John Locke. They had accepted the implication common to both thinkers that the universe was governed by natural laws that could be ascertained by the use of human reason, especially when applied to the acquisition of factual knowledge through controlled experiment. The philosophes accepted the scientific, rational attitude of mind as the foundation for future progress. That they did so unquestioningly was due to the great advances that science had made following the Renaissance, in what has been justly called the scientific revolution.

The Middle Ages had not entirely ignored science, though little new knowledge of scientific phenomena was acquired. The principal works of Greek science had been studied, usually after being obtained from the Arabs. Scholasticism had encouraged the use of logical inquiry and had insisted that the universe operated in accordance with specific laws, even if those laws could be set aside by God's intervention. But, especially after the establishment of a unified world view by Thomas Aquinas, which integrated Christian and pre-Christian thinking, it became dangerous to challenge the scientific explanations that the Church had accepted. Moreover, ordinary observation seemed to show the truth of most of these theories. For example in astronomy, it seemed clear, as Aristotle had said, that bodies fall to the center of the earth; that stars move, as Ptolemy had explained, in crystalline spheres; and that heaven, as the Church taught, lay outside the outermost sphere, the *primum mobile*, that kept the whole system turning. Even the explanation by chemistry that all matter was composed of earth, air, fire, and water seemed as reasonable as any other explanation before the apparatus for chemical experimentation had been invented.

Simultaneous advances in several spheres, however, made it possible for scientists in the sixteenth and seventeenth centuries first to challenge and then to overthrow most of the established authorities. First, the scientist and technician joined hands, inventing several important tools by which observation and experiment could be carried out. Of these the most

The Scientific Revolution and the Enlightenment

The Alchemist, by David Teniers the Younger (1610–1690)
The experimental methods of modern chemistry were founded in part on the attempts of alchemists to turn base metals into gold. (John G. Johnson Collection, Philadelphia)

important was the telescope, invented in Holland in the seventeenth century and used with great effect by the Italian astronomer Galileo (1564–1642). From the same skill in lensmaking came the microscope, which was seized on by biologists. The barometer, the pressure gauge for the measurement of air and gas pressure, the thermometer, the air pump, all were invented when the need of accurate measurement and tools for experimentation was felt.

Secondly, scientists realized that further explanation of the natural world was dependent on advances in mathematics. The language of the universe, wrote Galileo, "is written in the mathematical language, and its characters are triangles, circles, and other geometrical figures, without the aid of which it is impossible to understand a word of it, without which one wanders vainly through a dark labyrinth."[6] Arabic numerals had already been adopted in place of Roman numerals in the late Middle Ages. In the early seventeenth century, John Napier, a Scottish mathematician who had already invented the decimal system to deal with the problem of fractions, developed the system of logarithmic tables, cutting by half the time scientists spent in calculation. In 1637 Descartes made public his analytical geometry, a totally new branch of mathematics by which geometrical relationships could be expressed in algebraic equations, and vice versa. At the end of the seventeenth century, the German philosopher Leibniz and the English scientist Isaac Newton independently invented differential calculus. Without these mathematical tools, the scientific revolution would have been impossible.

Third, these new tools were used effectively because scientists developed the experimental method, whose principal popularizers were Francis Bacon in England and Descartes in France. "Neither the hand without instruments nor the unassisted understanding can do much," wrote Bacon. "We have good ground of hope, from the close and strict union of the experimental and rational faculty, which have not hitherto been united."[7]

Medicine was the first sphere to show the results that could be obtained from careful observation and experiment; and by the middle of the seventeenth century, many of the teachings of the Greek physician Galen had been thrown out, notably as a result of the anatomical treatises of Vesalius and the experiments of William Harvey (1578–1657), who in 1628 proved the circulation of the blood. But the most startling advances were made in astronomy because progress in the explanation of planetary motion involved an understanding of the nature of all motion and the relationship of all matter; and it was here that the established authority of Aristotle and Ptolemy was most firmly supported by the repressive instruments of the Catholic Church.

Change came relatively slowly. In 1542 a Polish clergyman, Nicolaus

---

[6]Cited in F. Sherwood Taylor, *A Short History of Science and Scientific Thought* (New York: Norton, 1963), p. 138.
[7]Ibid., p. 104.

Copernicus (1473–1543), in the search for a more perfect explanation of the universe that would agree with his conception of a perfect God, proposed that the earth moved around the sun. To his contemporaries, Copernicus seemed merely to have simplified astronomical explanation without producing any proof for the abandonment of the belief in a geocentric, or earth-centered, universe. The Dane Tycho Brahe (1546–1601), whose very accurate observations of the movements of the planets made possible the next advances in mathematical explanation of the heavens, was not convinced of the accuracy of Copernicus's view; and it was only in the early seventeenth century that Johannes Kepler (1571–1630), an erratic genius seeking the accurate description of the harmonies in the music of the spheres, made sense of Tycho's observations. In his three laws of planetary motion, Kepler not only proved that Copernicus was right but produced laws whose accuracy is still accepted. He showed, first, that planets travel around the sun in ellipses rather than circles and that the sun is one of the focuses of the ellipse. His second law states that planets do not travel at uniform speed, but that the motion can be described mathematically: a line drawn from the planet to the sun sweeps over equal areas in equal times. Finally, according to his third law, the time taken by all planets to complete their orbits can be described by a single mathematical formula: the squares of the period of the orbit are proportional to the cubes of their mean distances from the sun.

Isaac Newton (1642–1727), by Godfrey Kneller (1646–1723)

Newton exercised a formative influence on the French Enlightenment because his famous laws of motion, described in 1687, appeared to show that the whole universe is governed by laws definable by the application of human reason. (National Portrait Gallery, London)

The Italian physicist and astronomer Galileo took the attack upon the authority of Aristotle much further in his challenge of Aristotle's central concept of motion, namely that all bodies would remain at rest unless moved by some external force. Galileo showed that through "inertia" bodies would continue moving forever at the same speed as the planets unless stopped by some external force. But Galileo was determined to show that all aspects of the Aristotelian system were wrong; that the universe was heliocentric; that the cylindrical spheres were nonexistent; and that the old dynamics was disproved by observation. Galileo was writing, however, at a time when the Catholic Church was fighting off the Protestant challenge to its authority and when many of the European powers were locked in the Thirty Years' War. The Church thus felt that it could not ignore an attack on its world view, especially when Galileo expressed it in outspoken and widely comprehensible language in his *Dialogue Concerning the Two World Systems—Ptolemaic and Copernican*. At the age of seventy, he was called to Rome for trial by the Inquisition, threatened with torture, and compelled to make an abject renunciation of his views.

When Galileo died in 1642, many suspected that his soul had migrated into the body of Isaac Newton, born in England the same year. Newton was the genius who brought together all the findings in astronomy and physics of the previous two centuries and described them mathematically. By the time he was twenty-three, he was entirely the master of his age's scientific knowledge and had already hit upon most of his own contributions to scientific progress.

In the beginning of the year 1665 I found the method for approximating series and the rule for reducing any dignity [power] of any binomial to such a series [i.e. the binomial theorem]. The same year in May I found the method of tangents of Gregory and Slusius, and in November had [discovered] the direct method of Fluxions [the elements of differential calculus], the next year in January had the Theory of Colors, and in May following I had entrance into the inverse method of Fluxions [integral calculus], and in the same year I began to think of gravity extending to the orb of the Moon . . . and having thereby compared the force requisite to keep the Moon in her orb with the force of gravity at the surface of the earth, and found them to answer pretty nearly. All this was in the two years of 1665 and 1666, for in those years I was in the prime of my age for invention, and minded mathematics and Philosophy more than at any time since. [8]

In 1687, in the most influential book of the seventeenth and eighteenth centuries, *The Mathematical Principles of Natural Philosophy*, he explained in three laws of motion not only the movement of the planets but the relationship of all matter. He showed that all bodies attracted each other, and that the force of attraction is directly proportional to the product of their two masses and inversely proportional to the square of their distance apart. Here was a completely mechanical universe, explicable in simple, elegant mathematical laws. The effect of Newton's book was stunning. In Alexander Pope's famous lines,

> *Nature and Nature's Laws lay hid in night,*
> *God said, Let Newton be! and all was light.* [9]

And it was precisely with this feeling that the Frenchmen of the Enlightenment saw in the scientific revolution the proof of their optimism in the future achievements of the human understanding when working on the physical and the human universe.

Up to this point only one Frenchman, Descartes, could be numbered with the geniuses of the scientific revolution. But in the latter years of the reign of Louis XIV, science became enormously popular in France. Colbert had founded the Academy of Sciences in 1666 as a meeting place for scientists and amateurs who dabbled in science. Many middle-class scientists found social success in their public lectures on medicine or astronomy. Foreigners poured in to take the courses of prominent chemists. Even court ladies crowded the benches of the more popular lectures. Thus there was a receptive audience in France for the popularization of the great discoveries that culminated in the work of Newton. Most influential of the popularizers of science was Bernard de Fontenelle (1657–1757), secretary of the Academy of Sciences for forty-two years, habitué at all the major salons, and author of the very popular *Plurality of Worlds*, which set out to make clear for any intelligent person the content and meaning of the new sci-

[8]Ibid., p. 125.
[9]Alexander Pope, "Intended for Sir Isaac Newton," *Epigrams*.

ences. To the intelligentsia of Paris, the scientific revolution, and especially the work of Newton, promised the possibility of the complete comprehension of the working of the universe, including human psychology and the problem of human relationships. Thus, the main contribution of France in the eighteenth century was to apply the lessons of the scientific revolution to other spheres, even though the French did make direct contributions to science. Buffon, for example, director of the famous Jardin des Plantes, attempted a huge synthesis of all biological knowledge. Lavoisier founded modern chemistry, with his delimitation of basic chemical elements such as oxygen and hydrogen. But it was the belief in science rather than the involvement in the making of science that produced the most important results.

Comte de Buffon, by Louis Canogis
Buffon (1707–1788) directed the principal botanical garden in Paris for almost fifty years. He published an exhaustive synthesis called Natural History *in forty-four volumes. (A. Bernard Photographe, Chantilly)*

THE FRENCH ENLIGHTENMENT

887

Reform Program of the French Enlightenment

A good part of the work of the philosophes, like that of the early scientists, had to be destructive. They had to begin by clearing away the false knowledge and the mistaken authorities accumulated, as they thought, by centuries of error. A start had been made at the end of the reign of Louis XIV, when Charles Perrault, a poet and literary gadfly, split the intellectual world of Paris in the so-called "Quarrel of the Ancients and the Moderns," by arguing in a poem called "The Century of Louis the Great" that contemporary writers were better than those of Greece and Rome, who should no longer be treated as authority. The quarrel broadened, especially with the intervention of the rationalist philosopher Pierre Bayle in his *Historical and Critical Dictionary* (1697), whose many challenges to authority included the idea that the marriage of intelligent and educated women was a waste of national resources.

In the early eighteenth century, the criticism turned directly against the Christian Church, which, in all its various forms, the critics felt to be antipathetic to the progress of reason. Bayle's *Dictionary*, which quickly became one of the most influential books of the eighteenth century, had criticized religious persecution and had demanded universal toleration. But the attack was taken up in its most dramatic form by Voltaire (1694–1778), who used reason, ridicule, and pathos in his demand that the infamous thing be crushed: *Ecrasez l'infâme!* Here was a vague but powerful slogan that was to be used again and again to attack every form of institutional oppression against which the enlightened thinkers raged. When a Huguenot merchant, Jean Calas, was publicly killed with unspeakable tortures on the ludicrous grounds that he had strangled his eldest son to prevent his conversion to Catholicism, Voltaire made all Europe burn with anger against the organization that was permitted to carry out such barbarism in an enlightened age.

Even when the philosophes claimed to be defending the existence of God (most philosophes felt that a Creator was necessary for so perfectly conceived a world), they weakened the position of the established churches by arguing in favor of deism. God, they assumed, had stepped out of this universe once he had created it, leaving to humanity the power to know Him by using reason to understand the laws underlying the universe. Moreover, rather than see morality as a law laid down and interpreted by the churches, the philosophes assumed that man possessed in his own nature the capacity for moral judgment. To follow one's moral judgment, which was dependent on understanding the laws of nature, was thus a religious duty for the deists. "All that we do know is that the eternal Lord of nature," wrote Voltaire to Frederick the Great, "has given us the power of thinking, and of distinguishing virtue. . . . In the midst of all the doubts which we have discussed for four thousand years in four thousand ways, the safest course is still to do nothing against one's conscience." [10]

Voltaire, by Jean-Antoine Houdon (1741–1828)
Houdon, the leading French sculptor in the late-eighteenth century, portrayed Voltaire from a sketch made two days before his death. (The Fine Arts Museums of San Francisco, Gift of Mrs. Rose F. Magnin)

[10] Cited in Crane Brinton, ed., *The Portable Age of Reason Reader* (New York: Viking, 1956), p. 366.

This search for a new morality found a second target in the judicial system. Here the philosophes made a lasting contribution to human betterment. They excoriated the use of torture as a regular part of the judicial process, both for its cruelty and its ineffectiveness as a means of finding truth. "An ancient writer has also said quite sententiously," the *Encyclopédie* article on torture concluded, "that those who can stand the question [torture] and those who do not have enough strength to stand it lie in an equal way." Punishment, they wrote again and again, should be made to fit the crime, an extraordinary idea at a time when the death penalty was dealt out for minor theft, and imprisonment was regarded too expensive for the state.

This view of punishment was merely one ramification of a new approach to human psychology, whose origin lay in John Locke's *Essay Concerning Human Understanding* (1690), which had wide circulation in France. Locke had argued that all human knowledge is the product of sense impressions received by the mind and organized by reason into a coherent view of the outer world. At the basis of much French thinking was his famous paragraph describing the mind as a *tabula rasa*. French writers on psychology, especially Condillac and Helvétius, whose *On the Mind* appeared in 1758, felt that the character of a human being was entirely dependent on the environment in which one received early sense experiences. Helvétius even argued a doctrine that later became the basis of the theory called utilitarianism, that morality consisted in increasing human pleasure and decreasing human pain. A society in which this was the goal would be perfectly harmonious, he argued, because it would be in accord with the natural law that underlies human relationships and that had been ignored by previous societies.

It was evident to most of the philosophes that the relationship between the sexes was one in which the subordination of women was the result of custom and human law rather than natural law.[11] The Chevalier de Jaucourt, in an article in the *Encyclopédie* entitled "Woman (Natural Law)," argued that reason, which teaches the natural equality of humanity, also shows that a husband is not necessarily stronger or cleverer than his wife. Marriage, he felt, was a civil contract that should be drawn up to the mutual advantage of the two partners. Antoine Thomas, in *An Account of the Character, the Manners, and the Understanding of Women* (1772), severely criticized Periclean Athens for its seclusion of women and sought to show that women's attitudes and abilities at different periods of history were the result of the way they were treated by society. Since they were viewed as beings of great potentiality in Renaissance Italy, he argued, they became scholars and philosophers. Diderot felt, however, that Thomas had shown a lack of sympathy for the oppression of women by

---

[11] See Abby R. Kleinbaum, "Women in the Age of Light," in Renate Bridenthal and Claudia Koonz, *Becoming Visible: Women in European History* (Boston: Houghton Mifflin, 1977), pp. 219–235.

society; and he demanded an end of the tyranny of law over them. He even suggested a utopian society in which he envisioned women's lot being improved by membership in a community of wives and daughters. But many of the philosophes still reiterated the view that a woman's place was in the home; and Jean-Jacques Rousseau (1712–1778) in his influential novel *Emile* (1762), which deals with the perfect education of a human being who will live in political and moral freedom, returns to the Athenian ideal of the *gynaeceum* (see Chapter 3).

By the time of the publication of *Emile*, the philosophes had concluded, in the words of Helvétius, that "education can change everything" if dragged out of the hands of the Church. To them the expulsion of the Jesuits from France in 1762 seemed a good beginning. True education would permit a child to achieve the natural goodness and the power of reason with which he or she was born. By mid-century a host of books had explained how it should be done, books with titles like *New Maxims for the Education of Children*, *Treatise on the Education of Children*, and *General Principles for Use in the Education of Children*. But by far the most influential was Rousseau's *Emile*. A boy, Rousseau felt, should be entrusted for twenty years to the care of a tutor, sent out into the unsullied countryside to grow naturally into an understanding of himself and his relationship to nature, and brought through kindness to nurture the social instincts with which he was born. A girl should be raised at home by her mother rather than in a convent. Like a boy, she should be allowed to express her natural delight in play and in nature; however, she should be

Breakfast, by François Boucher
Within the harmonious architectural environment that the rococo designers sought to create in their Parisian townhouses, Boucher set an equally idyllic scene with his depiction of this tightly knit family circle. (Cliché des Musées Nationaux-Paris)

educated in practical subjects that would be of use when she was married. To Rousseau, the proud admirer of his native Geneva, the ultimate role of a woman, as for his heroine Sophie in *Emile*, was marriage and child-bearing. Nevertheless, for the education of both boys and girls, Rousseau had taught an important message that many eighteenth-century readers of *Emile* took to heart. They had come to accept that the child's emotions should be educated before the intellect; that kindness rather than discipline was the best tutor; that the life of the countryside was a better training in goodness than the life of the cities; and that the goal of education should be to achieve the child's own potential rather than imposed social homogeneity. Rousseau held that the realization of the individual began with childhood. Only under such circumstances could a person achieve the goal that Rousseau stated so proudly at the beginning of his *Confessions:* "Myself alone . . . I am not made like any one of those who exist. If I am not better, at least I am different."

In economics, too, the philosophes held that human beings should be allowed to follow their natural inclinations for the economic system to function in the most productive manner possible. The physiocrats (that is, those who believed in "government by nature"), as these economists came to be called, held that the state should leave things alone (*laissez faire; laissez passer*), avoiding the falsification of trade patterns that comes from tariffs, tolls, export bans, and unfair taxation. Trade should be free to follow its natural pattern, that is, the pattern created when each individual attempts to maximize personal profit from the production and sale of goods. But the physiocrats, and especially their acknowledged leader Quesnay, were unable to appreciate the importance of industry and commerce in the creation of wealth as it was expounded in England by Adam Smith (see Chapter 23), the true founder of capitalist economics. They were swept away by an emotional belief in the sanctity of the land. To Quesnay, agriculture was the source of the only true wealth, and the only genuine producers were the farmers. At the base of their theories was thus an ideological preference deriving from the "return to nature" rather than an economic rationale; but at least they publicized the harsh fact that the French economic system was vitiated by tax burdens laid on the peasantry and by ineffective systems of landholding and farm management. Moreover, in an age of inefficient government, they called for scientific administration, and thus provided one plank of the platform that was to bring the middle classes to accept the need for revolution.

The Economic Theories of the Physiocrats

Finally, in political theory, the philosophes took as their starting point the axioms that Locke had expressed in his *Two Treatises on Civil Government*, and that Jefferson was to define more succinctly in the American Declaration of Independence. All men are born with "unalienable rights" to life, liberty, and property; they enter into a contract with their government to preserve these rights in an organized society. The English too

Political Theories of the Enlightenment

seemed to have achieved this system in practice, as the philosophes attested who visited England in the early part of the eighteenth century. In Voltaire's *Philosophical Letters* of 1733, written during his stay in England, he painted an England that never existed, in which all natural rights were enjoyed by everyone, perfect religious tolerance prevailed, and harmony between the classes had been achieved. But Voltaire was setting an ideal for France, regardless of its applicability to England.

So too was the Baron de Montesquieu in his widely read *The Spirit of the Laws* (1748), although he was unaware of how he had failed to understand the compromises and corruption that made the English government work. Writing on a vast sociological scale, Montesquieu attempted to find all the laws that control the various forms of government. He was particularly impressed by the effects of climate. Cold countries produce moral people with a capacity for democracy; hot countries produce passionate and somewhat untrustworthy types, with a penchant for despotism, he felt. But his most important proposal, which he believed had been achieved in England, was that limited government should be organized by separation of powers, that is, by the mutual balancing of legislature, executive, and judiciary. Montesquieu was worshipped for a generation as the man who had shown, as the subtitle of his book said, "the relations which must exist between the laws and the constitution of each government, the manners, climate, religion, commerce, etc."

In 1762, however, in *The Social Contract*, Rousseau, whose uncomfortable passion for excessive honesty had led him to treat as enemies the majority of his friends, turned his scalpel to the question of freedom. To those who read the book inattentively, it appeared to move the doctrines of the philosophes from reform to revolution. "Man is born free, and everywhere he is in chains," Rousseau began. Human beings had natural rights that had been taken away by organized society; the institution of private property was the origin of social oppression. Then, with a realism that escaped many and infuriated more, Rousseau asked how human beings could be free, given the necessary constraints of living in close contact with each other. Here he parted company entirely with the Enlightenment. Each person, he said, had a double sense of what is right, an individual will, which is a feeling of self-interest regardless of the interests of other people, and an awareness of the "general will," a sense that all people living together in a community share of what is best for them as a group. You are only free when you harmonize your individual will with the general will, because otherwise you are only achieving part of what you regard as your well-being. The purpose of government is to interpret the general will. When it does so, each individual is directly represented by that government, and true democracy is operating. Where an individual fails to realize that the general will is being implemented, the government has the right to enforce the general will upon that individual. In short, in Rousseau's most famous paradox, the government has the right to force the individual to be free. Thus, two separate messages could be read

Jean-Jacques Rousseau (detail), by Allan Ramsay (1713–1784)

Rousseau's demand for a return to the natural life of the countryside is evident even in his choice of clothing. (National Gallery of Scotland, Edinburgh)

into the *Social Contract*, a call to revolution and a justification of the right of a small group of leaders to take totalitarian power to do what is best for society. The question Rousseau had posed was more important than his solution. He had recognized the inherent problem of democracy, that rule by the majority can imply suppression of the minority. He had asked, How can a minority be as free as a majority in a representative state? But his answer justified dictatorship by the few.

The Encyclopédie

The most effective instrument for the spread of the ideas of the philosophes was the *Encyclopédie*, whose twenty-eight volumes appeared between 1751 and 1772. The *Encyclopédie* was the most ambitious of a number of volumes attempting to illustrate all human knowledge that appeared in the middle of the century. Largely the work of Denis Diderot (1713–1784) and Jean d'Alembert (1717–1783), the *Encyclopédie* made an appeal to that technical-minded age by discussing at length and with fine

"Printing," from the *Encyclopédie*
The technical articles in the Encyclopédie were illustrated by detailed and extremely accurate engravings, such as this depiction of the preparation of type for printing. (Courtesy of French Embassy Press and Information Division)

THE FRENCH ENLIGHTENMENT

illustrations both the advances of science and industrial technology. It reproduced engravings, for example, on how to make Auvergne cheese, beat gold, prepare wigs, and manufacture glass. It even explained how to make gunpowder. But most of all it was a vehicle for the ideas of the philosophes in all the areas in which they saw the need for reform; and all the contributors wrote with a personal didactic passion that has distinguished few other encyclopedias. The article on government, for example, stated, "the greatest good of the people is in liberty. Liberty is to the body of the state what health is to each individual." Under "Press," it noted "the disadvantages of this liberty [of the press] are so inconsiderable compared to its advantages that this ought to be the common right of the universe, and it is certainly advisable to authorize its practice in all governments." Under "Political Authority," Diderot laid down that "the prince owes to his very subjects the *authority* that he has over them; and this *authority* is limited by the laws of nature and the state."[12] Attacked in France by the Church and censored by the state, the *Encyclopédie* found a surprising welcome in the courts of Catherine the Great of Russia and Frederick the Great of Prussia; and it was here, among the "enlightened despots," that the philosophes hoped to see many of their ideas put into practice.

Despotic Disciples of the Parisian Enlightenment

The great attraction of the philosophes to many rulers of the late eighteenth century was the philosophes' demand that government be scientific, as well as their belief that they had discovered those scientific principles that are applicable for effective government. Throughout Europe monarchs pored over the writings of the philosophes, sought their advice by letter, and begged or bribed them to appear in person. A similar attitude was displayed, not only by the rulers of the powerful states like Russia, Prussia, and Austria, but also by rulers in Spain, Portugal, Sweden, Tuscany, and many lesser German princely states.

The simpler reforms proposed by the philosophes, such as legal and judicial reforms, were applied at once without too much difficulty. Almost all the enlightened despots, for example, abandoned or restricted the use of torture and began a thorough reworking of the body of law in their countries. Many of them sought to follow the teachings of the physiocrats. They abolished internal tolls that hampered the movement of goods, cut down on external tariffs, and even occasionally tried a policy of free trade. A few, of whom Emperor Joseph II of Austria (reigned 1780–1790) was the most important, tried to put an end to serfdom and to restore the productivity of agriculture. All set out to restrict the power of the churches, and especially the influence of the Jesuits, in their states; but again, none went so far as Joseph, who proclaimed total religious freedom and equality, set up a secular system of education, and confiscated the vast wealth of many of the monasteries. Life undoubtedly became more tolerable for the subjects of the enlightened despots, in their relations with the law, the bu-

[12]Denis Diderot, *The Encyclopedia: Selections*, ed. Stephen J. Gendzier (New York: Harper Torchbook, 1967), pp. 125, 199, 186.

reaucracy, the Church, and the landlord. But it is also clear that the majority of the enlightened despots did not seek far-reaching change, and that those who did failed to achieve it. Frederick the Great (reigned 1740–1786), for example, retained most of the mercantilist controls over Prussia's economy, using all the instruments available to him, such as tariffs, subsidies, and heavy taxation, to direct economic planning from above. Catherine paid little attention to the representative assemblies she called, ignored the proposed legal reforms, strengthened the nobility's hold over Russia's serfs, and told Diderot that the philosophes had no understanding of the practical problems of government: "You work only upon paper which endures all things . . . but I, poor Empress as I am, work on the human skin which is irritable and ticklish to a different degree." As for Joseph, the best intentioned and most impatient of all the reforming monarchs, he was compelled to drop his plans for freeing the serfs against the opposition of his nobility, abandon his tax reforms, and moderate his plans

for integrating the peoples of his empire. He composed his own epitaph: "Here lies Joseph, who had the misfortune to see all his plans fail."

In foreign policy, even Joseph could not break with the cold calculation of national self-interest that gave the lie to the professions of Enlightenment of the despots, nor avoid the disastrous economic effects of the willingness to embark on almost constant war for territorial aggrandizement. Frederick the Great seized Silesia from Austria in 1740, when it became possible to contest the right of a woman, Maria Theresa, to inherit the Austrian throne. He thus plunged Prussia into two devastating wars (the War of Austrian Succession, 1740–1748, and the Seven Years' War, 1756–1763), in which the Russian armies occupied his capital Berlin and he came close to losing his own throne. The most cynical actions of the enlightened despots were, however, the three partitions of 1772, 1793, and 1795, by which they removed Poland from the map as an independent state. Poland was admittedly one of the worst governed states in eighteenth-century Europe, dominated by a hereditary nobility who chose

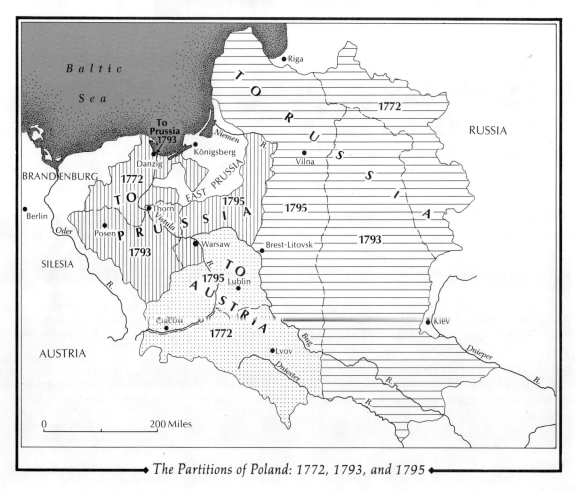

The Partitions of Poland: 1772, 1793, and 1795

their own monarch in elections that recurrently invited the intervention of the major states of Europe. The country was economically stagnant and politically chaotic. Thus, when Frederick and Catherine agreed in 1772 to help themselves to large portions of Poland and coerced the Austrians into participating for fear of upsetting the balance of power in eastern Europe, the Poles found no support either among the other states of Europe or among the philosophes themselves. In 1793 Russia and Prussia alone, and in 1795 the original three partitioners, divided the remainder of Poland among them.

The enlightened despots thus took from Paris only what suited them, creating a new style of monarchy but ignoring the message of liberty and equality that lay at the heart of the French Enlightenment. It is often thought that by alleviating the condition of their subjects they inoculated them against the contagion of the political message of the philosophes. But what of France itself? To what extent was the message of the philosophes heard in their own country?

ESTRANGEMENT BETWEEN PARIS AND FRANCE

The physiocrats had emphasized agriculture as the principal source of wealth; but they had done so with a definite awareness that the ruling elite in Paris and Versailles was impoverishing the rest of the country by its policy toward the agricultural population. If the role of Paris in eighteenth-century Europe was that of a beneficent donor of cultural largesse, its role in France was largely that of an exploiter. We must now examine what forms this exploitation took; what reaction it eventually provoked; and since only a small proportion of the Paris population belonged to the exploiting classes, what forms of social tension existed within the capital city itself. In short we must combine an analysis of the relationship of the urban to the rural population of France with an inquiry into the country's social structure.

Condition of the French Peasantry

A few statistics will point out the dual nature of the problem. The population of France at the beginning of the eighteenth century was about sixteen million, and it rose to perhaps twenty-two million by midcentury and twenty-six million by 1789. At that time, the peasantry or agricultural population numbered twenty-two million. The urban population may have reached two and a half million, with Paris by far the largest city, with about six hundred and fifty thousand inhabitants. The nonagricultural, rural population of lesser nobles, clergy, and artisans numbered about one and a half million. One important relationship, therefore, was between the peasant and the urban citizen, with the latter outnumbered at least nine to one.

A second relationship of perhaps greater importance was between the peasant and the landowning classes. The hereditary aristocracy, including

Old Peasant and Peasant Woman, by Georges de la Tour (1593–1652)

De la Tour sought to illustrate the simple dignity of peasant life, which he often used as the background for biblical scenes. (The Fine Arts Museums of San Francisco, Roscoe and Margaret Oakes Foundation)

the old "nobles of the sword," who had been ennobled by serving the king in battle, and the "nobles of the robe," who were bourgeois ennobled through royal service or purchase of office, owned about twenty percent of the cultivated land. The clergy held about fifteen percent of the land. The middle classes owned about thirty percent of the land, mostly in estates they had bought near the towns where they lived. The peasantry, of whom about half were landowners, were left with the remaining thirty-five percent. (Those who were not landowners worked the land of the other classes as renters, sharecroppers, or laborers.)

In the mind of the peasant, for very good reason, resentment at these two unequal relationships, of the country with the city and the peasant with the landowner, tended to merge. Paris and Versailles represented in the first place the insatiable eaters of state taxes that were squeezed in unjust proportion from the peasantry. The most important source of direct taxation was the *taille*, a land tax levied almost exclusively on the peasantry because most towns, including Paris, were exempt and most of the nobles and clergy paid only on land they let out to the peasants. Each parish was assigned a lump sum to collect; the collectors were fellow villagers, elected to the unpopular job and responsible themselves for failure to come up with the required amount. The collectors, wrote an eyewitness, "form a kind of army which wastes a whole year lounging about the place and collecting little but a thousand curses and insults, and all because as soon as the assessment has been made, it is the interest of those who have been taxed, and who can rely on no protection, to conceal all signs of wealth, and this involves a complete cessation of trade and all commercial transactions."[13] The indirect taxes, however, which were collected with terrible efficiency, were just as great a nightmare as the taille. The *gabelle*, or salt tax, was collected by thousands of *gabelous* and eluded by thousands of *faux-saulniers*, or salt smugglers. To buy for their families' needs, many risked imprisonment or the galleys. Excise taxes were collected on individual items, like wine, tobacco, and leather, so that a system of universal spying was adopted by the tax collectors to watch a peasant's consumption. Rousseau said he was once given a fine meal in secrecy by a peasant who told him "he had to hide his wine on account of the excise taxes, and his bread on account of the taille, and that he would be a lost man if any one began to doubt that he was not dying of hunger." Finally, the state imposed other burdens, such as the duty of working on the roads without payment, and the duty of doing military service if chosen by lot.

In return for these taxes the state provided very few services to the peasantry. There were very occasional efforts to alleviate famines, which occurred frequently until the 1740s, but there was no general effort at agricultural improvement of the type demanded by the physiocrats. The greater part of government expenditure went into support of the army and into payment of the public debt accumulated mostly in past wars. Most of the rest went for administrative expenses and for the court and nobles' pensions.

The majority of the peasants had little or no knowledge of the wars that were responsible for these taxes, but they could see evidence of the expenditures lavished not only on the nobility but on the clergy and bourgeoisie too. Here the peasants' resentment at royal taxation merged with their hatred of the dues enforced by the local lord, or *seigneur*. Even when a peasant owned land, he owed dues to a lord that went back to the medieval system of landholding. They included the right of the lord to hunt over the peasant's land and to graze his animals on parts of it; the duty of the peasant to use the lord's mill, oven, winepress, and market; and the payment by the peasant of various monetary fees, such as the *lods et ventes* when he sold land, or the *cens*, a kind of rent. The rights of the seigneurs were held by the bourgeois who had bought land as well as by the nobles, and the peasant made little distinction in his dislike. One may say that he had a vague and unfocused dislike of the state machinery that imposed the

[13]Ducros, *French Society*, p. 272.

direct and indirect taxes; but a clear, well-directed hatred of the local lord and of the local city.

The local lord could be an absentee, living in Versailles or Paris. In that case the peasant envied his ill-tended lands. "The quantity of waste land is surprising," wrote Arthur Young. "Much of these wastes belonged to the Prince de Soubise, who would not sell any part of them. Thus it is whenever you stumble on a Grand Seigneur, even one that was worth millions, you are sure to find his property desert."[14] The lord, however, was often present in the local château, where he became increasingly the target of peasant dislike, especially with the growth of rural overpopulation that occurred in the second half of the eighteenth century. But the peasant hated the towns too. In one of the complaints presented to the Estates General in 1789, the peasants were described as "bent over the earth which they water with their sweat, from the rising almost to the setting of the sun, and from which they bring forth by the labor of their hands that produce, that abundance, which is enjoyed by the citizens of the towns."[15]

It is true that the hierarchical division of the peasantry ran the whole gamut from *laboureurs*, wealthy rural capitalists with farms of up to several hundred acres, through the *manouvriers*, who held little or no land and had to work on the estates or in rural textile industry. But all peasants shared the desire for certain specific changes. They wanted a reduction in the burden of state taxation and abolition of seigneurial dues; and they wanted more land. The disaffection of the peasantry increased during the second half of the eighteenth century in spite of France's growing prosperity, or because they failed to share in it. The majority of the peasantry scraped a bare subsistence from the land, especially when rural population grew by two million in the fifty years before the Revolution, and they therefore had no surplus agricultural produce to sell. Moreover they were the main victims of the cyclical crises that invariably began with a poor harvest but precipitated other forms of rural unemployment, as among the textile spinners. The peasantry was ripe for a social revolution that would be directed against both the landlords and the cities.

Dangerous Isolation of the Upper Aristocracy

The peasantry, however, was not the only group in the French provinces that felt disenchanted with the French ruling class. Both the nobility and the clergy were divided into those who were the beneficiaries of France's social structure and those who felt exploited by it, and in a very real sense the division was again between those who enjoyed the amenities of Paris and Versailles and those who resented them.

Of the four hundred thousand members of the nobility, only a few hundred constituted *Les Grands*, the real aristocrats for whom the court life of Versailles and the social whirl of Paris were formed. Their way of

[14]Young, *Travels in France*, p. 59.
[15]Cited in E. N. Williams, *The Ancien Régime in Europe: Government and Society in the Major States, 1648–1789* (New York: Harper & Row, 1970), p. 199.

life was inordinately expensive, and many ran through fortunes trying to keep up with the requirements of society. Clothes and jewels, extravagant meals for hundreds of guests, carriages and servants, gambling and hunting—these absorbed ever-increasing sums as prices rose inexorably throughout the second half of the century. But presence in this social sphere was necessary to maintain one's wealth also, to receive the pensions and fees payable by the treasury, the governorships of wealthy provinces, or appointments to benefices in the Church. The wealthy stayed together by necessity as well as by inclination.

From about 1750 on, however, a vitally important change took place in the character of Les Grands. Both the nobility of the sword and the nobility of the robe, who had spurned each other for generations for the differences in origin of their wealth and social prestige, were prepared to draw together in common defense of their position. The upper nobility, which had always been open at the bottom to new blood as a result of newly acquired wealth or royal service, now sought to exclude new recruits, to maintain for those who had already been admitted to the happy circle of Les Grands a monopoly on all the major offices in the government, the army, the Church, and the law. In this effort to block the means of advancement into the upper ranks of society to the lesser nobility and to the middle classes, for whom acquisition of wealth would previously have made possible purchase of entrée into aristocratic society, the upper nobility was largely successful; and its success encouraged its members to undertake not merely a holding action but a conservative revolution, the attempt to replace royal absolutism as created in the seventeenth century by a more decentralized administration that they thought they could dominate.

This exclusiveness of Les Grands created a gulf between its members and the majority of the provincial nobility and those bourgeois who, though wealthy or talented enough to acquire the lesser titles of nobility, had not broken into the upper ranks before the middle of the century. Often the barrier was accepted with polite resignation. "I should like to pay you a visit," a provincial noble wrote his sister at court, "but to live in Paris I would have to be your valet. We have 10 to 12,000 livres revenue. With that one cuts a poor figure if one is a count or a baron. However, if you visit me, we will be high and powerful seigneurs."[16] But more frequently it caused bitter resentment. The country noble, barely squeezing a livelihood from an unwilling peasantry and an inefficient agriculture, often lived frugally in a broken-down château, unable to afford a carriage and avoiding visits even to the neighboring towns. His only hope of economic survival was to press more strongly for his seigneurial rights and to avoid unnecessary expenditure. Beaumarchais (1732–1799) expressed his outrage as a recently ennobled bourgeois—he himself was a watch- and harpmaker turned financier and government spy—in the two masterpieces

[16]Williams, *Ancien Régime*, p. 177.

Comtesse du Cayla, by Jean-Antoine Houdon
Houdon was deeply influenced by his study of the sculpture of ancient Rome, as can be seen in his fanciful use of the chain of leaves to suggest the statues of pagan goddesses. (Copyright the Frick Collection, New York)

of satire *The Barber of Seville* and *The Marriage of Figaro*. "Fancy following a woman to Seville when Madrid and the Court offer such a variety of easily won pleasures!" Count Almaviva remarks at the beginning of *The Barber*. "That's just what I'm trying to get away from. I'm weary of the conquests that self-interest or habit or vanity present us in endless succession!" But, once married, Almaviva rouses the anger of his valet Figaro, that epitome of social awareness, by pursuing Figaro's bride-to-be. In the monologue that made Louis XVI forbid the play's presentation, Figaro breaks out against all the abuses of aristocratic society:

No, my Lord Count, you shan't have her, you shall not have her! Because you are a great nobleman you think you are a great genius. . . . Nobility, fortune, rank, position! How proud they make a man feel! What have you done to deserve such advantages? Put yourself to the trouble of being born—nothing more! For the rest—a very ordinary man! Whereas I, lost among the obscure crowd, have had to deploy more knowledge, more calculation and skill merely to survive than has sufficed to rule all the provinces of Spain for a century! Yet you would measure yourself against me.

And Figaro glances back at the ironies of his life:

I study Chemistry, Pharmacy, Surgery, and all the prestige of a great nobleman can barely secure me the handling of a horse-doctor's probe. . . . I fudge up a play about the manner of the Seraglio. . . . Immediately, some envoy from goodness-knows-where complains that some of my lines offend the Sublime Porte, Persia, some part or other of the East Indies, the whole of Egypt, and the Kingdoms of Cyrenaica, Tripoli, Tunis, Algiers, and Morocco. . . . I was on the point of giving up in despair when it occurred to someone to offer me a job. Unfortunately I had some qualification for it—it needed a knowledge of figures—but it was a dancer who got it! Nothing was left to me but stealing, so I set up as a banker at. . . . Now notice what happens! I dine out in style, and so-called fashionable people throw open their houses to me—keeping three-quarters of the profits for themselves. . . . But since everybody was involved in some sort of swindle and at the same time demanding honesty from me, I inevitably went under again. [17]

The Split Within the Clergy

The clergy of the Catholic Church was equally split, the barrier again being the upper nobility's determination to monopolize the higher offices. In 1789 only one French bishop was not noble. A majority of the archbishops and bishops and of the abbots of the monasteries were absentees, drawing over half of the revenues of their office to support their life either in their country homes or, in the case of sons of the higher nobility, in Versailles and Paris. Frequently, a nobleman would make up his revenues by becoming abbot of three or four monasteries at once. Lacking any kind of religious vocation, many though by no means all of the upper clergy led comfortable social lives in Paris. To be sent to one's diocese by order of the

[17]Pierre-Augustin Caron de Beaumarchais, *The Barber of Seville; The Marriage of Figaro*, trans. John Wood (Harmondsworth, England: Penguin, 1964), p. 199–202.

king was known as "being exiled." Cardinal de Polignac was bishop of Auch for fifteen years and never once went there. The real work of caring for the rural multitudes was done by the village priest or curé, who had the ungrateful task of collecting the Church's tithe, usually an amount between one-twelfth and one-twentieth of the value of a peasant's produce, in order to send more than half of it to some absentee superior. The annoyance of the local priests was probably less great than the resentment of the aspiring clergy in the middle ranks, the bright young men of peasant or bourgeois background who had taken positions in monasteries or cathedrals or as professors in seminaries, and who found that the highest ranks of the Church were closed to them. This change in the character of a Church that had for centuries offered the main avenue of social mobility to a poor boy of talent had again infected one of the relatively healthy parts of the ancien régime.

The function of Paris and Versailles as the center of government and of privileged society—and thus as the source of taxes, seigneurial dues, and tithes—was therefore regarded with resentment by the majority of the peasantry, by the lower groups of the nobility, and by lower and middle ranks of the clergy. It was, however, the bourgeoisie who were to turn that resentment into support for revolution; and they, as an urban class that had come unwillingly to share the opposition of the nonurban French population to the royal government and the closed aristocracy, had to make a major propaganda effort to win over the disaffected groups of the French countryside.

THE RELUCTANT DISAFFECTION OF THE BOURGEOISIE

The French bourgeoisie, that variegated class engaged in finance, business, commerce, and the professions that lay between the nobility on the one hand and the manual workers on the other, was by far the most economically progressive class in French society. Until the late eighteenth century, it was also socially conservative. From the 1770s on, however, the bourgeoisie became annoyed at the combination of ineffective royal government and of the newly imposed barriers to upward social mobility. They then reluctantly concluded that the teachings of the philosophes on efficient administration could only be applied after political revolution.

The bourgeoisie was not large in number. In Paris at the middle of the century, it has been calculated to number only forty thousand out of a total population of over half a million. (At the time, there were in Paris about ten thousand clergy and five thousand nobles, the rest of the population being shopkeepers, artisans, laborers, and unemployed.) There were also marked differences of wealth and occupation within the bourgeoisie that

Character of the French Bourgeoisie

had great influence on political attitudes of its members. The main division was between those engaged in the professions, such as law, and those in business. There was, however, a constant movement between the business and professional groupings of the bourgeoisie, most notably because of the low social prestige attached to engaging in business. French economic development was hampered throughout the century by the distaste that many middle-class people felt for making money in trade or industry. Many who had prospered sent their sons into law or the Church or the army rather than into the family business; and instead of plowing their profits back into their companies, they preferred to invest in socially remunerative purchases of country châteaux, land, government bonds, or noble marriages for their children. In other words the middle classes were vitally interested in the social mobility that wealth could buy. In his play *Le Droit du Seigneur*, Voltaire summarized the social plans of a wealthy bourgeois:

I want everything to happen at my pleasure and in accordance with my wishes, for I am rich. So, father-in-law, listen: To dignify myself in my marriage, I am turning myself into a gentleman, and I am buying from the bailiff the flourishing office of royal receiver in the salt granaries: that's not bad. My son will be a counselor, and my daughter will raise herself to some noble family. My grandsons will be presidents: And the descendants of my lord will one day pay court to mine. [18]

Sources of the Bourgeoisie's Wealth

Throughout most of the eighteenth century, and especially in the years 1730 to 1770, the middle classes became increasingly prosperous. Many grew wealthy as a direct result of governmental inefficiency. The government's inability to collect its own taxes, and especially its need for an advance payment of taxes, enriched the farmers general and the thousands of tax collectors they employed. Other financiers supplied provisions for the army, sold the government the bullion it needed for the coinage, and provided the ships and capital for overseas colonization. These extremely wealthy men, with fortunes as great as any in the nobility and townhouses and country châteaux to match their fortunes, were able, even in the period of noble exclusivity in the later part of the century, to retain their place in the ranks of Les Grands.

But the widespread prosperity of the bourgeois class was due to the increasing productivity of the French economy. To some extent, governmental measures helped. The currency was stabilized in 1726; roads and canals were improved; loans and state subsidies were given to private companies considered of national importance, including not only such luxury manufacture as silks or velvet but iron foundries and coal mines too. Perhaps most important, the overseas empire, which the French had been acquiring piecemeal during the seventeenth century, became extremely

---

[18]Cited in Elinor Barber, *The Bourgeoisie in Eighteenth Century France* (Princeton, N. J.: Princeton University Press, 1970), p. 58.

lucrative. A few ships traded with Canada and Louisiana; but the real profits were made in the sale of slaves from the French colonies of Senegal and Gorée in West Africa, from the sugar and tropical products of the West Indian islands of Martinique and Guadeloupe, and from the fisheries off Newfoundland and Cape Breton Island. French merchants also opened up trade with the Ottoman Empire in the eastern Mediterranean and with the Mogul Empire in India. During the century, France's foreign trade quadrupled, and all its port cities showed evidence of the wealth their merchants had accumulated. France's provincial cities enjoyed a building boom unparalleled before the twentieth century. Nantes, which sent one hundred fifty ships and as many as thirty thousand slaves to the Caribbean each year, was almost completely rebuilt in the classical style. Bordeaux, the center of the new trade with India and a participant in the African trade, also maintained its old commerce in wine with northern Europe. Its commerce expanded sixfold, and its merchants not only built themselves fine houses but called in Gabriel to build a monumental square opening onto the river Garonne. Industry, however, lagged behind commerce, although a few large fortunes were made in textiles and iron manufacture. Most manufacturing was on a very small scale, tightly controlled by the guilds and subject to the most restrictive controls.

Until about 1770 the French middle classes were therefore quite content with their economic condition and with the social advancement that their wealth could obtain for them. From that point on, however, they became increasingly outraged at the damaging effects of governmental inefficiency to their economic status, and at the barriers to their upward social climb imposed by the nobility.

The Bourgeoisie Becomes Revolutionary

The most immediate effect of governmental inefficiency was the loss of most of the colonial empire in the wars with England. French colonial administrators, like Dupleix in India and Duquesne in Canada, had laid ambitious plans for restricting English colonial expansion and for annexing a good part of England's overseas possessions. In the War of the Austrian Succession (1740–1748) and the Seven Years' War (1756–1763), the French government tried to wage both a large-scale land war in Europe and a naval and colonial war in North America, the West Indies, Africa, and India. These undertakings proved completely beyond France's ability and resources. In the final campaigns of 1759–1763, the British took possession of almost all of France's overseas settlements in Canada, West Africa, and the Caribbean, and its Indian trading stations. Although the British returned a few of the possessions in the West Indies, Africa, and India, French activity was henceforth greatly restricted; and during the war and after, many merchants who were engaged in shipping and overseas commerce went bankrupt. But the effect of the wars upon French governmental finances was in the long run even more disastrous. As early as 1761 the French government had informed its continental allies that it was on the edge of bankruptcy.

"Equality Before Taxation"
The cartoon represents the three "estates" of nobility, clergy, and all other French citizens carrying an equal share of the burden of the national debt through a national territorial tax.
(Courtesy of French Embassy Press and Information Division)

The root cause was France's inefficient and unjust system of taxation, which left the wealth of the nobility and clergy largely untapped. Again and again, in the continuing financial crisis that ran from the defeats in the Seven Years' War until the Revolution, finance ministers sought a new system of taxation that would ensure that all Frenchmen would pay taxes in proportion to their wealth. In each case the privileged classes fought back until the king was persuaded to dismiss the reforming minister. French support of the American colonists in their revolt against England, financed exclusively by increased borrowing at interest rates of eight to ten percent, had the disastrous effect of bringing interest paid on the national debt to half the state's total revenues. Bankruptcy again threatened. The middle classes, who had made the greater part of the loans to the government by purchase of government bonds, thereupon felt themselves threatened by the financial calamity of the state. If one simple solution were followed—repudiation of the national debt—they would be the principal sufferers. If nothing were done, the state would go bankrupt and the result would be worse: not only would government bonds become worthless, but also the whole economic structure of France would be endangered.

This threat to the bourgeoisie's wealth coincided with their discovery that they could no longer buy their way upward in society. The upper ranks of the nobility and the Church had been closed to all except a few of the wealthiest bourgeois families. And this exclusion was being applied successfully in almost all parts of society. It had become almost impossible for lawyers to break into the nobility of the robe by gaining appointments in the Parlement of Paris. The upper levels of the bureaucracy were closed, as were the principal commands in the army and navy. At this point most of the bourgeois were converted into followers of the philosophes and were particularly sympathetic to the demand for a more egalitarian society. The bourgeois salons in Paris turned first to the demands of the physiocrats for a more efficient administration of the country's economy; but slowly, especially under the influence of the revolution in America, they began to demand institutional change. They were prepared in fact for the Revolution, which was to make France—briefly—a constitutional monarchy.

THE PARIS PROLETARIAT ON THE EVE OF REVOLUTION

Nine years before Parisian rioters stormed the state prison of the Bastille, Louis-Sébastien Mercier confidently asserted:

Dangerous rioting has become a moral impossibility in Paris. The eternally watchful police, two regiments of Guards, Swiss and French, in barracks near at hand, the King's bodyguard, the fortresses which ring the capital round, together with countless individuals whose interest links them to Versailles; all these factors make the chance of any serious rising seem altogether remote. . . . We are not practiced rioters, we Parisians, and possibly for that very reason an outbreak (if such a thing were ever to occur) would assume alarming proportions. Still, if it should happen, and were met at the outset with prudence and moderation, above all if bloodshed could be avoided, I maintain that the people's ill-humor would evaporate of itself.[19]

The Disaffection of the Parisian Worker

Mercier was, however, closing his eyes to the evidence of popular discontent continually ready to erupt into violence. In 1725 there had been serious uprisings that forced the dismissal of the minister responsible for Paris's food supply. In 1740 the chief minister had been mobbed. In 1752 the mob demonstrated against the archbishop of Paris and rioted for lower bread prices. In 1775 the central markets and granaries were ransacked by hungry crowds, which had to be put down by the troops. However, for twelve years after 1775 there was no uprising in the capital, and it appeared to many observers like Mercier that the fifteen-hundred-man Paris guard and the five to six thousand reinforcements stationed in barracks in the city itself were sufficient for any future emergency.

What was universally accepted, however, was the dangerous dissatisfaction of large sections of the Paris population. To many contemporary observers, the conditions of life in lower-class Paris were a sufficient explanation for the sense of grievance. Arthur Young visited the capital in 1787:

[19] Mercier, *The Waiting City*, pp. 108–109.

This great city appears to be in many respects the most ineligible and inconvenient for the residence of a person of small fortune of any that I have been; and by far inferior to London. The streets are very narrow, and many of them crowded, nine-tenths dirty, and all without foot-pavements. Walking, which in London is so pleasant and so clear, that ladies do it every day, is here a toil and fatigue to a man, and an impossibility to a well-dressed woman. . . . There is an infinity of one-horse cabriolets, which are driven by young men of fashion and their imitators, like fools, with such rapidity as to be real nuisances, and render the streets exceedingly dangerous, without an incessant caution. [As a result] all persons of small or moderate fortune are forced to dress in black, with black stockings; the dusky hue of this in company is not so disagreeable a circumstance as being too great a distinction; too clear a line drawn in company between a man that has a good fortune, and another that has not. [20]

Condition of the Sans-Culottes

To other observers and to many twentieth-century historians, it seemed that the discontent reached its height among the day-laborers, who were forbidden to organize into unions and who expressed their bitterness against the low wages paid by their employers by sporadic and ill-led strikes. The most notable of these were in the textile industry, which was the only type of manufacture in Paris to have anything resembling a modern factory organization. On the northern edge of the city there were a few companies that employed several hundred workers, though the average textile workshop still employed only a few. But most strikes occurred in the occupations where the lag of wages behind prices and the difficulty of getting advancement from journeyman to master provoked resentment. So there were strikes not only by stocking-frame weavers, journeymen hatters, and ribbon weavers, but also by bookbinders, carpenters, dyers, and especially the large numbers in the building trade. But these strikes were short in length and easily broken, and they were more symptoms of a generalized disquiet than proof that a distinctive class conflict existed between wage-laborer and capitalist employer.

If Paris did not provide factory employment for large numbers of wage-laborers, and did not do so until 1830–1848, it did offer jobs at just above the subsistence level for semiskilled or manual workers, and at a slightly higher level for independent craftsmen and masters of small workshops, and charity and menial jobs at a level that frequently fell below subsistence for a floating population of the displaced and unfortunate. All these groups composed the *sans-culottes* ("without knee breeches"), the working classes, who by the definition applied during the Revolution did not wear knee breeches and thus did not belong to the well-to-do classes. Some of them lived in localities devoted to specialized trades. The famous fishwives, or *poissardes*, lived around the central markets on the Right Bank or in the malodorous Place Maubert, where many riots began. Many artisans engaged in furniture making and other handicrafts lived on the eastern edge of the city beyond the Bastille state prison, in the Faubourg Saint An-

[20] Young, *Travels*, pp. 77–78.

A Woman Shopping, by Jean Siméon Chardin (1699–1779)
Although Chardin specialized in depicting scenes of everyday life in humble surroundings, his work was popular with the French aristocracy, and he was admitted to the conservative academy of art. His best-known paintings show household servants in the kitchen, surrounded by loaves of bread, fruit, bottles, bowls, and glassware. (Cliché des Musées Natonaux—Paris)

toine, which had a reputation for unruliness. The tenements of the Ile de la Cité and the neighboring quays lodged the workers from the river docks, the porters, and many of the masons employed by the cathedral. But in general the working-class population was spread throughout the city, although it was more concentrated in the eastern and northern districts than in the newer faubourgs in which the nobility and bourgeoisie had been constructing their new townhouses. Masters, craftsmen, and journeymen usually lived not only in the same street, but frequently in the same building; and they patronized the same wineshops and markets where political propaganda was exchanged and demonstrations were started. In spite of the strikes, there is little evidence of antagonism between the smaller masters and their workers and not much more of prolonged or organized opposition to large-scale employers. The working classes of Paris were united by one fear, that of hunger caused by their inability to buy bread.

Working-Class Grievances

All the working-class agitation of the eighteenth century has been shown to be directly related to rises in the price of bread. In normal times the Parisian worker spent one-half his income on bread. The riots of 1775, which spread throughout France, were known as the "flour war" because the rioters took over the sale of bread in the markets and reduced the price of a loaf from thirteen and a half sous to eight. The governments of Louis XV and Louis XVI were accused of "famine pacts," of buying up the grain to sell it at exorbitant profits when famine had been precipitated, although for fear of riots they did take elaborate if not always effective measures to ensure the bread supply of the cities through requisitioning, food convoys, and grain storage. In times of harvest failure, such as occurred in 1787 and 1788, these measures broke down completely. The price of bread in Paris doubled, at a time when a general economic depression had thrown up to half of the wage-earning population out of work and reduced the income of the rest.

The Paris working classes therefore had a political platform prescribed for them by their economic situation: they wanted a reliable bread supply at a reasonable price and regular work at reasonable wages. When they became politically active, and at times violent, during the Revolution, these goals remained predominant. But it was not the poorest and most depressed sections of the working classes that were most prepared to demonstrate for a change in their conditions; it was rather the more skilled and better educated among them, such as the shopkeepers, the artisans, and the masters. There is little evidence that these people were directly influenced by the philosophes or by the political writings that were agitating bourgeois Paris, except for a few slogans that seeped down to them. But they did have a strong dislike and distrust for the well-to-do, whom they came during the Revolution to group together as "aristocrats"; a feeling of their right to equality with all other Frenchmen, or more specifically with all other Parisians; and among a substantial minority, a sense of political awareness that was expressed directly by their involvement in the affairs of their own quarter of Paris. When Paris was divided into forty-eight "sections" in 1790, with assemblies and committees for each neighborhood, these working-class leaders would find the political instrument that corresponded to their almost instinctive belief in direct democracy in preference to representative democracy.

There were few Parisians, therefore, who would have agreed with Talleyrand that one had to have lived before 1789 to know how sweet life could be (*la douceur de vivre*). As early as 1753 Lord Chesterfield had predicted to his son:

The affairs of France ... grow serious, and, in my opinion, will grow more and more so every day. The King is despised, and I do not wonder at it; but he has brought it about to be hated at the same time, which seldom happens to the same man. His Ministers are known to be as disunited as incapable. ... The people are poor, consequently discontented; those who have religion are divided in their no-

tions of it; which is saying that they hate one another. . . . The French nation reasons freely, which they never did before, upon matters of religion and government, and begins to be spregiudicati *[free of prejudice]; the officers do so too; in short, all the symptoms which I have ever met with in history, previous to great changes and revolutions in Government, now exist, and daily increase in France. I am glad of it; the rest of Europe will be the quieter, and have time to recover.* [21]

SUGGESTED READING

There is no equivalent for eighteenth-century Paris of Orest Ranum's fine essay, *Paris in the Age of Absolutism* (1968), although much of Ranum's material is relevant to the later years of the ancien régime. Howard C. Rice, *Thomas Jefferson's Paris* (1976) is a beautiful introduction to the areas of Paris Jefferson visited just before the Revolution. Pierre Gaxotte, *Paris au XVIIIe siècle* (1968) is anecdotal, though based on many contemporary memoirs. Henry Bidou, *Paris* (1939) is a pleasant though superficial account (pp. 184–265). Two older books cover the state of Paris at the outbreak of the Revolution very thoroughly: A. Babeau, *Paris en 1789* (1889) and H. Monin, *L'Etat de Paris en 1789* (1889). Much the most interesting way to approach the study of the city is to read some of the fine memoirs by travelers, especially Arthur Young, *Travels in France During the Years 1787, 1788, and 1789* (1969); Carlo Goldoni, *Memoirs* (1877); Jacques Casanova, *Memoirs* (1922); Tobias Smollet, *Travels Through France and Italy* (1919); Horace Walpole, *Letters*, vol. 6; *The Diary of David Garrick Being a Record of His Memorable Trip to Paris in 1751* (1928); and Constantia E. Maxwell, *The English Traveller in France, 1698–1815* (1932). Louis-Sébastien Mercier's huge *Le Tableau de Paris* (1783–1788) is abridged in *The Waiting City: Paris 1782–88* (1933).

On the social structure of eighteenth-century France, that is, of the ancien régime, see the modern synthesis by Alfred Cobban, *A History of Modern France*, vol. 1, *Old Regime and Revolution 1715–1799* (1961); C. B. A. Behrens, *The Ancien Régime* (1968), a very suggestive and ambitious survey; Alexis de Tocqueville, *The Ancien Régime and the Revolution*, first published in 1856, for the brilliance of its insights; and Pierre Goubert, *The Ancien Régime. French Society, 1600–1750* (1974), for a survey by a fine contemporary French historian. Modern research has contributed many new findings. Franklin L. Ford, *Robe and Sword: The Regrouping of the French Aristocracy After Louis XIV* (1953) concluded that "the French aristocracy, if it did not have the strength to suppress revolution, had at least recovered enough strength to make revolution inevitable." Robert Forster, *The Nobility of Toulouse in the Eighteenth Century* (1960) provides a local case study. Elinor G. Barber, *The Bourgeoisie in Eighteenth Century France* (1970) found the "revolutionary" attitudes of the middle classes dependent on their attitude toward social mobility.

For the sans-culottes, one can turn to Olwen H. Hufton, *The Poor of Eighteenth Century France, 1750–1789* (1972) or Jeffry Kaplow, *The Names of Kings: The Parisian Laboring Poor in the Eighteenth Century* (1972). It is also useful to look ahead to the penetrating studies of the revolutionary period: George Rudé's

---

[21]Lord Chesterfield, *Letters to His Son* (London: Dent, 1929), pp. 274–275.

The Crowd in the French Revolution (1959) and especially Albert Soboul's The Parisian Sans-Culottes and the French Revolution, 1793–94 (1964). On the peasantry, the most important research in the provinces was done by Georges Lefebvre and is summarized in his The Coming of the French Revolution (1957) and The French Revolution from its Origins to 1793 (1962). Communal peasant agriculture is discussed in William N. Parker and Eric L. Jones, eds., European Peasants and Their Markets: Essays in Agrarian Economic History (1976).

Many historians have attempted to seek the similarities that existed among all European society in the eighteenth century. Useful international surveys include M. S. Anderson, Europe in the Eighteenth Century, 1713–1783 (1961); Albert Goodwin, ed., The European Nobility in the Eighteenth Century (1967); Robert Forster and Elborg Forster, eds., European Society in the Eighteenth Century (1969). Among the most useful national studies for comparative purposes are Hans Rosenberg, Bureaucracy, Aristocracy and Autocracy: The Prussian Experience, 1660–1815 (1958); Lewis B. Namier, The Structure of Politics at the Accession of George III (1957) and England in the Age of the American Revolution (1961); and Jerome Blum, Lord and Peasant in Russia (1961).

The Enlightenment has recently been a source of considerable controversy among historians. Carl Becker, The Heavenly City of the Eighteenth Century Philosophers (1969) argues that the philosophes were not as rational as they thought; Robert R. Palmer, Catholics and Unbelievers in Eighteenth Century France (1961) concludes that "the philosophers, to meet their own needs, reached a conception of nature which was in part that of science . . . and in part that of theology." For more straightforward and also admiring views see Kingsley Martin, French Liberal Thought in the Eighteenth Century (1954) and George R. Havens, The Age of Ideas (1955). An ambitious new synthesis is given by Peter Gay, The Enlightenment: An Interpretation (1966–1969). A difficult, schematic approach is followed by Ernst Cassirer in The Philosophy of the Enlightenment (1951), a much freer and more evocative approach by Paul Hazard in his book on the "crisis of the European consciousness," which he placed in the years 1680–1715, The European Mind (1963) and in his bubbly survey European Thought in the Eighteenth Century (1963). The writings of Quesnay and other physiocrats are analyzed in Elizabeth Fox-Genevese, The Origins of Physiocracy: Economic Revolution and Social Order in Eighteenth Century France (1976). On individual thinkers, consult the authoritative biography by Arthur Wilson, Diderot: The Testing Years, 1713–1759 (1957); Peter Gay, Voltaire's Politics (1965); Owen Aldridge, Voltaire and the Century of Light (1975), which is enlivened by many quotations from Voltaire's correspondence; and J. Salwyn Schapiro, Condorcet and the Rise of Liberalism (1963). And of course the best introduction to the philosophes is to read their own writings. Good selections from the Encyclopédie are chosen in Denis Diderot, The Encyclopedia: Selections (1967); Voltaire, Candide (1966) is a spicy modern translation by Joan Spencer; and Beaumarchais still sparkles in the new translation by John Wood, The Barber of Seville and The Marriage of Figaro (1964). Crane Brinton's The Portable Age of Reason Reader (1956) contains a wide variety of readings from most European countries. For Jean-Jacques Rousseau, one should read The Social Contract and, for his views on education, Emile; for Montesquieu, The Spirit of the Laws and The Persian Letters. Robert Darnton comments on the shift away from reason in Mesmerism and the End of the Enlightenment in France (1968).

The views of the principal Enlightenment thinkers on the position of women are summarized in Abby R. Kleinbaum, "Women in the Age of Light," in the previously cited Bridenthal and Koonz, eds., *Becoming Visible*, pp. 217–235. Rousseau's antifeminism is explained by Victor G. Wexler, " 'Made for Man's Delight': Rousseau as Antifeminist," *American Historical Review*, 81 (April 1976), 266–291.

For an excellent summary of the significance of the Enlightenment thinkers, see Robert Anchor, *The Enlightenment Tradition* (1979).

The enlightened despots are surveyed by John G. Gagliardo, *Enlightened Despotism* (1967) and E. N. Williams, *The Ancien Régime in Europe: Government and Society in the Major States 1648–1789* (1970). Useful works on individual rulers include Saul K. Padover, *The Revolutionary Emperor, Joseph the Second, 1741–1790* (1934); George P. Gooch, *Frederick the Great: The Ruler, the Writer, the Man* (1947); Gerhard Ritter, *Frederick the Great* (1968), with Peter Paret's introduction; G. S. Thomson, *Catherine the Great and the Expansion of Russia* (1962).

For the art and architecture of France, see Stéphanie Faniel, *French Art of the Eighteenth Century* (1957); the previously cited Lavedan, *Histoire de l'urbanisme*, vol. 2; Anthony Blunt, *Art and Architecture in France, 1500–1700* (1953); F. Kimball, *The Creation of the Rococo* (1943); and L. Hautecoeur, *Histoire de l'architecture classique en France* (1943–1945), vols. 3 and 4. On French cultural influence, the standard work is Louis Réau, *L'Europe française au siècle des lumières* (1933). Finally, after reading L. D. Ettlinger's article, "Taste and Patronage: The Role of the Artist in Society," in Alfred Cobban, ed., *The Eighteenth Century: Europe in the Age of Enlightenment* (1969), pp. 217–258, one could spend a few happy hours on the isle of Cythera by idly glancing at the book's sumptuous illustrations.

21

CITIES IN REVOLUTION

I n the late eighteenth and early nineteenth centuries, Western society was shaken, and eventually transformed, by forces so far-reaching in their effects that we are justified in calling them revolutionary. These forces—liberalism, nationalism, and industrialism—struck the predominantly rural, hierarchic, and slow-moving society of the ancien régime like a cyclone, totally changing the customary relationships of city to country, of citizen to government, and of individual to individual. Much of the history of Western civilization since the end of the eighteenth century can be interpreted as the working out of the effects of these three forces. As with so many drives within the West, these revolutionary movements were directly related to urban changes, for the cities provided much of their strength and suffered (or enjoyed) their most powerful consequences. The liberal revolution received its most succinct and perhaps most elegant expression in Philadelphia on July 4, 1776, when the Continental Congress declared that it held "these truths to be self-evident, that all men are created equal, that they are endowed by their creator with certain unalienable rights, that among these are Life, Liberty, and the Pursuit of Happiness." The American Revolution appeared to be direct proof that the Enlightenment's conception of political equality could be realized in practice. Liberalism, however, took on new meaning, or rather a series of new meanings, when revolutionary Paris explored the varieties of political system that could be created within the broad goals of a society based on liberty, equality, and fraternity. The spread of the revolutionary ideals of

Paris Mob Seizing Weapons from Armory on the Place Louis XV (now Place de la Concorde), 1792 *(Arch. Phot. Paris S. P. A. D. E. M.)*

Paris to the other states of Europe by force of arms, while at first welcomed by many would-be liberals, soon provoked disillusionment; and the conquest of the Revolution itself and then of most of Europe by Napoleon stimulated the forces of nationalism in all the states under French rule. In this chapter we shall consider the origins and development of liberalism and nationalism in cities in which their distinctive features can be most clearly appreciated: Philadelphia, for the first successful revolution for political equality; Paris, for the impact of liberal revolution in a hierarchic society; and Berlin and Naples, for the origins of the nationalist revolt in Germany and Italy. In Chapter 23, we shall observe the birth of the industrial revolution in Manchester, the spread of industrialism to the continent, and the development, in reaction to the blight of the new industrial city, of the theory of socialism.

PHILADELPHIA AND THE ATLANTIC REVOLUTION

The American Revolution was the first successful assertion of the right of colonies to independence from their "mother country." But it was far more than a war for independence, because its goal was to safeguard internal democracy, which Americans believed they largely possessed before the Revolution and considered to be threatened by the British crown. It is because the American Revolution had this character of a drive to secure political equality that some recent historians have regarded it as the beginning of a "democratic revolution," common to Europe and the American colonies, which was intended to assert "the principle that public power must arise from those over whom it is exercised."[1] In this sense it is justifiable to speak of the American Revolution as the first phase of "the Atlantic Revolution," as the French historian Jacques Godechot does, in spite of the considerable differences between the American and the French revolutions. The Declaration of the Rights of Man was issued in Paris only thirteen years after the Continental Congress subscribed to the Declaration of Independence in Philadelphia; and there was a direct connection between the two.

The English Colonies in North America

Up to the Revolution—and indeed until the city itself also succumbed to the impact of industrialization in the 1830s—Philadelphia symbolized for many Europeans the most attractive features of the American colonial environment. It possessed the dual charms of being both a well-planned city and a harmonious community.

When William Penn founded Philadelphia in 1682, the pattern of settlement in the British colonies was already well established. In the North

[1]Robert R. Palmer, *The Age of the Democratic Revolution: A Political History of Europe and America, 1760–1800. The Challenge* (Princeton, N. J.: Princeton University Press, 1969), I, 185.

the Puritan colonies of New England, founded primarily as refuges in which the saintly could create their own religious communities, had recognized the economic potential and restrictions of their rockbound territory. Farming was carried out by individual families on land assigned through their township. Along the coast, the towns concentrated on fishing, shipbuilding, and commerce with the West Indies. Through their assemblies and especially in the township meetings, New Englanders had developed the habit of administering themselves; and they fought vigorously as early as 1684 the first important royal attempt to restrict their self-government.

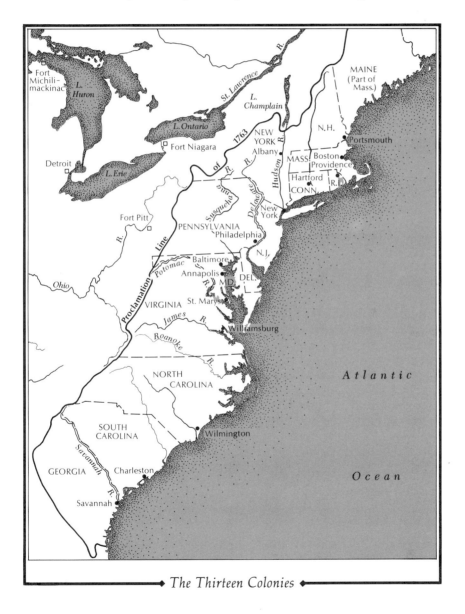

◆ The Thirteen Colonies ◆

"America," by Giovanni Battista Tiepolo (1696–1770)

In this fresco in the palace of the bishop of Würzburg, Tiepolo reflects the popular European notion of the American Indian as a "noble savage." *(Courtesy of the German Information Center)*

In the South, from Maryland to the Carolinas, the impetus to settlement had been mercenary rather than religious. Virginia had been founded by a trading company out to make money from gold and trade with the natives; after it became a royal colony in 1624, large estates were granted to anyone who would bring out settlers—fifty acres for himself as "headright" for each person he brought in. Concentration on tobacco, which could only be grown profitably on large estates, further encouraged the growth of plantations worked by slaves; and by the 1680s Virginia was in the control of a planter aristocracy that already included such families as the Byrds, the Randolphs, and the Washingtons. A similar social and economic pattern existed in the "proprietary colonies," that is, colonies, among them Maryland and the Carolinas, granted by the crown to a proprietor; and the individual farmer working his own land was never able, except in North Carolina, to take political power from the entrenched planter aristocracy.

In the so-called middle settlements, from New York to Delaware, there was a greater range of economic activity and social class. Large estates, such as those along the Hudson River, alternated with family farms. Religious faith and national origins were widely mixed, from Jew to Catholic, from Negro slave to Dutch aristocrat. Commerce, through the port of New York, encouraged the farmers of New Jersey to produce for the West Indian trade, and other entrepreneurs to go further afield in search of furs and whale oil. To this already variegated colonial scene, the foundation of Pennsylvania added new diversity.

William Penn (1644–1718) was a proprietor, like the duke of Baltimore, who was granted his huge province because of his admiral father's favor with the court. But he was also a Quaker, converted to that small offshoot of Puritanism in spite of his father's opposition and totally committed to the Society of Friends' belief that clergy and sacraments were an unnecessary impediment to the "inner light." In America he saw the opportunity to provide a refuge for the thousands of Quakers from throughout Europe and indeed from the other American colonies who were being persecuted for their beliefs. In a pamphlet called *Some Account of the Province of Pennsylvania*, which was translated into several European languages, Penn invited settlement of his colony and promised the two benefits that remained the lure of Pennsylvania throughout the eighteenth century: complete religious freedom and land on easy terms. Among the many natural advantages of the area, he noted that "the place lies six hundred miles nearer the sun than England, further south, that is, no mean lure to northern Europeans who, not having much of the sun, cherish it more than most."[2] The colonists he wanted, "industrious husbandmen and day laborers ... laborious handicrafts, especially carpenters, masons, smiths, weavers, taylors, tanners, shoemakers, shipwrights, etc. ... ingenious spirits," could rent a two-hundred-acre farm for a penny an acre or buy a large estate for only a hundred pounds. And as the main port and the capital of the province, Penn ordered his commissioners in 1681 to lay out the City of Brotherly Love, Philadelphia:

Let the rivers and creeks be sounded in order to settle a great towne. Be sure to make your choice where it is most navigable, high, dry and healthy. Let every house be pitched in the middle of its plot so that there may be ground on each side for gardens or orchards or fields, that it may be a green country towne that will never be burnt and always be wholesome.[3]

When Penn arrived to be his own governor in 1682, the little city had already been surveyed and an ambitious pattern of streets along the Delaware River laid out. Penn's was not to be an aristocratic, baroque city, but a modest town of simple proportions, designed like ancient Piraeus in a Milesian or gridiron pattern but with a market rather than a temple where the two main streets crossed. As the plan shows, people of different economic standing received lots of varying size, with the laboring poor clustered in the subdivided plots near the Delaware and Schuylkill rivers. A year after his arrival, Penn wrote back to London: "This I will say for the

The Foundation of Pennsylvania

William Penn, After an Original Painting, by Henry Inman (1801–1846) *(Loan Collection, Free Library of Philadelphia)*

Early Philadelphia

[2]Cited in Maxwell S. Burt, *Philadelphia: Holy Experiment* (New York: Doubleday, 1945), pp. 1–2.
[3]Ibid., p. 37.

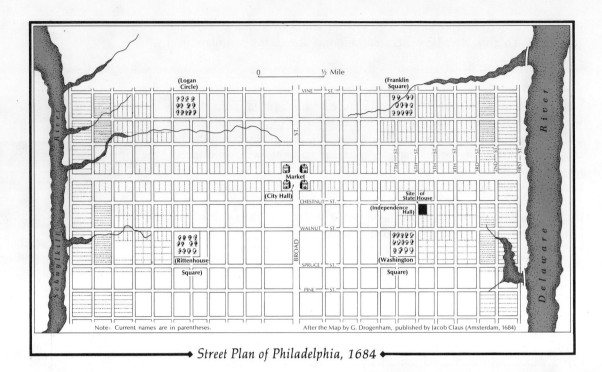

♦ Street Plan of Philadelphia, 1684 ♦

Note: Current names are in parentheses.

After the Map by G. Drogenham, published by Jacob Claus (Amsterdam, 1684)

Philadelphia in 1761
(Philadelphia Collection,
Free Library of Philadelphia)

good Providence of God, that of all the many places I have seen in the world, I remember not one better seated, so that it seems to me to have been appointed for a towne, whether we regard the rivers or the conveniency of the coves, docks, springs, the loftiness and soundness of the land and the air held by the people of these parts to be very good."[4]

Philadelphia and Pennsylvania prospered together. The colony by 1750 had a population of a quarter of a million people, composed largely of religious groups seeking freedom from the oppression of many parts of Europe: Quakers from England and Wales, Mennonites from Germany, Huguenots from France, Presbyterians from Northern Ireland, and many others. Their diversity was evident in the churches of Philadelphia, which an English clergyman described in 1759 as "eight or ten places of religious worship, viz. two churches [Anglican], three Quaker meeting-houses, two Presbyterian ditto, one Lutheran church, one Dutch Calvinist ditto, one Swedish ditto, one Romish chapel, one Anabaptist meeting-house, one Moravian ditto."[5] The economy was rich and varied, and through the port of Philadelphia the farmers shipped grain and flour, horses and cattle, tobacco, wool, lumber and staves, and bought English manufactured goods

[4]Ibid., p. 38.
[5]Andrew Burnaby, *Travels Through the Middle Settlements of North America* (New York: A. Wessels, 1904), p. 90.

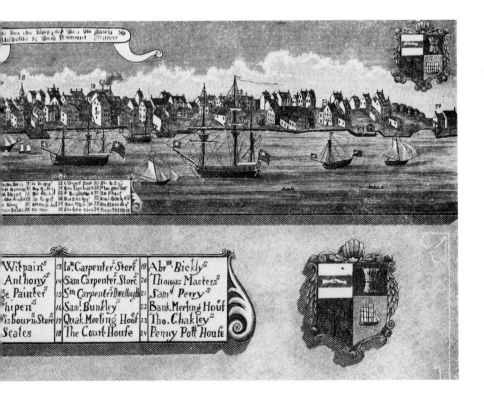

like hardware and clothing as well as West Indian products like sugar. The rural hinterland, constantly expanding in area of settlement as the immigrants poured in to take up the rich, inexpensive lands, provided a great stimulus to Philadelphia's growth. By 1760 Philadelphia had outdistanced Boston both in size and influence in the colonies; and in the urban world of the eighteenth century it had come to be recognized as the equal of most great European cities. "Its fine appearance," wrote a Swedish naturalist, "good regulations, agreeable situation, natural advantages, trade, riches and power, are by no means inferior to those of any, even of the most ancient towns in Europe."

Obstacles to Revolution

Many British observers felt that in this diverse American colonial society a revolution for political equality with Britain would be both unpopular and impossible, although internal struggles for control of political power between the different groups of the American population were inevitable. Because of the vast differences in the character of the economy and the social structure of the different colonies, it was felt that no common grievance could unite the colonists against Britain; and that even if such a grievance existed, the difficulty of organizing a revolt of people of so many different languages and backgrounds spread along twelve hundred miles of coast and scattered inland as far as the rough Appalachian range would be insuperable. "America is formed for happiness, but not for empire," wrote Andrew Burnaby.

The colonies, therefore, separately considered, are internally weak. . . . It appears to me a very doubtful point, even supposing all the colonies of America to be united under one head, whether it would be possible to keep in due order and government so wide and extended an empire, the difficulties of communication, of intercourse, of correspondence, and all other circumstances considered. . . . Fire and water are not more heterogeneous than the different colonies in North America. Nothing can exceed the jealousy and emulation which they possess in regard to each other. . . . In short, such is the difference of character, of manners, of religion, of interest, of the different colonies, that I think, if I am not wholly ignorant of the human mind, were they left to themselves, there would soon be a civil war from one end of the continent to the other; while the Indians and negroes would, with better reason, impatiently watch the opportunity of exterminating them all together.[6]

Internal divisions in each colony promised a further source of weakness. All the colonies felt the turbulence of internal conflict—between the coastal regions and the hinterland, between people of different national and religious origins, between the socially established and the social aspirants, between different factions within the legislatures themselves. But those who concentrated on the discord were misleading themselves and ended, like Burnaby, in being astonished to find that the American colonists should wish to revolt against Britain and be able to sink their differences sufficiently to do so.

[6]Ibid., pp. 152–153.

The American Revolution was made possible, in the long run, because of the positive features Americans felt they enjoyed on the new continent. Most obviously, whatever differences existed in wealth, almost no one was poor, with the exception of the tightly controlled slaves and a very few paupers in the cities. Except for the plantations, the feudal tradition had been left behind in Europe; and land was readily available for most of those who would work it. As a result no other eighteenth-century society enjoyed such economic independence; furthermore, no other society enjoyed such widespread political participation. The colonists had succeeded in whittling down the powers of royal intervention through the governors and of the colonial elites through the councils, which were usually twelve-man upper houses chosen by the governor. Power was largely exercised by the broadly representative lower house, which provided an organ within which ambitious new men of whatever class, national, or religious background could rise. The acquisition of wealth and the access to political power thus presented ways of upward mobility that were closed in eighteenth-century France. Moreover, until the 1760s the British government had adopted, almost unconsciously, a policy of "salutary neglect" toward its American colonies, trying only rarely to curb the growth of the political power of the colonial governments and permitting the colonies to evade the restrictive effects of the mercantilist laws officially governing the economic relations of the colonies and the mother country. The American colonists were largely satisfied with the structure of colonial life. Where dissatisfaction existed, they believed machinery existed for remedy, without recourse to internal revolution or external revolt. The Revolution occurred because a sufficiently large number of colonists, though far from a majority, came to feel, in the thirteen years after the defeat of their French rivals in North America in 1763, that the British government was attempting to destroy their satisfactory status within the empire.

Causes of Revolution in America

The changes introduced by the British government in 1763–1776 affected all sections of American colonial society, and for that reason the Revolution cannot be ascribed to any one source exclusively, either the cities or farms, the radicals or the planters, the merchants or frontiersmen. When the British attempted to solve the Indian problem by banning white settlement west of the Appalachian Mountains beyond a Proclamation Line, they annoyed not only the frontiersmen but many who had hoped to move west in search of new land. The Stamp Act, intended to raise revenue for support of the British army stationed in the colonies for their defense by the sale of stamps on all types of legal documents, newspapers, and even playing cards, was a heavy direct tax affecting everyone; it provoked both direct violence against the stamp sellers and more importantly the complaint that it was taxation without representation. The imposition of import taxes collected at the colonial ports on items such as tea annoyed all the city merchants as well as their customers. Finally, when resistance in Boston provoked the Coercive Acts, which included closing the port, all the colonists assumed this to be the final act of a gigantic conspiracy plotted by the British government to deprive them of their liberty.

Historians have uncovered many other motives as well as the desire to be rid of these new encroachments of British power. It has been suggested, for example, that the Southern planters saw revolution as a means of canceling their debts to English merchants, and that the smugglers of the seaports were outraged at the curtailment of their activities. But the overwhelming feeling was of repugnance for the political controls exercised by a corrupt and oppressive Britain. Benjamin Franklin summed up the feeling in 1775:

> When I consider the extreme corruption prevalent among all orders of men in this old rotten state, and the glorious public virtue so predominant in our rising country, I cannot but apprehend more mischief than benefit from a closer union. I fear they will drag us after them in all the plundering wars which their desperate circumstances, injustice, and rapacity may prompt them to undertake; and their wide-wasting prodigality and profusion is a gulf that will swallow up every aid we may distress ourselves to afford them. Here numberless and needless places, enormous salaries, pensions, perquisites, bribes, groundless quarrels, foolish expeditions, false accounts or no accounts, contracts, and jobs, devour all revenue and produce continual necessity in the midst of natural plenty. I apprehend, therefore, that to unite us intimately will only be to corrupt and poison us also.[7]

The Cities and the Revolution

The role of the cities was to convert this far-reaching dissatisfaction with Britain expressed by Franklin into a movement for independence. The grievances with the mercantilist system of empire were felt strongly in the colonial cities. In the 1740s, many of Philadelphia's merchants turned to smuggling rather than accept the restriction of the geographical area open to their trade. Its harbor, according to the governor, was soon swarming "with shallops unloading these illegal cargoes, bought at their return, and cheating the King of his duties, besides carrying provisions and ready money to the Enemy." Moreover, the opening of the inland regions provided a ready market for manufactured goods that the cities, rather than act as agents for British goods, preferred to supply themselves. Surplus capital from the cities also moved westward for land speculation, until blocked by the ban on settlement beyond the Appalachians. The cities too were accustomed to dominating the legislature of their colonies; and so the political elite of Philadelphia, Newport, and Boston enjoyed powers that were distributed geographically, if not socially, far more widely than in such rural states as Virginia, New Jersey, and Vermont. It was in the cities that the first counterattack against British policy, through trade boycott, could be most easily planned.

While directly aggrieved, the cities had prepared the theoretical basis for a break with Britain. The ideas of the Enlightenment, both in its Eng-

[7]Benjamin Franklin, cited in Bernard Bailyn, *The Ideological Origins of the American Revolution* (Cambridge, Mass.: Harvard University Press, 1967), p. 136.

lish origins and its French development, entered America through the cities. The club provided a substitute for the salon. Before the Revolution, Philadelphia had more than fifty; and they provided the organization for many of the militia groups formed when conflict began. Merchants met regularly in coffeehouses and taverns, where local politics was frequently settled; and it was here that the early revolutionary committees were formed. Habits of coordination were established and ideas exchanged easily. Through books published by Philadelphia's forty-two printers, through its seven newspapers, and through the importation of books from Europe, all the leading works of Enlightenment thought found their way into the colony; lending libraries dispersed them widely; and the meetings of the legislature in the State House on Walnut Street (soon to become Independence Hall) were enlivened with references to Locke, Montesquieu, and Voltaire. The ease with which men like Franklin could circulate in the salons of Paris provided proof of their acceptance into the inner circles of the Enlightenment.

The cities helped to provide not only the ideas of political equality but also the organization and the men to seek it. Coastwise shipping carried messages to correspondence committees that in turn circulated among the colonies news of acts of the British government and measures to combat

(Left) The State House, Philadelphia, in 1778, by Charles Willson Peale (1741–1827)
(Philadelphia Collection, Free Library of Philadelphia)

(Right) Independence Hall, Philadelphia, Today
In the state house, normally the meeting place of the Pennsylvania legislature, the Second Continental Congress approved the Declaration of Independence on July 4, 1776, and the Constitutional Convention drew up the Constitution of the United States in 1787. (Courtesy of the Convention and Visitors' Bureau, Philadelphia)

them. The Sons of Liberty, groups of middle-class citizens determined to use rabble-rousing techniques to block British measures like the Stamp Act as well as to create a spirit of insurgency, were predominantly a creation of the coastal cities; and in general, the most radical leaders of the independence movement came from the cities. And it was in the cities that the most far-reaching constitutional changes were carried out. The first Continental Congress, to which Philadelphia acted as host in 1774, was a revolutionary assembly, chosen illegally by revolutionary conventions or by committees of the legislatures, and it evolved during the next two years into a federal government.

But some colonies went even further in remodeling their own constitutions. A mass meeting of four thousand people in Philadelphia in May 1776 demanded a constitutional convention. It was called by irregular means. Dominated by democrats from the West and radicals from the city, it set up a constitution that gave all male taxpayers over twenty-one the right to vote and to be elected and imposed strict controls of the legislature over the other branches of government. The radicals too ensured that Philadelphia would remain faithful to the Revolution by seizing control of the city. In all the colonies, new constitutions were written, although most were not as radical as those of Pennsylvania and Massachusetts. Nevertheless, this "internal revolution" formed a significant part of the message of political equality that Europeans were learning from the American war of independence. Moreover, the principle that all power derives from the people (and not from the colonies, which had become states) was reaffirmed in the Constitutional Convention, which met in Philadelphia in 1787; and although the final Constitution compromised with the powers of the states, it provided further stimulus to the growing impatience in Europe for greater political equality in place of the ancien régime.

The popularization of the American Revolution in Europe was due to the drama of the war, enhanced by the constitutional changes of the immediate postwar years. But the American colonists were correct in thinking that they were fighting to safeguard an American political heritage that was already in existence in 1763 and was due to the transformation of institutions of British origin by a new people of multinational origins struggling with a completely new environment. Or, in John Adams' famous phrase, "the revolution was complete, in the minds of the people, and the Union of the colonies, before the war commenced in the skirmishes of Concord and Lexington on the 19th of April, 1775." But to Europeans the Revolution had a universal message. As one German poet wrote:

> And man was now again man; many noble beings
> Planted eagerly the seed of truth.
> Far on Philadelphia's shores there glowed
> A sweeter dawn. [8]

[8] Cited in Palmer, *Age of the Democratic Revolution*, I, 507. Translation modified.

PARIS AND THE EGALITARIAN REVOLUTION

Ιt was in Paris that the impact of the American Revolution was felt most deeply. To the philosophes of the Paris salons, it was an attempt to follow their own theories in an environment that was already favorable; for indeed a Frenchman, Hector St. John de Crèvecoeur, in his widely admired *Letters of an American Farmer*, had shown that in America man experienced "a sort of resurrection.... He now feels himself a man, because he is treated as such." This agreeable notion was fostered widely during the war of independence by no less a propagandist than Benjamin Franklin, who was appointed by the Continental Congress as its representative in Paris. Idolized by the salon society as the Enlightenment's ideal of intellectual sophistication and natural simplicity, Franklin skillfully passed on to Voltaire, Condorcet, Turgot, Helvétius, and his other salon acquaintances a somewhat distorted version of events in America; and

Benjamin Franklin Drawing Electricity from the Sky, by Benjamin West (1738–1820)
In his famous experiment of flying a kite in a thunderstorm, Franklin showed that lightning and electricity were identical. (Philadelphia Museum of Art, the Mr. and Mrs. Wharton Sinkler Collection)

it became fashionable in the highest society to show one's reverence for his cause by displaying his homely features on hats, watches, snuffboxes, and even handkerchiefs. Turgot wrote the famous epithet, "He stole thunder from the heavens and the scepter from tyrants."

The dream of American liberty penetrated all groups of French society. The future revolutionary, Brissot, founded a Gallo-American Society in 1787, with Crèvecoeur a founding member. Officers like the Marquis de Lafayette, returning from service in the French expeditionary force in America, spread the praises of the Revolution. Even the artists became involved. The great sculptor Houdon carved Franklin when he was in Paris and then accompanied him to Mount Vernon to make his uncompromising bust of Washington. Jacques Louis David (1748–1825), the protagonist of the classical revival, displayed his *Oath of the Horatii* in 1785, which many interpreted as a study in self-sacrifice *à l'américaine*.

Financial Collapse   Yet it was in less ethereal ways that the American Revolution pushed France into revolution. Helping the Americans win independence brought the French treasury to the edge of bankruptcy. It was a gesture that was reputed to have cost two and a half times the normal annual revenue. What was certain was that the borrowing by which the war was financed increased the interest on the national debt from 93 million livres in 1774 to 300 million in 1789, and that this sum was payable largely to the wealthier members of the bourgeoisie and the nobility of the robe. One controller-general followed another, every scheme for a reform of the system of taxation being blocked either by the nobility and the parlements, the twelve great law courts of Paris and the provinces that possessed the power to enforce or reject royal edicts, or by the tax collectors themselves. Finally in 1786, the charming, self-confident bureaucrat Calonne proposed to the king that he call an Assembly of Notables composed of nobility, clergy, and administrators who, he felt, could be persuaded to grant the king the right to tax them. The Notables met in February 1787, demanded a dispersion of governmental powers among provincial assemblies dominated by themselves, and refused otherwise the tax proposals. This meeting is often regarded as a backward-looking revolution of the aristocracy for restoration of the power they enjoyed before the time of Richelieu and Louis XIV. It compelled the king to try a second expedient, to decree a new land tax applicable to all classes and to force the Parlement of Paris to register the edict by appearing personally to hold a *lit de justice*, a session in which traditionally the Parlement accepted the king's wishes. The Parlement, the principal mouthpiece of the nobility of the robe, won a brief popular fame by refusing the edict. Instead they demanded that the king respect the principle of no taxation without representation and summon the one representative body in the nation that enjoyed the customary right of granting taxes, the Estates General, which had not met since 1614. Thus the nobility, both in the Assembly of Notables and the Parlement, called for a broader-based assembly, partly to postpone the day when they would be taxed but largely to provide a constitutional body, dominated by them, that would be a substitute for royal absolutism. They thereby opened the way for the middle classes to carry through their own constitutional reforms.

The ten years of revolutionary activity between 1789 and the seizure of power by Napoleon in 1799 can be divided, at some risk of over-simplification, into four main phases characterized by a turnover of leaders and programs. These four phases are: constitutional monarchy dominated by the bourgeoisie, in 1789–1792; provincial rule through the Girondin party in 1792–1793; a Reign of Terror by the lower bourgeoisie and working class of Paris in 1793–1794; and the restoration of bourgeois rule in 1794–1799. We may also very broadly summarize the goals of the different classes during this period. The aristocracy sought the return of their former political and economic privileges. The bourgeoisie wanted governmental efficiency, social mobility, and increased political power. The peasantry wanted an end to feudal dues, a reduction in the burden of taxation, and a larger share of the land. The working class of the cities wanted secure employment and cheaper food.

Character of the Revolutionary Movement

But class interest is only one of several influences in the Revolution. One has to recognize that no social class was homogeneous in composition or aims. No period of government was dominated by a single class. Revolutionary agitation was continuous until 1794 and intermittent afterwards, and this form of agitation seemed to produce its own momentum. Programs for change interacted. Bargains were concluded. Personal rivalries intervened. Psychological factors, like war-weariness, dislike or love of violence, and national pride, worked against purely material goals.

Perhaps the most far-reaching political division, which was to last throughout the Revolution, was between those who wanted to increase individual freedom by reducing state power and those who wanted to increase personal equality by augmenting it. These groups were to clash again and again, most notably in 1793 when the egalitarian Jacobins of Paris were able to take power from the libertarian Girondins of the provinces. Miscalculation and pure chance further complicated the conflict of interests. But there is one strand that runs through the whole tangled web of events: the predominant role of Paris, or rather of the group controlling Paris, in determining the course of the Revolution.

In August 1788 the king ordered the Estates General to be convoked for May 1789. Election procedures for election of the three houses—the First Estate of the clergy, the Second Estate of the nobility, and the Third Estate representing everyone else—were worked out haphazardly, according to jumbled notions of what had happened in 1614 when the Estates General had last met. But the combined pressure of self-seeking and liberal nobility and the middle-class reformers compelled an important concession—that the Third Estate should be twice the size of each of the other estates. En-

The Calling of the Estates General

1787	Feb.	Meeting of Assembly of Notables
1788		Parlement refuses to register law of taxation on landed income
	Aug.	Estates General summoned
1789	May 5	Meeting of Estates General
	June 17	Third Estate declares itself the National Assembly
	June 20	Tennis Court Oath
	July 14	Taking of the Bastille
	Aug. 4	Abolition of feudal rights
	Aug. 27	Declaration of Rights of Man and of the Citizen
	Oct. 5	March of the Fishwives to Versailles. Royal family brought back to Paris
	Nov. 2	Confiscation of property of Church and émigré nobles
1790		Paris divided into 48 sections
	July 12	Civil Constitution of the Clergy
1791	June 21	Flight of royal family and arrest at Varennes
	Aug. 27	Declaration of Pillnitz
	Oct.	Meeting of Legislative Assembly
1792	April 20	Declaration of war on Austria and Prussia
	July 25	Brunswick Manifesto
	Aug. 10	Storming of Tuileries Palace by Paris mob
	Sept.	Massacre of prisoners in Paris prisons
	Sept. 20	Meeting of National Convention. Victory at Valmy
	Sept. 21	Abolition of the monarchy
	Sept. 22	Proclamation of the Republic
	Nov. 19	Offer to aid other peoples seeking liberty
1793	Jan.	Execution of Louis XVI
	Feb. 1	Declaration of war on England and Holland
	March	Spain enters war against France
	June	Paris mob drives Girondins out of Convention
	Sept.	Rule by Committee of Public Safety
	Oct.	Execution of Queen Marie Antoinette
1794	July 27	Uprising of 9 Thermidor. Overthrow of Robespierre. End of the Reign of Terror
1795	June	Death of Louis XVII in Paris prison
		Constitution of Year III establishes government by Directory
	Oct. 5	Napoleon Bonaparte crushes Paris mob with "whiff of grapeshot" on 13 Vendémiaire
1796	May	Failure of "Conspiracy of Equals" of Babeuf (extreme left-wing plot)
		Napoleon's successful campaign in Italy
1797	Oct.	Treaty of Campo Formio. Austria cedes Belgium and Rhineland to France
1798		Napoleon's unsuccessful campaign in Egypt
1799	Nov.	Napoleon overthrows the Directory in the coup d'état of 18 Brumaire
	Dec.	Establishment of the Consulate, with Napoleon as first consul
1802	Dec.	Napoleon first consul for life
1804	Dec.	Napoleon emperor

couraged by this victory, the reformers flooded the country with model grievance petitions (*cahiers de doléances*), which the electors could send with their representatives to the meeting of the Estates.

When the members straggled into Versailles in May 1789, it became evident at once that the reformers enjoyed unexpected advantages. The First Estate, far from solidly supporting the upper hierarchy of the Church, included a majority of parish priests; the Second Estate did not represent the court but rather the poorer nobles of the countryside and the nobility of the robe; and sympathetic nobles and clergymen actually stood for election to the Third Estate, including its finest propagandist, Abbé Sieyès, whose pamphlet *What Is the Third Estate?* had wide circulation. To Sieyès, the problem was simple:

First   *What is the third estate? Everything.*
Second   *What has it been up to now in the political order? Nothing.*
Third   *What does it demand? To become something therein.*

The Third Estate itself was not composed of peasants or city workers, but of lawyers, bureaucrats, and intellectuals. They were well educated, with a knowledge of the law and the teachings of the Enlightenment. Royal errors during the first Estates' meetings unified them in a common opposition to their demeaning treatment. They were ordered to wear the same clothes as the Third Estate of 1614: hats without decoration, simple coats, muslin shirts, white stockings, knee breeches. In contrast, the nobility were to be resplendent in lace, feathers, gold braid, and the clergy to wear their finest robes. Members of the Third Estate were constantly kept waiting for hours, herded around by soldiers and ignored by the king. The king's opening speech warned of "an exaggerated desire for change," and he refused to compel the other estates to unite with the Third Estate in one assembly with common voting. The Third Estate replied by refusing to do any official business, although it met every day. On June 17 the Third Estate declared itself to be the National Assembly and invited the other estates to join it. A majority of the clergy voted to do so; and on June 20 the self-styled National Assembly, finding its meeting hall locked—for redecoration, according to the king; for intimidation, according to the deputies—moved to the nearby tennis court and took an oath never to disband "until the constitution of the kingdom is established and consolidated upon firm foundations."

A few days later the king capitulated, ordering the nobility to take part in the National Assembly. The assembly then renamed itself the National Constituent Assembly, as proof of its intention to write a constitution. It is clear, however, that the king's change of mind was not due to his conversion to the goal of establishing a limited monarchy. He was probably influenced by rumors that forty thousand armed brigands from Paris were preparing to march on Versailles and perhaps, too, by the growing numbers of riots in the countryside of peasants against landlords and the Church.

What was being glimpsed at Versailles, though far too mistily, was that the process of revolution was becoming self-perpetuating. The aristocratic revolution of 1777–1778 had made possible the middle-class revolution for a constitutional monarchy that was being successfully carried out by the Third Estate. But the successes of the Third Estate had provoked or encouraged two further revolutionary movements, the one in Paris and the other in the provinces. It was slowly to become clear that the master of Paris would be the eventual master of all the revolutionary movements.

The Taking of the Bastille (July 14, 1789)

On June 26, after a day spent observing the mood of the crowds in Paris, Arthur Young noted in his diary that the moderate constitutional change being considered by the assembly in Versailles was not likely to satisfy the Parisians. "Every hour that passes seems to give the people fresh spirit," he wrote. "The meetings at the Palais Royal are more numerous, more violent, and more assured; and in the assembly of electors, at Paris, for sending a deputation to the National Assembly, the language that was talked, by all ranks of people, was nothing less than a revolution in the government, and the establishment of a free constitution: what they mean by a free constitution, is easily understood—*a republic.*"[9]

Paris was in fact equipping itself with the organization of insurrection. The king's cousin Philippe, Duke of Orléans, had publicly sided with the Third Estate; and he had earlier opened to the people the grounds of his Palais Royal, where almost complete freedom of speech was permitted, seditious pamphlets circulated with impunity in the hundreds, and a large crowd was always available to stone a police spy or encourage a rebellious speaker. The electors of Paris, who had chosen the capital's members of the Third Estate, had constituted themselves the new municipal government of Paris and provided themselves with a volunteer, middle-class force, called later the National Guard. Like the other cities of the nation, Paris had thus spontaneously taken over its own government; and moreover, each of the electoral districts of the capital was continuing to run its own affairs through a district assembly. These districts were reorganized in 1790 into forty-eight sections, with assemblies and administrative committees; and the sections became henceforth the instrument of the adherents of direct democracy. In the early days of July 1789, the Parisian masses began to arm themselves, seizing knives from ironmongers and guns from gunsmiths and all the weapons and powder in the city hall and in the military Hospital of the Invalides.

At this crucial point, the king began to gather troops near Paris, mostly foreign, and dismissed the undeservedly popular finance minister, Necker. In Paris, Desmoulins yelled to the crowd the news of Necker's dismissal. "To arms!" he shouted. "Tonight the Swiss and German battalions are going to massacre the people of Paris." Part of the crowds who had been

---

[9] Arthur Young, *Travels in France During the Years 1787, 1788, and 1789* (Garden City, N.Y.: Doubleday Anchor, 1969), p. 130.

swarming around Paris for the last three days then extended their search for arms to the royal fortress of the Bastille itself and, after exchanging shots with its few defenders, were allowed inside, where they liberated its seven prisoners and murdered most of the guards. The rest were paraded in the gardens of the Palais Royal, and once they had declared their wish "to join the town and the Nation," were treated as welcome allies.[10] Paris quickly turned into a fortress. Spiked barricades crossed the streets. Trenches were dug. After a couple of days of hesitation during which his closest relatives set off into exile, the king decided to accept the advice of the National Assembly, and win Paris over with a personal display of good will. On July 17 he drove into the city where he was met by Bailly, the acting mayor. "Sire, I bring to your Majesty the keys of his good town of Paris," Bailly said. "They are the very keys that were presented to Henri IV. He had reconquered his people, and today the people have reconquered their king."

[10]Georges Pernoud and Sabine Flaissier, eds., *The French Revolution* (Greenwich, Conn.: Fawcett, n.d.), p. 29.

The Storming of the Bastille, July 14, 1789
The state prison of the Bastille was the symbol of royal oppression of the poor who lived in the slums at its base. When they stormed it, however, they found only seven prisoners inside.   (Arch. Phot. Paris/S. P. A. D. E. M.)

Reforms of August 1789

Up to this point Paris had gained very little from its skirmishings. The customs houses had been broken down, and some prices were lowered as a result. But the great shortage of bread was not alleviated. The officials in charge of the food supply were massacred by a mob in late July. It was, however, disorder in the provinces that provoked the first deep-reaching changes in the structure of French society. The peasants, nearly as hungry as the Paris crowds, had for weeks been burning down châteaux, destroying feudal records, and seizing grain supplies. During the so-called Great Fear, rumors that the nobility were employing brigands to attack the peasants produced even greater rioting, which was reported to the National Assembly by one of its committees. On August 4, in a dramatic all-night session, the Assembly made an emotional gesture of appeasement. Led by a few liberal nobles, the Assembly voted to end serfdom without compensation and to abolish all other feudal rights in return for a cash payment. The clergy was to receive no further tithes. All citizens were to pay taxes. Legal offices could not be sold. And promotion to officer rank in the army and navy was open to all. Thus, the first grievance of the peasantry had been dealt with through the abolition of feudal rights; but the peasants possessed no more land than before. Some were, however, to increase their holdings by buying up land confiscated from the Church and from émigré nobles during the next four years; and it is probably true that these peasants, by 1793–1794, sought only to conserve their gains and opposed any further revolutionary changes. It is likely that the poorer peasants suffered more in 1790–1795 as a result of the revolutionary changes because of the end of charity and employment by the Church and because many of the common lands were sold.

The Assembly returned to the more congenial task of turning France into a constitutional monarchy. On August 27 it issued the Declaration of the Rights of Man and of the Citizen, which marked the high point of the libertarian, as opposed to the egalitarian, trend of the Revolution. It emphasized the freedom of the individual from arbitrary arrest; freedom of speech, press, and assembly; and freedom to enjoy possession of one's property as a "sacred and inviolable right." Since these rights were not explicitly granted to women, and many property-related rights remained denied to them, a woman playwright named Olympe de Gouges published a parallel Declaration of the Rights of Woman and the Citizen in 1791, calling for equal property rights as well as government employment for women.

March of the Fishwives (October 5, 1789)

Paris remained restive. On a nasty, wet October dawn, a crowd of women, mostly from the central markets, trudged the three or four blocks to the city hall to demand cheaper bread. During the morning the crowd swelled; church bells were rung in the tocsin, to call the citizens forth to insurrection; the district assemblies debated; and in the afternoon a crowd of several thousand set off to Versailles to wring the beloved king away from his evil counselors and bring him bodily back to Paris. The supposed leader of the march was Renée-Louise Audu, known as Queen of the Markets, who

was arrested the following year for causing this insurrectionary action and sent to jail for a year. The crowd spent an uncomfortable night on the wet cobblestones and draughty passageways of Versailles, watched by the National Guard who had followed them from Paris; and the next morning, in a sour mood, they broke into the palace, killed a few royal guards, and demanded that the king return to Paris with them. With the huge courtyard before the palace filled with a furious crowd chanting "We want the King in Paris—the King in Paris," Louis XVI gave in to their wishes. That afternoon a vast procession of National Guards, disarmed bodyguards, wagons of grain, guns with marketwomen riding on their barrels, the royal coach, and a hundred members of the National Assembly made a slow journey into Paris, where the king was deposited in the Tuileries Palace. Thus the Paris crowd in one act of physical power impaired the royal despotism that Louis XIV had seen could only function effectively out of reach of Paris. But who was master of Paris?

Rule of the National Assembly, 1789–1791

For two years Paris permitted itself to be governed by the National Assembly, which with some misgivings had transferred its meetings to the riding salon of the Tuileries Palace in late October. There was a marked improvement in the food supply and an increase in employment as the economy picked up; and those who favored the work of the Assembly set the tone of the city. The work of the Assembly's constitutional lawyers was slow, but by September 1791 they had written a new constitution based on the separation of powers; but the political control of the middle classes was assured by requiring high property qualifications for the all-male voters and deputies, who were ingenuously labeled "active citizens" as compared with the

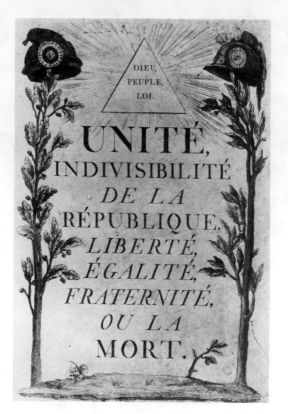

Goals of the French Revolution
Beneath a triangle containing the words God, People, Law, *a poster designed shortly after France became a republic in 1792 proclaims: "Unity, indivisibility of the Republic. Liberty, equality, fraternity, or death."* (Arch. Phot. Paris/S. P. A. D. E. M.)

poorer "passive citizens." A series of other important reforms followed. France's hopelessly antiquated administrative system was reworked. The country was divided into eighty-three departments of roughly equal size, with elected officials at every level of government. Equality of rights was given to Protestants and later to Jews. Torture was forbidden, and new legal procedures drawn up. Barriers to free movement of goods inside the country were abolished.

To solve the pressing financial problem, the lands of the Church were confiscated in November 1789 and the proceeds from their sale used to back a new paper currency. By the Civil Constitution of the Clergy of July 1790, the Catholic hierarchy was to be elected by all active citizens, not merely by Catholics; the clergy was to be paid state salaries; and all clergy had to swear to accept the Civil Constitution. The pope denounced the Civil Constitution and suspended all clergy who accepted it. The attack on the Church, so consonant with the teachings of the Enlightenment, was one of the worst errors of the Assembly. It weakened the national finances when the paper currency became drastically inflated; it made sincere Catholics enemies of the revolution; and, by satisfying the demand for land of many bourgeois and well-to-do peasants, it turned them into conservatives who felt no further need for the revolution.

This great surge of reforming activity was, however, heady medicine for many French people, and for foreigners too. The sense of a glorious new day dawning was captured most vividly in Wordsworth's famous lines:

Bliss was it in that dawn to be alive,
But to be young was very Heaven! O times,
In which the meagre, stale, forbidding ways
Of custom, law and statute, took at once
The attraction of a country in romance!
When Reason seemed the most to assert her rights
When most intent on making of herself
A prime enchantress to assist the work,
Which then was going forward in her name!
Not favored spots alone, but the whole earth,
The beauty wore of promise. [11]

Rise of the Jacobins

Meanwhile, however, less starry-eyed revolutionaries were preparing to profit from the anarchy that the impracticality of the new government was encouraging. The Assembly's grant of total freedom of the press and political meetings saw the creation of many newspapers and political clubs. Constitutional monarchists joined the Feuillant Club, while the radical members of the Assembly were active in the highly influential Jacobin Club. Women took advantage of this new opportunity to engage in political action. Many attended the Jacobin Club. More moderate admirers of the Enlightenment writer Condorcet, who in his essay *On the Admission of Women to the Rights of Citizenship* (1790) had argued for their equal political rights, had joined the Friends of Truth; and hundreds of similar clubs were formed in the provinces.

The Jacobin Club, by distributing food and money and by throwing its debates open to the public, won the largest popular following in Paris; and, through correspondence, the Paris Jacobins created a close-knit network of Jacobin clubs throughout the country, perhaps as many as two thousand in number, which were very close to a conspiratorial underground. With a membership of moderately prosperous middle-class people, the Jacobins sought ideological rather than class goals—the creation of an egalitarian society through their political activity as an elite which, in Rousseau's sense, could understand the general will and must eventually be entrusted with the task of implementing it. In the early years, however, the meetings of the clubs and of the Assembly itself were chaotic. A noisy audience interjected its comments, shouted down unpopular speakers, and occasionally joined in the voting.

Governmental chaos was compounded when the king, who still exercised important executive functions and whose collaboration was essential to the success of the constitution being written, fled from Paris in June

[11] William Wordsworth, *The Prelude*, xi, lines 108–118.

Marie Antoinette, by Elisabeth Vigée-Lebrun (1755–1842)
Vigée-Lebrun's flattering portraits were highly prized by the leading aristocrats of all the European courts. (Editorial Photocolor Archives/Alinari)

1791. He and his family were caught near the Luxembourg border at Varennes and brought back through leering crowds to undisguised imprisonment in the Tuileries. The soldiers lining the streets reversed their arms, as though they were at a funeral!

The Collapse of Limited Monarchy, 1791–1792

The flight of the king to Varennes greatly weakened the position of those who had hoped to create an effective constitutional monarchy in France; but the new constitution nevertheless came into force in September 1791. A new Legislative Assembly, elected shortly afterwards, was completely inexperienced, since the members of the Constituent Assembly were not permitted to seek election to the new assembly. Only about a third of the

Legislative Assembly's members were moderates who wanted to make the limited monarchy work; and a struggle for power ensued between the followers of Jacques Brissot, a propagandist and intriguer from the provincial city of Chartres, and the more extreme members of the Jacobin Club.

The Brissotins, or Girondins as they came to be called because many of their leaders came from the Gironde department near Bordeaux, were ideological hotheads. They demanded a war to sweep the ideals of the Revolution into the tyrannical states on France's borders and beyond; and they expected popular uprisings in those countries to welcome the French armies of liberation. They sought strict enforcement of the Civil Constitution of the Clergy, and repressive measures against the emigrant nobility. Although many Girondins were originally members of the Jacobin Club and, like the more extreme Jacobin leaders, belonged to the relatively affluent middle classes, they differed from them in finding their support in the provinces, especially among the lower professional classes and the craftsmen, artisans, shopkeepers, and more prosperous peasants. They wanted the subordination of Paris to the provinces and the reduction of governmental interference in the economy, which would inevitably redistribute the wealth of the country in favor of the Parisian working classes, given the continuing pressure of the Paris crowds.

The Jacobins became the party of the Paris radicals, possessing, in the elected political assemblies and committees of the districts or "sections" into which Paris was divided, the means of organizing instant insurrection and in the Jacobin clubs of the smaller cities the means of spreading their orders throughout France. The Jacobin leaders, Robespierre, Danton, Marat, Saint Just, and Couthon, believed in effective, interfering government manipulated by a ruthless elite prepared at any time to sacrifice liberty to the needs of equality. Again, in the battles between the factions, it was the ability to manipulate the Paris mob that would ensure victory.

During the winter of 1791–1792, the Girondins succeeded in whipping up war fever against Austria and Prussia. In August 1791 the rulers of Austria and Prussia had offered to use force to restore the absolute rule of Louis XVI if other states would aid them. Nobles fleeing from France were finding a ready welcome in the smaller German courts and in Austria, where most French people believed they were enlisting support for an armed attack on the Revolution. Above all the Girondins argued that the success of the Revolution in France would only be assured when similar revolutions had been carried out against the conservative monarchies in Austria and Germany, with the aid of France. Louis XVI, convinced his own plight would be helped by the defeat of France, agreed in April 1792 to the Legislative Assembly's declaration of war on his brother-in-law, the emperor of Austria, who was quickly aided by the king of Prussia.

The raw French armies, lacking officers, arms, and training, were easily defeated, and took flight. Defeats on the frontiers, fear of foreign invasion, worsening inflation, a new food crisis, and the urging of professional agitators brought Paris again to the boil.

On August 9, 1792, the old municipal government was replaced by a revolutionary one called together by craftsmen from the agitated Faubourg Saint Antoine, and the new government threw the city hall doors open to the crowd throughout the sultry night. The tocsin was sounded from the churches, and in the morning radical leaders led the mob against the Tuileries Palace. When fighting broke out between the king's guards and the crowds, the king and the royal family took refuge in the Assembly chamber. Six hundred guards and four hundred attackers lost their lives, however; and the Assembly suspended the king and called new elections for a National Convention.

With the king transferred to the Temple prison in the control of the Paris Commune, the mob went wild again at news of further advances of the Austrian and Prussian armies into France. Reacting spontaneously to the atmosphere of hatred and fear enveloping the city, in September 1792 the crowd began an indiscriminate massacre of all the prisoners it could find in the city. In more than a week of slaughter over half the prisoners in Paris perished, including only a small minority of aristocrats. The elections, held concurrently with the massacres, not surprisingly were ill-attended. Less than one-tenth of those eligible voted, and Parisian voters did so publicly in the Jacobin Club in front of howling onlookers. Paris thus returned a strongly Jacobin delegation headed by Danton, but the provinces again returned the Girondins, who were greatly encouraged by the first victory won by the revolutionary army at Valmy on September 20.

Siege and Taking of the Tuileries Palace, August 10, 1792
Outraged by threats of the general commanding the Austrian and Prussian armies attacking France that he would destroy Paris if the royal family was harmed, the Paris mob stormed the Tuileries Palace. The king and queen escaped to the protection of the Assembly but were later transferred to prisons controlled by the new city government of Paris. (Arch. Phot. Paris/S. P. A. D. E. M.)

On September 21 the new assembly, called the National Convention, abolished the monarchy. On September 22 France became a republic. France's constitutional monarchy had lasted exactly one year.

In the National Convention, the Girondins were the most conservative social group represented, and were known, from the section of the riding school where they sat, as the Right. They relied for support on a number of independent members, known as the Plain because they sat in the center of the assembly hall at ground level. The Jacobins bunched together on the left, high in the back of the room and were known as the Mountain, or the Left.

The Domination of the Girondins, September 1792– June 1793

The Girondins favored the extension of the political reforms of the early years of the Revolution into the provinces through a strengthening of the local governments in a kind of federal decentralization of France; and they extended to women certain civil rights, including the recognition of divorce, the right to take a share of family property, and the right of inheritance. The Girondins were, however, deeply worried by the activism of many of the lower-class women of Paris, who seemed to them natural allies of their rivals the Jacobins and who were constantly agitating against high prices and the shortage of food. Surprisingly enough, however, the Jacobins did not welcome women as political activists, especially as their leader Robespierre was a convert to Rousseau's views on the subordination of women; and they were suspicious of women's representation in the assemblies of the different sections of Paris, which had been granted in 1792. The great error of the Girondins was to seek to broaden the war, because the demands of the war were certain to force the acceptance of stringent central controls, to which they were opposed on principle. At first it seemed that their war policy was totally successful. General Dumouriez, who had defeated the Prussians at Valmy in September, crushed the Austrian army in Belgium at Jemappes in November. On November 19, 1792, the Girondin-dominated convention proclaimed a crusade throughout Europe, promising the aid of France to any people seeking "to recover their liberty." Their troops occupied Belgium, the Rhineland, and Savoy, and threatened Holland.

Carried away by revolutionary fervor, the Convention tried the king for treason in December and had him guillotined on January 21, 1793 in the Place de la Concorde. This execution caused a shock wave throughout Europe, especially in England, where more material sensibilities had been ruffled by the French decision to reopen navigation on the Scheldt River to permit Antwerp to challenge London's trade. Forestalling the English, the Convention declared war on England and Holland in February 1793, and a month later on Spain also.

The French had drastically overreached themselves, however, and in the spring of 1793 their armies were driven back from the Rhineland and Belgium. Moreover, a violent royalist uprising in the Vendée region of western France appeared as a threat to the revolution from within. This chaotic situation provided the opportunity for the Jacobins to seize power. On June 2, 1793, a mob, supplied with lists of suspected Girondins and armed with cannon, surrounded the Convention building and demanded the arrest or resignation of most of the Girondin faction. The majority of Girondins lost their nerve and fled home. A few were arrested, leaving the Jacobins in control not only of Paris but of the official constitutional authority of the whole country.

The Reign of Terror, June 1793–July 1794

The Reign of Terror that followed was nothing less than the dictatorship of the radical leaders of Paris, working through a tight-knit system of committees, of which the most important were the Committee of Public Safety and the Committee of General Security. They were supported by many radical groups in Paris, including the Club of Republican Revolutionary Women, which took an active role in pressing for increased terror, patrolling the streets in workingmen's clothes and the revolutionary red cap of liberty, and brawling with the marketwomen who objected to the price controls. The most significant member of the Committee of Public Safety

The Cells of the Conciergerie, Paris
During the Reign of Terror, the most important state prisoners, including Marie Antoinette, were imprisoned in the Conciergerie in the months before their trial and execution on the guillotine. (Courtesy of French Embassy Press and Information Division)

**Maximilien Robespierre,
by an Unknown Artist**
(*Cliché des Musées Nationaux-Paris*)

was the tough, dogged, dogmatic Maximilien Robespierre, the "sea-green incorruptible," a fanatic devoted to the establishment of a reign of virtue. The Terror was both a desperate effort to save the country from disaster in war and at the same time a determined plan to remodel French society and even the French themselves. Both goals seemed to require the apparatus of terror—the use of the guillotine and other less rapid methods of annihilation such as mass drownings in which up to twenty thousand people died; "representatives on mission," sent to the provinces to ensure their loyalty; and open civil war against regions like the Vendée that remained royalist. The war had to be won by organization, however. Universal military draft, the *levée en masse*, was adopted for the first time in history. Strict economic controls to ensure the food supply of the civilian population and the armies, apportionment of resources to provide weapons and uniforms, food rationing, and maximum-price laws followed rapidly.

The Republic of Virtue was to be achieved by both practical and symbolic reforms. In place of Christianity, reason and later a supreme being were ordered worshipped. A new calendar, adopted in September 1793, threw out the old months and replaced them with such charming names as Fructidor, or fruitful month, and Ventôse, or windy month; and, abolishing the Christian Sabbath, the government instituted instead a ten-day week, with provision for such civic holidays as Maternal Tenderness Day.

The war measures were overwhelmingly successful, and by 1794 the French armies were again in possession of Belgium, the left bank of the Rhine, and Savoy. But success provoked internal scissions in the Jacobin leadership. Robespierre met the challenge to his authority at the hands of the followers of Danton, who wanted to relax the terror, and the followers of Hébert, who wanted to intensify it, by executing them all for treason.

Overthrow of Robespierre (July 26, 1794)

Robespierre and his few remaining followers, however, had lost the support of the Paris mob that had given them their lease on power. The successful war had not provided bread; the deflection of popular discontent against traitors through the bloodletting of the guillotine was no longer effective, especially as it was obvious to any observer that a majority of the victims were peasants and workers. When the Convention voted to arrest Robespierre on July 26 (8 Thermidor), only three thousand people turned out in his support, while the moderates of the Convention put together a force of six thousand from the wealthier Paris sections. Two days later Robespierre and twenty-two of his followers were beheaded. Paris at once became its pleasure-loving self again, in reaction against the virtue that had been bought at such price. Restaurants, cafés, theaters, and parks soon filled with crowds in extravagant new fashions. But a visitor from Geneva, arriving in September, found Paris greatly changed from "the place that [he] had so long idolized":

There are some quarters of Paris which seem entirely deserted and you will easily guess that the most abandoned of all is that of the Faubourg Saint-Germain, where among whole streets flanked by Palaces, the only occupied mansions are those occupied by new government departments. . . . In every house into which a revolutionary committee has found its way one seems to recognize the traces of an army of Huns or Vandals. Nor must one forget the great houses transformed and laid waste by the forty-four sections of the Commune of Paris, who grabbed, one after another, the finest houses, which they found unoccupied in their quarters and set up in them their offices and guard rooms. . . . It is when the entertainments are over, toward ten o'clock at night, that the stranger is especially struck by the gloom and destitution of Paris, especially if he has known the city in happier days.[12]

The Directory and Napoleon Bonaparte

The Convention and the middle-class Directory that had taken over in 1795 quickly brought Paris under control. The remaining Jacobins were hunted down. The National Guard was restricted to men of property, and only the guard of the wealthy western sections was used against demonstrations that broke out in April and May 1795. The army was brought into the city and, under a young general named Napoleon Bonaparte, was used to mow down a mob led by royalist agitators with a "whiff of grapeshot" on 13 Vendémiaire (October 5). Paris had thus lost its radical leaders. The Committee of Public Safety was disbanded. The sections were

[12]Pernoud and Flaissier, *French Revolution*, pp. 335–338.

reorganized to prevent their developing into centers of future insurrection, and the revolutionary Commune government was suppressed. After six years of efforts to direct the course of the Revolution, the majority of the citizens of Paris had probably gained less and suffered more than any other segment of the French population.

It was Napoleon Bonaparte who was to restore the dominance of Paris over France, but only when he had made himself the undisputed master of both capital and country, a position for which neither his origins nor his age appeared to equip him. Napoleon was born in Corsica only a year after it had been acquired by France, and he spoke Italian better than French. He won a scholarship to military school in France and, like other bourgeois, found his advance in the army of the ancien régime blocked by his lack of noble birth. The Revolution removed those barriers and provided employment for a soldier of talent. In 1793 he made a brief splash as an artillery officer by compelling the British fleet to abandon the port of Toulon. After the whiff of grapeshot endeared him to the Directory, he was entrusted in 1796–1797 with the army fighting Austria in northern Italy. There, in a brilliant campaign, he utterly routed the Austrian forces; and in a treaty he wrote himself, he made northern Italy a republic and the left bank of the Rhine part of France. He was sent to Egypt in 1798 to break

The Madeleine, Paris
In 1805 Napoleon ordered the construction of this temple, which was modeled upon the Parthenon, as a memorial to the victories of his Grand Army. It was to be one of the most important buildings of his planned reconstruction of Paris as a new Rome. (Peter Menzel)

the British hold on the eastern Mediterranean. Although his campaign was disastrous and Admiral Nelson of Britain destroyed his fleet in the mouth of the Nile, he was fortunate in the even worse performance of the French generals in Europe. In 1799 France was not only losing its previous conquests but was again threatened by invasion. Approached by ambitious politicians inside the Directory, who wished to use a popular general and his loyal troops to forestall both royalists and Jacobins, Napoleon agreed to overthrow the government. He deserted his army, rushed back to France before the news of his debacle in Egypt had been assimilated, and in a quick, bloodless coup overthrew the Directory. His move was welcomed by the majority of the French people, who gave an overwhelming vote of confidence to the new constitution of the Consulate, which established a barely disguised dictatorship under the first consul, Napoleon himself.

The Consulate, 1799-1804

Napoleon at once set about providing the benefits the voters had hoped to receive. Within two years he had defeated the Austrians and persuaded the Russians and the British to make peace. His popularity by then was so great, and arrests of possible enemies in Paris so numerous, that in 1802 he was made consul for life by an even larger majority; and no one was surprised when in 1804 a plebiscite sanctioned his change of title from first consul to emperor.

It was during the five years of the consulate that Napoleon carried through the internal reforms that guaranteed the permanence of many of the changes made by the Revolution. He did so by subordinating the rest of the country to Paris. The chaos of governmental administration by the ancien régime, with which the revolutionary governments had begun to deal, was finally cleared up; and a coherent group of ministries was created, including those two vitally important instruments of central control, the Ministry of Finances, which controlled taxation, and the Ministry of the Interior, which ensured internal security. Napoleon accepted the administrative division of the country into departments, cantons, and communes, but made every one responsive to Paris by appointing all officials from the center rather than having them elected. To assure the integration of the governmental programs, he formed the Council of State, a body of legislative experts who were a kind of central cabinet responsible only to him; and he followed their advice in seeking the immediate economic restoration of the country. Revenues were restored by the reimposition of many indirect taxes and by a less successful effort to ensure that everyone paid direct taxes. Financial centralization was achieved by the foundation of the Bank of France, whose two hundred major shareholders, constituting its governing body, were the elite of Paris's financial bourgeoisie. Centralization of the legal system was furthered by the issuing of the *Code Napoléon*, a new codification of law that abolished the different provincial laws of France and created an all-embracing body of laws based not on precedent but on reason. Even the centralization of religion was made workable when the pope accepted a concordat giving the state the right to nominate the clergy.

Napoleon Points out the Course for the St. Quentin Canal

Napoleon won middle-class support by a vast program of road and canal building.

Thus, it is true that Napoleon bound all France together under the control of the government ministries in Paris and that this control was to be perhaps his most lasting legacy to France. But it is also true that by these controls he justified his claim to have been the heir and the guarantor of the Revolution. To the middle classes, he offered the financial stability, orderly administration, and social mobility for which they had entered the Revolution. To the peasants, he guaranteed the land they had already acquired, accepted in his Code the end of the feudal dues, and restored the Catholic Church. To the working classes, he provided employment, not least because of the demands of his armies for labor, supplies, and bread. To democrats of all classes, he guaranteed equality before the law and equality of opportunity, religious toleration, the abolition of torture and cruel punishments, and educational opportunity for the intelligent; and he promised the far wider spread of these benefits behind his eagles than had been achieved by the Revolution. To all nationalists, he promised not only national security but territorial expansion and military glory. It was for all these reasons that during the years of Napoleon's hegemony, Paris ceased to be a city of revolution. It was beyond the French borders that cities were in revolution after 1799.

BERLIN AND NAPLES: HARNESSING OF THE NATIONALIST REVOLUTION

The effects of the French Revolution and Napoleon's rule on the rest of Europe were paradoxical. The overthrow of the ancien régime in France undoubtedly stimulated great liberal enthusiasm among would-be reformers in other parts of Europe. Yet it was the despotic governments, such as those of Prussia and Austria, that became the most determined advocates of the introduction of certain reforms passed by the National Assembly in France. "Your Majesty!" wrote the reforming minister Hardenberg to the king of Prussia. "We must do from above what the French have done from below." Liberalism thus found some unexpected supporters. The stimulus to nationalism provoked by the conquests first of the revolutionary armies and then of Napoleon was equally paradoxical. Nationalism was fired by the positive reforms instituted both by the revolutionary armies and the governments they helped install, and by the governmental reforms introduced by Napoleon in the countries he conquered. At the very same time, however, it was stimulated from above by the conservative governments of countries against which Napoleon had fought as a weapon against him. Nationalism was thus encouraged by those governing classes who had the most to lose if nationalism should turn truly liberal.

Influence of the French Revolution in Europe

Both Berlin and Naples lay well beyond the early expansion of the revolutionary armies. When the Legislative Assembly made war on Austria and Prussia in 1792, it promised the spread of liberty; but France annexed Savoy and Nice in 1792, Belgium in 1795, and the left bank of the Rhine in 1797. Agitation by minorities of democrats, mostly middle-class in origin, gave the French an excuse, or perhaps a justification, for aiding the establishment of republics in Holland, Switzerland, and northern Italy (the Batavian, the Helvetic, the Cisalpine, and the Ligurian republics). Within this area of direct French control, reaction to the Revolution was already mixed. There was a genuine welcome for the introduction of such reforms as the abolition of feudal rights, the modernization of central and local administration, equality of access to legal and governmental positions, freedom of speech, and a reduction in the wealth of the Church. But there was widespread resentment at the annexations and bitterness at the exactions and the general behavior of the French armies. It became increasingly difficult, even for the most uncritical admirers of the change in Paris, to regard the revolutionary armies as altruistic liberators. It was thus quite easy for the king of Prussia to ignore the ideological threat to his own power from the Revolution; and his ministers were already claiming in 1791 that the aim of the king to reduce the power of his own nobility made him a "democrat in his own way." After the unsuccessful though inexpensive campaign of 1792–1795, Prussia remained neutral until 1806.

1792 April   Declaration of war on Austria and Prussia. War of First Coalition
September   Battle of Valmy (defeat of Prussia)
November   Battle of Jemappes (defeat of Austria)
1793 February   Declaration of war on Britain and Holland
March   Declaration of war on Spain
French driven back from Belgium and Rhineland
August   Jacobins decree *levée en masse* (mass conscription)
1794 French reconquest of Belgium and Rhineland
1795 April   Prussia withdraws from war
1796 March   Opening of Napoleon's campaign in Italy. Establishment of Cisalpine and Ligurian republics
1797 October   Treaty of Campo Formio with Austria. Austrian recognition of French annexation of Belgium and Rhineland. Austria annexes Venice
1798 July   Napoleon's victory in Egypt at Battle of Pyramids
August   Nelson destroys Napoleon's fleet at Battle of Aboukir Bay. Napoleon's army isolated in Egypt and Syria.
1799 War of Second Coalition (England, Austria, Russia, Turkey, Naples, Portugal). French driven out of Italy by Marshal Suvorov
December   Napoleon seizes power in France
1800 June   Napoleon defeats Austria at Battle of Marengo in Italy
1801 February   Treaty of Lunéville. Austria reaffirms territorial cession made at Treaty of Campo Formio
1802 March   Treaty of Amiens. Peace with England
1803 May   War of the Third Coalition (Britain, Austria, Russia, Sweden, later Prussia). Preparation for invasion of England from Boulogne
1805 October   Napoleon defeats Austria at Ulm
October   Nelson destroys French and Spanish fleets at Battle of Trafalgar
December   Napoleon's crushing victory over Austria at Battle of Austerlitz
1806 October   Prussia defeated at Battles of Jena and Auerstedt. Napoleon occupies Berlin. Decree ordering continental blockade against England.
1807 February   Stalemate Battle of Eylau with Russia
June   Defeat of Russia at Friedland
July   Treaty of Tilsit between Napoleon and Russian Tsar Alexander. Creation of Grand Duchy of Warsaw and Kingdom of Westphalia
1808 March   French invasion of Spain
July   Spanish defeat French at Battle of Baylen. British expeditionary force to Portugal. British enter Spain. Napoleon places brother Joseph on Spanish throne
1809 April   Austria declares war on France
July   Napoleon defeats Austria at Battle of Wagram
October   Austria makes peace at Treaty of Vienna
1812 June   Napoleon's invasion of Russia with army of 450,000
August   Capture of Smolensk
October   Retreat from Moscow
1813 February   Defeat of Prussia at Battles of Lützen and Bautzen
October   Combined German armies defeat Napoleon at Leipzig (Battle of the Nations)
October   Duke of Wellington invades France from Spain
1814 March–April   Allied armies occupy Paris
April   Napoleon forced to abdicate; in exile on Elba. Opening of peace conference in Vienna
1815 March   Napoleon lands in France
June   Napoleon's reconstituted army defeated at Waterloo by English and German armies. Second abdication.
October   Napoleon in exile on St. Helena

**Reform in Italy,
1789–1799**

In Italy, however, the threat of the Revolution could not be ignored so easily, if only because the French armies had resumed their traditional exploitation of the political division of the peninsula by defeating the small states individually. In the 1790s Italy was in as bad a state of political disintegration and military impotence as it had been at the end of the fifteenth century. In the north, the two mercantile republics of Genoa and Venice were run by torpid oligarchies; Milan and Modena were governed directly by the Habsburg emperor of Austria. Tuscany was ruled with enlightened ducal despotism by another branch of the Habsburgs. The Papal States were stagnant because the papacy rightly equated modernization with an attack on the Church. The Kingdom of Naples was controlled by a repressive monarchy and an exclusive landowning aristocracy. Only the king of Piedmont-Sardinia was showing any inclination to modernize, as the price of survival for a state squeezed between the grindstones of France and Austria. The peasants, who composed the mass of the population, were discontented but politically apathetic, unwilling to take direct action against the city-dwelling aristocrats and gaining a greater share of the land only by hacking out pitiable farms on the inhospitable mountainsides. All reform movements—which in the 1790s meant all movements for the overthrow of the governing classes—for the establishment of efficient state government and for the union of the Italian states came from a small, active middle class within the cities. As in Paris, this reforming bourgeoisie was able to bring out onto the streets the mass of workers in the large cities of Milan, Venice, Genoa, Rome, Naples, and Palermo. But they could only take power with the aid of the French armies. For example, a revolt in Naples in 1792 was encouraged by a visit of a French naval squadron that fraternized with the reformers and helped the formation of two revolutionary societies; but the revolt was broken easily with the arrest and imprisonment of its leaders.

After Napoleon's victories in Italy in 1796, new encouragement for the reformers in Naples was given by the foundation of the Cisalpine Republic, which united around Milan portions of several of the small states of northern Italy. In the three years before the Austrians returned, Milan was the center of republican influence in Italy, a citadel of reform to which revolutionaries from all over the peninsula gravitated, a symbolic nucleus for unification, an example of successful constitutional and administrative modernization. It was disillusioning that Napoleon handed the ancient republic of Venice over to Austria in 1797, since, as Wordsworth remarked, Venice was the "eldest child of liberty"; but the example of Milan gave hope for the "Cisalpinizing" of the rest of the peninsula.

Following the murder of a French general in Rome, French troops occupied the city, ousted the pope, and set up a Roman republic. When King Ferdinand of Naples attempted to overthrow this republic, the French army moved south to Naples itself, defeated Ferdinand's army with ease, and set up the Parthenopean republic. As usual in times of stress, Ferdinand retired to Sicily, where the British fleet could defend him. The republic in Naples survived only six months, but its brief life highlighted all the problems of liberalism in southern Italy. The king, Ferdinand IV, a Spanish Bourbon, and his queen, Maria Carolina, an Austrian Habsburg, were blindly opposed to change. The Church was the only institution that could reach the peasantry or indeed even speak their dialect; and it was a peasant army led by a Catholic cardinal that overthrew the republic. The city poor, living in conditions of deprivation unequaled in western Europe, lacked any sympathy for the well-educated, affluent reformers from among the city's professional classes and absentee landlords. Nationalism was nonexistent among the mass of the population, since most did not even know what the Kingdom of Naples was, not to mention Italy, a country that had never existed. Nevertheless, this isolated reforming minority prepared the way for change in Italy since, during the short republican experience, they drove out the king, wrote a constitution, took over the administration, and began to analyze if not yet to solve the problems of Naples.

Napoleon and Germany

After Napoleon's seizure of power in 1799, France's influence both as a force encouraging liberal change and as an oppressive occupier stimulating nationalist reaction increased greatly in Germany. In the short months of peace in 1802–1803, Napoleon made far-reaching changes in Germany. Winning the cooperation of the larger German states by dangling before them the prospect of territorial accessions, Napoleon persuaded the Germans to abolish most of the ecclesiastical states, most of the free cities, and all of the principalities of the imperial knights. The political geography of Germany was greatly simplified, and thus the number of vested interests opposing its future unification was reduced; and by granting Prussia new territories, Napoleon further strengthened the state that would eventually drive Austria out of Germany.

When fighting again broke out in May 1803, Napoleon concentrated his forces for two years along the English Channel in preparation for an invasion of England. Faced by the danger of attack from the armies of Austria and the smaller German states in the autumn of 1805, however, he suddenly transferred his forces to Germany. He handed the Austrians a minor defeat at Ulm in October, and then, after occupying Vienna, annihilated their principal armies in his most brilliant military victory, at Austerlitz in December. Prussia was bought off with the cession of Hanover.

Napoleon, however, continued his remodeling of German geography with the formation in 1806 of the Confederation of the Rhine, a federal union of fifteen German states that included Bavaria, Baden, and Württemberg. This section of Germany, proud to have been part of the Roman Empire, conscious of its cultural affinity with France, and suspicious of the militaristic Prussian state, had a greater sense of affinity of its peoples than any other region; and, if unification through the absorption of the rest of Germany by one of its most powerful states were to be avoided, the expansion of this confederation into a federal union of all Germany was a fea-

Napoleon Receiving the Queen of Prussia at Tilsit, by F. L. N. Gosse
(Editorial Photocolor Archives/Alinari)

sible alternative. But the confederation offered a direct threat to the ambitions of Prussia and to the self-esteem of Austria; and in 1806 the Prussian king, Frederick William III, finally decided to join the Russians against Napoleon. Outnumbered, outgunned, and outmaneuvered, the Prussians suffered humiliating defeats in the twin battles of Jena and Auerstedt; and Napoleon entered Berlin in triumph. When Russia too was defeated the next year, the mercurial Tsar Alexander met with Napoleon on barges at Tilsit in the river Niemen. Together they settled the fate of Europe, while Frederick William rode up and down the opposite bank of the river in the rain. Napoleon finally decided not to wipe Prussia off the map. (The blandishments of the Prussian queen Louise apparently had not effected this as some suggested; "I am made of oil-cloth, and all this just slides off," Napoleon wrote to his wife Josephine.) It did, however, lose half its territory and population. Its Polish acquisitions were made part of a new duchy of Warsaw. Part of its German territories and the lands of other princes who had unwisely fought Napoleon were put together as the Kingdom of Westphalia as a throne for Napoleon's brother Jerome. Frederick William returned to a profoundly humiliated Berlin, to embark on a renovation of what remained of his state.

Revolution from Above in Prussia

The philosophy of the revolution carried out in Prussia mostly under the chief ministers Stein in 1807–1808 and Hardenberg in 1810–1822 was summarized by Hardenberg as early as 1794:

The French revolution . . . has brought the French people a new vigor, despite all their turmoil and bloodshed. . . . It is an illusion to think that we can resist the revolution effectively by clinging more closely to the old order, by proscribing the new principles without pity. . . . Thus our . . . guiding principle must be a revolution in the better sense, a revolution leading directly to the great goal, the elevation of humanity through the wisdom of those in authority and not through a violent impulsion from within or without. Democratic rules of conduct in a monarchical administration, such is the formula. [13]

Karl, Freiherr von und zum Stein
As chief minister in Prussia in 1807–1808, Stein began the reform of Prussia's economic and social system that enabled it to take a leading part in the final defeat of Napoleon. (Courtesy of the German Information Center)

In short, the revolution that was to be carried out in Prussia from above was to achieve the modernization of the Prussian state. The reforms were to make possible a greater sense of identification of the people with the state. "We must train the nation to manage its own affairs," wrote Stein, "and to grow out of this condition of childhood in which an ever-restless and officious government wishes to keep the people." [14] Modernizing measures were numerous and effective. One of Stein's first actions was the decree emancipating the serfs and granting them part of the land. Physiocratic doctrines were followed in the abolition of the medieval corporations. All professions were opened to all classes, so that nobles were able at last to engage in commerce and industry. A new and extremely effective bureaucracy was founded in 1808. In this way Stein and Hardenberg hoped to break the ossified structure of Prussian society, enabling the nobles and middle classes to make a greater contribution to the state without impairing its despotism. But it was the military reforms that were the most significant. The French revolutionary army was the model. Noble privileges were ended. The planning committee laid down as the new goal: "From now on a claim to officer rank shall in peacetime be warranted only by knowledge and education, in time of war by exceptional bravery and quickness of perception. From the whole nation, therefore, all individuals who possess these qualities can lay title to the highest positions of honor in the army." [15] The draft was adopted, after a struggle with the nobility; and service in the army became more humane. To evade the peace treaty's ban on maintenance of any army of more than forty thousand men, troops were called for a month's training at a time and kept in permanent reserve afterward.

To make effective in Prussia reforms that were so obviously borrowed from the French, it was felt necessary that the people should be inspired with a feeling of nationalism that could be directed against the French; and here writers, philosophers, poets, and journalists were to be used. A very large number of German intellectuals had welcomed the revolution in France, and many, like the philosopher Kant, remained admirers to the

Karl August, Freiherr von Hardenberg
As chancellor from 1810 to 1822, Hardenberg carried on the modernization of the Prussian state. (Courtesy of the German Information Center)

[13] Cited in Koppel Pinson, *Germany: Its History and Civilization* (New York: Macmillan, 1954), p. 33.
[14] Cited in Peter Paret, *Yorck and the Era of Prussian Reform, 1807–1815* (Princeton, N.J.: Princeton University Press, 1966), p. 118.
[15] Ibid., p. 133.

end. Even Beethoven, who had decided against his first impulse to dedicate the *Eroica* Symphony to Napoleon, returned to the ideals of the revolution at the end of his life, in the Ninth Symphony, by setting to music Schiller's ode to joy, by which he implied freedom.

> All men will be brothers
> In the shelter of thy wing.

But the violence and naked self-interest of the conquests disillusioned most of the revolution's former supporters. "Our golden dream is shattered," wrote Klopstock. In Berlin, in his famous *Addresses to the German People*, Fichte called for "the devouring flame of higher patriotism, which embraces the nation as the vesture of the eternal, for which the noble-minded man joyfully sacrifices himself, and the ignoble man, who only exists for the sake of the other, must likewise sacrifice himself."[16] In Berlin the deepest emotions of German Romanticism were focused on the national struggle—the hatred of reason and of France as the land of the Enlightenment, the worship of the national community and of the subordination of the individual in the nation, the admiration of the Middle Ages when German society was at its purest. By 1813, at least among the intellectuals and especially among the students and professors of the newly founded University of Berlin, there was a burning feeling of nationalism that had been harnessed in support of the reforms of the Prussian state. It was important because it had inspired the future leaders, but it had not created much of a response in the masses of the German people, in Prussia or outside. The final campaigns in 1813, in which the armies of the German states fell on Napoleon's forces after his defeat in Russia, were not a national war of liberation (*Befreiungskrieg*) by volunteer forces from an aroused German nation but rather successful attacks by well-trained professional armies on a weakened and demoralized Napoleonic army.

Napoleonic Rule in Italy

The spread of nationalist feeling in Italy, while even less widespread among the masses than in Germany, was equally important in its effects on the politically active minority in the cities. The most lasting effect of French rule was to persuade this minority that internal reform could never be carried out by their former rulers, whose stagnant administrations contrasted unfavorably with the reforms introduced under the French.

The kingdom of Italy, created by Napoleon in 1804 and composed of much of northern and central Italy, was the finest example of the benefits of modernization. Under the viceroy, Eugène de Beauharnais, it was given effective financing, the Code Napoléon, improved education, large-scale public works, expanded exports in agricultural goods, and public order. Moreover, by uniting for a number of years the inhabitants of several formerly independent states, it gave to administrators the experience of work-

[16]Pinson, *Modern Germany*, p. 35.

Pauline Bonaparte, by Antonio Canova (1757–1822)
Napoleon married his favorite sister, Pauline, to a leading Roman aristocrat of the Borghese family and then, after they separated, made her princess of the tiny Italian state of Guastalla. (Courtesy of the Italian Government Travel Office)

ing together in a unified administration. There was no revolt against Eugène in 1814, even after the fall of Napoleon; and many in his kingdom would have been pleased to recognize him as king in his own right. The major part of the Papal States were eventually annexed to France, and the pope deposed; and the improved administration won a certain grudging admiration from the Roman populace.

But it was in Naples that the French rulers attempted the most ambitious appeal to Italian nationalism. Ferdinand, who had mistakenly invited the Russians and British to use his ports, was forced to flee to Sicily once more by a French army that invaded in 1806. His territories in continental Italy became the Kingdom of Naples, which was given to Napoleon's elder brother Joseph, a kindly, though vague, administrator. Joseph's legacy to Naples from his brief rule, which ended in 1808 when Napoleon sent him to be king in Spain, was a new constitution, the Code, improved roads, and better bureaucrats. His successor as king was Marshal Joachim Murat, Napoleon's brother-in-law, a vainglorious, shortsighted, but glamorous leader of cavalry.

Murat, while carrying on with Joseph's policies, made a deliberate attempt to court the reformers and slowly came to consider himself the "liberator of Italy." His own Gascon origins, his rise through the army, and his lack of ease with aristocrats gave him a natural egalitarianism, while his unrestrained exuberance in manner and dress won him a popular following among the Neapolitan crowds. Perhaps suspicious of the ambitions of his wife, Caroline Bonaparte, as defeats crowded in, he became determined to separate his own fortunes from those of the emperor; he courted the tiny revolutionary groups of the Carbonari and turned increasingly to those Neapolitan councilors in his government who favored a united Italy. Reconciled to Napoleon when he was given command of the cavalry in the invasion of Russia, Murat decided to abandon him after the retreat from Moscow; and in 1813 he returned to Naples to bargain with the Austrians for a reward for deserting Napoleon. He told his army it would fight henceforth for Italian independence; and finally, after hanging on to his throne until Napoleon escaped from exile on Elba, he declared war on Austria in March 1815 for the ostensible purpose of liberating Italy from foreign rule. Only a few intellectuals supported him, however, and the peasantry ignored his pleas to volunteer. The Austrians quickly defeated his forces, and he finally fled to France, where his last hopes were dashed by Napoleon's defeat at Waterloo. In a final gesture he gathered two hundred men in Corsica and invaded Naples, where he was immediately captured and, on Ferdinand's orders, executed. Murat's own career was an ignominious farce and probably did disservice to the cause of Italian nationalism. It was only in retrospect, when the conservative regimes had been restored throughout the peninsula, that the memory of the changes brought by France became a stimulus to the desire for improved government and national unity.

THE ATLANTIC REVOLUTION REACHES
LATIN AMERICA

Napoleon's actions in Europe also provoked the final phase of the Atlantic Revolution, the spread of liberal and national revolution to the Spanish and Portuguese colonies in Central and South America. During the second half of the eighteenth century, the ideas of the philosophes had become well known among the wealthy Creoles (as Spaniards born in America were called), especially after the successful revolution in the British colonies in North America had led to the adoption of many of these views in the constitution of the United States. Merchants in Latin American cities like Caracas, Buenos Aires, and Rio de Janeiro, as well as planters in the countryside, felt aggrieved by the same mercantilist restrictions on their trade that the inhabitants of the thirteen British colonies had resented. Their anger at their subordination to Europe was increased by the precedence in government and society accorded in the colonies to the European-born "peninsulars."

Toussaint L'Ouverture (c. 1744–1803)
Toussaint led a slave revolt against the Creole planters in the French colony of Haiti in 1791. Although at first supported by the French republican government, he was captured by Napoleon's forces in 1802 and died in captivity in France. (The New York Public Library)

The brief attempt of the Spanish monarchy to improve colonial conditions in the late eighteenth century had seemed too little and too late. Nevertheless, the slave revolt in Haiti against the French, begun by Toussaint L'Ouverture in 1791 and finally successful in 1803, discouraged the thought of radical revolution in Latin America among the well-to-do, especially in the islands of the Caribbean and in Brazil, where a majority of the population were slaves. The revolution they envisaged would be a change of government, but to only a small degree a change of society. In 1807–1808 Napoleon gave them the opportunity for just such a revolution. Determined to punish the Portuguese monarchy for failing to collaborate in his boycott of trade with Britain, he crossed Spain with a large army in order to attack Lisbon. The Portuguese royal family fled to Rio de Janeiro in Brazil, and Napoleon himself took the Spanish royal family prisoner and installed his brother Joseph as king of Spain. These actions set off the movement in Latin America that culminated within twenty years in the end of Spanish and Portuguese rule on the American continent.

Although the Spanish American colonies at first proclaimed their loyalty to the deposed king Ferdinand VII, revolutionary sentiments soon triumphed. In 1810 the municipal council of Caracas placed the forces of

Venezuela under the command of Francisco de Miranda, a veteran revolutionary leader; and the next year a congress declared Venezuela independent. Miranda's forces were weakened by internal dissension, especially between himself and his former friend Simón Bolívar, who finally turned him over to the Spanish. Meanwhile, a disastrous earthquake persuaded many of Miranda's followers that his cause was unholy. Bolívar, however, returned from Colombia with a new army in 1813, captured Caracas, and proclaimed a new Venezuelan republic. It too was defeated within a few months, and Bolívar fled to Jamaica. Buenos Aires, which had become the center of a new revolt in Argentina, immediately became absorbed in quarrels with forces seeking independence for Paraguay and Uruguay and in a military expedition against Spanish-controlled Peru.

A third center of rebellion against Spain was formed in Mexico in 1810, when a Creole priest, Father Miguel Hidalgo, raised a mixed army of Indians and *mestizos* (people of mixed Indian and Spanish blood) against the Spanish authorities. After Hidalgo's capture and execution in 1811, another priest, José Morelos, again declared Mexico independent; but he too was captured and executed in 1815. Thus, when Ferdinand VII was restored to the Spanish throne following Napoleon's defeat in 1815, the independence movement in Spanish America seemed to have been abortive. Only in Brazil, where the arrival of the royal court had brought de facto independence from Portugal as well as a more enlightened economic administration, had local discontent been assuaged.

After 1815, however, the Spanish monarchy resumed its old policies of exploitation of its colonies and discrimination against their leaders, thus reviving the demands for independence. In 1817 Bolívar returned to Venezuela, where he built up a large army that defeated the Spanish in Colombia. In 1819 he became president of a Republic of Colombia that included Venezuela and to which Ecuador was added in 1822 to form the Republic of Gran Colombia.

In Argentina the revolt had been taken over by a brilliant military commander, José de San Martín, who led his army across the Andes to defeat the Spanish near Santiago in Chile in 1817 and captured Lima, Peru, in 1820. San Martín left for Europe in 1823, probably after disagreeing with Bolívar on the future of the new Latin American states; and Bolívar completed the defeat of the Spanish forces in South America in 1825. Meanwhile, Augustín de Iturbide, a professional soldier and adventurer, had declared himself emperor of an independent Mexico in 1822, only to be driven out by republican forces in 1823.

Brazil became independent more painlessly. The former regent, John, who had become king on his mother's death in 1816, was summoned back to Portugal following a liberal revolution there in 1820. His son Pedro, left behind as regent, simply proclaimed Brazil independent in September 1822 and was crowned emperor the following December, receiving widespread support since the Portuguese had reinstituted in 1821–1822 the old policy of economic exploitation.

THE NATIONALIST REVOLT AGAINST NAPOLEON

Whereas the nationalist revolt in Latin America, stimulated by Napoleon's invasion of the Iberian peninsula, was to drag on for two decades, the nationalist revolt against Napoleon in Europe led to the emperor's final defeat within eight years. The principal cause of Napoleon's defeat was his inability to persuade the British to give up their unrelenting struggle against him. The English had concluded during the peace of 1802–1803 that their interests and Napoleon's were irreconcilable. Napoleon had campaigned in Egypt, the British felt, with the intention of

The Shooting of the Third of May, 1808, by Francisco Goya
Goya watched from a distance the execution of the Spanish rebels by the French troops of Joseph Bonaparte and returned at night to sketch the bodies by moonlight. (The Prado, Madrid)

challenging their rule in India. He controlled the Low Countries, which the British considered the key to London's security. Furthermore, he was preparing the military force to extend his domination into central Europe and beyond.

Admiral Nelson put an end to the potential for an invasion of England by destroying the combined French and Spanish fleets off Cape Trafalgar in October 1805. In 1806, in retaliation, Napoleon attempted to force the British to sue for peace by ordering all the ports of Europe closed to trade with Britain. This so-called Continental System proved far more damaging to the European countries than to Britain and provoked the resistance to Napoleon within Europe that eventually led to his downfall.

Like most Europeans, including the French themselves, Italians eluded the Continental System by smuggling. It was, however, the refusal to coop-

→ *Europe in 1810* ←

erate of Portugal in 1807 and of Russia in 1810 that led Napoleon into the military adventures that brought about his final defeat. Both the Portuguese and the Spanish rose in revolt to oppose his invasion. Peasants, led by juntas of priests and nobles, proved useful allies of the regular armies and of the British troops under Arthur Wellesley, the future Duke of Wellington; and large French forces were held down in Spain for the next six years. From that point on Napoleon was unable to gain any respite. The Austrians declared war on him again in 1809, and he had to scratch together an army of three hundred thousand men, half of them disloyal foreign conscripts, to defeat the Austrians at Wagram. His success disturbed the Russians, who withdrew from the Continental System and massed troops on the Polish border. Napoleon then made his greatest error. With an army of four hundred fifty thousand men he invaded Russia in June 1812. He was able to bring his troops to battle only once in the march to Moscow across the "scorched earth" the Russian army left behind it, found Moscow in flames, and retreated in growing disorder back to Poland as the winter cold decimated his troops. Only thirty thousand of the Grand Army reached Poland by December. His weakness was the chance for which the Prussians and Austrians had been waiting, to throw their reorganized armies against the green troops he was desperately raising in France. After several indecisive battles, he was badly defeated at Leipzig in

Tomb of Napoleon, Church of the Invalides, Paris
The body of Napoleon was brought back to Paris from St. Helena for burial in 1840. The funeral monument was cut from red porphyry obtained from Russia because that stone was used in the burial of Roman emperors. (Peter Menzel)

1813; when he returned to France in 1814 to wage a last campaign, his marshals demanded that he abdicate. Napoleon sailed in April for the island of Elba, to which his enemies had ceded him sovereignty; and Louis XVIII, the younger brother of Louis XVI, was returned to Paris as king. (Louis XVI's son, Louis XVII, had died in a Parisian prison in 1795, thus leaving his uncle the legitimate claimant to the throne.) The victorious allies moved to Vienna where, under the chairmanship of the Austrian chancellor Prince von Metternich, they deliberated on what they should do with France and the Europe it had so drastically reorganized.

In March 1815, however, their deliberations were interrupted by Napoleon's escape from Elba. After landing in the south of France, Napoleon was welcomed back by his former troops. Louis XVIII fled to Belgium, and Napoleon, who had attempted to win greater popular support by issuing a new liberal constitution for the restored empire, set off with an army of little more than one hundred thousand men to meet the British and Prussian armies just south of Brussels. There, at the Battle of Waterloo (June 18, 1815), the emperor was decisively defeated and compelled once more to abdicate, thus ending the adventure known as the Hundred Days. The British exiled him to the remote island of Saint Helena in the South Atlantic Ocean where he dictated his memoirs and perhaps, it has recently been suggested, died of a slow-acting poison in 1821.

In Vienna the conference resumed; and it became clear that the statesmen had not merely to change boundaries and apportion indemnities but to find methods to deal with intangible enemies—the revolutionary forces of liberalism and nationalism. If the unity of the period 1776 to 1815 lay in the unleashing of those forces, the unity of the years 1815 to 1848 lay in the unsuccessful attempt to restrain them.

SUGGESTED READING

Samuel Bass Warner, Jr.'s *The Private City: Philadelphia in Three Periods of Its Growth* (1968) argues that "the Revolution left the city a tradition of democratic forms and democratic goals grafted upon a society of private economic aspirations." A more optimistic view of Philadelphia as "one of the outstanding urban communities of the century and a center of civilization and culture for the continent" is documented by Carl and Jessica Bridenbaugh, *Rebels and Gentlemen: Philadelphia in the Age of Franklin* (1962). The grievances of one group in the working class are shown by Charles S. Olton, *Artisans for Independence: Philadelphia Mechanics and the American Revolution* (1975) to be directly related to the Stamp Act. On the colony of Pennsylvania, see the reliable survey by Joseph E. Illick, *Colonial Pennsylvania: A History* (1976); and for a comparison study, read about the character of the nearby colony of New York in Michael Kammen, *Colonial New York: A History* (1975). Carl Bridenbaugh's two masterful studies on the colonial cities, *Cities in the Wilderness* (1955) and *Cities in Revolt* (1955) provide a rich survey of life in the five principal colonial cities. A short survey is given by Charles N. Glaab and A. Theodore Brown, *A History of Urban America*

(1967), pp. 1–24. Infighting among Philadelphia's political factions is described by William S. Hanna, *Benjamin Franklin and Pennsylvania Politics* (1964), with no little disparagement of Ben himself. For the revolutionary years in Philadelphia, see David Hawke, *In the Midst of a Revolution* (1961) and Robert L. Brunhouse, *The Counter-Revolution in Pennsylvania 1776–1790* (1942). Maxwell S. Burt, *Philadelphia: Holy Experiment* (1945) makes easy reading.

Among the many delightful travel books, try Andrew Burnaby's *Travels Through the Middle Settlements of North America* (1904) or Marquis de Chastellux, *Travels in North America* (1963). For a thoroughly jaundiced view, see Gottlieb Mittelberger, *Journey to Pennsylvania* (1960).

On the Revolution itself, see Robert R. Palmer, *The Age of the Democratic Revolution. A Political History of Europe and America, 1760–1800: The Challenge* (1969), which presents the thesis that the American and French revolutions were parts of one great movement. Palmer is supported by Jacques Godechot, *France and the Atlantic Revolution of the Eighteenth Century, 1770–1799* (1965). Bernard Bailyn, *The Ideological Origins of the American Revolution* (1967) argues that colonists saw the changes in British policy as "a deliberate assault launched surreptitiously by plotters against liberty both in England and in America." The approach of the Revolution can be followed in detail in two volumes in the New American Nation Series, Lawrence H. Gipson, *The Coming of the Revolution, 1763–1775* (1954) and John R. Alden, *The American Revolution, 1775–1783* (1962).

Richard M. Andrews analyzes the character of the different areas of revolutionary Paris in an excellent article, enhanced by statistics and maps, "Paris of the Great Revolution: 1789–1796," in Gene Brucker, ed., *Peoples and Communities in the Western World*, II, (1979), pp. 56–112. The most recent study published in French is Marcel Reinhard, *Nouvelle histoire de Paris: La Révolution, 1789–1799* (1971).

The atmosphere of revolutionary Paris can be felt dramatically in many eyewitness reports, such as Arthur Young's *Travels in France* (1969); Gouverneur Morris, *A Diary of the French Revolution by Gouverneur Morris, 1752–1816, Minister to France During the Terror* (1939); Oscar Browning, ed., *Despatches from Paris, 1784–1790* (1910), vol. 2; and especially in the fine collection by Georges Pernoud and Sabine Flaissier, *The French Revolution* (n.d.). All the main documents of the Revolution are to be found in John Hall Stewart, *A Documentary Survey of the French Revolution* (1951). Primary materials have been thoroughly exploited in John Fisher's entertaining *Six Summers in Paris, 1789–1794* (1966). For scholarly analyses of the Paris crowds and their motives, one should again consult George Rudé, *The Crowd in the French Revolution* (1959) and Albert Soboul, *The Parisian Sans-Culottes and the French Revolution, 1793–94* (1964).

Attempts to explain the French Revolution by use of an analytical framework into which events are made to fit, more or less, are innumerable; and new attempts at analysis have brought us fresh insights into the complexity of the Revolution. The historiography of the Revolution is summarized by Gordon Wright in *France in Modern Times: 1760 to the Present* (1960), pp. 107–114. One could also dip into Albert Mathiez, *La Révolution française* (1922–1927) for a left-wing rehabilitation of Robespierre or into Soboul's study of the *sans-culottes* for a contemporary Marxist view. A persuasive analysis of the Revolution as a series of class revolutions by aristocracy, bourgeoisie, city crowds, and peasants is given by

Georges Lefebvre in *The Coming of the French Revolution* (1947), and in *The French Revolution from its Origins to 1793* (1962). This analysis is equally convincingly dismissed by Alfred Cobban in *The Social Interpretation of the French Revolution* (1964) and in his brilliantly concise survey, *A History of Modern France*, vol. 1: *1717–1799* (1961). Crane Brinton, *The Anatomy of Revolution* (1952) seeks a common pathology in the English, American, French, and Russian revolutions. Palmer's *Twelve Who Ruled: The Year of the Terror in the French Revolution* (1970) looks at the terror from above and not like Soboul and Rudé, from below.

The Directory's return to bourgeois rule is covered in two sound studies, Georges Lefebvre's *The Directory* (1965) and Martyn Lyons, *France Under the Directory* (1975). The latter shows that the continuing conflicts after 1795 were largely the same as those before the Terror.

For the economic background to the coming of the Revolution, see Tom Kemp, *Economic Forces in French History: An Essay on The Development of the French Economy, 1760–1914* (1971) and the far more specialized study of J. F. Bosher, *French Finances, 1770–1795: From Business to Bureaucracy* (1970). The condition of the poor throughout France is documented in the massive study of Olwen Hufton, *The Poor of Eighteenth Century France, 1750–1789* (1974). Richard Cobb throws light upon the position of the Girondins in *Paris and Its Provinces, 1792–1802* (1975), which emphasizes the distrust between town and country. See also his *Police and the People: French Popular Protest 1789–1820* (1972). Georges Lefebvre describes the peasant uprisings in the summer of 1789 in *The Great Fear of 1789: Rural Panic in Revolutionary France* (1973).

The role of France's women in the Revolution has received new attention from Olwen Hufton, "Women in Revolution 1789–1796," *Past and Present* no. 53 (November 1971), pp. 90–108, and Jane Abray, "Feminism in the French Revolution", *American Historical Review*, 80 (April 1975), pp. 43–62. Gita May writes entertainingly of the life of the great Girondin and her behind-the-scenes influence in *Madame Roland and the Age of Revolution* (1970). Marat's murder by Charlotte Corday is blood-curdlingly described, and Corday's motives analyzed, in Stanley Loomis, *Paris in the Terror, June 1793–July 1794* (1964). For a brief introduction, see Ruth Graham, "Loaves and Liberty: Women in the French Revolution," in Bridenthal and Koonz, eds., *Becoming Visible*, pp. 236–254.

With Napoleon, it is best to begin with a quick survey of the innumerable conflicting opinions of his career, in Pieter Geyl's *Napoleon: For and Against* (1949). Georges Lefebvre's *Napoleon* (1969) is very thorough. J. M. Thompson, *Napoleon Bonaparte* (1952) draws heavily on his published correspondence. A new synthesis of the impact of Napoleon's conquests in Europe is made by F. H. M. Markham, *Napoleon and the Awakening of Europe* (1954) and by Geoffrey Bruun, *Europe and the French Imperium* (1963).

On the impact of the Revolution and Napoleon on Prussia, see George P. Gooch, *Germany and the French Revolution* (1920) for a general introduction and Herbert A. L. Fisher, *Studies in Napoleonic Statesmanship: Germany* (1903). The military reorganization in Berlin is explained in Peter Paret, *Yorck and the Era of Prussian Reform, 1807–1815* (1966), required reading for those who do not know the difference between line battalions and light battalions or why Prussian rifles used plaster bullets. For the bureaucrats, see Hans Rosenberg, *Bureaucracy, Aristocracy and Autocracy: The Prussian Experience, 1660–1815* (1958) and G. S. Ford, *Stein and the Era of Reform in Prussia, 1807–1815* (1922). For a different point of view, see Walter M. Simon, *The Failure of the Prussian Reform Movement, 1807–1819* (1955). The nationalist reaction is described by Eugene N. Anderson in *Nationalism and the Cultural Crisis in Prussia 1806–1815* (1939).

The changes in Italy in 1789–1815 are surveyed by Emiliana P. Noether, *Seeds of Italian Nationalism, 1700–1815* (1951) and A. Fugier, *Napoléon et l'Italie* (1947). Eugène de Beauharnais's Kingdom of Italy is described in Owen Connolly, *Napoleon's Satellite Kingdom* (1965), which has a superb bibliography. For Naples, see R. M. Johnston, *The Napoleonic Empire in Southern Italy and the Rise of the Secret Societies* (1904), 2 vols.; Harold Acton, *The Bourbons of Naples* (1956); Owen Connolly, *The Gentle Bonaparte: A Biography of Joseph, Napoleon's Elder Brother* (1968).

The intellectual origins of the Atlantic revolution in Latin America are examined in A. P. Whitaker, ed., *Latin America and the Enlightenment* (1961), the revolutions themselves by John Lynch, *The Spanish-American Revolutions, 1808–1826* (1973). Gerhard Masur, *Simon Bolivar* (1969) is an adequate biography of the great liberator. For the revolution in Mexico, see M. C. Meyer and W. L. Sherman, *The Course of Mexican History* (1979), which is perhaps the most reliable survey of that country's tortuous past.

Finally, to gain a visual impression of how Napoleon conceived himself as another Roman emperor, see the photographs and sketches of his public works in Paris, which included a column like Marcus Aurelius's, arches of triumph, and plans for a palace for his baby son that would outdo the Palatine, in Marie-Louise Biver, *Le Paris de Napoléon* (1963).

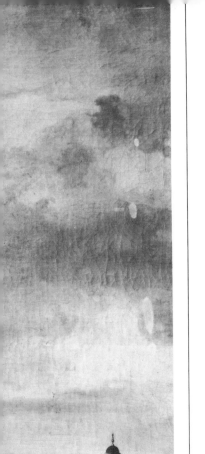

22

THE VIENNA OF METTERNICH

Vienna, on which I first set my eyes again on a fine bright Sunday, enchanted me—I admit it! I found Paris again, only more beautiful, more gay and German.—Richard Wagner, during the 1848 revolution. Cited in Vienna, *by Martin Hürlimann. English edition copyright 1970 by Thames and Hudson Ltd. Reprinted by permission of The Viking Press.*

During the first half of the nineteenth century, Vienna was the dominant European city in two distinct and possibly contradictory, senses. Until the revolutions of 1848, it molded the diplomacy of the great powers, inspiring a conservative policy of repression of the forces of liberalism and nationalism that had been earlier unleashed by the French Revolution. Yet at the same time it stimulated one of the greatest outpourings of musical genius that Europe has ever experienced.

From the chancery in the Ballhaus at the center of the Old City in Vienna, Prince Clemens von Metternich directed the diplomacy of Europe. In 1815, in his offices, the sovereigns and diplomats attending the Congress of Vienna attempted to restore the prerevolutionary society as it had existed before 1789, by a mutual agreement to hold down the

(Left Page) Vienna from the Upper Belvedere Palace (Detail), by Bernardo Bellotto (1720–1780) *(Kunsthistorisches Museum, Vienna)*; (Inset) Metternich *(Bildarchiv d. Ost. Nationalbibliothek)*

fermenting pressures of liberalism and nationalism. For Metternich, such a policy of repression was essential to Austria's self-interest, because the absolutist, multinational Austrian Empire of all the European states was least capable of withstanding the demand for political change voiced by liberal and nationalist leaders. This policy was largely successful until, in 1848, liberal and national movements joined hands in almost every state of Europe in a dramatic but ultimately unsuccessful attempt to overthrow the regimes that had been so carefully safeguarded by the fine diplomatic hand of Metternich.

But the other Vienna dominated Europe in a more lasting sense. In the great hall of the university, in the Theater an der Wien, or in the ballroom of the palace of Count Rasumowsky, the orchestras and choirs, the opera companies, and the quartets performed the works of Vienna's composers, most of them adopted citizens who found the city's atmosphere congenial to their talent. Mozart was buried in Vienna in a pauper's grave in 1791, the year of the first production of *The Magic Flute*. Franz Josef Haydn returned in 1790, to give Vienna *The Creation* and *The Seasons*. When Beethoven died in 1827, Schubert, Czerny, and the playwright Grillparzer were his torchbearers; Schubert was buried near Beethoven in a Viennese grave only a year later. But others settled during the coming years—Brahms and Bruckner, and on toward the end of the century Mahler, Hugo Wolf,

◆ *The Vienna of Metternich* ◆

Period Surveyed	Chancellorship of Prince Clemens von Metternich (1809–1848)
Population	232,000 (1800); 260,224 (1820); 356,869 (1840)
Area	Old City, 0.54 square miles; city and suburbs within the Line Wall, 8.64 square miles
Form of Government	Absolute monarchy: Emperors Francis I (1792–1835); Ferdinand I (1835–1848)
Political Leaders	Metternich; Count Kolowrat; Archduke Lewis
Economic Base	Imperial bureaucracy; production of luxury goods (especially textiles); banking; tax revenues from Austrian Empire
Intellectual Life	Drama (Grillparzer); Biedermeier painting (Amerling); music (Beethoven; Schubert; Czerny; Johann Strauss, Sr. and Jr.; Lanner)
Principal Buildings	St. Stephen's Cathedral; baroque palaces (especially Hofburg, Upper Belvedere, Schönbrunn)
Public Entertainment	Open-air concerts; opera and symphony concerts; wine parlors in Vienna Woods
Religion	Roman Catholic

Richard Strauss. Meanwhile the taverns of the Vienna Woods and the bandstands on the city wall where the regiments of the City Guard performed rang to the waltzes of the Johann Strausses, father and son, and their rival Joseph Lanner. In orchestral music, Vienna had no rivals; and in opera, it acknowledged only the rivalry of Italy.

Robert Schumann, who had just found Schubert's *Unfinished* Symphony among his unpublished manuscripts, commented in 1840:

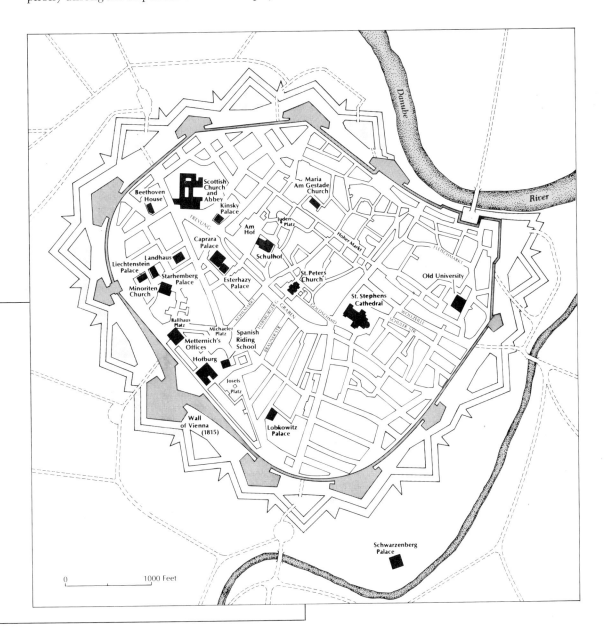

It is true: this Vienna, with its St. Stephen's tower, its beautiful women, its air of pageantry, girdled by the countless convolutions of the Danube and reaching out to the lush plain which rises gradually into the towering mountains beyond, this Vienna with all its memories of the great German masters, must be fruitful ground for the musician's imagination. . . . In a Schubert symphony, in the clear, rich, romantic vitality of it, I am reminded of Vienna more vividly today than ever and I realize again why this particular environment should have produced such works.[1]

How are we to explain the contradictions in the character of Viennese preeminence? Why should this city, at least during this particular half-century, have produced such superb music but almost no art or architecture of more than superficial charm, little science or philosophy, and only one writer of more than local interest? And why should Vienna's other distinction during this period be the leadership of conservative forces throughout the continent?

To find an answer to these questions we will examine first the nature of the Austrian Empire and Vienna's role in it; second, the character of the diplomacy that Metternich dictated from Vienna; and third, the social structure and cultural ideals that evolved from Vienna's distinctive position in the Austrian Empire and in the diplomacy of Europe.

THE BAROQUE LEGACY

Medieval Vienna

During Metternich's years as Austrian chancellor (1809–1848), the city of Vienna still showed strong evidence of its six-hundred-year history, although much of its character was later lost through the industrialization and rebuilding in the late nineteenth century. Vienna was beautifully located on the rich plain of the river Danube, at the foot of the Vienna woods, where little farming and wine-producing villages nestled in the folds of the last outcroppings of the Alps. The most striking feature in Metternich's time was the wall that surrounded the inner, medieval city, a brick rampart some fifty feet high that had been extended outward in the seventeenth century in a complicated pattern of spearheaded bastions for defense against artillery. Here Vienna had blocked the advance of the Turks into Europe, from 1529, during the siege by Suleiman the Magnificent, to 1683, when the Grand Vizier Kara Mustapha was compelled to withdraw his forces by a joint imperial-Polish army. A new line of fortifications, the Line Wall, built in 1704, encircled the outer suburbs; but it was only twelve feet high, intended to protect the newer Viennese settlements from Hungarian marauders who disliked their subjection to the Habsburgs, and used mainly for the collection of customs duties on all goods consumed by the Viennese. The inner wall had been abandoned as a defense and was used for Sunday walks, bandstands, and coffee shops.

[1]Cited in Martin Hürlimann, *Vienna* (London: Thames and Hudson, 1970), p. 74.

Viewed from above, the inner city still seemed to possess a maze of medieval streets, with the great Gothic tower of the cathedral of Saint Stephen providing the main point of orientation. The appearance was misleading, however. Vienna during the twelfth and thirteenth centuries had been controlled by its trading classes and merchant guilds, and their houses, shops, and churches had given it its cramped appearance. But by Metternich's day the ground plan and a very few churches were all that remained of medieval Vienna. From the fourteenth century on, the city had been taken over increasingly by the monarchy, the aristocracy, and the Church. At the same time, the urban bourgeoisie had been restricted to an ever smaller role in the city's economic life and architectural planning. The Habsburgs had decided that the city they had chosen as their capital in 1278 could not be permitted autonomy like that of the patriciates of South Germany; the Turkish occupation of Hungary blocked Vienna's east-west trade route along the Danube; and the religious wars of the sixteenth and seventeenth centuries damaged its commercial ties with Germany. Worst of all for the Viennese middle classes, who had mostly become Protestant, the Habsburg leadership of the Catholic Reformation in central Europe led to persecution and, for many, emigration.

Origins of Viennese Baroque

During the late sixteenth and the seventeenth centuries, Vienna was given the indelible mold of the Catholic Reformation and the baroque civilization that accompanied it. The Jesuits were called to Vienna in 1551 to

Bird's-Eye View of Vienna, 1769–1774, by Josef Daniel Huber

This extraordinarily accurate view, unrivaled before aerial photography, was the work of a professional artillery officer. (Bildarchiv d. Ost. Nationalbibliothek)

establish control of higher education and, to a large extent, of architectural style in church building. Vienna welcomed hundreds of Italian architects, painters, stucco-workers, and sculptors, whose domed churches and bulbous towers, built for new and old religious orders, were visible proof of the dominance of Catholic Reformation religion.

The transition from a purely Italian style to a native Viennese, and from the Catholic Reformation to the Enlightenment, was provided by Johann Bernard Fischer von Erlach, the first of the great Viennese baroque architects. Fischer, after studying for sixteen years with Bernini in Rome, settled in Vienna in 1678 and proceeded to place a more personal imprint on the city than any other architect except, perhaps, his rival, Lukas von Hildebrandt. Fischer and Hildebrandt were the architects most responsible for shaping the face of Metternich's Vienna, a city of aristocratic palaces— urban palaces with flamboyant facades on the narrow, dirty streets of the inner city, and country palaces in the green belt that lay within the Line Wall. The sudden flurry of palace building occurred in the fifty years following raising of the Turkish siege of 1683: the Lobkowitz Palace in 1685, the Liechtenstein in 1694, the winter palace of Prince Eugen of Savoy in

1695, the Schwarzenberg Palace in 1697, the Rasumowsky Palace in 1706, the Kinsky Palace in 1713 in the inner town, and a galaxy of summer palaces including the two Belvedere palaces of Prince Eugen and imperial Schönbrunn. Besides these luxurious palaces, whose interior decorations brought the arts of rococo to a theatrical climax unexcelled even in Paris, the lesser nobility and the wealthier bourgeois constructed less ambitious but perfectly harmonious private houses of five or six stories, with the same monumental facade and frequently a similar sweeping staircase, but adaptable to leasing to a number of families of different income levels. Thus the aristocratic style spread from the noble quarter throughout the inner city, giving a coherence that impressed visiting foreigners like Dr. Burney, who had come from England in the 1770s to study the state of Viennese music:

The streets of Vienna are rendered doubly dark and dirty by their narrowness and by the extreme height of the houses; but as these are chiefly of white stone [stucco] and in a uniform, elegant style of architecture, in which the Italian taste prevails, as well as in music, there is something grand and majestic in their appearance, which is very striking; and even many of those houses which have shops on the groundfloor, seem palaces above. Indeed, the whole town, and its suburbs, appear, at first glance, to be composed of palaces, rather than of common habitations. [2]

[2] Cited in Ilsa Barea, *Vienna: Legend and Reality* (London: Secker and Warburg, 1966), pp. 61–62.

Vienna from the Belvedere, by Jakob Alt
Terraced gardens link the Upper and Lower Belvedere palaces, which were built by Lukas von Hildebrandt as the summer residence of Prince Eugen of Savoy. To the left in the painting is the baroque Charles Church, while the Gothic spire of St. Stephen's Cathedral marks the heart of the old city of Vienna. (Bildarchiv d. Ost. Nationalbibliothek)

Class Structure of the Habsburg Empire

The multinational nobility in Vienna rested its wealth on ownership of vast landed estates. The Habsburgs themselves were originally archdukes of Austria; and from a nucleus of what is approximately modern Austria, they succeeded in adding, mostly by marriage but occasionally by war, a disparate series of regions bound together only by allegiance to the Habsburg ruler. Of the regions the dynasty still possessed at the end of the eighteenth century, it had acquired Bohemia in the fifteenth century, reconquered Hungary and Croatia from the Turks at the end of the seventeenth century, retained the Austrian Netherlands and Lombardy in 1713, and taken Polish Galicia in the partitions of 1772 and 1795. The nobility of Poland and Italy was a pre-Habsburg creation; but in all the other regions, the great families, like the Esterhazy in Hungary and the Kolowrat in Bohemia, owed much of their fortune to the land grants of the emperors. Moreover, the empire was based on a fairly simple agricultural system—at least since the reforms of Joseph II—a division of the land between a free-holding peasantry and the great aristocracy. The peasants who worked the nobles' estates were almost entirely under the nobles' control, in spite of Joseph's abolition of serfdom. In Hungary alone was there a compromise that permitted the native nobility control over local affairs; in the rest of the empire, the rule of the imperial bureaucracy was complete. Thus the great aristocrats (*Hochadel*) formed a tacit alliance with the emperor, who supported their rule over the peasantry and provided openings for their younger sons in the army, the Church, or even the bureaucracy. The aristocracy felt itself part of an international society that revolved around the emperor and found its natural habitat in the court of Vienna.

If the great aristocracy was linked by a membership in court society that transcended national origins, the bureaucratic class that developed in Vienna in the eighteenth century was united in its exclusively German origins. The building of the chancery by Lukas von Hildebrandt in 1719 and its extension later by Fischer von Erlach marked the beginning of the bureaucratization of the rule of the empire, and the establishment in Vienna of what soon became its most populous class. Vienna dominated the administration of the rest of the empire through the cities, also largely German in population; even in Prague and Budapest there were many more Germans than Czechs or Hungarians. The tie was of German language and culture which were willingly accepted by new recruits to the bureaucracy. For the Viennese middle class, the bureaucracy was the main road to social advancement into the ranks of the professional aristocracy (*Briefadel*), a second level of aristocracy considered below the Hochadel. A climb in social status could easily be charted by checking an individual's position in the system of ranks; but no one felt a career had been launched until his title began with the letters K. K., for *Kaiserlich-Königlich* ("Imperial-Royal")!

The rest of the city's population, who lived in the upper stories of middle-class houses, in tenements in the less fashionable quarters, or in more healthful village houses within or beyond the Line Wall, worked in

Therese, Countess Kinsky, by Elisabeth Vigée-Lebrun
After the Revolution, the French court painter Vigée-Lebrun fled from Paris to find new patrons among the nobility of France's enemies. (Norton Simon, Inc., Museum of Art, Pasadena)

small shops, craftsmen's houses, or an occasional mill to supply the needs of the court, the bureaucracy, the church, and the army. They were shoemakers, silk weavers, porcelain workers, builders, the variety of professions that supply the needs of any large city. Only remarkable was the fact that a city almost exclusively devoted to the supply of a court and aristocracy could support a population of almost three hundred thousand people. Yet it soon became clear that the whole city revolved around the Hofburg, the rambling palace of seventeen different buildings that stretched along the southwestern edge of the inner city. Here were combined the remains of a medieval fortress, a late Gothic chapel, a sixteenth-century mansion, and the great series of baroque buildings built by Fischer von Erlach and Hildebrandt. These superb buildings included the Spanish Riding School, which was often borrowed for gala state dinners; the imperial library, with the leatherbound volumes of Prince Eugen's private collection; the long row of state apartments on the Josefsplatz; and the imperial chancery on the Ballhausplatz. Except when the court moved to Schönbrunn for the summer, all ceremonies, entertainments, and governmental decision-making were carried on in this complex of buildings.

Metternich's Vienna was therefore different from the other large capital cities in Europe. It had, at least until the 1830s, only slight commercial and almost no industrial importance. It was almost exclusively a social and administrative capital. But the two classes that controlled its life, the multinational aristocracy and the German bureaucracy, were both in their own way alien to the majority of the inhabitants of the empire from which their economic support was drawn; and therefore two possibilities of revolutionary change existed. The one was social revolution by the peasantry against the great aristocratic landlords and against the emperor, whose power rested on the aristocrats. The other was nationalist revolution, which was most likely to be led by the economically depressed lower nobility or by an aroused peasantry against German-Austrian dominance. Both fears weighed on Metternich when he assumed the office of chancellor after Austria's disastrous defeat by Napoleon at Wagram in 1809.

The Library, Hofburg Palace, Vienna

The sumptuous library in walnut and stucco was built by Fischer von Erlach in 1722–1737 to house the great book collection of Prince Eugen of Savoy. (Bildarchiv d. Ost. Nationalbibliothek)

METTERNICH AND THE CONSERVATIVE RESTORATION

It is easy enough to explain the preeminence of Metternich among Europe's diplomats; the difficulty is to understand the weight accorded the Austrian Empire.

Metternich was the supreme exponent of the doctrine of conservatism in internal and foreign relations at a time when the sovereigns of Europe were grasping desperately for some means to inoculate their subjects, and the subjects of neighboring powers, against the dangerous notion spread by the French Revolution and Napoleon that long-established societies can be remodeled by their less privileged members. "Unmoved by the errors of our time—errors which always lead society to the abyss," Metternich wrote in his *Memoirs*, "we have had the happiness in a time full of danger to serve the cause of peace and the welfare of nations, which will never be advanced by political revolutions."[3] He was admirably equipped for this effort. His father was a wealthy Rhineland count who served the emperor in various diplomatic posts, including governing the Austrian Netherlands. His youthful experiences—study at the universities of Strasbourg and Mainz, stays with his father at Brussels where he moved among French émigré society, a long visit to England where he met the leading politicians—gave him a knowledge of several European languages and of many leading statesmen; and at the age of twenty-one, he was sent on a mission to Holland for the emperor. Only in 1794 did he see Vienna for the first time, when his parents arranged an advantageous marriage for him with the granddaughter of Chancellor Kaunitz. Then and later, Metternich was realistic about the city in which he was to spend most of his life:

> Lamentable illusions hang like a thick cloud over the poor city of Vienna. She believes that she holds the same position that Paris occupied in France; she thinks she can dictate to the Empire. It is a gross error. Vienna is merely the outer shell of a nut which constitutes the main body. She is only the leading town in the smallest province of the Empire and she only becomes the capital of it if the Emperor remains Emperor and lives there with the government of the Empire. For her to be the capital it is, therefore, necessary that there should be an Emperor and an Empire.[4]

Fortunately for Metternich, he found the emperor to be a man after his own heart. Francis II had reigned as Holy Roman emperor since 1792, but in 1804 he became Francis I of the Austrian Empire, giving up the title of Holy Roman emperor in 1806. To Metternich he appeared "a true father to his subjects . . . in everything loving and seeking only the truth, firm in his

Metternich's Character and Opinions

Metternich, by Klemens Wenzel Lothar
Brilliant, good-looking, elegant, and humorous, Metternich epitomized for many the continuance into the nineteenth century of the aristocratic ideals of the ancien régime. To the discontented millions seeking political and social change, however, the Metternich system of repression was the principal obstacle to attainment of their goals. (Bildarchiv d. Ost. Nationalbibliothek)

---

[3]Prince Clemens von Metternich, *Memoirs* (London: Bentley, 1888), I, 175.
[4]G. de Bertier de Sauvigny, *Metternich and His Times* (London: Danton, Longman, and Todd, 1962), p. 165.

principles and just in his opinions." To others, however, Francis was a born conservative, though perhaps not a reactionary, who amused himself by making chain mail and toffee, refused to make use of the bureaucracy left him by Joseph II, ignored recommendations for change—even from Metternich—and relied on red tape in place of decisiveness. Metternich's opponents felt that he had found a perfect master; for Metternich himself, according to the revolutionary Mazzini, was "immobility personified, the Chinese principle in its highest expression, the Status Quo incarnate." Francis gave the elegant, almost too handsome young man a rapid series of promotions: as ambassador to Saxony; then to Prussia; and in 1806–1809 at Napoleon's request, to Paris. The dangers to Austria that Metternich was to confront changed during the next half-century, but Metternich's conviction as he assumed his post in Paris did not: "Napoleon seemed to me the incarnation of the Revolution; while in the Austrian Power which I had to represent at his court, I saw the surest guardian of the principles which alone guaranteed the general peace and political equilibrium."[5]

The Congress of Vienna

This was Metternich's conviction when the victorious powers assembled in Vienna in the fall of 1814. Peace with France would take the shape of either revenge or an attempt to establish "the greatest political equilibrium between the Powers." To persuade the powers to accept his views, a propitious setting had to be arranged; Vienna, except for the intermission of Napoleon's Hundred Days, was to be a gigantic festival for the aristocracies of Europe. In the Hofburg, the emperor entertained the tsar of Russia, the kings of Prussia, Denmark, Bavaria, and Saxony, and a host of lesser nobles. Forty tables were laid for dinner each night. Fourteen hundred horses, with barouches or sleighs, were at their disposition. Colorful military pa-

[5]Metternich, *Memoirs*, I, 65.

Ceremonial Return to Vienna of the Emperor Francis II, June 16, 1814, by Johann Nepomuk Höchle (1790–1835)
(Bildarchiv d. Ost. Nationalbibliothek)

rades, equestrian displays in the riding school, fireworks, ice parties, balls in the Grand Hall of the Hofburg, weekly dances at Metternich's, lotteries, amateur theatricals, concerts conducted by Beethoven, and a new performance of *Fidelio* convinced the Viennese that their city was the most romantic in Europe. The pomp also disguised the fact that serious discussions of the Congress were being conducted by Metternich, British Foreign Secretary Castlereagh, Tsar Alexander I, the Prussian minister Hardenberg, and the persuasive French delegate Talleyrand, who successfully urged that the Congress would assure stability in Europe by making the restored Bourbon king Louis XVIII popular with his subjects. Saddling France with a punitive treaty would not endear to his subjects a monarch they knew had returned home in "the baggage train of the allies." (Wine lovers have asserted that Metternich served to the Congress the great Riesling wine, Schloss Johannisberg, from the family estate near Mainz, to counteract the influence of Talleyrand, who served his own Chateau Haut-Brion, one of the greatest of the red Bordeaux wines.)

To achieve equilibrium, a "balance of power," the great states agreed to roughly equal territorial annexations, so that no one of them would become a threat to the others. Their first decision was not to return indiscriminately to the situation of 1789. Metternich was convinced that Austria's primary concern was in Italy, where Napoleonic reforms had left a dangerous residue of both liberal and national resentments. Austria regained Lombardy, which it had lost in 1797, and annexed Venetia and the Illyrian provinces along the Dalmatian coast; and relatives of the emperor Francis were handed other Italian states. In Germany Metternich wanted the formation of a confederation under the presidency of Austria that would replace the Holy Roman Empire; but to win Prussia's agreement to this Germanic confederation, he had to accept the doubling of the size of Prussia through the acquisition of territory of its immediate neighbors and of a large part of the left bank of the Rhine. Russia took over an enlarged share of Poland, to which it was supposed to grant internal autonomy as a kingdom of Poland; and it annexed Finland. Britain returned most French colonial possessions, but held on to Malta in the Mediterranean and Heligoland off the North German coast and also a line of trading and supply stations on the route to India: Cape Colony on the tip of South Africa, Mauritius in the Indian Ocean, and Ceylon. The Allies decided to compel France to give up all its territorial annexations in Europe but not to dismember it as the Prussians were demanding.

The second principle underlying the political changes was to establish a number of buffer states around the French borders to prevent future French aggression. The former Austrian Netherlands (Belgium) was united to Holland under the rule of the House of Orange; the Prussians were given the watch on the Rhine; and the kingdom of Piedmont-Sardinia was enlarged by annexation of the former Republic of Genoa, part of Savoy, and Nice. These were the most important decisions made at the Congress of Vienna, and not one was intended to set the clock back. They were con-

"In Vino, Veritas"
The cartoon, printed on a playing card, shows Metternich as the alien Schloss Johannisberg wine (which he owned) being driven out during the 1848 revolution by a humbler Viennese bottle. (Bildarchiv d. Ost. Nationalbibliothek)

sidered necessary, in Castlereagh's words, "to bring the world back to peaceful habits." The third principle, "legitimacy," which implied the restoration to power of rulers whose right to their thrones had been demonstrated by long tenure and conservative philosophy, was invoked to justify the return of Louis XVIII to the throne of France, Ferdinand VII to Spain, and Ferdinand IV to the Kingdom of the Two Sicilies.

To ensure the permanence of these agreements, Britain, Austria, Prussia, and Russia signed a Quadruple Alliance, in which they agreed to take up arms if the French attempted new aggression or a Bonapartist restoration and to meet periodically to consider measures "for the repose and prosperity of peoples, and for the maintenance of peace in Europe." The aims of the Quadruple Alliance became blurred in the minds of liberals and perhaps also of conservative sovereigns, with those of the Holy Alliance, a mystical-sounding agreement that Tsar Alexander I forced the Austrian emperor and the Prussian king to join him in signing. Under the influence of Baroness Kruedener, a religious fanatic, the tsar had wanted a high-sounding declaration of repentance for past failings, and a return by the monarchs to "an order of things based on the exalted truths of the eternal religion of our Savior." After Metternich had skillfully intervened, he was given, amid the moralistic declarations, the very down-to-earth statement that "regarding themselves as compatriots [the three monarchs] will lend aid and assistance to each other on all occasions and in all places." When the periodic meetings of the great powers led in the following years to the repression of liberal movements, it was generally assumed that it was the principles of the Holy Alliance that were being invoked.

Signatures from the Congress of Vienna, March 13, 1815

French support for Napoleon upon his escape from Elba led the statesmen at the Congress of Vienna to abandon the lenient treatment of France to which they had agreed by the protocol of March 13, 1815. Among the signatories were Metternich for Austria, Talleyrand for France, and the Duke of Wellington for Britain. (Bildarchiv d. Ost. Nationalbibliothek)

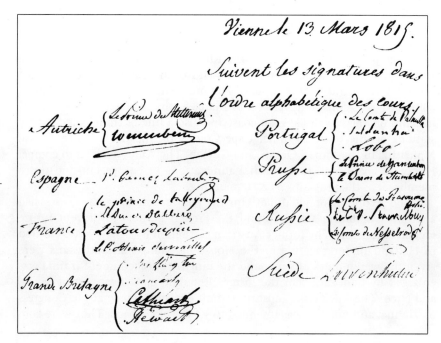

Thus, the basis of what came to be called, to Metternich's annoyance, the "Metternich system," as constructed at the Congress of Vienna, was his concept of the solidarity and interdependence of states. Revolutionary change within one state affected all other states. "No peace is possible with a revolutionary system, whether with a Robespierre who declares war on châteaux or a Napoleon who declares war on Powers," Metternich wrote. In the maintenance of a world free of revolutions, the Austrian Empire had to play a central part, both in the prevention of revolution beyond its borders and in the preservation of its own internal stability. Metternich was far more successful in the former aim. "Europe I may have governed," he remarked. "But never Austria."

THE DOCTOR OF REVOLUTION

Metternich's power base was the Austrian Empire, which in 1815 had a population of about thirty million, of which a quarter were German-speaking. Prussia's population by comparison was only eleven million, Russia's forty million, and France's twenty-eight million. In none of the continental countries had industrialization begun on a large scale; and thus the strength of all lay in agriculture and trade. Austria, after much needed military reforms under General Radetzky, was able to maintain an army that could easily defeat any of the smaller powers of Europe but none of the larger. Metternich was fully aware of the limitation on Austria's action this implied and of the further justification it supplied for the maintenance of a system of consultation among the major powers. He constantly opposed any further territorial annexations by Austria, especially adventures to profit from the weakening of the Turkish Empire in southeastern Europe. This "saturated" Austrian Empire, far from threatening the other great powers, was justified in its international position as a barrier against revolution. In this sense, it was a "European necessity."

Repression of Liberalism in Italy and Spain

Austria's primary international task was to hold down Italy, the country most infected by French revolutionary ideas and the continuing interference of France itself. In part, Austria's dependence on Italy was economic. Lombardy in the Po valley included the empire's richest agricultural land and was the earliest region to industrialize. Trieste was built up as Austria's main port, linked directly with Vienna. But the whole peninsula was ripe for revolution. The restored regimes seemed backward after the Napoleonic reforms, particularly the papal administration and the repressive Bourbon rule in Naples. Revolutionary secret societies abounded, especially the Carbonari before 1830 and Mazzini's Young Italy later. Young army officers, professional classes, and business leaders were in agreement on the need for modernization, including the adoption of more liberal constitutions. And the presence of Austrian occupation troops in Lombardy and Venetia, and of Austrian secret police everywhere, made the revolutionary movement anti-Austrian, and, by necessity, nationalist. It was revolution in Italy that eventually led the powers to use the Congress system to authorize armed intervention for the suppression of liberalism.

The members of the Quadruple Alliance met in 1818 at Aix-la-Chapelle (Aachen) to formalize the end of the military occupation in France and to expand their coalition into a Quintuple Alliance by admission of France. Two years later army officers and liberal business leaders carried out a successful coup in Spain, where they forced the king to proclaim a new constitution. Intervention by the Quintuple Alliance was, however, blocked by the British. But when revolutionaries in Naples followed the Spanish example, Metternich persuaded the Prussians and Russians at the Congress of Laibach in January 1821 that Austria should be authorized to crush the Neapolitan revolution before the contagion of revolution spread. This fear seemed justified when an uprising also broke out in Piedmont. The Austrian army, however, had little difficulty in subjugating the rebel forces in Naples and Piedmont. Encouraged by these successes, Austria, Russia, and Prussia decided to ignore any further British protests against intervention in Spain; and at a meeting in Verona in October 1822, they authorized the French to invade Spain. By the spring of 1823 a French army of one hundred thousand men had defeated the Spanish revolutionaries, and the Spanish king was able to rescind the liberal constitution he had granted three years earlier.

Suppression of German Discontent

In Germany, Metternich felt the threat of liberal agitation among army officers, students and professors, and middle-class merchants to be almost as dangerous as the turbulence in Italy. In particular, he feared that the German-speaking people in the Austrian Empire might be willing to abandon the empire to become part of a unified Germany. Germany, in Metternich's view, was as ripe for revolution as Italy—in particular a social revolution to overthrow the noble control of the land; a liberal revolution, beginning in the universities, to attain the political changes of France; and a nationalist revolution to unify the German people in one state. Napoleon had encouraged the nationalists by reducing the number of German states from about five hundred to thirty-nine; but Metternich attempted at the Congress of Vienna to prevent any further reduction in number by linking these thirty-nine states in a German Confederation. The Confederation was to establish common policies, mainly for defense, at meetings in Frankfurt of a Confederate Diet composed of diplomats representing the member governments. The Confederation was thus a disappointment to those nationalists who had hoped to use it to increase Germany's political unity by reduction of the power of the individual states.

Nationalist agitation continued, however, particularly in the universities, where in 1817 student organizations called *Burschenschaften* got out of hand; students burned antinationalist books and celebrated the murder by a student of a conservative dramatist. Metternich persuaded the Prussian king and the leading German princes to suppress the student associations. By the Carlsbad Decrees of 1819, the German Confederation banned the Burschenschaften, set up a rigid censorship of the press and the universities, and employed inspectors to find subversives. The next year, the few parliamentary assemblies in Germany were severely restricted in their competence. When several South German rulers were compelled in the uprisings of 1830 to grant constitutions, the Confederate Diet acted again, under Metternich's pressure, to reduce their powers; and thus until 1848, German liberal and national movements found themselves under such severe police controls that they had little opportunity to seek wider support.

Throughout central Europe, therefore, in that band of states comprising the German principalities, the Austrian Empire, and the states of Italy, which Metternich considered the key to European stability, the forces of nationalism and liberalism were suppressed. In this area Metternich had secured the establishment of a police regime symbolized by the great jails for political prisoners such as the Spielberg in Vienna, where the Italian revolutionary Silvio Pellico wrote one of the most influential indictments of Metternich's regime, *My Prisons*.

First Cracks in the Metternich System

Outside central Europe, Metternich wrestled with less success to maintain the political equilibrium. In Greece, France, and Belgium, he was forced to accept the overthrow of established governments by armed revolt inspired either by nationalism or liberalism; and the settlement of all three crises largely as a result of conferences in London under British sponsorship was an indication that during the 1830s and 1840s Metternich's role would be that of an observer rather than an instigator of European diplomatic events.

The Greeks had been under Turkish rule since the mid-fifteenth century. Although some of the better educated Greeks had made careers in the Turkish administration and in the upper ranks of the Greek Orthodox Church, and some of the richer merchants had profited from the economic opportunities offered within the Turkish Empire, most Greek peasants as well as the lower middle classes of the cities felt oppressed by the increasing exactions of the Turks from the early seventeenth century on. To these discontented groups, the French Revolution was an inspiring example; and they had formed secret societies to propagate the message of self-government and national autonomy. In 1821 they rose in revolt and declared themselves independent. For the first four years the struggle was fairly evenly balanced; but in 1825 the intervention of Egypt, a vassal-state of Turkey, appeared to promise victory for the Turks. Russia determined to intervene on behalf of the Orthodox Christians of Greece in spite of Metternich's entreaties to remain neutral; and Britain and France thereupon decided to intervene as well, partly because of sympathy for the Greeks and partly to prevent the new Greek state from becoming totally dependent on Russia. In 1827 the French and British destroyed the Turkish fleet; and in 1828–1829 the Russian army invaded the Balkans. Turkey was compelled to sue for peace; and in 1829 at the Treaty of Adrianople, it granted autonomy to Moldavia and Wallachia, the nucleus of the future state of Rumania, under Russian suzerainty. In 1830, in the London Protocol, Turkey recognized the independence of Greece.

Metternich, however, did not feel that Greek independence, even though won by a nationalist movement, infringed upon the system he had formed, since Turkey had never been regarded as part of the Concert of Europe. In France, however, the revolution of July 1830 was directed against the Bourbon family, which had been restored by armies that defeated Napoleon. King Louis XVIII (reigned 1814–1824) had been put on the throne as the only candidate on whom the allies could agree; but in spite of his unprepossessing appearance and unquestioned indolence, he was intelligent enough to make constitutional concessions by grant of a royal charter. Although the king retained executive power, France was permitted an elected Chamber of Deputies. The form of government, however, was intended to restrict power to the landed aristocracy, both the old nobility of the ancien régime and the new nobility created by Napoleon. The electorate, restricted to a hundred thousand voters, chose conservative majorities, revived the powers of the Catholic Church, and restricted civil liberties. Nevertheless, after a first phase of repression in 1814–1815 called the White Terror, Louis XVIII succeeded in keeping the extreme conservatives or Ultras out of power until two years before his death. With the accession of his brother Charles X (reigned 1824–1830), however, the Ultras were given a free hand in France. They proceeded to indemnify the old nobility for their losses during the Revolution, to reinforce the hold of the Church over education and to stiffen punishments for offenses against the Church, and to further restrict the suffrage. In 1830 Charles X provoked revolution by handing down several decrees that cut press freedom, disbanded the Chamber, and reduced the electorate to a mere twenty-five thousand voters. In July the Paris mob came out on the streets and set up barricades. Charles X fled to England. Although a few of the revolutionaries attempted to create a republic, the liberal monarchists, a coalition of rich landowners, industrial and financial capitalists, and members of such professional groups as lawyers and journalists, triumphed. In a rapid move of great skill, they placed on the throne their own nominee, Louis Philippe of the Orléans branch of the Bourbon family, who had himself fought with the revolutionary armies. It quickly became clear that the "middle-class monarchy" of Louis Philippe did not represent a serious challenge to Metternich's conservative principles. The new constitution broadened the electorate to two hundred thousand voters only, through a cleverly written law that gave the franchise to well-to-do business owners and less wealthy but politically reliable doctors, lawyers, and professors. Almost all members of the government were recruited from the bankers and industrialists of the upper bourgeoisie. State interference in the economic system was almost eliminated, except for the suppression of workers' uprisings and the planning of the railroad network. Few laws to reform working conditions were passed, and none were enforced. Elections were corruptly managed and all changes in the electoral system refused. Paris seemed to have become the plaything of the aristocrats of the new society—the bankers, railroad builders, textile manufacturers, and manipulators of government bonds.

In September 1830 the Belgians revolted against their union with the Dutch. Both French-speaking and Flemish-speaking Belgians objected to the predominance given in the new kingdom to its Dutch-speaking subjects. Economic policy was felt to discriminate against Belgium. The Catholics complained of Calvinist interference in the schools. The Belgians, who were almost twice as numerous as the Dutch, had the same number of representatives in the States General. Metternich, as well as the Prussian and Russian rulers, would gladly have aided the Dutch king in suppressing the revolt; but both the British and the French objected. Before any decision could be taken, the tsar found himself confronted with revolt in Poland, and Metternich with uprisings in several of the smaller Italian states. Russian troops quickly extinguished the uprising in Poland, and Austrian troops invaded Parma, Modena, and the Papal States to end the revolution there. Meanwhile, however, the French had intervened in Belgium on behalf of the revolutionaries; and in July 1831 the powers recognized Belgian independence under the kingship of Leopold of Saxe-Coburg-Gotha, thus accepting the first important breach of the decisions of the Congress of Vienna.

After the successful Belgian revolt, however, there were no further triumphs for liberalism or nationalism until 1848. Metternich could congratulate himself on the negative achievement that he had sought:

Let anyone look at the situations which Austria and all of Europe confronted between 1809 and 1848 and let him ask himself whether one man's insight could have transformed these crises into health. I claim to have recognized the situation, but also the impossibility of erecting a new structure in our Empire . . . and for this reason all my care was directed to conserving that which existed.[6]

UNREST IN THE AUSTRIAN EMPIRE

The Austrian Empire itself was extremely fragile. Two major changes were transforming the empire from within. The first and most important was the rise of nationalism; the second was the beginning of industrialism.

The Impact of Nationalism and Industrialism

About one-quarter of the empire's population was German. This segment was concentrated in the Alps, in the plains around Vienna, in cities throughout the empire, and on the fringes of Bohemia. Germans had a

[6]Cited in Henry A. Kissinger, *A World Restored* (New York: Grosset & Dunlap, 1964), p. 213.

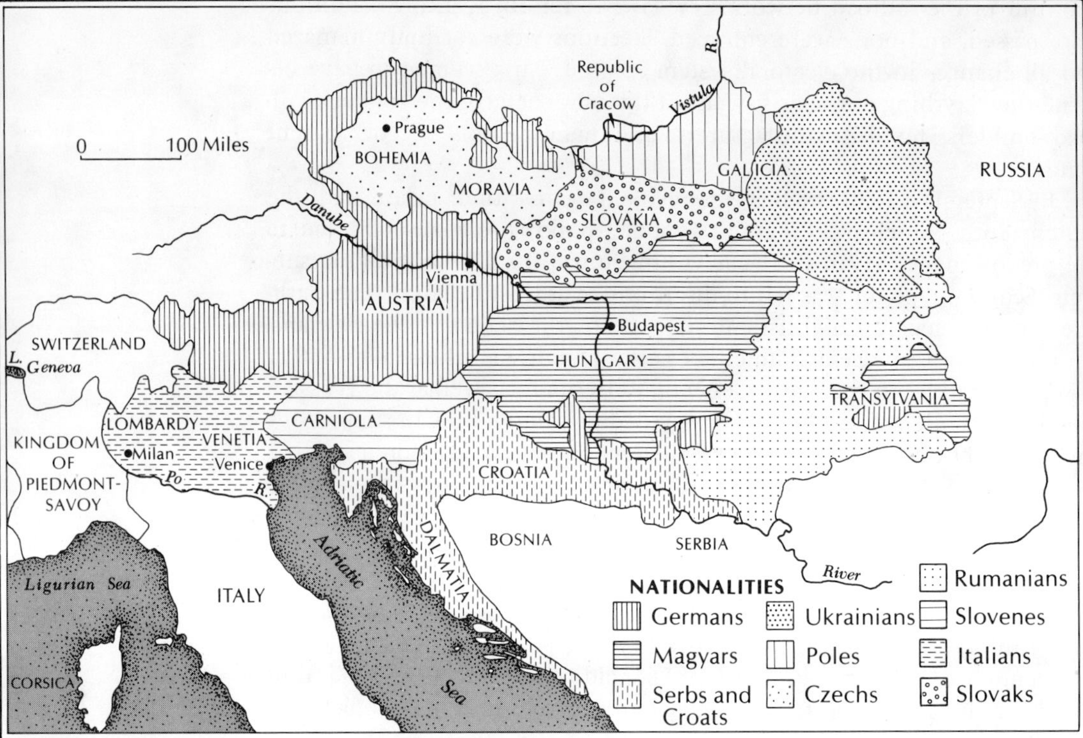
Republic
of
Cracow
Vistula
R.
0
100 Miles
Prague
BOHEMIA
MORAVIA
GALICIA
RUSSIA
SLOVAKIA
Danube
Vienna
AUSTRIA
Budapest
SWITZERLAND
L. Geneva
HUNGARY
TRANSYLVANIA
LOMBARDY
CARNIOLA
VENETIA
KINGDOM
OF
PIEDMONT-
SAVOY
Milan
Venice
Po
R.
CROATIA
BOSNIA
SERBIA
DALMATIA
Adriatic
Sea
Ligurian Sea
ITALY
CORSICA
River
NATIONALITIES
Germans
Magyars
Serbs and Croats
Ukrainians
Poles
Czechs
Rumanians
Slovenes
Italians
Slovaks

Austrian Empire, 1815

stake in the preservation of the empire because of their dominance in the bureaucracy and commerce; but many were sympathetic to the idea of linking Austrian Germans with the rest of the German states at the expense of abandoning the non-German regions of the empire.

The Magyars of Hungary were made up of half a million aristocrats and almost eight million peasants; they retained a strong sense of national identity, encouraged by their national diet and by control of their own local administration. In the great noble Széchényi, Metternich found a Magyar diplomat with whom he could collaborate. Like Metternich, Széchényi wanted to encourage the economic development of Hungary within the unity of the Austrian Empire. His policy was to compel the landed aristocracy and growing middle class of the Hungarian cities to work together, and pay together, for the roads, bridges, and railroads that would modernize the country. Against him, however, Széchényi found the most vital and persuasive propagandist of the new nationalism, a political journalist of genius named Louis Kossuth. Kossuth set out to harness the national pride of middle-class Hungarians against German dominance in trade and the professions. Moreover, he succeeded in creating opposition to the Magyars among the Croats and among the Rumanians of Transylvania, whom the Magyars felt they themselves should be governing.

The Poles of Galicia, annexed only at the end of the eighteenth century, felt no sympathy for the Austrian Empire; and their nationalism was stimulated by the teaching of the intellectuals at the university in Cracow, the ancient Polish city on the northern border of the Austrian Empire that had been made an independent republic in 1815. The influence from Cracow was so disruptive that Metternich finally annexed the city in 1846. The Czechs remembered the independent kingdom of Bohemia whose great Hradčany palace still dominated the skyline of Prague, while in Lombardy and Venetia the doctrines of Mazzini's Young Italy were making great progress among the young people of the cities.

The Austrian government's answer to the nationalist movement was suppression; and this was quite successful until 1848 because the movement was concentrated among the intellectual classes, the students and professors, and the artists and writers, who thought of nationalism in terms of history of linguistics or literature—that is, for whom nationalism was a cultural phenomenon before it became a political movement. Metternich himself was contemptuous of professors as revolutionaries:

There are no clumsier conspirators than professors, individually or in groups. Conspiracy is only profitable when it is directed against things and not against dogmas. . . . When political dogmas are involved they must be supported by action, but action means the overthrow of every existing institution and the application of the principle 'out of my way and let me in!' Savants and professors are incapable of this; it is the lawyers who are best suited to it. [7]

But the spread of nationalist ideas in the period before 1848, in conjunction with the desire of liberals to overthrow absolutist regimes that had been restored after the French Revolution or had survived it, was extremely dangerous to the survival of an inefficient empire.

What provided the final recruits for revolution was the coming of industrialism in the 1830s and 1840s. Vienna's population had expanded by almost a hundred thousand in the period after 1815, the increase composed primarily of immigrants from the rural parts of the empire.

The railroad had reached the small towns outside the Line Wall, and led to the creation there of manufacturing plants for the construction industry as well as large breweries and textile mills. Indeed, the whole city felt the ferment of economic change with the development of many joint stock companies, the great expansion of the activity of the stock market, and the formation of chambers of commerce and societies for agricultural and industrial development. Similar growth was taking place in Budapest and the western plains of Hungary, Prague, the mining regions of Bohemia, and the cities of Lombardy, where by 1848 industrialization had created both an urban proletariat and an industrial bourgeoisie.

Deep but generally undirected discontent was prevalent in many parts of the Austrian Empire by 1848—dissatisfaction with the distribution of

[7]Bertier de Sauvigny, *Metternich*, p. 60.

the land, factory conditions, absolutism and the police-state regime, and the lack of national independence. The very variety of the forms of discontent was, however, regarded by the Austrian government as a source of its own strength. When the Polish gentry and intellectuals revolted on nationalist grounds in 1846, the peasants used the opportunity to turn on their own landlords, in some instances with the encouragement of local Austrian officials. Rioters in the Prague factories in 1844 attacked not the Austrian administration but the machines they regarded as responsible for their misery. And even in 1848, when revolutions broke out over the whole continent, the revolutionaries within the empire failed because of their division. Metternich himself could probably have survived even that great series of upheavals if he had not been attacked at the point where he was most vulnerable, by the imperial family itself.

Administrative Immobility in Vienna

Metternich was aware that Austria required a more effective form of government to deal with these dangerous new forces, and he made several efforts to improve Austrian internal administration. Each time, he was blocked: first by the procrastination of Francis I and then by the paralyzing committee government, instituted to cover the imbecility of his successor Ferdinand I (reigned 1835–1848). Metternich admired the Napoleonic system of government; and lacking an emperor of Napoleon's genius, he proposed that a council of state, or *Reichsrat*, should exercise centralized control of the empire from Vienna. To vitalize such a body, he wanted it broadly representative of the bureaucracy, the aristocracy, and even the provincial assemblies. Moreover, Metternich recognized that the national problem within the empire could not be solved by mere repression. He wanted to compromise, by giving the local assemblies in the empire more power, at least to advise the emperor. At one point, Metternich even proposed that the Austrian Empire be governed through a chancery divided into six national groups—Austria, Italy, Bohemia-Moravia-Galicia, Illyria, Hungary, and Transylvania. But none of his schemes progressed very far. Metternich himself described what happened to the proposal for a council of state that he had first made to Francis I in 1811. The emperor put a new version of the plan in his drawer in 1817; ten years later, after a serious illness, Francis told Metternich he had felt guilty of a serious crime toward his chancellor and would take up the reform program when he was convalescent. Seven years later, on December 31, 1834, in Metternich's words,

I went to see the Emperor to present my good wishes for the New Year. "Again you see in me a repentent sinner," the Emperor said, interrupting me. "Your work still has not left my drawer. I give you my word of honor that the year 1835 will not pass without this institution being created." Two months later, the Emperor was dead. [8]

Ferdinand I had epilepsy and rickets and was mentally unstable. Government was placed in the hands of a committee consisting of his younger

"Ferdinand I as the Foundling of the Aristocracy"
This political cartoon shows the imbecilic emperor as an abandoned baby fallen into the hands of the aristocracy. (Bildarchiv d. Ost. Nationalbibliothek)

[8]Ibid., p. 143.

brother Lewis, Metternich's bitter rival Kolowrat, and Metternich himself. Paralysis of action was inevitable, and the already stagnant bureaucracy excelled in the slow amassing of memoranda on which the committee remained deadlocked. Everyone in Vienna became aware of a sense of waiting for an inevitable breakdown, a feeling described after the revolution began in March 1848 as the *Vor-März*, the pre-March years.

VIENNA IN THE BIEDERMEIER ERA

To most Viennese the Metternich system provided the kind of tranquility they seemed to want. The years from the Congress of Vienna to the revolution of 1848 were the Biedermeier era, a time of cozy and somewhat cloying sentimentality, middle-class comfort, family virtues, and kindly self-satisfaction. (The name *Biedermeier* was first applied in a satire by a German writer who put into the mouth of a naive bourgeois schoolteacher called Gottlieb Biedermeier a number of comic poems expressing simple-minded satisfaction in everyday pleasures. The word soon came to be used to describe the forms of taste of the period in all the German-speaking countries.) To one would-be revolutionary, the Viennese were irresponsibly escapist.

The people of Vienna seem to any serious observer to be revelling in an everlasting state of intoxication. Eat, drink, and be merry are the three cardinal virtues and pleasures of the Viennese. It is always Sunday, always Carnival time for them. There is music everywhere. The innumerable inns are always full of roisterers day and night. Everywhere there are droves of fops and fashionable dolls. Everywhere, in daily life, in art, and in literature, there prevails that delicate and witty jesting. For the Viennese the only point of anything, of the most important event in the world, is that they can make a joke about it. [9]

The attitude was a natural reaction to the strain of the years of war with Napoleon, during which Vienna had twice been occupied by French troops. But the self-indulgence took a form totally different from that of London in the 1660s or Paris after the Terror, for example. The Viennese withdrew into the family circle. Their pleasures became those of the family: in the evening daughters played the piano (Vienna being the principal center in Europe for the manufacture of that instrument) or a group of friends sang from newly printed songsheets. Many of Schubert's songs were written for groups like these. The weekly outing was a trip to the Prater, a parkland to the east of the city sprinkled with cafes and dance halls, where the aristocrats rode in formal procession in their coaches. Furniture too took on the comfortable, upholstered character of the period, curved and even protuberant, decorated with black lacquer and peasant designs. Greet-

[9]Cited in Edward Crankshaw, *The Fall of the House of Habsburg* (New York: Viking, 1963), p. 23.

Biedermeier Greeting Card

The refrain reads: "May your life be spent in flowering meadows, made happy by the blessings of sweet nature." (Bildarchiv d. Ost. Nationalbibliothek)

A Child's Portrait, by Friedrich von Amerling (1803–1887)

The sweet innocence of childhood was a favorite theme of Biedermeier artists. (Bildarchiv d. Ost Nationalbibliothek)

ing cards with simple rhymes called down the blessings of art and nature on their recipients. Fashionable paintings showed inordinately delightful children or exquisitely charming lovers, or they idealized nature, as in the coveted works of Friedrich von Amerling and Friedrich Gauermann. The theater followed the same pattern. Farces and fairy tales, simple stories of peasants making good and being laughed at for their pretensions, and especially plays idealizing the legendary Vienna were very popular. In 1822 a comedy with music called *Aline, or Vienna in Another Continent* fea-

The Three Precious Things: Wine, Woman, and Song, by Friedrich von Amerling
Amerling was the most popular painter in Biedermeier style. (Bildarchiv d. Ost. Nationalbibliothek)

tured a lilting song with the refrain: "Yes, only one Imperial City; Yes, only one Vienna." And the greatest escapism of all was the waltz. The dance probably originated among the peasants of southern Germany; but at the end of the eighteenth century it appeared on the stage—best of all in Mozart's *Don Giovanni*—and soon all the composers, including Haydn, Mozart, and Beethoven, were being called on to write dances for the balls in the Hofburg and at Schönbrunn, especially waltzes. "The people of Vienna were in my time dancing mad," wrote a friend of Mozart's. "For my own part I thought waltzing from ten at night until seven in the morning a continual whirligig; most tiresome to eye and ear—to say nothing of any worse consequences."[10] In the post-1815 period, however, Schubert, writing slow, regular waltzes for dances in the open-air taverns of the Vienna woods or for winter parties in the homes of his friends, created one of the finest of Biedermeier forms—warm, pure, rustic, and immediately intelligible. In the 1830s, the dance orchestras became far more elaborate with the enormous success of Josef Lanner and Johann Strauss the Elder. At first playing together, then splitting up to form two rival orchestras, both were fine showmen and musicians. Lanner remained gently Biedermeier, delicate, sweet, charming; but Strauss became the demon king of the waltz, frenzied, exotic, irresistible. Lanner and Strauss became the chief tourist attractions of Vienna until 1844, when Strauss's son and namesake formed his own orchestra and began to compose the most popular waltzes of all.

Absolutism à la Viennoise

Behind the scenes of Biedermeier revelry was the constant presence of the secret police. No absolutism has ever succeeded like the Viennese because no other has persuaded its citizens that spontaneous enjoyment is in the interests of the state. The repression of free thought and the arrest of native agitators and the exclusion of foreign were certainly successful. The dramatist Grillparzer was forced to keep much of his writing concealed. "The French have driven out their king," Grillparzer noted in his secret diary, "who tried . . . to break the constitution and turn them into a sort of—Austrians, which, civically and politically, seems to be the worst that can happen to anyone." To Metternich it was desirable that science be encouraged and the humanities kept down; but even science was unable to transcend the kinds of bonds that prevented Austria from producing any philosophy or political science except that of Metternich and his brilliant adviser, Gentz, or any theology or history of merit. The creative urge, and even the desire for enjoyment, were channeled by the state into directions that would release enthusiasms harmlessly. The police department had insisted that the Theater an der Wien stay open after the bread riots of 1805, on the grounds that the "people are accustomed to theatrical shows. . . . In times like these, when the character of individuals is affected by so many sufferings, the Police are more than ever obliged to cooperate in the diver-

[10]Mosco Carner, *The Waltz* (New York: Chanticleer Press, 1948), p. 18.

sion of the citizens by every moral means. The most dangerous hours of the day are the evening hours. They cannot be filled more innocently than in the theater." And what could be more harmless and moral than music? Metternich himself adored it.

Nothing affects me like music. I believe that after love, and above all with it, it is of all things in the world the one that makes me a better human being. Music excites and calms me at the same time. It has the same effect on me as something remembered, it takes me outside the narrow framework in which I live. My heart unfolds; it embraces at one and the same time the past, the present, and the future. Everything comes to life: trouble and enjoyment that is past, thoughts and pleasures to which I look forward with yearning. Music rouses me to gentle tears. It draws my sympathy on to myself, it does me good and it hurts me which in itself is good. [11]

Here at least is a partial explanation as to why the age of Metternich is also the age of Beethoven, and a partial answer to the question as to how the great rebel in music, the passionate lover of human freedom, could work with the master of the Spielberg.

THE MUSIC CAPITAL OF EUROPE

Many factors strengthened Vienna's interest in great music in addition to the desire of the secret police for a harmless diversion for the masses and the emotional needs of an overworked chancellor. The patronage of the Habsburg family for many generations was probably the most important of all. The founder of the dynasty, Rudolf of Habsburg, was a friend of the medieval troubadors, the minnesingers; and one of the greatest among them, Walter von der Vogelweide, declared, *"In Österreich lernt ich singen und sagen"* ("I learned to sing and declaim in Austria"). By the sixteenth century, there was a large court orchestra and choir; and from the seventeenth century almost every emperor was not only a proficient musician but a composer as well. Even Metternich's emperor, Francis I, played second violin in a weekly quartet; his aunt, Queen Marie Antoinette, had lessons from Gluck before her marriage to the dauphin of France. Both Gluck and Mozart were appointed to the position of Royal and Imperial Court Composer but received only a pittance. Until the end of the eighteenth century, the great aristocrats followed the musical example of the Habsburgs, maintaining their own orchestras and employing their own *Kapellmeister*, or resident musician. The most famous example was the Esterhazy family, at whose estate forty miles from Vienna Haydn spent thirty years in uninterrupted intellectual growth. All the great families, such as the Lobkowitz, the Starhemberg, and the Schwarzenberg, gave

Vienna as Music Patron

[11]Bertier de Sauvigny, *Metternich*, p. 8.

entertainments at which the symphonies and concertos of composers in their employment were performed, although many composers also found it necessary to perform as virtuosi as well. Beethoven's powers of improvisation, one of Vienna's favorite diversions, took him into the palace of Prince Lichnowsky, who, Beethoven laughed, "would like to enclose me in a glass ball so that neither the unworthy nor their breath would touch me." As aristocratic patronage declined in the early nineteenth century, the middle classes became increasingly important as patrons, through attendance at public concerts (like those of the Vienna Philharmonic Orchestra) and opera performances, and the purchase of sheet music, although Vienna never offered composers the financial possibilities of London or Paris. Yet it was significant that throughout Austrian society, from the country towns to the court, there existed the habit of not merely listening to but also performing music. In the 1770s the English musical writer Charles Burney commented over and over on the counterpoint singing of scholars in his inn, of glees sung by soldiers on guard, and especially of the music teachers in the provincial towns: "I went into the school, which was full of little children of both sexes, from six to ten or eleven years old, who were reading, writing, playing on violins, hautbois, bassoons, and other instruments."

Vienna's patronage thus encouraged the influx of musicians from all over Europe. "Vienna is so rich in composers and encloses within its walls such a number of musicians of superior merit," Burney went on, "that it is but just to allow it to be, among German cities, the imperial seat of music, as well as of power." These musicians learned from each other and thereby increased the overall quality of Viennese music. Again, the most outstanding example was the relationship of Haydn and Mozart, from which Haydn, twenty-four years the senior, profited most. Only after he had studied Mozart's work was Haydn able to achieve the purity of his later string quartets, a debt that Haydn willingly acknowledged; but Mozart repaid it with six great quartets that he dedicated to Haydn. Beethoven arrived in Vienna in 1792 to study with Haydn, but, impatient from the start, he soon transferred to lesser musicians. Beethoven taught Czerny, Schubert studied with the court composer Salieri, and so on. Vienna, however, acted as a fuser of musical styles in a far broader sense, owing to its geographical and cultural position as the meetingplace of the Germanic and Italian worlds.

Early Development of European Music

Until the Renaissance, music had been largely vocal, the few existing instruments being used to accompany the voice. Advances had been made through polyphony, the interweaving of several melodic lines, an art which reached one climax in the works of Palestrina in the sixteenth century and another, enriched by the use of harmony and colored by full exploitation of the possibilities of the organ and of the infant orchestra, in the vast output of Johann Sebastian Bach. Polyphony had ruled at the Habsburg court in the sixteenth century; but with the visit in 1618 of the first Italian opera company, Viennese music was dominated for a century and a half by the Italian pursuit of melody, both in the voice and the orchestra that accompanied it. Italian opera was the most baroque of all the arts, combining illusion, sensuality, grandeur, and display. Its high point in Vienna was the production in 1666 of Cesti's opera *The Gold Apple* at the marriage celebration of the emperor; the performance, which lasted five hours, took place in a specially built imperial opera house. The stories were usually classical myths, fairly static in performance but allowing to the human voice, in the arias, great liberty to develop flowing lines of melody and infinite decoration of trills and flourishes. It was the Viennese Gluck who brought this style of opera to perfection in the 1760s with *Orfeo* and *Alceste*. The orchestras had improved in parallel with the development of opera for both technical and stylistic reasons; and this too was essential preparation for Vienna's classical age. The most popular keyboard instrument used to provide continuo in the opera house was the harpsichord, in which the strings were plucked by quills. But the pianoforte, in which the strings were struck by hammers, was invented in 1709 and had been perfected by the late eighteenth century. Bach approved of it, but Haydn and Mozart wrote great concertos for it.

Most important, however, was the development of the orchestral stringed instruments. The violin and other instruments of the same family, the viola and the violoncello, had already been developed by the sixteenth century; but their manufacture was brought to perfection by such craftsmen as Stradivari and Guarnieri, and their possibilities for melody, harmony, and tonal color were more fully exploited when the first eighteenth-century virtuosi, like Tartini, took them up. The oboe and bassoon came into regular use at the end of the seventeenth century, the clarinet and the flute at the end of the eighteenth century. By the time of Haydn, therefore, the instruments and their combination in the form of the modern orchestra had been achieved.

The form in which the Viennese composers achieved their greatest writing for the orchestra was the symphony. In the seventeenth century, pieces of music written for instruments were called sonatas, which meant that they were played; pieces written for the voice were called cantatas because they were sung. By the eighteenth century, the word *sonata* was applied more exclusively to a composition written according to specific rules and usually designated a piece in three movements—normally fast (*allegro*), slow (*adagio*), faster (*presto*). Sometimes a minuet or a scherzo was added before the last movement. Moreover, in the first movement, two separate themes or melodies were presented, developed into more complicated forms, and finally recapitulated. This form gave to orchestral music a strongly intellectual framework, and it enabled music to achieve the respect of universally recognized laws of composition, a goal that was in accordance with the aims of the other intellectual fields, such as economics and psychology, in the eighteenth-century Enlightenment. Music of the late eighteenth century is known as classical because that word implies respect for rules, unified design, restraint, and avoidance of excessive emotionalism. As was suitable to an age of reason, listeners had to think as well as allow the sounds to wash over them. When composers like Mozart and Beethoven applied the sonata form to the symphony, played by a full orchestra, they were able, by use of key change, rhythm, tonal coloring, harmony, and the reintroduction of polyphony, to achieve enormous variety; and it was in the working out of the full range of the symphonic form that Vienna's composers established their supremacy in the world of music. These forms were used, moreover, with great effect in the string quartet, the violin and the piano concerto, and the keyboard sonata.

Mozart (1756–1791) and Haydn (1732–1809)

In the second half of the eighteenth century, Viennese music began to break away from Italian supremacy by drawing on elements from other parts of the Austrian Empire and from Germany. Mozart, for example, who had written his first opera, the unsuccessful *Idomeneo*, on the Italian pattern, turned his attention to the German *Singspiel*, a lighthearted combination of song, speaking, and rapid action. The result was *The Abduction from the Seraglio*. When he combined this convention with that of Italian comic opera, *opera buffa*, he created a series of characters of unforgettable individuality. In *Don Giovanni* above all, he created one of the greatest of all operas, perhaps the greatest. Every character is memorable: the timid rogue of a manservant, Leporello, with his list of the Don's amorous conquests ("But in Spain, a thousand and three"); the seduced Donna Elvira, who loves Giovanni in spite of his villainy; the flirtatious country girl, Zerlina, and her boob of a fiancé; the powerful figure of Giovanni himself, with such panache in his fights, his parties, and his love affairs that one feels the identification that is essential to great tragedy. And when the statue of the Commendatore whom Giovanni has murdered comes terrifyingly onto the stage to claim the Don for hell, Mozart drops all pretense of gaiety and, in the darkest of all music, presents the inevitability of damnation.

Commendatore: *You invited me to supper.*
Now you know what you must do in turn.
Give me your answer, give me your answer,
Will you come to supper with me?

Don Giovanni: *No one shall ever be able*
To accuse me of cowardice.
I have decided!

Commendatore: *Will you come, then?*

Don Giovanni: *My heart is strong within me,*
I have no fear of you.
I will come.

Commendatore: *Give me your hand to prove it.*

Don Giovanni: *There it is! Oh!*

Commendatore: *Why do you shudder?*

Don Giovanni: It is as cold as death.

Commendatore: Repent, repent your life of sin.
Your last moment is near.

Don Giovanni: No! No! I'll not repent.
Get away from me.

Commendatore: Repent! Repent!

Don Giovanni: No! No! No![12]

Finally, at the end of his life, Mozart combined the opera buffa with another Viennese institution, the fantastic fairy tales of the popular suburban theater; and in Papageno, the cheerful, down-to-earth birdcatcher of *The Magic Flute*, he transformed the humble traditions of the Viennese pantomime.

It was Haydn who first displayed the richness that could be achieved in the developing form of the symphony, moving in more than a hundred symphonies from charming studies of the morning and night to the depth of those he wrote in London toward the end of his life. Mozart was to carry on Haydn's use of the orchestra to present complex melodic relationships, as well as Haydn's mastery of counterpoint, which he brought to even greater levels of subtlety, as in the fugue to the *Jupiter* Symphony. But it was Ludwig van Beethoven (1770–1827) who made the symphony the supreme expression of human greatness and human loneliness.

Beethoven first came to Vienna at the age of seventeen, possibly to study under Mozart; but he returned to his post in the court chapel of Bonn on the death of his mother. He went again, aged twenty-two, to study under Haydn, and stayed there the rest of his life. By the time he was thirty, he had established himself as the undisputed successor of Haydn and Mozart, patronized by the wealthiest aristocrats; but he differed from Haydn and Mozart in being entirely his own master. With Beethoven, the rights of genius were respected for the first time as greater than those of birth. "Prince," Beethoven told his patron Lichnowsky, "what you are, you are by accident of birth; what I am, I am of myself. There are and there will be thousands of princes. There is only one Beethoven."

Beethoven had always been rough and self-assertive, even in the early period of his success as a pianist and composer; but in 1802, he gave expression, in the will he wrote in the Viennese suburban village of Heiligenstadt, to the deep despair and loneliness that were to give unparalleled intensity to his greatest works of the next decade. He was going deaf from sclerosis of the inner ear. "What a humiliation," he wrote, "when anyone standing near me could hear at a distance a flute that I could not hear, or anyone heard a shepherd singing and I could not distinguish a sound!" The deafness grew progressively worse, compelling him to give up public

The Supremacy of Beethoven

[12] Author's translation.

performances and to withdraw inside himself to compose music he would never hear. In his notebooks he began to elaborate the largest, most intellectually complex, and most emotionally intense of all the symphonies he would ever compose—first, a drama of changing keys, then the melodic themes and their development, then a coda of extraordinary length, to complete, in the first movement of the *Eroica* Symphony, a total change in the ambitions of instrumental music. In this, his third symphony, Beethoven was concerned with the nature of heroism seemingly in the lightning successes of Bonaparte but in reality in his own struggle with infirmity. Throughout the symphony there is a feeling of explosive energy, recalling his famous saying, "I will take fate by the throat." The second movement is a funeral march, but it pulses with an unforgettable rhythm that prepares one for the wild syncopation of the scherzo that follows. The last movement gains its power from development in the base by means of a fugue, a polyphonic method of playing themes against each other. In the *Eroica* it provided a sense of completeness, of integration of the move-

Manuscript of *Fidelio* by Beethoven

In his only opera, Fidelio, *Beethoven used the story of Leonora's strivings to free her imprisoned husband to explore two of his favorite themes—the need for freedom and the nature of heroism.   (Bildarchiv d. Ost. Nationalbibliothek)*

Ludwig van Beethoven, by August von Klöber
When he sat for this 1818 drawing, Beethoven had been totally deaf for a year; but he was working on some of his most complex and profound compositions, including his great Ninth, or Choral, Symphony. (By permission of the Beethoven-Haus, Bonn)

ments, that had never been heard before. Beethoven had overcome the inherent difficulty of presenting as a unity four movements that differed in structure, theme, and mood.

Beethoven had done for the sonata what the thirteenth-century architects had done for the cathedral—he had created a form in which the profoundest human emotions and thoughts could be expressed as an artistic unity. And he was fully aware that each symphony had to be created as a whole. "I alter a great deal, discard and try again until I am satisfied. And then inside my head I begin to work it out, broadening here and restricting there. . . . And since I am conscious of what I am trying to do, I never lose sight of the fundamental idea. It rises up higher and higher and grows before my eyes until I hear and see the image of it, moulded and complete, standing there before my mental vision."[13] Alternating between works of serenity and repose (the Fourth, Sixth, and Eighth symphonies) and works of storm and conflict (the Third, Fifth, and Seventh symphonies), Beethoven plunged into a decade of driving work, increasing the range of his orchestra with new instruments and putting new demands on old ones, widening the relationships between the keys he employed, broadening the emotional range he wished to express. By 1815, at the end of what is called his "middle period," Beethoven succumbed to his deafness, bad health, and loneliness, and he wrote little. Then, at the end of his life, he wrote his *Choral* Symphony, a work on a scale even larger than his *Eroica*, and his last quartets, difficult works in which he explored his own deep, spiritual sufferings.

[13]Cited in Ralph Hill, ed., *The Symphony* (Harmondsworth, England: Penguin, 1949), p. 94.

**Franz Schubert
(1797–1828)**

Franz Schubert, the last of this great generation of Viennese musicians, died in 1828, at the age of thirty-one, a year after Beethoven. Unlike Beethoven, Schubert was not fully appreciated for his genius until years later. The Viennese knew him as a writer of songs (he wrote 603); but only in the 1840s did they realize that they had failed to appreciate another master of the symphony, the quartet, and ballet music. The *Unfinished* Symphony was found by Robert Schumann when he started going through Schubert's unpublished papers in 1838; and the *Rosamunde* ballet music was discovered in an old cupboard by Sir Arthur Sullivan in 1868.

Schubert's symphonic music was a superb continuance of the classical tradition. However, it was the lyricism of his songs that pointed the way to the new form of music that was soon to conquer Vienna—Romanticism.

**The Romantic
Movement in Music**

Romanticism had begun in the late eighteenth century as a reaction against the excessive reliance on reason and the belief in the universal existence of natural law that characterized the thinkers of the Enlightenment. Its first artistic expression was in the poetry and novels written in Germany in the last twenty years before the French Revolution by Goethe, Schiller, and others, although Rousseau's *Emile* had provided an intellectual foundation. These writers extolled, often in an exaggerated form, the expression of human emotions and the search for realization of one's own individuality; and their message was carried into France by the writings of Madame de Staël, especially her influential book *On Germany*. In France, in the plays and poems of Victor Hugo and particularly in his flamboyant drama *Hernani* (1830), it took the form of worship of heroes of unrestrained self-righteousness and self-pity. "I am a moving force," Hernani

Franz Schubert (1797–1828)
Although many of Schubert's contemporary musicians recognized his brilliance, his work was largely unknown to the general public before his death. He lived in poverty, composing incessantly and taking pleasure primarily in the conviviality of musical evenings with his many friends. (Courtesy of the German Information Center)

Robert and Clara Schumann
Clara Wieck, one of the most brilliant pianists of the nineteenth century, married composer Robert Schumann in 1840. After his death in 1856, she not only cared for their eight children but also continued to give concerts throughout Europe and to teach at the Frankfurt Conservatory until a few years before her death in 1896.   (H. Roger-Viollet)

exclaims, "a blind and deaf agent of funereal mysteries, a soul of misery formed of darkness." Such heroes, historians have pointed out, were most likely to be found in the past, especially in periods like the Middle Ages.

In the early nineteenth century, Romanticism entered the world of music, introducing a new range of sound and subject; and it quickly conquered the Viennese public. The virtuoso performer and conductor filled the concert halls with audiences avid for sensation. The idol of the violin was Nicolò Paganini (1782–1840), who not only introduced new bowing and fingering techniques of enormous complexity and wrote pieces so fiendishly difficult that he was considered in league with the devil, but also used such flourishes as ending a piece on one string after cutting the other three with a pair of scissors. On the piano Franz Liszt was the great showman, creating frenzy by carefully staged demonstrations of his ability to create previously unheard sonorities from the new metal-frame pianos. As a public favorite he was followed by Clara Schumann, wife of composer Robert Schumann and a former child prodigy who developed into one of the continent's finest performers. Even the composer became a virtuoso: when German composer Carl Maria von Weber picked up the conductor's baton, he started a tradition that was to be followed by such other fine composers as Berlioz and Wagner.

The technical perfection of these performers allied itself with the goal of the composers—that of using music to create new forms of experience for the audience. Nationalism, for example, was enhanced by Liszt's use of

Hungarian motifs in his piano and orchestral pieces. The sensation of the supernatural was created in Weber's opera *Der Freischütz*. These composers and performers resided in Vienna only for short periods of time, however; and in the 1830s and 1840s it was Paris that attracted such musical giants as Berlioz, Chopin, Rossini, Cherubini, and Meyerbeer. For at the height of the Biedermeier period, Vienna had turned to Strauss and Lanner and to the gaiety of Rossini's *Barber of Seville* and Nicolai's *Merry Wives of Windsor*. Viennese creativity in music went into a temporary dormancy or at least set its sights lower.

"How different our feelings were at leaving Vienna from what they had been when we came," wrote Robert Schumann's wife Clara in 1846. "Then we thought we had found our future haven of refuge, and now all our desire for it has vanished." Two years later, Vienna had overthrown Metternich, and the composer Richard Wagner thought the city was reborn:

During the sixteen years that have passed since I last saw Vienna the whole city has been renewed: its half million inhabitants, all dressed in German colors, poured through the streets on Sunday as if in celebration—on the Saturday a wavering, incompetent Ministry had been forced out by the People's Committee! You should see the faces of these people: everything that disgusts you in the people of Dresden would appeal to you here. . . . And now this opulence! This life! The strange costumes they wear, an entirely new type of hat with feathers and tricolor German hat-bands. On almost every house a German flag. . . . And so it goes on. But everything is gay, calm, and youthful. [14]

THE REVOLUTIONS OF 1848

Causes of the Revolutions of 1848

In the spring of 1848, revolutions broke out in a kind of chain reaction in almost every country of Europe. Britain, which had broadened the suffrage in 1832 to meet the demands of the liberal middle class, and Russia, where opposition was scattered and repression well organized, remained largely immune. But in the rest of Europe almost fifty individual revolutions occurred; they were due to the final failure of Metternich's attempt to enforce in the rest of Europe a policy of procrastination in meeting widely supported demands for political and social reform. Forces of change common to most of Europe had combined with factors of discontent particular to individual regions to produce universal, though short-lived, revolution.

The demands of the revolutionary leaders immediately made clear their belief in the forces of liberalism and nationalism that the Metternich system had attempted to subdue. The supporters of liberalism were divided. The most influential group, the intellectual classes and the commercial and industrial middle class, wanted the abolition of such police controls as censorship and political imprisonment; the grant of a con-

[14]Cited in Hürlimann, *Vienna*, p. 93.

stitution; the right of freedom of speech and assembly; and the end of aristocratic privilege. When these demands were satisfied, as occurred in many countries during the first weeks of the revolution, this group withdrew from further revolutionary activity and directly opposed any further liberalization. A second group, representing the radical wing of liberalism, demanded universal suffrage rather than property-owning democracy, and social reforms for the benefit of the working class.

The nationalists were especially prominent in regions like Germany and Italy, where a nation was divided into several political units, or in the Austrian Empire, where several nations were incorporated in one political unit dominated by one nationality. Here the revolutionaries demanded the formation of nation-states, or at least of a new state dominated by their own particular nationality. Because both liberalism and nationalism were intellectual theories, almost ideologies, they were preached largely by the intellectual classes of the cities, specifically university teachers, lawyers, and journalists. In this sense, far more than the first French Revolution, the revolution of 1848 was a "revolution of the intellectuals."

More material causes of dissatisfaction impelled the working classes to risk their lives in street demonstrations and on the barricades and brought the peasantry to share in the revolution. Rapid population growth produced social dislocation in both countryside and city. Europe's population grew from 192 million in 1800 to 274 million in 1850. The populations of both France and Austria grew by a third. This increase was due to improved medical care, especially of infant children and older people; to an increased food supply through better agricultural methods and better transportation; and to freedom from civil and religious war and internal disorder. In the agrarian lands of eastern Europe, the pressure of population on limited resources of land produced a stronger resentment of remaining feudal privilege and labor services; throughout Europe it made efficient farming profitable and encouraged consolidation of estates by purchases and the move of former owners into the cities, which grew in size at a far higher rate than the total population. In the cities the former peasants found inadequate housing, social discrimination, and, except in England and Belgium, few jobs. In the Austrian Empire, where most of the newcomers to the cities were Slavs, they found racial discrimination as well. They were more vulnerable than ever to the periodic recessions within the capitalist system of production and especially to the harvest failures like those in potatoes and grain in 1846–1847. For the first time the workers expressed their grievances in a specific economic demand upon the state, the right to a job.

The year of revolution began with a January uprising in Palermo in Sicily against Ferdinand II, which was followed by similar revolts in most of the larger Italian cities. In France, where the revolution of 1830 (see pages 984–985) had disappointed the middle-class groups that had hoped for a genuine widening of political democracy and where working-class organizers had been pressing for social reform, revolution was more far-reaching.

The Wave of Revolution in Italy and France

After the government had banned a political banquet, which radical reformers had planned to hold in a working-class district of Paris, crowds began demonstrating on the evening of February 22. The next day the king dismissed his prime minister Guizot in the hope of satisfying the mobs, which had begun erecting barricades. After a number of demonstrators were killed in a clash with troops loyal to the monarchy, the crowds turned against the king himself. On February 24 he fled into exile, and France became a republic again. Its new cabinet, however, was divided between bourgeois leaders who were satisfied with a broadening of the suffrage and other political reforms, and Socialists who favored immediate economic reforms. From February 25–28, the provisional government bowed to the social reformers, guaranteeing a minimum wage for workers, providing work for the unemployed by setting up "national workshops," and establishing a special Luxembourg Commission to prepare labor legislation.

Revolution in the Austrian Empire

News of events in France acted as a catalyst to revolutionary activity in the Austrian Empire. On March 3 the popular Hungarian nationalist leader Kossuth gave a dramatic speech in the Hungarian Diet demanding Hungarian autonomy and constitutional reform in the Austrian Empire. On March 11 an assembly of Czechs met in Prague to make similar demands for constitutional reform and autonomy for Bohemia. On March 13 in the early afternoon, a crowd of students and professors from the University of Vienna gathered in the courtyard of the Landhaus, where the provincial diet of Lower Austria was meeting to discuss a reform petition they wished to present to the government. Together students and deputies made their way to the Ballhausplatz, the square outside Metternich's chancery building, where a few people began to shout, "Down with Metternich." When workers from the depressed suburbs filtered into the inner city, the crowd became large enough to frighten the Viennese military commander, and he ordered his troops to clear the square. They fired point-blank into the crowd, killing five and turning a good-tempered crowd into a furious mob. The students broke into the city armory and armed themselves; workers denied entry into the inner city at the closed gates returned to burn down their factories near the Line Wall; and several factions of the crowd presented ultimatums to the government, demanding Metternich's resignation by that evening. The state council met in indecision, but Metternich's enemies in the court banded against him, delighted to sacrifice him for their own supposed advantage. The chancellor reminded them that the empire was absolute and that he could be dismissed only by the emperor. The emperor's reply was absolute in its concessions: "I am the Emperor, and it is for me to decide; and I yield everything. Tell the people I consent to all their demands." Metternich at once resigned; and the next night he left Vienna with a false passport and a loan of a thousand ducats from the banker Rothschild. A few days later he explained his fall with the same mixture of perception of administrative reality and blindness to social

The Ouster of Metternich
This political cartoon of March 15, 1848, illustrates the delight of the Viennese masses in the ignominious flight of Metternich. (Bildarchiv d. Ost. Nationalbibliothek)

change that characterized his whole chancellorship: "You know what I have wanted without being able to achieve it. Above all I insisted upon establishing a *governing power* without which a state cannot be."

After Metternich's ouster, the emperor agreed to the constitutional changes demanded by the Hungarians; and in April he made the same concessions to the Czechs. Meanwhile, in the Austrian-held province of Lombardy in Italy, revolution had broken out in Milan between March 18 and 23, and this insurrection had been followed by an uprising against the Austrians in Venice. Austrian troops were compelled to withdraw from both cities. Seizing this opportunity to pose as the savior of Italian liberalism and national self-rule and to extend the borders of his own state, the king of Piedmont-Savoy, Charles Albert, declared war on Austria and invaded Lombardy.

Revolution in Germany

The king of Prussia attempted to forestall the revolutionaries in his kingdom by promising internal reforms and dismissing his conservative ministers. On March 18, however, huge crowds demonstrating outside the palace were fired on by the soldiers. Faced, as a result, with a city in complete insurrection, the king ordered the troops out of the capital and promised a liberal government and elections by universal suffrage. The news from Prussia spurred uprisings in many of the smaller German states. In May, a nationally elected parliament met in Frankfurt to draw up a constitution for a united German state.

Thus in the spring of 1848, it appeared that Metternich's Europe had disappeared with the archconservative. *"Eh bien, mon cher, tout est fini"* ("Well, old friend, everything is finished"), Metternich remarked after the revolution in Paris.

**Reaction Against
the Revolutions**

During the first phase of the revolutions, most of the liberal demands were satisfied, and a beginning was made in satisfying the nationalists. By May new constitutions had been written or were being prepared in France, Prussia and many German states, Austria, Hungary, Bohemia, and several Italian states. Hungary and Bohemia had been promised autonomy; an elected national parliament was meeting in Frankfurt to draw up a federal constitution for the whole of Germany; and the king of Piedmont-Sardinia had been supplied with troops from most other Italian states to fight a war of national liberation against Austria. During the following six months, more radical demands were made by extremists among liberal leaders. The wealthier among those who had formerly supported the revolutions, as well as the peasantry, turned against the extremists and supported the governments in their decision to crush the revolutions by use of the army. By the end of the year, a new period of reaction had begun in most European countries.

In Paris, the liberal government that took over in February had broken with its working-class supporters by ordering the suppression of the national workshops it had created to provide jobs for the unemployed; and in June, when the Paris crowds seized the working-class quarters, they used the regular army and mobs of peasants to bring Paris into submission. The ultimate victor in this political struggle was Napoleon's nephew, Louis Napoleon Bonaparte, who was elected president of the Second Republic in December because an overwhelming majority of the French peasants and bourgeoisie saw in him a "symbol of order."

In Berlin in November, the king ordered the return of the regular army to barracks in the city from which they had been withdrawn during the March riots, suspended the meetings of the Prussian Parliament, and in

**The Ceremonial Entry of the
Frankfurt Parliament into the
Paulskirche, 1848**
*As a free city, Frankfurt was able to host
the nationally elected parliament, whose
goals were opposed by most hereditary
German rulers.   (Courtesy of the German
Information Center)*

March 1849 contemptuously turned down the Frankfurt Parliament's request that he become "emperor of the Germans." The Frankfurt Parliament itself, an assembly of impractical scholars, lawyers, and merchants, had written a fine charter of fundamental rights and an advanced constitution, and it had finally brought itself to accept the probable exclusion of Austria from the unified German states; but it had no armed forces and no authority recognized by the larger German states. When the king of Prussia ordered the Prussian delegates home, several other states followed his example; and the few remaining members finally dispersed in June. With Prussia under control, the king dispatched his army to Dresden to restore the king of Saxony, and to Baden and the Rhenish Palatinate to suppress rebellions in western Germany. It was, however, with the aid of the Russians that Austria was to bring its own empire and the rest of Italy under control.

Revolution à la Viennoise

In Vienna, after the departure of Metternich, the revolution developed a party atmosphere. "It was the gayest revolution imaginable," wrote Grillparzer. "Favored by the most beautiful spring weather, the whole population filled the streets all day long."[15] When the emperor announced on March 15 that he was granting a constitution, the whole inner city was illuminated. But the new cabinet was full of reactionaries, the new constitution was issued without consultation with the diet, and the city's garrison had been doubled with troops who were advertising their arrival by pitching tents in the open land around the wall of the inner city. Even a more liberalized constitution issued in May stated: "Workmen paid by the day or by the week, domestic servants, and persons receiving public assistance are not eligible to vote for candidates standing for the Chamber of Deputies." A huge crowd of workers, students, and the National Guard marched on the Hofburg on May 15 to present a new petition, during which the army terrified the court by fraternizing with the marchers. The emperor was then removed to the imperial palace in Innsbruck by the leading courtiers, to get him away from the influence of the Viennese revolutionaries; but the government felt compelled to agree to universal suffrage and a one-chamber legislature for the whole empire. Meanwhile, the workers had been slightly appeased with a public works program of road construction and waste reclamation, a concession to their demand for the "right to work."

The success of the Viennese revolution was, however, dependent on concurrent success of the revolutions in the other parts of the empire; and there the Austrian forces were commanded by ruthless, efficient, conservative soldiers. General Windischgrätz pulled his troops out of Prague in June, leaving the city in the hands of students and workers. A week later he bombarded the city into submission. In Italy Field Marshal Radetzky defeated the king of Piedmont at the decisive Battle of Custozza on July 26;

[15]Cited in Barea, *Vienna*, p. 194.

Viennese Fashions in 1848
(Bildarchiv d. Ost. Nationalbibliothek)

then he broke the revolt in Lombardy by taking Milan. The Magyars of Hungary, who in the section of the empire they controlled had refused to grant any form of national autonomy to the Serbs and Croats, were faced by revolt, supported by the new governor of Croatia, Colonel Jellachich. In September Jellachich began to march on Budapest. To support him, the imperial government in Vienna ordered part of the Viennese garrison to Hungary, to help crush the government of Kossuth, which most of the Viennese revolutionaries felt to be their indispensable support. Demonstrations to stop the trains leaving with the troops for Hungary began on October 6; railroad lines were pulled up, and telegraph wires cut; and when the government turned loyal troops against the crowds, the mob succeeded in lynching the minister of war. Windischgrätz and Jellachich were then ordered to march against Vienna.

For three weeks, Vienna, besieged by the imperial armies, was defended only by bands of university students, impoverished workers and craftsmen, and a few idealistic bourgeois. At first the defenders tried to hold the Line Wall, converting the poorhouses along it into bastions. But Windischgrätz repeated his Prague tactics, bombarding the central city for several days. A Hungarian army sent to relieve the city was beaten back without difficulty. In the final assault on October 30 the imperial armies broke through the Line Wall in the morning; and in the afternoon, after severe fighting at the Burgtor near the imperial palace, the inner city was taken. Windischgrätz then turned his troops loose on the population, permitting looting and indiscriminate savagery. Although only twenty-five people were officially executed, it is probable that several thousand were killed. Martial law was imposed, thousands were jailed, and informers were encouraged to denounce the untrustworthy. The city thus suffered from the worst kind of civil war, a kind of family struggle—symbolized by the split in the Strauss family. Johann Strauss the Elder wrote his "Radetzky March" to celebrate the fall of Milan; Johann Strauss the Younger played his "Revolution March" and "Songs of the Barricades" on the ramparts of the inner city daily during the October siege.

The new imperial cabinet under Prince Schwarzenberg moved to restore efficiency to Austrian absolutism. The emperor Ferdinand was persuaded to abdicate in favor of his eighteen-year-old nephew, Francis Joseph, who was to govern for the next sixty-eight years. New law courts and government ministries were instituted. Internal customs barriers were ended, making the Austrian Empire into one of the world's largest economic units and thus encouraging capitalist industrial development. And most important of all, the remaining feudal rights of landlords, such as judicial powers over the peasants and the right to demand forced labor, were abolished, so that the peasant became free to own land and equally free to be forced by economic necessity to sell his land and move to the cities. A new, efficient absolutism based on an alliance with the upper middle class was thus the first internal result of the Viennese revolution. In dealing with the rest of the empire, no progress was made toward a solution of the nationality question. The constituent assembly's suggested constitution providing national and local autonomy was ignored. The demands of German nationalists were foiled by reintroduction of the German Confederation of 1815. And the remaining centers of revolt were soon defeated. The aid of one hundred forty thousand Russian troops was needed to bring about the defeat of the Hungarians; and in Italy, Radetzky besieged Venice by land and sea, driving it into defeat with starvation, cholera, and shelling. Rome, where a republic had been set up in 1849, led by Mazzini and defended by the charismatic guerilla hero Garibaldi, was captured by a French army dispatched by the new French president, Louis Napoleon Bonaparte.

Restoration of Absolutism

Thus liberalism and nationalism had failed after all to triumph over the Metternich system. Liberal leadership had been idealistic but impractical. Nationalism had proved to be a divisive force, since quarrels among different nationalities had been one decisive cause of the failure of the revolutions. Industrialism had been sufficiently far advanced to create an impoverished proletariat in certain large cities but insufficiently advanced for the working classes to be powerful enough to create a revolutionary movement of their own. Industrialism indeed had provided the railroad and the telegraph and the big guns by which the reactionary government forces could subdue the revolutions. Would-be organizers of liberal, nationalist, or social revolutions were thus forced into a period of reassessment of both aim and technique, which is one of the main themes of the next half-century. The restored court society of Vienna had little appeal to the statesman it had so gladly sacrificed at the beginning of the revolution. Metternich was perfectly at home in London, where he found a society surprisingly attuned to his own ideals, "a calm of which the continent has lost even the memory, and for which it ought in its own interest to find a taste again." But his wife was restless, and in 1851 he returned to Vienna, from which he continued to offer the governments of Europe his own suavely reasoned advice, which was sought by everyone from the British foreign secretary to the sultan of Turkey. Nothing had changed, he felt, with his fall from power: "My disappearance from the stage has not influenced things; it may be reduced to this: There is one man less but not one need or one necessity less."

SUGGESTED READING

Ilsa Barea, *Vienna: Legend and Reality* (1966) is a delightful reconstruction of the city's social history, combining literary sources with sound historical documentation; the Biedermeier period receives specially sympathetic treatment. Arthur May describes the physical appearance of Vienna in 1848 in the opening chapter of *Vienna in the Age of Franz Josef* (1966). A brief history with fine photographs is given by Martin Hürlimann, *Vienna* (1970). The intellectual background of eighteenth-century Vienna is painstakingly dissected in Robert A. Kann, *A Study in Austrian Intellectual History: From Late Baroque to Romanticism* (1960). Patricia Drake provides a good definition of Biedermeier literature in *Grillparzer and Biedermeier* (1953). For a delightful contemporary memoir, see Frances Trolloppe, *Vienna and the Austrians* (1838).

Among the general works on Austrian history, A. J. P. Taylor's *The Habsburg Monarchy, 1809–1918* (1948), though concentrating almost exclusively on political and diplomatic history, is still the most useful. Arthur May, *The Age of Metternich, 1814–1848* (1963) is brief but old-fashioned. There is no good economic history of the Austrian Empire in English, but some information can be gleaned from Shepard Clough and Charles W. Cole, *An Economic History of Europe* (1952). The agrarian situation is profoundly analyzed in Jerome Blum, *Noble Landowners and Agriculture in Austria* (1948).

On Metternich there is an abundance of material, too much of it polemical. The chancellor is his own best advocate in his *Memoirs*, edited by Prince Richard Metternich (1888) and in the superbly chosen quotations that form the major portion of G. de Bertier de Sauvigny, *Metternich and His Times* (1970). Helene du Coudray, *Metternich* (1936) and Constantin de Grünwald, *Metternich* (1953) are a bit romanticized but have useful primary materials. Alan Palmer, *Metternich* (1972) is weak on diplomacy but has much detail on the private life of the chancellor, while Henry A. Kissinger's *A World Restored* (1964) is an exciting and evocative analysis of the diplomacy through 1829. Enno E. Kraehe, *Metternich's German Policy*, vol. 1, *The Contest with Napoleon, 1799–1814* (1963) is a standard treatment of the early years. The Congress of Vienna is reconstructed by Harold Nicolson, *The Congress of Vienna, A Study in Allied Unity, 1812–1822* (1946) and Charles K. Webster, *The Congress of Vienna, 1814–1815* (1934). The atmosphere of the year can be sampled in John Fisher, *Eighteen Fifteen: An End and a Beginning* (1963), which describes a football match organized by Walter Scott and the breakthrough across the Blue Mountains of Australia as well as the Congress. The repressive side of the regime can be studied in Donald E. Emerson, *Metternich and the Political Police* (1968).

Musical Vienna can be enjoyed in Egon Gartenberg's *Vienna: Its Musical Heritage* (1968) and Hans Gal, *The Golden Age of Vienna* (1948). For scholarly analysis of the Viennese Classical age of music, see Alec Robertson and Denis Stevens, eds., *The Pelican History of Music*, vol. 3, *Classical and Romantic* (1968); W. H. Hadow, *The Oxford History of Music*, vol. 5, *The Viennese Period* (1904); and Paul Henry Lang, *Music in Western Civilization* (1941). In *The Classical Style: Hayden, Mozart, Beethoven* (1971), Charles Rosen argues that Beethoven was a true Classical composer and that the Romantic composers were reacting against him. The gulf between aristocrats and bourgeois as patrons of music is demonstrated in William Weber, *Music and the Middle Class: The Social Structure of Concert Life in London, Paris, and Vienna* (1976).

On individual composers, there are fine biographies by Alfred Einstein— *Gluck* (1945) and *Schubert* (1951). See also Einstein's *Music in the Romantic Era* (1947). For Haydn consult Karl Geiringer, *Haydn: A Creative Life in Music* (1946). For Beethoven's life but not his music, Alan Pryce-Jones has a short biography, *Beethoven* (1957); J. W. N. Sullivan, *Beethoven* (1949) is a fine analysis of the music. Frida Knight, *Beethoven and the Age of Revolution* (1973) is superficial but makes good use of contemporary quotations. Mosco Carner, *The Waltz* (1948) compares the dance kings.

But there is no substitute for listening to the music. Of Haydn's more than one hundred symphonies, a fine introduction is the *Clock* Symphony (no. 101), whose second movement simulates the ticking of a clock. The *Drum-Roll* Symphony (no. 103) gets its title from the kettledrum that opens the first movement. One of the most complex of Haydn's symphonies was his last, the *London* Symphony (no. 104). The full development of Mozart's genius as a symphonic composer came with the *Jupiter* Symphony (no. 41). His most admired opera is probably *Don Giovanni*, but *The Magic Flute* and *The Marriage of Figaro* are near-rivals. Two piano concertos written to display his own sparkling technique are the Concertos in B-flat (K. 450) and D (K. 451). Of Beethoven's nine symphonies, the most immediately charming is the *Pastoral* Symphony (no. 6). His explosive energy is most evident in the *Eroica* (no. 3). In the *Choral* Symphony (no. 9), his ambitions have become so great that the finale becomes a kind of oratorio for soloists and chorus. His love of freedom is best expressed in his one opera, *Fidelio*. His reconciliation with personal tragedy is most movingly expressed in the last quartets, for which Opus 132 in A Minor would be a fine introduction. Schubert's song cycle *Die Winterreise* ("The Winter's Journey") is considered by many critics to be his finest achievement for the voice.

The revolutions of 1848 throughout Europe are ably dissected in Priscilla Robertson, *The Revolutions of 1848* (1952); and in François Fejtö, ed., *The Reopening of an Era, 1848: A Historical Symposium* (1948), in which Robert Endres (pp. 253–280) deals with the revolution in Vienna. Jean Sigmann, *1848: The Romantic and Democratic Revolutions in Europe* (1973) is for those who adore detail, covering the revolution in every single country of Europe. For a detailed study of events in Vienna, see R. John Rath, *The Viennese Revolution of 1848* (1957). Arnold Whitridge covers the fall of Metternich in *Men in Crisis: The Revolution of 1848* (1949). Lewis B. Namier, *1848: The Revolution of the Intellectuals* (1946) is particularly good on Germany. For France, see G. Duveau, *1848: The Making of a Revolution* (1966); or, far better, read Gustave Flaubert, *A Sentimental Education* (many translations).

23

THE INDUSTRIAL REVOLUTION

The political history of the years from the American Revolution to the revolutions of 1848 was marked by the rise of liberalism and nationalism and the unsuccessful attempts to suppress them. The economic history of this period was shaped by the completion of the first phase of Europe's industrialization, the revolution in textiles, coal, and iron, which began in England in the late eighteenth century and spread to the continent in the three decades following the Congress of Vienna. Industrialization involved changes greater than Western society had ever undergone. Human and animal power were replaced by machinery of infinitely greater effectiveness. Largely unused resources, especially those in the subsoil, were exploited. The factory supplanted the craft worker and greatly reduced the importance of domestic production carried out by the family group within the home. The laboring population changed from a peasantry to an urban proletariat. Relative to industry, agriculture declined continually in importance as the source of economic wealth. As a result, the countryside in many areas was depopulated, and urban life became the norm rather than the exception. Furthermore, the impact of industrialization and of urbanization changed the roles of men, women, and children within the economic structure. Women, for example, found profitable though often debilitating work in the textile factories, or lower-paying employment as domestic servants. With improvements in food and medical care as the century progressed, populations grew at unprecedented rates.

New means of transportation and communications helped unify the world. An entrepreneurial middle class replaced the aristocracy as the pos-

Slum, Manchester, England *(Courtesy of the City of Manchester Cultural Services, Manchester, England)*

sessor of the major portion of society's wealth. Antagonism between employer and worker extended from union-owner bargaining to open class war. Finally, and perhaps most important of all, the development and application of new political ideologies conceived as a solution to the problems inherent in industrial society began to transform the nature of politics.

In this chapter we shall consider first the coming of the industrial revolution to Manchester, the city universally recognized in the early nineteenth century as the prototype of the new society. Then we shall study the spread of industrialization to the continent of Europe. Finally, we shall examine the political ideologies that were developed in response to the problems of industrialization.

MANCHESTER AND THE ORIGINS OF THE INDUSTRIAL REVOLUTION

From this foul drain the greatest stream of human industry flows out to fertilize the whole world," wrote Alexis de Tocqueville after visiting Manchester in 1835. "From this filthy sewer pure gold flows. Here humanity attains its most complete development and its most brutish, here civilization works its miracles and civilized man is turned almost into a savage."[1] The reason Manchester enjoyed and endured this mixed blessing was obvious to all observers: Lancashire, with Manchester as its industrial heart, had adopted the modern factory system. Everything Tocqueville observed was the result of that one essential change.

Manchester lay on the edge of the plain of southwestern Lancashire, where the prevailing westerly winds from the Atlantic hurled rain-heavy clouds against the steep slopes of the Pennine range. It was for long a pleasant market town bringing a taste of urban amenity to a backward agricultural region. A sixteenth-century visitor called it "the fairest, best buildid, quikkest and most populous toun of all Lancashire," but then it had little competition in attractiveness from the scrawny fishing village of Liverpool or the gloomy fortress of Lancaster. The changes in the rest of Britain made it possible for Manchester, from the 1770s on, to capitalize on its natural if hitherto unappreciated advantages—its humid climate, its access to water power, the availability of labor from its depressed countryside, its outlet to the sea through the great natural harbor of Liverpool, perhaps even the thrifty and uncompromising Protestantism of its inhabitants.

Prerequisites for Industrialization in Britain

By 1700 Britain alone possessed all the factors necessary for an "industrial revolution," a phrase first used in the 1820s to show that the industrial changes taking place were of the same magnitude as the political changes introduced by the French Revolution. Geographically, it was ideally suited

[1]Cited in E. J. Hobsbawm, *Industry and Empire: An Economic History of Britain Since 1750* (London: Weidenfeld and Nicolson, 1968), p. 27.

The Industrial Revolution in Britain, c.1840

to becoming a great industrial power. No point in Britain is more than seventy miles from the sea. Fine harbors exist on every coast. Distances were so small and natural barriers so negligible that where rivers were inadequate for inland transportation by water, canals could be constructed with relative ease and profit. Rich, accessible deposits of raw materials were awaiting exploitation: coal in Tyneside near Newcastle, in Lancashire near Manchester, in Staffordshire near Birmingham, and in South Wales; iron ore along the eastern and southern slopes of the Pennines; even the clay that was to be made into the Wedgwood pottery of Etruria. Easily harnessed water power was provided by the steep streams of the Pennine range, such as the Ribble, the Tees, and the Irwell.

Economically, it possessed the instruments necessary for making use of these natural advantages. In the two centuries since it had first chal-

Coal Miners at Work, 1871
Mining conditions improved very slightly during the nineteenth century. Coal was still dug by hand, but light was provided by a safety lamp, and children drove pit ponies instead of pulling the carts of coal themselves.
(The Graphic, January 28, 1871)

lenged the Spanish on the seas, Britain had built the largest merchant marine in the world, perhaps as many as six thousand ships employing a hundred thousand seamen; and these ships were engaged in a regular trade not only with the British colonial empire but with the Baltic, the Turkish Empire, the Spanish and Portuguese colonies, and West Africa. The East Indiamen were even sailing to China. With great commercial expertise, the merchant classes of England had thus accumulated capital, for which insufficient investment opportunities existed in commerce itself. So too had the enterprising noblemen who, through the "enclosure" of the open fields and common pasture, were converting English agriculture from predominantly subsistence farming to capitalistic agriculture geared to profit-making through sale on a nationwide market. This conversion incidentally had changed the social structure of English farming from a landowning peasantry to a threefold structure of landowning aristocracy, tenant farmer, and hired laborer. The excess capital in the hands of the mercantile and the agrarian nobility was mobilized through the development of a fine banking system—a central national bank in the Bank of England founded in 1694, and a large number of private banks, including such long-lived institutions as Barclay's and Martin's. The function of the banking system in the industrialization of Britain was to transfer money accumulated largely in the south and west to the north, especially from the 1820s, when large-scale investment in iron, coal, and railroads seemed inviting. Experience in the formation of joint-stock companies for such trading ventures as the Muscovy company and even for the Bank of England had provided financial knowledge and safeguards that could be applied in the formation of industrial companies, and indeed had accustomed many to the uses that could be made of "risk capital."

Not only did the agricultural improvements provide surplus capital for reinvestment; their most significant effect was to make possible greater productivity both per worker and per acre. With the improved crop rotation, fallow was no longer necessary, especially because of the growing use of clover and turnips, which not only restored fertility of the soil after wheat growing but also provided fodder for animals. The wasteful strips in the open fields were gone, and the laborer no longer lost hours in moving between scattered holdings. Improved breeding of animals, especially cattle and sheep, enormously increased the contribution of livestock to agricultural income. By the mid-eighteenth century, only one-third of Britain's population worked in agriculture, and it was only in the 1780s that Britain for the first time was unable to feed its population from home production. As a result of the agricultural changes and the continual rise in the total population caused principally by improved diet and medical care, large numbers of the rural workers lost their jobs; and since they no longer lived on family farms, they were unable to remain underemployed at home like their counterparts on the continent, but went on poor relief or sought employment in city industries. The agrarian changes thus provided both laborers for the factories and much of the food to feed them.

Finally, the political and social climate, an intangible but significant factor, was conducive to industrialization. As a result of the constitutional struggles of the seventeenth century, the government was stable and in the hands of the upper classes. The upper classes, however, respected and encouraged through legislation the talent for making money; and possession of wealth was a guarantee of upward social mobility, though not always at the pace its owner might have wished. The power of the state, to some extent its army but largely its navy, was available for the extension overseas of Britain's economic interests. This was clearly displayed when, in the Seven Years' War, the government accepted that it was in Britain's national interest to prevent the East India Company from being ejected from Bengal. All of these factors contributed to the success of that dour, self-confident, forceful capitalist who became known throughout England as the Manchester Man.

The First Textile Inventions

Manchester had been a textile town at least since the sixteenth century; but it was mostly woolen goods, spun and woven in the cottages of the neighboring villages by peasant families, that constituted the bulk of trade. Slowly the product became more varied with the introduction of linen from Ireland and silk from Damascus, and especially of cotton. Fustians (a mixture of cotton from Cairo and linen), calico (cloth of cotton from Calicut), and muslin (manufactured from cotton of Mosul in Iraq) were exported to many parts of Europe and especially to Africa. The cotton merchants in Manchester at the beginning of the eighteenth century were aware of the potential market for cotton goods, based on the comfort and wearing quality of cotton cloth compared with those of wool; and they saw the inability of spinners, almost exclusively women working for low pay in their own cottages, to keep up with weavers, especially those who had started to use a weaving machine called the Dutch loom, imported from Holland in 1660. The industrial revolution began when inventors in or near Manchester invented machines for speeding up the process of spinning and weaving and northern businessmen then put them into use in factories.

This first phase of industrialization did not require great scientific knowledge from the inventors nor large capital investment from the manufacturers. The first of the Lancashire inventors, John Kay, was a weaver who magnified the imbalance between the efficiency of spinning and that of weaving by inventing the "flying shuttle," an ingenious combination in which the operator was able, with one hand, to control two hammers that tapped a shuttle on wheels from side to side across the lengthwise threads of the loom. Not only could cloth be woven faster, but for the first time a piece could be made wider than the operator's outstretched arms. When the flying shuttle was widely adopted in the 1760s, the Society for the Encouragement of Arts and Manufactures of London was so struck by the need of comparable productivity in spinning that it offered two prizes for "the best invention of a machine that will spin six threads of wool, flax, cotton, or silk, at one time, and that will require but one person to work it and to attend it." The desired invention was patented in 1770 by James Hargreaves of Blackburn, a cotton town near Manchester, who turned his dual skills as carpenter and weaver to making a machine that could spin eight threads at once. Within twenty years, twenty thousand of these

A Manchester Cotton Mill, 1842

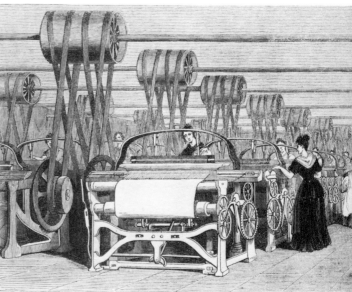

(Left) Spinning Cotton, from *Michael Armstrong*, by Frances Trollope (1780–1863)
Frances Trollope, mother of the novelist Anthony Trollope, wrote many travel books and several novels. Michael Armstrong is a slashing indictment of the working conditions for women and children in the cotton factories of northern England.

(Right) Weaving Cotton
In a Manchester factory like this one, frequent accidents were caused by the unprotected belts of the power looms.

"spinning jennies" were in use in England, and the spinning wheel had almost disappeared from Lancashire. (Hargreaves does not seem to have won the Society's prize, however, and his invention was pirated by others.)

The application of water power to spinning followed shortly after, when Richard Arkwright invented the "water frame" at Preston, twenty miles from Manchester. Arkwright was a barber and wigmaker, whose business acumen drove him to not only the invention but also the large-scale merchandising of his product. For Thomas Carlyle, whose popular writings in the 1830s blackened the fame of Manchester's capitalists for all England, he was typical of the industrial exploiter, a "plain, almost gross, bag-cheeked, pot-bellied Lancashire man, with an air of painful reflection, yet also of copious free digestion. . . . Oh, reader, what a historical phenomenon is that bag-cheeked, pot-bellied, much enduring, much inventing barber!" Arkwright went on to become the richest cotton spinner in England; his factories became the model for the whole textile industry. When Samuel Crompton of Bolton invented his "mule," a combination of the water frame and the spinning jenny, the spinners at last exceeded the output of the weavers and moreover were able to produce all varieties of cotton thread from coarse and strong to the most delicate muslin. Thus the first phase of the revolution in cotton production was in cotton spinning and weaving; and by 1800 Manchester had become the leading city to apply the inventions in factory production. Arkwright himself built the first spinning mill in Manchester in the 1780s; by 1802, there were fifty-two such mills. Twenty years later, one-quarter of all the cotton spindles in Britain were in Manchester. Since women working their own spinning wheels in the cottages could not compete with the new machines, rural families lost an important source of income, at a time when fewer laborers were needed in the fields. Thus the cities received both women and men from the farms for work in the factories.

From 1820, weaving sheds were added to the spinning mills to accommodate the final major invention of this technological revolution, the power loom of Edmund Cartwright, a Leicestershire clergyman who was stimulated by conversation with some Manchester businessmen to invent the needed weaving machine. His own ingenuous description shows just how amateurish such an inventor might be:

It struck me that . . . since there could only be three movements which were to follow each other in succession, there could be little difficulty in producing and repeating them. . . . To my great delight, a piece of cloth, such as it was, was the product. As I had never before turned my thoughts to anything mechanical, either in theory or practice, nor had even seen a loom at work, or known anything of its construction, you will readily suppose that my first loom was a most rude piece of machinery. The warp was placed perpendicularly, the reed fell with the weight of at least half a hundredweight, and the springs which threw the shuttle were strong enough to have thrown a rocket.[2]

Canals, Steam Engines, and Railroads

The growth of Manchester's cotton industry stimulated other forms of industrial progress. As early as 1759, the duke of Bridgewater, whose estate at Worsley a few miles to the north had rich coal deposits, determined to become the main supplier to the growing city by cutting a canal from the underground galleries in Worsley to the heart of Manchester. He called in James Brindley, a brilliant though almost illiterate engineer, who in two years organized the cutting of the canal, even though the first stages were 550 feet below ground and an aqueduct had to be built to carry the canal 40 feet above the river Irwell. The canal, the first true canal in Britain, halved the price of coal in Manchester and was regarded by contemporaries as a marvel of engineering. Brindley followed it by linking Manchester to the river Mersey and thus to the port of Liverpool with the Bridgewater Canal, 42 miles long. Manchester thus started the rest of the country on a mania of canal building, which by the beginning of the nineteenth century had linked the chief industrial centers of Britain with each other and with their ports, and, perhaps most important of all, had connected northern and southern England with the Grand Trunk Canal. This canal and its branches, Brindley's greatest and last undertaking, linked Manchester, the Midlands, London, and the western ports on the river Severn.

Apart from good transport, the cotton industry required power. Steam engines had been in use since the early eighteenth century to pump water out of coal mines; but in 1769 James Watt, a scientific-instrument maker at the University of Glasgow, invented the first engine that used steam power rather than atmospheric pressure to drive the piston. It economized greatly on the use of fuel and, as he later showed, could be converted from

[2]Cited in John Sanders, *Manchester* (London: Rupert Hart-Davis, 1967), p. 66.

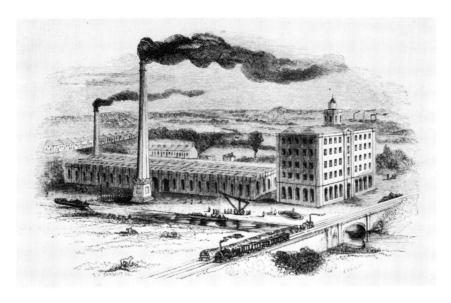

The Bridgewater Factory
The factory was located where the Liverpool and Manchester Railway crossed the Duke of Bridgewater's Canal.

up-and-down to rotary motion. In a long and profitable partnership with a Birmingham businessman, Matthew Boulton, Watt sold engines to most of the mining districts of Britain, and especially to the cotton mills of Lancashire. In the last quarter of the eighteenth century, three times as many steam engines were used in the textile mills as in the mines.

Manchester too stimulated the most far-reaching application of the steam engine—to railroad transportation. Railways, that is, parallel metal rails on which trucks were pulled, had been used in the mines since the 1700s, and a complicated steam locomotive had been used in a few cases. In 1829, George Stephenson, an engineer from the Tyneside mines, perfected a locomotive called the Rocket, in which steam pressure was applied in rotary motion to drive a piston connected directly to the wheels. Stephenson was commissioned by the Liverpool and Manchester Railway Committee to link the two cities by railroad; and at a famous competition on a specially built piece of track at Rainhill, halfway between Liverpool and Manchester, he demonstrated that his Rocket could travel at twenty-nine miles an hour pulling a thirteen-ton load. (At the official opening of the railroad a year later, attended by the whole government, the Rocket had the unfortunate distinction of running down and killing the Home Secretary in the first fatal railroad accident.) As with the Bridgewater Canal, the success of the Liverpool and Manchester Railway set off a drive for improved transportation. By 1843 nineteen hundred miles of railroad had been constructed in Britain, and all the main cities were linked more effectively than they had ever been by canal.

Manchester's Overseas Trade

Overseas, too, the influence of Manchester's cotton merchants was strongly felt. Vast quantities of the raw material were needed. In 1785 ten million pounds of cotton were imported; in 1850 five hundred and eighty-eight million. At their peak cotton imports accounted for one-fifth of all

British imports. For most of the eighteenth century, the West Indian islands supplied the bulk of Lancashire's needs; and the cotton trade thus increased the need for African slaves on those islands and magnified the profits of the merchants of nearby Liverpool who supplied them. From the 1790s, however, the southern United States of America became the main cotton supplier, after Eli Whitney's invention of the gin had made possible the use of the American brand of short-stapled cotton. By 1830 three-quarters of the cotton imported by Britain was grown on the slave plantations of the southern United States. The British cotton industry was largely responsible both for the spread of cotton plantations from the Old South into the Gulf states and Mississippi valley in the early nineteenth century, and for making slavery pay.

The effect of exports of cotton goods was also considerable. In Europe, the preponderance of British cotton goods effectively delayed the growth of native European cotton industries for half a century. But war and trade barriers restricted the growth of British exports to Europe; and the cotton industry became largely dependent on exports to the underdeveloped parts of the world, many of which were part of the British Empire or were soon to be. Latin America took more British cotton than Europe after gaining its independence from Spain; the native Indian industry collapsed before Lancashire's competition; and Lancashire shirts were worn by West Africans (those at home and the slaves in the West Indies), by the citizens of the Turkish Empire, and even by Chinese peasants. Cotton established a form of economic imperialism, in which native industries of unprotected countries were severely restricted and concentration on production of raw materials for the industry of the developed countries encouraged. Some writers have held that the British government sought an extension of its territorial empire to secure the market for cotton; but even in India, it has been hard to prove that the cotton manufacturers could not have extended their sales without political controls.

The Manchester Businessman

What most impressed contemporary observers about the growth of Manchester's industry was the entirely new type of society it seemed to have created. Manchester was divided into two social classes, between which there appeared to be no bond of any kind except what Carlyle called the cash nexus. And what is more, both classes in Manchester—the millowners and the workers—were new to England. To many, the millowner represented a vital, sound new force in English life. Without the cotton plants, wrote one of them, "those majestic masses of men which stretch, like a living zone, through our central districts, would have had no existence; and the magic impulse which has been felt during that period in every department of national energy, which has affected more or less our literature, our laws, our social condition, our political institutions, making us almost a new people, would never have been communicated."[3] Such self-made men

---

[3]Cited in Asa Briggs, *Victorian Cities* (Harmondsworth, England: Penguin, 1968), p. 100.

included the early socialist theorist Robert Owen, who began in Manchester with £100 and eventually was able to supply £84,000 in cash to pay off his factory. But they were probably represented better by the industrialist whom Friedrich Engels described in a famous anecdote:

One day I walked with one of these middle-class gentlemen into Manchester. I spoke to him about the disgraceful unhealthy slums and drew his attention to the disgusting condition of that part of the town in which the factory workers lived. I declared that I had never seen so badly built a town in my life. He listened patiently and at the corner of the street at which we parted company, he remarked: "And yet there is a great deal of money made here. Good morning, Sir!" [4]

The Manchester businessmen were deeply and personally involved in the production of the factories. Many had begun their careers as spinners or weavers themselves, others as manufacturers of textile equipment, still others as brokers of raw cotton or the finished goods. They knew every detail of the process of manufacture, worked exceedingly long hours themselves, took risks with their capital, and demanded very high profit margins from their investment. Their driving energy impressed the older landed aristocracy when it saw the great propaganda machine that Manchester erected in the 1840s to force Parliament to end protection of England's wheat farmers. And they so impressed contemporary novelists in the 1840s and 1850s that some of the most unforgettable figures, perhaps because they were so exaggerated, were the northern business owners in such novels as Disraeli's *Coningsby*, Mrs. Gaskell's *Mary Barton*, and Charles Dickens's *Hard Times*. In Josiah Bounderby of Coketown, Dickens sought to isolate through exaggeration the extraordinary character of the new businessman:

He was a rich man: banker, merchant, manufacturer, and what not. A big, loud man, with a stare, and a metallic laugh. A man made out of coarse material, which seemed to have been stretched to make so much of him. A man with a great puffed head and forehead, swelled veins in his temples, and such a strained skin to his face that it seemed to hold his eyes open, and lift his eyebrows up. A man with a pervading appearance on him of being inflated like a balloon, and ready to start. A man who could never sufficiently vaunt himself a self-made man. A man who was always proclaiming, through that brassy speaking-trumpet of a voice of his, his old ignorance and his old poverty. A man who was the Bully of humility. [5]

To most contemporary social critics, Dickens's picture rang true. The well-to-do of Manchester lived in Alderley Edge, on the outskirts of town and facing the lovely moorland countryside. Henry Adams described the

[4]Cited in E. J. Hobsbawm, *The Age of Revolution: Europe, 1789–1848* (London: Weidenfeld and Nicolson, 1962), p. 182.
[5]Charles Dickens, *Hard Times* (Boston: Houghton Mifflin, 1894), p. 14.

area in 1861 as "all country houses on the outskirts of the town, so that for miles about one meets long and very pretty roads lined with villas and parks, which leave the city proper very dull and gloomy, from the want of handsome private houses."

Condition of the Workers

The rest of the town had spread haphazardly in acres of slums, built for a quick profit by local builders. The worst was Irish Town, built for immigrants in a valley below the level of the rest of the city; but little of the working-class housing was better. An early nineteenth-century economist described how Irish Town and the other sections of Manchester were built:

These towns . . . have been erected with the utmost disregard of everything except the immediate advantage of the speculating builder. A carpenter and builder unite to buy a series of building sites (i.e. they lease them for a number of years) and cover them with so-called houses. In one place we found a whole street following the course of a ditch, because in this way deeper cellars could be secured without the cost of digging, cellars not for storing wares or rubbish, but for dwellings of human beings. Not one house of this street escaped the cholera. In general the streets are unpaved, with a dungheap or ditch in the middle; the houses are built back to back, without ventilation or drainage, and whole families are limited to a corner of a cellar or a garret.[6]

Working conditions in the factories were as bad, as a series of governmental inquiries in the early 1800s proved. Early on, child labor was regarded as essential to profitable operation. At first apprentices were picked from orphans on parish relief. Then child labor spread more widely among the children of the millworkers. The children usually began work at the age of six, spending from 6 A.M. to 7 or 8 P.M. in the factories, with half an hour for lunch and an hour for dinner, six days a week. They were used to join broken threads in the spinning machines, to sweep up waste cotton, or to replace bobbins of thread. Children were regularly beaten to keep them awake; they had constant lung trouble from breathing the fine cotton fluff. The first important attempt to remedy their condition, the Factory Act of 1819, was itself a comment on attitudes on child labor because it merely forbade the employment of children under nine years of age and restricted the working hours of children under eighteen to ten and a half hours a day. Inspection was left to the local justices, who were frequently retired factory owners.

Conditions for women were as bad, particularly in the textile factories, which by 1871 were employing almost four hundred thousand women, in part so high a number because they were brought in to replace children after the Factory Acts cut down child employment. Women worked from twelve to fourteen hours in dirty, stuffy, overcrowded buildings. In linen

[6]Nassau Senior, cited in J. L. and Barbara Hammond, *The Town Labourer, 1760–1832: The New Civilisation* (London: Longmans, 1932), pp. 43–44.

Child Labor

As this popular London magazine shows, half a century after the first Factory Act, very young children were still employed in unhealthful, heavy work at the mines. (The Graphic, June 10, 1871)

Outside the Factory, from *Michael Armstrong*, by Frances Trollope

Exposure by Britain's novelists of the suffering of the poor in the industrial cities led Parliament in the 1840s to cut down the working hours of women and children and to supervise their conditions at work. Progress was, however, extremely slow.

Slum Neighborhood, Liverpool, c. 1895
Liverpool was the principal port for the export of the products of the northern industrial cities of England. Its vast slums spread for miles along the dockland of the river Mersey. (BBC Hulton Picture Library)

factories, the temperature might be over 120 degrees. In most textile factories, the air was filled with fibers, while in metal polishing plants, women breathed fine metal dust. Women in Oldham, a town near Manchester, had triple the national rate of tuberculosis in the 1850s. Pay was well below that of men, and failure to obey posted rules was punished by monetary fines. Married women frequently could not keep up with the schedule or the duties in addition to running a home and looking after children, and most were compelled to take only temporary jobs. Women found too that they received little training; therefore, they were unable to compete with men for the skilled positions. Some were even aggrieved when the Factory Acts of the 1840s cut down their working hours and their access to dangerous jobs because simultaneously they lost the chance for increasing their pay. However, certain writers have argued that the factory system, for all its exploitation, offered advantages to women—the opportunity of gaining work experience and a personal income, the provision of social contact not only with other women but with prospective husbands, and the sense of personal independence within the family. But the price was high.

In the 1830s and 1840s, many commissions appeared in Manchester and the other industrial cities to study working conditions of all laborers, produced a large number of case studies and some statistics, and publicized the appalling conditions they found. The most famous report, *On the Sanitary Condition of the Labouring Population of Great Britain in 1842*, showed that the average age of death of "mechanics, labourers, and their families" in Manchester was seventeen, compared with thirty-eight in a completely rural area taken for comparison. And even the well-to-do of Manchester suffered from the unsanitary condition of the city, since "professional persons and gentry, and their families" died at an average age of thirty-eight compared with fifty-two in the rural county.

Recently, economic historians have shown that real wages in England were rising during the nineteenth century—by twenty-five percent between 1800 and 1825 and by forty percent between 1825 and 1850. But this did little to palliate the discontent of the working classes. Manchester was known as a caldron constantly ready to boil over. Frequently the workers smashed the machines they held responsible for their condition. Occasionally, particularly during the wars with France after the Revolution, they rioted for bread. Elementary unions were formed among the cotton spinners as early as the 1790s, and they organized sporadic and fairly ineffective strikes. But widespread mob disorder was common. The worst occurred in 1819, when troops fired into a crowd of demonstrators, killing ten and injuring hundreds, in what came to be known as the Peterloo massacre; and in 1842, when the city was given over entirely in the Plug Plot riots to a vast mob augmented by rioters who had swarmed in from all the neighboring cotton towns. There was thus, during the first half of the nineteenth century, the constant fear of genuine insurrection in Manchester. "Here there seems no sympathy between the upper and lower classes of society," wrote a Manchester newspaper in 1819. "There is no mutual confidence, no bond of attachment." It was this vision of Manchester that Engels was to present to Karl Marx in their talks in Paris in 1844; and it was Manchester more than any other place they had in mind when they penned *The Communist Manifesto:*

Our epoch, the epoch of the bourgeoisie, possesses, however, this distinctive feature: it has simplified the class antagonisms. Society as a whole is more and more splitting up into two great hostile camps, into two great classes directly facing each other: Bourgeoisie and Proletariat.

In Manchester and the other great industrial cities of northern England, especially during the first fifty to seventy years of their expansion, a new form of urbanization had thus occurred. Here were cities devoted entirely to economic production. Until the 1850s, almost all building in Manchester itself consisted of factories, warehouses, and mass housing; and its social structure was equally simple. That is to say, two-thirds of its population were wage earners, mostly engaged in the cotton industry; the rest

Character of the Industrial City

were a service population of shopkeepers, lawyers, doctors, and "merchants," comprising not only the millowners but owners of engineering companies and trading companies and the bankers. From the 1840s on, when Manchester's character as a Coketown was irrevocably formed, the city began to receive a few of the urban amenities that had made life in Constantinople or Paris constantly interesting and at times even pleasant for the mass of inhabitants. Three public parks were opened in 1846. Manchester's university employed its first five professors in 1851, and a year later a free library was started. An exhibition of paintings from private collections was held in 1857 and attracted over a million visitors; and the city's musical director, Charles Hallé, stayed on to found in Manchester one of the world's great symphony orchestras. Finally in 1868–1877, the town fathers spent a million pounds for the construction of a monstrous Gothic town hall that would symbolize the city's devotion to local self-government. Manchester thus slowly and belatedly built a cultural life for itself amid the gloom of its factory chimneys; and its evolution was typical of the industrial city.

This haphazard evolution can be explained in part by the lack of governmental controls. Manchester had no municipal government and no representation at all in Parliament until the 1830s. No form of zoning or even of sanitary controls was exerted over the early builders, and so expansion was completely dictated by the desire to make a quick profit. Moreover, until the first Factory Act, no form of governmental control regulated working conditions, and the efforts of workers to better their own condi-

Town Hall, Manchester, England

Constructed in 1868–1877, the Gothic town hall was modeled on the wool halls of medieval Flanders, like that of Ypres. (BBC Hulton Picture Library)

tions by unionization were forbidden by law. Most house building had to cater to a working population paid close to subsistence wages. Here the philosophy of laissez-faire, accepted sincerely by the industrialists, played an important part. Britain's economic theorists from the time of Adam Smith had taught that the economic system followed its own natural laws and that when it was left free from governmental interference the greatest economic productivity resulted. The industrialists believed in the simple lessons taught by the economists. Adam Smith had proved the value of free trade. Ricardo had taught the "iron law of wages," that "the natural price of labor is that price which is necessary to enable the laborers, one with another, to subsist and perpetuate their race, without either increase or diminution." Malthus had shown that improvement in the standard of life increases population, which negates the rise in the standard of life, and that therefore population, or at least the working-class population, will always be at subsistence level. These comfortable theories were summarized in Ricardo's statement, "The pursuit of individual advantage is admirably connected with the universal good of the whole."

Moreover, the traditional elements that had made city life more refined and more humane were largely lacking. The churches played a very subordinate role. The nonconformists (that is, Protestants who did not accept the Church of England) built their chapels in functional red brick, like warehouses; and their preachers, especially the Methodists with their visions of a heavenly paradise that would follow this earthly hell, were often deemed more effective at quenching the desire for revolutionary change than the police forces. The Church of England, comfortably entrenched in the rich livings of the rural South, barely penetrated the North. The aristocracy, the force that had given the baroque city so much of its character, kept its townhouses in London, but saw no reason for building similar homes in Manchester or Liverpool, even when it owned large parts of the city's acreage, as Lord Derby did in Liverpool or the duke of Bridgewater in Manchester. The industrial cities augmented the agricultural income of the aristocrats, who were thus able to extend through the whole nineteenth century the lavish life on their country estates without the need to penetrate the maelstrom of the northern cities.

The flourishing industry ravaged the natural environment. The use of coal for power and for home fires filled the air with grime and the mining towns near Manchester with mountains of slag. The rivers were polluted with chemicals from the dyes used in printing the textiles and with every other kind of waste. The river Irwell at Manchester was graphically described by a mid-nineteenth-century novelist:

The hapless river—a pretty enough stream a few miles up, with trees overhanging its banks and fringes of green sedge set thick along its edges—loses caste as it gets among the mills and print works. There are myriads of dirty things given it to wash, and whole wagon-loads of poisons from dyehouses and bleachyards thrown

The Ecological Disaster of Industrialization

Contrasts, by Augustus Welby Pugin (1812–1852)
(Above) "Catholic Town in 1440." (Below) "The Same Town in 1840." Pugin sought to show that the ruin of the English city was due to Protestantism as much as to industrialism.

into it to carry away; steam boilers discharge into it their seething contents, and drains and sewers their fetid impurities; till at length it rolls on—here between tall dingy walls, there under precipices of red sandstone—considerably less a river than a flood of liquid manure.[7]

The factories needed the best sites along the rivers for water power or transportation. The railroads followed the river valleys for ease of construction, slashed gashes through hillsides, and cut vast swathes right into the center of town. And the whole city reechoed constantly to the sound of the mills, the steam engines, and the trains. Noise pollution had become normal.

Manchester had become the prototype of the unplanned industrial city, the creator of wealth and the producer of material goods on a scale unknown in history, and—at least until the mid-nineteenth century—one of the ugliest of man's creations. "Every day that I live," wrote an American in 1845 after visiting Manchester, "I thank Heaven that I am not a poor man with a family in England."

[7]Cited in Lewis Mumford, *The City in History* (New York: Harcourt, Brace & World, 1961), pp. 459–460.

SPREAD OF INDUSTRIALISM TO THE CONTINENT

On the continent of Europe, industrialization lagged behind the British pace; but by the middle of the nineteenth century, Belgium, parts of France, the Rhineland and Saxony, some cities in Lombardy, and a few small regions of the Austrian Empire were enjoying the mixed blessing of the eruption of their own Coketowns. Engels had seen the waters of the Wupper River polluted with textile dye from the mills of Elberfeld, where Germany's first spinning jenny had been installed, and watched the disappearance of "the fresh and vigorous popular life, which existed almost all over Germany." The city of Lyons in southern France was seized by thirty thousand silk weavers in 1831 in protest against their inadequate wages. Belgian mining towns like Liège and Namur were as foul as any in the Rhondda valley of south Wales, and no factory acts had been passed to alleviate intolerable working conditions.

Certain factors common to all Europe helped retard the beginning of industrialization; and to these disadvantages individual countries added their own peculiar impediments. War and internal revolutions had thrown the European economy into recurrent chaos, discouraging the investment of risk capital or the movement of the labor force from the land. Most governments had regarded the growth of cities as a danger to public order and had tried to discourage it. Communications by land were atrocious, as few new roads had been built since the time of the Roman Empire. Water transport was hindered by political barriers, which also discouraged the canalization of rivers crossing borders. Customs duties hampered not only foreign trade but internal trade as well; and governments were reluctant to give up one of their most reliable sources of income. Whereas luxury goods, as medieval trade proved, can be sold at many times their original cost and can thus absorb the large price of transportation and duties, the products of the industrial revolution that are intended for the mass consumer market cannot; and thus the large-scale sale of heavy goods like coal and iron and of manufactured goods only became possible on the continent with cheap transportation and the reduction of supplementary costs in tolls or customs. In a broader sense, this implied that the industrial revolution was only possible when a large, unified market existed; and the political fragmentation of Germany and Italy was thus an economic impediment as well as a nationalist grievance. Political fragmentation was particularly disastrous to the development of the European coal industry, because Europe's greatest coal deposits lay in a great crescent stretching from northern France to the Ruhr in Germany, broken up among France, Belgium, the Netherlands, Luxembourg, and Prussia. The only significant deposit of iron ore on the continent, in French Lorraine, was cut off from the coal deposits of the Saar by the national hatred between French and Germans and from the French coal of the Channel coast by lack of transportation. The continuing restrictions placed on new economic activity by

Drawbacks to Industrialization on the Continent

the guilds, which were still powerful through much of Europe, prevented the introduction of the factory system in the older cities, while the genuine preference of many peasants, like those in France, to go hungry on their own land rather than in the cities prevented the growth of a large labor market. Even the attitude of the middle classes who made money in commerce discouraged industrialization, since most preferred to put their profits into the more socially remunerative investment of land, while those who did invest in industrial projects wanted to keep them small, in their family possessions, and stable rather than expansive. But the most discouraging factor was Britain's industrial progress, which had given it an enormous lead in capture of markets, in technical improvements, and in mobilization of capital. It was hard for any other country to compete with the British in quality or price or well-established market organization.

Beginning of Industrialism in Europe

In a small way after 1815, and on a large scale after 1830, certain regions of the continent underwent an industrial revolution of their own because conditions were more favorable than in the eighteenth century. No major war disturbed the continent's stability. Population growth was as rapid as in England and overpopulation increased, as thus did the underemployment of the villages. Consequently, poverty-stricken farm laborers began drifting into the cities. Many governments, determined to emulate the effective administration enforced by Napoleon, wished to stimulate the modernization of their economies by state action. Foremost among these were the governments of the united Netherlands, Prussia, and France after the 1830 revolution. Such governments sponsored industrial expositions, subsidized inventors, founded technical and scientific schools, and paid for official inspection tours abroad. Capital was more easily mobilized for investment in industrial enterprises with a great improvement in the banking system, partly the foundation of national banks but especially of joint-stock banks. Moreover, the British, seeking lucrative investment for the profits of their own industrial revolution, began to make large funds available for continental industrialization, especially for investment in the supposedly secure profits from railroad building.

Transportation seemed to many the key to the creation of an industrial revolution on the continent, and a start was made in road building, river dredging, and canal construction. For example, France had twelve hundred kilometers of canal by the time of the abdication of Napoleon I, the canal builder; the restored Bourbons added another nine hundred; and the middle-class government of Louis Philippe added two thousand before the 1848 revolution. The introduction of the steamboat was especially important for use in river transportation and short sea crossings. As in England, however, it was the railroad that linked the continental suppliers and markets. The Belgian state took the lead by constructing two intersecting lines across the country. France and Germany were somewhat slower; but in the 1840s the French produced an ingenious plan whereby the state would provide the roadbed, tunnels, and bridges, and private companies

The North Sea area, showing Major Industrial Areas and Railroads.

Liverpool, Manchester, Birmingham, Amsterdam, London, Calais, BELGIUM, RUHR, PAS-DE-CALAIS, LOR-RAINE, Frankfurt, Paris, Danzig, Berlin, SAXONY, BOHEMIA, Vienna, Munich, Lyons, Bordeaux, Venice, LOMBARDY, Marseilles, Barcelona, Madrid, Lisbon, Rome, Naples, Constantinople, St. Petersburg, Moscow, Danube River, North Sea, Atlantic Ocean, Black Sea, Mediterranean Sea

◆ *The Beginning of Industrialization of Europe, c. 1850* ◆

the rolling stock and rails. A centrally planned system, with Paris at its hub, was well under construction by 1848 and was completed by the 1860s in spite of early fears that frightened cows would give no milk and passengers in tunnels would catch pleurisy. Less anxious about such perils, the Germans created their network a decade earlier than the French, so that the philosopher Treitschke could boast: "It was the railroads which first dragged the nation from its economic stagnation. . . . With such power did they break in upon all the old habits of life, that already in the forties the aspect of Germany was completely changed." The rural East of Germany, now united to western Europe, found new markets for its agricultural pro-

**The Great Hammer
"Fritz," Krupp Factory,
Essen, Germany (1861)**

*Factory owner Alfred Krupp
designed this hammer to
forge steel ingots weighing
up to fifty thousand pounds
for use in very large pro-
pellor shafts and other pieces
of heavy machinery.
(Courtesy of the German
Information Center)*

duce and felt a psychological impact that had never before penetrated the
aristocratic estates of the broad eastern plains.

The economic environment was therefore more favorable to industrialization; but the most difficult phase in a process of economic growth, in
Walt Rostow's phrase, is the "takeoff" into sustained growth, "the interval
when the old blocks and resistances to steady growth are finally overcome." In Europe, a first stimulus was provided by the acquisition of British machines and skills. In part this was achieved by industrial espionage—
since the export of the most important machinery, except steam engines,
was forbidden by law until 1842—or by study of British technical periodicals. But many British skilled workers emigrated to the continent to enjoy
the high wages paid them for instructing native workers in their skills, including the operation of the flying shuttle and the spinning jenny and the
new techniques in iron manufacture like puddling. British managers and
entrepreneurs saw that they could make a fortune more rapidly in the un-
competitive continental environment than in Britain. Business-minded
British engineers built the railroad from Paris to Rouen, opened the great
Hibernia coal mines in the Ruhr, modernized the cotton industry of Normandy, and built the largest engineering concern in the world in the 1830s
at Seraing in Belgium.

Europeans were very soon making their own inventions or improving
on those brought from England; and among these pioneers were some of

the founders of the great industrial fortunes of the nineteenth century. Friedrich Krupp of Essen, for example, made crucible cast steel in the early 1800s; the Borsig company of Berlin developed an improved locomotive in the 1830s; the de Wendels of Lorraine pioneered in introducing the integration of the various stages of iron making. These were only a few of the greatest names among the thousands of entrepreneur capitalists who were determined to become continental counterparts of the Manchester Man.

Thus by the middle of the century, the relative economic position of Britain and the continental countries had shifted, although not yet dramatically. Britain was still producing one-half of the iron and cotton cloth and two-thirds of the world's coal; and half of its population lived in towns. Belgium, however, the most thoroughly industrialized country on the continent, greatly resembled Britain. It had a highly developed coal mining and iron manufacturing industry in the central towns from Mons to Liège, and a large-scale textile industry for both cotton and woolen goods. The French had developed the coal mines of the Channel coast and were beginning to exploit the rather poor quality iron ore of Lorraine; and they had several isolated but highly organized centers of iron production, such as Le Creusot in central France, as well as a thriving textile industry in Alsace. Agriculture, however, remained the main employer, and the most usual form of business was the family firm. (Curiously enough, the reason why the same proportion of women were employed in France as in England was that they largely remained on the family farm or else were employed in the family business.) In Germany, a start had been made in opening up the coal mines and developing an iron industry in the Ruhr and Saar and in Saxony, but textile manufacture was still spread throughout the country among millions of small craftsmen. Small-scale industry, especially textiles or iron, had begun in northern Italy, Bohemia and western Hungary, and around Vienna.

The change in the character of society affected Europeans in various ways. To those who had loved the placid life of the eighteenth century, it was depressing. "Wealth and speed are things the world admires and for which all men strive," wrote the seventy-six-year-old Goethe.

Social Impact of Industrialism in Europe

Railways, express mails, steamboats, and possible means of communication are what the educated world seeks. . . . Actually this is the century of clever minds, of practical men who grasp things easily, who are endowed with a certain facility, and who feel their own superiority to the multitude, but who lack talent for the most exalted tasks. Let us as far as possible retain the ideals in which we were raised. We and perhaps a few others will be the last representatives of an era which will not soon return.[8]

[8]Cited in Theodore S. Hamerow, *Restoration, Revolution, Reaction: Economics and Politics in Germany, 1815–1871* (Princeton, N.J.: Princeton University Press, 1966), p. 3. Reprinted by permission of Princeton University Press.

Industrial Landscape, by Vincent van Gogh (1853–1890)

Although industrialism came later to the continent than to England, its effects were no less ravaging to the landscape. (Stedelijk Museum, Amsterdam)

To others more attuned to the spirit of enterprise, it was a time of unlimited possibilities. Even the German railroads had romantic possibilities:

> *For these rails are bridal bracelets,*
> *Wedding rings of purest gold;*
> *States like lovers will exchange them,*
> *And the marriage-tie will hold.* [9]

But industrialization on the continent was producing the same problems that had shocked the observers of Manchester. The Prussian king was informed in 1828 that early work in the factories of the Rhineland had so stunted the population of his western provinces that they could no longer fill their quota of army recruits; eleven years later, the employment of children under nine in Prussia was forbidden. In 1840 Louis Blanc had begun his famous indictment of early French capitalism, *The Organization of*

[9] Ibid., p. 8.

Work, with the startling announcement: "The other day a child was frozen to death behind a sentry-box in the heart of Paris, and nobody was shocked or surprised at the event." Europeans, like the British, had realized belatedly that industrialization was a phenomenon whose social consequences were so disruptive that they required widespread political action. But there were irreconcilable differences of opinion on the action needed.

POLITICAL PANACEAS FOR INDUSTRIALIZATION

Liberalism

The most natural reaction to industrialization on the part of those who profited from it was to justify its workings. The upper middle classes adopted the doctrine of liberalism, whose principal tenet, at least so its opponents claimed, was summarized in the French premier Guizot's advice to those who wanted a lower property qualification for voting: *Enrichissez-vous* ("Get rich"). This helpful doctrine had been given a convincing formulation by the great English economist Adam Smith (1723–1790) in his book *The Wealth of Nations*, published in 1776. Smith had argued that individuals had the unique ability to trade, that is, to exchange material goods in order to increase the well-being of both parties to the bargain. In a state of perfect freedom from interference, some people realize that certain goods are more in demand than others and exert themselves to profit from that demand. These entrepreneurs develop new resources or create new patterns of trade for the purpose of bettering themselves by satisfying demand. Competition among suppliers increases quality and prevents excessive profitmaking. When one demand is satiated, the entrepreneurs seek new demands to satisfy. The consumer, with the ability to buy or not to buy, is therefore king of the economic system. The worker, with the ability to sell his labor or not sell it, is also theoretically master of the wage structure, since competition among employers for labor enables the worker to choose satisfactory wage rates. Yet the consumer too is protected, since the demands of the workers must not force the price of goods above what the consumer can afford to pay. Therefore a harmony of interests of consumer, employer, and worker exists, Smith argued, when the working of the economic system is not falsified by government interference, tariffs or other restrictions on international trade, or monopolies of producers. The role of government is to protect society from foreign attack, to ensure internal order and justice, and to create large-scale public works, such as roads, that the individual cannot erect alone.

Adam Smith, from the Plaster-Cast of the Medallion by James Tassie *(National Portrait Gallery, London)*

This theory was incorporated into David Ricardo's *Principles of Political Economy* published in 1817, which became the gospel of the early nineteenth-century liberals. Ricardo, however, was convinced that Smith had been too optimistic in thinking this natural system to be harmonious. Ricardo saw that the classes of society were of necessity antagonistic, and that in particular the wages of the working class would always remain at the approximate level necessary for subsistence alone. Taking up the theory of Thomas Malthus in his *Essay on the Principle of Population* (1798), Ricardo showed that an expanding economy merely supports an expanding population, and that the natural tendency is for the expanding population to exceed the food supply. Faced with starvation, the working class is compelled to reduce its size so that its share of the wealth of society is always exactly what is needed for subsistence. But the landlord receives rent and the capitalist profits from the wealth produced by labor; and these two groups are also in conflict over their share of society's wealth. Ricardo's sympathy lay with the capitalist, whose enterprise produced wealth, and not with the landowner, who in his view did little to justify his share.

Radicalism

The so-called radicals or democrats believed that the liberals' mistake was their restriction of the suffrage to their own class. They held that the solution of society's ills was the extension of universal suffrage and the taking of political power by the people. This program, advocated in England by a brilliant political pamphleteer, William Cobbett, received widespread popular support in the difficult times following the end of the Napoleonic wars. The government's answer was repression—the Peterloo massacre of 1819 and the Six Acts that restricted public meetings and the freedom of the press. In the renewed distress of the 1830s and 1840s, these demands were voiced again by the Chartists (named after the People's Charter,

Mary Wollstonecraft (1759-1797)
Wollstonecraft was one of the first women in England to campaign for equal rights for women. She moved to Paris during the French Revolution and came to know many of its leaders. She later married the political philosopher William Godwin and died giving birth to their first child, Mary, the future wife of the poet Shelley. (The Walker Art Gallery, Liverpool)

which they drew up in 1838), a working-class group that demanded universal manhood suffrage, annual parliaments, equal electoral districts, and payment of the members of Parliament. The Chartists twice presented petitions to Parliament with millions of signatures, held huge demonstrations, and promised general strikes. A violent confrontation in Wales between Chartist miners and British troops led to the arrest of the Chartist leaders in 1839; but by the late 1840s the movement had lost much of its support. When a last attempt was made, in London in 1848, to organize a mass demonstration, the leaders called off their procession through the city when the government refused them a permit.

The radicals' demands for greater individual freedoms encouraged women to seek improvement in their own legal and social positions. A start had been made by Mary Wollstonecraft, the friend of such radical English writers as Thomas Paine and William Godwin, whom she later married. In 1792 whe wrote *A Vindication of the Rights of Women*, in which she argued the natural equality of men and women and the justification for women to receive as complete an education as men. Attacks on the legal disadvantages of women in England led a reluctant Parliament in the first half of the nineteenth century to institute numerous changes. Lady Caroline Norton, whose husband had refused to allow her to see her children after their separation, had written every member of Parliament and composed a large number of pamphlets, pleading the right of a mother to have control over her young children. Parliament responded by giving to women separated from their husbands custody of the children, but only to the age of seven. Demands for legal divorce finally led in 1857 to the Matrimonial Cause Bill, which however made it more difficult for a wife than a husband to sue for divorce: and only in 1884, with the grant of financial support to a wife who successfully sued for divorce, was it genuinely possible for her to consider divorce. A third demand by women, greater control over their property, was refused in Parliament in 1855, though women were finally granted equal property rights with their husbands. The feminist movement of the first half of the nineteenth century in England, like the radical movement, was however largely middle-class. Only in the future would the few gains made be of interest to working-class women, whose poverty was more of a burden than their legal disabilities.

Paris became the center of radicalism on the continent, welcoming exiled reformers of every description. In France the lower middle classes were most frustrated by the restriction of the suffrage, and they found leadership among the intellectual classes—notably the poet Lamartine and the political journalists—in demanding a republic. In 1847–1848, the radicals created the French equivalent of the Chartist petitions, a series of "reform banquets" in which leading opposition deputies called for a broadened suffrage and salaries for deputies. With industry in depression the radical leaders were able, in February 1848, to overthrow the liberal government and to turn France briefly into a republic with universal suffrage. Lamartine himself took office as president of the provisional government of

Alphonse de Lamartine (1790–1869)
Turning from poetry to radical politics, Lamartine briefly headed the provisional government established in France by the revolution of February 1848. (Cliché des Musées Nationaux-Paris)

the Second French Republic on February 24. In June, when he was compelled to use the army to suppress the workers of Paris, it was made dramatically clear that for one section of the population political solutions of the radical variety were inadequate for dealing with social problems. Social problems required socialist solutions.

Early Socialist Theory

The theory of socialism had existed long before the industrial revolution. In *The Republic*, Plato had suggested common ownership of property, including wives and children; and the early Christians laid considerable emphasis on the sharing of wealth. In the sixteenth century, writers of books about perfect lands, such as Sir Thomas More in *Utopia*, frequently refused to allow private ownership of property; and Rousseau blasted private ownership of land in one of his most famous passages:

The first man who, having enclosed a piece of land, took it into his head to say: "This belongs to me," and found people simple enough to believe him, was the true founder of civil society. What crimes, wars, murders, what miseries and horrors would have been spared the human race by him who, snatching out the stakes or filling in the ditch, should have cried to his fellows: "Beware of listening to this imposter; you are lost if you forget that the fruits belong to all and that the earth belongs to none." [10]

The French peasants demonstrated how little Rousseau had understood them by using the Revolution to stake themselves a plot of land rather than to communalize it; and the only genuine opponent of private property during the Revolution, Gracchus Babeuf, who led an insurrection in 1796 to achieve a communistic society in place of the Directory, was denounced by informers and executed. Only when the progress of industrialization had begun to create the large agglomerations of factory workers, a proletarian class, and an equally identifiable class of bourgeois employers, who actually practiced the doctrine that the workers can never rise above subsistence level, did modern socialist theory begin.

Utopian Socialism

Socialism began as an emotional reaction against the results of the industrial revolution and the inequity in the sharing of the products of industrialism between worker and capitalist. It was also a reaction against the worthlessness of the industrial way of life in the new cities, where freedom was given to the individual to seek profit regardless of the public good and thus to some extent even of his own. It was not a reaction against industrialization itself but a demand for its better regulation and use.

One of the first and most influential socialists was factory owner Robert Owen, who made a fortune by the age of twenty-eight from spinning mills in Manchester and then bought the largest mill in Scotland, New Lanark, which he attempted to make into a model socialist community.

[10]Cited in Alexander Gray, *The Socialist Tradition: From Moses to Lenin* (London: Longmans, Green, 1947), p. 81.

Owen showed, to the amazement of industrialists all over Europe who came to see his achievement, that a factory could be attractively designed, that workers could be given decent homes and free schools, and that wages could be higher than the competitors', without a loss of profits. In New Lanark and later in the United States at New Harmony, Indiana, he set up working examples of reconciliation between the classes; and he tried to show that the new industrial society could be created by the gradual proliferation of communities of this type. These two ideas were widely popular among the socialists of the first half of the nineteenth century, who for their unrealistic idealism were called by Karl Marx the "utopian" socialists. Owen himself became disillusioned and went on to attempt better working-class conditions through a national trade union organization and later through the establishment of consumers' cooperatives.

Owen's ideal of the voluntary organization of society into harmonious industrial communities was taken up by the French writer Charles Fourier (1772–1837), an eccentric traveling salesman with a passion for amateur mathematics. Fourier held that society should be organized in groups of 1,620 people because in such a group the work to be done can be matched to the natural inclination of the members. (Children, who like playing in dirt, would clean the streets.) In these groups, called *phalanstères*, all work would be cooperative but the profits would be shared unequally among labor, capital, and "talent."

Fourier followed the English socialists Owen and William Thompson in believing that socialism ought to improve the status of women. Thompson had written a strong appeal for female suffrage in his *Appeal of One-Half of the Human Race Against the Pretensions of the Other Half* (1825); in his phalanstères, Fourier provided day care for children in order to give mothers the same freedom of activity as men, and he made divorce easily available. Like Thompson, he also held that neither men nor women could be free in a capitalist society, and that a society's level of freedom was to be judged by women's progress toward equality. Nevertheless, Fourier appealed to any capitalist of good will to invest in his communities; but, although he reportedly went home at noon every day for ten years to meet prospective investors, no one ever came.

Far more influential in France were the followers of Claude de Saint-Simon, a nobleman who had fought in the American Revolution and had turned to science and history to find a more harmonious method for organizing society. Saint-Simon was an important theorist because he taught his followers that industrial society could be collectively planned for the benefit of all. He felt that the French Revolution had done good work by destroying obsolete institutions; the moment had come to create new ones. For that, *les oisifs* ("the lazy"), who were the nobles and soldiers, should be overthrown; control of administration and government should be placed in the hands of *les industriels* (manufacturers and bankers), who would work in favor of the unpropertied class, "the class which is the most numerous and the most poor"; and the general moral and intellectual well-being of society was to be safeguarded by an elite of intellectuals and artists. In this way, society would be run for the benefit of the poor by those most capable of providing those benefits. Saint-Simon also came up with countless other ideas that were taken up by the bankers and industrialists who served Louis Napoleon Bonaparte when he became emperor (1852–1870)—the building of the Suez Canal, the founding of credit institutions, the employment of technocrats in government. After his death his followers turned his creed into a wild messianic religion, with a universal father who spent a somewhat unwholesome length of time in search of the universal mother.

The transition to the view that the working class cannot be reconciled to the bourgeoisie but must overthrow it was made by Pierre Joseph Proudhon (1809–1865), the only utopian theorist in France of working-class origins. Like Rousseau's *Social Contract*, Proudhon's main work, *What Is Property?* (1840), made his fame with its opening paragraph:

If I were asked to answer the following question: What is slavery? *and I should answer in one word, It is* murder, *my meaning would be understood at once. No extended argument would be required to show that the power to take from a man his thought, his will, his personality, is a power of life and death; and that to enslave a man is to kill him. What, then, to this other question:* What is property? *may I not likewise answer, It is* theft, *without the certainty of being misunderstood; the second proposition being no other than a transformation of the first?*[11]

Property must disappear; possession should be given to those who do the work, but only for as long as they work. Society would become a group of federations of producers; and as later anarchists would hold, the power of the state would become unnecessary.

In such a society, the French socialist writer and labor organizer Flora Tristan urged, both the exploitation of the worker and the exploitation of women could be ended together. Yet her effort to enlist women in the cause of socialism and men in the cause of feminism was premature. "I have nearly the whole world against me," she wrote. "Men because I demand the emancipation of women, the owners because I demand the emancipation of the worker."

Louis Blanc and the National Workshops

Among the utopian socialists, Louis Blanc (1811–1882) was the only one to find a government willing to put his ideas into practice. In his *Organization of Work* (1840), he had satirized the supposed freedom of the worker to offer his labor to the employer who would pay him best.

What is competition, relative to the workers? It is work put up to auction. An entrepreneur has need of a worker: three present themselves. . . . How much for your work? . . . Three francs: I have a wife and children. . . . Good, and you? Two

[11]Cited in Albert Fried and Ronald Sanders, *Socialist Thought: A Documentary History* (Garden City, N.Y.: Doubleday, 1964), p. 201.

*and a half francs: I have no children, but I have a wife. . . . Marvellous. And you
. . . Two francs are enough for me: I am single. . . . You get the job. The transac-
tion is over: the bargain is concluded. What will become of the two proletarians
who are excluded? It is to be hoped that they will allow themselves to die of hunger. But suppose they become thieves? Have no fear; we have policemen. And
murderers? We have the hangman. As for the most fortunate of the three, his
triumph is only provisional. If there should come along a fourth worker sufficiently sturdy to fast every other day, wages will slide down to the bottom;
there will be a new pariah, a new recruit for the convict-prison, perhaps!*[12]

The worker, Blanc claimed, had the right to work; the state's duty was to
help him to do so by creating "social workshops." The workshops would
receive their initial capital from the state, would provide ideal working
conditions and good wages, and would therefore attract the best workers
away from private industry. The private capitalist, finding himself uncom-
petitive with the social workshops, would turn his business over to the
state, and thus in time the whole of industry would be organized into prosperous, cooperative units.

During the February revolution of 1848 in Paris, Blanc and another
working-class leader became members of the provisional government, and
pressed Lamartine and the democratic members to provide work for the
unemployed through national workshops. But the democrats, who had
little faith in social reform, sabotaged the scheme by refusing to put Blanc
in charge and by providing meaningless work. When one hundred twenty
thousand unemployed flocked into Paris to join the workshops, the government lost its nerve and ordered their dissolution. When the Parisians
again took to the barricades, the regular army was assembled against them.
In the bloody June Days, the first confrontation took place between the
democrats who wanted political reform, and the social reformers; and in
this battle of the streets, the conservatives and liberals joined forces with
the democrats in crushing the proletarian Reds. The June Days effectively
killed utopian socialism as a method of solving the evils of industrialism;
class reconciliation and the gradual adaptation of society to industrialization through cooperative units of production were regarded as idealistic
relics of little use in the class war that had been laid bare by General Ca-
vaignac's reconquest of Paris. The doctrine for the new age was "scientific"
socialism, better known after its founder as Marxism.

MARXISM

Perhaps the most important event of the year 1848 was the publication,
by a small group of German socialists, of a short pamphlet called *The
Communist Manifesto*, written by Karl Marx (1818–1883) and Friedrich Engels (1820–1895). Although at the time only a few hundred people
read the manifesto, it is now part of the official political philosophy of

---

[12]Cited in Gray, *Socialist Tradition*, pp. 221–222. Translation modified.

more than a billion people. Marx and Engels had provided the socialist movement with a theory of history, a materialist philosophy, an economic explanation of class conflict, and a blueprint for a new society. And they had given the working-class leaders a specific role in hurrying along the process of history, in exacerbating class conflict, and in realizing the new society.

The Philosophy of Marx

Marx was born in Trier on the Franco-German border, the son of a Jewish lawyer who had converted to Christianity when his son was six; but Marx was marked by a sense of messianic isolation that many have attributed to generations of rabbinic ancestors. Although he studied law at the Universities of Bonn and Berlin, he was swept away by the attractions of Hegelian philosophy. He soon changed fields, and after receiving his doctorate sought unsuccessfully a university post in philosophy. The first principles of Marxism were formulated in his argument with the followers of Hegel on the philosophy of history. Marx agreed with Hegel that history is a dynamic process, or dialectic, that moves forward through a series of conflicts: any given state of society (the thesis) produces its own opposite (the antithesis), and the conflict between the two leads to their amalgamation (the synthesis). Hegel, however, had seen the process of history as the working out of God's purpose, the realization of the Absolute Idea, which, Hegel apparently decided, had been achieved in the Prussian state. Such abstractions dissatisfied Marx, and he found the antidote in the materialist philosophy of Feuerbach. The dialectical process of history, Marx decided, was determined by economic forces, not by abstract ideas.

Dialectical Materialism

By 1845 Marx had formulated the two key ideas by which to apply this theory to actual historical events. The method of production at any time dictates the character of social relationships and the politics, law, and even the values and spiritual beliefs of a society. Medieval society, for example, believed in chivalry, the Church, and so on because it was based on agricultural production by unfree labor. Moreover, in the productive process there have always been two classes, the exploiter and the exploited, who are in political terms the ruler and the oppressed. The conflict of classes is the dialectic of history. The constant change in the means of production through technological advance, pressure of population, and so on, ensures that new classes will constantly arise to challenge the dominance of the established ruling class. Plebeian had challenged patrician; the journeyman, the guildmaster; the serf, the baron. But the most important challenge had been the attack of the commercial and manufacturing bourgeoisie on the feudal ruling class, which was an attack of a moneyed class on a landed class.

Here Marx's acquaintance with Engels, whom he met in 1842 but only got to know while Engels was working on *The Condition of the Working Class in England*, was invaluable. After failing to get a university post, Marx took up newspaper writing for a couple of years. But, hounded by the censors, he moved on to Paris and later to Brussels, and finally, after the failure of the Rhineland revolution in which he participated, to London. His knowledge of the proletariat before meeting Engels was slight, although he was burning with moral outrage. Engels provided him with the details of factory life, of slum conditions, of cyclical crises, that fed the passion with which, in the late 1840s, Marx analyzed the character of the proletariat. The working class, "instead of rising with the progress of industry, sinks ever deeper beneath the social conditions of [its] own class. The laborer becomes the pauper, and pauperism increases even more rapidly than population and wealth." Marx, however, much more than a polemicist, wanted to explain the condition of the proletariat in the broadest economic conditions. The poverty of the worker was explained by the labor theory of value. A product was only "so much congealed labor-time"; but the capitalist sold the product for several times more than he paid the worker in wages. The difference, "surplus value," the capitalist took for himself, a blatant form of exploitation. As a result of competition among the capitalists, however, their numbers were being constantly reduced, while the size of the proletariat was constantly increasing. While the proletariat was thus growing in strength, the capitalists themselves would find that the crises in the system would swell in number and intensity, thereby preparing the moment when the proletariat would be able to seize power itself.

Karl Marx (1818–1883)
Although delicately poetic in appearance when young, Marx later developed the girth and beard befitting the strong-willed patriarch of a revolutionary workers' movement. (Tass from Sovfoto)

The Proletarian Revolution

The Marxist theory of revolution was already complete in *The Communist Manifesto*. The process of economic change was inevitably working toward the victory of the proletariat over the bourgeoisie because industrial ownership was becoming restricted to fewer and fewer enormously wealthy capitalists, who by competition were weakening themselves. Once the bourgeoisie was overthrown, the working class would set up a dictatorship of indefinite length, which would set about putting an end to the dialectical process of history by creating a classless society. When no classes existed, presumably there could be no further conflict of classes. Slowly the workers' attitude to material things was to be transformed. During the stage when ideas carried over from capitalism were still prevalent, wages would be paid in accordance with the amount of work done, although already, since the state would have taken possession of all means of production, no capitalist would exist to appropriate surplus value for himself. When the new society was a reality, the slogan would be "from each according to his ability, to each according to his need." Women, too, would be liberated from their subjection within the family structure that had arisen as a result of the private ownership of property, Engels pointed out in an essay entitled *On the Origins of the Family, Private Property, and the State*. In this new society, therefore, human beings would be transformed in their very nature. Such institutions as the police and the army would become unnecessary. The organs of the state would be gradually allowed to wither away. "The government of persons is replaced by the administration of things and the direction of the process of production."

**A German Workers'
Meeting in 1890**
*(Courtesy of the German
Information Center)*

To Marx and Engels, the industrial revolution and, in fact, the rise of
the bourgeoisie, had been of enormous benefit to the human race because
they had destroyed the feudal society and simplified the class relationship
to the point where the proletariat could take power. In the classless society
they envisaged, the vast productive power of industrialism would be used
for the benefit of the workers, who alone produced the wealth.

There have been many criticisms of the theories of Marx and Engels.
They have been accused of overemphasizing the materialist motivation of
human beings and of ignoring such driving forces as patriotism and religion and even chance. It has been suggested that when they founded their
dialectic on changes in the means of production they were in fact linking
it to human initiative rather than to material forces. Their emphasis on
surplus value has been held to ignore the contribution of the capitalist to
the creation of wealth. Some historians have pointed out that the Marxian
assumption of the coming of an inevitable crisis of capitalism and of a reduction in the number of capitalists has not been borne out by events. Finally, many have objected that class war and violent revolution is an inhuman way to rescue humankind from inhumanity. Nevertheless, the
doctrine had a revolutionary appeal and an intellectual logic that was lacking in earlier Socialist theory, and the spread throughout Europe of Coketowns was providing Marx and his followers with the vast proletarian army
to which they had spoken in the *Manifesto*.

SUGGESTED READING

Nineteenth-century Manchester is considered a symbol of the new industrial city by Asa Briggs in *Victorian Cities* (1968), pp. 88–138. In this superb introduction, Briggs weighs particularly the reasons for the fictional treatment of Manchester and the value of such an approach. For graphic portrayals of industrial life, see Charles Dickens, *Hard Times*; Elizabeth Gaskell, *Mary Barton*; Benjamin Disraeli, *Coningsby*; and Kathleen Tillotson's study, *Novels of the Eighteen-Forties* (1954). Friedrich Engels's slashing study, written when he was twenty-four, *The Condition of the Working-Class in England*, is still a fascinating document of Manchester's contribution to the formulation of communist attitudes. For an introduction to Engels's experiences in Manchester, see Steven Marcus, *Engels, Manchester, and the Working Class* (1975).

For some scholarly inquiries into the character of Manchester business, there are Arthur Silver, *Manchester Men and Indian Cotton, 1847–1872* (1966); Michael M. Edwards, *The Growth of the British Cotton Trade, 1780–1815* (1967); and Arthur Redford, *Manchester Merchants and Foreign Trade, 1794–1858* (1934). The impact of Jewish immigration after the 1840s is traced in Bill Williams, *The Making of Manchester Jewry, 1740–1875* (1976).

For Manchester's economic theories, see W. D. Grampp, *The Manchester School of Economics* (1960). A fine overview of Manchester's history and geography is given in C. F. Carter, ed., *Manchester and Its Region* (1962); especially useful is W. H. Chaloner's chapter, "The Birth of Modern Manchester," pp. 131–146, which also, like Briggs, has a useful bibliography. Leon S. Marshall discusses the public reaction to the coming of industrialization in *The Development of Public Opinion in Manchester, 1780–1820* (1946). Frances Collier, *The Family Economy of the Working Classes in the Cotton Industry, 1784–1833* (1964) shows how individual families coped with industrial wages. Life in Salford, a suburb of Manchester, is movingly portrayed in Robert Roberts, *The Classic Slum* (1971). Michael Anderson, *Family Structure in Nineteenth Century Lancashire* (1971) is a quantitative sociological study of the family under the impact of industrialization in the nearby city of Preston. Josiah Slugg wrote his graphic impressions of Manchester during the early industrial revolution in 1881, in *Reminiscences of Manchester Fifty Years Ago* (new ed., 1971).

For the origins of the industrial revolution in England, brief surveys are provided by Arthur Redford, *The Economic History of England (1760–1860)* (1957) and T. S. Ashton, *The Industrial Revolution, 1760–1830* (1964). Paul Mantoux, *The Industrial Revolution in the Eighteenth Century* (1961) is still the fullest and most serviceable account and has much incidental detail on Manchester. Fine synthesis from the left-wing point of view is given by E. J. Hobsbawm in *Industry and Empire: An Economic History of Britain Since 1750* (1968) and in more abbreviated form in *The Age of Revolution: Europe 1789–1848* (1962), pp. 27–52. For the early nineteenth century, see John H. Clapham, *An Economic History of Modern Britain: The Early Railway Age, 1820–1850* (1930) and W. O. Henderson, *Britain and Industrial Europe 1750–1870* (1965) for the British influence on European industrialization. Modern economic techniques are applied to the study of economic growth in Phyllis Deane and W. A. Cole, *British Economic Growth, 1688–1959: Trends and Structure* (1962) and Patrick O'Brien and Caglar Keyder, *Economic Growth in Britain and France 1780–1914: Two Paths to the Twentieth Century* (1978). Many case studies are evoked in J. L. Hammond and Barbara

Hammond, *The Town Labourer, 1760–1832: The New Civilisation* (1932), and relevant anecdotes are cited by John Sanders, *Manchester* (1967). Enid Gauldie discusses living conditions in the slums in *Cruel Habitations: A History of Working-Class Housing, 1780–1918* (1974).

W. O. Henderson, *Britain and Industrial Europe 1750–1870* (1965) traces the direct influence of British inventions, entrepreneurs, and capital in creating industrialization on the continent. Henderson deals more fully with the industrial revolution in France, Germany, and Russia in *The Industrial Revolution on the Continent* (1967). Among the old-fashioned economic histories that are still useful and that one could profitably consult are Herbert Heaton, *Economic History of Europe* (1936), for continentwide treatment of various economic sectors, such as transportation, banking, and currency; and Shepard B. Clough and Charles W. Cole, *Economic History of Europe* (1952) on business organization. David S. Landes, *The Unbound Prometheus: Technological Change and Industrial Development in Western Europe from 1750 to the Present* (1969) is a fine up-to-date survey with a particularly useful analysis of "continental emulation" of British industrialization. Landes's book is an enlarged version of his chapter in the valuable *Cambridge Economic History of Europe*, vol. 6, *The Industrial Revolutions and After: Incomes, Population and Technological Change* (1965), in which W. A. Cole and Phyllis Deane (pp. 1–55) assess the impact of industrialization on the growth of national incomes. Arthur Birnie's short *An Economic History of Europe 1760–1939* (1962) is useful on social reform. Everyone should read Walter W. Rostow's little book, *The Stages of Economic Growth: A Non-Communist Manifesto* (1960), which presents his theory of the "takeoff" into sustained economic growth.

Much recent work in economic history, and particularly in the history of the industrial revolution, has drawn so heavily from economics that it claims to be the "new economic history." To sample this approach, see R. M. Hartwell, ed., *The Causes of the Industrial Revolution* (1967) and Simon Kuznets, the economist on whose studies the new economic historians have depended so largely, *Modern Economic Growth: Rate, Structure, and Spread* (1966). Phyllis Deane considers the first century of industrialization in the new economic framework of theories of growth in *The First Industrial Revolution* (1965).

John H. Clapham, *The Economic Development of France and Germany 1815–1914* (1963) is urbane and very readable; Rondo E. Cameron, *France and the Economic Development of Europe, 1800–1914* (1966) emphasizes international finance. Two basic accounts of France's slow industrialization are A. L. Dunham, *The Industrial Revolution in France, 1815–1848* (1953) and Shepard B. Clough, *France: A History of National Economics, 1789–1939* (1939). Theodore S. Hamerow relates economic development to political change in *Restoration, Revolution, Reaction: Economics and Politics in Germany, 1815–1871* (1966). The importance of the German customs union is assessed in W. O. Henderson, *The Zollverein* (1959).

The doctrines of nineteenth-century liberalism are ably abbreviated in John Plamenatz, ed., *Readings from Liberal Writers, English and American* (1965); but the most persuasive approach is to go directly to Adam Smith, *Inquiry into the Nature and Causes of the Wealth of Nations* and John Stuart Mill, *On Liberty* (many editions). Guido de Ruggiero, *The History of European Liberalism* (1927) contrasts the different versions in France, Germany, and Italy. On the political democrats, see Asa Briggs, ed., *Chartist Studies* (1960); Mark Hovell, *The Chartist Movement* (1925), old but reliable; and John Plamenatz, *The Revolutionary Movement in France, 1815–1871* (1952).

Jürgen Kuczynski, *The Rise of the Working Class* (1967) is a fascinating dissection, from a left-wing point of view, of the nature of the working class, presenting international similarities and national differences. E. P. Thompson, *The Making of the English Working Class* (1963) analyzes the structure of the laboring class and its sense of class consciousness. An excellent selection of documents of socialist theory is made by Albert Fried and Ronald Sanders, eds., *Socialist Thought: A Documentary History* (1964); one should, however, read *The Communist Manifesto* somewhere, perhaps in Karl Marx and Friedrich Engels, *Basic Writings on Politics and Philosophy* (1959), edited by Lewis S. Feur. Early socialist theory is surveyed, but with inadequate commentary, in G. D. H. Cole, *Socialist Thought*, vol. 1, *The Forerunners, 1789–1850* (1955); and Alexander Gray, *The Socialist Tradition: From Moses to Lenin* (1947). Edmund Wilson, *To the Finland Station: A Study in the Writing and Acting of History* (1940) is incisive in relating personal experiences to social history, particularly for Marx and Engels. Two fine lives of Marx are Isaiah Berlin, *Karl Marx* (1948) and Franz Mehring, *Karl Marx* (1962).

Louise A. Tilly and Joan W. Scott, in *Women, Work, and Family* (1978), discuss the transition in England and France from a "family economy" in the preindustrial period to a "family wage economy" in the industrial revolution to a "family consumer economy" in the twentieth century. In *Working Women in Nineteenth Century Europe* (1979), they show that the separation of work and home as a result of industrialization increased women's dependence upon men as wage earners. Patricia Branca's *Women in Europe Since 1750* (1978) is an admirably succinct account of the changing roles of women at work and in the home and of the rise of the women's movement. Ivy Pinchbeck, *Women Workers and the Industrial Revolution, 1750–1850* (1930, 1969) is a pioneering study in women's history that is still of value. Theresa M. McBride, *The Domestic Revolution: The Modernization of Household Service in England and France, 1820–1920* (1976) weighs the advantages and disadvantages for the millions of young women employed as household servants.

24

THE LONDON OF VICTORIA

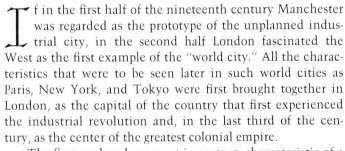

He did notice one peculiarity about it worth remembering. London was still London. A certain style dignified its grime; heavy, clumsy, arrogant, purse-proud, but not cheap; insular but large; barely tolerant of an outside world, and absolutely self-confident.—Henry Adams in 1858

If in the first half of the nineteenth century Manchester was regarded as the prototype of the unplanned industrial city, in the second half London fascinated the West as the first example of the "world city." All the characteristics that were to be seen later in such world cities as Paris, New York, and Tokyo were first brought together in London, as the capital of the country that first experienced the industrial revolution and, in the last third of the century, as the center of the greatest colonial empire.

The first, and perhaps most important, characteristic of a world city is a very large population distributed over a very large area. By 1900 Greater London had a population of over six million inhabitants spread over more than seven hundred square miles. This expansion had been made possible by the mechanization of transport. Middle-class commuters moved out to newly developed suburban areas after con-

(Left Page) Crystal Palace, Sydenham, South London, c. 1853 (*Greater London Council Photograph Library*); (Inset) Victoria, 1852 (*BBC Hulton Picture Library*)

struction of the railroads in the 1830s. The dispersion of the poorer classes was brought about by the construction of the underground railroad in 1865 and the advent of street rails for horse-drawn trams (and later electrically powered streetcars) in the 1880s.

Second, the world city's population is drawn from the whole world. London's population was constantly augmented by the influx of great numbers of migrants from within Britain and abroad. The railroads brought into London the dispossessed and the ambitious of the countryside and the northern cities, as well as the poor and politically oppressed from the south and east of Europe; the steamship brought migrants from the empire, Indians and Chinese above all.

Third, the world city has direct industrial and commercial ties to the rest of the planet. The steamships brought into the Port of London eight million tons of goods in 1880, compared with only eight hundred thousand at the beginning of the century; and Baedeker was sending visitors to

◆ *The London of Victoria* ◆

Period Surveyed	Reign of Queen Victoria (1837–1901)
Population	County of London: 1.9 million (1841); 2.8 million (1861); 3.8 million (1881); 4.14 million (1901)
Area	County of London, 117 square miles, including City of London (1.05 square miles) and City of Westminster (3.91 square miles)
Form of Government	Constitutional monarchy; Houses of Parliament as legislature (hereditary House of Lords, elected House of Commons); executive (prime minister and cabinet). City government: public works through Metropolitan Board of Works after 1855, local administration by London County Council after 1888.
Political Leaders	Queen Victoria and Prince Consort Albert; prime ministers Peel, Palmerston, Disraeli, Gladstone
Economic Base	National and imperial bureaucracy; law courts; banking and stock exchange; international commerce; light industry; freight and passenger transportation by water and rail
Intellectual Life	Novel (Thackeray, Dickens, H. G. Wells); poetry (Wordsworth, Tennyson, Browning); painting (Turner, Rossetti, Morris); theology (Newman); science (Joule, Darwin)
Principal Buildings	Tower of London; St. Paul's Cathedral; Westminster Abbey; Buckingham Palace; townhouses of aristocracy; houses of Parliament; railroad stations
Public Entertainment	Soccer and cricket matches; horse racing; theater (opera, symphony, plays, vaudeville); dance halls, public houses (beer, gin); royal and military processions
Religion	Church of England; many Protestant sects; Roman Catholic minority; Jews

"London Going Out of Town—Or—The March of Bricks and Mortar," by George Cruikshank (1792–1878) *Cruikshank's engraved caricatures made mordant comment on the ecological disaster of uncontrolled urban expansion.*

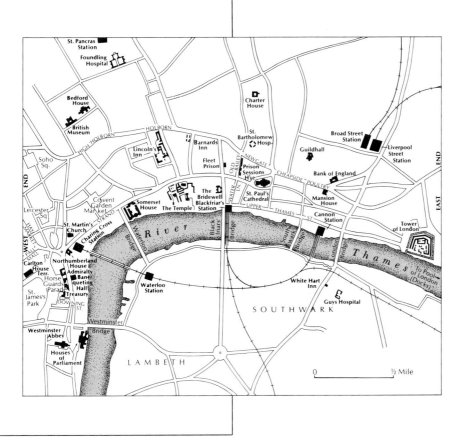

see the warehouses that could store two hundred thousand tons of goods. "Nothing will convey to the stranger a better idea of the vast activity and stupendous wealth of London," he wrote, "than a visit to the warehouses, filled to overflowing with interminable stores of every kind of foreign and colonial product."

Fourth, the world city is deeply involved in the internal affairs of other nations. For Victorian London this involved a dual responsibility. It was the administrator of a growing colonial empire and the undisputed leader of a group of self-governing dominions; and as its industrial supremacy and its naval might made it, at least until about 1870, the major power in the world, it was a necessary participant in all important world affairs. Indeed at times its attitude seemed well summed up by the popular music hall song:

> *We don't want to fight*
> *But by Jingo, if we do*
> *We've got the men, we've got the ships,*
> *We've got the money too.*

SOCIAL TENSION IN BRITAIN, 1815–1848

The years between the defeat of Napoleon at Waterloo and the continentwide revolutions in 1848 were not years of social peace in Britain. The predominant mood was disquiet about the future of British society, brought on by distrust of British institutions on the one side and fear for their survival on the other. It is true that the industrial revolution was continuing unabated, and that production rose at an average of thirty-seven percent each decade. Yet the working classes were continuously discontented and intermittently riotous.

In the 1830s and 1840s, bad harvests combined with the tariff on imported wheat to keep food prices high; downturns in the business cycle, uncontrolled by government action, produced severe unemployment; and there was even a fall in the real wages of those who had jobs. The reform measures that were finally passed in the 1840s, such as the Factory Acts, were little more than palliatives. Barely surviving in the squalid poverty of the great northern industrial cities and in the slums of London itself, the British urban poor felt little benefit from the industrial revolution that had transformed their lives and little hope of improvement from the activity of the men who governed them.

Political Aims of the Tory and Whig Parties

Discontent with Britain's policies and institutions provoked continuous conflict in Parliament between the two main parties, the Tories and the Whigs. The Tories, composed of the aristocratic landlords, the Church of England, and the army, represented the conservative groups in British society; they held office from 1815 to 1830. The general attitude of the

Tories was to favor agriculture (especially by passing and upholding the Corn Laws of 1815, which banned importation of foreign wheat until the English price rose to eighty shillings per quarter) and to maintain a mercantilist economic policy.[1] The Whigs, representing mainly but not exclusively the liberal groups in British society, were composed of the older commercial classes, the new industrialists from the North, and many of the professional classes. They wanted cheap food for the working classes (and thus lower wages) through abolition of the Corn Laws, and an end to all forms of state interference in the economic system, such as tariffs. But they also demanded a change in the British electoral system, which was a strange hodgepodge of anachronisms inherited from the Middle Ages. The new industrial cities like Manchester and Birmingham had no parliamentary representation. Many boroughs sending members to Parliament had little or no population and were in the "pocket" of some great landowner. No constituency had more than a few thousand voters, and they were usually bribed. The liberal demand, however, was for a property-owning democracy; Parliament had to be made responsive to the wishes of the industrial middle class, which was described by one of its principal theorists as "the wisest part of the community."

Power seesawed between the Tories and Whigs; but on many crucial issues, conscience or self-interest drove large numbers to cross party and even class lines. The Tories repealed the Combination Acts forbidding

[1] The word *corn* is used to denote a country's principal grain crop. In England, corn is wheat; in Scotland, corn is oats; in the United States, corn is maize!

Westminster Bridge, the Houses of Parliament, and Westminster Abbey, by John Anderson
The neo-Gothic Parliament building was erected after a fire in 1834 destroyed the palace where the House of Lords and House of Commons had met since 1547. (Museum of London)

workers to form trade unions, and Tories were the leaders of the movement for reform of working conditions in the factories. In 1846, Whig pressure and fear of an uprising in Ireland following famine compelled Sir Robert Peel, the Tory prime minister, to repeal the Corn Laws. The Whigs focused their demands for reform upon the country's electoral system. In 1832, they forced through Parliament a reform bill, which at last gave representation to the industrial cities and gave the wealthier middle class the suffrage. But only one man in five was enfranchised; and no women were given the vote. The Reform Bill of 1832 was, however, of great significance for the future of British democracy: it showed that greater degrees of self-government could be won piecemeal without revolution.

Disillusionment with the Monarchy and the Empire

The general discontent with the nature of parliamentary representation had even, in the early part of the century, extended to include the monarchy itself. George III had been totally insane in the last years of his reign. His son George IV (reigned 1820–1830) was interested only in buildings, food, and clothes. William IV (reigned 1830–1837) was, in the words of *The Spectator*, "a weak, ignorant, commonplace sort of person." Little more was expected of Victoria when she ascended the throne in 1837 at the age of eighteen, unprepared by education or background for her new responsibilities.

As for the empire, which was to become the chief source of national pride by the end of Victoria's reign, no popular enthusiasm was felt for colonial possessions. The loss of the American colonies after seven years of fighting had provoked in the general public a mood of disillusionment that still persisted in the middle of the nineteenth century. Since colonies were, in the much-quoted phrase of a French diplomat, "ripe fruit that fall from the parent bough," it hardly appeared worth the sacrifice of soldiers and money to found them. Only the working classes showed any interest in the remaining colonial possessions. In the 1830s, over one hundred thousand persons emigrated annually; and the number increased to two hundred thousand annually in the 1840s. The usual destination was Canada, Australia, New Zealand, or southern Africa, but large numbers also migrated to the United States. But it was economic necessity and not imperial patriotism that motivated the migrants. Their exodus was yet another sign of the widespread discontent with British society at the beginning of Victoria's reign.

THE TWO LONDONS: WEST END AND EAST END

London itself in the early nineteenth century was a graphic illustration of the gulf that existed between the poor and the well-to-do in British society. To the east of the Tower of London, stretching on both banks of the river Thames, was the East End, where by 1841 over half a million people lived in conditions of appalling deprivation. To the west, beyond

Ludgate Hill, by Gustave Doré (1833–1883). Engraving for Blanchard Jerrold's *London: A Pilgrimage* **(1872)**

the predominantly business district of the old City of London, were the aristocratic and middle-class squares and terraces of the West End. The contrast between the two sections of the city, at least until the 1870s or 1880s, became increasingly stark.

The West End

London had developed from two nuclei, Westminster, where the king resided and Parliament met, and the City of London, where the port, trading companies, and financial offices were situated. By the end of the eighteenth century, when London had a population of about eight hundred thousand, the two nuclei were joined in a continuous band of buildings, with a thoroughfare called the Strand joining the older sections. After a period of slow growth between 1700 and 1750, the West End had been vastly expanded by the creation of a number of large squares, with terraced houses on all four sides and miniature parks in the middle, which were joined up by long, terraced streets composed of less expensive houses. Great aristocrats like Lord Burlington created whole sections of the city around their own townhouses and leased them to others of acceptable rank and fortune. The houses were usually of red brick, with delicately columned doorways, high, stuccoed ceilings, and tall windows. All were solid and comfortable, with ample provision of space in the basement and the attic for a number of servants. All too were within easy reach of the great parks like Hyde Park. The one monumental riverfront development was the Adelphi, near the Waterloo Bridge, the creation of the great architect Robert Adam; but Londoners seemed to have little taste for grandiose housing of the type favored in Paris. The houses in the Adelphi terrace had to be sold by lottery.

At the end of the eighteenth century, however, the taste of the aristocrats and middle class became more luxurious. Whole new areas were developed, such as Belgravia in the neighborhood of Buckingham Palace, the ultimate aristocratic quarter of London. The most favored architect was John Nash, whose white stuccoed terraces were erected along the monumental mall that led to Buckingham Palace, overlooking the picturesque new Regent's Park, and along the great curve of Regent's Street north from Piccadilly Circus. Nash's abandonment of red brick radically changed the appearance of the West End:

> *Augustus at Rome was for building renowned*
> *And of marble he left what of brick he had found;*
> *But is not our Nash, too, a very great master,*
> *He finds us all brick and leaves us all plaster.*

But no one style predominated. The nineteenth century was the heyday of period revivals; and for this the Romantic movement was primarily responsible. With the rejection of industrialism by the supporters of Romanticism, any period before the industrial revolution appeared aesthetically valuable. King George IV, while still prince regent, even introduced Indian Mogul architecture in the fanciful pavilion he built on the seacoast in Brighton. For such sober buildings as the British Museum or Euston railroad station, a neo-Greek style of architecture was used. The great London clubs and many of the banks were disguised as Florentine palaces. But the most popular style was a Gothic revival.

The leader of the Gothic revival was Augustus Welby Pugin, who had shown in his *True Principles of Pointed or Christian Architecture* that Christian morals and Gothic art went together. By the mid-nineteenth century, Victorian London was in a fervor for medievalism. The art critic John Ruskin in *Seven Lamps of Architecture* was praising the medieval centuries for their purity of faith as reflected in their art. Thomas Carlyle was directing the historians back to the heroes of the Middle Ages, while novelist Walter Scott was thrilling his readers with the broad sweep of distant battles and crusading kings. Many, like John Henry Newman, who later

Sussex Terrace, London, by John Nash (1752–1835)
John Nash's monumental terraces, which overlooked the lawns of Regent's Park and lined the streets of central London near Buckingham Palace, imposed a sense of urban order on the city's confused growth. (Greater London Council Photograph Library)

Royal Pavilion, Brighton, England
Nash built this fanciful adaptation of a Moslem temple in India as a seaside villa for the prince regent, the future king George IV, at a time when sea bathing was first becoming fashionable. (BBC Hulton Picture Library)

became a cardinal, took the Gothic apostasy to its ultimate conclusion and were converted to Catholicism. Some of England's leading painters even rejected the High Renaissance and sought to return to the supposed purity of the Italian painters before Raphael. In 1848, a group under the leadership of Dante Gabriel Rossetti founded the Pre-Raphaelite Brotherhood, setting the style for the 1850s with bright colors, affectedly innocent tableaux of religious or rural scenes, and grotesque recreations of scenes from medieval chronicles. Thus when the Houses of Parliament burned down in 1834, it was no surprise that the winning design for the new buildings along the Thames riverfront should have been in Gothic Revival style.

The East End

London had already possessed slum areas in the eighteenth century that appalled and fascinated painters like William Hogarth. But they were small in comparison with those that sprang up in the first forty years of the nineteenth century, when London's population increased by a million as a result of better medical care and greater employment openings in the huge new docks and London's expanding industries like foodstuffs, drink, building materials, and soap. The bulk of the new population lived in the

Over London—by Rail, by Gustave Doré

The Southwark
Waterworks, by George
Cruikshank

"Salus populi suprema lex"
("The people's health is the
highest law") is Cruik-
shank's comment on the use
of the polluted Thames
River for London's drinking
water.

boroughs to the east of the City, in Stepney, Poplar, Bethnal Green, Bermondsey, and Southwark. The squalid conditions in these districts were
described in 1842 by the great reformer Edwin Chadwick, in his *Report on
the Sanitary Conditions of the Labouring Classes*; and his exposés were
followed over the next half-century by a proliferation of official and unofficial reports, of which the most influential was the seventeen-volume *Life
and Labour of the People in London*, published between 1886 and 1903, by
Charles Booth, a philanthropic Liverpool shipowner.

The contrast of West and East ends, which increased during the century, fascinated both English and foreign observers. The reason was obvious. "I was yesterday . . . over the cholera districts of Bermondsey," the
novelist Charles Kingsley wrote his wife in 1849. "And, oh God! what I
saw! People having no water to drink—hundreds of them—but the water of
the common sewer which stagnates full of . . . dead fish, cats and dogs, under their windows." Owing to an almost total lack of public administration
in the newer areas—London did not get a city government until 1888—
there were few public services. Water, often polluted, was supplied by nine
private companies at a profit, and usually was turned on only a few hours a
day three times a week. Drainage was inadequate; uncovered ditches emp-

Night in the East End, by Gustave Doré

tied the cesspools into the river Thames, which became, in *Punch's* words, a "foul sludge and foetid stream." Cemeteries were overcrowded, and bodies buried above street level; shallow graves were inadequately provided, in pest fields and plague pits, for victims of the epidemics. No controls were extended to housing contractors, who threw up the slums called rookeries. The author of one report found 1,465 families in an area near London's most fashionable church, living in 2,174 rooms with only 2,510 beds among them. But it was Dickens, in *Bleak House*, who permitted the London bourgeois to follow Kingsley's advice: "Go, scented Belgravian, and see what London is."

Jo lives—that is to say, Jo has not yet died—in a ruinous place, known to the like of him by the name of Tom-all-Alone's. It is a black, dilapidated street, avoided by all decent people; where the crazy houses were seized upon, when their decay was far advanced, by some bold vagrants, who, after establishing their own possession, took to letting them out in lodgings. Now, these tumbling tenements contain, by night, a swarm of misery. As on the ruined human wretch, vermin parasites appear, so these ruined shelters have bred a crowd of foul existence that crawls in and out of gaps in walls and boards; and coils itself to sleep, in maggot numbers, where the rain drips in; and comes and goes, fetching and carrying fever, and sowing more evil in its every footprint than Lord Coodle, and Sir Thomas Doodle, and the Duke of Foodle, and all the fine gentlemen in office, down to Zoodle, shall set right in five hundred years—though born expressly to do it.

The vast numbers of poor were compelled to seek work in conditions of great hardship. The worst exploitation did not take place in factories but among small employers, particularly in the clothing trade where so-called sweated labor was normal. Women and children worked at sewing in their homes for very small wages; they received four shillings and sixpence for sewing a dozen shirts. As a result of the lack of regular employment, thousands turned to trades like hawking and others less legal. Henry Mayhew, in his very influential book *London Labour and the London Poor* (1861), estimated that there were thirteen thousand street traders, many of whom he interviewed. They included the children called mud-larks, who scraped the Thames mud for scraps of coal dropped by the barges; sellers of sheeps' trotters, ham sandwiches, flowers, and birds' nests; and costermongers, who sold fish, fruit, and vegetables. There were also the dredgers, who went into the river for dead bodies, and the sewer hunters, who searched for bottles or iron that could be sold. Mayhew's books became a mine for novelists like Kingsley and Dickens; but Mayhew's own ear for the language of the interviewed and the illustrations he published were as effective as any novel in waking the conscience of London. His twenty-two-year-old birds'-nest seller told him:

Mother died five years ago in the Consumption Hospital at Chelsea, just after it was built. I was very young indeed when father died; I can hardly remember him. He died in Middlesex Hospital: he had abscesses all over him; there were six-and-thirty at the time of his death. . . . I'm a very little eater, and perhaps that's the luckiest thing for such as me; half a pound of bread and a few potatoes will do me for the day. If I could afford it, I used to get a ha'porth of coffee and a ha'porth

Dudley Street, Seven Dials, by Gustave Doré

of sugar and make it do twice. Sometimes I used to have victuals given to me, sometimes I went without altogether; and sometimes I couldn't eat. I can't always.[2]

It was hardly surprising then that crime, especially theft, was rampant. The police believed that some twenty thousand children were being trained in thieving in the 1860s, in the way Dickens described in *Oliver Twist*. Prostitution was widespread. Gambling was a full-time profession for ten thousand people. By the 1880s, it was common for reformers to compare the London slums unfavorably with the jungles of central Africa being described contemporaneously by England's explorers and missionaries. General William Booth's *In Darkest England and the Way Out* began with the comment, "The lot of the Negroes in the Equatorial Forest is not, perhaps, a very happy one, but is it so very much worse than that of many a pretty orphan girl in our Christian capital?"[3]

Metropolitan Reform   The authors of the reports on London were clear on the reforms needed to remedy the problems of unplanned urban growth. They did not condemn the whole structure of capitalist society, as the Socialist reformers were doing, but, as practical people, they suggested practical reforms. London needed public construction and maintenance of a network of drains and sewers, and public provision of pure water. Slums had to be cleared and decent public housing provided. Public asylums for the insane and public hospitals for the indigent sick had to be built. Above all London needed a metropolitan government to deal with the problems of the whole sprawling area in a unified way. Slowly the reformers gained their way. In the 1850s there was established a Metropolitan Board of Works, which began a large-scale building program and sanitary improvements. Parks were purchased. Burial boards, an asylums board, a school board, and finally in 1888 a London County Council were created. Life was still hard for the London poor, as the riots known as Bloody Monday in 1886 and Bloody Sunday in 1887 demonstrated. But a start at least had been made in remedying the most blatant grievances.

CHARLES DICKENS: THE NOVELIST AS SOCIAL REFORMER

If any one person should be given greatest credit for awakening the conscience of the British to the conditions of the slums and the poor who dwelled there, it is the novelist Charles Dickens; and in the English novel he had the ideal instrument for spreading his message of outrage and sympathy.

[2]John L. Bradley, ed., *Selections from London Labour and the London Poor* (Oxford: Oxford University Press, 1965), p. 116.
[3]Cited in Asa Briggs, *Victorian Cities* (Harmondsworth, England: Penguin, 1968), pp. 313–314.

With the publication in 1740 of Samuel Richardson's *Pamela*, the modern form of novel was invented. There had been storytelling in prose for two millennia at least, in Apuleius's *The Golden Ass*, for example, and the Arabian *Tales of a Thousand and One Nights*. But in London in the mid-eighteenth century, writers used the story in prose to probe human motivation, explore individual character, and present a reconstruction of all the varieties of contemporary life, as they engaged in a dramatic form of infinite complexity. With Henry Fielding, who was a magistrate in the Bow Street law court and the head of the equivalent of the London police, the great variety of the London underworld first entered the English novel; and in his masterpiece *Tom Jones*, after delighting in the rollicking scenes of bucolic life in the West Country, we are thrown into the rough slums of London that Hogarth depicted in his painting *Gin Lane*. By 1836, when Charles Dickens had swept his way to fame by depicting the meeting of Mr. Pickwick and his inimitable valet, Sam Weller, in the fifteenth number of the serialization of *The Pickwick Papers*, the novel had won a vast following among the middle-class patrons of the monthly magazine and the lending library. With Jane Austen, it had explored the art of showing subtleties of character through the niceties of conversation. With Walter Scott, it had spread itself over past panoramas of time and space, becoming the instrument for the Romantic movement's recreation of the imagined dramas of medieval life. With Disraeli, it had begun to explore the nature of English class distinction. But Dickens was able to create a world in his

The English Novel

St. Pancras Hotel and Station, by John O'Connor
The grand Gothic railroad station and hotel stand in sharp contrast to the drab workers' homes of northern London. (Museum of London)

novels that for many had a greater reality and coherence, and a more poignant message than the necessarily restricted sphere of their own daily lives.

Dickens's London

For his readers, Dickens described parts of London they had never known, or gave meaning to the parts they knew. In *Bleak House*, it was the law courts along the Strand and the lawyers' chambers in Lincoln's Inn Fields, characterized by the fog that penetrates everything. "Fog everywhere. Fog up the river, where it flows among green aits and meadows; fog down the river, where it rolls defiled among the tiers of shipping and the waterside pollutions of a great (and dirty) city. Fog on the Essex marshes, fog on the Kentish heights. . . . And hard by Temple Bar, in Lincoln's Inn Hall, at the very heart of the fog, sits the Lord High Chancellor in his High Court of Chancery." In *Oliver Twist*, it was the dark recesses along the riverbank where Fagin's gang lurked, where "the old smoke-stained storehouses on either side rose heavy and dull from the dense mass of roofs and gables, and frowned sternly upon water too black to reflect even their lumbering shapes." And there was the den in the slums where Fagin trained his boys as pickpockets, "these foul'd and frowsty dens, where vice is closely packed and lacks the room to turn." Mr. Pickwick was consigned to a debtors' prison, just as Dickens's own father had been:

"Ohr," replied Mr. Pickwick, looking down a dark and filthy staircase, which appeared to lead to a range of damp and gloomy stone vaults, beneath the ground, "and those, I suppose are the little cellars where the prisoners keep their small quantities of coals. Unpleasant places to have to go down to, but very convenient, I dare say." "Yes, I shouldn't wonder if they was convenient," replied the gentleman, "seeing that a few people live there, pretty snug." . . . "My friend," said Mr. Pickwick, "you don't really mean to say that human beings live down in those wretched dungeons?" "Live down there! Yes, and die down there, too, very often!" replied Mr. Roker; "and what of that? Who's got to say anything agin it?"

The Londoners of Dickens

But even more than he did with places, Dickens brought alive a vast gallery of London characters. His anger blazed against the heartless and irresponsible among the middle classes. Mr. Snawley abandons his stepchildren to Mr. Squeers's nightmarelike school of Dotheboys Hall, in *Nicholas Nickleby*:

"Not too much writing home allowed, I suppose?" said the step-father hesitating.
"None, except a circular at Christmas, to say they never were so happy, and hope they may never be sent for," rejoined Squeers.
"Nothing could be better," said the step-father, rubbing his hands.

Unscrupulous lawyers abound in his pages. It is through the machinations of the firm of Dodson and Fogg that Mr. Pickwick finds himself in the Fleet Prison. In *Bleak House*, the trial of *Jarndyce* v. *Jarndyce* has been prolonged for years, the symbol of the profitable legal procrastination of the court of chancery, "which has its worn-out lunatic in every madhouse and its dead in every churchyard." The bureaucrats who froze an army to death in the Crimean War appear as the Tite Barnacles of the Circumlocution Office in *Little Dorrit*. There is the cheap, hypocritical crook, like Uriah Heep in *David Copperfield*; and in *Oliver Twist* the violent, unthinking thief, like Bill Sikes, and Fagin, the almost likable trainer of pickpockets and psychological master of outcast children. Only occasionally is there an oasis of quiet and good will, like Pickwick's Christmas with the Wardles at Dingley Dell. Usually Dickens's characters cannot avoid the great swelling tide of social injustice and the human malice that grows in such a system. For all his humor, Dickens's London was a place where the sufferings of human beings needed remedy. His method, which was to create innumerable scenes from the great macrocosm of metropolitan life and then to intensify the effect by showing those scenes through the eyes of a large number of characters, was perfect for his task.

Dickens was able to bring alive the different worlds of London but especially those in need of reform—the prisons, hospitals, mortuaries, slums, poorhouses, schools, countinghouses, law courts, hustings, ministries, factories, shipyards, cab stands, fishmarkets. "Heart of London," he wrote, "I seem to hear a voice within thee that sinks into my heart, bidding me, as I elbow my way among the crowd, to have some thought for the meanest wretch that passes, and, being a man, to turn away with scorn and pride from none that wears the human shape." In spite of his sentimentality and sensationalism, or perhaps because of them, Dickens impressed on his huge reading public his own vision of a London in which the mechanism of society had not kept up with the needs of its diverse humanity. He was the reformers' finest ally.

VICTORIAN RELIGION

The reformers had another ally, however, that spread through Victorian society even more pervasively than the writings of Dickens—the sense of the obligations of religion.

In the early years of the century, the reforming forces within organized religion were to be found in the dissenting sects (that is, those branches of Christian worship, such as the Methodists or Congregationalists, who dissented from the beliefs or form of worship of the Anglican and the Catholic churches) or in the evangelical, or reformist, wing of the Anglican Church. By Victoria's reign, "evangelicalism" had come to denote an attitude of moral rectitude, an emphasis on the sense of sin and the need for self-improvement, and a reliance on Bible reading and strict religious observance regardless of whether the evangelical was an Anglican or a dissenter. The most famous of the early evangelicals had been the Clapham

Evangelicalism and the Oxford Movement

A Victorian Family at Home, c. 1860

Victorian morality viewed the cohesion of the family as the safeguard of social stability. For the middle classes, the prime responsibility of a wife or a daughter was the smooth running of the home. (BBC Hulton Picture Library)

Sect, named after the village just outside London where the members met. Their leaders, especially William Wilberforce and Lord Shaftesbury, had successfully fought a number of crusades for social reform that had culminated in the abolition of the slave trade in 1807 and slavery in the British Empire in 1833; in the Factory Acts of the 1830s and 1840s; and in the banning of all public amusement on the Sabbath. The changes that accompanied the parliamentary reform of 1832 and the establishment of municipal governments after 1835 strengthened the evangelical movement, bringing its adherents to power in the local districts and increasing their influence in Parliament.

"Evangelical morality," as Noel Annan has shown, "was the single most widespread influence in Victorian England. . . . It spread through every class and taught a clear set of values."[4] The evangelicals felt that they

---

[4]Noel Annan, *Leslie Stephen* (London: McGibbon and Kee, 1951), p. 110.

experienced God personally, in their daily emotional communication with Him; they knew from their conversion that they were saved; and they were confident that they had the power, and knew they had the duty, to go into the world to do God's work.

In the 1830s, however, the main body of the Church of England was stirred from a somnolence due to anachronistic organization and clerical indifference by a very different type of religious enthusiasm from evangelicalism, the Oxford Movement. Many of the leaders of the movement sprang from the evangelical groups, found in their upbringing a sense of religious certainty, and then rejected evangelicalism for its inability to accept the Catholic origins of the Anglican Church, or even Catholicism itself. In *Tracts for the Times*, the preachers of the Oxford Movement demanded a return to the deep devotion of the seventeenth-century Church, with its emphasis on authority, ritual, liturgy, and ecclesiastical decoration. By 1840 this "High Church" revival had roused great interest, which was not dissipated when several of its most influential leaders, like Newman, converted to Roman Catholicism.

Popular Attitudes Toward Religion

When a religious census was taken in England for a Sunday in 1851, it showed that over seven million people attended church that day, of whom just over half went to Anglican services. The census, which shocked many by showing that so few of the population had gone to church, proved conclusively that religious attendance was a matter of class standing or even of income. The reaction was a new effort from the 1850s by all denominations to reach the poor through church building, increases in the number of clergy, the founding of church schools and Sunday schools, and genuine missionary activity, which included the support of revivalist preachers from the United States and in the eighties the founding of the Salvation Army. Thus from the 1860s there was a strong religious revival that affected the poorer sections of society and combined with the movement for the simultaneous improvements of their material conditions. It is ironic that the most dramatic example of the strength of the religious revival was the Victorian Sabbath. In many middle-class homes, diversions like cards, music, dancing, and reading anything other than the Bible were forbidden. Screens were even put in front of pictures in Ruskin's house. All public amusements were closed, which caused more hardship on the poor than on anyone else, as Dickens complained in *Little Dorrit*.

Everything was belted and barred that could possibly furnish relief to an overworked people. No pictures, no unfamiliar animals, no rare plants or flowers, no natural or artificial wonders of the ancient world—all taboo with that enlightened strictness, that the ugly South Sea gods in the British Museum might have supposed themselves at home again. Nothing to see but streets, streets, streets. Nothing to breathe but streets, streets, streets. Nothing to change the brooding mind, or raise it up. Nothing for the spent toiler to do but to compare the monotony of his seventh day with the monotony of his six days, think what a weary life he led and make the best of it—or the worst, according to the probabilities.

There are many possible explanations for this religious enthusiasm. Religion brought a sense of hope and self-importance to many who felt ignored by the political and economic systems. It provided emotional release—to some through the vestments and rituals of the High Church or of Catholicism, to others through revivalism or evangelicalism. It canalized the moral forces that sought remedy for social injustice. For women it provided socially approved activity in charity and philanthropy outside the home; many Victorian women, like Mary Carpenter and Octavia Hill, worked toward a reduction in juvenile delinquency and an upgrading of housing and living conditions for the poor. For some, like the architect Pugin, it was a reaction against the values of an industrial age. For most it coincided with the Victorian belief in self-improvement preached by everyone from the self-made businessman to the costermonger of Mayhew. Above all, the religious revival succeeded because it was led by a number of people of extraordinary personality and often of great intellect, such as John Keble, who began the Oxford Movement; the Catholic converts Newman and Manning; William Booth, who founded the Salvation Army; Thomas Arnold, who made religion a bulwark of boarding-school education; the novelist Charles Kingsley, who preached Christian socialism; and Charles Spurgeon, who brought the poor of the London borough of Southwark into the Baptist Church by the thousands.

THE SELF-CONFIDENCE OF THE MID-VICTORIAN AGE, 1848–1873

The religious sobriety and sense of purpose of the Victorian middle classes were admirably personified in the royal family, especially after Victoria's marriage in 1840 to the earnest young German prince, Albert of Saxe-Coburg-Gotha. As she slipped under the influence of Albert, Victoria slowly found a political role consonant with the new functions of the monarchy in the nineteenth century, a role that Albert had perceived as combining a small amount of political manipulation with unlimited responsibility as the British people's emotional and ceremonial focus. At least until Albert's death, the royal family took an important part in fostering the new feeling of self-confidence and even self-righteousness that characterized the mid-Victorian age and that lasted until the economic crash of 1873.

Character of the Mid-Victorian Age

After 1848 the discontent with industrialism and with the country's political institutions was alleviated, and the first glimmerings of interest in empire were being roused by the activities of antislavery groups and explorers. From about 1848 to the crash of 1873, the mid-Victorian age knew steady and real prosperity. Its basis was the expansion of the heavy industries linked to coal, iron, and steel, especially for the building of railroads, steamships, and other forms of heavy engineering. The beginning of

A Summer Day in Hyde Park, by John Ritchie

Hyde Park, the largest public park in the center of London, was favored by the Victorian middle classes for family picnics. Originally owned by the monks of the Abbey of Westminster, the land was turned into a deer park by Henry VIII. In the eighteenth century, Queen Caroline had a little river dammed to create the charming Serpentine Lake. (Museum of London)

industrialism on the continent made the developing countries there major importers of British coal, iron and steel, and heavy engineering products until they themselves, from the 1870s, could challenge Britain's position as the workshop of the world. Capital accumulated in the earlier phases of the industrial revolution now sought openings for profitable investment in new forms of industry and in overseas investment. Britain became the world's banker as well as its manufacturer. Even the farmers found that they could profit from the growing home market by capital investment in land or mechanical improvements, and ceased to regret the repeal of the Corn Laws. Free trade was welcomed as the common philosophy of both industrial and agricultural classes, and a climate of opinion thus came to exist that was favorable to the capitalist expansion. Even working-class wages rose faster than the rising prices that were themselves acting as an inflationary stimulus to the economy. Money wages probably rose fifty-six percent between 1850 and 1874. Taken in relation to the rise in prices, the average working-class family probably received about ten percent more in real wages.

One important factor strengthening faith in Britain's political institutions was the sense of relief at having avoided the upheavals that rocked the continental capitals in 1848. British governments, even if elected by a minority of the country's population, had answered demands for reform with bills ranging from the abolition of slavery in the British Empire (1833) to the institution of a ten-and-a-half-hour working day in the factories (1847). Moreover the predominant liberal ethic was against the increase in state controls, and hence minimized the significance of widespread political participation. London itself lacked an effective local government, and even an adequate water supply and sanitation system, and efforts to provide them received little public support. "We prefer to take our chance of cholera and the rest," wrote *The Times*, "than be bullied into health." Even minor attempts at parliamentary reform in the 1850s died for lack of interest.

To this renewed acceptance of the validity of Britain's political institutions, Victoria herself had contributed substantially. From the moment of her accession, Victoria showed the qualities that were to remain with her throughout her reign: a sense of duty, a conviction of moral righteousness, and a deep feeling for her country. "Since it has pleased Providence to place me in this station," she wrote in her diary, "I shall do my utmost to fulfil my duty towards my country; I am very young, and perhaps in many, though not in all things, inexperienced, but I am sure that very few have more good will and more real desire to do what is fit and right than I have." But it was Prince Consort Albert who forced Victoria to take an interest in matters that had previously bored her, such as science and literature and even industrial progress. Indeed nothing gave her greater cause for adoration of her husband than Albert's plunge into the world of British industry.

The Great Exhibition of 1851

In 1849 Albert hit upon the idea of holding a "Great Exhibition" in London, "to give us a true test and a living picture of the point of development at which the whole of mankind has arrived in this great task of applied science and a new starting point from which all nations will be able to direct their further exertions." The nations of the whole world were to be invited to send exhibits of their industrial and artistic skills for display in the first international exhibition ever held. As one poet showed, the Exhibition was to serve some revealingly Victorian purposes:

> *Gather, ye Nations, gather! From forge, and mine, and mill!*
> *Come, Science and Invention; Come, Industry and Skill!*
> *Come with your woven wonders, the blossoms of the loom,*
> *That rival Nature's fairest flowers in all but their perfume;*
>
> *Come with your brass and iron, Your silver and your gold,*
> *And arts that change the face of earth, unknown to men of old.*
> *Gather, ye Nations, gather! From ev'ry clime and soil,*
> *The New Confederation, the Jubilee of toil.* [5]

The prince's idea was approved by the Royal Society and won the financial backing of industry and the general public, who subscribed £200,000 as guarantee. A Royal Commission of architects and engineers

[5] John W. Dodds, *The Age of Paradox: A Biography of England, 1841–1851* (Westport, Conn.: Greenwood Press, 1952), p. 443.

was appointed to plan the building and exhibits. Out of 234 plans submitted, the commission, urged by the prince, eventually picked the most original concept of all, a massive greenhouse designed by the head gardener of a northern duke. Joseph Paxton, however, was no mere gardener, but an engineer, railroad director, newspaper promoter, and imaginative architect in glass and iron. He offered a building 1,848 feet long, 408 feet broad, and 66 feet high, tall enough to cover the old elm trees already occupying the chosen site in Hyde Park. It was composed of mass-produced and standardized parts, including over 6,000 15-foot columns and over one million square feet of glass. It could be erected in seventeen weeks; and it could be, and was, dismantled and reerected in another part of London when the exhibition was over. In spite of many fears expressed over the building's durability, it survived until 1936. The completed building found few detractors. All of the thirteen thousand exhibitors had ample space; and so did six million visitors from all over the world, who gazed in fascination, on

> . . . the giant aisles
> Rich in model and design;
> Harvest-tool and husbandry,
> Loom and wheel and enginery,
> Secrets of the sullen mine,
>
> Steel and gold, and coal and wine,
> Fabric rough or fairy-fine . . .
> And shapes and hues of Art divine!
> All of beauty, all of use,
> That one fair planet can produce.[6]

[6]Lord Tennyson, cited in Nikolaus Pevsner, *High Victorian Design: A Study of the Exhibits of 1851* (London: Architectural Press, 1951), p. 12.

To Victoria, it was Albert's greatest triumph, "the *greatest* day in our history, the most *beautiful* and *imposing* and *touching* spectacle ever seen, and the triumph of my beloved Albert." The queen was right in thinking that the exhibition epitomized the aspirations of her time. She had little idea how diverse would be the judgments of later ages on the contents of her Crystal Palace and on the state of mind and taste that they revealed.

Purpose of the Great Exhibition

The mixed motives of the Victorians, the unselfconscious combination of altruism, moral striving, and material selfishness that the Great Exhibition illustrated, were summarized by Albert himself when he tried to win the support of London's business and civic leaders for his idea.

We are living at a period of most wonderful transition, which tends rapidly to accomplish that great end, to which, indeed, all history points—the realization of the unity of mankind. . . . The products of all quarters of the globe are placed at our disposal, and we have only to choose which is the best and cheapest for our purposes, and the powers of production are intrusted to the stimulus of competition and capital.

The exhibition was a monument to the belief in progress, to humanity's inevitable upward drive to self-improvement and material productivity under God's guidance, which, as the Archbishop of Canterbury ingenuously noted, had brought "peace within our walls and plenteousness within our palaces." The exhibition's organizers in fact genuinely believed that the display would convince foreigners of the good sense of peace and international collaboration through the doctrine of free trade. But the exhibition was also intended to promote internal peace in England by glorifying honest work and the trustworthy laborer. The prince was president of the Society for the Improvement of the Labouring Classes, and he had a model home for the working classes erected near the entrance to the exhibition.

Prince Albert's Model Lodging House
The Society for the Improvement of the Labouring Classes erected this workers' house opposite the exhibition as an example for employers. (Illustrated London News, June 14, 1851)

Interior of the Crystal Palace, London, 1851
Numerous special concerts and ceremonies were held inside Paxton's glass and iron pavilion, which housed the Great Exhibition. Millions of visitors were attracted from all over the world.
(H. Roger-Viollet)

The workers were encouraged to come from their northern slums by special excursion train to see the wonders of the exhibition after the entrance price had been reduced to a shilling; and their good humor and behavior delighted the city's well-to-do and reinforced their satisfaction with England's social system.

For all its moral messages, the exhibition was above all a display of the application of artistic taste to objects of utility. The exhibition was divided into four categories: raw materials, machinery, manufactures, and fine arts. Even in the first category there had been a lapse of taste, with exhibits of glass imitating wood, clay as artificial marble, and papier-mâché substituting for brass. But the machinery category produced the most extraordinary, and the most popular, examples of extravagance. This display included some functionally designed machinery like McCormick's reaping machine, gas cooking ranges, electric clocks, and the electric telegraph. However, there were also steam engines in ancient Egyptian style, others with Greek Doric columns, yet others in cast iron Gothic. No style appeared pure, but elements of many crept together in jovial juxtaposition, as in the example of a partially Elizabethan sideboard made entirely of rubber by the gutta-percha company that had just started tapping the sap of Malayan trees. The Exhibition, in short, was a demonstration of the damage an excessive love of history had done to Victorian taste. While taking pride in their material achievements in industrial production and in the huge spread of their cities, the Victorians failed to develop an architecture or an art or a functionalism of design that would be in harmony with their new technology and materials.

It is thus not surprising that Queen Victoria should have found pleasure in the gloom of Pugin's Medieval Court in the Crystal Palace. Years later, when the last traces of the Crystal Palace had been removed from the lawns of Hyde Park, and a memorial to Albert, dead in 1861 at the age of forty-two, was to be erected on its site, it was in Victorian Gothic that the 175-foot-high canopy with its 178 life-size figures was designed. Albert was to look forever over the scene of his greatest triumph.

IMPERIALISM IN THE LATE VICTORIAN AGE, 1873–1901

The Late Victorian Malaise

Mid-Victorian prosperity came to an abrupt halt with the financial crash of 1873, which was followed by fifteen years of depression in agriculture, greatly reduced profits in industry accompanying a decline in the rate of economic growth, and violent antagonism between workers and employers. But by the beginning of the 1870s there were many other signs that the late Victorian period would be very different in character from the two stable decades ushered in by the Great Exhibition. Economically, Britain was being challenged by foreign competitors, both abroad and in the home market itself. The United States and Germany especially threatened Britain's world monopoly of cheap, mass-produced manufactured goods; and at that very time the British working classes, organizing through trade unions and moving toward Socialist political leaders, were determined to better their own conditions of life and to gain a greater share of the national revenue. The Reform Bill of 1867, which had extended the vote to the working classes of the cities, had provoked a new uncertainty not restricted to the well-to-do; and the adoption of the secret ballot in 1872 and the extension of the vote to the rural workers in 1884 put squarely before Britain the challenge of making its newly democratic system work. In the political sphere, considerable changes followed: a vast increase in the duties of local government, a democratization and increase in the powers of the central bureaucracy, the extension of public education, the abandonment of many of the dogmas of liberalism. The right of women to vote, which had been demanded by the Chartists, again became a burning issue. The most famous statement of the arguments for giving women the vote was John Stuart Mill's *The Subjection of Women* (1869), but in 1870 Parliament again refused women's suffrage. Operating first on a local level, women's suffrage groups united in 1897 in a national organization called the National Union of Women's Suffrage Societies, whose president was Millicent Garrett Fawcett. Six years later, the more militant Emmeline Pankhurst founded the Women's Social and Political Union to agitate for the vote. The members dramatized their cause by smashing

Communist Working Men's Club, London
The left-wing parties provided the workers, many of whom were exiles, not only with the radical newspapers of the continent but with a social meeting place as well. (Illustrated London News, Jan. 6, 1872)

windows, setting fire to buildings, breaking up political meetings, and going on hunger strikes when arrested. In 1913 Pankhurst was arrested and set free twelve times, on each occasion going on a hunger strike until her release. It was not, however, until 1928 that British women were given the vote, on the same conditions as men. The tranquility of Parliament, shocked by the presence of a Socialist in tweed jacket and cap, was further disturbed by the speed with which reformers in the early twentieth century clamored for social change and by the widespread strikes that backed these demands. The refusal of the House of Lords to accept a proposed redistribution of income through capital gains taxes and supertaxes in 1911 was the culmination of a rearguard action fought by conservatives against the reformers; and their opposition was broken only by the threat of swamping the House of Lords with new, reform-minded peers. The movement for home rule in Ireland, which became increasingly violent at the end of the century, further exacerbated the political divisions in the country.

In this atmosphere of economic and political tension, only one endeavor seemed to catch the imagination and swell the pride of the majority of the country's population. The acquisition of a new empire between 1870 and 1890 appeared to advance the cause of science and to extend to benighted lands overseas the solicitude of a revivalist religion. Acquisition also provided investment opportunities for the nation's surplus capital, captive markets for its industrial production, ports for its warships, and an infusion of national pride at a time of external challenge to Britain's hegemony. The new imperialism was for the late Victorians an escape from their problems at home.

Origins of the New Imperialism

The first and lasting imperial love of the Victorians was for the colonies settled by Britons. Until the 1870s, the overseas territorial expansion of which they most approved was in Canada, Australia, New Zealand, and southern Africa. These territories, the Victorians felt, were inhabited by people of British tastes and political experience, with comprehensible desires as consumers, realistic goals as exporters, and reliable habits in business. These areas—and the former British colonies that had become the United States—were the principal recipients of British overseas emigration and capital investment. Moreover, the grant of self-government to these territories had proved a completely satisfactory way of ending the burden of colonial rule without breaking any valuable ties. The Dominion of Canada had been formed in 1867; Australia had four self-governing colonies by 1861; New Zealand received its autonomy in 1854, and Cape Colony in South Africa in 1872. This pleasing and mutually profitable relationship helped preserve a certain affection for empire during the long period of questioning that followed the American Revolution.

The possession of India, however, taught a very different imperial lesson. It showed that a country, alien in race and religion and unsuitable for British settlement or for anglicization, could be a profitable area for investment provided that military and administrative control was firmly maintained. One-fifth of Britain's overseas investments had been made in India by the 1880s, and almost one-fifth of Britain's exports were sold there. Possession of India gave the British a controlling position in most of the local trade of East Asia. India provided an army of two hundred fifty thousand men, with limitless reserves, that was used without compunction to enforce British wishes throughout Asia; and from its ports the British navy patrolled the great trade routes from East Asia and Australia to Britain. And, perhaps the most magnetic of all India's inducements to imperialism, it conferred a strange, exotic glamor on the nation and the monarch that possessed it.

India appealed to the imagination of the imperialist. Benjamin Disraeli (prime minister, 1874–1880), an exotic creature himself, flamboyant in appearance and baroque in language, had proclaimed the monarchy as the center of a new imperialism in a famous speech in the Crystal Palace in 1872. Three years later, as premier, one weekend when the banks were

Benjamin Disraeli, Earl of Beaconsfield (1804–1881), by John Millais (1829–1896)
Disraeli's subtle flattery as much as his support for the new imperialism won him the lasting favor of the aging Queen Victoria. (National Portrait Gallery, London)

The British Army on the March in India

Britain maintained control of the vast subcontinent of India with only several thousand British officers and administrators by using Indians in subordinate positions in the army and civil service. (Illustrated London News, Oct. 7, 1848)

closed, he had borrowed four million pounds from the Rothschild family to buy the controlling shares in the Suez Canal to safeguard the route to India; and he had handed it to the aging Victoria as a personal trophy: "It is just settled. You have it, Madam." And in 1876, he had persuaded Parliament to name her empress of India. That night, she came out of her widow's mourning, having decked herself in huge, uncut jewels sent her by the Indian princes of her new empire. It was the Indian contingent that raised the excitement of the crowd watching the great Jubilee procession make its colorful way to Saint Paul's Cathedral in 1897 behind a band playing *Three Cheers for India*—the squadron of Indian Lancers manned by bearded Sikhs and Pathans; forty princes of the native states who cantered three abreast; diamond-clad rajas, their wives in golden cloth. And it was an Indian-born Englishman, Rudyard Kipling (1865–1936), who did most to bring alive for the English the colorful scenes and intoxicating scents of their Indian possession. His first stories of life of the English in India, *Plain Tales from the Hills* and *Soldiers Three*, and his rollicking, colloquial poems like *Barrack-Room Ballads*, caused a sensation. With his deep, simplistically moral commitment to empire and his ability to conjure up battles on the sultry plains of India, depict the tough, unromantic chores of the young Englishman struggling to bring law beyond the reaches of civilization, and sketch sympathetic portraits of Indians like Gunga Din, Kipling made India the best known part of the empire.

The fact that they already possessed an empire prepared and in some ways predisposed the British to imperial action. Far more, however, than the example of India was driving the British into Africa and the Far East by the 1870s. With Africa, the leading impulses during the preceding two decades had been missionary activity and scientific curiosity. The former was of course linked with the antislavery movement. Largely as a result of the continuing pressure of the evangelicals and the humanitarian societies, British ships patrolled the coasts of eastern and western Africa to intercept slave traders. But the philanthropists were aware that they would have to strike inland if they were ever to put an end to the sale of Negro slaves by Arabs along the valley of the Nile and in the markets of Zanzibar, or by na-

The Slave Market of Zanzibar

The island of Zanzibar off the coast of east Africa was the chief market for slaves captured in the interior by Arab traders, until it was made a British protectorate in 1890. (Illustrated London News, *June 8, 1872*)

tive chieftains along the rivers of western Africa. After the British government set up the Gold Coast Colony in 1874, for example, the Aborigine Protection Society of London persuaded it to put an end to slavery in the surrounding regions. Among the hundreds of missionaries sent out to bring Christianity to the Africans, the most famous was Dr. David Livingstone, who penetrated the unknown heart of Africa as a medical missionary in the 1840s. His books, like *A Narrative of an Expedition to the Zambesi*, told of the sufferings of the slaves in the hands of the Arabs and brought his readers a personal glimpse of massacres like that in a tiny village on the Congo River by Arab slavers:

Shot after shot continued to be fired on the helpless and perishing. Some of the long line of heads [of Africans in the river] disappeared quietly: whilst other poor creatures threw their arms high, as if appealing to the great Father above, and sank. . . . As I write I hear the low wails on the left bank over those who are slain, ignorant of their many friends now in the depths of the Lualaba river. Oh, let Thy kingdom come! No one will ever know the exact loss this bright sultry summer morning. It gave me the impression of being in Hell.[7]

Most explorers, however, were patronized not by the missionary societies or by the newspapers but by scientific societies, such as the Royal Geographic Society of London. As early as 1866, Burton and Speke embarked on one of the first important explorations of eastern Africa with the aim of discovering the sources of the Nile. During the next thirty years, expedition after expedition brought back to England increasing knowledge of the great lake region of eastern Africa and the Nile valley and of the torrid hinterland that lay up the broad river valleys of western and central Africa. No region of the world interested the scientists of Victorian London more than this heart of the Dark Continent, which was supplying the biologist and the ornithologist with new specimens, the anthropologist with data on unspoiled tribes, and the geologist with new access to the mineral wealth of the earth.

Business soon joined science in exploring the potential of the opening region; and many people came to believe that business investors were the principal gainers from empire. In 1902, an English economist named John A. Hobson argued in the influential study *Imperialism* that the primary forces behind imperialism were the industrialist and the finance capitalist. The industrialists needed captive markets for "the excessive capitalist production over the demands of the home market." The inequitable division of the national revenue left in the hands of the capitalists a surplus that they could not use at home because of the restriction on consumption and that they therefore sought to invest in the newly acquired colonies. "Manchester, Sheffield, Birmingham, to name three representative cases," Hobson wrote, "are full of firms which compete in pushing textiles and hardware, engines, tools, machinery, spirits, guns, upon new markets. . . .

[7] Alan Moorehead, *The White Nile* (New York: Harper, 1960), pp. 108–109.

Advertisement for Lipton's Tea

Large British companies established tea plantations on the hills of Ceylon, which had been brought under British control in 1833.
(Illustrated London News, November 27, 1897)

Certain sectional interests . . . usurp control of the national resources and use them for their private gain." These ideas were even more widely popularized by Lenin, in his *Imperialism: The Highest Stage of Capitalism* (1916). For Lenin, this stage was marked by the struggle of monopoly companies growing constantly fewer in number and engaged in a feverish search for raw materials and profitable investment, which ends in a mutually destructive confrontation. "The economic essence of imperialism," he concluded, "must be characterized as capitalism in transition, or, more precisely, as dying capitalism." In assessing the validity of these arguments, historians have little difficulty in showing that most of the colonies acquired at the end of the nineteenth century were not profitable. They accounted for little of the increase in trade during the period 1870–1914; barely one-eighth of Britain's investments at that time went to the dependent colonies, including even India; and very few British people chose to migrate to Africa or Asia. But it is also clear that the business community expected colonies to be profitable and that therefore the desire for profit, if not its actual achievement, was a definite motivating force in the new imperialism.

It was rare, however, to find even a private business owner engaging in the colonial venture without a firm conviction of national pride, national superiority, and mission. These forces made him conceive of his business ventures as a contribution to national glory and human betterment. Statesmen and businessmen joined in the pursuit of economic self-interest in the name of national power and glory. Disraeli had forced his Conservative party to endorse imperialism as a matter of policy, and had inextricably involved Britain in the affairs of Egypt. Furthermore, the colonial secretary, Joseph Chamberlain, a tough, imaginative Birmingham business leader, had in 1895–1903 worked on the principle, he said, that the job of the Colonial and Foreign Office was to find new markets and defend old markets, and the task of the War Office and Admiralty to protect commerce on land and sea. He sincerely thought that Britain was the trustee of civilization, and he had joined with the South African premier, Cecil Rhodes, in seeking to bring all Africa from the Cape to Cairo under British control.

All these impulses to empire—religious philanthropy, scientific curiosity, economic self-interest, national assertiveness—were gathered together in the city of London. London, like seventeenth-century Amsterdam, possessed the institutions that could turn national impulses into governmental policy, and its ruling class was still sufficiently small and homogeneous for the ideas of one group to penetrate rapidly. In London were the offices of the most important missionary organizations, all of which acted as pressure groups in forcing the government into the realization that Christianity and commerce could only extend securely with governmental protection. In close contact with the missionaries were both the scientific societies, like the Royal Geographic Society, and blatantly expansionist groups, like the Imperial Federation League. These societies gained

London as an Imperial Capital

Traffic Congestion, Oxford Circus, London, 1888
Oxford Circus was formed at the intersection of two of the busiest arteries of Victorian London: Regent's Street, oriented north-south, and Oxford Street, running east-west. Its congestion increased with the opening in the area of many of London's best stores. (BBC Hulton Picture Library)

strong support in both major political parties, especially when it became clear to Parliament that, startled by the rise on the continent of great new powers like Germany, the British public was turning its affections and ambitions toward the colonial empire.

By 1870 imperialism had become good politics. "Our great empire has pulled us out of the European system," declared one Conservative leader. "Our foreign policy has become a colonial policy." But the politicians who voted the rapidly increasing funds for imperial expansion and defense were not merely responding to the pressure of their constituents. They were products, almost without exception, of the boarding-school training devised by Dr. Arnold, the famous headmaster of Rugby School. Employees of the Indian civil service and commanders of the colonial armies, they viewed themselves as Christian gentlemen disciplined from youth for command of colonial peoples. Such a feeling gave a moral veneer to the more down-to-earth interests in empire expressed by the business leaders of the city. Grouped within a mile of the Bank of England were the most significant of all London's pressure groups, the companies who demanded the profitability of empire and whose very solidity seemed to guarantee it. Here were the great commodity exchanges, such as those for rubber and tea on Mincing Lane, diamonds in Hatton Garden, wool on Coleman Street; the Royal Exchange, where much insurance was issued by firms like Lloyd's; the Foreign Exchange, which dealt in all the world's currencies as well as gold and silver; and the Metal Exchange, which established the world price for most metals. Nearby in the maze of narrow streets were foreign banks, joint-stock companies, shipping offices, insurance companies, stockbrokers, and shipping suppliers, all of whom in some way participated in the imperial venture.

The combination in one place of all these institutionalized interest groups provided the main impetus to imperialism. "The key of India is not Herat or Kandahar," said Disraeli. "The key of India is London."

Acquisition of a New Colonial Empire

Britain, however, was far from unique in its desire to acquire new colonies; and in its attempt to expand into Africa and eastern Asia it found itself in competition with the French, the Belgians, the Portuguese, the Italians, and the Germans. Even the United States decided to "take up the White Man's Burden," as Kipling bade it to do, at the end of the century; and Russia began to put pressure on Iran, Afghanistan, and China. The same motives, though in differing degrees, affected all these would-be imperialists. All believed that it was necessary to acquire raw materials, markets, and outlets for population while they were still available. All believed they needed strategic bases, additional sources of labor, and even the imponderable advantages of prestige provided by the acquisition of colonial territory. The European powers were sending out missionaries, such as the French White Fathers and the Belgian Catholic missions in the Congo, and subsidizing explorers such as Karl Peters, who explored the Congo, and De Brazza, who penetrated equatorial Africa. Additionally, the European gov-

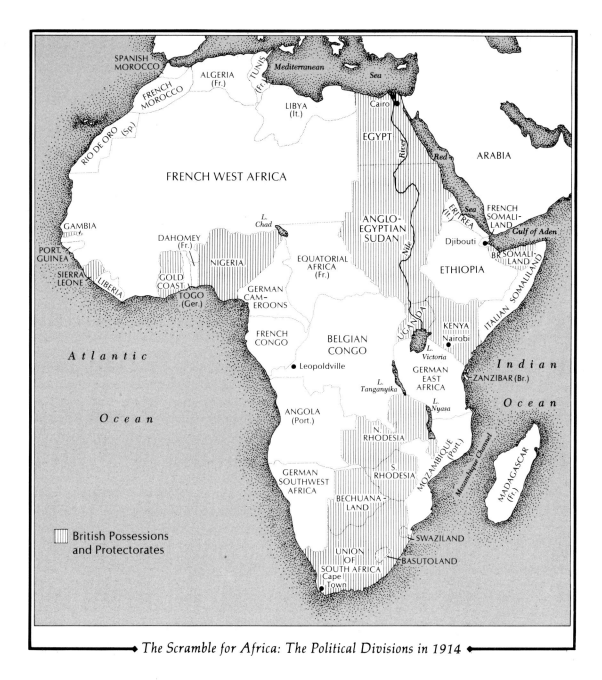

SPANISH
MOROCCO
ALGERIA
(Fr.)
TUNIS
(Fr.)
Mediterranean   Sea
FRENCH
MOROCCO
LIBYA
(It.)
Cairo
EGYPT
Red
ARABIA
RIO DE ORO (Sp.)
FRENCH WEST AFRICA
L.
Chad
ANGLO-
EGYPTIAN
SUDAN
ERITREA
(It.)
Sea
FRENCH
SOMALI-
LAND
Gulf of Aden
GAMBIA
DAHOMEY
(Fr.)
Djibouti
BR. SOMALI-
LAND
PORT.
GUINEA
NIGERIA
EQUATORIAL
AFRICA
(Fr.)
Nile
ETHIOPIA
SIERRA
LEONE
LIBERIA
GOLD
COAST
TOGO
(Ger.)
GERMAN
CAM-
EROONS
UGANDA
KENYA
Nairobi
ITALIAN SOMALILAND
Atlantic
FRENCH
CONGO
BELGIAN
CONGO
L.
Victoria
Indian
Leopoldville
GERMAN
EAST
AFRICA
ZANZIBAR (Br.)
L.
Tanganyika
Ocean
Ocean
ANGOLA
(Port.)
L.
Nyasa
N.
RHODESIA
MOZAMBIQUE (Port.)
Mozambique Channel
MADAGASCAR
(Fr.)
GERMAN
SOUTHWEST
AFRICA
S.
RHODESIA
BECHUANA-
LAND
SWAZILAND
BASUTOLAND
British Possessions
and Protectorates
UNION
OF
SOUTH AFRICA
Cape
Town

◆ *The Scramble for Africa: The Political Divisions in 1914* ◆

ernments were under pressure from colonial societies, such as Germany's
Society for Commercial Geography and the Promotion of German Interest
Abroad and the Pan-German League.

But Britain was easily able to outdistance its rivals. To maintain its
control of the Suez Canal, it established a protectorate over Egypt in 1882,

and soon extended its rule southward to the Sudan. From Cape Colony in South Africa, which Britain had taken from the Dutch in 1806, the British pushed northwards, interrupting the Portuguese attempt to join up their territories of Angola and Mozambique. Bechuanaland was taken in 1885, Rhodesia in 1889, and Nyasaland in 1893. In 1899–1902, in three years of brutal fighting in the Boer War, the British forced the independent states of the Transvaal and the Orange Free State, inhabited by descendants of the original Dutch settlers of southern Africa, called Boers, to join in a Union of South Africa. Since the British had also established themselves on the eastern coast in British East Africa and Uganda, it seemed that the dream of controlling Africa from Cape to Cairo was near realization. The German East Africa Company, however, succeeded in establishing itself in East Africa; and Germany also took a large area of West Africa and the arid wastes of German Southwest Africa. The Congo valley with its great deposits of copper, lead, and gold and its valuable rubber, cotton, and ivory, had been annexed as the Congo Free State under the personal control of the Belgian king Leopold II. Although the British were able greatly to expand their holdings in the Gold Coast and Nigeria, the French became the masters of most of North and Central Africa, while the Italians took Libya and a scrap of Somaliland. By 1900 only one-tenth of Africa had not been annexed by the European powers, whereas twenty-five years earlier only one-tenth was in European possession.

In the Far East, the attention of the imperialists was divided between the South Pacific and China. In both areas, Britain took the lead. It annexed the Fiji Islands in 1874, and it shared in the division of New Guinea with the Germans and the Dutch in 1885. By the end of the century, Germany was in possession of the Marianas and the Caroline Islands. France had extended its hold from Tahiti to include the whole of the Society Islands and the Marquesas, and was sharing the New Hebrides with Britain. And the United States, after the Spanish-American War of 1898, had not only annexed Porto Rico in the Caribbean but had also, somewhat unwillingly, acquired the Philippine Islands. In China, Britain had gained possession of Hong Kong in 1842, following a brief war, and had forced open a number of ports to European trade. Moreover by taking Burma, it shared in the amputation from China of tributary states. The French had completed their conquest of Indochina in the 1880s, and the Japanese, who had defeated China in 1894–1895, annexed Korea and Formosa.

Thus, in the last thirty years of the nineteenth century, the European powers vastly increased their colonial possessions. Britain, the greatest gainer, added to its empire over four million square miles with a population of sixty-six million. In the outburst of self-congratulation with which the propagandists of imperialism dazzled public opinion at home, the problems that had been acquired along with the new colonies were largely ignored, and, for Queen Victoria's Diamond Jubilee in 1897, the British organized the most glamorous celebration of the imperial age.

For weeks London was filled with the representatives of empire—princes from India, gold diggers from Australia, Chinese police from Hong Kong, overweight Maoris and Dyak headhunters, Sudanese horsemen, Fijian princesses, and eleven prime ministers of the self-governing colonies. The conquerors of empire were accorded a suitable precedence, especially Lord Roberts, who had subdued Afghanistan; and the power of empire was emphasized with a special demonstration of the new Maxim gun. For the last time, before their self-confidence was swept away by the First World War, the people of London gave themselves up to an imperialist euphoria so explosive that even Rudyard Kipling was moved to rebuke them:

> *If drunk with sight of power, we loose*
> *Wild tongues that have not Thee in awe,*
> *Such boastings as the gentiles use,*
> *Or lesser breeds without the Law—*
> *Lord God of Hosts, be with us yet,*
> *Lest we forget—lest we forget!*[8]

This ill-timed moralizing merely reduced Kipling's popularity. In 1897, Londoners believed with some reason that theirs was the greatest of world cities.

Four years later, Victoria was dead. The adjective *Victorian*, which had been coined in the euphoria of 1851 to indicate the glory of the new age, soon became a word of opprobium; and London gave itself up under the leadership of King Edward VII (reigned 1901–1910) to its own *belle époque*, to the uninhibited pleasures of the Edwardian age.

[8] *Rudyard Kipling's Verse: Definitive Edition* (London: Hodder and Stoughton, 1940), p. 329.

British and Indian Princes in the Jubilee Parade
The great parade composed of units from all Britain's empire celebrated the six-tieth anniversary of Queen Victoria's accession. (Illustrated London News, June 26, 1897)

SUGGESTED READING

Francis Sheppard's *London 1808–1870: The Infernal Wen* (1971) is a fine reconstruction of all aspects of the city's life, with special attention to the money market, the transport revolution, and public health questions; the bibliography is indispensable for further study. Aldon D. Bell, *London in the Age of Dickens* (1967) has many details of the aspects of the city that interested Dickens, such as the law courts and the slums. Different quarters of the city are examined in more specialized fashion by H. J. Dyos, *Victorian Suburb: A Study of the Growth of Camberwell* (1961); F. M. L. Thompson, *Hampstead: The Building of a Borough, 1650–1964* (1973); Ruth Glass, ed., *London: Aspects of Change* (1964), which concentrates on the role of the Irish immigrant; James Bird, *The Geography of the Port of London* (1957); and Peter Hall, *The Industries of London Since 1861* (1961). Gareth Stedman Jones studies the consequences of unemployment on day labor in *Outcast London: A Study in the Relationship Between Classes in Victorian Society* (1971). On crime before and after the institution of uniformed police forces, see Ted Robert Gurr, Peter N. Grabovsky, and Richard C. Hula, *The Politics of Crime and Conflict: A Comparative History of Four Cities* (1977), the four being London, Stockholm, Calcutta, and Sydney; and Wilbur R. Miller, *Cops and Bobbies: Police Authority in New York and London, 1830–1870* (1977). A good overview is provided by the essays in H. J. Dyos and Michael Wolff, eds., *The Victorian City: Images and Reality* (1973), which include studies of Dickens as a Londoner and of the East End as a literary subject.

The best introduction to the Victorian age is perhaps G. M. Young's *Victorian England: Portrait of an Age* (1936); and for good textbooks one can turn to David Thomson, *England in the Nineteenth Century* (1950); Asa Briggs, *The Making of Modern England, 1783–1867: The Age of Improvement* (1959); and Robert K. Webb, *Modern England: From the Eighteenth Century to the Present* (1968). For portraits of the leading Victorians, one can savor the malice of Lytton Strachey in *Five Victorians* (many editions); Asa Briggs, *Victorian People* (1954) is especially good on Thomas Hughes, headmaster of Rugby School, and on Benjamin Disraeli, who is treated more fully in the fine biography by Robert Blake, *Disraeli* (1967). Two strong-willed women are admirably described by Elizabeth Longford, *Queen Victoria: Born to Succeed* (1965) and Cecil Woodham-Smith, *Florence Nightingale* (1951). Prince Consort Albert is best understood through the Great Exhibition, as analyzed in Nikolaus Pevsner, *High Victorian Design: A Study of the Exhibits of 1851* (1951).

The social reformers' achievements are weighed by David Owen, *English Philanthropy 1660–1690* (1965). The motives of the evangelicals are sparklingly outlined in Noel Annan's *Leslie Stephen* (1951). The great work of Henry Mayhew can be sampled in John L. Bradley, ed., *Selections from London Labour and the London Poor* (1965).

The literature on Charles Dickens is even more voluminous than his own writings. Good introductions that deal specifically with the London scene as perceived by Dickens are J. Hillis Miller, *Charles Dickens: The World of His Novels* (1959), and Angus Wilson, *The World of Charles Dickens* (1970), which is beautifully illustrated. Dickens's own essays dealing with London are collected by Rosalind Valance, ed., *Dickens' London* (1966), with illustrations by George Cruikshank. But it is better to turn to the novels themselves, especially *The Pickwick Papers* for the debtors' prison; *Bleak House* for the law courts; *Oliver Twist* for the slums called rookeries; *Nicholas Nickleby* for the private schools; and *Little Dorrit* for the government bureaucracy.

The role of religion in Victorian life is reassessed in J. Kitson Clark, *The Making of Victorian England* (1962) and K. S. Inglis, *Churches and the Working Class in Victorian England* (1963). Augustus W. Pugin, the Gothic reviver, showed in *Contrasts* how architecture should incorporate the medieval Catholic spirit, and Cardinal John Henry Newman described his spiritual pilgrimage to Catholicism in *Apologia pro Vita Sua*.

The position of women in Victorian society is discussed in Lee Holcombe, *Victorian Ladies at Work: Middle-Class Working Women in England and Wales, 1850–1914* (1973); Janet Dunbar, *The Early Victorian Woman* (1953); Duncan Crow, *The Victorian Woman* (1972); and Wanda Neff, *Victorian Working Women* (1929). In *Silent Sisterhood: Middle Class Women in the Victorian Home* (1975), Patricia Branca uses manuals for housekeeping and child care as sources for the realities of Victorian life. She summarizes many of her findings in her essay "Image and Reality: The Myth of the Idle Victorian Woman," in Mary S. Hartman and Lois Banner, eds., *Clio's Consciousness Raised: New Perspectives on the History of Women* (1974), pp. 179–191. Barbara Kanner provides two excellent bibliographies on women in nineteenth-century Britain in the two books edited by Martha Vicinus, *Suffer and Be Still* (1972) and *A Widening Sphere: Changing Roles of Victorian Women* (1977).

The most delightful introduction to imperialism without shame, or at least with nostalgia, is James Morris, *Pax Britannica: The Climax of an Empire* (1968), which contains a glorious exposé of life in India's summer capital of Poona. More conventional histories of the empire include D. K. Fieldhouse, *The Colonial Empires* (1966) and his *Economics and Empire, 1830–1914* (1973), and Ronald Hyam, *Britain's Imperial Century, 1815–1914: A Study of Empire and Expansion* (1976). The decline of empire is the main focus of Bernard Porter, *The Lion's Share: A Short History of British Imperialism, 1850–1970* (1976). The best history of imperialism in Africa is Robin Hallett, *Africa Since 1875: A Modern History* (1974). The intellectual roots of imperialism are analyzed by A. P. Thornton, *The Imperial Idea and Its Enemies: A Study in British Power* (1959). The economic basis of imperialism is denied by L. H. Gann and Peter Duignan, *Burden of Empire* (1967); the strategic significance of Africa is emphasized by John T. Gallagher and Ronald I. Robinson, with Alice Denny, *Africa and the Victorians* (1965). The explorers of eastern Africa fight every kind of misfortune and each other in Alan Moorehead, *The White Nile* (1971). But one understands the spirit of empire best by reading the poems of Rudyard Kipling or the novels of George A. Henty (choose any of his eighty best sellers).

For the relief that set in after Victoria passed on, that outburst of Edwardian good spirits, see James Laver, *Manners and Morals in the Age of Optimism, 1848–1914* (1967); J. B. Priestley, *The Edwardians* (1970); and the more scholarly study of Paul Thompson, *The Edwardians: The Remaking of British Society* (1975).

25

THE AGE OF THE NEW COLONIALISM, 1815–1914

For the Western powers imperialism was a source of self-congratulation and self-enrichment. For the peoples affected by imperialism, however—both those in territories directly annexed and those more indirectly influenced by the political, economic, and at times military pressures of the West—imperialism had a different face. In the previous chapter we considered imperialism from the viewpoint of the imperial powers. In this chapter we shall look at imperialism as part of the changing experience of the peoples of the non-Western world, seeking in particular the transformations within their civilizations that were brought about during the nineteenth century by the impact of, and their reactions to, the overwhelming new challenge from the West.

We shall look first at the civilizations of India, Southeast Asia, the Pacific, and Africa that were incorporated, usually by military force, into the empires of the Western powers. Second, we shall consider the debilitating impact of the West on the failing Manchu Empire in China. Third, we shall study the stimulating influence of Western modernization on Japan. Finally, we shall examine the progress of the Latin American countries in their attempts to create states that were both politically and economically independent, in the aftermath of their liberation from the colonialism of Spain and Portugal.

Victoria Memorial, Calcutta   (G. R. Richardson/Taurus Photos)

INDIA UNDER THE BRITISH RAJ

Decline of the Mogul Empire

The decline of the Mogul Empire after the forced abdication of Shah Jahan in 1658 permitted the British to gain the toehold in India that they converted, in the eighteenth and nineteenth centuries, into domination of the whole subcontinent. Shah Jahan's son, the emperor Aurangzeb (reigned 1658–1707) devoted most of his life to successful but expensive campaigns in the south of India, neglecting the cultural life of his capital at Delhi, although strengthening Mogul administration. At the end of his life Aurangzeb became a religious recluse, devoting himself to study of the Koran and to his plans for Islamization of India. Meanwhile, his rivals—the Hindu tribes of the Maratha federation in the Deccan, the Sikhs of the Punjab, and the Rajput princes—grew stronger.

After Aurangzeb's death the title of Mogul emperor was disputed frequently among many factions in the Delhi palace. Although under these eighteenth-century emperors there was a brief revival of Moslem poetry and painting and the building of palaces reminiscent of the rococo era in contemporary Paris, many emperors preferred the diversion of acrobats and dancing girls; and the economic and administrative weakness of the Moguls became palpable. In 1739 the aggressive Nadir Shah of Persia invaded India and captured Delhi with little effort. The city was savagely sacked and vast booty carried back to Persia, including the famous Peacock Throne of Shah Jahan and the Koh-i-Noor diamond. Less than twenty years later the city was sacked by Afghan armies, and many of its inhabitants were executed. In short, by the mid-eighteenth century the power of the Mogul emperors had vanished, although they continued to

Astronomical Observatory, Jaipur
The Hindu Maharaja Jai Singh founded Jaipur as his new capital city in 1727. An astronomer and mathematician, he built a huge outdoor observatory that included this ninety-foot-tall gnomon, or sundial, which keeps completely accurate time. (F. Roy Willis)

maintain the semblance of authority until the last emperor was finally ousted by the British in 1857.

In the early eighteenth century the principal European trading posts in India were the Portuguese fortress of Goa; the French settlements of Pondicherry, Masulipatam, and Chandernagore; and the British holdings in Bombay, Madras, and Calcutta. The Portuguese showed little interest in expanding their territorial holdings, and British defeats of the French in the Seven Years' War (1756–1763) enabled them to confine the French within their trading posts.

With no other European power to hinder their action, the British were left free to determine how best to profit from the weakness of the Indian states. The East India Company, which was the sole representative of Britain in India, felt compelled to begin a policy of taking direct control of whole Indian states when, in 1757, the nawab of Bengal seized their trading post at Calcutta. At the Battle of Plassey, an army of British soldiers and Indian mercenaries under Robert Clive defeated the nawab's far larger army and replaced him with a more pliant ruler.

With the rich province of Bengal in its hands, during the next century the East India Company—in a series of haphazard, largely unplanned moves—brought under its rule several other Indian states that either presented a military threat or offered economic opportunity to the company. The most important of these annexations were the takeover of the Maratha Empire in central India in 1818, of Sind at the Indus mouth in 1843, of the Sikh state in the Punjab in 1849, and of the rich state of Oudh in 1856. At the same time the company concluded agreements with the hun-

Tiger Mauling a British Official
The wooden model, equipped to emit piercing moans, was made for Tipu, sultan of Mysore. Tipu allied with the French against the British and was killed in battle in 1799. (The Victoria and Albert Museum, London)

INDIA UNDER THE BRITISH RAJ

dreds of local princes in the rest of India, promising them secure incomes and British aid against internal rebellion, but allowing them to remain nominally autonomous although under the supervision of a British "resident."

The East India Company's policy began as exploitative and ended as inefficient. Many eighteenth-century officials went out to India to get rich as quickly as possible, either from a share of the land revenues being squeezed from the peasantry by local Indian tax collectors, or from a share of the profits of trade, or by receipt of bribes. Parliament slowly began to take a greater role in the government of India, however. In 1814 it ended the company's trade monopoly in India; the company reacted by expanding its cultivation on its Bengal estates of opium for export to China, where it retained monopoly of British commerce until 1834.

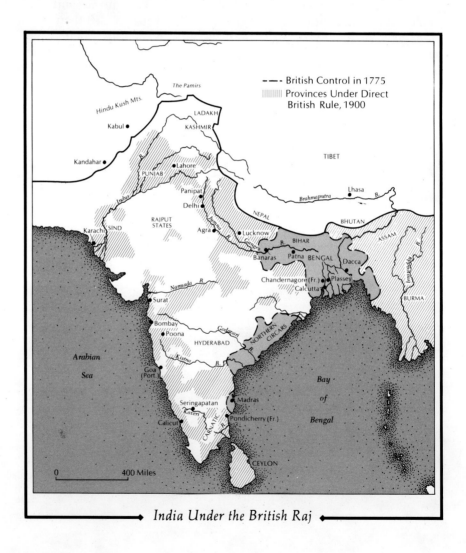

India Under the British Raj

Session of an East India Company Court
In the provinces controlled directly by the East India Company, its officials administered law through an institution called a cutcherry, or court, as depicted in this painted wooden model. (Victoria and Albert Museum, London)

Parliament also made greater efforts to change what the British regarded as the immoral customs of the Indians themselves. *Sati*, the burning of widows on their husband's funeral pyres, was banned. Slavery and infanticide were abolished. Both the caste system and religious discrimination were challenged by the declaration in the Charter Act of 1833 that "no native of India ... shall be disabled from holding any place, office, or employment by reason of his religion, place of birth, descent or colour."

Anger built up by British annexations of princely states like Oudh and fear that interference with India's religious customs was a prelude to forced conversion to Christianity combined in 1857 to turn a military mutiny into a widespread revolt. Indian troops near Delhi refused to bite off the fat-smeared tips of the cartridges for their new Enfield rifles, for fear of religious defilement—the Moslems by pig fat, the Hindus by cow grease. They seized Delhi, executed the British civilians who had taken refuge in the Red Fort, and claimed to restore the Mogul emperor Bahadur Shah to actual rule. Similar uprisings destroyed British control of most of the Ganges Valley and parts of the Deccan, but most of the princely states remained loyal to the British.

British troops, outraged at atrocities against captured British men and women, engaged in vicious reprisals against captured villages; when Delhi was retaken after a long siege, large numbers of Indians were bayoneted and the rest driven out to live in the countryside for months before being allowed to return. When the Mutiny was finally defeated in July 1858, the British government drew the conclusion that the end of both the Mogul

The Indian Mutiny, 1857–1858

Lucknow After the Indian Mutiny
Some of the heaviest fighting in the Indian Mutiny occurred during the five-month-long siege of the British garrison of Lucknow in the state of Oudh. Much of the city was in ruins when it was relieved in November 1857. (BBC Hulton Picture Library)

Empire and the rule of the East India Company was necessary. In the Government of India Act of August 2, 1858, the British government assumed full control, acting in India through a governor-general who was also viceroy, but establishing policy in London through a secretary of state for India and an advisory council. For the next half century the new institutions functioned with increasing efficiency, and an effective program of reforms was instituted.

India Under the Crown, 1858–1914

The most immediate reform was of the army. The percentage of British troops was increased to one-third, and the officer corps was kept almost entirely British. Native troops were recruited from those groups like Sikhs and Gurkas who had remained loyal; and, although regiments were composed of troops from only one region or sect, they were usually stationed far from their own provinces. Technologically, the new regime sought to unite the country, building 25,000 miles of railroad and stringing almost as many miles of telegraph wire by 1900. In a conscious attempt to rival Rome, the British laid out over 170,000 miles of roadway, of which 37,000 miles were surfaced in macadam. Irrigation brought 30 million acres of land into cultivation; even though most of India's production of cotton and jute was shipped unprocessed to Britain, the textile industry did revive. Finally, an effort was made to improve public health, with the result that the population rose from 150 million in 1850 to 250 million in 1881. Not surprisingly, the food supply failed to keep up with the population growth, and famines broke out at frequent intervals. Nevertheless, the British were convinced of the success of their new policies, and in 1876 Queen Victoria agreed to celebrate the triumphs of direct rule by assuming the title of empress of India.

For the next thirty years the bureaucratic and military machine of British rule lumbered effectively on. Campaigns waged on India's borders were mainly successful. The annexation of Burma, which had begun after the First Burmese War of 1824–1826, was completed in 1885. Afghanistan became dependent on Britain, its allegiance being purchased by an annual subsidy. Finally, Tibet recognized British predominance over its foreign policy after an expedition captured Lhasa in 1904.

In India the civil service was manned by four thousand British university graduates chosen by competitive examination; half a million Indian civil servants carried out their commands at the local level. There was even in the first decade of the twentieth century the beginning of Indian representation in the Central Legislative Council and in provincial legislatures. Hence it was possible for many of the British living in India to delude themselves, from their mansions in the hills at the summer capital of Simla or in their all-white clubs in the backcountry, that they had won the heart of India. But the decision to move the government of British India in 1912 from the increasingly volatile cauldron of Calcutta to a newly constructed capital at New Delhi was clear evidence that an impatient Indian population would eventually put an end to the anomaly of alien rule.

THE CALCUTTA OF THE TAGORES

Calcutta, founded in 1690 when an East India Company agent named Job Charnock turned three mud-brick villages on the banks of the Hooghly River in Bengal into a trading post, soon became the economic center of the Ganges Delta. It expanded even more rapidly after 1773, when the Regulating Act gave Warren Hastings, the governor-general of Bengal, control over the other British-held territories in Madras and Bombay, thus giving Calcutta the position of capital of British India, which it held until 1912. By 1820 it had a population of over 200,000. By 1910 the population was almost 1 million, and Calcutta was the largest city in India. As a totally new creation of the British Raj, Calcutta portrayed in microcosm the British conception of how an empire should be administered and how a ruling elite should live in its conquered land. Since, however, Calcutta also attracted many of the most energetic and cultivated Indians of the whole region of Bengal, which was noted for the strength of its intellectual tradition and for the vigor of its economic life, the city must also be studied for evidence of the flowering of both economic and cultural genius of the Indians under the British Raj. No family more clearly typifies this genius than the Tagores, who generation after generation played a leading part in Calcutta's economic and intellectual life and whose most celebrated member, Rabindranath Tagore (1861–1941), won world recognition for Bengali literature with the receipt of the Nobel Prize in 1913. Finally, Calcutta became in the nineteenth century one of the leading centers of opposition to British rule; there one can see the growth of the

Rabindranath Tagore
(United Press International, Inc.)

campaign for *swadeshi* (boycott of British goods) as a means to ultimate *purna swaraj* (independence). The great riots of Calcutta in 1905 were a portent of the end of imperialism in India.

The Creation of Calcutta

Almost every visitor and most residents agreed throughout Calcutta's history that its location could not have been worse. Built on mud flats on a tropical river, over eighty miles from the Bay of Bengal, it was difficult of access and perpetually threatened by malaria and other swamp-bred diseases. Except for a few winter months, its climate is enervatingly hot and humid, especially in the nerve-racking days before the monsoons strike in May, bringing up to sixty-four inches of rain in four months. Once Charnock had built the first warehouse, however, trade boomed; and no further

◆ *The Calcutta of the Tagores* ◆

Period Surveyed	Period of Calcutta as capital of British India (1773–1912), especially the lifetime of Dwarkanath Tagore (1794–1846); Debendrenath Tagore (1817–1905); and Rabindranath Tagore (1861–1941)
Population	Calcutta City: 229,704 (1837); 896,867 (1911) Metropolitan Calcutta: c. 1 million (1837); 2 million (1912)
Area	Calcutta City: 8 square miles (1834) Metropolitan Calcutta: 220 square miles (1912)
Form of Government	1773–1858: Administration by British East India Company, through a governor-general in Calcutta under supervision of Board of Control and Court of Proprietors in London 1858–1912: Administration by secretary of state for Indian affairs and council of India in London and by viceroy–governor general in Calcutta. Partial city administration by Calcutta Corporation after 1876
Political Leaders	British: Governor-generals: Warren Hastings (Bengal, 1774–1785); Lord William Bentinck (Bengal, 1828–1833; India, 1833–1835); Earl of Dalhousie (India, 1848–1856). Viceroy: Lord Curzon (1899–1905) Bengali: Surendranath Banerjea; Lal Mohan Ghose; Romesh Kayastha Dutt
Economic Base	Bureaucracy; tax collection; banking; international trade (jute, cotton, textiles, coal, indigo)
Intellectual Life	Novel (Bankim Chandra Chatterji, Michael Madusudan Dutt); poetry (Rabindranath Tagore); philosophy (Ram Mohun Roy); theology (Ramakrishna Paramahansa, Vivekananda)
Principal Buildings	Government House; Fort William; Writers' Building; Victoria Memorial
Public Entertainment	Horse races; religious festivals; river excursions; bazaars
Religion	Hindu; Moslem; Christian

effort was made to select a better site. Rudyard Kipling described Charnock's mistake:

> *Thus the midday halt of Charnock—more's the pity!*
> *Grew a City*
> *As the fungus sprouts chaotic from its bed*
> *So it spread*

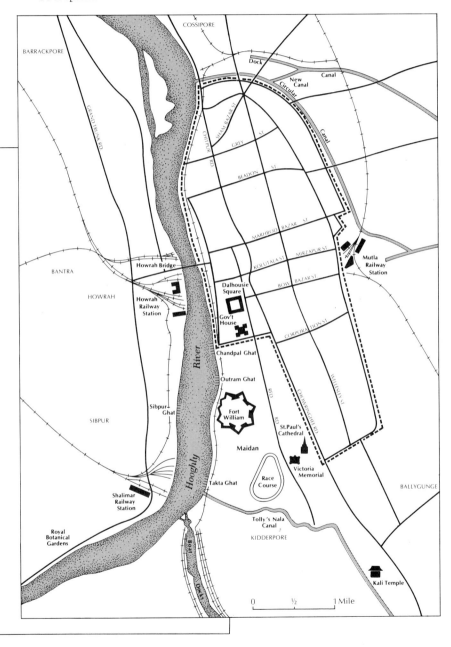

Government House, Calcutta (1798–1803)

Governor-General Arthur Wellesley modeled his official residence in Calcutta on the great English country house Kedleston Hall, one of the finest buildings constructed by the architect Robert Adam. Its classical style set the pattern for other residences and administrative buildings of the East India Company. (India Office Library and Records)

Chance-directed, chance-erected, laid and built
On the silt
Palace, byre, hovel—poverty and pride—
Side by side;
And, above the packed and pestilential town,
Death looked down.[1]

The first significant building of the East India Company was Fort William. However, from the time of Warren Hastings a classical English city, modeled on the contemporary buildings of London and Bath, was created on the left bank of the Hooghly. Hastings himself had built a mansion in white marble in one of the suburbs; other officials and merchants followed his example, making Calcutta known as the City of Palaces. Fort William itself was rebuilt further south, and a huge "field of fire" was created around it by hacking down the jungle. This esplanade, two miles long and a mile wide, became the Maidan, the city's favorite park, containing a racecourse and sports fields; the broad road beside it, the Chowringhee, became the principal residential area of the well-to-do whites. The company created the business center of town around the Tank Square, later called Dalhousie Square, by building there the massive Writers' Building, where their clerks from England could live and work.

Between Tank Square and the Maidan, Governor-General Wellesley built a massive Government House modeled on one of the great aristo-

---

[1] Excerpt from "A Tale of Two Cities" from *Rudyard Kipling's Verse: Definitive Edition*, by Rudyard Kipling. Reprinted by permission of Doubleday & Company, Inc.

cratic mansions of England. It cost so much—about $250,000 at that time—
that the company recalled the governor-general; but its beautiful Ionic columns, set in four projecting wings that caught the breezes from the river,
dominated the architecture of the city from then on. Well-to-do Indian tax
collectors, merchants, and manufacturers did not lag behind the British in
the grandeur of the homes they built, although they were restricted to the
Indian sections of town. The Marble Palace, for example, was built in 1835
by a family of tax collectors who had once served the Mogul emperor and
who now copied the taste of the British rulers by filling their new home
with English ceramics, Italian sculptures, and paintings by Rubens and Ti-
tian. One of the sights in the countryside nearby was the mansion of one
of Calcutta's first Indian capitalists, Dwarkanath Tagore, the grandfather of
Rabindranath. Tagore's entertainments included elephants on the lawn,
ices in the summerhouse, dancing girls in the salon, and even the sacrilege,
in Hindu eyes, of roast beef in the dining room.

For most Indians, however, Calcutta was always a place of extreme poverty.   ***"The Black Town"***
Many Indians lived on the right bank of the Hooghly in acres of shanties
in the area called Howrah, which was redeemed only by the large expanse
of the Botanical Gardens. Here the construction of the railroad in the
1850s led to the building of the famous Howrah Station, which became
(and still remains) home to a dispossessed population of thousands. In the
city itself the Indian quarters expanded to the north and west. Almost no
urban improvements were made, however. No sewers were constructed.
Streetlights were almost nonexistent. Bodies—sometimes partially burned
on funeral pyres—were thrown into the river, which was the main source
of the city's water supply. An observer noted in 1863:

*Should business or curiosity call [the visitor] to the native town, he will see or
rather feel by the jolt of his carriage, streets than which the natural paths of the
forest are better fitted for travelling. He will have his nose assailed by the stench
of drains which have not felt the ministering hand of man since the last rains, his
affrighted horse will obstinately back from pits in the thoroughfares wide enough
to bury all the rubbish in the adjoining houses. . . . After a heavy shower of rain
he will in some places deem it more pleasant and advantageous to hire a boat
than swim his horse.*[2]

Congestion in these northern areas of the city was worsened by the fact
that no bridge was built across the river until pontoons were strung across
in 1874, and no controls at all were laid down for required widths for
streets. In 1914 a British civil engineer reported that 250,000 people were
living in houses that anywhere else would have been condemned as unfit
for human habitation. "Nearly all the working-class families can afford but
a single room in which they have to live, eat, sleep, propagate their species
and die. . . . Usually it is ill-lit and badly ventilated and is in a slum or

---

[2] Cited in Geoffrey Moorhouse, *Calcutta* (London: Weidenfeld and Nicolson, 1971), p. 258.

chawl. Often two families exist in one room."[3] At this time, in startling contrast, the viceroy, Lord Curzon, was erecting, on the edge of the Maidan, the Victoria Memorial, one of the most colossal monuments to the Victorian empire, built in dazzling white marble in 1906–1921, in which all the events of the conquest and rule of India were to be commemorated.

Thus British and Indians together had created in Calcutta a city of extremes: of architectural elegance and urban degradation, of economic opportunity and social deprivation, of aristocratic privilege and racial discrimination. Yet the British were proud of their achievement. Lord Curzon declared in a speech to Calcutta's business community in 1903:

> To me, Calcutta is the capital, not merely of a province, great as that province is, but of the Indian Empire. As such, it appears to me fitly to symbolise the work that the English have done, and are doing in this country. . . . A glance at the buildings of the town, at the river and the roar and the smoke, is sufficient to show that Calcutta is in reality a European city set down upon Asiatic soil, and that it is a monument . . . to the energy and achievements of our race.[4]

The Indians were slow and seemingly reluctant to criticize that achievement. To understand nineteenth-century Calcutta is to penetrate to the nature of the imperialism that produced such great cities as Hong Kong, Singapore, and Nairobi in the British Empire; Saigon, Brazzaville, and

[3]Cited in ibid., p. 263.
[4]Cited in ibid., pp. 260–261.

Lord Curzon (1859–1925)
As viceroy of India from 1899 to 1905, Curzon was responsible for numerous reforms in education, finances, and administration. His decision to partition Bengal, however, caused the great riots in Calcutta in 1905. (BBC Hulton Picture Library)

Dakar in the French Empire; or Leopoldville in the Belgian Empire. Such cities could be created only with the collaboration of the colonial peoples who were eventually to drive out the colonialist.

Collaboration of imperialist and Bengali was closest during the first half century of British rule; and the Indian who most typified the advantages of such a relationship was Dwarkanath Tagore (1794–1846), grandfather of the great writer Rabindranath. During this period, many of the British administrators, merchants, and missionaries were fascinated by Indian culture, mastered one or more of the Indian languages, and encouraged a synthesis of British and Indian culture. In the college founded at Fort William for the education of the young company officials, Asian languages were taught and large numbers of books in the Indian languages published. Within two generations this "Oxford of the East" became one of the principal centers of Asian studies, and through contact with young Indian scholars its graduates helped encourage what became known as the Bengal or Hindu renaissance of scholarship in Calcutta.

Dwarkanath Tagore: The Hindu Brahman as Merchant Prince

The leader of this movement was a Calcutta brahman named Ram Mohun Roy (1772–1833), who formed a group of educated Indians to discuss theology and philosophy. This "friendly association" studied the original texts of the Hindu classics and sought to reach a purer understanding of the worship of Brahma, in keeping with the rational approach to religion that the British Unitarians were teaching in India. Out of these meetings came a new Hindu sect, the Brahmo Samaj, founded in 1828, which for the rest of the century was to encourage the pride of Hindus in their own culture and was to prepare the way among India's leaders for the campaign for independence from Britain.

Dwarkanath Tagore was one of Roy's earliest associates. His family controlled the tax collection in part of Bengal, and Dwarkanath used his profits to help found Calcutta's Union Bank. Diversifying his holdings, he bought up jute plantations, silk factories, and indigo mills; in 1834 he joined with British capitalists in transforming one of Calcutta's basic economic institutions, the Managing Agency or private export-import company, into a diversified company with holdings in collieries, transportation, indigo plantations, and banking. Throughout his career Dwarkanath envisaged an ongoing partnership of British and Indians that would revitalize both the economic and the cultural life of his country. In helping to found Calcutta's Hindu College and in supporting the young intellectuals of the Brahmo Samaj, he sought to create a new Indian elite that would cooperate with the British. His own reputation became so high among Europeans that on a tour to Europe he was entertained by Queen Victoria in London and by King Louis Philippe in France.

During the lifetime of Dwarkanath's son, Debendranath Tagore (1817–1905), this collaboration soured. In 1835, in his *Minute on Education*, Lord Macaulay had persuaded the British administration in Calcutta

Debendranath Tagore: Partnership Soured

that Indians should be educated in English, which was to become the official language of India. Macaulay admitted he had no knowledge of Sanskrit or Arabic, but he concluded that "all the historical information which has been collected from all the books written in the Sanskrit language is less valuable than what may be found in the most paltry abridgements used at preparatory schools in England. In every branch of physical or moral philosophy the relative position of the two nations is nearly the same." In 1857 the Mutiny further weakened the desire of the British to understand their Indian subjects, especially the Bengali of Calcutta. "Large promises, smooth excuses, elaborate tissues of circumstantial falsehood, chicanery, perjury, forgery, are the weapons, offensive and defensive, of the people of the Lower Ganges," Macaulay stormed.[5] In response, Debendranath Tagore led many of the members of Brahmo Samaj in a return to Hinduism and a rejection of British ideals, including even a refusal to use the English language. He established primary schools for Hindu children from which Christianity could be excluded. The protest against the British remained at the level of religious and social protest, however. Only at the end of the century did it take political shape.

Rabindranath Tagore: Poetry and Protest

In the 1880s and 1890s Indian resentment at the exploitation and arrogance of British rule, which reached its culmination while Lord Curzon was viceroy (1899–1905), began to take the form of a nationalist revolt. The leaders of the new movements were middle-class Indians, mostly products of the universities of Calcutta and Bombay that had been founded as part of the post-Mutiny reforms; and their centers of organization were the cities of Bombay, Poona, Madras, and Calcutta. The principal instrument of the nationalists was the Indian National Congress, founded in Bombay in 1885 for the purpose of pressuring the British to give a larger share in government to Indians and a greater share of the revenue to economic development. Several British sympathizers participated in the early meetings, and an attempt was made to include Moslems. The congress was even welcomed by the British administration as a harmless safety valve.

In 1895–1905, however, India was struck by economic depression, famine, and bubonic plague; at the height of the suffering, the viceroy, Lord Curzon, decided to make the Bengali more governable by partitioning their province in two. To the nationalists of Calcutta and to the Congress, the partition seemed an ill-disguised effort to destroy the political power of the Bengal Hindus. Calcutta took the lead in violent opposition to British rule. A boycott of all British goods (swadeshi) was begun with the public burning of British-made cloth. New Indian schools were founded throughout the city. Homemade bombs were set off by groups of young terrorists, the first killing two English women. The British replied with repression, arresting hundreds and exiling others; in 1912, in what amounted to a punishment of Calcutta, they moved the capital to Delhi.

[5]Cited in Leonard A. Gordon, *Bengal: The Nationalist Movement, 1876–1940* (New York: Columbia University Press, 1974), p. 6.

It was this period of agitation that brought Rabindranath Tagore into political involvement. The eighth son of Debendranath, he had been given his family's traditional combination of literary education in both Calcutta and England and practical experience in administering the family plantations. However, he soon became poet, playwright, novelist, and musician, combining his love of the physical world with a deep philosophical and spiritual probing. Bengal fascinated him, especially the Ganges:

Every day there was the ebb and flow of the tide on the Ganges; the various gait of so many different boats; the shifting of the shadows of the trees from west to east; and, over the fringe of shade-patches of the woods on the opposite bank, the gush of golden life-blood through the pierced breast of the evening sky.[6]

Calcutta, too, where he grew up in the rambling family home, remained with him.

> *Dark, dense rain,*
> *Train fares go up,*
> *Wages go down.*
> *The lane is littered*
> *With rotting mango peels, jackfruit kernels,*
> *Scraps of fish bones,*
> *Dead kittens—*
> *All kinds of rubbish.*
> *My umbrella is full of holes,*
> *Like my pay, after they've cut the fines.*
> *My office dress?*
> *Rain-drenched*
> *Like the heart of Gopikana Gosai wet with elegant wit.*
> *Dark shadows of rain*
> *Enter my damp room.*
> *Like a beast, trapped in a machine,*
> *Fallen in a faint,*
> *Day and night, I feel I am*
> *Chained hand and foot to a half-dead world.*[7]

During the 1880s he had developed his own original verse forms, composed like the Indian music in which he also excelled in long, plaintive incantations; and his deep originality, with its sources in his love of the Hindu classics and of the writings of the fifth-century playwright Kalidasa, infused the great collection of poems known as *Gitanjali*, which he wrote in 1904–1912 and which was primarily responsible for his receipt of the Nobel Prize for literature in 1913.

[6] Cited in Edward Thompson, *Rabindranath Tagore, Poet and Dramatist*, 2nd ed. (Oxford: Oxford University Press, 1948), p. 21.
[7] Rabindranath Tagore, "The Flute," in Subhoranjan Dasgupta and Sudeshna Chakravarti, eds., *Bengali Poems on Calcutta* (Calcutta: Writer's Workshop, 1972). Copyright by individual poets.

As his literary reputation in Bengal grew, Tagore became more occupied with political questions. He had briefly joined a revolutionary youth group when he was young, and in the 1890s he began to brood on the national character first of Bengal and then of India itself. He saw the denial of nationalism as the British rejection of the internationalism of which he approved, since only in mutual national respect could international harmony be achieved.

In 1905 the partition controversy made Tagore a leader of Calcutta's protest. He led processions through the city to dramatize the boycott movement, and he would link people's hands with thread to symbolize the unity of one Bengali to another. The divisions within the leadership of the revolt disturbed him, however, as did the growing violence. Eventually he withdrew to the countryside, to a school he had founded in the Ganges Delta. Although he remained a spiritual inspiration to the independence movement, his one further gesture in the struggle was his return of the knighthood the British had granted him after his receipt of the Nobel Prize. He continued to write poetry and philosophy and to lecture throughout the world on internationalism; he even took up painting with his usual creativity. The poem by the Bengali novelist Bankim Chandra Chatterji (1838–1894), which Tagore had set to music, was to become the rallying song of the nationalist movement:

> Hail to thee, Mother!
> Rich with thy hurrying streams,
> Bright with thy orchard gleams,
> Cool with thy winds of delight,
> Dark fields waving,
> Mother of might,
> Mother free.[8]

Tagore's gentle humanism was to remain a potent influence in support of the nonviolent road to independence that would culminate in the final, successful struggle launched by Mahatma Gandhi in the 1920s.

The Significance of Calcutta

Calcutta in the nineteenth century thus symbolized in an extreme form the experience of India under British colonial rule. British rule had brought to India both the advantages and the worst burdens of the modern industrial age. Calcutta, as the dynamo of the Indian economy, showed in its factories, port, and slums the mixed results of industrialization. In no other Indian city had the local middle class so profited from the opportunities offered by the new regime, and in no other city had so large or poor a proletariat gathered. British rule had stimulated an Indian intellectual revival in which Bengal, with Calcutta as its focus, had played a leading role. The three generations of the Tagore family represented by Dwarkanath, Debendranath, and Rabindranath typify the change of attitude of

[8]Cited in Stanley Wolpert, *A New History of India* (New York: Oxford University Press, 1977), p. 274.

many of India's intellectuals toward British rule from an early appreciation of its stimulus, through a period of passive disapproval and distrust, to open and active opposition.

Finally, Calcutta offered a very early example of rapid urbanization in a relatively underdeveloped country. Like many of the expanding cities of the Third World in the twentieth century, it possessed a well-planned center of elegance and luxury, where well-to-do British and Indians could lead an urbane, civilized existence. Its employment opportunities in industry, trade, and personal service made Calcutta a magnet for both the ambitious and the dispossessed from the whole surrounding region. But the influx of would-be workers far exceeded the creation of openings for work, and the poor in the outer districts and especially in the totally unplanned slums across the river found that the city was incapable of meeting their minimal needs for housing or public services. Calcutta thus represented both a promise of the potential benefits of modernization and a frightening portent of the results of the failure, through demographic pressure, to share those benefits among the population that demanded them.

EUROPEAN EMPIRES IN SOUTHEAST ASIA

The British in Burma

Burma's weakness in the nineteenth century lay in the continuing animosities between the dominant Burman groups, centered on the Irrawaddy River valley, and the many unassimilated ethnic groups, of which the most important were the Mons in the south, the Shans in the north, and the Karens in the east. The different groups had been politically unified in 1758 by King Alaungapaya, founder of the last Burmese royal dynasty, who moved the capital to the coastal city of Rangoon. The pressure of his successors on the borders of India in the early nineteenth century, however, gave the British East India Company a military reason for intervention in Burma; and the country's rich rice lands in the Irrawaddy Delta, its deposits of tin, and its forests of teak attracted the interest of British merchants. Hence, in the first Burmese war (1824–1826) the British seized part of the coast.

Finding that the Burmese government was still restricting their access to the main seaports, the British provoked a second war in 1852. Rangoon was bombarded by a British warship, and British troops from India moved inland to defeat the Burmese army. The Burmese king, compelled to cede the entire coast including Rangoon and part of the hinterland, withdrew to establish a new capital at Mandalay. Rangoon expanded into one of the major cities of Southeast Asia, acting as the principal port for the import of British manufactured goods and for the export of Burma's teak, tin, and rice. However, British realization of the importance of the Irrawaddy Valley as an access route to southwestern China's raw silk provided an incentive to overthrow the Burmese dynasty in the third and last Burmese war (1885). The king was exiled to India, and Burma was placed under direct British rule by the viceroy in Calcutta.

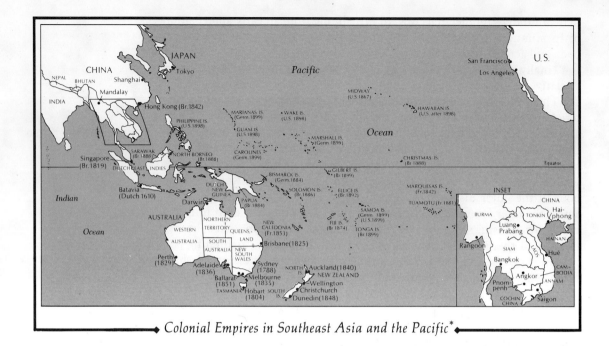

The British immediately moved to develop Burma's economic resources. Using Burmese taxes, they constructed an efficient railroad network whose main purpose was to allow export of Burma's agricultural produce and raw materials. The Irrawaddy Delta became a major rice-producing region, with irrigation and flood control; but the land was held

*Year in parentheses: foundation date of city in Australia or New Zealand; country and year in parentheses: colonial power, date of colony acquisition.

British Capture of Rangoon, 1824
The British seized Rangoon during the First Burma War and occupied it for three years. After its recapture by the British army in 1852, it was transformed into a modern banking and commercial metropolis. (India Office Library and Records)

largely by absentee owners, most of them British. Oil production in central Burma was rapidly expanded, and taxes on teak production became the principal source of state income. Thus, although small numbers of the Burmese merchant class of the cities and some landowners profited from British rule, the majority of the peasants found their conditions of life ever more precarious, and relations between the different racial groups in Burma were worsened by the British administration's encouragement of their rivalries.

Worst of all, however, was the growth of chronic lawlessness, especially among the thousands of unemployed persons roaming the country. British rule had deprived many of their land and had broken the strict discipline of the village communities. Large numbers of Indians had been introduced to work in the rice fields, the factories, and public transport, thereby denying work to the Burmese. Respect for authority declined as the local police abused their powers. Violent crime became endemic, especially in Lower Burma. Petty theft by individuals was followed by gang robbery known as *dacoity*. Thus, although some had profited from British rule, for many its principal effect before 1914 was to precipitate the breakdown of a previously well-ordered society.

On the small island of Singapore, lying on the narrow straits between the Malay Peninsula and Indonesia through which the great trade route from China passed to India and Europe, the British constructed one of the world's finest trading cities. The almost empty island had attracted the attention of Stamford Raffles, an East India Company official who had been working at the British-held port of Penang and, during the Napoleonic wars, in the British occupation of the island of Java. Raffles was able to gain Singapore's transfer to Britain in 1819, and it was made into a free port. As a result, immigrants poured in from the Malay Peninsula and from China. Within one year the island had a population of 10,000. Raffles himself paid his last visit to Singapore in 1824 and, in nine months, laid down ambitious plans for new roads, harbors, housing, swamp drainage, law codes, and separate towns for Malays and Chinese.

For the next fifty years the British were satisfied to retain control of only three ports—Singapore and the cities of Penang and Malacca on the Malay Peninsula—which were jointly known as the Straits Settlements and were ruled by the governor-general in Calcutta. Inland, the local sultans maintained a shaky hold over a turbulent population of feuding Malay peasants, Chinese tin miners, and Indian rubber workers. When their battles, many of which were provoked by Chinese secret societies, began to reduce the production of tin and rubber exported from the Straits Settlements, the British finally acted. In 1874 they compelled the sultans of the four states of the central Malay Peninsula to accept the political control of a British resident and paid them a British salary. In 1896 these states were renamed the Federated Malay States, and a new capital was constructed at Kuala Lumpur, on the site of a Chinese tin-mining camp. The remaining five sultans were all persuaded to join the new union by 1914.

Singapore and the Malay Peninsula

Waterfront Warehouses, Singapore, Late Nineteenth Century
The vast commercial potential of Singapore, which controls the straits between Indonesia and the Malay Peninsula, was recognized by Sir Stamford Raffles, who in 1819 obtained control of the island for Britain from the local sultan. (Popperfoto)

Thus in Malaya the British had succeeded in gaining control relatively peacefully, and the exports of tin and rubber were used to pay for a sound infrastructure of roads, railroads, hospitals, utilities, and schools. Although the native Malays remained primarily occupied in agriculture and felt little of the new prosperity, the Chinese and Indian immigrants undoubtedly did well under British rule; and there was remarkably little opposition to colonialism until the Second World War.

The French in Indochina

One motive of the British in moving into Burma and the Malay Peninsula had been to forestall the French, who were creating a new colonial empire in Indochina (present-day Vietnam, Cambodia, and Laos). French interest in Indochina had originally been spurred by Catholic missionaries in the late eighteenth century; and they were able to gain a political foothold by giving military aid to Nguyen-Anh, a general who in 1802 united the northern Vietnamese state of Tonkin, named after its capital city (present-day Hanoi), with the central Vietnamese state of Annam, whose capital was Hué. Nguyen-Anh chose Hué as the capital of his new Vietnamese Empire and soon established a protectorate over Cambodia. The French were ceded territory off the tip of Cochin China, the southernmost state of the Vietnamese Empire.

The new dynasty in Hué proved xenophobic and oppressive, most notably to Vietnamese converts to Christianity, who were often executed or branded and sent into exile. French fleets roamed the coasts, seeking to protect the Christians by threat of bombardment. In 1858–1859 they finally seized the coast of Cochin China, including the port of Saigon; and in 1867 they were ceded the rest of Cochin China by the Vietnamese emperor. Cochin China became a French colony; and, as the center of France's trading and financial interests, Saigon expanded rapidly. Cambodia became a French protectorate the same year. The independence of the remaining parts of the Vietnamese Empire lasted only until 1883, when the French, determined to open up trade with southern China along the Red River valley, made protectorates of both Annam and Tonkin. In 1887 Cochin China, Tonkin, Annam, and Cambodia were formed into the Union of Indochina under a French governor-general. Laos was added to the union in 1893.

Two indigenous groups profited from French colonialism in Indochina: the Chinese mercantile population of the booming cities like Saigon and the well-to-do Vietnamese landlords of the efficiently exploited rice lands of the Mekong River Delta. Taxes—mostly levied on the peasantry in the form of a head tax, a salt tax, and customs duties—helped produce the revenues that built a fine road and railroad system and good harbors. Peasant labor on European-owned estates grew the rubber, coffee, and tea that provided a good living for the colonial aristocracy. The resentment of the peasantry against the French was finally expressed by a small intellectual group to whom the colonial authorities extended the opportunity of French education in secondary schools in Indochina and in France itself. From them were eventually to come such leaders as Ho Chi Minh (1890–1969); but before 1914 the resentment was largely mute.

Dutch Indonesia

The most exploitative regime in Southeast Asia was that of the Dutch in Indonesia. After ousting the Portuguese from the islands of Indonesia by 1610, the Dutch fought off efforts by the British to gain a share of the spice trade there. Over the next two centuries the Dutch East India Company established its hold over the native inhabitants. From the start the peasants found that Dutch rule meant a new kind of feudalism in the countryside, with local administrators compelling them to give fixed shares of their rice and later of their coffee beans for taxes. Batavia (present-day Djakarta), the principal port and administrative center, represented to the Indonesians an alien implantation whose primary function for the Dutch was to keep open the commerce with the Far East and whose secondary function was to squeeze greater taxes from them.

The situation became worse after 1830, when the Dutch introduced the so-called Culture System, following the suppression, after five years of desperate fighting, of a popular revolt against their rule. The peasants were compelled to set aside one-fifth of the land for planting of crops specified by the authorities—mostly coffee, sugar, tea, and cotton—and were required to work half the time on those lands for the authorities. Within a few years the system produced a vast financial surplus, which was sent back to the Netherlands for reinvestment.

Investors in the Netherlands, however, began to demand an opening in Indonesia, which had been governed directly by the Dutch government as the Dutch East Indies since 1799. Between 1862 and 1917 the Culture System was slowly dismantled, and a new program called the Forward Movement was implemented, in which private capitalists were permitted to buy up huge plantations and to sink mines in which Chinese immigrants, as in Malaya, were employed. The result was urbanization on a rapid scale, especially with the growth of Batavia; but the cities provided an opportunity to the leaders of an anticolonial revolt to organize, disregarding a new Dutch program of pacification known as the Ethical Policy (1901), by which Indonesians were slowly to be given a share in power. Meanwhile the desperation of the peasantry was seen in two attacks mounted against the Dutch forts on Bali in 1906 and 1908, as well as in a guerrilla war on Sumatra that lasted for thirty-five years.

**Independent
Thailand**

The only country of Southeast Asia to remain independent of the European colonialists was Thailand (known as Siam until 1937). After the Burmese destruction of its old capital of Ayudha, a Thai general had seized power, founded the Chakkri dynasty, created a new capital at Bangkok, and renamed himself Rama I (reigned 1782–1809). Under Rama III (reigned 1824–1851), Thailand, which had been closed to the West since

The Grand Palace Compound, Bangkok
Some of the finest of Bangkok's three hundred Buddhist temples cluster in the walled enclosure of the royal palace. The tapering towers, or prangs, are derived from the stupas of India, whereas the curved gables of the prayer halls are influenced by Cambodian and Chinese architecture. (F. Roy Willis)

1688, was partially opened to modernization. Trade treaties were signed with Britain and the United States, and some Western advisers were welcomed. Under Mongkut, or Rama IV (reigned 1851–1868), and his son Chulalongkorn, or Rama V (reigned 1868–1910), Westernization became state policy. Roads and railroads were constructed, new laws enacted, and a more efficient administration introduced. English as well as Thai was the language of instruction in the schools, and American missionaries ran many private schools.

Bangkok became the glory of the new monarchy. The palace compound on the banks of the Chao Phya River was ablaze with the multi-colored tile of the roofs of Buddhist prayer halls, with the bright gilt of innumerable bell-shaped shrines known as *prangs*, and with the blue and pink ceramics of its palaces. Rama I placed the lovely Emerald Buddha, a thirty-one-inch figure carved in jasper, in the principal temple, the Wat Phrakeo; across the river Rama III created the rival Wat Arun, with pagodas in the style of ancient Cambodia and a prang 260 feet tall that dominated the city. Only in the 1860s, however, did Bangkok receive its first street, which ran inland parallel to the winding river, because most of the city's inhabitants moved themselves and their goods by small boat on the city's many canals.

NEW EMPIRES IN THE PACIFIC

For a century after Magellan's Spanish-sponsored expedition (1519–1522) had crossed the vast reaches of the Pacific Ocean, the only European peoples to explore and settle the lands of the Pacific basin were the Spanish and the Portuguese. The Spanish settled in the Philippine Islands, which Magellan had reached in 1522 but which were not conquered until 1564. Their city of Manila, rebuilt in 1571, became one of the major trading centers of East Asia, linking China and the Spanish colony of Mexico; but although the Spanish explored some of the Pacific islands, the only one they made into a colony was Guam. The Portuguese remained satisfied with their bases in the East Indies.

The only other European power to penetrate the Pacific basin in the seventeenth century was the Dutch who, in the process of creating a trade empire based on Indonesia, explored the South Pacific and discovered Australia in 1606. Later expeditions explored other parts of the Australian coast, which the Dutch found too uninviting for settlement, although they named the continent New Holland. In 1642 their sea captain Tasman, who had been investigating Australia, found a large new island which was named New Zealand, after a Dutch province. However, the Dutch, who were interested primarily in gaining access to the existing trade networks, especially with the Spice Islands (Moluccas), made no attempt to settle.

In the eighteenth century both the British and the French began serious scientific exploration of the Pacific, partly in the interests of pure research but primarily as part of their search for new sources of wealth and for political hegemony. By far the most significant of these voyages were the three expeditions of Captain James Cook in the late eighteenth century, which not only led to the British annexation of Australia and New Zealand but also gave the British knowledge of almost every part of the three Pacific island groups, Polynesia, Melanesia, and Micronesia. A French expedition around the world under Louis de Bougainville had given France a special interest in Tahiti, whose Polynesian inhabitants were enthusiastically described by Bougainville as the noble savages that the contemporary Enlightenment writers claimed all human beings would be if untrammeled by the constraints of society.

Australia

In 1787 the British moved rapidly to settle Australia by shipping to Botany Bay, at the site of the city of Sydney, a group of convicts punished for such crimes as bankruptcy, vagrancy, larceny, and sheep stealing. Other groups of convicts were sent out over the next forty years; and private settlers opened up sheep farms, primarily along the east coast, to which the convicts were often released to work off their sentences. Exploration of the other coastal areas, as well as journeys into the interior, was slowly followed by new settlements, often by squatters moving onto vacant land before government officials could take possession. By 1840 the nucleus already existed of most of Australia's principal cities, notably Sydney, Perth, Melbourne, Hobart, and Brisbane.

In 1851 the discovery of gold in New South Wales added a new element to an economy primarily based on sheep and wheat production. The gold rush to Australia was as large as that to California had been two years earlier, and Australia's population shot from 400,000 in 1850 to 1.1 million in 1860. As the gold ran out, however, the governments of the six colonies into which Australia had been divided (New South Wales, South Australia, Tasmania, Victoria, Queensland, and Western Australia) were compelled to undertake large-scale public works, such as irrigation and road building, in order to permit the unemployed miners to move into farming. The new farmers, however, found great hostility from the sheepherders, whose flocks roamed over vast ranges that the arable farmers wanted to open to the plough.

Problems of unemployment also raised the question of the racial composition of the Australian population, especially since there had been riots between Asian and European workers during the gold rush itself. At first preference was given to European and especially British stock by offering monetary assistance to emigrants from Europe to pay their passage. In the 1880s and 1890s increasingly restrictive legislation made it extremely difficult for the Chinese and later for all Asians to settle in Australia. The final problem facing Australians after the gold rush was the relationship among the six self-governing colonies, all of which were jealous of their autonomy. The solution was adoption of a constitution on the United States pattern, delegating to the former colonies, now renamed states, a large share of

Sydney, Australia
Sydney, Australia's largest city and principal port, grew up around the original British penal colony at Botany Bay. Its harbor is dominated by the soaring rooflines of the Opera House, completed in 1974.   (Russell A. Thompson/Taurus Photos)

power, but also forming a central, federal government with a parliament of two houses (Senate and House of Representatives) for such tasks as defense and foreign policy for the new Commonwealth of Australia. After approval of the constitution by the British Parliament, the new state came into being in 1901.

Settlement of New Zealand after Cook's visit in 1769 proceeded more slowly than that of Australia, despite the country's temperate climate and excellent potential for arable farming and animal raising. Fear of the cannibalistic Maoris, the original Polynesian settlers of the islands, who numbered over 200,000, discouraged all except missionaries and a mixed group of temporary visitors ranging from whalers and sealers to purchasers of timber. In 1840, however, the British government officially annexed the country and permitted Edward Gibbon Wakefield to send out a group of colonists sponsored by his New Zealand Company. The British bought peace with the Maoris by guaranteeing them possession of their lands under the sovereignty of the British crown. Over the next two decades settlers poured into New Zealand, many of them determined to get rich quickly by land acquisition. In 1854, when the British government permitted the colony to become self-governing through an appointed Legislative Council and an elected House of Representatives, there was a white population of over 40,000, mostly from Britain or Australia.

New Zealand

For the Maoris, however, European settlement was disastrous, both stripping them of their lands and reducing their numbers through European diseases. They fought back desperately between 1860 and 1872, especially as the discovery of gold had brought in even larger numbers of Europeans. When finally defeated, the Maoris numbered only 100,000; their numbers continued to decline, to only 40,000 in 1896. The survivors sold off large portions of their ancestral lands, and many took work as laborers on the sheep farms or in building the roads and other public works that opened up the interior they had once controlled.

For the white New Zealanders the three decades after the end of the Maori wars saw the establishment of a largely rural economy based on export of agricultural products to Great Britain that remained unchanged into the 1970s. Widely shared landholding was encouraged by the breakup of the large estates created during the period of settlement, and political reforms running in parallel with the economic change brought universal suffrage to males over twenty-one in 1879 and to women over twenty-one in 1893. A social security system was created as early as 1898 with the establishment of old age pensions. Under the leadership of their chiefs, the Maoris themselves began to revive, and by the 1970s numbered 225,000 out of New Zealand's total population of 2.8 million.

Tahiti and Hawaii

The Maoris of New Zealand formed part of a racial group called Polynesian, who in the early nineteenth century were virtually the only inhabitants of the hundreds of islands that stretch across the Pacific in a great triangle from Hawaii in the north, New Zealand in the south, and Easter Island in the east. (*Polynesian* means "many islands" in Greek.) This racial group originated in Asia, perhaps in Malaysia, and had settled the Pacific islands by long, daring canoe expeditions that extended from about 1000 B. C. to the final establishment in Hawaii about A. D. 750.

When European sailors visited them in the eighteenth century, they found somewhat similar societies and economies throughout the area of Polynesia. The principal social tie was the kinfolk, linked by descent from a common ancestor and by worship of the same ancestral deities. Tribal chiefs were believed to be descended from the deities and thus to possess *mana*, or supernatural power. The kins were grouped in tribes with claims to specific territorial sovereignty, which they often disputed by war. Economic life was largely communal, based on fishing, growing the basic foods (taro, breadfruit, coconuts, and sweet potatoes), and raising pigs, chickens, and dogs. Tapa cloth was made from the bark of a mulberry and a fig tree. The Europeans were astounded at the simple geniality of this society, in spite of its warfare; but almost immediately they began to wreak fundamental changes in the ways of Polynesia that had so attracted them. Tahiti and Hawaii present two of the most interesting examples of this interaction.

After the islands of Tahiti had been explored by the British and French expeditions of the 1760s and 1770s, no attempt was made to enforce political controls until the 1840s. A few French and, to a lesser degree, British government ships continued to visit for scientific research. But the larger number of vessels visiting were British, French, and especially American whalers and sealers, as well as merchant ships seeking sandalwood and pearl shells for which they exchanged cloth, metal tools, and guns. A London missionary society attempted in 1797 to convert the islanders to Protestantism, principally by aiding one of the Tahitian dynasties, the Pomare family, to win supremacy over the other tribes. King Pomare II took power after 1803 with missionary support, and after his official conversion in 1812 the rest of the population became superficially Protestant.

The papacy, however, decided in the 1830s to win the Pacific islands back to Catholicism and sent to Tahiti French priests whom the French government backed with gunboats. The English missionaries who were acting as the real government of Tahiti behind the throne of Queen Pomare (reigned 1827–1877) were left without support by the British government; in 1843 the French warships, by threatening to bombard the capital, Papeete, compelled the Tahitians to accept a French protectorate and, shortly afterward, to convert to the Catholic religion. Queen Pomare adapted with grace to this new situation. She received a salary from the French but shared it widely among her family and servants. She took a personal interest in the administration of the islands, making frequent tours to inspect the working of the courts and to prevent the French from taking arbitrary action against the district chiefs.

Freed of the puritanical approach of the London missionaries, the islanders reverted to their less inhibited ways and their subsistence economy. Attempts to found cotton plantations failed even though Chinese laborers were imported; the only crops the Polynesians adopted for export were copra and vanilla, which they grew on their own holdings. Only after the death of Queen Pomare did the French finally decide the islands were worth annexing, principally because of their suspicion of German and American penetration of the region. In 1880 the French forced the abdication of Queen Pomare's son, Pomare V (reigned 1877–1880), and formally annexed Tahiti as a colony. Ironically, the painter most responsible for portraying the romance and beauty of Tahiti and its islanders—Paul Gauguin (1848–1903)—arrived there in 1891 to protest French colonialism by attending the funeral of Pomare V, the last Tahitian king. By then, the islands of the Pacific had been partitioned almost entirely among Britain, France, Germany, and the United States.

Although Hawaii had been discovered by Captain Cook in 1778, American influence rather than British became predominant almost immediately. The discovery of sandalwood in 1790 brought many American traders who, for the next twenty-five years, shipped the wood to China. The Hawaiian king Kamehameha I (reigned 1790–1819), who had unified all the islands by conquest in 1810, was able to gain considerable revenue by establishing a royal monopoly on sandalwood supplies; but traders' de-

Queen Liliuokalani of Hawaii on Her Coronation Day (1891)
Liliuokalani was dethroned in 1893 by a revolt led by American sugar planters. After the annexation of the Hawaiian Islands by the United States, she was eventually given a small pension, but her claims for compensation for the loss of her kingdom were denied by the American government.   (Hawaii State Archives)

mands became so excessive that the forests were wiped out. By then diseases brought by the sailors were already reducing the Hawaiian population, which declined from 300,000 in 1770 to 140,000 by 1825. The ancient Hawaiian religion was under attack by Kamehameha's own successor. Thus, when the first American Protestant missionaries arrived in 1820, led by the Reverend Hiram Bingham, they found it easy to establish their influence, especially during the reign of Kamehameha III (reigned 1825–1854). The missionaries brought schools, Christian books printed in Hawaiian, and puritanical rules of behavior.

In 1839–1840 the king gave Hawaii a bill of rights and a constitution, creating a legislature, abolishing feudalism, and recognizing that God had "given alike to every man, and every chief—life, limb, liberty, the labor of his hands, and productions of his mind." Although the United States had officially recognized the independence of the Hawaiian kingdom in 1842, two of the chief ministers of the new government were former American missionaries who had become Hawaiian citizens. For the next forty years American economic influence increased rapidly. Whaling replaced the sandalwood trade as the primary source of income until the 1860s. Sugar plantations expanded, often owned by missionary families in huge estates. With the decline of the native Hawaiian population to only 70,000 in 1853, it became increasingly necessary during the sugar boom of the 1870s and 1880s to bring in large numbers of Chinese and Japanese laborers.

As early as 1852 negotiations began for the annexation of the islands by the United States; but European and Japanese objections, as well as the reluctance of the American government, delayed action until the 1890s, when a group composed of native-born Americans and sons of American missionaries overthrew the last Hawaiian monarch, Queen Liliuokalani (reigned 1891–1893), and demanded annexation to the United States. When the Senate balked, they turned Hawaii into a republic in 1894–1898, under the presidency of Sanford P. Dole.

Liliuokalani, held a prisoner in her Iolani palace, was compelled to sign abdication papers making it possible for President William McKinley and Congress to approve the annexation. Hawaii became a territory in 1900, with Dole appointed as its governor. The annexation of Hawaii was not, however, primarily a response to the actions of powerful citizens of American stock in the islands. For the United States it was part of the process of becoming a major Pacific power that had been undertaken at the end of the Spanish-American War of 1898 with the annexation of the Philippine Islands and Guam.

The Philippines

The Philippines, a group of 7,000 islands in the southwest Pacific, were linked by easy sea journeys and, up to 30,000 years ago or even later, by land bridges with Borneo, Sumatra, and the Malay Peninsula. It is thought that the earliest inhabitants of the Philippines, the Negritos (negroid pygmies) who form 5–10 percent of the present population of the islands, crossed these land bridges. They were followed by successive waves of peoples of Malay stock and language, who at first crossed the land bridges (which had disappeared by about 8,000 B. C.) and then came by sea, forming the vast majority of the Philippine population.

The history of the islands before the Spanish conquest is shadowy. Some contact was made with the Sri Vijaya Empire and with the later Madjahpahit Empire between the eighth and fifteenth centuries, and a little Hindu influence may have been felt in the islands as a result of a small amount of commercial exchange. China during the Sung dynasty was interested in obtaining the islands' exports of pearls, shells, cotton, and wax; and the Filipino people took from the Chinese some knowledge of metallurgy, gunpowder, and textiles, and perhaps even a primitive ancestor worship. The Chinese expanded their trading posts and some married Filipinos. By the fourteenth century the Chinese emperor considered the Philippines a tributary state. The southern Philippines were also exposed to Moslem influence from Arab traders and Malay settlers moving there in the fourteenth and fifteenth centuries from the Indonesian islands. Many of the inhabitants of Mindanao and the Sulu Peninsula were converted to Islam, and their descendants form the Moslem minority (5 percent) of the Filipino population today.

Magellan's Spanish expedition reached the Philippines in 1522. Although Magellan himself was killed in a skirmish with a local chief in the islands, one of his ships returned to Spain with spices and news of the potential value of the islands in opening up trade with China. Several Spanish expeditions failed to gain a foothold, although the leader of the 1542 expedition named the islands the Philippines after Philip, the heir to the Spanish throne. The islands were finally conquered, after fierce opposition from the inhabitants, by an expedition sent from Mexico in 1564 under López de Legaspi. Manila was made the Spanish capital in 1571 and became the center of Spanish trading and missionary activities. Manila flourished as the port where an annual galleon from Acapulco exchanged a cargo of silver for Chinese silks and a few other Asian products, although English privateers made dependence on the arrival of the silver fleet precarious. Rebuilt in the early seventeenth century in stone and tile, surrounded by a strong defense wall, Manila became a city of luxurious living, at least for an upper class of merchants and administrators. Chinese settlers, on whom much of the commercial life of the islands came to depend, lived in a separate enclave on the edge of the city and were often subject to persecution, which reached its height in the massacre of thousands in 1603.

For the Filipinos the worst aspect of Spanish rule was the land-grant or *encomienda*, by which Spanish soldiers and settlers were given not only ownership of land but also the right to exact tribute and labor service from its inhabitants. Spanish missionary monks and friars helped consolidate the new regime by converting the majority of the population by the end of the sixteenth century. Both locally and at the Spanish court, many Church leaders attempted to mitigate the exploitative nature of the Spanish occupation; and their priests became the principal Spanish authority with whom most Filipinos had contact.

During the eighteenth and early nineteenth centuries the Spanish regime became increasingly corrupt and ineffectual, although the local authorities were still able to put down frequent uprisings led by aggrieved local chiefs and by the Moros, the Moslems of the southern islands. From the 1830s and 1840s, however, Filipino grievances grew. The Manila-Acapulco trade stopped in 1815, and China's grant of treaty ports to the European powers ended Manila's role as an intermediary in the China trade. At a time of economic distress, new missionary orders, especially the Jesuits, were sent from Spain to revive the fervor of the Philippine Church. Meanwhile, Spanish trading groups sought compensation in the Philippines for their losses in Central and South America.

Filipino resistance to the new policies was stimulated by the brilliant writer José Rizal, who, after rebellion began in August 1896, was executed by the Spanish. His execution brought great popular support for the rebellion which, under Emilio Aguinaldo, soon spread to all the islands. Aguinaldo had signed a truce with the Spanish—which neither side appeared ready to keep—when a U.S. fleet under Commodore George Dewey destroyed the Spanish fleet in Manila Bay in May 1898. This action, which broadened the scope of the Spanish-American War that had begun in Cuba earlier in the year, was followed by a U.S. request to Aguinaldo to gather a

Filipino force to attack the Spaniards in the interval before an American army could arrive. Aguinaldo was able to seize most of Luzon and besiege Manila, and his forces declared the Philippines an independent democratic republic.

The peace settlement included the grant of the Philippines to the United States in return for payment of $20 million. This annexation drove Aguinaldo to rebel against the new master of the islands in a bloody war that took more lives than the entire Spanish-American War. The rebellion helped to inspire a debate in the United States over the wisdom of retaining the new possession, which lasted for most of the U.S. occupation. The Republican party in particular felt that recent American territorial acquisitions in the Pacific (Midway and Alaska in 1867; the Philippines, Guam, Wake Island, and Hawaii in 1898) were a necessary counterpart to the trading concessions that had been won in China and Japan. The Democrats argued that the Philippines at least lay beyond the sphere of U.S. interest. Although it was decided to retain the islands, constant efforts were made to persuade the Filipinos that they had a share in their own government—by the establishment of an elected lower house in 1907 and an upper house in 1913, with power of approval of appointments made by the American governor-general. In 1934 the Tydings-Macduffie Independence Act, which was ratified by the Philippine legislature the following year, provided for independence in 1946 after self-rule under American tutelage. A Commonwealth of the Philippines was established in November 1935, with Manuel L. Quezon its first president. Although the Philippine government had to flee into exile in the United States during the Japanese occupation of 1942–1944, the new president, Sergio Osmeña, who had taken office on Quezon's death in 1944, returned to the islands with the first

Captives in the Philippines During the Spanish-American War, 1898
Although the Spanish were ousted from the Philippines with little difficulty, the decision by the United States to annex the islands provoked a bloody revolt by the Filipinos that was not put down until 1901. (Library of Congress)

American invading force. Independence was granted as scheduled, on July 4, 1946.

The forty years of U.S. control had major effects on Philippine society and economy. Social reforms included the institution of a free, universal, and secular system of private education, as well as much improved standards of public health. A more impartial judicial system was created; penal laws were made more humane; and guarantees of political rights improved continually, especially under the Commonwealth. A large-scale program of public works—notably in road and railroad construction, port development, and electrification—gave the island the basis of a modern infrastructure. Many of the economic reforms also pleased the Filipinos— most notably the purchase of the vast landholdings of the friars and their redistribution in small holdings among the local population. But U.S. control of the Philippine economy has also been criticized as a form of colonial exploitation. The economy of the island was oriented to supply the United States with raw materials, such as gold, silver, manganese, and copper, and with agricultural products like hemp, sugar, and lumber. Little effort was made to establish local industry where it might compete with products from the United States, which flooded into the country under a regime of free trade. Perhaps the worst aspects of the occupation were the control of the major companies in shipping, banking, and the export trade by American interests, and the concentration in large estates owned by Americans in cooperation with a small upper class of wealthy Filipinos of much of the country's agricultural land.

SUB-SAHARAN AFRICA BEFORE AND DURING PARTITION

Most of sub-Saharan Africa was formally annexed by the European powers between 1875 and 1900; but between 1800 and 1875, in every part of the continent, the political power and social stability of the African states were already being eroded by forces from within the societies themselves and from countries beyond the continent. Thus the first three-quarters of the nineteenth century was for Africa a period of transition from a society in which indigenous influences were predominant, if not exclusive, to a period of colonial subordination that lasted until independence was restored after World War II.

The Savanna States of the Western and Central Sudan, 1800–1875

For the states of the northern savanna, stretching from the middle Niger Valley to Lake Chad, the principal cause of unrest after 1800 was a widespread Moslem revival that frequently took the form of *jihad* or holy war. Until the beginning of the nineteenth century, Islamic penetration of the savanna lands of the western and central Sudan had been largely superficial. Rulers had been converted and had used the educated Moslems of the cities as administrators. However, they had recognized that their real power over the majority of their subjects in the countryside derived from recognition of their spiritual powers as kings and priests under the traditional religious beliefs of the African peoples. After the fall of Songhai at the end of the sixteenth century, the rulers of the many smaller states that replaced it were often openly pagan or merely paid lip service to Islam.

One principal exception was the Fulani peoples, the main African cattle nomads who had spread two thousand miles eastward from their original home in Senegal. As pastoralists, they had never felt the need to compromise with the pagan animism of the settled agricultural peoples; and their Moslem clerics had encouraged them to despise the compromising attitude of the nominally Moslem rulers of the agrarian states, against whom they felt constant grievance for the taxing of their cattle during their migrations. The Fulani were therefore prepared to take the lead in the Islamic revivalist movement of the early nineteenth century, especially since they were under the influence of the Qadiriyya brotherhood, a fundamentalist group that advocated a restoration of the purity and the theocracy of Islam.

In a series of jihads, the Fulani created several Moslem empires, incorporating many of the Hausa city-states and controlling many of the greater cities of the earlier empires in the Niger Valley, such as Jenne and Timbuctu; the most powerful of these states was the Sokoto caliphate. The Fulani penetrated into the rain forest of West Africa to defeat the Yoruba kingdom of Oyo and capture their capital, from which thousands of refugees were driven out. Many of these gathered in Ibadan, which had been founded by Oyo soldiers in 1829 and rapidly grew into an important city

Nineteenth-Century Timbuctu
Timbuctu was one of the principal centers of Islamic learning in sub-Saharan Africa in the fifteenth and sixteenth centuries. It never fully recovered from its sack in 1593 by invaders from Morocco. (The New York Public Library)

capable of holding back further Fulani attacks. After the decline of Oyo, however, the Yoruba continued to fight among themselves and thus left open the way for British intervention. Between 1848 and his death in 1864, al-Hajj Umar of the Tokolor created an even larger empire that controlled the area from the city of Masina in the east to Segu in the west, an empire almost equal to the earlier Songhai Empire. (The Fulani and Tokolor spoke the same language, Fulfulde; the Tokolor were sedentary, the Fulani nomadic.) Finally, yet another Moslem ruler, Samori Toure, won an empire for himself between 1860 and 1870 on the headwaters of the Niger River.

Although at times these Moslem empires appeared to be efficient, autocratic states that restored the glory of Islamic learning and offered an ideologically unified resistance to European encroachments, in reality they weakened the capacity of their regions to react. They enhanced the antagonism between the Moslems and the animistic pagans in their empires, creating enmities that still wrack countries like Chad today. They fought against each other, despite their proclamation of the jihad, and even sought the aid of the British and French against other Moslems. Finally, they weakened such states as Kanem-Bornu and Oyo, which might have been centers of opposition to the Europeans.

West Africa, 1800–1875

In West Africa the principal forces for change in the period 1800–1875 were the abolition of the slave trade, the establishment of settlements of freed slaves along the coast, and the decline of once-powerful native states like Benin and Oyo. The abolition of the slave trade was spearheaded by humanitarian groups, often Quakers, in western Europe and the United States, and by other Europeans who had seen the trade firsthand as sailors or physicians on the slave ships. Moreover, by 1800 the trade was becoming less profitable, as the plantations of the United States and the Caribbean islands supplied part of their own needs by the natural increase of their own slave populations. At the same time, European capitalists saw more profit to be made by a shift of their commerce from human beings to raw materials needed for the new industrial factories. Thus self-interest aided conscience in the decisions to forbid their citizens to engage in the slave trade that were made by Denmark in 1805, Britain in 1807, and the United States in 1808. The institution of slavery, however, was not made illegal in the British colonies until 1833, in the French colonies until 1848, or in the Portuguese colonies until 1869. Slavery was finally abolished in the United States by the Thirteenth Amendment to the Constitution in 1865. In Latin America slavery was abolished as early as 1819 in Argentina and 1829 in Mexico, but it was maintained in Brazil until 1888.

The British took the lead after 1807 in using their gunboats to patrol the Atlantic off West Africa to prevent the trade in slaves, although their effectiveness over so vast an area was questionable; and until the 1840s many slaves were smuggled out. The Spanish, Portuguese, and Brazilians continued to trade openly in slaves and to transport them to South America. The jihads and the civil war among the Yoruba continued to make it easy to capture slaves in the interior, and the West African states such as Dahomey traded in slaves as long as possible. The center of the trade moved south, however, to the coast between Cabinda and Luanda, where Spanish and Portuguese ships, unmolested by British patrols, shipped many slaves from eastern Africa to Brazil, Cuba, and Puerto Rico at least until 1870. For the West African states that had been dependent on the slave trade, the decline of the trade after 1822, the year in which the highest number of slaves ever was shipped across the Atlantic, compelled an economic reorientation that only a few were able to make fully. In addition to the traditional export items such as gold, spices, and skins, increasing amounts of ivory and especially of palm oil nuts, which were used to provide lubrication in the factories and for soap manufacture, were sold. Senegal developed an export trade in peanuts, and the Gold Coast shipped out timber. Inland, the city of Kano became an important textile center whose humane system of home production deeply impressed a German visitor in the 1850s: "This industry is not carried on here as in Europe, in immense establishments degrading man to the meanest conditions of life . . . [Since] it gives employment and support to families without compelling them to sacrifice their domestic habits, we must presume Kano to be one of the happiest of countries." The damage done to the African trading system by four centuries of the slave trade was not easy to repair, however, and many states proved unable to make the transition. Moreover, the new trading pattern required Africa to become increasingly a supplier of raw materials and a purchaser of finished goods, thus helping to destroy the native handicraft system.

The British were the first to settle freed slaves in Africa. In 1797 a philanthropic group shipped several thousand freed slaves from England to Sierra Leone, which became a crown colony in 1808. From then on the British navy brought to Sierra Leone slaves their patrols had freed from trading ships, and by 1850 the colony had a population of 50,000. Similarly, philanthropists in the United States sent a small number of freed slaves from the Northern states to Monrovia in Liberia in 1822; the colony eventually received about 20,000 freed slaves from the United States or from the slave ships. Liberia was made independent in 1847 by the society that founded it. In the 1840s the French too formed a colony for freed slaves, around the town of Libreville in Gabon. These settlements had considerable difficulty in establishing good relations with the indigenous Africans there, especially as they were used by the British and French as bases for encroachment into the interior. The American government made almost no official contact with Liberia, and very few freed slaves chose to go there from the United States.

The British and French governments were becoming convinced that, for economic and political as well as humanitarian reasons, it was essential for them to increase the number of their footholds on the African continent as a preliminary to extending their influence into the interior, especially as their explorers were making known the potential wealth that lay up the valleys of the Niger and the Senegal rivers. The French base was the colony of Senegal, where between 1854 and 1865 the ambitious governor, Louis Faidherbe, transformed a somnolent backwater into a flourishing entrepôt. He embellished the old colonial capital of Saint Louis, built a new port at Dakar, and linked them by telegraph. Schools based on French culture were founded, and a strong army of native recruits was formed. The British not only developed their existing forts but also took over the coastal settlements of the Dutch and the Danes; in 1861 they annexed the island of Lagos, ostensibly to end its role as the center of the remaining slave trade. Lagos eventually was used to increase British influence in the Yoruba territories and became the base from which the whole of Nigeria was taken. British and French military action thus hastened the decline of the native states of West Africa that had begun with the ending of the slave trade and the increase of warfare among themselves. The end of their independence was to come in the scramble for Africa after 1875.

East Africa, 1800–1875

The Arabs of Oman, a powerful principality on the southeastern coast of Arabia, had established their dominance over the Swahili cities in East Africa at the end of the seventeenth century. Under their ambitious sultan, Sayyid Said (reigned 1806–1856), they compelled each of the coastal cities to recognize their overlordship, which they exercised from the island-city of Zanzibar, to which they had transferred their capital in 1841. Said placed the financial administration in the hands of Indian bankers, using his Arab merchants to penetrate inland toward the lake country of East Africa, where they purchased slaves, ivory, and copper. He kept many of the slaves himself for work on vast clove plantations on Zanzibar. He even made agreements with the European powers to restrict the extent of his slaving activities, in order to persuade them to open merchant houses and consulates in Zanzibar and to extend their protection to his trading empire.

The interior of East Africa was thus opened to the inhumanity of the slave trade as well as to the slaughter of elephants and rhinoceros for their tusks. Moreover, the traders sold vast numbers of guns in exchange for slaves, precipitating decades of savage fighting among the many inland peoples. Occasionally, however, powerful inland states were formed by leaders who learned to turn the trade with Zanzibar to their own profit. One of the largest was the kingdom of Buganda on the shores of Lake Victoria, whose absolute ruler, Mutesa I (reigned 1854–1883), shocked European explorers with his arbitrary punishments and his daily executions. Farther south, a military adventurer known to Europeans as Tippu Tib, the son of a Zanzibar merchant, created an empire in the eastern Congo that prospered on trade and raiding by its well-equipped army.

Both in the interior and on the coast, however, the European penetration of East Africa had begun. Even the empire of Sayyid Said was informally controlled by the British through their fleet and consul, and after his death they split his state into two and totally banned the slave trade

(1873). All the interior states became known through the visits of explorers and missionaries and would remain independent only until the 1890s.

The Dutch had settled Table Bay (Capetown) at the Cape of Good Hope in 1652, as a supply base for their fleets to the Indies; more settlers followed who opened up the grasslands beyond the city for cattle and slaughtered the native population of San (Bushmen) and Khoikoi (Hottentots). The British seized the Cape in 1795 and retained it at the peace congress in 1815. The Dutch colonists, known as Boers, became increasingly restive under British rule, especially because of the abolition of slavery in 1834, British administration of criminal justice, and British land taxation. These grievances drove fourteen thousand Boers to set off on the so-called Great Trek in 1855, traveling in covered wagons drawn by oxen to found small Boer republics to the northeast of the British frontiers along the Vaal and Orange rivers. In the mid-1850s the British, who had briefly brought the Boers back under their rule by force, recognized the independence of the Boers living beyond the Vaal River in the two republics of the Transvaal and the Orange Free State.

Both the Boers and the British had frequently fought with the many African chiefdoms into which they were penetrating. Of these the most powerful was the Zulu kingdom, created early in the nineteenth century by its ruler Shaka as a strong military federation. Shaka invented a new form of warfare, using highly disciplined regiments equipped with short stabbing spears in place of the more traditional throwing spears. His regiments advanced behind a wall of cowhide shields, which deflected the

Southern Africa, 1800–1875

Zulu Warriors, c. 1900
Their short, stabbing spears and cowhide shields gave the Zulus military superiority over neighboring African peoples in the early nineteenth century. They were able to defeat British troops armed with rifles and artillery on several occasions before finally capitulating in 1879. (BBC Hulton Picture Library)

spears thrown by their adversaries, who were then massacred at close range. Shaka also reorganized Zulu society by governing through his own regimental leaders rather than the highborn local chiefs; and he created barracks throughout his state where a military caste was formed in deep loyalty to the ruler and to the Zulu state.

The Zulus compelled many other Nguni-speaking tribes to flee northward into the interior of East Africa, where in turn, using the military methods of the Zulu, they caused havoc among the indigenous peaceful pastoral tribes. The Zulus ambushed the Boers in 1838, and in response the Boers slaughtered 3,000 Zulus in 1840 at the Battle of Blood River. Thus southern Africa experienced several disruptive experiences after 1800—conflict of the British and the Boers; constant warfare of the organized forces of the Europeans and the black Africans; dispossession of black Africans from many of the grasslands on which their herds had pastured; and struggles of black Africans among themselves—all of which caused further migrations.

African Resistance
By 1914 all of Africa except four states (Ethiopia, Liberia, Egypt, and South Africa) had been annexed by the European powers. For the Africans the experience of annexation had three facets—military repression of native resistance or rebellion, economic exploitation, and political administration by Europeans either directly or indirectly through native rulers.

The European powers had avoided fighting each other over the partition of Africa by agreeing at the Conference of Berlin (1884–1885) to rather vague assignment of the territories within which each European power might extend its rule. African resistance to European annexation proved unexpectedly strong, however. Far from welcoming Europeans desirous of taking up the "white man's burden," the Africans fought desperately against technologically superior forces; and their losses in lives were very high. The Germans appear to have provoked the most resistance, possibly because their military were less restrained by missionary or commercial interests than were the forces of the other powers. In German Southwest Africa (Namibia) they encountered sharp resistance from the Herero people who in 1904–1906, armed only with bows and spears, lost more than 60,000 (two-thirds of their total population) in vain. In German East Africa the Germans met opposition from the Swahili coastal cities, which were defeated in 1890 with the aid of the British and French fleets. Almost immediately the inland peoples revolted, and thousands were killed as German troops burned villages and destroyed crops; but in 1905–1908, resentful at forced labor and taxes, the inland peoples again joined in massive attacks on German settlements. In the German counterattack, between 75,000 and 125,000 Africans were killed.

French ambition to create an empire that would include the savannas stretching from the Senegal and Niger rivers to Lake Chad brought them to war with the Tokolor Empire created by al-Hajj Umar, which they defeated in 1893, and with the empire of Samori Toure to the south of the

Tokolor Empire. Samori fought skillfully against the French for twenty years in perhaps the most effective resistance to European encroachment mounted by any African ruler. A master of guerrilla warfare, he purchased modern breech-loading rifles and had them copied by his own craftsmen. He even moved his kingdom hundreds of miles to the east in a vain effort to create a new center for resistance. He was finally captured in 1898 and exiled to an island off the coast, where he died in 1900. Dahomey offered stubborn resistance, even attacking a French gunboat, but was overwhelmed in 1894. In fact, no part of the French Empire was acquired without bloodshed, and resistance on the edges of the Sahara continued for half a century.

The British, too, came up against well-organized African states determined to fight for their independence. Some of their most punitive actions were taken against the Ashanti federation, which was not subdued until 1896 and was made part of the Gold Coast colony in 1901. Benin fought back by massacring British investigators trying to stop human sacrifices. The British burned the city of Benin in 1898, exiled the oba (king), and made the country part of the Niger Coast protectorate. In East Central Africa they faced a joint uprising of the Shona and Matabele peoples in Nyasaland (Malawi), Southern Rhodesia (Zimbabwe), and Northern Rhodesia (Zambia), who forced the white settlers back into the safety of the larger towns, only to be defeated by armies sent from South Africa. African losses in that war were 10,000. In the Sudan—where armies of a self-proclaimed *mahdi*, a religious savior whom Sunni Moslems believed would appear to restore universal Islam at the end of time, was fighting to eject Egyptian forces—the British intervened in 1898–1900. Their army under Herbert Kitchener killed 20,000 Sudanese at the Battle of Omdurman and thus brought the Sudan under British control. Britain's greatest losses—over 5,000 killed—occurred when they subdued the two independent Boer republics of the Transvaal and the Orange Free State in 1899–1902, because they then met Europeans equipped with arms and techniques similar to their own.

The Italians were successful in establishing themselves along the Red Sea coast, where the colonies of Eritrea and Italian Somaliland had been established by 1895; and in 1911–1912 they were able, against strong resistance, to take the Mediterranean territories of Tripolitania and Cyrenaica (modern Libya). When they attempted to conquer the kingdom of Ethiopia in 1895–1896, however, they came up against a state whose rulers had been successfully adopting Western military techniques for forty years. Their invading army was outgunned, outnumbered, and outmaneuvered in the Battle of Adowa (1896), and Ethiopia maintained its independence until the Italian armies returned in 1935–1936 at the orders of Benito Mussolini.

In the Congo Free State, which from 1884 to 1908 was the personal fiefdom of the Belgian king Leopold II (reigned 1865–1909), approximately half (1.5 million) of the Congo's population either were killed or died of

Bronze Memorial Head of a Deceased King, Benin
The kingdom of Benin was probably founded in the thirteenth century. Its last oba, or king, was deposed by the British in 1898, and Benin soon after became part of the British colony of Nigeria. (Peabody Museum, Harvard University)

starvation during the pacification. Leopold's exploitation of the Congo was the most naked and brutal of all the European regimes. The population was dragooned into labor battalions to build railroads, ports, and roads. Government monopolies were created for ivory and wild rubber, and concessions were sold to European companies for opening up the mineral deposits, especially the vast copper resources of the province of Katanga. Eventually news of the terror became known in western Europe and the United States, and Leopold was forced to hand over his control of what became the Belgian Congo to the Belgian government.

The other European governments sought to gain economic profit from their new possessions by persuading or compelling the African farmers to turn to cash crops for export, as was already being done in the coastal regions where the Europeans had been present for centuries. The French encouraged the development of groundnuts and cotton in the savanna areas of French West Africa, which they had formed as a federation of military territories and colonies in 1895. French West Africa's coastal areas (Guinea and the Ivory Coast) were encouraged to produce coffee, palm nuts, and cocoa. The British were interested in the mineral resources of their new territories, especially the copper of Northern Rhodesia and the gold and diamonds of Southern Rhodesia. Where the land was suitable, as in Kenya and Southern Rhodesia, they encouraged the immigration of white settlers and gave them the finest farmland. Elsewhere they followed the French pattern of encouraging the most profitable cash crops for sale on the European market.

The economic results of imperial rule for the African population have been much disputed. The bad effects of heavy taxation, forced labor, dispossession from much of the better land, destruction of subsistence farming, and concentration on export of raw materials at low prices are obvious. Equally clear are the long-term benefits of the construction of an efficient road and railroad system, the foundation of schools and universities (primarily by the British and French), the modernization of farming techniques, and the training of the labor force for at least semiskilled jobs. Yet the supposed value of even these benefits must be qualified. Education was inadequate for the masses of the population, since except in the capitals far too few schools were constructed. Moreover, the education was too frequently based on the European curriculum, which in most cases was quite unsuitable for training the Africans to work in their own environment and which made no effort to instruct them in their own culture or history. Although agricultural research on tropical export crops was well funded, research into tropical food crops lagged behind. Transportation links were excellent only between the coast and the interior owing to the colonial government's desire to facilitate the export of raw materials. Since the different areas of Africa were not linked together, trade within Africa failed to develop.

It was evident from the refusal of the African populations to reconcile themselves to European rule for more than brief periods that they regarded the benefits as far outweighed by the disadvantages. The British believed they could win over African resistance by indirect rule, governing inexpensively through reliable native rulers as they did in large parts of India. This system worked best in their Northern Nigerian protectorate, which corresponded roughly to the Sokoto caliphate, because there they permitted the local Moslem emirs to carry on most of the work of government. In other areas, such as the Gold Coast, they attempted to increase the competence of local chiefs under British guidance. Only in white-settled areas such as Southern Rhodesia did they give almost no power to local African rulers. The French were willing to work with those Africans who had absorbed French culture and spoke the French language; in general, however, they preferred direct rule through their own bureaucrats and military personnel sent from France. As a result, almost all the great empires they had defeated disappeared, to be replaced by artificial administrative units like the eight territories into which French West Africa was divided. The Belgians, Germans, Italians, and Portuguese carried direct rule to an extreme, making almost no effort to create an educated class of Africans to aid them in administration and destroying the existing African political structure.

EUROPEAN ENCROACHMENT AND MANCHU DECLINE: CHINA, 1800–1912

During the nineteenth century, as the Manchu dynasty entered its final decline, the vast empire of China lay open to Western exploitation. The most obvious encroachments were the annexation of Chinese national territory or of China's tributaries or vassal states, countries nominally under the suzerainty—though not the sovereignty—of China. The British annexed the island of Hong Kong in 1842. The Portuguese, who had paid tribute for permission to reside in Macao for over three hundred years, took formal sovereignty over the city in 1887. In 1858–1860 the Russians compelled the Manchus to cede to them all land north of the Amur River, as well as the territory that was to become Russia's Maritime Province, where the new port of Vladivostok was founded. Russia also occupied Ili in Chinese Turkestan in 1871, although the region was partially returned to China in the Sino-Russian treaty of 1881. The French threw off Chinese suzerainty over Indochina in the war of 1884–1885, prompting the British to take sovereignty over Upper Burma. Finally, the Japanese defeated China in a short but decisive war in 1894–1895, after which they increased their influence in Korea and annexed the island of Taiwan. Korea was recognized as a Japanese protectorate in 1905 and was annexed in 1910.

Although China had thus lost territory on its periphery, it was not seriously weakened by these losses. Far more important was the European and, to a lesser degree, American exploitation of the economic wealth of

China by more indirect means, including the establishment of "treaty ports" and foreign-policed "settlements," the grant of commercial privileges, and (after 1895) the leasing of ports and naval bases and the creation of "spheres of influence."

Although Western dominance thus exacerbated China's internal troubles, it should not be regarded as the exclusive or even the primary cause of them. The internal unrest and rebellion that were rampant by the mid-nineteenth century were caused chiefly by economic and social strains resulting from population pressure and administrative decay.

The Canton System of Trade, 1759–1842

Britain took the lead in opening China to Western trade, using the East India Company as its sole representative until 1834. However, other European powers, notably the Portuguese and the French, also sought a share. Since 1759 the Europeans had been allowed to trade only through the port of Canton on the Pearl River in the south of China. Trade was supervised by a Chinese official called the *hoppo* and was carried out on the Chinese side by government-licensed merchant firms known collectively as *cohong*, which monopolized the staple trade in tea and silk. The government levied taxes on all imports and exports and habitually added irregular charges to the tariff; the officials also collected fees from the monopoly merchants, who tried to recoup by overcharging the Europeans for goods and services. However, the trade was run amicably until the 1830s. The Europeans obtained shipments of tea, silk, and cotton textiles, on which they could make large profits, and at first supplied a variety of manufactured goods and raw materials such as cotton. The balance owing the Chinese was covered with silver and, increasingly, with opium.

By the 1830s the British had reversed this trade balance and were being paid in silver for huge exports of opium from India, which were bought by China's increasingly large number of addicts. The Chinese government had banned the importation or production of opium in 1796 and had appointed a special commissioner to stop the smuggling of the drug into China, which had increased from 400,000 pounds in 1816 to 5.6 million pounds in 1835. In 1839 Commissioner Lin Tse-hsü, a hero in modern Chinese history, seized and burned almost 3 million pounds of opium owned by foreign traders, after confining them for six weeks in their factories in Canton. Shortly afterward the British refused to hand over to a Chinese law court sailors who had killed a Chinese peasant, on the grounds that the Chinese system of justice was incompatible with (and presumably inferior to) British justice. Hostilities in what became known as the Opium War (1839–1842) began with naval skirmishes, but the British soon landed an expeditionary force that took a number of Chinese coastal cities and sent modern naval vessels that sank the outdated Chinese war junks. In treaties in 1842 and 1843 the Chinese were compelled to abandon the Canton system. The British were granted freedom to trade in five Chinese ports (Canton, Amoy, Foochow, Ningpo, and Shanghai). They were paid a large indemnity and were allowed to annex the island of Hong Kong as a colony.

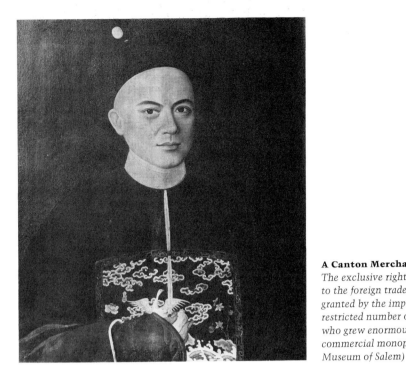

A Canton Merchant
The exclusive right to sell silks and tea to the foreign traders in Canton was granted by the imperial government to a restricted number of Chinese merchants, who grew enormously wealthy from this commercial monopoly. (Peabody Museum of Salem)

Similar treaties were then granted to the United States and France, whose citizens, like the British, were to have the privilege of "extraterritoriality"—that is, to be under their own legal system administered by their consuls, even though on Chinese soil. The "most favored nation" clause gave the rights gained by one treaty power to each of the others.

After the Opium War relations between Westerners and Chinese were regulated by this "treaty system," which the Chinese called the "unequal treaties." The Chinese, not unreasonably, were especially dissatisfied at the continuance of opium smuggling but were also annoyed at the activity of Christian missionaries and at the demands of the European governments for diplomatic equality with the Chinese. The Europeans were disturbed at the breakdown of Chinese administration, especially during the Taiping rebellion; in 1854 they began to take over the administration of their own sectors of Shanghai, which they later converted into two virtually autonomous areas within the city known as the International Settlement (British and American) and the French Concession. Annoyed at the corruption within the customs collection, the Europeans also won the right to have foreigners administer the Chinese maritime customs as employees of the Chinese government. In 1855 the Foreign Inspectorate of Customs, which collected all duties on China's trade paid by foreign vessels, including trade between treaty ports, was headed by a British citizen in Chinese service.

Friction Under the Treaty System

In 1856–1860 warfare again broke out between the Chinese and Anglo-French forces, primarily because the Europeans saw no hope of expanding trade in China without gaining foreign diplomatic equality and thus the right to maintain representatives in Peking itself, where authority over the empire lay. In the final year of the war British and French armies marched on Peking and punished the Manchus for their resistance and imprisonment of British officials by burning down all the buildings of the beautiful eighteenth-century Summer Palace. The Manchus then agreed to treaties permitting the Western nations to have diplomatic envoys residing in Peking (although none of those who arrived was to succeed in having an imperial audience for thirteen years). Eleven more treaty ports were opened. Foreigners were free to travel throughout China, and the British were granted a lease on the Kowloon Peninsula facing Hong Kong Island.

Dynastic Decline and Internal Rebellion

The treaty system forced on China by the West, though humiliating to Manchus and Chinese, did not do the dynasty irreparable damage. On balance, it was the weakness of the Chinese government and society itself that led to the eventual collapse of the dynasty. Throughout the nineteenth century, reformers within the Chinese administrative structure and rebels without had sought the renovation of government and society; but the Manchus had done almost nothing in the way of basic change, partly because they had taken over a governmental system deeply rooted in China's past, within which such weaknesses as court factionalism and intrigue had long precedent.

Many factors accounted for the inertia of the administrative structure of the late Manchu period. The traditional examination system as administered in the nineteenth century encouraged conservative views on all subjects examined, from culture to politics. Officials were discouraged by their superiors from taking any initiative. Moreover, the attitudes of the bureaucratic class were profoundly opposed to policies that favored economic enterprise and development. They regarded trade and industry as ungentlemanlike activities that were to be relegated to the less respectable classes of merchants and artisans. They were convinced that a self-sufficient China based largely on agricultural production would be socially stable, and they felt that economic activity should always remain at the same level rather than expand.

The reality of the system was that the peasant was exploited for the support of a large class of officials inured to institutionalized corruption and of large landlords of gentry status who were taxed at a lower rate than ordinary farmers. Moreover, the Chinese elite's deep conviction of the superiority of Chinese civilization over that of the "barbarians" made it difficult for them to learn from the West. Change might be possible in the new port cities where Western influence was growing; but nationwide change could come only from the imperial rulers themselves. Even the Taiping rebellion, perhaps the greatest civil war in history, failed to end their inertia.

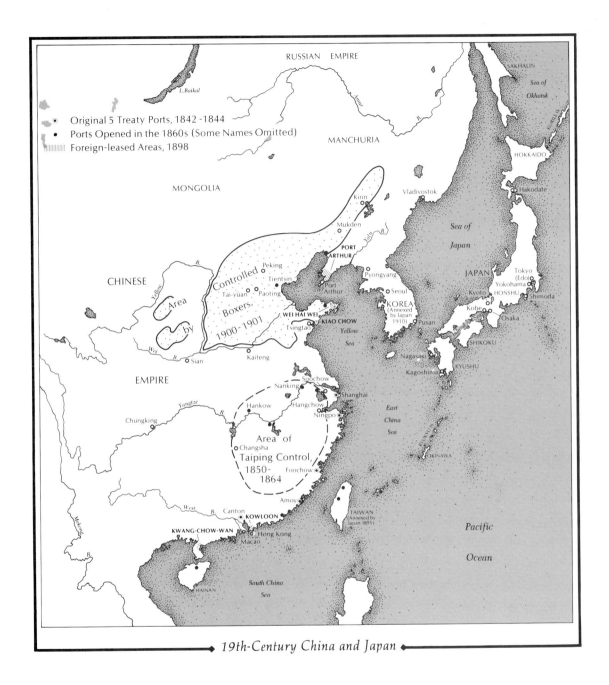

Original 5 Treaty Ports, 1842-1844
Ports Opened in the 1860s (Some Names Omitted)
Foreign-leased Areas, 1898

RUSSIAN EMPIRE

L.Baikal

MANCHURIA

MONGOLIA

Kirin

Mukden

CHINESE

Peking

Tientsin

Tai-yüan   Paoting

Yellow R.

Area   by

Controlled   by   Boxers   1900-1901

PORT ARTHUR

Port Arthur

WEI HAI WEI

KIAO CHOW

Tsingtao

Pyongyang

Seoul

KOREA (Annexed by Japan 1910)

Pusan

Vladivostok

Sea of Japan

JAPAN

Tokyo (Edo)

Yokohama

Kyoto   HONSHU

Kobe   Shimoda

Osaka

SHIKOKU

Sea of Okhotsk

SAKHALIN

HOKKAIDO

Hakodate

EMPIRE

Wei R.

Sian

Kaifeng

Yellow Sea

Nagasaki

Kagoshima   KYUSHU

Yangtze R.

Chungking

Hankow

Nanking

Soochow

Hangchow

Ningpo

Shanghai

Area of Taiping Control, 1850-1864

Changsha

Foochow

East China Sea

OKINAWA

West R.

Amoy

Canton   KOWLOON

KWANG-CHOW-WAN

Hong Kong

Macao

TAIWAN (Annexed by Japan 1895)

Pacific Ocean

Mekong R.

HAINAN

South China Sea

19th-Century China and Japan

This cataclysm, which lasted from 1850 to 1864 and probably took twenty million lives, was the most threatening to the dynasty of a number of rebellions that broke out in China in the 1850s and 1860s. The leader of the rebellion was Hung Hsiu-ch'üan (1814–1864), a village schoolteacher from the area near Canton, who had grown resentful at the Manchus after failing the examinations several times. Early acquaintance with Christian tracts in Chinese, as well as an extraordinary dream while he was seriously ill, had led him to believe that he himself should update Christian teachings and that he was the younger brother of Jesus Christ. The God Worshippers Society he founded in hilly Kwangsi Province attracted thousands of discontented peasants of the Hakka minority from which Hung himself came. To them, Hung preached his vision of a "Heavenly Kingdom of Great Peace" (T'ai-p'ing t'ien-kuo), from which the rebellion took its name of Taiping. Community feuds developed into conflicts with the local gentry. Hung's followers took up arms and drove north to central China and thence down the Yangtze River to Nanking, the capital of the early Ming dynasty.

The Taiping army, which grew from the twenty thousand who set out from Kwangsi to two million who arrived at Nanking, was composed mainly of peasants without land or means of livelihood. When the Taipings settled down in Nanking in 1853, they issued a land reform program that called for redistribution of farmland and placed units of twenty-five families under the administration of a military-religious hierarchy that extended to the village level. The leaders of the Taiping government, consisting of Hung Hsiu-ch'üan as the Heavenly King and a few "brother Kings," including the powerful Yang Hsiu-ching, ruled as a theocracy. Yang, who came from a charcoal burner's family, acted as a kind of shaman who claimed to speak for Jehovah. These leaders were attracted by the luxuries of Nanking, which they decided to make their "celestial capital," and formed harems there despite their claim to believe in equality of the sexes. They sent small expeditions toward Peking in the north but were continually locked in battle with the imperial forces in the Yangtze Valley. Nanking itself frequently came under siege. Meanwhile, in North China rebels called the Nien, who prided themselves on their bandit ethics, engaged in widespread attacks on the imperial forces. A revolt by Chinese Moslems in Yunnan was followed in the 1860s by an even larger uprising of Chinese Moslems in Shensi and Kansu, which spread to Chinese Turkestan in the far northwest.

The dynasty was able to put down the Taiping and the other rebellions because the Chinese scholar-gentry continued to identify themselves with the dynasty and because a group of remarkably able scholar-officials successfully raised new private armies in south-central China for service throughout the country against the Taiping. Europeans also played a small part. Although in 1860 Anglo-French forces invaded Peking itself to demand new commercial and diplomatic advantages, once the new treaties had been granted, they cautiously gave the Manchus aid. A Taiping attack on Shanghai in 1862 was repulsed by a small European force. Shortly afterward the British assisted American and British mercenaries enlisted by the Chinese government, who were led at first by an American, Frederick Townsend Ward, and later by the British hero Charles Gordon. Although the mercenary forces were small, their howitzers and mortars, which could breach city walls, contributed to imperial victory over the Taiping in 1864.

The Chinese scholar-generals who supervised the mercenaries, notably Li Hung-chang (1823–1901), were so impressed that they persuaded the Peking government to approve the establishment of a modern Chinese arsenal in Shanghai to manufacture rifles and howitzers. With these weapons and others purchased from the Europeans, the Manchu dynasty was able to survive into the twentieth century.

Attempts at Modernization

Following the building of this first arsenal in 1865, the scholar-generals who had suppressed the Taiping rebellion embarked on an effort to adopt Western technology known as the Self-Strengthening Movement. In 1866–1867 two modern shipyards were founded to construct vessels for the Chinese navy, and schools in which Western sciences and languages were taught were attached to the arsenals and shipyards. A Chinese educational mission even operated for about nine years in Hartford, Connecticut, to which more than a hundred Chinese boys were sent for Western schooling; but it had to be closed as a result of conservative opposition at home. In the 1870s there were also some efforts at economic modernization and industrialization, especially by creation of textile mills, mechanically operated mines, and steamship lines. These efforts at modernization were, however, of far less significance than the influence exerted on the Chinese economy by the rapid growth of the European-controlled ports like Shanghai.

After 1860 Westerners were able to operate almost freely throughout China. Their ships took part in local carrying trade. Foreigners manned the Chinese Imperial Customs Service, which regulated foreign trade. Onerous inland taxation for foreign trade goods was partially avoided by special permits. Catholic and Protestant missionaries sought converts in even the remotest regions. The treaty ports became bustling metropolises in which the local Chinese sought to emulate the economic practices of the dominant European merchant and administrative class. Shanghai became the epitome of this new, modernizing China.

The Growth of Shanghai

Shanghai was located on a swampy peninsula to the south of the mouth of the Yangtze River, where drainage works and the building of a seawall had created some of the richest farmland in China. Ideally located to control the trade of the rich Yangtze Valley, it had expanded from a small walled town in the sixteenth century to a commercial center of 270,000 people by 1842, when it was made one of the treaty ports. After 1842 the city grew primarily by extension of the areas controlled by Westerners. The British and Americans combined their separate concessions in 1863 into the International Settlement, which was vastly extended in 1899 to include most of the northern part of the city. The city's principal street, called the Bund, ran along the Whangpu River and was the site of the major banks, agency houses, hotels, and European clubs, guarded by Sikh policemen recruited from India. The French Concession lay immediately to the south of the International Settlement.

Within these areas the foreigners enjoyed extraterritoriality and virtually governed the Chinese living in the concessions without reference to the Chinese government. All the work of municipal administration, such as roads, ports, police, and sanitation, was done by the foreign-controlled Shanghai Municipal Council; expenses were covered by levying municipal taxes. The foreign consulates, as holders of land in the concessions technically leased from the Chinese government by payment of lump sums of money, rented out parcels of land to the Chinese in ninety-year contracts.

Within this system both Chinese and foreign capitalists flourished. Foreign banks in Shanghai, especially the Hong Kong and Shanghai Banking Corporation (founded 1865), gained an increasing hold on the Chinese commercial economy. Beginning in the 1870s, however, Shanghai also became the center of Chinese newspaper and book publishing and hence a magnet for patriotic reform writers as well as disaffected intellectuals—from early Chinese journalists accepting appointment in British-financed Chinese newspapers to twentieth-century radicals, including the early Chinese Communists, who founded their party there in 1921.

Although the British and Americans early constructed shipyards in China to repair the steamships that sailed the China coast and the Yangtze River, not until China's defeat by Japan in 1895 were foreigners given the

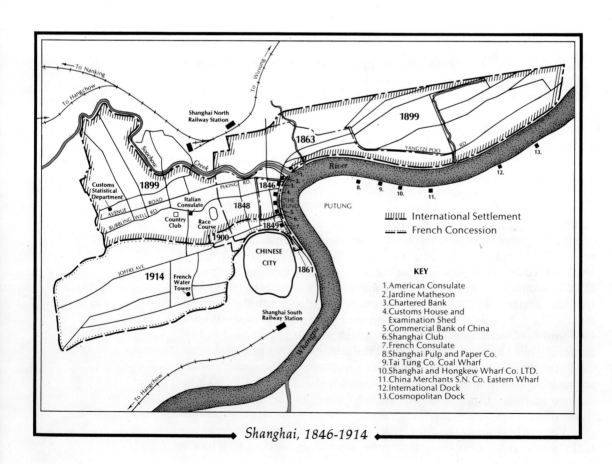

Shanghai, 1846-1914

European Buildings on Soochow Creek, Shanghai
The principal European factories, offices, hotels, and clubs were located along the Bund, a street following the north bank of the Whangpu River, and on both sides of Soochow Creek, the Whangpu's main tributary. (Bruno Barbey/Magnum Photos, Inc.)

right to establish manufacturing enterprises in the treaty ports. Foreign textile factories and flour mills then competed with enterprises owned by Chinese industrialists trained in the commercial world of Shanghai. Cheap industrial labor was recruited for these factories, and the discrepancy increased between the living conditions of the rich and the poor of the city. As a result, Shanghai came to represent for many Chinese both the enormous economic potential and the deep social cost of Western capitalism, operating under Western law without the social controls of Chinese tradition.

The Spheres of Influence System

The encroachment on China by the Western powers entered a new phase after 1895 with China's ignominious defeat by Japan in the Sino-Japanese War (1894–1895). China was compelled to accept the punitive Treaty of Shimonoseki, which called for it to pay a vast indemnity, to cede to Japan the islands of Taiwan and the Pescadores and the Liaotung Peninsula, and to authorize Japanese activity in Korea. Japan's territorial gains were so great, in fact, that the German Kaiser, fearing the prospect of an East Asia united under Japan, persuaded the Russians and the French to join him in pressuring Japan to give up the Liaotung Peninsula. Nevertheless, the European powers, believing that the disintegration of the Chinese empire was imminent, abandoned the treaty system, under which they had collaborated in allowing impartial opportunity for trade, and began to stake out geographical areas known as spheres of influence, in which individual nations would acquire by special treaty preeminence in certain ports or provinces.

The French were the first to demand new privileges, in return for their assistance in the regaining of the Liaotung Peninsula and for the provision of loans from Parisian bankers to enable the Chinese to pay their indemnities. The French were granted the right to build a railroad from Vietnam into Yunnan, China's southwest province, and to work the rich mines there. In 1897 the Germans seized Kiaochow Bay and were granted economic concessions in the surrounding Shantung province. A year earlier the Russians had invited a Chinese envoy to the tsar's coronation to negotiate a secret treaty granting a Russian company the right to build a railroad across Manchuria to Vladivostok. In early 1898 the Russians further acquired the concession to extend this railroad to Port Arthur in southern Manchuria, which was to be leased to Russia as a naval and commercial base.

The scramble for concessions had thus begun in earnest. The French and British navies won leases on new ports, and the British won the concessions to build several railways in the Yangtze Valley. Feeling isolated by the triple intervention of Russia, Germany, and France over the Liaotung Peninsula, the British decided to safeguard themselves against their three major imperialist competitors, especially against Russia—which was challenging British power on its southern borders all the way from the Middle East to East Asia—by concluding an Anglo-Japanese alliance in 1902.

By the beginning of the twentieth century the area and the nature of the spheres of influence the powers were taking in China was clear. The French were pushing into southwest China from Indochina. The Germans were penetrating Shantung. The Russians had surrounded Manchuria on three sides and were using railroad construction to increase their economic influence there. The British were determined to dominate the Yangtze Valley from Shanghai and the Pearl River valley from Canton. These spheres of influence were not colonies, however. The control of the foreign powers extended only to operation of railroads, exploitation of mines, administration of police and local justice, and regulation of tariffs. The Chinese were afraid, nevertheless, that control of the railroads and mines and leasehold of ports and naval bases might easily be used as a step toward the partition of China just as similar concessions had been used in India, Africa, and elsewhere as the first step toward annexation.

Reform Frustrated

These fears gave new stimulus to the reformers in China. Desire for change, which had been growing for several decades among officials and intellectuals, was now more freely expressed. There were demands not only for industrial and commercial development and for the technology on which military strength was founded but also for institutional change.

Dowager-Empress Tz'u-hsi

As the dominant force in Chinese government from 1861 until her death in 1908, Tz'u-hsi bears much of the responsibility for China's failure to modernize. She is shown wearing a yellow dragon dress, sable hat, and tall Manchu shoes. (Courtesy of the Freer Gallery of Art, Smithsonian Institution, Washington, D.C.)

The cautious efforts at what was called "self-strengthening" gave way to a political movement championing reform in the examination and civil service systems and drastic alteration of the governmental structure, including even the calling of a deliberative assembly. The leader of the reform movement that emerged in 1895, the year of Japan's victory, was a young scholar, K'ang Yu-wei (1858–1927), who had written an iconoclastic book entitled *Confucius as Reformer*, in which he argued that Confucius had meant to encourage each person to achieve the "right to autonomy" through democratic institutions such as an elected parliament.

The greatest obstacle to these reform plans was the dominance of the dowager empress Tz'u-hsi (1835–1908). She had been admitted to the palace as a concubine at the age of sixteen, but in 1856 she had borne the emperor his first son and on the emperor's death five years later had become regent for her son. From then until 1908 she was almost uninterruptedly the principal force in the Chinese government, using guile and cruelty to maintain a regime opposed to reform. She also increased her personal wealth by receiving gifts from regional officeholders and, in her most celebrated piece of extravagance, shifted the funds earmarked for modernization of the Chinese navy in the vital decade after 1885 to construction of a beautiful new Summer Palace. Tz'u-hsi had previously allied with conservatives in the palace and the administration to frustrate reform efforts;

her own solution had been an attempt to restore efficiency through a revival of the Confucian governmental system, as a result of a genuine effort to find the men of talent the regime needed. After 1889, however, she had gone into semiretirement at the Summer Palace in the outskirts of Peking, permitting her nephew, the emperor Kuang-hsü, to attend to state business. (He had been nominally emperor since his accession at age four in 1875.)

Kuang-hsü, deeply aware of the danger that China might be partitioned and resentful at the conservative policies that the dowager empress still insisted he implement, suddenly embarked on a "hundred days of reform" in June–September 1898, employing K'ang Yu-wei as his principal adviser. In some two hundred decrees he ordered the modernization of the army and navy; the founding of new schools; the encouragement of industry and mining; improvements in agriculture; changes in the examination system; and, most provocative of all, the appointment of a commission to study the restructuring of government and the calling of a parliament. The dowager empress put an end to these plans by secluding the emperor in semiarrest on a lake within the palace grounds. K'ang and some of his supporters fled to Japan, and others were executed.

The dowager empress resumed the regency, and the reform edicts were rescinded. She surrounded herself with ultraconservative officials and Manchu clansmen who led her to believe that the Europeans who were carving out spheres of influence in China were also plotting to put Kuang-hsü back in power. Tz'u-hsi was therefore prepared to accept the advice of some of her advisers that she throw her support to the antiforeign rising of the secret society known as Boxers.

The Boxer Rising, 1900–1901

Since the 1860s there had been over two hundred cases of violent action against Christian missionaries and their converts, many of which had been instigated by officials and gentry and carried out by secret societies. The most powerful of the societies was the Society of Righteous and Harmonious Fists. Its members engaged in a kung-fu type of boxing, from which they gained the name of Boxers. They also believed that breathing exercises, charms, and spells could render them invulnerable to bullets. The disastrous economic conditions of 1898–1899—precipitated by floods in Shantung and drought in North China, as well as industrial depression believed to be caused by importation of foreign goods—vastly increased the social disorder. A widespread sense of frustration thus increased the support received by the Boxers as they lashed out at what they considered disruptive forces in their traditional society. At first the Boxers were opposed to the Manchus, but in the late 1890s they allied with conservative Manchu officials against the missionaries and their converts and against all foreign intervention in China.

In 1900 large groups of Boxers rampaged from Shantung to within reach of Peking itself. The dowager empress, who had been given a forged document, supposedly an ultimatum from the British minister demanding the restoration of the rule of Kuang-hsü, authorized the declaration of war against all the treaty powers. The Boxers entered Peking, where they besieged the staffs of the foreign embassies in the hastily fortified Legation Quarter for fifty-five days before a rescue force of Japanese, British, French, Russian, and American troops could reach them from the coast.

When the 19,000-man army had freed the besieged diplomats, it entered the Forbidden City to burn and plunder. A German force arrived later and, following the Kaiser's admonition to behave like the Huns of Attila, plundered large numbers of North Chinese cities. In the peace settlement, known as the Boxer Protocol (1901), the Chinese were compelled to mortgage customs receipts of the future to pay a huge indemnity; to execute officials connected with the uprising; to destroy their forts between Peking and the sea; and to permit the foreign powers to maintain a fortified, garrisoned Legation Quarter inside Peking. Although the dowager empress returned from Sian, to which she had fled, and proclaimed her total innocence of all involvement in the Boxer excesses, the prestige of her dynasty plummeted among Chinese as well as foreigners. It lasted only ten more years.

Bengal Lancers Entering the Forbidden City
An international force ended the eight-week siege of the Peking Legation Quarter by the Boxers in August 1900. The force was later placed under a German commander, who is seen being escorted into the Forbidden City by a company of Bengal Lancers from India.   (Library of Congress)

The Revolution of 1911

After the suppression of the Boxer Rising, the dowager empress had no choice but to turn to more enlightened advisers than the discredited conservatives. Many of the reform decrees of 1898 were revived or given a new form. Schools were established, and the examination system itself was abolished in 1905. Chinese in the port cities and provincial capitals were encouraged to start industrial enterprises. German and Japanese instructors were brought in to train the army recruits. Thousands of Chinese students went abroad, especially to Japan, where, rather than supporting China's absolute dynasty, they divided between constitutionalists seeking a parliamentary style of monarchy and revolutionaries determined to overthrow it. Before her death in 1908, which followed by only one day the announcement of the death of Kuang-hsü, the dowager empress had proclaimed a number of principles of constitutional government, according to which, during a nine-year period of preparation, China would be given consultative local assemblies and finally a consultative parliament. The reform measures had, however, merely opened the floodgates of change. China's new ruler, another child monarch guided by the dowager empress's nephew as regent, could not close them.

Constitutionalism was welcomed by many prominent gentry and merchants, who from 1906 were authorized to form elected provisional provincial assemblies. They sought greater control over taxation and over local affairs through these bodies. The younger radicals, notably those from Shanghai and other Chinese cities and those who had studied in Japan, turned to more drastic remedies under the leadership of Dr. Sun Yat-sen (1866–1925), the head of a federation of anti-Manchu forces called the Revolutionary Alliance. Sun Yat-sen had studied in Hawaii and received medical training in Hong Kong; as early as 1895 he had received overseas Chinese support for the founding of an anti-Manchu society. His first attempts to stage uprisings in Canton and elsewhere had ended in failure, but Sun's radical followers managed to infiltrate the new provincial armies while Sun went to the United States and Europe to raise funds for revolution from Chinese emigrants. Sun, moreover, had attempted to give the anti-Manchu forces an ideology by proclaiming three principles—nationalism, democracy, and "people's livelihood" (by which he meant moderate social reform but not socialism).

On October 10, 1911, a radical group within the provincial army at the city of Wuchang in central China staged a mutiny. The Manchu governor fled by gunboat down the Yangtze, and some of his officers took over command of the forces and won financial support from the provincial assembly. Together, the new military commanders and the local merchant-gentry formed a temporary provincial government and called for the establishment of a republic in China. Within two months similar uprisings took place in thirteen other provinces, and a revolutionary congress was called. On January 1, 1912, the provisional government at Nanking declared China a republic and appointed Sun Yat-sen, who had hurriedly returned to China from Denver at the outbreak of the revolution, the first provisional president.

The provinces of North China continued, however, to be dominated by Yüan Shih-k'ai, the most powerful official during the last years of the dowager empress Tz'u-hsi, who enjoyed the esteem of the principal northern commanders because of his success in rebuilding the imperial armies. Although given extensive powers by the Manchus to suppress the revolt, Yüan was regarded by most Chinese as the one leader who could avoid plunging China into prolonged civil war. Yüan persuaded the last Manchu emperor to abdicate in February 1912, with guarantees of an annual subsidy, but demanded the presidency for himself. To reunite the different regions of the country, Sun Yat-sen resigned the presidency in favor of Yüan, whom the national assembly, called by the Manchus in Peking, had previously named prime minister. The new republic thus got off to a very shaky start by appointing as its president the chief minister of the empire it had just destroyed.

THE MODERNIZATION OF JAPAN, 1868–1912

B y the mid-nineteenth century Japan's policy of isolation from the rest of the world, which had been valuable in promoting domestic harmony in the seventeenth century, was no longer tenable. The Western powers, which had already encroached on China, were determined to force open the Japanese economy; and as a result of the industrial revolution they possessed both the economic strength and the military technology to compel the Japanese to accept their demands. The officials of the shogunate, partly as a result of information received from the Dutch in Nagasaki, were well aware of their weakness relative to the Western powers. They even possessed samples of the unequal treaties that the Chinese had been compelled to accept and that were likely to be thrust on them in turn. Yet the shogun's authority had declined to the point where little could be done to prepare Japan to repel the interference of the Western powers. The outer daimyo had been restive under shogunal authority for two centuries, and by the nineteenth century even the traditionally loyal inner daimyo were proving unreliable. When the U.S. government decided to use a display of force to compel the Japanese to open their country to trade, the shogunate could do little but accept at least a minimal part of the demands.

The "Black Ships"

On July 8, 1853, the inhabitants of Uraga on the Bay of Edo saw four warships steam into the roadstead against the wind, with their huge guns trained on the small cannons of the coastal batteries. The American commodore Matthew Perry, who had been sent to Japan around the Cape of Good Hope and across the Indian Ocean at the orders of President Millard Fillmore, demanded that a letter from the president requesting commercial and diplomatic relations be delivered to the emperor, whom he erroneously believed to govern the country from Edo.

Perry's demand precipitated a national debate within Japan among the shogunal officials, the outer and inner daimyo, and even the imperial

A Japanese View of a "Black Ship" in Perry's Fleet (1854)
When the American commodore Matthew Perry returned to Tokyo Bay in 1854 to receive the shogun's answer to his demands for U.S. trading rights in Japan, the firepower and maneuverability of his expanded fleet compelled the Japanese to accede. (Courtesy of the Mariners Museum, Newport News, Virginia)

court in Kyoto. The shogun's chief adviser, Abe Masahiro, exacerbated the internal situation by formally seeking the advice not only of the inner daimyo, who had traditionally been consulted, but also of the outer daimyo, whose advice had never previously been asked. The inner daimyo were outraged at his affront to them. The outer daimyo, most of whom had advised that isolation be maintained and the Americans driven off by force, were furious when the shogunate signed a treaty with Perry on his return in 1854, granting the United States the right to trade through two small, isolated ports, and followed this concession by signing similar treaties with the British, Dutch, and Russians. Under pressure of the American consul, Townsend Harris, the Japanese signed a new commercial treaty in 1858, permitting American trade through several more ports, reducing tariffs, and giving extraterritorial privileges. Once again, the British, French, Dutch, and Russians quickly obtained similar concessions.

The Meiji Restoration

The decision of the shogunate to open Japan to the foreigners—or rather the shogunate's inability to do otherwise—brought to fever pitch all the hostilities and rivalries within Japan. The two most important groups opposed to the new policy and to the shogunate itself were the samurai of Satsuma and Choshu, two of the major outer daimyo domains. The principal castle town of Satsuma had been bombarded by British gunboats as punishment for the murder by samurai of an Englishman who had failed to dismount in the presence of a retinue from their domain. After Western shipping had been fired on from Choshu, it had been bombarded by a combined fleet of European and American ships. Thus Satsuma and Choshu had learned firsthand that isolation was no longer a viable policy and that the only alternative, if the foreigners were to be met on equal terms, was the modernization and strengthening of the country. In their view the shogunate represented the main obstacle to such a program of modernization.

The leaders of Satsuma and Choshu therefore conspired together and with members of the imperial court in Kyoto to gain control of the teen-aged emperor. In January 1868 they had him demand that the shogun restore authority to the emperor himself. The shogun acquiesced, although some of his followers undertook a halfhearted military resistance that was soon overcome. The new leaders moved the capital from Kyoto to Edo and changed the city's name to Tokyo, or "eastern capital." The emperor himself was installed in the shogun's palace in the center of Tokyo. In accordance with the East Asian custom of giving names to new eras, the name of Meiji ("enlightened rule") was assigned to the new era that began in 1868; the emperor Mutsuhito (reigned 1867–1912) became known as the Meiji emperor and the regime as the Meiji restoration.

The first task of the new regime was the abolition of the antiquated feudal system. The dismantling began in 1869 when two key leaders, Kido in Choshu and Okubo in Satsuma, persuaded their daimyo voluntarily to turn over their domains; similar actions were taken by the daimyo in Tosa and Hizen. Other lords, fearing that they might lose the chance for government position and the assumption of their debts, also returned their domains. By 1871 the government felt strong enough to order the remaining daimyo to do the same. In place of the daimyo, new prefectures were created for local government.

The Program of Reforms

Mutsuhito, the Meiji Emperor (reigned 1867–1912)
Although he never wielded great personal power in spite of the so-called "restoration" of the emperor after the end of the shogunate in 1868, Mutsuhito came to symbolize the modernization of Japan that took place during his long reign. (BBC Hulton Picture Library)

Second, after careful study of the European military organizations, the armed forces were modernized. Britain was the model for the new navy and Germany for the army, which was expanded by adoption of universal conscription for three years. The distinction between samurai and commoners was ended at one stroke. When some samurai, annoyed at the loss of their feudal privileges, revolted in 1877, the new conscript army mowed them down with their rifles.

Third, a new constitution was issued in 1889 that was an amalgam of the constitutions of West European countries but closest to that of imperial Germany. A diet or parliament, consisting of a House of Peers and a House of Representatives elected by about 2.6 percent of the male population, according to amount of taxes paid, was given powers of legislation, although these were restricted regarding the budget and the military. The emperor (or, in reality, his advisers) remained in supreme command of the army and navy, could legislate when the diet was not in session, and was directly in charge of foreign policy. A bill of rights promised freedom of speech and religion, providing public order was not disturbed. The constitution, despite its democratic form, put real power in the hands of the emperor and a number of leaders who had formulated the ideas of the Meiji restoration, and left open the way for the military leaders to form a powerful clique with direct access to the emperor in the making of policy. Nevertheless, political parties did develop in the 1880s, especially the Liberal party and the Progressive party, both of which demanded greater powers for parliament and a more responsive cabinet.

Fourth, a determined effort was made to Westernize the Japanese economy. At first foreign scholars were employed in Japan to teach science, medicine, and technology; but they were soon replaced by Japanese trained in foreign universities or by institutions in Japan itself such as Tokyo Imperial University. The Ministry of Education, founded in 1871, created a modern, nationwide system of schools modeled on the centralized pattern of France. Through strict government supervision of textbooks, curriculum, and teachers' performance, the government was able to indoctrinate the new generation with the ideals of the new nationalism, as well as a reaffirmation of the Confucian notion that Japan was a hierarchical society with a basis in the family unit. The government was equally involved in the fostering of new industry, which it encouraged indirectly by loans and subsidies and directly by itself building the needed roads, railroads, ports, telegraph, and factories for arms and textiles. The great firm of Mitsubishi, for example, was begun by an entrepreneur who was encouraged by the government to create a shipping line for Japan in order to end the control exercised by foreign vessels over the country's trade. By the 1890s a new capitalist class had been created. Some of its members were older merchant families such as the Mitsui, who had opened a dry goods store in Kyoto two centuries earlier and who now plunged into banking, foreign trade, and retail merchandising. A few samurai broke into industry by use of their government indemnity payments.

Japan's successes in its war with China in 1894–1895 and its war with Russia in 1904–1905 were due to the ability of the new army and navy to draw on the country's modernized industrial machine. The wars themselves exercised a further stimulating effect, not only by the demands for weapons, uniforms, transportation, and foodstuffs, but also by opening up Asia to Japanese trade. The victories also made the Western powers realize that Japan would soon force them to give up the privileges they had extorted before 1868, unless these were relinquished voluntarily. By 1911 the Western powers had given up their extraterritorial privileges and their power over Japanese tariffs. Britain, seeking an ally against Russia in 1902, was the first to sign a treaty of alliance on equal terms. Japan, in fact, had become one of the imperialists itself, especially with its annexation of Taiwan in 1895 and of Korea in 1910. In 1914 Japan entered World War I on the Allied side in order to add the German possessions in China and the Pacific islands to its territorial empire.

ECONOMIC DEPENDENCE IN INDEPENDENT LATIN AMERICA

Although most Spanish and Portuguese colonies in Latin America had won their independence by 1825, their political instability, social injustice, and economic weakness exposed them to outside exaction as surely as the decay of the Manchus left China prey to Western imperialism.

Nowhere in Latin America did independence bring political stability. The large states created by the liberators soon broke up. Bolívar's state of Gran Colombia had split into Venezuela, Ecuador, and Colombia. Mexico failed to unite Central America; and small, barely viable states were created in Guatemala, Honduras, El Salvador, and Costa Rica. The territory of Uruguay had been occupied by Portuguese troops from Brazil in 1816 and annexed to Brazil as the Cisplatine Province in 1821. With the help of Argentina, the Uruguayans won their independence from Brazil in 1825–1828.

Uncertain boundaries led to frequent border wars throughout the century. Even the smaller countries failed to find a coherent political system. Throughout Spanish America the urban Creoles, who had headed the independence movement, found that they were unable to control the *caudillos*, leaders of armed bands who came to dominate much of the inland regions and often the government in the capital as well. Mexico, for example, was governed between 1832 and 1854 by a conservative military adventurer, López de Santa Anna, as a barely disguised dictatorship. Where political parties existed, they theoretically represented liberal and conservative ideologies but only too often were mere facades hiding the rule of a strong man. Brazil was plagued with provincial revolts, some of them demanding separatism, for a quarter of a century. None succeeded, but the

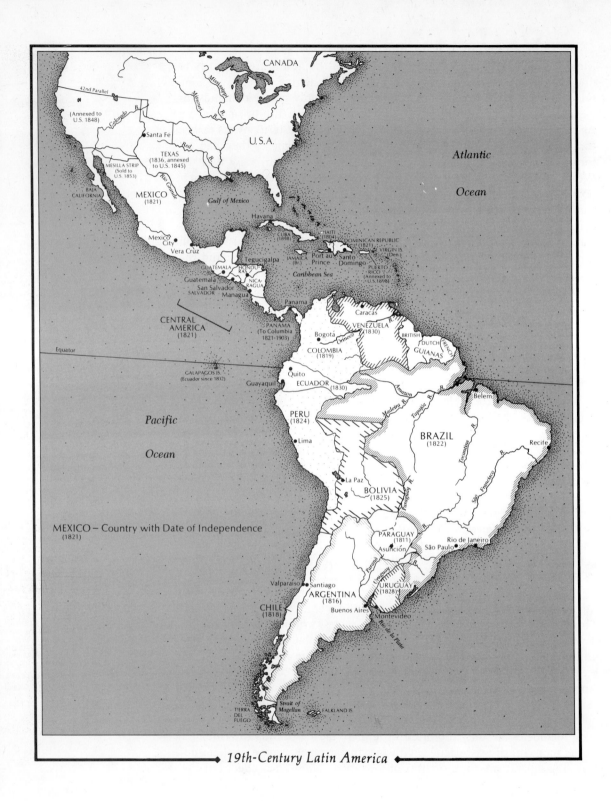

◆ *19th-Century Latin America* ◆

most serious, in Rio Grande do Sul, lasted for ten years (1835–1845). Following the failure of the last revolt, in Pernambuco in 1849, Brazil enjoyed almost half a century of peace under the strong rule of Emperor Pedro II (reigned 1840–1899). Indeed, Pedro II's reign seemed to prove that San Martín had been right in 1822 in pressing for the retention of monarchy in the new states, since Pedro was able to manipulate his parliamentary regime to maintain a semblance of orderly government.

Social and economic injustices were far more deep-rooted sources of instability than the nature of the parliamentary regimes. At independence the new rulers had made no effort to alter the structure of land and property ownership, which left the wealth in every country in the hands of a small Creole elite, numbering no more than two to three million in Spanish America and less than a million in Brazil. Worse, by requiring individual landownership, the new governments in the western countries destroyed Indian communal landholding and made possible the purchase of Indian lands by the Creoles at low prices. Thus the Indian peasant became a peon on the great *haciendas*, or estates, that stretched along the Andean chain from Chile to Mexico. Only rarely was an attempt made to better the conditions of the Indian poor, the most ambitious being the *reforma*, or reform program, of Benito Juárez in Mexico in the 1850s and 1860s. So great was the opposition to Juárez's attempts to redistribute the land, reduce the power of the Church, and bring the mestizos and Indians into the political system that a savage three-year civil war (1857–1860) had to be fought before the reforms could be implemented.

Slavery added its poison to the social system. Although abolished in most of Spanish America in the 1820s, it was not abolished in Puerto Rico until 1873, in Cuba until 1886, or in Brazil until 1888. Emancipation left an impoverished, illiterate population of ex-slaves whose integration into the social and political structure offered enormous difficulties. Although many individual church leaders worked for the social betterment of the poor, the Church as an institution helped prolong the injustices because of its own share in the great estates, its alliance with conservative political forces, and its opposition to intellectual change.

Disunited politically and socially and wracked by economic discontent, the Latin American countries found it difficult to fight off encroachments by the Western powers. Most obvious were the attempts at territorial annexations. Britain took the Falkland Islands from Argentina in 1833, and Spain again made Santo Domingo a colony in 1861–1865. The French attempted unsuccessfully in 1862–1865 to make Mexico into a puppet state under the emperor Maximilian. It was the United States, however, which in the Monroe Doctrine (1823) had warned the European powers to avoid further colonization in the Western Hemisphere, that seized the greatest territory. Florida was acquired in 1811 and 1821, Texas in 1845, and the rest of Mexico's possessions north of the Rio Grande in 1848. At the end of the Spanish-American War in 1898, Puerto Rico was annexed and Cuba made into a form of protectorate. In 1903 the United

Buenos Aires, Argentina
During the rapid growth of Buenos Aires in the late nineteenth century as a port and a manufacturing and food-processing center, its new streets and buildings were modeled on those of Paris. (Russell A. Thompson/Taurus Photos)

States was granted the Panama Canal Zone "in perpetuity" after supporting a revolt in Panama against the government of Colombia.

Before 1875 the British took the lead in opening Latin America to Western economic penetration. Occasionally, as in China, they resorted to gunboat diplomacy. In 1845, for example, they joined with the French in blockading the Rio de la Plata to support Uruguay in a dispute with the dictator of Argentina. They also collaborated with the French in 1862 in sending troops to compel the Mexican government to pay its foreign debts. Mostly, however, penetration took the form of investment on favorable terms, which gave the British enormous leverage in directing Latin American economic development. The British were primarily interested in gaining control of the merchant houses that dominated the import and export trade, the banks, the railroads, the ports, and the utilities.

Argentina became one of the principal centers of British investment, especially with the growing European demand for Argentinian beef in the second half of the century. British capital took over the meat-packing houses, the docks, and the most profitable railroads, thus contributing to the extraordinary growth of Buenos Aires, which had reached a population of 500,000 in 1889 and 1.2 million in 1909. The favorite residence of the native Creoles, of the large European immigrant population, and of many of the dispossessed from the back country, Buenos Aires became the most European of the Latin American cities in both architecture and style of life. Its residents took pride in considering their city the Paris of the Western Hemisphere.

After 1875 the export trade of all Latin America was increasingly directed to the supply of raw materials and primary commodities to the advanced industrial countries in exchange for manufactured goods. The result was the dangerous concentration by each country on one or two products only. Argentina and Uruguay exported wheat and beef, Brazil coffee and sugar, Chile nitrates and copper. The most precarious forms of monoculture, however, were introduced to the Central American countries by U.S. companies, which were able to buy up vast estates such as the sugar plantations of Cuba and the banana plantations of Honduras. Mexico under Porfírio Díaz was especially welcoming to American financial interests, who took over much of the country's copper, lead, and tin mines; its oil; and its sugar, tobacco, and banana estates.

In many countries the prospect of quick profit from exports led the Creole ruling class to press for the expropriation of the Indians as well as the sale of Church and other national lands at bargain prices to the cronies of the ruling elites. By 1914 the great estates, worked by an impoverished, brutalized peasantry, were a greater scandal than even the *latifundia* that had been created by the original conquistadores. The price of neo-colonialism, as this system of economic exploitation is sometimes called, was being paid by the vast Indian, black, and mestizo majority of the Latin American population.

The first attempts to overthrow not merely the government but the system of oppression—as in China, where a similar exploitation of the poverty-stricken majority had been carried out by a native landowning class backed by a repressive authoritarian regime and by a native mercantile class pressed by foreign capitalist interests—occurred in 1910. In that year Mexico embarked on its long, troubled revolution, which heralded the opening of a new era of social and political upheaval in Latin American history, in which the institutions established in the century since independence would prove increasingly fragile.

SUGGESTED READING

Well-balanced estimates of the character of British influence on India are given in P. E. Roberts, *History of British India Under the Company and the Crown* (1921, 1958) and Percival Griffiths, *The British Impact on India* (1965). For more detailed studies of the policies of the various viceroys, turn to Philip Woodruff, *The Men Who Ruled India* (1954) or such excellent surveys as Stanley Wolpert, *A New History of India* (1977) or Michael Edwardes, *A History of India from the Earliest Times to the Present Day* (1961). Reliable biographies of the more interesting or colorful of the governor-generals and viceroys include Penderel Moon, *Warren Hastings and British India* (1962); Paul E. Roberts, *India Under Wellesley* (1929); and David Dilks, *Curzon in India* (1969–1970). Amusing details of British life in India are related in Dennis Kincaid, *British Social Life in India, 1608–1937* (1938, 1971); Michael Edwardes, *Bound to Exile: The Victorians in India* (1969); Reginald Reynolds, *White Sahibs in India* (1973); and Charles Allen, ed., *Plain Tales from the Raj: Images of British India in the Twentieth Century* (1975).

Geoffrey Moorhouse, *Calcutta* (1971), a lively and sympathetic introduction to both historic and contemporary Calcutta, should be supplemented with Pradip Sinha, *Nineteenth Century Bengal: Aspects of Social History* (1965) and R. C. Majundar, *Glimpses of Bengal in the Nineteenth Century* (1960). The economic life of early nineteenth-century Calcutta is analyzed in Blair B. Kling, *Partner in Empire: Dwarkanath Tagore and the Age of Enterprise in Eastern India* (1976). Dwarkanath and Debranath Tagore's involvement with the Hindu renaissance can be followed in David Kopf, *The Brahmo Samaj and the Shaping of the Mod-*

ern Indian Mind (1979). Kopf turns to the educational foundations of the Hindu renaissance in *British Orientalism and the Bengal Renaissance: The Dynamics of Indian Modernization, 1773–1835* (1969), which details the achievements of the College of Fort William, the "Oxford of the East." Rudyard Kipling described the late nineteenth-century city with lurid distaste in *City of Dreadful Night*, republished in *The One Volume Kipling* (1928), pp. 187–251.

Amiya Chakravarty, ed., *A Tagore Reader* (1961) presents a broad selection of Rabindranath Tagore's poems, stories, and lectures. Edward Thompson, *Rabindranath Tagore: Poet and Dramatist* (1926, 1948) relates the poetry to the evolution of the writer's thought, whereas his political activity is placed in its Bengali setting in Leonard A. Gordon, *Bengal: The Nationalist Movement* (1974).

For a contrast with the modernity of Calcutta, Percival Spear, *Twilight of the Mughuls: Studies in Late Mughul Delhi* (1951) writes feelingly of the last tragic years when the imperial court was a mere shadow. The remnants of grandeur in the Red Fort may be compared with the new ostentation of the British rulers in Mark Bence-Jones, *Palaces of the Raj: Magnificence and Misery of the Lord Sahibs* (1973) which describes Government House in Calcutta and the viceroy's country retreat at Barrackpore up the Hooghly River.

The economic and political development of Australia and New Zealand are detailed in C. Hartley Grattan, *The Southwest Pacific to 1900: Australia, New Zealand, the Islands, Antarctica* (1963) and *The Southwest Pacific since 1900: Modern History* (1963). For the individual countries, see A.G.L. Shaw, *Australia* (1955); Brian Fitzpatrick, *The Australian People, 1788–1945* (1946); and Keith Sinclair, *A History of New Zealand* (1959). The history of Australia's cities can be approached through the detailed histories of the separate states, such as H. G. Turner, *A History of the Colony of Victoria, 1797–1900* (1904) and J. S. Battye, *Western Australia* (1924); a brief introduction is given in A. J. Brown and H. M. Sherrard, *Town and Country Planning* (1951) and Morton Herman, *The Early Australian Architects and Their Work* (1954). For Melbourne, see Maie Casey et al., *Early Melbourne Architecture, 1840–1888* (1953).

An excellent economic analysis of the structure of Tahitian commerce and production is given in Colin Newbury, *Tahiti Nui: Change and Survival in French Polynesia, 1767–1945* (1980). Patrick O'Reilly, *La Vie à Tahiti au temps de la reine Pomaré* (1975) provides details of daily life from the hours of postal service to the price of oranges, in addition to describing the fifty-year reign of Tahiti's queen. The standard study of the Hawaiian monarchy is the three-volume history of Ralph S. Kuykendall, *The Hawaiian Kingdom* (1938, 1966, 1969). Ruth Tabrah, *Hawaii: A Bicentennial History* (1980) describes the demographic disaster and economic dispossession suffered by the native Hawaiians in the nineteenth century, while showing sympathy for the problems and aspirations of all Hawaiians from Kamehameha and his successors to the indentured Asian laborers on the great plantations. A lively survey is provided by Gavan Daws, *School of Time* (1968).

Robert W. July, *A History of the African People* (1980) has full treatment of the independent African states before the scramble for Africa. The end of slavery is weighed in Basil Davidson, *The African Slave Trade* (1961). For more detailed treatments of individual countries of West Africa, see Michael Crowder, *The Story of Nigeria*, 4th ed. (1978); David Kimble, *A Political History of Ghana; The Rise of Gold Coast Nationalism, 1850–1928* (1963); and C. Daryll Forde and Phyllis M. Kaberry, eds., *West African Kingdoms in the Nineteenth Century* (1967). An excellent analysis of the economic background is given in Anthony G.

Hopkins, *An Economic History of West Africa* (1973). On the settlements for freed slaves, see Christopher Fyfe, *A History of Sierra Leone* (1962) and P. J. Staudenraus, *The African Colonization Movement, 1816–1865* (1961). The early years of colonialism in West Africa are scrutinized in Michael Crowder, *West Africa Under Colonial Rule* (1968) and his *West African Resistance* (1971). Reliable studies of East Africa include Kenneth Ingham, *A History of East Africa* (1963) and Basil Davidson, *East and Central Africa to the Late Nineteenth Century* (1967). For examples of the most exploitative phases of colonialism, see Ruth M. Slade, *King Leopold's Congo* (1962) and John Iliffe, *Tanganyika Under German Rule, 1905–1912* (1969). The evolution of South Africa is analyzed at great length in the three-volume *Oxford History of South Africa* (1969, 1971, 1973), edited by Monica Wilson and Leonard Thompson. The policies and goals of the different European powers may be compared by consulting Ronald Robinson and John Gallagher, *Africa and the Victorians: The Climax of Imperialism in the Dark Continent* (1961); Henri Brunschwig, *French Colonialism, 1871–1914* (1966); and Prosser Gifford and William R. Louis, eds., *Britain and Germany in Africa: Imperial Rivalry and Colonial Rule* (1967).

For a fine combination of primary sources and historical survey, see David N. Robinson and Douglas Smith, *Sources of the African Past* (1979).

Chinese history in the nineteenth century is surveyed in Li Chien-nung, *The Political History of China* (1956) and *The Cambridge History of China*, vol. 10, *Late Ch'ing, 1800–1870*, part I (1978), edited by John K. Fairbank and vol. 11, *Late Ch'ing, 1800–1911*, part II (1980), edited by John K. Fairbank and Kwang-Ching Liu. On the rebellions, see Franz Michael, *The Taiping Rebellion: History* (1972); Victor Purcell, *The Boxer Uprising: A Background Study* (1963); and, for the 1911 revolution, Mary C. Wright, ed., *China in Revolution: The First Phase, 1900–1913* (1968) and H. Z. Schiffrin, *Sun Yat-sen and the Origins of the Chinese Revolution* (1968). Rather specialized articles on Chinese urban history give a good deal of information on Shanghai, in G. William Skinner, ed., *The City in Late Imperial China* (1977) and Mark Elvin and G. William Skinner, *The Chinese City Between Two Worlds* (1974). The economic impact of the treaty ports is analyzed in Rhoads Murphey, *The Outsiders: The Western Experience in India and China* (1977). On Shanghai itself, see his *Shanghai: Key to Modern China* (1953), which includes a good analysis of the city's development in the late nineteenth century.

The standard work on the reforms of the late nineteenth century in Japan is W. G. Beasley, *The Meiji Restoration* (1973). Economic modernization is described in Thomas C. Smith, *Political Change and Industrial Development in Japan: Government Enterprise, 1868–1880* (1955) and William W. Lockwood, *The Economic Development of Japan: Growth and Structural Change* (1954). David Kornhauser discusses the impetus industrialization gave to urban growth in *Urban Japan: Its Foundations and Growth* (1976).

The economic dependence of Latin America in the nineteenth century is analyzed in Celso Furtado, *The Economic Development of Latin America* (1970). On the leading countries, see M. C. Meyer and W. L. Sherman, *The Course of Mexican History* (1979); E. B. Burns, *A History of Brazil*; José Maria Bello, *A History of Modern Brazil, 1889–1954* (1966); Henry S. Ferns, *Argentina* (1969); and Jay Kinsbruner, *Chile: A Historical Interpretation* (1973). City growth is analyzed in Warren Dean, *The Industrialization of São Paulo, 1880–1945* (1969) and James R. Scobie, *Argentina; A City and a Nation* (1971).

26

FIN DE SIECLE

In the 1870s and 1880s, Europeans were sharply aware of an acceleration in the pace of change. A new epoch, both exciting and frightening in its promise, was opening. After centuries of disunity, Germany and Italy were each united as nation-states in 1871; and their future role in the European balance was still uncertain. The European powers were beginning to scramble for control of the undeveloped regions of the world, in a movement that promised immense returns but also the possibility of war among the imperialists. But the average European was more aware of the social and economic changes that impinged upon his own daily life; and these were enormous. A population explosion was taking place that increased the total number of Europeans from 274 million in 1850 to 460 million in 1914, in spite of the emigration between 1870 and 1914 of 25 million. This rise in population caused a vast increase in the size and number of cities in western Europe and Russia. The urbanization of life, the grouping of huge populations in modern industrial cities composed largely of factories, offices, and houses, was perhaps the most marked phenomenon in social history; and this concentration of population was made possible by revolutionary technological advances and the reorganization of the capitalist method of running the economy. At the same time, however, the working classes became far less willing to tolerate the conditions of life in the factory and the city slum; and they expressed their demand for change through increasingly effective trade unions and political parties. Accompanying these changes, and undoubtedly greatly influenced by them, was an intellectual transformation as far-reaching in its effects on science, medicine, music, painting, and philosophy as any in Western history. The magnitude of the leap forward is evident if one considers some

Avenue de l'Opéra, Paris   (H. Roger-Viollet)

of the intellectuals active in this period—Einstein, Freud, Picasso, Schoenberg, Max Weber, and Proust. These years were among the most seminal in all Western history; and although every part of the continent contributed to the general achievement, two cities were universally recognized as the most exciting embodiments of the end-of-the-century spirit, of *fin de siècle*. In the Vienna of the aging emperor Francis Joseph and in the Paris of the Belle Epoque, the nineteenth century came to a resplendent climax and the twentieth century made a fittingly iconoclastic debut. "The world has changed less since Jesus Christ," commented the French poet Charles Péguy in 1913, "than it has in the last thirty years."

URBANIZATION OF THE WEST

The Population Explosion

During the nineteenth century, the European population expanded faster than that of any part of the globe except those regions inhabited by European migrants. In 1800 Europe's population was one-fifth of the total population of the world; by the end of the century it was one-quarter. This growth affected all parts of the continent. Between 1850 and 1914, Russia's population increased 89 percent, to reach 142 million. Italy's population increased from 26 million to 36 million, giving it a density of 118 people per square kilometer. Britain, whose population increased from 26 million to more than 40 million, reached a population density of 172 per square kilometer.

The most important factor in this rise in population was the fall in the death rate. Great medical advances were made in the last quarter of the century, especially in the prevention of typhoid, cholera, typhus, and plague. The provision of more and better hospital care, the use of anesthesia, increased hygienic control in operations, improved laboratory techniques for the diagnosis of bacteria, new public health codes—all raised the life expectancy. Between 1880 and 1900 in France, for example, the mortality rate of infants was reduced from 184 per thousand to 159. Food supply too was greatly improved. The railroad and the steamship made it easier and cheaper to supply the population with food from distant areas and in greater variety. In the early part of the century cultivation of the potato provided food for the poor, although even the potato crop could fail, as the Irish famine of 1846 showed. By the end of the century even the working classes were buying fats made of vegetable oils, more and varied vegetables, citrus fruits, and pasteurized milk and cheese. Better-built houses and apartments supplied with running water and with coal heating cut the impact of winter epidemics, although in some of the densely packed slums of the larger cities mortality rates among the very poor may even have increased. At least until 1880, there was also an increase in the birth rate, which rose in some countries by as much as a half; and a large family became the rule in most parts of the West. But beginning in France quite early in the century, in Britain about 1880, in the United States about

Vaccination in the East End of London, 1871
Smallpox vaccination helped reduce the death rate in England by one-fourth in 1850–1900. (The Graphic, April 8, 1871)

1900, and in Germany about 1910, there was a marked fall in the birth rate as a result of voluntary family planning. Although this process was at first most evident in the upper and middle classes, the habit of keeping down the size of the family spread among the less well-to-do as they realized that their young were going to survive more frequently. The average size of the family in Britain, for example, fell from 5.9 to 2.8 persons between 1870 and 1914.

The great mass of this new population was either born in the cities or made its way there. In Germany, the increase in the population of the cities equaled exactly the increase in the total population. In France, where

◆ City Growth in the Nineteenth Century ◆
(Population in Millions)

City	Year					
	1800	1820	1840	1860	1880	1900
London	0.86	1.2	1.9	2.8	3.8	4.1
Paris	0.55	0.71	0.93	1.7	2.3	2.7
Berlin		0.20	0.33	0.55	1.1	1.9
Vienna	0.23	0.26	0.36	0.48	0.78	1.9
Budapest	0.06	0.08		0.18	0.36	0.72

the population was growing more slowly, the increase in the size of Paris alone was the equivalent of half the country's total increase. The vast expansion of the cities was not restricted to western Europe or even to the industrialized areas. By 1900 there were already seventeen cities in European Russia with over a hundred thousand inhabitants.

Mechanization of City Transport

There was a great similarity of character in the development of the new centers and the expansion of the older cities. The most novel feature of the city in this period was the mechanization of its transport. First came the steam railroad. In London, a great swathe of railroad cuttings, viaducts, sidings, and freight yards had been inflicted by the construction of the London and Birmingham Railway, which was finished in 1838. By the end of the century the iron roads snaked off in every direction from the huge Gothic or classical railroad stations. The stations had even begun to acquire a certain glamor of their own. In *Howard's End* (1910), the novelist E. M. Forster spoke of the meaning for his heroine of the different stations:

Like many others who have lived long in a great capital, she had strong feelings about the various railway termini. They are our gates to the glorious and the unknown. . . . In Paddington all Cornwall is latent and the remoter west; down the inclines of Liverpool Street lie fenlands and the illimitable Broads; Scotland is through the pylons of Euston; Wessex behind the poised chaos of Waterloo. Italians realize this, as is natural; those of them who are so unfortunate as to serve as waiters in Berlin call the Anhalt Bahnhof the Stazione d'Italia because by it they must return to their homes. And he is a chilly Londoner who does not endow his stations with some personality, and extend to them, however shyly, the emotions of fear and love. [1]

But much the same could be said of any of the great metropolises. In Paris, the Gare Saint Lazare meant trips to the Channel resorts or to England; the Gare de Lyon, an escape to the Riviera. In Vienna, the Südbahnhof meant journeys to Budapest and the Balkans. In Saint Petersburg, the overnight express from Moscow arrived at the Nikolaevsky Station, which Leo Tolstoy, in his novel *Anna Karenina*, used as the setting for the first parting of the infatuated Anna from the glamorous Prince Vronsky; and it was at the Finland Station that the Bolsheviks met Lenin in April 1917 on his return from exile in Switzerland, a moment that immortalized that railroad station in the history of Communism. In all, Europe's railroad mileage increased from 66,000 to 172,000 in the last thirty years of the nineteenth century. Every major city and most minor ones entered the transportation network.

The railroad exercised a direct effect on the character of the city itself, not only by linking its factories to distant sources of raw materials and markets, but by making possible a dispersion of the population from the heart of the historic city to nearby villages and towns. At first the middle

[1] E. M. Forster, *Howard's End* (New York: Knopf, 1951), p. 16.

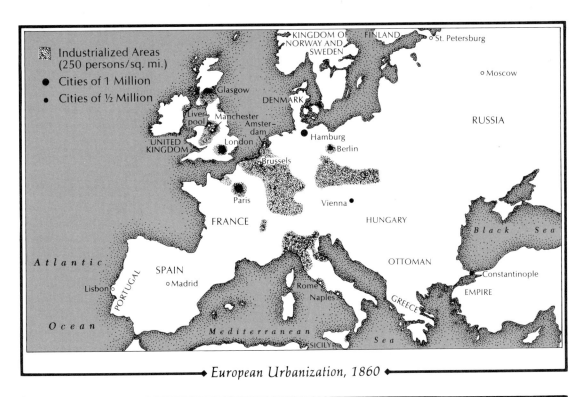

Legend:
- Industrialized Areas (250 persons/sq. mi.)
- Cities of 1 Million
- Cities of ½ Million

KINGDOM OF NORWAY AND SWEDEN
FINLAND
St. Petersburg
Moscow
RUSSIA
DENMARK
Glasgow
Liver-pool
Manchester
Amster-dam
Hamburg
Berlin
UNITED KINGDOM
London
Brussels
Paris
FRANCE
Vienna
HUNGARY
Black Sea
OTTOMAN
Atlantic
PORTUGAL
SPAIN
Madrid
Lisbon
Rome
Naples
GREECE
Constantinople
EMPIRE
Ocean
Mediterranean
Sea
SICILY

European Urbanization, 1860

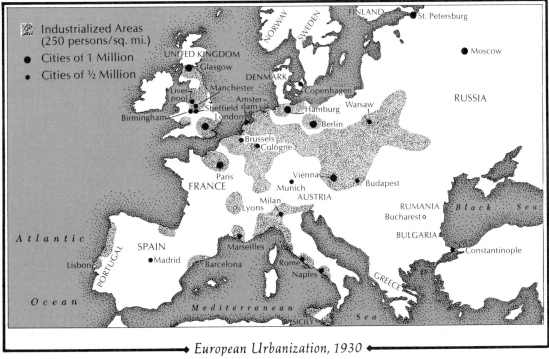

Legend:
- Industrialized Areas (250 persons/sq. mi.)
- Cities of 1 Million
- Cities of ½ Million

NORWAY
SWEDEN
FINLAND
St. Petersburg
Moscow
UNITED KINGDOM
Glasgow
DENMARK
Manchester
Liver-pool
Sheffield
Birmingham
London
Amster-dam
Copenhagen
Hamburg
Warsaw
Berlin
RUSSIA
Brussels
Cologne
Paris
Vienna
Budapest
FRANCE
Munich
AUSTRIA
Milan
Lyons
RUMANIA
Bucharest
Black Sea
BULGARIA
Atlantic
SPAIN
Marseilles
Constantinople
Lisbon
PORTUGAL
Madrid
Barcelona
Rome
Naples
GREECE
Ocean
Mediterranean
Sea
SICILY

European Urbanization, 1930

classes and then, with the introduction of commuter fares toward the end of the century, the more prosperous of the workers began to take the train to work, thus establishing a physical separation of the classes on a scale never known before. For most of the city population, however, a far more important change was the laying down of rails for omnibuses, which were horse-drawn from the 1860s and driven by electricity from the 1880s. In very large cities, the surface transportation was supplemented by the underground railroad. London built the first underground line, most of it only a few feet below the ground; twelve million passengers were carried in 1864. Other cities were slower in following London's example. Boston constructed its system in 1895, Paris in 1900, New York in 1904. Many cities, particularly in the United States, found it cheaper, if more unpleasant for nearby inhabitants, to build elevated railroads above existing streets. In the elevated railroad and the subway, the most inexpensive and effective forms of public transport had been invented, since the trains could carry between forty and sixty thousand passengers an hour.

The transportation revolution created the working-class suburb. Huge new areas of closely packed tenements grew up on the edges of all the large cities of the West. These were no longer restricted to the linear development, forced by the railroad line, that had created an aristocracy of commuters—the Main Line of Philadelphia or the London-to-Brighton commuters, for example. With little municipal control, free enterprise builders threw up blocks of flats. In Berlin, six- and seven-story tenements were built around tiny courtyards with little provision for air or light. In Vienna, it was legally permissible until 1929 to build an eight-story building covering eighty-five percent of the land site. Areas that had been pre-

Traffic on the Leipzigerstrasse, Berlin, in 1914
The first motorbus, with a 22-horsepower engine, was introduced in Berlin in 1905, and proved considerably faster and more comfortable than horse-drawn vehicles. By 1914, however, Berlin was already suffering from traffic jams and air pollution. (Courtesy of the German Information Center)

Workers' Tenements, Kreuzberg, Berlin
The borough of Kreuzberg developed rapidly in the mid-nineteenth century, after the construction of the Landwehr Canal linking the upper and lower sections of the Spree River. Kreuzberg was densely populated, with an average of 130 inhabitants per acre. (Courtesy of the German Information Center)

viously left as uninhabitable because they were low lying, subject to flood or disease, or marshy, were developed as the sites of working-class housing. Budapest, for example, extended from the charming hill settlement of Buda, with its palaces, churches, and medieval houses, across the Danube to the flatlands of Pest, which soon became the industrial, commercial, and working-class section of the city. The spatial separation of the different classes of the population undoubtedly slowed the demand for urban improvements in sanitation, public health, housing, education, and cultural amenities. The inhabitants of the villas of Hampstead on the edge of London or of the chalets of the Buda hills could isolate themselves morally and physically from the smoke and grime. Physical separation became an alternative to municipal improvements for a laissez-faire society.

The Boulevard Builders

Not all cities developed at this time without planning, however, nor were all population movements centrifugal. Since the development of military technology had made the city walls useless for defense, in the mid-nineteenth century most large continental cities began to pull down their fortifications. As the land laid bare was usually municipally or nationally

The Ringstrasse, Vienna
When the massive fortifications surrounding the inner city of Vienna were demolished in 1858–1865, a complete circle of tree-lined boulevards was constructed in their place. The first of the new public buildings erected on the "Ring" was the State Opera House (right), which opened in 1869 with a performance of Mozart's Don Giovanni. *(H. Roger-Viollet)*

owned, large-scale plans of rebuilding and often of urban beautification were adopted, with results very beneficial to the inner city's inhabitants. A glance at the map of almost any European city will show an encircling band of broad roads, or boulevards, which are usually tree-lined and backed by substantial middle-class houses or apartments built on the site of the walls. The most lavish example of redevelopment was in Vienna, where the walls' demolition began in 1858. In their place a wide series of boulevards encircled the medieval city. This Ringstrasse, opened in 1865, was sixty yards wide and two and a half miles long, lined with trees and illuminated with gas burners. Between the boulevards were pathways for pedestrians, and on the outer edge, many public gardens. The Ringstrasse became the setting for a grandiose, though occasionally unprepossessing, display of Habsburg imperial architecture. For the next quarter of a century, a medley of massive architectural styles was developed along the Ring—first the neo-Renaissance opera house and university, then a Gothic town hall and a classical imperial parliament, and finally two imposing hybrids for art and science. "The entire Ringstrasse affected me like a fairy tale out of the Arabian Nights," Adolf Hitler commented after living there a generation later.

Improvements in Urban Amenities

There were many other ways in which the quality of the urban environment was improving. Gas and electricity were introduced for street lighting between 1880 and 1900. Clean water from reservoirs and aqueducts was made available in all parts of the city. Public baths were built, and private enterprise began to cater on a large scale to the enjoyment of the working classes. The end of the nineteenth century saw the building of the great popular theaters, and the music halls and vaudevilles, along Shaftesbury Avenue in London, the Boulevard Montmartre in Paris, and Broadway in New York. After 1895, when the first movie was shown in Paris, increasing numbers of movie houses appeared.

Catering to an even larger audience were the sports fields. Sports had been encouraged by both public and private organizations in the nineteenth century for a wide variety of motives. In Germany, gymnastics clubs had been started to prepare German youth for the war of liberation against Napoleon I; they were later made an integral part of the German school system. Trade unions and other workers' organizations turned to athletics and other open-air sports to counteract the ill effects of slum and factory, and even, in the minds of some labor organizers, to build a sense of working-class solidarity. In England, sport, in particular rugby football, was regarded by private school headmasters as part of the training for future administrators of empire, while soccer was applauded by many social reformers as a way of counteracting the appeal of drinking in the public house. Soccer games in London as early as 1900 attracted over a hundred thousand people. In the United States, baseball became the first important spectator sport in the new industrial cities; by 1876, when the National League was formed, most large American cities sported a baseball arena. In France the greatest number of spectators turned out for the horse races. A third of a million Parisians would tramp out to the races at Longchamps and Auteuil in the Bois de Boulogne for an afternoon's gambling and picnicking.

Parisian Aristocrats at the Races (*Photo Desoye*)

Galleria Umberto I, Naples, Italy

In the late nineteenth and the early twentieth centuries, Italian architects glorified the shopping arcade, roofing it with a cast iron frame and glass, and laying down a floor of multicolored marble. Like the imperial forums of ancient Rome, the gallery at once became a favorite meeting place, pleasant in sunshine or rain. (Peter Menzel)

Perhaps the most appreciated amenity to be introduced into the new cities was the department store. Until the nineteenth century, shops either carried highly specialized goods or, in the small towns, offered just about everything. Early in the nineteenth century, the ingredients of the department store were put together. Price labels in shop windows appeared for the first time in 1820. Plate glass windows had been introduced by 1850.

Drapers led the way by diversifying their stock and were followed closely by the large-scale food sellers. Gaslight and the plate glass window gave scope to the window dressers, giving rise to the new phenomenon of the window shopper. First in the great capital cities, and then in the provinces, the department store became a palace of light. Already by 1900, enchanted emporia had been created on Fifth Avenue in New York, Regent Street in London, the Boulevard Haussmann in Paris, the Leipzigerstrasse in Berlin, and the Nevsky Prospekt in Saint Petersburg. It was still, however, the factory and the office building that gave the predominant character to the new urbanism. The creators of wealth created the urban landscape.

THE OLD AND THE NEW INDUSTRIALISM

Coal, Iron, and Textiles

The first industrial revolution had been based on coal, iron, and textiles. Its principal source of power had been the steam engine. Its main form of transportation had been the canal and then the railroad. As a result, the cities that grew up during that first industrial revolution had been massed around the sources of coal and iron or near water power. Up to 1870, the agglomeration of the industrial population in Europe had taken place principally around the Pennine chain in England and the coal mines of South Wales and along the great belt of coal deposits that ran from the Ruhr valley in Germany across Belgium and Luxembourg into the Channel region of northern France. Because of their large working-class population and their position as the arbiters of financial and commercial power, most capital cities, too, had expanded, and all had acquired large industrialized suburbs. In all these places the pattern of urbanization had been similar. The factories had been constructed where possible near water, monopolizing the lake or river frontage; water washed or cooled their products and swept away their effluent. Otherwise, they were grouped near the freight yards of the railroads or the slag heaps of the mines. Workers' homes were scattered in the unused spaces between them or on hillsides too steep for factory construction.

Between 1870 and 1914, the first industrial revolution continued its vertiginous expansion. In countries where it was already established, such as Britain, France, Germany, and the United States, it achieved new heights of productivity. Furthermore, it spread rapidly to other parts of Europe and to restricted areas of South America, Africa, and Asia. Thus the basis of the industrial growth of the late nineteenth century was primarily a continuation of the first industrial revolution. Coal remained central to the expansion. British coal production, for example, increased 150 percent; French, 300 percent; German, 800 percent; and American, 1,700 percent. Pig iron production expanded at a similar rate, and new ore mines were opened in areas like Lorraine after its annexation to Germany in 1871. While Britain maintained its supremacy in textile production, new competitors such as Italy and Russia appeared. Finally, railroad construction was vastly expanded, especially in countries like the United States, Canada, and Russia, with the opening up of vast hinterlands. The first transcontinental railroad in the United States was opened in 1869, in Canada in 1875, and in Russia in 1905. This expansion produced in the cities conditions similar to those in Manchester half a century earlier. Houses, factories, marshaling yards, and urban amenities in Pittsburgh, Saarbrücken, or Dnepropetrovsk were little different from their English forerunners.

The Second Industrial Revolution: Steel

Nevertheless, largely by the application of new scientific knowledge, the scale of industrial production was increased, and its output greatly diversified during this period. The character of the industrial cities changed, in some instances for the better. An important series of new industries arose, probably the most significant of which was the manufacture of steel.

Steel was an enormously versatile metal, far tougher than the wrought iron used in the first half of the nineteenth century. It was made by combining iron and carbon, and its qualities could be varied by the addition of small quantities of other metals such as tungsten and manganese. Subsequent to improvements in the blast furnace used to convert iron ore into pig iron, in 1856 an English scientist named Henry Bessemer developed an inexpensive method of making steel by blowing air through molten pig iron in a lined steel container. Then, to remedy the lack of quality controls

Bessemer Steel Plant, Krupp Factory, Essen, Germany, 1862
Four egg-shaped Bessemer converters can be seen at the base of the chimney vents. Mounted on pivots turned by wheels, they could tilt to receive the pig iron, stand upright while air was blown through the spherical base to burn out impurities, and tilt again to pour out the molten steel. (Courtesy of the German Information Center)

in the Bessemer process, the open-hearth, or Siemens-Martin, process was invented in the 1860s. Scrap iron was mixed with pig iron in a reverberatory furnace in which air and a gaseous fuel were introduced at very high temperatures. The process was slow, but it produced high-quality steel and moreover had the advantage for countries short of ore of using scrap metal. In 1878 the Thomas Gilchrist process was perfected to permit the use of high-phosphorus ores such as those of Lorraine. Finally, at the beginning of the twentieth century, the electric furnace process, in which steel was produced by passing an electric current through the resistant mass of materials inside an electric furnace, was adopted in countries poor in coke and rich in hydroelectric power.

World steel production had reached more than sixty million tons by 1914, a one-hundred-twentyfold increase from half a century earlier. Steel replaced iron for railroads, steam engines, cable, and most forms of machinery. It was used in the construction of larger and lighter steamships, which finally replaced sailing ships as the principal vehicles of ocean transportation. It made possible the sewing machine, which had replaced handsewing by the 1870s, and it was soon applied to the mechanization of shoe production. It transformed the office with the typewriter in 1878 and the tabulating machine in 1890. Steel made it possible for Daimler-Benz to develop the first gasoline-driven automobile in 1886, although the effects of this invention were felt on a large scale only after the First World War. And steel also changed the basic form of city building, making it possible to replace wood, brick, and stone with the steel beam and girder and with ferro-concrete.

There had been suggestions of the advent of a new form of architecture in the first half of the century when engineers rather than architects were called on to design iron suspension bridges, like Adam Clark's bridge across the Danube at Budapest, and when Paxton designed the Crystal Palace in iron and glass. The United States took the lead in recognizing the potential of steel architecture. The first use of a steel skeleton for a facade was in Chicago's Home Insurance Company Building of 1884. The style was ideal for warehouses, department stores, and factories; and in the work of Louis Sullivan (1856–1924), Chicago led the world in architectural innovation. The Marshall Field wholesale warehouse (1895) in Chicago was a model of the use of steel framing to create large interior spaces. The great innovator Walter Gropius had designed a steel and glass frame factory in Germany as early as 1911.

It was the use of steel in the skyscraper that most changed the appearance of the American city. The first electric elevator had been used in 1889, and from then American buildings could, as the French said in awe, become "sky-scratchers." Since the 1850s Americans had been building solid stone skyscrapers up to twenty stories using hydraulic elevators. By the 1890s riveted steel frames had been developed, and in 1913 the Woolworth Building in New York City, then the tallest building in the world, reached sixty stories.

Woolworth Building, New York
The 792-foot-tall tower, the highest building in the world when completed in 1913, was built for the five-and-ten-cent store tycoon Frank W. Woolworth (Fine Arts Commission, The National Archives)

Electricity

Electricity was second only to steel in changing the appearance of the city. Electricity had been known in classical times, but its only application before the nineteenth century had been in shocking guests at parties in eighteenth-century salons. Benjamin Franklin, however, had caught electricity from the skies with his lightning conductor, and he and several Italian scientists had begun serious experiments as to the nature of this mysterious force. But electricity could only be used as a source of power when the relationship between magnetism and electricity was understood.

The Englishman Michael Faraday produced the first electrical motor by applying the principle of electromagnetic induction; he used a magnet spinning inside a wire coil to produce a current of electricity. Shortly after, American inventor Samuel Morse was able to apply such a motor to the invention of the electric telegraph. In the 1870s an important advance came with the invention of the turbine for generating electricity. The turbine, which converted moving water or steam into mechanical energy, had been used on a large scale in the Alps to harness water power. Water turbines of this kind were linked to electrical generators; by them, the mechanical power generated in the water turbine was converted into electrical energy.

The Advantages of Electricity (Left), The Disadvantages of Electricity (Right)

As electricity came into wide public use in the 1880s, the streets of all Western cities were festooned with innumerable wires and cables.

Even more power was produced, however, when Charles Parsons in the 1880s used steam to drive a turbine, a process that was soon used to power ships. Other machines made it possible to supply electrical power to factories in the safer form of alternating current, and to carry it over long distances. Although the invention of the incandescent gas mantle in 1886 prolonged the use of gas lighting for another generation, the use of electricity as the main form of lighting was assured with the development by Joseph Swan in England in 1860 and by Thomas Edison in the United States in 1879 of the electric light bulb, based on the principle that electricity passing through a filament of metal can be made to heat the filament to incandescence. Electricity, in short, had become an important source of power and of light for the expanding industries.

By 1914 the use of electricity was evident in every part of the city, not least in the innumerable wires that crisscrossed the skies. Streetcars drew their power from trolleys attached to overhead electric wires. Streets, factories, theaters, and many houses were illuminated with the new light bulbs, prolonging the hours of business, making urban life cleaner and safer, and removing the drudgery and inconvenience of the oil lamp and candle; and there were signs, small as yet but pregnant with promise, of the transformation in everyday life that would occur when the household electrical appliance was brought within the reach of the average consumer. The radio, the phonograph, the refrigerator, the washing machine, and the electric heater had all been invented by 1914.

It was, however, the telephone that most captured the imagination of the fin de siècle generation. To the exquisite sensibility of the French novelist Marcel Proust, writing in an age when all calls were handled by female operators, it was an "angel-voice":

We are like the person in the fairy-tale to whom a sorceress, on his uttering the wish, makes appear with supernatural clearness his grandmother or his betrothed in the act of turning over a book or shedding tears, of gathering flowers, quite close to the spectator and yet ever so remote in the place in which she actually is at the moment. We need only, so that the miracle may be accomplished, apply our lips to the magic orifice and invoke—occasionally for rather longer than seems to us necessary, I admit—the Vigilant Virgins to whose voices we listen every day without ever coming to know their faces, and who are our Guardian Angels in the dizzy realm of darkness whose portals they so jealously keep; the All Powerful by whose intervention the absent rise up at our side, without our being permitted to set eyes on them; the Danaids of the Unseen who without ceasing, empty, fill, transmit the urns of sound; the ironic Furies who, just as we were murmuring a confidence to a friend, in the hope that no one was listening, cry brutally: "I hear you"; the ever infuriated servants of the Mystery, the umbrageous priestesses of the Invisible, the Young Ladies of the Telephone.[2]

[2] From *Remembrance of Things Past*, Vol. V, by Marcel Proust, translated by C. K. Scott Moncrieff. Copyright 1932 and renewed 1960 by Random House, Inc. Reprinted by permission of Random House, Inc., the translator's literary estate, and Chatto & Windus Ltd.

Chemistry

The inventions in chemistry were less evocative in their appeal but no less pervasive in their effects. The main industrial use of chemistry in the first half of the nineteenth century had been in the adaptation of sulfuric acid and chlorine to heavy industry and textile production. In the second half, however, chemistry advanced over a broad front. Paper was made from wood pulp instead of from linen and rags. Rayon (artificial silk) was also developed from wood pulp. Metal alloys diversified the forms of metal available, especially the different kinds of steel. Black-and-white photography was invented in 1870, and cameras were marketed commercially in the 1880s. But the two chief developments in the chemical industry were the production of cheap alkalis and the invention of synthetic dyestuffs. Alkalis, especially soda ash, were needed on a very large scale for soap and textile manufacture, as well as for the bleaching powder used in papermaking. The Solvay process, perfected in the 1870s, reduced the cost of the manufacture of soda ash and prevented the wastage of by-products. The first synthetic dyestuff, mauve, was isolated in England in 1856, and thereafter German scientists produced a whole series of artificial colorings that were far more reliable and lasting than natural dyes. Vast sales of dyestuffs made the German chemical industry boom, to become the largest in the world.

The impact of chemistry was most obvious in the inexpensive products it made possible. It was no longer necessary for city dwellers to wear black as now the colors of their ready-made clothes would not fade. Cheap paper spurred the development of a vast new communications industry, including inexpensive newspapers and the magazines—which became even more popular when in the 1880s they could carry the latest photographs that ubiquitous journalists had snapped with their Kodak or Zeiss cameras. Improvements in canning made wider supplies of fruit and vegetables available at all times of year, improving the diets of the poor. But as always there was a heavy price to be paid. The destructive power of the new chemistry was made plain in the explosives developed by the Swede Alfred Nobel. The environmental damage was also extensive, for few chemical factories controlled the disposal of their waste products. In the neighborhoods of the industrial cities, chemical factories spewed out sulfur, hydrochloric acid fumes, and calcium. Chemical-producing cities like Widnes on the river Mersey in northern England were topped with a noisome dome of blue and yellow fumes, and their houses were filmed with sulfur powder.

The Change in Business Organization

The new industrial techniques, the improvement in the transport of heavy and bulky products, the growing competition, and the speed with which supply was overtaking demand on the world market made anachronistic the small family-owned firm or partnership, which had been the basis of most industrial firms until the 1870s. Industrial production and distribution had now to be carried out by large-scale organizations. The most obvious industry in which concentration was necessary was the manufacture of steel. By combining in one series of interlocked operations the production of iron into pig iron in the blast furnace, the conversion of pig iron into steel, and the stamping or shaping of the final products, heat loss was minimized and waste products utilized; and to these basic processes could be added the coking of coal. Cost could be further reduced by the ownership of mines for coal and iron ore and of ships, cokeries, freighters, and sales agencies. This combination was the secret of the success of the Krupp Company in Germany, which expanded from a work force of 16,000 in 1873 to 70,000 by 1913, of Schneider-Creusot in France, and especially of Andrew Carnegie in the United States.

Very frequently many companies in comparable lines of production merged in what is known as horizontal integration. Companies in similar lines of business joined together in holding companies or trusts, such as the Standard Oil trust of John D. Rockefeller or the dynamite trust of Alfred Nobel. The financial advantages of the collaboration of firms competing for the same markets were often achieved without merger. Informal groups called cartels were formed to fix prices and to eliminate costly competition by the sharing of markets among the participating companies. The lead was taken by the steel companies of northern Europe and was followed rapidly by other cartels among bankers, shipping owners, munitions manufacturers, chemical and metal producers, and even whiskey distillers. In this way the number of industrial units and thus the number of individual owners declined drastically.

A major change in the character of banking from industrial to financial capitalism accompanied the change in industrial organization. In the early years of the industrial revolution, most capital for expansion had been provided by the capitalists themselves from their profits. Short-term working capital to buy raw materials had been provided by merchant banks. But in the nineteenth century, companies appealed to the people directly for their savings, through the sale of stock. These joint-stock companies could only be created on a large scale when the government permitted them the principle of limited liability, which meant that the management of the company was not held personally responsible for the debts of the company for which it worked. Britain was the first to grant limited liability in 1825 and was followed by the United States, France, and Germany. From the time of the 1870s, joint-stock manufacturing companies were created for public utilities and for insurance companies, banks, and most forms of transport. From 1900, the joint-stock company extended to most forms of manufacture, and thus enabled the small investor and the insurance companies and savings banks to channel their investment into the business sector. Management of the larger companies was increasingly divorced from control by their stockholders, who often preferred to have their capital handled by investment banks that took a controlling role in company administration. As a result, the great investment banks—some of them in the hands of private families like the Rothschilds; others, vast enterprises drawing on the savings of millions of people, like the Darmstädter Bank in Germany—wielded enormous power, not only over finance but over industry as well.

The Aristocracy of Wealth

The profits accumulated in the hands of leading industrialists and bankers dwarfed those of any previous period of history. Every branch of industry, commerce, and finance produced its elite of wealth, who, in an age of increasing nationalism among the masses, formed a kind of supranational aristocracy that met constantly in the pursuit of business and pleasure; and slowly the industrialists and bankers amalgamated with the older landed aristocracy to form a relatively homogeneous European ruling class. The United States was prolific in the production of this new type of capitalist. When Scottish immigrant Andrew Carnegie sold out his steel holdings to the United States Steel Corporation, he was paid $250 million. The railroads produced great fortunes, like those of the Vanderbilts of the New York Central Railroad or the Stanfords of the Southern Pacific; and the banking empire of John Pierpont Morgan made its founder a Midas among financiers as a result of his wizardry in moving among investments in steel, shipping, communications, insurance, mining, and munitions. These capitalists were, of course, the builders of the banks, offices, factories, and working-class housing that composed most of the new urban expansion. But the great capitalists, although they all possessed vast country estates, were still city dwellers, like the Parisian aristocracy of the eighteenth century or the Florentine patriciate of the fifteenth century. With their city mansions, they added variety, and even at times charm, to the landscape of the city. In New York City, their townhouses advanced northward from Washington Square to the upper reaches of Fifth Avenue; in San Francisco they looked down on their business enterprises from the heights of Nob Hill; in Paris, they overlooked the Bois de Boulogne or the Avenue Foch.

These nouveaux riches were not, however, divorced from the older landed aristocracy. In some cases the older aristocracy became involved in industry themselves: Lord Derby in England, for example, owned most of the riverfront in Liverpool and a number of mines in the South Lancashire coalfield. Others, such as the old families of the Austro-Hungarian Empire or the aristocrats of Russia, remained extremely wealthy from the exploitation of their agricultural estates, and could equal in wealth and outshine in blood the upper bourgeoisie. In many cases, wealth brought social equality. Queen Victoria happily accepted the hospitality of the Rothschilds. Often equality was the result of marriage, especially of American heiresses to impoverished European nobility. Usually fusion was the result of the mingling of social mores—education at the same schools, membership in the same regiment and club, attendance in the restricted balconies at the horse races or opera.

The whole of Europe became the playground of this elite of wealth and breeding. During the social season the capital cities were transformed with balls, plays, banquets, and horse races. The English season set the pattern and was emulated by all the capitals of Europe. In July, as one French visitor commented, it seemed as if "a race of gods and goddesses descended from Olympus upon England ... to live upon a golden cloud, spending

Boat Races at Henley
The annual regatta at Henley was the occasion for London society belles to display their newest summer costumes. (Illustrated London News, June 27, 1874)

their riches as indolently and naturally as the leaves grow green."[3] To the novelist John Buchan, looking back on it, it seemed like a dream:

London at the turn of the century had not yet lost her Georgian air. Her ruling society was aristocratic till Queen Victoria's death and preserved the modes and rites of aristocracy. . . . In the summer she was a true city of pleasure, every window box gay with flowers, her streets full of splendid equipages, the Park a show ground for fine horses and handsome men and women. The ritual went far down, for frockcoats and top-hats were common wear not only for the West End, but about the Law Courts and in the City. . . . Looking back, that time seems to me unbelievably secure and self-satisfied. The world was friendly and well-bred as I remember it, without the vulgarity and the worship of wealth which appeared with the new century.[4]

Out of season the well-to-do entertained each other at their country homes for grouse shooting or else met for a round of parties at their favorite vaca-

<hr>

[3]Cited in Barbara Tuchman, *The Proud Tower* (New York: Macmillan, 1966), p. 16.
[4]John Buchan, *Memory Hold the Door* (London: Hodder and Stoughton, 1940), pp. 92–94.

tion towns. Most favored were the spas: Aix-les-Bains in the Alps of France, Marienbad and Karlsbad in the Sudeten highlands of what is now Czechoslovakia, and Baden-Baden on the edge of the Black Forest. But the seaside resorts, especially those of the French and Italian Riviera, drew their clientele to the gingerbread fantasies of seafront hotel and casino. The Americans and Russians shared in these passions. The wealthy of America took their waters at Hot Springs, Virginia, and relaxed by the ocean in the mansions on the cliffs of Newport, Rhode Island. Russians sunned themselves at Yalta and safeguarded their livers at Piatigorsk, although they were often to be found also in the playgrounds of western Europe.

The Advance of the Trade Unions

In spite of improvements in the conditions of urban life, the working class continued to feel that it was being denied just returns for its labor and in fact being exploited for the benefit of the aristocracy of wealth. In the half-century before the First World War, its discontent was far more effectively organized through trade unions and political parties.

The first associations of workers had been mutual-aid societies of day-laborers or "journeymen," who had pooled their resources to help each other in case of illness, accident, or death. They were usually tolerated by the governments as long as they took no political action and did not organize against their employers. Unions of workers, formed to compel their employers to grant more favorable conditions through collective bargaining, were only slowly given the right to exist by governments controlled by the industrial and landed classes. In Britain, trade union activity in peaceful ways was permitted in 1824–1825; but most continental countries were unwilling to follow the British example. Complete freedom of organization was only permitted, after long struggles, in Austria-Hungary in 1870, in Germany in 1890, and in Russia in 1906. After 1886 the unions began to give up their emphasis on self-help through accident and sickness insurance programs, and to take strike action against their employers on a large scale. Long bitter strikes were carried out by such groups as the London match girls and dockworkers; and at the end of the century it looked for a short time as though the French trade union movement would attempt to seize power through a general strike, as advocated by "syndicalist" writer Georges Sorel. Syndicalists held that the trade union rather than any form of governmental body was the basic unit of society, and that paralysis of the instruments of the state through a general strike, involving violence where needed, would permit the workers to take power through their unions. Syndicalist strikes, however, were usually badly organized and quickly suppressed, although they played a part in forcing the Belgian government to grant universal male suffrage in 1893 and in compelling the Russian tsar Nicholas I to agree to establishment of a constitution in 1905.

From the 1880s on, the trade unions changed character. Whereas previously they had been mostly craft unions enrolling the more skilled members of the working class, they now enlisted the masses of less skilled workers. There was a proliferation of different types of union. The Catholic Church encouraged the formation of Catholic unions. Others followed the different trends within the Socialist movement. In England more than thirty local women's unions were founded by the Women's Trade Union League (1874–1921), partly because of the unwillingness of many unions to admit women. The barriers eventually crumbled, however, for by 1914, 6.5 percent of British union members were women. The fragmentation often weakened the labor movement; in Britain, there were over a thousand unions. As a result, efforts were made to form national federations of labor unions, and some of these organizations became powerful pressure groups at the national level, like the British Trades Union Congress, formed in 1868. Finally, the national federations came together in 1913 to form the International Federation of Trade Unions, to coordinate planning on a European scale.

The working classes had turned to the doctrines of Utopian Socialism in the first half of the nineteenth century (see Chapter 23), and a small number had followed Karl Marx after his enunciation of the doctrines of scientific Socialism, or Marxism, in *The Communist Manifesto* of 1848. But after the failure of the 1848 revolutions and the discrediting of the experimental national workshops in France, socialism made only small numbers of converts for the next three decades. Marx himself retired to the reading room of the British Museum, where he concentrated on the great theoretical exposition of his views in *Capital*, the first volume of which appeared in 1867, and on a number of analyses of the revolutionary struggles he had witnessed in France. He helped set up the first International Workingmen's Association, or First International, in London in 1864, whose purpose was to spread socialist ideas among workers' organizations throughout the world; but after quarreling bitterly with Michael Bakunin (1814–1876), whose anarchist followers believed that the state should be replaced in a violent upheaval by associations of producers, Marx allowed the International to die peacefully in 1876.

Formation of Working-Class Political Parties

Anarchism never became a serious rival of Marxism, in spite of the magnetic personality of Bakunin himself. It did find followers in the less developed countries of Europe, and a few individual terrorists in the developed nations adopted it. Assassinations of leading statesmen that were supposed to be the prelude to the abolition of the state machinery became common toward the end of the century—the murders carried out by anarchists included those of the president of France in 1894, the prime minister of Spain in 1897, the empress of Austria in 1898, the king of Italy in 1900, the president of the United States in 1901, and another prime minister of Spain in 1912. Anarchism's greatest strength was among the Spanish agricultural and industrial workers, and anarchists dominated the anti-Fascist forces in the province of Catalonia during the Spanish civil war (1936–1939). Elsewhere, however, anarchism never made significant gains over socialism or communism.

A far more important challenge to Marx's teachings than anarchism came from moderate working-class leaders who sought to ameliorate the condition of the workers without destroying the capitalist system by violence. The first important organization pledged to parliamentary activity on behalf of the workers was Ferdinand Lassalle's German Workingmen's Association of 1863, which merged in 1875 with a more revolutionary group from southern Germany called the German Social Democratic Labor party. By their Gotha program, the two groups agreed to found a German Social Democratic party to engage in a campaign for representation in the new German Reichstag, where by parliamentary means they proposed to advance the socialist cause. They were very successful, in spite of the harassment of Bismarck's antisocialist laws. Under the leadership of the former carpenter August Bebel, the party enrolled a million members and built up a huge organization that included publishing houses, newspapers, beer halls, insurance companies, and educational clubs. In 1903 it received twice as many votes as any other party in the Reichstag, although it did not gain the greatest number of deputies until 1912. Its parliamentary successes persuaded many of its members, led by the theorist Eduard Bernstein, to demand that the party "revise" its ideology, to accept openly what they were tacitly recognizing—that Marxism was out of date. In particular, the "revisionists" demanded that the party give up talk of inevitable class war, of the dictatorship of the proletariat, and of the revolutionary seizure of power, and concentrate instead on the gradual transformation of society. The party refused to make this open break with Marx's teachings, yet continued to act as though Bernstein were correct. As a result, it unnecessarily lost the support of many members of the middle classes who were offended by the revolutionary oratory and failed to realize that the practice of the party was more akin to that of the reformist socialists in Britain and Scandinavia.

In Britain a small Marxist party had been formed in 1883, called the Social Democratic Federation and patronized by the poet William Morris. This group never became important, however, until it joined with the reformist socialist groups (namely the Independent Labour party founded by Keir Hardie in 1893, the Fabian Society formed by a number of left-wing intellectuals in 1894, and the trade unions) to found the British Labour party in 1900. In France the warring factions among the Socialists were finally brought together in 1905 under the leadership of the fine organizer and orator Jean Jaurès; and by 1913 the French Socialist party had seventy-six deputies in the Chamber. Thus before 1914, the majority of socialists in the large industrial countries of Europe had come to accept the doctrine of gradual reform of the capitalist system as a result of their participation in extension and administration of parliamentary democracy. Orthodox Marxism, in accordance with the tenets of *The Communist Manifesto*, appeared to be restricted to a vocal but uninfluential fringe of fanatics until in 1917 the collapse of the Russian monarchy gave the Bolshevik movement of Lenin the opportunity to take power in the largest state in Europe (see Chapter 28).

THE WRITER AS SOCIAL ANALYST

The Realist and Naturalist Schools

The rapid pace of industrial, scientific, and social change stimulated the writers of the late nineteenth century to undertake a rigorous analysis of their changing world. European novelists of the Realist school of the 1850s and 1860s had already begun a searching inquiry into the character of the new industrial society and especially the problems of the bourgeoisie in struggling upward in the pursuit of material success. Deeply impressed by the progress of science and technology, they had rejected the exaggeration, the sentimentality, and the unreality of the writers of the Romantic school, and had determined instead to apply scientific methods in their approach to human beings, their physical settings, and their social relationships. They considered their method experimental, an attempt to combine all data, ugliness as well as beauty, corruption as well as heroism, to place human beings in an exactly described situation and to observe the results. They were convinced that the philosopher Auguste Comte (1798–1857) had correctly described the progress of human society as passing through three stages—primitive theological; more advanced metaphysical; and final scientific, or positivist, a stage wherein, by the observation of phenomena and the collection of scientific fact, exact laws for all knowledge from mathematics to sociology (a word he invented) could be established. In 1857, when Gustave Flaubert published *Madame Bovary,* the unsentimental portrayal of an intelligent woman trapped in the inanity of provincial life, he created the first genuine masterpiece of Realism. After Flaubert, the Realist novelists insisted on absolute accuracy and enumeration of physical details of the environment, the painstaking portrayal of human emotions and thoughts, and the analysis of such influences as heredity and social restriction.

Emile Zola (1840–1902) brought the Realistic approach to its most extreme. He explained his theories in 1880 in *The Experimental Novel,* in which he argued that "the writer is part observer and part experimenter. In him the observer provides the facts as he has seen them, decides the point of departure, establishes the firm ground on which the characters will move and phenomena develop. Then the experimenter appears and sets up the experiment, I mean to say causes the characters to move and act in a particular story in order to show that the succession of facts will be such as the determinism of the phenomena that are being studied demands."[5] With Zola, the Realist school of novelists merged in the Naturalist.

The Naturalist school held that all human action should be explained in terms of the working of natural forces, such as heredity, physical environment, or human drives. Zola himself set the pattern of analysis by studying not a few individuals but a whole family, in twenty novels that he called the Natural and Social History of a Family under the Second Em-

---

[5]Cited and translated by Eugen Weber, *Paths to the Present* (New York: Dodd, Mead, 1962), p. 167.

**Gustave Flaubert
(1821–1880)**
Although his health compelled him to live in the peacefulness of a small provincial town, Flaubert won both fame and blame for his exposure in Madame Bovary *(1857) of the emptiness of provincial life. (A. Harlingue)*

Thomas Mann (1875–1955)
After chronicling the life of a German bourgeois family in Buddenbrooks *(1900), Mann turned increasingly to psychological problems, in such novels as* Death in Venice *(1911) and* The Magic Mountain *(1924). (Karsh/Woodfin Camp and Associates)*

pire. But in spite of the prolific material details, these novels still rang with the outraged morality of a Dickens, as when Zola dealt with prostitution in *Nana* or the sufferings of the workers in *Germinal*.

It was only in the last two decades before the First World War that the Naturalist novelists produced their most balanced and searching works, when the reaction against the excesses of social Realism had combined with a greater interest and knowledge regarding the human character. The playwright Anton Chekhov (1860–1904) explored the vacuity and ineffectiveness of the provincial Russian gentry. The Norwegian dramatist Henrik Ibsen (1828–1906) laid bare the false values of the middle classes, as in *An Enemy of the People,* when a whole town whose livelihood is dependent on its spa rises up against the conscientious doctor who has discovered that the waters are harmful to the spa's visitors. At the end of the century the brothers Heinrich Mann (1871–1950) and Thomas Mann (1875–1955) gave classic portrayals of the decadence of the bourgeois class. They had been brought up in Lübeck, a city that had slipped into irretrievable decay because its middle classes had failed to keep up with modern progress. For Heinrich Mann, the middle class deserved savage satirization. In his novel *Der Untertan (Little Superman),* he followed the progress of Diederich Hessling, whose hapless infatuation with the upper-class Germans symbolizes the willingness of the upper middle class to seek a kind of feudalization of their own social values in late nineteenth-century Germany. At the moment when Diederich has sold out his factory to the local governor, at a ridiculously low price, he is rewarded with an imperial medal, the Order of the Crown Fourth Class.

A blue ribbon could be seen hanging from Karnauke's pointed fingers, and beneath it a cross, whose gold rim sparkled. . . . Ah, what an uproar and congratulations! Diederich stretched out his two hands, an ineffable joy flowed from his heart to his throat, and he began to speak involuntarily, before he knew what he was saying: "His Majesty . . . unprecedented graciousness . . . modest services . . . unshakable loyalty." He bowed and scraped, and as Karnauke handed him the cross, he laid his hands on his heart, closed his eyes, and sank back, as if another stood before him, the Donor himself. Basking in the royal approval Diederich felt that salvation and victory were his. . . . Authority kept its pact with Diederich. The Order of the Crown, fourth class, glittered. It was an event, foreshadowing the William the Great monument and Gausenfeld, business and glory! . . .

Like a man of iron he stood before her [his wife], his order hanging on his breast; he glittered like steel. "Before we go any further," he said in martial tones, "let us think of His Majesty, our Gracious Emperor. We must keep before us the higher aim of doing honor to His Majesty, and of giving him capable soldiers." "Oh!" cried Guste, carried away into loftier splendors by the sparkling ornament, "is it . . . really . . . you . . . my Diederich?"[6]

[6]Heinrich Mann, *Little Superman* (New York: Creative Age), pp. 241–242.

Marcel Proust (1871–1922)
After 1905, Proust withdrew from fashionable society to recreate that world in the seven volumes of Remembrance of Things Past. *(A. Harlingue)*

In 1913, however, in the work of the great French writer Marcel Proust (1871–1922), the novel that had portrayed the peculiarities of society was enriched with an exploration of the role of the unconscious and of the changing experience of time. Proust, the son of rich parents who spoiled him, had made a vigorous and fairly successful attempt to reach the upper levels of Parisian society. Before the death of his mother in 1905, he wrote a few unimportant sketches. A chronic invalid, he cloistered himself after 1905 in a bedroom lined with cork, probing in his writing the character of a society that had disillusioned him, and the nature of his own self. The first volume of his massive novel, *A la recherche du temps perdu (Remembrance of Things Past)*, caused little sensation; the second volume, published in 1919, was recognized as a modern classic. The succeeding volumes, published mostly posthumously, won him acclaim as one of the greatest novelists in all French literature. At one level, Proust's novel was a superb portrayal of the weaknesses and the idiosyncrasies of French middle and upper classes at the turn of the century. He created an unforgettable gallery of portraits of the minor nobility and the rising bourgeoisie: the graceful aristocrat Saint Loup, the petulant hostess Madame

Marcel Proust

Verdurin, the witty Marquis de Villeparisis, the fanatically prideful Baron de Charlus. But above all there is the duke of Guermantes, with his wealth and his vanity and his vulgarity, and the duchess of Guermantes, who floats through so much of the novel as if a character in a distant dream:

> Mme de Guermantes had sat down. Her name, accompanied as it was by her title, added to her corporeal dimensions the duchy which projected itself round about her and brought the shadowy, sun-splashed coolness of the woods of Guermantes into this drawing-room, to surround the tuffet on which she was sitting. I felt surprised only that the likeness of those woods was not more discernible on the face of the Duchess, about which there was nothing suggestive of vegetation, and at the most the ruddy discoloration of her cheeks. . . . Her eyes . . . held captive as in a picture the blue sky of an afternoon in France, broadly expansive, bathed in light even when no sun shone; and a voice which one would have thought, from its first hoarse sounds, to be almost plebeian, through which there trailed, as over the steps of the church at Cambrai or the pastry cooks in the square, the rich and lazy gold of a country sun.[7]

But Proust had done far more than pick up the social analysis of Thomas or Heinrich Mann. He helped change the whole character of novel writing by displaying the unconscious workings of the mind, the forgotten memories that can be touched off by a sudden, unimportant event, as when the taste of a little cake called a madeleine soaked in tea evoked for him the whole of his childhood. But above all he examined the character of time, the elasticity of its nature relative to the emotions and experiences of the individual, the fusion of the past with the present. With Proust it was the inner world that was worth knowing, and it too could only be understood in relation to the experiences in time that remained perpetually in one's unconscious memory.

Robert Comte de Montesquiou-Fezensac, by James McNeil Whistler (1834–1903)
This prominent society figure is now best remembered as one of the models for Baron de Charlus in Proust's Remembrance of Things Past. *(Copyright The Frick Collection, New York)*

Sigmund Freud

THE ANALYSIS OF HUMAN BEHAVIOR

The novelists had sapped the faith in bourgeois society by exposing its hypocrisies and the shallowness of its pretensions. The new science of psychology, with its emphasis on the unconscious motives of the mind, undermined even more the belief that reason can control the environment.

Since the mid-nineteenth century, medical experimenters had made considerable progress in understanding the mind by concentrating on the relationship of physiology to psychology. The French doctor Philippe Broccart had shown that the front lobe of the brain controls speech. Other psychologists who were called behaviorists had experimented on the behavior of animals, attempting to find physical stimulations that would produce

[7]Proust, *Remembrance of Things Past*, V, 278.

psychological responses. The most famous of these was Ivan Pavlov (1849–1936), who had conditioned dogs to salivate every time a bell rang to indicate the presence of food. But it was essential to get beyond the physiological and the rational factors in human behavior. The explanation of the unconscious mind was undertaken by Sigmund Freud (1856–1939), a Viennese doctor whose ideas took a formative role in twentieth-century culture because he combined scientific genius, literary skill, and stubborn ambition. He was the child of a German-Jewish family from Moravia that, after financial troubles, had moved to Vienna when Freud was four years old. Although Freud lived in Vienna until the last years of his life, he claimed never to like the city. "I never felt really comfortable in the town. I believe now I was never free from a longing for the beautiful woods near our home in which," he wrote, linking his feelings immediately to the Oedipus complex, "(as one of my memories from those days tells me) I used to run off from my father, almost before I had learned to walk."[8] Although constantly short of money, he entered the university as a medical student. Finding that he disliked the physical aspects of medical practice, he devoted himself to neurology. Slowly, under the influence of professors he worked with in Vienna and Paris, he abandoned the physical explanation of nervous disorder. In the famous case of Anna O., who was paralyzed by hysteria, he succeeded in curing his patient's physical symptoms by persuading her through hypnosis to dredge up unhappy events of her childhood.

It was essential for the physician, Freud decided, to discover in the unconscious the thoughts or wishes that, being incompatible with the "ethical, aesthetic and personal pretensions of the patient's personality," had been repressed. Since those repressed ideas were still active, causing pain and even physical symptoms, Freud advocated not only the free association of ideas stimulated by the questions of the doctor or by hypnosis, but also the interpretation of dreams and unconscious acts, such as forgetting names or making random body movements. But, as Freud was well aware, he had to explain the origin of the memory that remained in the unconscious. He had already decided that the primary impressions, which he thought to have existed in earliest childhood, were sexual. "He found in himself love of the mother and jealousy of the father," and claimed that it was universal in early childhood. This, he said, was why the play *Oedipus Rex* was so gripping. The Greek myth "seizes upon a compulsion that everyone recognizes because he had felt traces of it in himself. Every member of the audience was once a budding Oedipus in fantasy, and this dream-fulfillment played out in reality causes everyone to recoil in horror, with the full measure of repression which separates his infantile from his present state."[9] He went on to theorize that personality could be understood in an

Theories of Freud

[8]O. Mannoni, *Freud* (New York: Pantheon, 1971), pp. 8–9.
[9]Ibid., p. 46.

almost physical sense as the conflict between the *ego*, the reason that directs a person's adaptation to the environment, and the *id*, the primary instinct that drives an individual to erotic and aggressive thoughts. The ego was the rider, the id the horse that had to be directed. But the ego had also to deal with the *superego*, the sublimation of the image of the parent that a child had constituted inside itself as a set of moral goals. For Freud, the task of the ego was enormous because it had to sublimate or direct into permissible or socially useful channels the drive of the id; and, where it failed, the suppression of those drives could produce neuroses.

Influence of Freudian Psychology

Freud's main psychological ideas were quite well known by the First World War. Freud went much further, attempting to relate the whole development of society to the work of the unconscious, but few people would accept him as the analyst of all human development. As the analyst of the individual, however, he soon gained widespread acceptance. His ideas were the starting point for other psychologists, such as Carl Jung (1875–1961), who eventually substituted the will for power as the primary drive in place of the sexual urge. The influence of the new psychology was deeply pervasive. In the widest sense, it sapped the liberal belief in the rationality of human beings and their ability to govern themselves through rational processes. It destroyed much of the Victorian belief concerning such matters as parent-child relations. Although some followers of Freud used his theories of the separate sexual identity of the male and the female to reinforce traditional notions of the woman's self-fulfillment through motherhood and dependence on the male, his work undoubtedly acted as a liberating force from many of the more puritanical Victorian notions about female character.

To some political theorists, the new knowledge was the beginning of a wiser theory of the state. To social reformers, it was a key to a healthier society. To the creative mind, it offered an enormous hope; it was the long-dreamed-of key to human motivation. By presenting a character's stream of consciousness, it became possible for the novel to break out of its established narrative form. To painters like the Surrealists (see Chapter 29), it provided a challenge to represent on canvas the free association of ideas and the working of the unconscious mind. For novelists like Proust, James Joyce, and Virginia Woolf, poets like T. S. Eliot and W. B. Yeats, and painters like Salvador Dali and René Magritte, the psychologist had uncovered a startling new world.

THE NEW SCIENCE

The climax of a century of advances in all fields of science came in the discoveries of the great physicists between 1890 and 1914, which destroyed the very concept of nature as described by laws that scientists like Newton had so successfully uncovered. Nature implied the existence of absolute and distinct space, time, matter, energy, and velocity. By 1914 it had been demonstrated that matter and energy are interchangeable; that matter is not composed of indivisible atoms but that all atoms are themselves composed of electrically charged particles; and even that mass increases with velocity.

Progress in Chemistry

In the early nineteenth century the scientific field in which the most significant breakthroughs occurred was chemistry, largely because of refinements in laboratory experimentation. Chemists like the French pioneer Antoine Lavoisier and the English experimenter Joseph Priestley concentrated on Aristotle's theory that matter comprised four elements (earth, air, water, and fire), and they were able to prove, after oxygen had been isolated in 1774, that phenomena such as burning and rusting involved a combination of some element with oxygen. By 1800 Aristotle's concept had been thrown out, and the scientists were successfully beginning to draw up a list of the basic chemical elements. Lavoisier himself had identified thirty-two; Priestley had discovered many of the basic combinations, such as sulfur dioxide, carbon monoxide, and many acids.

After 1800, however, a major advance was made by considering the elements as composed of atoms. John Dalton, an English schoolteacher, suggested in 1802–1808 that the nature of compounds (that is, combinations of elements) could be described by ascertaining the weight of the atoms of the elements forming each compound. Dalton was correct in assuming that future progress lay in ascertaining the exact atomic weight of the different elements, although he mistakenly assumed that the simplest compound of two elements would contain only one atom of each element. During the following sixty years, chemists were able to designate the atomic makeup of a large number of compounds, both by letters (CO_2 = carbon dioxide = a molecule made up of one atom of carbon and two atoms of oxygen) and by structures based on the grouping of the atoms in the molecule. The practical uses of chemistry won it instant acceptance in industry. Although its principal uses became apparent after 1850, before that time chloride of lime had been used for bleaching textiles, coal gas for illumination, ether and chloroform occasionally as anesthetics, carbolic acid for cleansing, vulcanized rubber for waterproofing. High explosives evolved through the discovery of nitrocellulose in 1846. Organic chemistry was one basic force in industrial progress in the second half of the nineteenth century.

The Study of Energy

Equally important advances were made in the study of energy. In the eighteenth century, scientists had been unable to find the connection between heat, light, electricity, and magnetism, namely, that they were all forms of energy that could be transformed into mechanical work. Instead, they assumed that heat, electricity, and so on were substances—material fluids that flowed in and out of other material substances but were weightless. These weightless substances were called imponderables. A hot body was said to contain the imponderable called calorific fluid; an electrified body, electric fluid; a magnetic body, magnetic fluid. The idea of calorific fluid was rejected after the experiments of Benjamin Thompson, Count Rumford, at the end of the eighteenth century. Rumford was able to show that heat in unlimited quantities could be produced by friction, and that since matter cannot be produced limitlessly, heat cannot be matter. By the 1830s it was generally conceded that light was not a substance but rather a wave motion of energy. And in the 1840s, through the work of an English physicist, James Joule, and a German, Hermann von Helmholtz, the convertibility of one form of energy into another, such as electricity into heat, was demonstrated quantitatively. Helmholtz then formulated the important law of the conservation of energy, that energy can be changed from one form into another but the total amount of energy in the world will always remain the same. This concept was especially useful for industrial chemistry, where the transformation of one form of energy into another was basic to many processes; and it reached its most effective use in the twentieth century with the harnessing for destructive as well as peaceful uses of the energy contained within the atom.

Darwin and the Theory of Evolution

Advances in biology in the mid-nineteenth century caused a public furor because they challenged the description of creation given in the Bible in the Book of Genesis—that the earth and all living things were created by God in six days (about 4000 B. C. according to many church leaders). The work of the English naturalist Charles Darwin brought down on him the wrath of the churches because he (1) challenged the notion that God had created immutable species; (2) opposed the idea that man had always been the highest form of creation; (3) disagreed that change in the biological world was the product of a purpose, and especially of a divine purpose.

Darwin, at the age of twenty-two, had signed on as naturalist with the surveying ship *Beagle*, which for five years (1831–1836) sailed in the South Atlantic and South Pacific and eventually circumnavigated the globe. From the start he made vast collections—of fossils dug from the cliffs of the Cape Verde Islands, of extinct toxodons as large as elephants in Argentine riverbeds, of the fish of the South Pacific. But it was in the Galapagos Islands off the coast of Ecuador that he found the most startling evidence of the mutation of species. On these small islands many species bore close resemblance but also marked differences to species on the coast six hundred miles away. Even more remarkable, in his view, was the subtle but clear variation from island to island in animals like the tortoises and birds like the finches. Darwin devoted the rest of his life to working out a theory that would explain these differences and in fact impose an intelligible pattern on the origin of all living and all extinct things and their relation to each other and to their environment. His theory was finally presented in 1859 in his book *On the Origin of Species by Means of Natural Selection, or the Preservation of Favoured Races in the Struggle for Life.*

Darwin began by pointing out that species do change, as can be shown by considering domestication of animals and plants. But species also vary in nature; and this, he felt, could only be explained as the outcome of a

Charles Darwin (1809–1882)
(National Portrait Gallery, London)

struggle for existence that is the result of the tendency of all living groups
to multiply their numbers.

*As many more individuals of each species are born than can possibly survive; and
as, consequently, there is a frequently recurring struggle for existence, it follows
that any being, if it vary however slightly in any manner profitable to itself, under the complex and varying conditions of life, will have a better chance of surviving, and thus be naturally selected. . . . Natural Selection almost inevitably
causes much Extinction of the less improved forms of life, and leads to what I
have called Divergence of Character.*[10]

This divergence Darwin felt was due to the existence of "variants," or variations, which made a plant or animal adapt to its environment more effectively. Birds that had coloring that camouflaged them survived; others did
not. These variations were extremely small, "accidental" differences of
one organism from another, whose origin Darwin could not explain but
whose accumulation in those species that proved fittest in the struggle for
survival was apparent. The theory suggested that all life was being continually perfected in its adaptation to the environment.

    The notion of a divine purpose in the universe was unnecessary, at
least from the biological point of view. The most startling consequence of

[10]Cited in Philip Appleman, ed., *Darwin* (New York: Norton, 1970), p. 103.

Darwin's theory that species evolved from a common ancestor was its application to human beings. To his demolition of the literal interpretation of the Bible, Darwin had added as a final ignominy the assertion that human beings were biologically related to all invertebrates, and especially to monkeys. A storm of protest arose on publication of the *Origin of Species*, led by the bishop of Oxford, who accused Darwin of "a tendency to limit God's glory in creation." The theory of natural selection, the bishop claimed, "contradicts the revealed relations of creation to its Creator." Catholic Cardinal Manning remarked that Darwin's view was "a brutal philosophy—to wit, there is no God, and the ape is our Adam." For once, in their denunciation, Protestants and Catholics seemed to be in agreement. The controversy dragged on for more than thirty years, during which ecclesiastical opposition gradually lost its fervor. By the 1890s Darwin's views had come to be generally accepted among the educated groups

"Man is But a Worm"
The attack on Darwin for his views on evolution—led by the churches—was frequently supported in the press with viciously satirical cartoons.

MAN·IS·BVT·A·WORM·

in society; and, in the thinking of many, Darwin had taken his place beside Newton as a person who had provided the laws governing a whole field of scientific knowledge.

The advances in physics at the end of the nineteenth century transformed the study of matter and created a totally new field of knowledge. The new physics was the product of simultaneous progress in many fields of experiment and theory. Experiments on the nature of radioactivity were carried out in the 1890s by Wilhelm Roentgen, who discovered X rays, and by the French scientists Pierre and Marie Curie, who showed that radium emits energy. By 1913 several scientists had demonstrated that the atom, far from being solid, was constructed something like a solar system, with a positively charged proton, or nucleus, surrounded by negatively charged electrons. Ernest Rutherford was able to prove the truth of his ideas experimentally by bombarding a nitrogen atom to reduce the number of its electrons in such a way as to change it into a hydrogen atom. He thus succeeded in changing one element into another, the dream of the medieval students of alchemy. Knowledge of the behavior of the electron was dependent on Max Planck's quantum theory, which he set forth in 1905. Planck held that energy is emitted in small groups, or quanta, in a series of discontinuous ejections rather than in a continuous stream; moreover, because of the extremely small size and rapid movement of these particles, it is impossible to state their precise position but only the probability of their being in a particular place. Science would have to accept the uncertainty principle, that one cannot observe the exact position or speed of particles but only predict the probability of a certain result.

Albert Einstein, a German-Jewish theoretical physicist, in his special theory of relativity of 1905 and general theory of relativity of 1916, succeeded in producing a unified explanation of the phenomena of the physical world. There is no such thing as absolute space, time, or motion, Einstein held. Space is not filled with a weightless substance called ether against which motion can be measured, as scientists had theorized, and thus there is no absolutely stationary space. All motion is relative to the speed at which the observer himself is traveling. Einstein showed, moreover, that even mass is dependent on velocity, since it increases as its speed increases. Finally, Einstein concluded that mass and energy are interconvertible, and that their relationship is defined by the equation, $E = mc^2$ (energy equals mass multiplied by the square of the speed of light). He deduced that the conception of space and time would have to be replaced by a four-dimensional space-time continuum. Meanwhile, his ideas on the curving nature of space received wide, if uninformed, popular admiration when his prediction was proved correct that in a solar eclipse light rays passing near the sun would be bent. Thus, by 1914 physicists had played a major part in disturbing humanity's conception of itself. If space, time, and motion no longer could be accepted as external realities, what certainties were left?

Einstein and the Theory of Relativity

Albert Einstein (1879-1955)
Einstein formulated his special theory of relativity in 1905 while working in the patent office in Bern, Switzerland. He later accepted professorships at Zürich and Berlin, but settled at Princeton University after the Nazi takeover in Germany in 1933. (National Archives)

THE ANALYSIS OF SOUND

In music and painting, Vienna and Paris continued to exert their predominance. Artists and musicians were drawn to these bustling, exciting cities, which offered easy communication with other artists, a good living, and enthusiastic audiences.

In Vienna, there was a sense of the brilliant end of a great epoch. In part, the tone was set by the emperor Francis Joseph himself (reigned 1848–1916), unbendingly determined in the face of continual personal tragedy to act out the kindly, aloof role of father of his people. Tall, upright, white-mustached, *der alte Herr* reigned in Vienna for almost seventy years, and the occasional glimpses of him brought alive a memory of an older empire. When the emperor appeared briefly at aristocratic balls, noted a Russian diplomat, "it was not to lead for a fleeting moment the life of a mere mortal but to represent the majesty of the sovereign." All the inhabitants of Vienna gave themselves up to nostalgia, created in a self-deception so patent as to be doubly charming. Johann Strauss died in 1899, but his place was taken by Franz Lehar, an equally effective dream-maker, whose *Merry Widow* was produced in 1905. Even more than in the Biedermeier era, Vienna lived in the charm of self-admiration, its houses decorated with engravings of its own streets, its winegardens echoing to songs celebrating its own beauty, its conversations filled with stories of memorable Viennese characters.

Brahms, Bruckner, Mahler

Audiences who filled the new opera house on the Ringstrasse after 1869 were satisfied that they too were carrying on and developing to fulfillment the great tradition of classical music their grandfathers had patronized. Johannes Brahms (1833–1897), who had settled in Vienna in 1863, was regarded as having mastered the counterpoint of Bach and the symphonic structure of Beethoven. His First Symphony won him the highest praise possible for Viennese audiences. This, wrote a critic, was a "Tenth Symphony, alias the First of Johannes Brahms. . . . But I believe it is not without the intelligence of chance that Bach, Beethoven, and Brahms are in alliteration."

Four years after Brahms's arrival, Anton Bruckner (1824–1896) came to Vienna from the Austrian provinces. A disciple of Richard Wagner, he was a writer whose boundless cadences and spaciousness appealed to the audiences of the 1870s. His orchestration was so lush that Brahms found it offensive. Bruckner sought to create whole forests, rollicking rustic dances of peasants in iron-soled boots, gigantic storms, and galloping huntsmen. With him, the emotional coloring of Romantic music reached a new immensity that could only be accepted by a spacious age.

And after Bruckner came the even more expansive music of Gustav Mahler (1860–1911). As the conductor of both the opera and the philharmonic orchestra, he had a far more expert knowledge of orchestral instruments than Bruckner; and in his Eighth Symphony, known as the

Emperor Francis Joseph of Austria *(Hoover Institute)*

Symphony of the Thousand because it required a huge orchestra and chorus, he seemed to be reaching out to introduce into symphonic music that combination of voice and instrument that found an ideal in opera. However, in spite of all the choral and orchestral embellishments of his music, Mahler was developing a new form of symphonic expression. Especially in the Ninth Symphony of 1909, he plunged deep inside his personality, writing music at once cynical, overbearing, wistful, delicate, and tragic.

Mahler's work nevertheless lay within the accustomed tradition of Western music, which was written on a seven-tone scale with major and minor keys. The revolt against tonality was begun by Arnold Schoenberg (1874–1951), a widely talented composer from a middle-class Jewish family. Schoenberg was dissatisfied with everything, from the way babies were brought up to the local streetcars; and he suggested remedies for all of society's shortcomings. He began as a composer with a sparsely orchestrated tone poem, *Transfigured Night*, a morality play in which a man forgives a woman for bearing a child that is not his own, and by his generosity transfigures the night. The eery clarity of the moonlit night is suggested by a new form of harmony, which, together with the nature of the story, shocked the first audience in 1899 into uproarious ridicule. By 1908 Schoenberg and two young followers, Alban Berg and Anton Webern, had begun to abandon altogether the traditional conception of keys. The result was the strange, disturbing sound of atonality that Schoenberg preferred to call "floating tonality." Schoenberg argued that the traditional sounds based on rules giving preference to specific notes, such as the tonic, and the laying down of rules for the progression from key to key, were stifling. All notes should be equal, he argued, and that would be achieved if a twelve-tone scale were used. The notes would be related to each other in a "series," or tone row, in which none of the twelve notes could be repeated until the other eleven had been played. This tone row in a set sequence would be repeated with various changes of orchestration or volume and could be used with all kinds of mathematical variants, such as backward or upside-down configurations. It was impossible for most people to distinguish the tone row being used, and the music seemed to the uninitiated to have a completely shapeless character. But Schoenberg had in fact created a totally new sound, which, he argued, the audience should learn to hear.

Atonal Music: Schoenberg

But it was Berg, a student of Schoenberg from 1904, who won for the new music its widest, though still restricted, audience. In his operas *Wozzeck*, a savage attack on the savagery of war, and *Lulu*, a Freudian fantasy littered with the dead bodies of ineffectual lovers, Berg showed that the action of the operatic stage could emphasize the drama inherent in the moderate use of atonality. Webern, with a doctorate in musicology from the University of Vienna, was a natural disciple of Schoenberg. To him the atonal

Berg and Webern

scale appealed because of its ability to express in the most compressed form the deepest of emotions. His total written work can be played in three hours; one string quartet lasts one minute. With the same mathematical ability and the same fascination with the nature of numbers as Schoenberg, he was able to create works of extraordinary ingenuity. The twelve-tone scale appealed to him, he said, because one does not need a chord to end the music; and in accordance with this principle, after surprising his listeners by the fact that no note seems at first to relate to any other note, his music simply stops.

Der Rosenkavalier

But even the young had to recognize that Vienna had found itself again not in Schoenberg or Berg, but in the collaboration of its finest poet, Hugo von Hofmannsthal (1874–1929), and its new operatic genius, Richard Strauss (1864–1949). Strauss was unrestrainedly and successfully romantic. Hofmannsthal belonged to a group of writers called Young Vienna, who met nightly in the Café Griensteidel to reinvigorate Viennese literature, drawing to it the analysis of human motives and mental aberration. They called themselves expressionists because they wished to reveal the mental states of their characters. It was the miracle of Viennese music that Hofmannsthal was able to write an operatic libretto that, in the character of the Marschallin, summed up that moment of fragile beauty and self-awareness when a charming woman feels the first cold breath of age. It is hardly fanciful to think that the immense popularity of *Der Rosenkavalier* in Vienna was due to the fact that the Viennese saw in the Marschallin, and heard in the elusive waltzes of Strauss, the dilemma of their own aging city:

> *I too can remember a young girl*
> *Who, fresh from the convent, was ordered into holy marriage.*
> *Where is she now? Yes,*
> *Look for the snows of yesteryear!*
> *How can I say it so lightly?*
> *But how can it really be*
> *That I was that little Resi*
> *And that some day I shall be an old woman.*
> *An old woman, the old Marschallin!*
> *"Take a look, there she goes, old Princess Resi!"*
> *How can this happen?*
> *How can our dear God do this to us?*
> *When I am still the same as ever.*
> *And if He must do this*
> *Why does He let me see the change*
> *Ever so clearly? Why doesn't He conceal it from me?*
> *That's all such a secret, such a very great secret.*
> *And yet we are here to endure it.*
> *And in the "How"—*
> *There is what makes the difference.* [11]

[11] Hugo von Hofmannsthal, *Der Rosenkavalier*, Act I. Author's translation.

PARIS DURING LA BELLE EPOQUE

A golden glow suffuses all reminiscences of Paris at fin de siècle, as though then more than at any other time in its role as the incubator of the European intellect Paris had combined intense creativity with the most seductive charm of daily living. To the Austrian novelist Stefan Zweig, who arrived there in 1904 at the age of twenty-three, it was an "exhilarated and exhilarating Paris":

Nowhere did one experience the naive and yet wondrously wise freedom of existence more happily than in Paris, where all this was gloriously confirmed by beauty of form, by the mildness of the climate, by wealth and tradition. Each one of us youngsters took into himself a share of that lightness and in so doing contributed his own share; Chinese and Scandinavians, Spaniards and Greeks, Brazilians and Canadians, all felt themselves at home on the banks of the Seine. . . . Oh, how easily, how well, one lived in Paris, particularly if one were young. . . . The only difficult thing was to stay home or to go home, especially when it was spring and the lights shone soft and silvery over the Seine, and the trees on the boulevards were beginning to bud, and the girls were wearing bunches of violets which they had bought for a penny. But it was not necessarily spring that put you in a good mood in Paris.[12]

Paris was truly the artistic heart of Europe, and few artists or writers could stay away for long. In Paris, they fed on each other, stimulating one another to new experiments and to more sustained effort of imagination and relaxation. From America came Henry James and Gertrude Stein; from Russia, Stravinsky, Diaghilev, and Kandinsky; from Belgium, Maurice Maeterlinck; from Italy, Modigliani; from Switzerland, Le Corbusier; from Spain, Pablo Picasso; and from Germany, Rainer Maria Rilke. Thus, Paris led the West in painting and poetry and was second only to Vienna in music.

The Appeal of Paris

Paris was the unparalleled setting for a society of extraordinary individualism and complexity. In spite of the industrial expansion, the painters of Paris could still appreciate the unique clear, grey light of the Ile-de-France, not only in the surrounding towns like Barbizon but in the very heart of Paris itself, as the street scenes of Camille Pissarro showed. But the city's population was part of the fascination. The almost total centralization in Paris of French government, commerce, banking, publishing, theater, and scientific and medical research had siphoned off into the city an extraordinary proportion of the country's talent. It had also concentrated there a great proportion of the country's wealth; and much that was not earned in Paris was spent there. Hence the first impression Paris presented was of a well-to-do city, supporting a uniquely large number of great restaurants, boutiques, race courses and racing stables, playhouses, international exhibitions, and art galleries and museums. This was all due of course to the very widespread extravagance of the era, uninhibited and self-

[12]Stefan Zweig, *World of Yesterday* (New York: Viking, 1943), pp. 127–128, 130.

congratulatory. This spate of spending provided a regular source of entertainment for most of Paris, and it was surprisingly hard for reformers to rouse resentment against it. With Edward VII at Maxim's, Sarah Bernhardt at the Théâtre de la Nation, and the king of Serbia at the Jockey Club, even the intellectuals had to enjoy the spectacle; painters like Degas and Renoir in particular delighted in portraying the rich fabrics of a couple in an opera box or the bright panorama of the races in the Bois de Boulogne.

But this immoderation of life was only tolerable because there was a general improvement in the standard of living of the whole Parisian population, which became especially marked after 1900. For all except the poorest working-class districts, wages provided a little money for entertainment, and the general Parisian population was as determined as the well-to-do to enjoy itself. Working-class Parisians attended the races, although they observed from the grassy oval in the middle of the track rather than the stands. As Renoir showed, they enjoyed boating parties on the river

Au Moulin Rouge, by Henri de Toulouse-Lautrec (1864–1901)
In the famous Montmartre cabaret, the artist is seated at the right of the table with his friends, while in the background, the dancer La Goulue knots her orange hair. (Courtesy of the Art Institute of Chicago)

Seine, or, as Seurat portrayed in his *pointilliste* paintings, a swim at the island of Grande Jatte. They filled the great open-air dance halls like those operating on the slopes of Montmartre, especially the Moulin de la Galette where Toulouse-Lautrec found them waltzing beneath the gas lights. Everyone attested to the joy in being alive, the *joie de vivre* that permeated Paris. It was especially in the music hall and the café that Paris achieved a kind of social unity. The café, its tables scattered across the sidewalks of the newly opened boulevards, became a substitute for the declining salon. Although there were still a few *grandes dames* to carry on the traditions of the eighteenth century, it was in the famous cafés, like the Napolitain and the Weber, that the intellectuals held court. Impressionist painting worked out its credo around the tables of the Café Guerbois and the Nouvelle Athènes, where the composer Eric Satie later became café pianist. There was little opportunity for conversation in music halls like the Moulin Rouge or the Chat Noir, where a throaty-voiced singer called Yvette Guilbert was singing for Émile Zola and his friends and a cancan dancer known as La Goulue was being drawn by Toulouse-Lautrec.

It was perhaps this intermingling in conditions of almost total artistic freedom—combined with a mildly open-handed government generous in the provision of low-paying sinecures to artists and writers, and an interested if not exceptionally open-handed audience—that brought the talented to Paris. They lived in small, inexpensive apartments, some in the streets leading up to Montmartre, others in the maze of the Left Bank. In *The World of Yesterday*, Stefan Zweig described the group he had known in 1904 and emphasized the stunning impression of genius created on him by the sculptor Rodin:

Rodin was so engrossed, so rapt in his work that not even a thunderstroke would have roused him. His movements became harder, almost angry. A sort of wildness or drunkenness had come over him; he worked faster and faster. Then his hands became hesitant. They seemed to have realized that there was nothing more for them to do. Once, twice, three times he stepped back without making any changes. Then he muttered something softly in his beard, and placed the cloths gently about the figure as one places a shawl around the shoulders of a beloved woman. . . . In that hour I had seen the eternal secret of all great art, yes, of every mortal achievement, made manifest: concentration, the collection of all forces, all sense, that ecstasis, that being-out-of-the-world of every artist. I had learned something for my entire lifetime. [13]

Paris in short appeared to offer an immensity of experience, as Guillaume Apollinaire showed:

But ever since then I've known the flavor of the universe

I'm drunk from having swallowed the entire universe
On the quay from which I saw the darkness flow and the barges sleep

[13]Ibid., pp. 134, 136, 148–149.

Listen to me I am the throat of all Paris
And I shall drink the universe again if I want

Listen to my songs of universal drunkenness. [14]

The vitality became less coherent as the twentieth century advanced; but for the poet Cendrars in 1913, the sights and sounds of Paris were still symbolic of a whole universe of experience:

It's raining electric light bulbs
Montrouge Gare de l'Est subway North-South river boats world
Everything is halo
Profundity
In the Rue de Buci they're hawking l'Intransigeant *and* Paris-Sports
The airdrome of the sky is on fire, a painting by Cimabue [15]

It was in this exhilarating atmosphere that the writers, painters, and musicians of Paris embarked on half a century of experimentation at an ever-increasing tempo, leaving behind not only the more conservative patrons of art but the majority of the public as well.

FROM IMPRESSIONISM TO CUBISM

Impressionism

During the first three-quarters of the nineteenth century, Paris had seen three major artistic movements rise to general acceptance and then fall before their critics—Romanticism, Realism, and Naturalism. In the 1870s, the exponents of the Naturalist school, such as Zola in the novel or Gustave Courbet in painting, were still defending an approach to art that was almost scientific in character. A number of young painters who had gathered around Courbet in the 1860s were determined, however, to carry the study of reality beyond Courbet's view that "painting is essentially a concrete art and does not consist of anything but the representation of real and concrete things." The camera alone could achieve this goal only too well.

The first big step away from the accurate representation of concrete objects was taken by the group of painters who became known as Impressionists, a word first used as abuse but later taken as an accurate description of their attempt to capture the immediate impression on their visual sense of external reality. Above all they were interested in the effect of light and color in the creation of an impression. The leading Impressionist painter, Claude Monet, showed how little he was interested in a specific scene—his real subject matter was the change of light in different atmospheric conditions—by painting several pictures of the same scene under

[14]Roger Shattuck, *The Banquet Years* (New York: Random House, Inc., 1968), p. 313.
[15]Ibid., p. 337.

Gare Saint-Lazare, Paris, 1877, by Claude Monet (1840–1926)

(Courtesy of the Fogg Art Museum, Harvard University. Bequest–Collection of Maurice Wertheim.)

differing light conditions, using such subjects as haystacks, water lilies, Saint Lazare railroad station, or the South Church at Amsterdam. He and Alfred Sisley were especially interested in the play of light upon water, where disassociation from the concrete is most striking. Sisley profited from the widespread flooding in the Seine valley in 1876, for example, to paint a series of pictures of flooded streets and meadows. The technique of the Impressionists was to avoid sharply drawn design using lines, and instead to lay down broad dabs of color, which seen from a distance would fuse in the eye of the onlooker to give him both a sense of perspective and an enhanced sense of the scintillating character of the colors themselves. This technique could be transferred from the landscapes outside Paris to the city streets themselves, as Camille Pissarro demonstrated; or to the beauty of the female body, clothed or unclothed, as Auguste Renoir showed. But it was also effective in giving the true sparkle of the Paris haunts the Impressionists so loved—the cafés, the theater, the skating rink.

The first exhibitions of the Impressionists were met with either disbelief or scorn at their apparent inability to finish a painting properly; and it was a rare critic, like Jules Laforgue, who understood at once what they were trying to achieve:

The Impressionists abandoned the three supreme illusions by which the academic painters lived—line, perspective, and studio lighting. Where the one sees only the external outline of objects the other sees the real living lines, built not in geometric forms but in a thousand irregular strokes which, at a distance, establish life. Where one sees things placed in regular perspective planned according to theoretical design, the other sees perspective established by a thousand trivial touches of tone and brush and by the varieties of atmospheric states. [16]

The heyday of the Impressionists lay between their first independent exhibition in 1874 and their last joint show in 1886. By then their conception of the artist's task as the recorder of fleeting sense impressions had been challenged by several painters who are known collectively as the Post-Impressionists. Paul Cézanne, the leader of the new school, argued that the artist must go beyond the transitory moment to the eternal. Through mental discipline he must impose his own conception upon a subject he is painting. This implied, in part, a return to line, form, and strict design; in part, the intellectual involvement of the painter in his scene. Cézanne, increasingly determined to discipline his subject matter, became convinced that the answer lay in geometry, in the reduction of nature's vastness of form to the elementary shapes of the sphere, the cone, and the prism. In his landscapes of the Provence hills, one sees the Impressionist vision slowly evolve from painting to painting until a landscape is viewed that is almost an abstract design.

For Paul Gauguin, the son of a well-to-do bourgeois family, who abandoned the artificial world of France altogether to find his own reality among the unspoiled primitive landscapes and peoples of the South Seas, the essential task of the painter was to create an understanding of humanity by an appeal to its most deep-rooted emotions. "Where do we come from? What are we? Where are we going?" he would constantly ask. His answer was an almost mythical presentation of the life of the South Sea islanders, in whose innocence he claimed to see a sense of reality that civilized Europe had lost. Henri Rousseau, known as Le Douanier Rousseau because he was a customs official, found a similar purity in the countryside outside Paris, which he depicted with a childlike sense of the primitive forces at work even in a suburban meadow. But it was Vincent van Gogh, a Dutchman who spent the last tormented years of his life in the south of France, who was most successful in making the basic elements of painting, the colors themselves, into symbols expressing an inner view

[16]Cited in Phoebe Pool, *Impressionism* (New York: Praeger, 1967), p. 178.

Haystacks, by Vincent van Gogh (1853–1890)
Even in a black and white drawing, van Gogh could present the intense, vibrant heat of a landscape in Provence. (Philadelphia Museum of Art. Samuel S. White III and Vera White Collection)

of truth. "To express the feelings of two lovers by a marriage of two complementary colors, their mixture and their oppositions, the mysterious vibrations of tones in each other's proximity. To express the thought behind a brow by the radiance of a bright tone against a dark ground. To express hope by some star, the ardor of being by the radiance of a setting sun."[17] But as the illustration above shows, van Gogh could express the same intensity of insight even in a black and white drawing, where the sharp flare of emotion might be caught in the movement of branches or the waving of grass. Van Gogh came close, as he intended, to the nature of both music and poetry, at the time when both were striving to achieve reality through Symbolism.

Symbolism

The Symbolist school of poetry was a French creation, another aspect of the attack on Realism. To escape the detailed, concrete presentation of a purely rational perception, its members hit upon the qualities of the symbol, which they valued for its intensity. The Christian Church had used heaven and hell as symbols; the poet would achieve a similar effect, for himself at least, by using words that *evoked* for him certain passionate experiences, memories, or unconscious reactions. Wagner, they felt, had succeeded in doing this in music, not least by his use of the *leitmotiv*. The

[17]Cited in Weber, *Paths to the Present*, p. 202.

poet must use words in the manner of a musician. *De la musique encore et toujours* ("Music ever and always"), wrote Verlaine.

> *Music ever and always*
> *Let your verse be the object flying on high*
> *That one feels to be fleeing from a soul in freedom*
> *Toward other skies and other loves.*
>
> *Let your verse be the great adventure*
> *Flying high on the sharp wind of morning*
> *Which floats scented with mint and with thyme . . .*
> *And the rest is literature.* [18]

Fauvism, Cubism

By 1900, in short, there seemed to be a kind of common purpose among the artists, poets, and musicians at work in Paris. As usual, the victory of an idea—illustrated by the admission of the Impressionists and Post-Impressionists to the Great World Exhibition of 1900 and their ready sales to American collectors, if not yet to French—was followed by a reaction. The artists in revolt were nicknamed *les fauves*, or "the wild beasts," because the violence of their approach to art was something entirely new. The leader of the Fauves was Henri Matisse, who explained their daring use of brutal discordant colors as a search for expression:

Expression to my way of thinking does not consist of the passion mirrored upon a human face or betrayed by a violent gesture. The whole arrangement of my picture is expressive. The place occupied by the figures of objects, the empty spaces around them, the proportions, everything plays a part. Composition is the art of arranging in a decorative manner the various elements at the painter's disposal for the expression of his feelings. [19]

If Paris found the colors of Matisse and Georges Rouault disconcerting, it was even more shocked by the first exhibition of Cubist painting in 1907, in which Pablo Picasso, an émigré from Spain, displayed *Les Demoiselles d'Avignon*. Picasso, at the time influenced by Cézanne's geometric landscapes, had adapted the geometric approach to the human figure. Not only did Picasso and the other Cubists who joined him at this time, including Georges Braque and Fernand Léger, seek out geometric structures, but they deliberately fragmented their subjects, as though they were being viewed in a mosaic of mirrors. From this they moved to the even greater distortion of the collage, which made possible a representation of the unconscious mind. Fernand Léger explained what they were trying to achieve:

Trees cease to be trees, a shadow cuts across the hand placed on the counter, an eye deformed by the light, the changing silhouettes of the passers-by. The life of

---

[18] Author's translation.
[19] Cited in Herbert Read, *A Concise History of Modern Painting* (New York: Praeger, 1968), p. 38.

Les Demoiselles d'Avignon, by Pablo Picasso (1881–1973)
Picasso first exhibited his picture of the young women of Avignon at the Cubist exhibition of 1907. Although he had reverted to the geometric patterns of Cézanne, the distortion of the bodies represented his attempt to solve the problem of presenting all aspects of the human figure simultaneously. (Collection, Museum of Modern Art, New York. Acquired through the Lillie P. Bliss Bequest)

fragments: a red finger-nail, an eye, a mouth. The elastic effects produced by complementary colors which transform objects into some other reality. He fills himself with all this, drinks in the whole of this vital instantaneity which cuts through him in every direction. He is a sponge: a sensation of being a sponge, transparency, acuteness, new realism. [20]

What had been achieved was in fact the takeoff point for all modern art. The picture had been finally liberated from its relationship to its subject. The painter had passed from the representation of an object to the interpretation of an object and finally to the idea suggested by an object; and the painting now existed in its own right as a free association of images from the artist's own mind with their own objective reality in the painting. From this point it became possible to embark on even more revolutionary forms of art. Even before 1914, the principles of Surrealism, Dadaism, Futurism and abstract art were being worked out.

[20] Ibid., p. 88.

For Paris, however, its artists were now increasingly an isolated and incomprehensible coterie. When Stravinsky's *Rite of Spring* brought its wild rhythms and disturbing story of human sacrifice to the stage in 1913, the music could not be heard for the jeers of the audience.

SUGGESTED READING

Adna F. Weber supplies the statistics of urban growth, and suggests reasons for the vast expansion, in *The Growth of Cities in the Nineteenth Century* (1963), while E. A. Wrigley relates population growth to industrialism in *Population and History* (1969). Excellent surveys of the economic growth of all western Europe are given by David Landes, *The Unbound Prometheus: Technological Change and Industrial Development in Western Europe from 1750 to the Present* (1969), and Alan S. Milward and S. B. Saul, *The Development of the Economies of Continental Europe, 1850–1914* (1977). Peter N. Stearns, *European Society in Upheaval: Social History Since 1800* (1967) is useful on the composition of the working classes. Class structure is entertainingly analyzed in Edward R. Tannenbaum, *1900:The Generation Before the Great War* (1976), which contains fine contemporary quotations and photographs. For insight into the improvements in city life, one should consult the studies of individual cities, such as Sheppard's *London, 1808–1870: The Great Wen*, which does look beyond the carbuncular aspects; David H. Pinckney, *Napoleon III and the Rebuilding of Paris* (1958); and Gerhard Masur, *Imperial Berlin* (1970). The technology of mass transport, but not its social consequences, is described in John P. McKay, *Tramways and Trolleys: The Rise of Urban Mass Transport in Europe* (1976). Nineteenth-century urban growth is explained in Robert E. Dickinson, *The West European City: A Geographical Interpretation* (1951) and dramatized in Arnold Toynbee, *Cities on the Move* (1970). Urban improvements are questioned in Lewis Mumford, *Technics and Civilization* (1934) and also in his *The City in History* (1961).

The technology of the second industrial revolution is described in S. J. Singer et al., eds., *A History of Technology, vol. 5: Late Nineteenth Century, 1850–1900* (1958) and T. K. Derry and T. I. Williams, *A Short History of Technology* (1961). On steel, see N. G. B. Pounds and W. N. Parker, *Coal and Steel in Western Europe* (1957); on electricity, Singer, *History of Technology* cited above, pp. 177–234; and on chemistry, L. F. Haber, *The Chemical Industry in the Nineteenth Century* (1958). The changes in business organization can be followed in H. J. Habbakuk, *American and British Technology in the Nineteenth Century* (1962); William C. Cochran and William Miller, *The Age of Enterprise* (1961); and C. J. H. Hayes, *A Generation of Materialism, 1871–1900* (1941).

Among the many novels that deal with the social changes of fin de siècle, see Marcel Proust's *Remembrance of Things Past* translated in 1951 by C. K. Scott Moncrieff; E. M. Forster, *Howard's End*; Heinrich Mann, *Little Superman*; Thomas Mann, *Buddenbrooks*; Roger Martin du Gard, *Jean Barois*; John Galsworthy, *The Forsyte Saga*; and of course the vast output of H. G. Wells, including *Kipps* and *Tono Bungay*, which, if prolix, at least gives his view of the evolution of London. For a succinct and often biting summation of this society, see Barbara W. Tuchman, *The Proud Tower* (1966).

For an introduction to the intellectual currents of this period, one might begin with H. Stuart Hughes, *Consciousness and Society: The Reorientation of Eu-*

ropean *Social Thought, 1890–1930* (1961) or George L. Mosse, *The Culture of Western Europe: The Nineteenth and Twentieth Centuries* (1961). Freud's life is succinctly explained, with ample quotations from the doctor himself, in O. Mannoni, *Freud* (1971); the standard biography is Ernest Jones, *The Life and Work of Sigmund Freud*, which has been abridged by Lionel Trilling and Steven Marcus (1961). Darwin's great work *On the Origin of Species* is placed in its position in the evolution of scientific thought in Philip Appleman, ed., *Darwin* (1970), while his intellectual development is assessed in Jacques Barzun, *Darwin, Marx, Wagner: Critique of a Heritage* (1958) and Gertrude Himmelfarb, *Darwin and the Darwinian Revolution* (1959). For the battle over evolution, see W. Irvine, *Apes, Angels, and Victorians* (1959). For a biographical approach to the new physics, which is perhaps the best method for a layman to cope with the complexity of relativity and quantum theory, there is Leopold Infeld, *Albert Einstein: His Work and Its Influence on Our World* (1950) and B. L. Cline, *The Questioners* (1965). A stimulating introduction to late-nineteenth-century French society is provided in Theodore Zeldin, *France, 1848–1945*, vol. 1, *Ambition, Love and Politics* (1973) and vol. 2, *Intellect, Taste and Anxiety* (1977).

The Belle Epoque is charmingly evoked through the lives of Alfred Jarry, Henri Rousseau, Erik Satie, and Guillaume Apollinaire in Roger Shattuck, *The Banquet Years* (1968). The journey of the writers from Romanticism to Naturalism is traced by Cesar Graña, *Modernity and Its Discontents: French Society and the French Man of Letters in the Nineteenth Century* (1967). On Symbolism, see Edmund Wilson, *Axel's Castle: A Study in the Imaginative Literature of 1870–1930* (1943) and C. M. Bowra, *The Heritage of Symbolism* (1943). Stefan Zweig describes the intoxicating effect of Paris on a young writer in *The World of Yesterday* (1943); Igor Stravinsky relates his explosive experiences in the unreceptive world of Parisian music in *Autobiography* (1936). On the Impressionist painters, see the solid work of John Rewald, *The History of Impressionism* (1962) or the lighter Phoebe Pool, *Impressionism* (1967). Late developments from Cézanne through Surrealism are explained by Herbert Read, *A Concise History of Modern Painting* (1968). Finally, to enjoy the full overromanticized feeling of the *gaieté parisienne*, one could browse in the music halls described by Jacques Castelnau, *Belle Epoque* (1962), or glance at the fine old photographs in Jean Roman's *Paris: Fin de siècle* (1960), with a delightful text translated by James Emmons.

27

THE BERLIN OF THE KAISER

Since 1870, when Berlin had changed from the rather small, sober, and by no means rich capital of the Kingdom of Prussia into the seat of the German Emperor, the homely town on the Spree had taken a mighty upswing . . . The large concerns and the wealthy families moved to Berlin, and new wealth, paired with a strong sense of daring, opened to the theater and to architecture greater opportunities than in any other large German city . . .

It was just at this period of its transition from a mere capital to a world city that I came to Berlin—Stefan Zweig, on Berlin in the early 1900s. Cited in The World of Yesterday *by Stefan Zweig. Copyright 1943, © renewed 1970 by The Viking Press, Inc. Reprinted by permission of The Viking Press.*

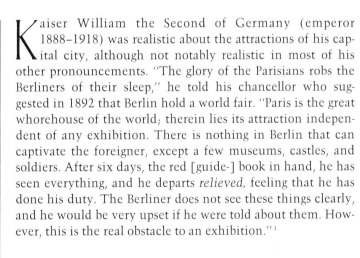

Kaiser William the Second of Germany (emperor 1888–1918) was realistic about the attractions of his capital city, although not notably realistic in most of his other pronouncements. "The glory of the Parisians robs the Berliners of their sleep," he told his chancellor who suggested in 1892 that Berlin hold a world fair. "Paris is the great whorehouse of the world; therein lies its attraction independent of any exhibition. There is nothing in Berlin that can captivate the foreigner, except a few museums, castles, and soldiers. After six days, the red [guide-] book in hand, he has seen everything, and he departs *relieved*, feeling that he has done his duty. The Berliner does not see these things clearly, and he would be very upset if he were told about them. However, this is the real obstacle to an exhibition."[1]

[1] Gerhard Masur, *Imperial Berlin* (New York: Basic Books, 1971), pp. 125–126.

(Left Page) The Cathedral, Berlin *(H. Roger-Viollet)*; (Inset) Kaiser Wilhelm II *(Courtesy of the German Information Center)*

The Kaiser's Berlin, whatever it may have lacked in the more obvious tourist attractions, had progressed considerably since the mid-fifteenth century, when one of its first Hohenzollern family rulers had chosen it for the capital of his Mark of Brandenburg. At that time it consisted of little more than twin trading settlements, Berlin-Kölln on the two banks of the insignificant Spree River, and a castle that provided protection against marauding barons and served as an outpost for the drive against the Slavs across the sandy wastes of the North German plain. It had been laid in ruins during the Thirty Years' War, and was saved from insignificance only by the forceful genius of the Great Elector, Frederick William I (reigned 1640–1688). He gave his state of Prussia, now enlarged to include

◆ The Berlin of the Kaiser ◆

Period Surveyed	Chancellorship of Bismarck (1862–1890) and reign of Kaiser William II (1888–1918)
Population	657,690 (1865); 964,240 (1875); 1.5 million (1889); 1.9 million (1900); 2 million (1910)
Area	Inner city, 2.9 square miles; including suburbs, 29 square miles (1910)
Form of Government	Authoritarian empire. Two-house legislature (Bundesrat, chosen by state governments; Reichstag, elected by universal manhood suffrage). Executive (chancellor appointed by emperor). City government by mayor and city council
Political Leaders	Emperors: William I, William II. Chancellors: Bismarck (1862–1890), Caprivi (1890–1894), Hohenlohe-Schillingsfürst (1894–1900), Bülow (1900–1909), Bethmann-Hollweg (1909–1916). Party leaders: August Bebel (Social Democrat); Ludwig Windthorst (Center); Eduard Lasker, Rudolf von Bennigsen (National Liberal)
Economic Base	Imperial and Prussian administration; banking and stock exchange; heavy engineering; electrical appliances; chemicals; publishing
Intellectual Life	Music (Hans von Bülow, Johannes Brahms, Richard Strauss); drama (Gerhart Hauptmann); novel (Theodor Fontane); poetry (Stefan George, Georg Heym, Rainer Maria Rilke); painting (Oskar Kokoschka, Käthe Kollwitz); science (Max Planck, Albert Einstein)
Principal Buildings	Pre-1871: Forum Fredericianum, Brandenburg Gate, Neue Wache, Old Museum, City Palace, Charlottenburg Palace Post-1871: Museum Island, Cathedral, Kaiser William Memorial Church, Reichstag, General Staff
Public Entertainment	Military parades and maneuvers; gymnastics, hiking, bicycle riding; theater (drama, opera, and symphony); beer halls
Religion	Lutheran, Catholic, Jewish

territory on the Rhine and the province of East Prussia on the Baltic, a large standing army, adequate revenues, a peasantry submissive to their aristocratic landlords, and a thriving industrial base that was mainly the work of French Calvinist refugees and Dutch immigrants. The role of Berlin as the garrison center of the Prussian state was further emphasized by King Frederick William I (reigned 1713–1740), a rough brute whose pet ambition was to possess the tallest regiment in Europe and who despised the refinements of French culture that his son, Frederick II (reigned 1740–1786) appeared to prize above military virtues. Frederick, as we saw earlier, was adept in combining military adventures and territorial aggrandizement (notably in Silesia and western Poland) with the patronage of the

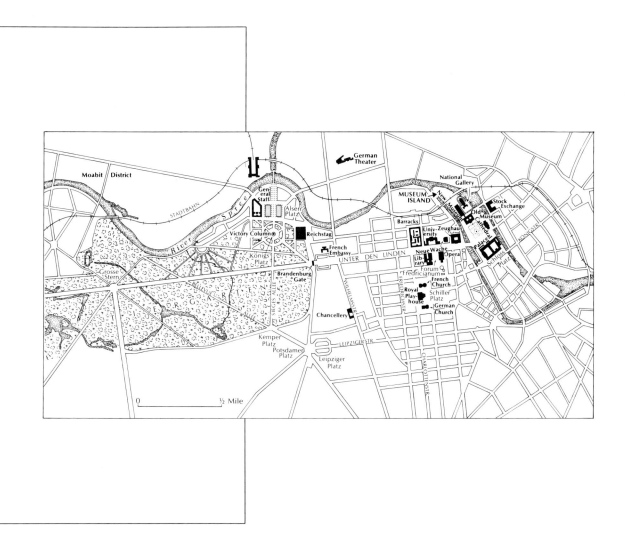

arts and music; and by the end of his reign, Berlin and the neighboring town of Potsdam shared in a small, subdued way in the architectural and artistic advances of the rococo age.

By 1786, Berlin, with a population of almost 150,000, was a moderately attractive representative of the many princely capitals of a Germany divided into more than three hundred states. Each of the rulers of the previous century and a half had left an imprint on the growing city. The wife of the Great Elector had laid down the city's most famous avenue, Unter den Linden, that led westward from the castle. The castle itself received a new baroque facade when the Great Elector's successor, Frederick I, who had won the title of king, decided to let Germany's finest architect and city planner, Andreas Schlüter, make Berlin worthy of its new royal status. Frederick II, however, created on both sides of the Unter den Linden one of the great eighteenth-century squares, the Forum Fredericianum. On one side of the street was the classical facade of his brother's palace, which was soon converted into the University of Berlin. Facing it was the new opera house, a domed Catholic church, and the curving facade of the royal library. With the completion of Frederick's Forum, Berlin possessed a monumental center of great dignity; and the preeminent importance of Unter

Berlin in 1815
In 1815, the most notable landmarks of Berlin visible from the meadows surrounding the city were the new baroque royal palace and the neoclassical cupolas of the French and German churches.   (Courtesy of the German Information Center)

City Palace, Berlin
The great baroque architect Andreas Schlüter designed the principal facade for this palace, which was the residence of the Hohenzollern family from 1470 to 1918. The building was demolished after the Second World War. (Courtesy of the German Information Center)

den Linden was emphasized with the construction in 1788–1791 of the Brandenburg Gate at its western terminus.

For the next generation, the classical revival replaced the rococo, and the style was created that was to dominate the 1800s. Monumental Berlin of the nineteenth century was to be, its architects hoped, a synthesis of Athens and Rome, an idea that corresponded to some extent to the rulers' belief that Berlin could be a combination of spirit (*Geist*) and strength (*Macht*). The Brandenburg Gate was a Doric version of a Roman triumphal arch. The guardhouse, or Neue Wache, had a Parthenon-like portico as entry to a square Roman fortress. The Old Museum, built by the architect Karl Friedrich Schinkel, who was perhaps more responsible than any other person for the appearance of the heart of Berlin, was a long basilica, like Julius Caesar's in Rome, masked by a facade of Ionian columns. The Museum Island in the Spree River, dedicated by the king as "a sanctuary of Art and Learning" and developed during the next hundred years into one of the three or four greatest museum complexes in the world, was a totally new concept for Berlin and other cities.

For most of the nineteenth century, however, Berlin's development, though extensive, was lackluster. After the brief period in which Prussia led the national revolt against Napoleon, and the political life of Berlin itself was reinvigorated by the reforms of Stein and Hardenberg and the intellectual life by the Humboldt brothers, it slumped into its own Biedermeier quiescence. Germany's intellectual life was centered still in Weimar, where Goethe held sway until 1832, although in Berlin Hegel and his disciples were teaching (to Karl Marx, among others) the philosophy of the dialectic and the embodiment of the absolute in the Prussian state.

In Prussia, after the king had dismissed the reforming ministers in 1819, those who sought change had to find it in economics rather than politics. In the Rhineland provinces Prussia had acquired in 1815, the first great ironworks and engineering companies were created in the 1830s and 1840s. In Berlin itself, the Borsig locomotive works was the forerunner of several large engineering plants, stimulated especially by the construction of railroads and by the formation of a customs union, or *Zollverein*, joined by most German states. By 1848 Berlin's population had reached 400,000, many of whom lived in dismal slum conditions in the new suburb of Moabit. Neither industrialization nor political repression had turned the Berliners into effective revolutionaries, however, as the anarchist Bakunin complained in 1840:

Berlin is a fine town, excellent music, cheap living, very passable theater, plenty of newspapers in the cafes. . . . In a word, splendid, quite splendid—if only the Germans weren't so frightfully bourgeois. Yesterday I noticed a sign outside a shop: the Prussian eagle above and below a tailor ironing. And underneath the following couplet:

> *Under thy wings*
> *Quietly, I can do my ironing.* [2]

The failure of the 1848 revolution in Berlin and the concurrent collapse of the attempt to unify Germany through the Frankfurt Parliament were, however, the necessary prerequisites to Berlin's seizure of its role as the unifier of Germany, and thus to its transformation into the imperial capital of a country unified by Prussian military might.

But throughout the 1850s, the Prussian government seemed unwilling to recognize that the failure of the Frankfurt Parliament was its own opportunity. The king, Frederick William IV (reigned 1840–1861), was slowly succumbing to the mental sickness that made it necessary for him to relinquish power to his brother William I (reigned 1861–1888) three years before his death. The highest positions in society and politics were held by the landed aristocracy, and especially by the semifeudal gentry from East Prussia and the Mark of Brandenburg, who had little interest in western or southern Germany. The middle classes, elated by the rapidity of Prussia's economic growth under the stimulus of vast railroad construction, were increasingly aware of the benefits of economic unification in Germany but disoriented as to possible methods of achieving it. In the Prussian constitution, issued by the king after the defeat of the revolutionary forces in

[2]Cited in John Mander, *Berlin: The Eagle and the Bear*, trans. modified (London: Barrie and Radcliff, 1959), p. 76.

Berlin, the wealthiest members of the middle class had been given the predominance in the Lower House, or Landtag, of the legislature, through an electoral system that favored those paying the highest taxes. But the aristocracy had been entrenched in the Upper House or House of Lords, which was appointed by the king, and the king retained control over the executive, including the vitally important direction of foreign policy and the army. The liberals in the Lower House, profiting from Prussia's rapid economic advancement in the 1850s, remained acquiescent in this system, although they made muted protests at the extension of police powers that seemed necessary to enforce the paternalism of the Prussian bureaucracy and its aristocratic overlords.

In 1860–1861, however, the liberals in the Lower House, who formed the Progressive party, opposed a reorganization of the army that would have increased the term of conscription to three years, doubled the army's size, and drastically reduced the importance of the civilian militia. The liberals rightly charged that the government's aims were to reduce the importance of the middle-class officers of the militia, imbue the population with a more military sense of discipline and a stronger admiration for the monarchy, and expand the military role of the landed aristocracy. In 1862 the Lower House refused to pass an increased general budget that included expenditures for the army reorganization. A situation of constitutional deadlock resulted, in which the king and his conservative advisors accused the liberals of attempting to gain control of the state and were regarded in turn by the liberals as seeking to militarize it. King William's resolution of the impasse was the appointment of a new chief minister, Otto von Bismarck, who in nine years converted Berlin from the capital of a Prussian kingdom of eighteen million to the capital of a German empire, the Second Reich, with almost forty million inhabitants.

FROM ROYAL TO IMPERIAL CAPITAL, 1862–1871

Prussia is henceforth absorbed into Germany," the Prussian king had declared in 1848. By 1871, on the contrary, it was Prussia that had swallowed up Germany, preferring to follow Bismarck's own maxim that in Germany pike eats carp. To carry through this design Bismarck had to overwhelm the liberal opposition inside Prussia, create a modernized army, harness the nationalism of North Germany behind Prussia, defeat Austria and eject it from Germany, and stimulate the South German states to seek unification under Prussia by leading them to victory in a war against France. But he had perhaps unguardedly summed up his program more pithily two weeks before he dismissed the recalcitrant parliament. "It is not by speeches and majority resolutions that the great questions of our time are decided," he said. "That was the great mistake of 1848 and 1849. It is by blood and iron."

The genius of Bismarck as an international politician lay in his astute manipulation of the ambitions and rivalries of the other powers of western and central Europe. Where Metternich had used his diplomatic skills to discourage change, Bismarck used his equally adroit mastery throughout the 1860s to institute change that would benefit Prussia and weaken its enemies. Of these opponents, the most threatening to his plans for the unification of Germany were the France of Emperor Napoleon III and the Austria of Emperor Francis Joseph; but fortunately for Bismarck, these two powers were also pitted against each other because of French support for the formation of a united Italian state.

The French Second Empire

In the 1850s the most powerful state in Europe appeared to be the Second Empire of Napoleon III. Louis Napoleon Bonaparte had been elected president of the French Second Republic in December 1848 as a result of the growing disillusionment of large sections of the French population with the excesses and the inefficiency of the radicals and socialists in the republican government. He had promised order and economic revival, and had hinted that, like his uncle the emperor Napoleon I, he would be able to restore French prestige abroad. For three years he had manipulated the political parties in the Chamber to isolate the fervent republicans from a more conservative coalition that extended from monarchists and Bonapartists through moderate republicans; and he had appointed loyal supporters to run the army and the Paris police. In December 1851, in a quick coup d'état, he overthrew the constitutional system of 1848 and made himself president for ten years with complete control over the executive. A year later, the French public overwhelmingly supported a plebiscite making him emperor of France. (He took the title Napoleon III because Napoleon I had abdicated in 1815 in favor of his son Napoleon II, who died in 1832.)

As emperor, Napoleon III made great efforts to stimulate French economic growth. He transformed the French banking system by encouraging the foundation of several large banks that would extend credit to new industry, to peasant farmers and urban dwellers, and to railroads and shipping lines. The mobilization of the savings of many small investors made possible loans to foreign governments for large capital projects. Enormous progress was made in the completion of the French railroad network. Fifteen thousand kilometers of new track were laid down, and a special effort was made to bring isolated regions into the national transportation system. To increase the stimulation of foreign competition and to help open foreign markets to French exports, Napoleon III adopted a policy of free trade and negotiated treaties of tariff reduction with most of France's important trading partners. The upshot of these policies was an economic boom that substantially increased the living standards of the French population. The output of coal and metal products tripled, as did the volume of foreign commerce. Most of the economic benefits of the new prosperity were received by the financial and industrial bourgeoisie and to a lesser extent by

Napoleon III (1808–1873)
(H. Roger-Viollet)

the middle classes in the professions and administration; but even working-class wages rose slowly, while improved transportation and technology helped some of the farming population.

The most dramatic demonstration of the prosperity of the new regime was to be seen in the rebuilding of much of central Paris, a project undertaken by the emperor and his prefect of the Seine, Georges Haussmann. Haussmann used the dictatorial powers of the empire to override property rights, the demands of historic or aesthetic preservation, and financial difficulties, to open up the malodorous medieval heart of the city. Haussmann built eighty-five miles of new streets, imposing on them a uniformity of height and style; many of them struck directly through working-class slums where barricades had been erected during previous revolutions. He reduced the incidence of cholera by supplying pure water to replace that drawn from the polluted Seine River. Beneath the city, he dug vast storm drains that could later be used for underground utilities. And on the edges of the city he created new parks, especially the Bois de Boulogne on the western side and the Bois de Vincennes on the eastern side, that were to become the city's lungs.

Paris thus became, more than ever before, the tourist capital of Europe. The imperial court in the Tuileries, presided over by the emperor and his beautiful Spanish empress Eugénie, was the most glittering in Europe. French fashions dictated style throughout Europe and North America. The great new department stores, such as the Bon Marché and the Samaritaine, offered an enticing array of French and foreign products. The new opera house attracted Europe's finest singers, while an equally appreciative horde thronged to the light operas of Offenbach or to the newly founded Folies Bergères. To demonstrate the achievements of his empire, Napoleon organ-

The Opera, Paris
In his designs for the imposing opera house that was to be one of the focal points of Haussmann's reconstruction of central Paris, Charles Garnier attempted to create a new "Napoleon III style" derived from baroque. Although it is the largest theater in the world, the Opera seats only twenty-two hundred people. (Peter Menzel)

ized two splendid exhibitions on the pattern of London's Crystal Palace display of 1851, the first in 1855 and the second in 1867.

Abroad, Napoleon III intended to become the arbiter of European diplomacy. His two constant aims, discernible in spite of frequent hesitations and changes of direction, were the support of nationalist movements throughout Europe (with the exception of Germany) and the winning of glory (*la gloire*) like his uncle Napoleon I by annexation of territory to France, especially along its eastern frontiers. Napoleon III's first major military adventure, intervention in the Crimean War (1853–1856), was his greatest triumph in international affairs. Russian armies invaded the principalities of Moldavia and Wallachia, the nucleus of modern Rumania, in ostensible support of their claim to safeguard Orthodox Christians in the Turkish Empire, in July 1853; and the Russian navy sank a Turkish fleet in November. Napoleon joined with the British government in declaring war on Russia, to prevent the establishment of Russian hegemony in the Balkans. The war was bungled on both sides, but half a million men were killed in the fighting on the Crimean peninsula that culminated in the Franco-British capture of the fortress of Sebastopol. Russia eventually accepted the French and British terms for peace; and in a grandiose peace conference in Paris in 1856 Napoleon took the opportunity of posing as the patron of the autonomy of the Rumanians of Moldavia and Wallachia. Moreover, he ensured that a prominent hearing at the Congress be given to the demand of Piedmont-Savoy for Austrian ouster from its Italian province of Lombardy, even though Piedmont had made only a small contribution of soldiers to the Crimean fighting. For Austria, France had thus become the most immediate danger to the preservation of its multinational empire, because Napoleon had unmistakably declared himself the supporter of the expansion of Piedmont-Savoy into the Austrian territories of northern Italy.

The Unification of Italy

The French government's ally in Italy, the state of Piedmont-Savoy, was under the rule of leaders far more realistic than such earlier revolutionaries as Mazzini and Manin. Count Camillo Cavour, who became chief minister of Piedmont-Savoy in 1852, coldly and painstakingly planned Italy's unification by his own state and its royal family, the one native dynasty in the peninsula. He groomed Piedmont for stardom, modernizing its industry and seeking reliable allies against Austria. After years of bargaining with Napoleon and of skillful propaganda among the various nationalist groups inside Italy, Cavour provoked Austria into war with Piedmont, in April 1859. At once his carefully laid plans were implemented. France came to the aid of its aggrieved ally Piedmont and on its behalf defeated the Austrian armies in Lombardy. Well-orchestrated nationalist uprisings took place in the central states of Italy, whose populations demanded unification with Piedmont. When Garibaldi conquered Naples and Sicily without Piedmont's support or authorization, a Piedmontese army was sent to compel him to hand over his newly won possessions—which, to Cavour's relief, he did peacefully and with panache. By

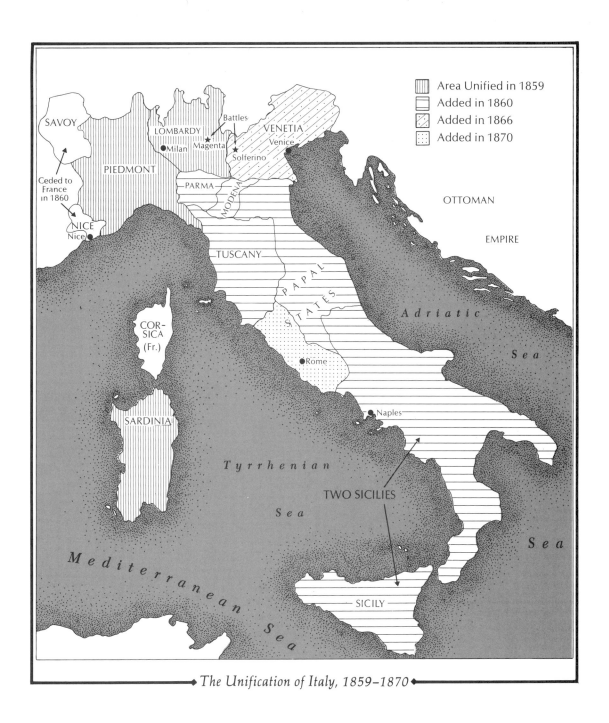

Legend:
- ▦ Area Unified in 1859
- ▤ Added in 1860
- ▨ Added in 1866
- ▦ Added in 1870

SAVOY

LOMBARDY

Battles

VENETIA
Venice

Milan Magenta
Solferino

PIEDMONT

Ceded to
France
in 1860

PARMA

MODENA

OTTOMAN

NICE
Nice

EMPIRE

TUSCANY

P A P A L

S T A T E S

A d r i a t i c

COR-
SICA
(Fr.)

Rome

S e a

SARDINIA

Naples

T y r r h e n i a n

TWO SICILIES

S e a

S e a

M e d i t e r r a n e a n   S e a

SICILY

◆ *The Unification of Italy, 1859–1870* ◆

1860, Piedmont had thus been able to unite all Italy except Venice and part
of the Papal States under its king, Victor Emmanuel I; the price paid had
been the cession of Savoy and Nice to France. Austria, the great obstacle to
Italian unification from the year 1815, had collapsed ignominiously.

Bismarck Unifies Germany

Prince Otto von Bismarck (1815–1898)
Even as chancellor of a united Germany, Bismarck prided himself on preserving the simplicity and directness of a Pomeranian Junker. (Courtesy of the German Information Center)

Bismarck saw that the events of the 1850s had been very favorable to the cause of the Prussian unification of Germany. In the new Italian state he saw a potential ally against Austria, especially as Austria was still holding the province of Venetia. The rapid defeats of the Austrian armies by the French had demonstrated the military inefficacy of the troops of Emperor Francis Joseph. But above all the success of Piedmont had provoked a fervor in Germany for its unification by Prussia. Much of the outpouring of nationalist feeling in 1859–1862 in favor of Prussian leadership was liberal rather than conservative or militarist in orientation. Bismarck, the most sagacious of political observers, was prepared to profit from the nationalist atmosphere created by the liberals while at the same time denying their aspirations within Prussia, secure in the belief that they would eventually return to his support after success.

Bismarck was clear both as to methods and goals for Germany's unification. In background and in character, he stood for authoritarianism. "I am no democrat and cannot be one!" he said. "I was born and raised as an aristocrat." He was also unshakably though realistically loyal to the Prussian monarchy. "I take the king in my own way, I influence him, trust him, guide him, but he is the central point of all my thinking and all my action, the Archimedes point from which I will move the world." Far from being isolated as a rural squire, however, Bismarck had studied law in Göttingen and Berlin, and had gained international political experience as a Prussian representative to the German Confederation in Frankfurt and later as ambassador to Saint Petersburg and Paris. From this experience he had drawn the conclusion that Germany was too small to include both Prussia and Austria and that eventually the outcome would be settled on the battlefield. He prepared for that day with extraordinary skill.

When parliament refused the olive branch he offered it (he literally offered an olive branch that he had brought from Avignon), he ordered the state's tax collectors to collect the taxes anyway, and gave the army organizers, Albrecht von Roon and Helmuth von Moltke, the credits to supply the army with the needle-gun and steel-barreled artillery from the Krupp factory. He manipulated Austria with great skill. After winning Russian friendship by encouraging Russia to crush a revolt in its Polish territories in 1863, he lured Austria into a war against Denmark to prevent the incorporation into the Danish kingdom of the two largely German-inhabited duchies of Schleswig and Holstein, and then persuaded the Austrians to administer Holstein while Prussia ran Schleswig.

Meanwhile, he set about isolating Austria diplomatically. He sensed that Napoleon III's humiliation in Mexico—where his attempt in 1861–1867 to establish a satellite state of France under the archduke Maximilian of Austria was failing as a result of Mexican military resistance and pressure from the United States—had made him desperate for some prestigious gain in Europe. In vague but plausible promises in a meeting with Napoleon at Biarritz in October 1865, he indicated that French neutrality in a war between Prussia and Austria might be rewarded with territory along the Rhine. He astounded, and to some extent disarmed, the German liberals by proposing that the German Confederation be given an all-German parliament elected by universal suffrage. He made a secret treaty with the Italian government, promising it Venetia if it attacked Austria from the south in the event of an Austro-Prussian war within three months' time. And he reassured world opinion that his aim was not to bring Austria or southern Germany into Prussian control, merely "that part of Germany which is united by its genius, its religion, manners, and interests to the destiny of Prussia—the Germany of the North."

When military preparations for a war with Austria were complete, he sharply criticized Austrian administration in Holstein and seized the province. Austria and the German Confederation declared war on Prussia for occupying Holstein, even though the Austrian army was badly armed and hampered by inadequate railroads. Austria and its allies were defeated within seven weeks at the decisive Battle of Königgrätz. Bismarck, who had sat with King William I on horseback watching his rising excitement and

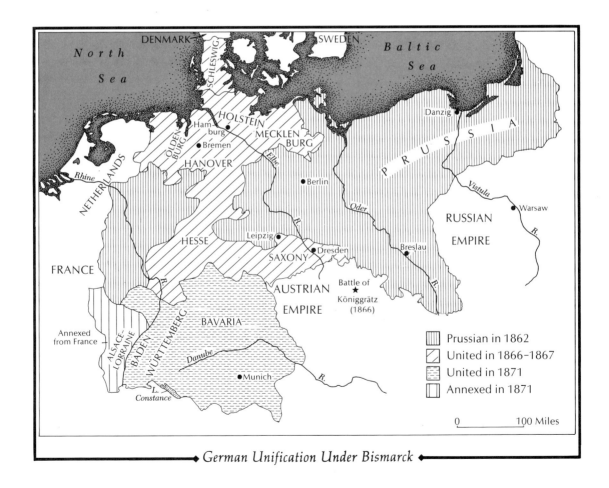

◆ German Unification Under Bismarck ◆

disregard for danger, found that the martial experience had given the king and his general staff an unwise desire to humiliate the Austrians with an occupation of Vienna and annexation of Austrian territory. "We are just as quickly intoxicated as discouraged," he wrote to his wife, "and I have the ungrateful task of pouring water in the foaming wine, and to make them see that we are not living alone in Europe, but with three neighbors still." He was successful in winning light terms for Austria, although he insisted that Italy, which had entered the war as stipulated only to be defeated, should be given Venetia. For the North German states, however, he demanded unification with Prussia in a new North German Confederation with Berlin as its capital. By 1866, the territory under Prussian control had increased by four and a half million people, while Austria was definitively driven out of internal German affairs.

In the flush of victory, Bismarck took the opportunity of ending the constitutional crisis that had brought him to power originally. He introduced in the Prussian parliament an indemnity bill, which provided for passage of the budgets of 1862–1864 from which Bismarck had collected revenues without parliamentary authorization, declared that the actions of Bismarck during those years had not been illegal, and provided for government accounting for expenditures to parliament. The bill passed the Lower House by a massive majority, and was followed by a vote of confidence in the conduct of foreign affairs by the government. Although some liberals voted against both measures, the vast support marked the abdication by most German parliamentarians of their attempts to gain a greater share in the running of the state. Military success had bred political resignation.

France remained the principal obstacle to the unification of the South German states with Prussia after the defeat of Austria. A successful war against France would end the territorial ambitions in Europe of Napoleon III, quash French opposition to German unification, and entice the Catholic states of South Germany to join with the largely Protestant North German Confederation under the leadership of Prussia in a military alliance that would be the prelude to political unity. In 1870, Bismarck incited Napoleon III to declare war on Prussia. He did this by publicizing his demands for compensation in Luxembourg or in Belgium for Prussia's expansion in Germany, by promoting the candidacy of a member of the Hohenzollern family for the throne of Spain, and by doctoring a telegram from William I at Bad Ems to make it appear that the Prussian king had rudely snubbed the French ambassador. The telegram arrived on July 13, 1870, when Bismarck was dining with his army leaders, Moltke and Roon. All were despondent that, with plans for the invasion of France in complete readiness, the French seemed unwilling to give them the desired declaration of war. According to Bismarck:

In the presence of my guests I reduced the telegram by deleting words, but without adding or altering a single word. . . . The difference in the effect of the shortened text of the Ems telegram as compared with that of the original was not the result of stronger words but of the form, which made the announcement appear decisive.

After I had read the condensed version to my two guests, Moltke said:

"Now it has quite a different ring. In its original form it sounded like a parley. Now it is like a flourish of trumpets in answer to a challenger."...

I went on to explain:

"If, in execution of his Majesty's order, I immediately communicate this text, which contains no changes in or additions to the telegram, not only to the newspapers but also by wire to all our embassies, it will be known in Paris before midnight. Not only on account of its contents but also because of the manner of its distribution, it will have the effect of a red flag on the Gallic bull..."

This explanation drew from both generals a metamorphosis into a more joyous mood, whose liveliness surprised me. They had suddenly recovered their desire to eat and drink. [3]

This masterful manipulation of public opinion brought the crowds out on the streets of Paris and Berlin in a war-hungry mood. The French declared war; the South German states placed their armies at the disposal of the Prussian command; within three months, the main French armies were defeated and Napoleon was captured. After organizing makeshift armies in the provinces, a new republican government in Paris, established on September 4, 1870, succeeded in prolonging the war until January 1871. Peace was finally made only after Paris had been bombarded by the Germans and hundreds of civilians killed. By the treaty of May 1871, France ceded Alsace-Lorraine to Germany and agreed to pay an indemnity of five billion francs.

Meanwhile, in January Bismarck had prevailed on the South German states to unite with the North German Confederation and to accept without essential change its constitution. He had thus created a unified German state under the traditional Prussian monarchy. Even then he had difficulties persuading the king to any compromise in form in return for this victory of substance. William objected vehemently to the title "German Emperor," which the German princes had declared him in the Hall of Mirrors in the Palace of Versailles; and, since he blamed Bismarck for not winning their agreement to the stronger title of "Emperor of Germany," he blatantly ignored his chancellor at the ceremony. In spite of these personal tensions, Bismarck ensured that the ceremony have the requisite grandeur for the recreation of the German Empire. He delighted in the symbolism of using the palace of the French kings, the recognition of the emperor by the German ruling houses and not by a parliamentary assembly, and especially the presence of the army, which supplied officers from all sixty of the units surrounding Paris. The new emperor returned to Berlin on June 16, 1871,

[3]Cited in Louis L. Snyder, *The Blood and Iron Chancellor: A Documentary Biography of Otto von Bismarck* (Princeton, N.J.: Van Nostrand, 1967), pp. 185–186.

The Proclamation of William I as German Emperor, 1871, by Anton von Werner (1843–1915)

The Prussian king William I was proclaimed German emperor in the Hall of Mirrors of the Palace of Versailles on January 18, 1871, to dramatize for the South German states then joining the new state the tremendous strength that a united Germany would possess. (BBC Hulton Picture Library)

passing through a garlanded Brandenburg Gate to a vast cheering welcome from the crowds in Unter den Linden. Berlin, the imperial capital, was about to enjoy the exhilarating economic boom of the *Gründerjahre* ("founding years") of the new empire.

BERLIN DURING THE GRÜNDERJAHRE: CREATION OF AN IMPERIAL CAPITAL

A capital city is essential for the state, to act as a pivot for its culture," Heinrich von Treitschke proclaimed in his self-appointed role as guide to the new nation's position in history. "No great nation can endure for long without a center where its political, intellectual, and material life is concentrated, and its people can feel united." That center could only be Berlin. Some cities, such as Leipzig and Frankfurt, were better located; others, such as Munich and Dresden, were more beautiful and more cultivated. But since Prussia had absorbed Germany, Prussia's capital would have to be transformed into a capital worthy of the Reich.

Preparation had already been made in the 1860s for the replanning of Berlin. Until then the city had been surrounded by a wall some eighteen feet high, which had been erected during the wars with Napoleon and used for collecting local tolls. With its demolition the expansion of the city to engulf nearby villages became possible. Several great avenues already existed that could become the axes of future development, notably the Kurfürstendamm, which led from the beautiful Tiergarten Park on the edge of the old city to the lovely woods of the Grunewald, and the Charlottenburgerstrasse, which prolonged Unter den Linden toward Charlottenburg Palace, originally a country residence of the Hohenzollern family. Berlin was even given a general development plan in 1863, the last it was to have for more than half a century; to this the newer sections owed their wide tree-lined streets. Undoubtedly, the example of Haussmann's transformation of Paris inspired many of the city planners, although they could do little with the inner city itself. Here only piecemeal improvements were made: a huge city hall in an odd mixture of native Brandenburg and Italian Renaissance styles; a monumental square called the Königsplatz, whose central feature was a tall, ugly Victory Column (*Siegessaüle*) begun in 1864 to celebrate

Unter den Linden, Berlin, in the 1930s
This fine avenue, called "Under the Lime Trees," was lined with baroque palaces and churches in the late eighteenth century. (Courtesy of the German Information Center)

Statues from Victory Avenue, Berlin

William II intended that Victory Avenue commemorate the glories of the Hohenzollern family; he personally paid for its statues. Among those that survived the Second World War are, from left to right, Emperor William I, Elector Frederick II, Elector Frederick I, and Elector Johann Georg. (Courtesy of the German Information Center)

the defeat of Denmark and further elaborated to immortalize the victories over Austria and France; and a number of vast, half-classical railroad stations around the old city boundary, such as the Lehrter Station of 1869 and the Potsdam Station of 1870, which helped link the capital to its new possessions.

There was surprisingly little monumental building carried out to accommodate the demands of imperial administration or even imperial pretensions. The most grandiose building erected was a new home for the imperial parliament, the Reichstag, on the edge of the Königsplatz—a vast neoclassical building completed in 1894. William I made no pretense of seeking to enhance the glamor of a title he had never wanted; but his grandson William II sought in his own idiosyncratic way to give a little monumental sparkle to the subdued setting bequeathed him by his ancestors. Leading to the Victory Column he laid out a new Victory Avenue, which he flanked with thirty-two marble statues of the principal rulers of the House of Hohenzollern, from Albert the Bear to William I. Although William paid for it himself as a gift to his people and thought it made Berlin the most beautiful city in the world, most Berliners found it a masterpiece of grotesquely bad taste. The two huge churches he erected were little better. The cathedral, built near the palace on the site of Frederick the Great's cathedral, which had been pulled down, was intended to outdo Michelangelo's Saint Peter's in size, color, and decoration but failed except in scale; the Kaiser William Memorial Church built in commemoration of his grandfather at the head of the Kurfürstendamm was a massive, neo-Romanesque creation, which many later felt looked more picturesque after 1945, in ruins. Only the new museums added to the Museum Island managed to harmonize with the older Schinkel buildings; and in them Wilhelm Bode, the director of the Berlin galleries, accumulated one of the greatest collections of world art, including the findings of the great German archaeologists who were laying bare the buried cities of the Near East. These treasures included the Altar of Pergamum, the Processional Way and Ishtar Gate of Babylon, and the Market Gate of Miletus; and their acquisition was directly favored by the Kaiser, who admired and understood archaeology.

But the main changes in Berlin's appearance were the result of the economic and commercial expansion that followed unification. The population of Berlin increased at great speed. It had reached a million by 1875, 1.5 million by 1889, and two million by 1910. As was true of all big cities of the late nineteenth century, a physical separation of the classes occurred. The new workers moved into overcrowded tenements in the area to the north of the Spree River, first in the slums of the Moabit district and then, as the big factories moved into the countryside, in the outer districts to the north and east. It was in these areas of working-class discontent that the Socialist party found ready support. Most of the aristocracy came to Berlin only for court functions, preferring to remain on their country estates, where they could still cultivate the old Prussian virtues of discipline and thrift; in Berlin they composed only a small percentage of the population. The middle classes included the *Bildungsbürgertum* (intellectual middle class) and the *Besitzbürgertum* (propertied middle class); and they too were minutely subdivided according to the social prestige of their employment. The former included university professors, bureaucrats, and other professionals, many of whom liked to live in what was called the Old West, a quiet, charming area on the edge of the Tiergarten Park. They were thus separated from the money-making middle class, whose most successful members bought themselves plots in the wooded suburbs of Grunewald and erected elaborate mansions in Gothic or Renaissance style. The majority of the business people lived in new, stuccoed apartment buildings near the Kurfürstendamm, in an area that one industrialist labeled "Chicago on the Spree."

A great rash of offices and factories was erected by this middle class during the Gründerjahre. After unification, the financial center of Germany passed from Frankfurt to Berlin. This was due in part to the fact that the 5-billion-franc indemnity paid by France was channeled through Berlin, where much of it remained. It was also due to the foundation of new banks by industrial companies already in Berlin, and the transfer of central bank offices to the seat of political power and the home of the new imperial bank, the Reichsbank. Berlin thus became the center of the great speculative mania that gripped the German people in the euphoria of uni-

Economic and Commercial Expansion

fication and led them to shift capital from savings banks into stocks, real estate ventures, and railroads, only to lose much of it in the crash of 1873. Berlin too was becoming the chief manufacturing city in Germany, and, by the time of the great industrial exhibition in 1886, it produced seven percent of the nation's industrial output. The greatest Berlin industries were the heavy engineering industry, which turned out enormous steam engines, locomotives, and machine tools; the electrical appliance industry; and the chemical industry. But there were many others, including textiles, rubber, printing, and food processing. Hence Berlin became a great industrial city, the majority of whose inhabitants had no connection at all with its function as a capital.

The economic expansion of Berlin was possible only because of the enormous boom felt throughout Germany during the Second Reich. By 1914 Germany had become the greatest industrial power in Europe. The country was rich in natural resources, especially coal from the Ruhr basin and iron ore from newly acquired Alsace-Lorraine. It had a superb transportation network: readily navigable rivers, fine canals, and a railroad system linking the agricultural east with the industrial west. It had a good supply of well-educated laborers; in fact, with the increase in population

Stock Exchange Berlin
The stock exchange, built in 1859–1864, had a fine Doric colonnade overlooking the river Spree. It was demolished after 1945. (Courtesy of the German Information Center)

from 40 to 68 million between 1870 and 1914, many Germans felt compelled to emigrate overseas in search of work. Its banking system had been designed to further industrial growth. The banks put little money into government bonds but invested in long-term operations that they themselves could supervise. As small banks were merged into larger by the 1890s to produce several giants, especially the four "D Banks" (Deutsche Bank, Diskonto Gesellschaft, Dresdener Bank, and Darmstädter Bank), bankers were able to encourage the formation of trusts in industrial production, especially in those large-scale operations such as mining and engineering where great capital investment was required. Trusts were supplemented by the great cartels, which claimed to maintain stability of production and employment by their rigid supervision of prices and markets. Between 1871 and the First World War, coal production rose from 30 million tons to 191 million, steel production from almost nothing to 13 million tons. Moreover the average German had profited personally from this growth. Real per capita income had risen from 352 marks a year to 728, a remarkable achievement in view of the increase in population. This vast economic growth was the foundation for the growth of Berlin; and it was the awareness of the power of this newly acquired wealth that inspired much of the rhetoric of Berlin, both official and unofficial, in the years before the war.

Berlin's mood was satirized as early as the 1870s by an English visitor, who found *Berlin wird Weltstadt* ("Berlin will be a world city") on everyone's lips. The orators of the beer halls, he wrote, were boasting:

We have vanquished the modern Babylon. . . . Paris is at our feet like the dragon beneath the lance of St. George. She was the capital of the world; she is fallen. Berlin will take her place. The mode of Paris will become that of Berlin. . . . We will inundate the world with Moltke cravats, and Bismarck collars, manufactured in Berlin. The products of Paris and Vienna are condemned for the future. We have already 800,000 inhabitants, next year we shall have 900,000, and the year after that a million. We have outdistanced St. Petersburg and Vienna, we shall soon pass before Constantinople, then Paris, and afterwards commence to compete with London.[4]

Bismarck and the Creation of a Political Capital

Economic power gravitated naturally toward political power; and Bismarck had determined that political power should be concentrated in Berlin. He had been forced to make numerous concessions to persuade the rulers of South Germany freely to join a united Germany; the separate states of the federal union ran their own law courts, police, education, and most fiscal matters, and in time of peace the South German states controlled their own armies. But the central government ran foreign affairs, the navy and the wartime army, customs, and colonies. And Bismarck had ensured above all that Prussia, and specifically its king and chancellor, should control the central government. The king of Prussia was the hereditary emperor. In the upper house, or Bundesrat, Prussia had seventeen out of the

[4]Henry Vizetelly, *Berlin Under the New Empire*, vol. 1 (London: Tinsley, 1879), pp. 164–165.

fifty-eight seats. The lower house, or Reichstag, elected by universal manhood suffrage, appeared to be a genuine legislative body. However, it had no power over foreign policy, could not force the resignation of the chancellor, and was able to influence the military only through its control of the budget. Most power lay in the hands of the imperial chancellor, appointed by the emperor and dismissible only by him. Bismarck had thus created a constitutional structure in which he himself appeared indispensable, except for the seemingly remote chance of his dismissal on the whim of an emperor.

Bismarck proposed to run this constitutional system by playing one element within the Reichstag against another. In the Reichstag elected in 1871, he allied with the Free Conservatives, who were supported by the industrialists, the financiers, and the great non-Prussian landowners, and with the National Liberals, who represented the interests of the professional and industrial middle classes. To please them, he introduced a program of measures geared to economic unification of the new German state, including internal free trade and a uniform coinage, and began a campaign known as the *Kulturkampf* ("the culture struggle") to reduce the powers of the Catholic Church in Germany. His repressive measures only created vast opposition in the Catholic South, and the Catholic Center party grew in number of deputies from sixty-three in 1871 to one hundred six in 1890. Bismarck thereupon changed course abruptly, allying with the Catholic Center party and with the Conservative party, which represented the Prussian landowning classes. In 1875, in place of the liberal economics he had previously backed, he embarked on a policy of protection through high tariffs on industrial and agricultural goods. Fearing that the resulting high prices would drive the working classes into the arms of the Social Democratic party, he decided to use both force and persuasion to win over the workers. After the election of 1877, in which the Socialists received almost half a million votes and elected twelve deputies to the Reichstag, Bismarck used the pretext of two assassination attempts on the emperor (neither of which was carried out by a Socialist) to ban the party. Many of its leaders went into exile, its newspapers were suppressed, and all Socialist meetings were forbidden. Yet Socialists were still permitted to run for election to the Reichstag; and the Socialist vote increased continually during the 1880s. The chancellor therefore tried to win the workers over to his paternalistic state by passing a program of state socialism. Between 1883 and 1889 he gave Germany some of the most advanced welfare legislation in the world, including sickness insurance, accident insurance, and old age and disability insurance. Nevertheless, when the Reichstag allowed the anti-Socialist law to lapse in 1890, the Social Democratic party received 1.4 million votes. In 1903, with 3 million votes, it received almost twice as many as the second most popular party, the Center, even though it received fewer seats in the Reichstag. Finally, in 1912, with a popular vote of 4.2 million, it became the largest party in the Reichstag, with one hundred ten seats.

William I (Reigned as King of Prussia 1861–1888 and as German Emperor, 1871–1888)
(Courtesy of the German Information Center)

Bismarck and the Socialist Jack-in-the-Box

Although German chancellor Bismarck had the Social Democratic party banned in 1878, the voters continued to elect socialists to the Reichstag. The ban expired in 1890. (Punch, Sept. 28, 1878)

The effect of Bismarck's policies was to harm German democracy. The weakness of the Reichstag brought it into disrepute with the people at large and ensured that few first-rate men would seek election to it. Moreover, Bismarck's personal control of executive power had a similar effect on recruitment to the highest ranks of government. Bismarck had made Berlin the political capital, but he had so restricted the exercise of political power that large numbers of Germans thought of themselves as unpolitical. "Bismarck has broken the nation's backbone," wrote the Liberal historian Theodor Mommsen. "The injury done by the Bismarck era is infinitely greater than its benefits. . . . The subjugation of the German personality, of the German mind, was a misfortune that cannot be undone."

Bismarck's Diplomacy, 1871–1890

After the defeat of France, Bismarck became the foremost proponent of the maintenance of the status quo in Europe. His principles for running European diplomacy were simple and realistic, based on Realpolitik, or the clear-headed calculation of relative positions of power. Germany, he told Europe's uneasy governments, was a "satiated" power. The new German state, he implied, had no intention of seeking the incorporation within it of the Germans living in any other European states. Germany's role as the greatest economic and military power on the continent was to dominate the structure of alliances by which the major states assured themselves of military backing in the event of war. There were only five powers that Bismarck considered important: Germany, Russia, Austria-Hungary, France, and Britain. Germany must therefore always be "one of three on the European chessboard"; and it must try, as a subsidiary goal, to prevent the remaining two from allying. One of those two would inevitably be France, which was smarting not only over its defeat but also over the German annexation of Alsace-Lorraine, which Bismarck was slowly coming to see as a mistake. France must therefore be isolated at all costs.

The most natural alliance appeared to be between the three authoritarian emperors of central and eastern Europe. In 1872, the suspicious tsar intimated to Bismarck that he would like to be invited to Berlin during the state visit of the emperor Francis Joseph of Austria. The city was thus able to give a first demonstration of its ceremonial function as Europe's new arbiter. The monarchs feasted in the royal palace, enjoyed a ballet in the opera house, and heard an open-air concert in Unter den Linden. Military display predominated, some of it theatrical—the German emperor wore an Austrian uniform with a Russian scarf, and his son a Russian uniform with an Austrian medal—but most of all it taught the lesson of German might, especially in the parade of the regiments that had defeated Austria in 1866. The Three Emperors League was duly concluded the next year as an agreement to put down internal subversion and to consult on problems in Europe.

The Congress of Berlin in 1878 was a more effective demonstration of Germany's new prestige in international affairs. During the previous year, the Russians had defeated the Turks, ostensibly in support both of the independent Slavic states of Serbia and Montenegro and the Greek Orthodox Bulgars, who were under Turkish rule. Although the Russians were stopped before they could take Constantinople, which appeared their main goal, they imposed crushing peace terms that forced Turkey to recognize the creation of a large Bulgarian state and to cede other territories to Russia and its allies. To Austria-Hungary this settlement imposed a threat to its own ambitions to expand in the Balkans, and to Britain it was a dangerous disturbance of the balance of power. Fearful of the possibility of war between Austria-Hungary and Russia, and convinced, he said, that the Balkans were not worth the bones of a single Pomeranian grenadier, Bismarck invited the powers to meet in Berlin, with the chancellor himself in the position of an "honest broker."

For the city of Berlin, the Congress of 1878 had much the same distinction the Congress of 1815 had for Vienna, or the Congress of 1856, which ended the Crimean War, for Paris: it recognized the central position of Germany in the international system. Bismarck dominated the negotiations and in many ways dictated the terms of the final settlement. Moody, sick, and bloated, he appeared to many a man unnecessarily petulant and outspoken; he provoked considerable resentment, especially from the Russians, whom he compelled to give up many acquisitions and to settle for the creation of a much smaller Bulgarian state. The Austrians were conciliated somewhat with the administration of Bosnia and Herzegovina, which Serbia had hoped to annex. The British were handed Cyprus because it was on the route to the Suez Canal. The French, whom Bismarck openly courted at the congress, were encouraged to move into Tunisia, which would bring them into conflict with the Italians and divert them from Europe.

From the high point of his diplomatic influence in 1878, Bismarck's strategy went rapidly downhill. Although he continued to seek an alliance with the Russians, as in the Reinsurance Treaty of 1887, he had decided to base Germany's security on a secret alliance with Austria, signed in 1879, and on the German army, which was expanded in 1873, 1880, and especially in 1887, when the standing army was increased to almost half a million men. With his policy predicated on a possible conflict with Russia and a certain confrontation with France, he made the mistake of·agreeing to go along with the demand of some sections of the commercial classes for a share in the colonial world. Inevitably this move into Africa and the South Pacific would bring Germany into conflict with Britain and would drive the German government eventually to challenge Britain on the seas. Bismarck thus invited the formation of the anti-German alliance he most feared—France, Russia, and Britain—which occurred in 1907.

Bismarck had long expected that the son of William I, Crown Prince Frederick, would eventually appoint a chancellor of a different political caste from himself. But when William I died in 1888, his son was already struck by cancer and ruled for only ninety-one days. He was succeeded by his son, William II, whose grossly inflated sense of his own abilities gave him the courage to dismiss Bismarck in March 1890. That night at dinner, Bismarck declared that William II was "the man who will certainly ruin the Empire."

THE SCHIZOID BERLIN OF WILLIAM II

Under the reign of the new Kaiser, Berlin showed a divided personality, which was an exaggerated form of the character of the whole of the German Reich. During these years the intellectual and cultural life of the city achieved a kinship in quality and inventiveness with that of the other great Western capitals. But at the same time, the government of the Reich remained under the influence of the military, whose massive forces were placed at the disposal of an irresponsible emperor and mediocre politicians. Under Bismarck there had been little of this schizophrenia. Berlin had remained the somber, hard-working, disciplined city it had been as capital of Prussia; and its imperial dignity had done little to improve the quality of its intellectual life. Under William II, however, the question could be seriously raised: which was the real Berlin—the Berlin of Albert Einstein and Max Planck, of Gerhart Hauptmann and Stefan

George, of Max Reinhardt and Oskar Kokoschka? Or was it the Berlin of Admiral von Tirpitz, Count von Schlieffen, and General von Moltke?

Intellectual Liberation of Berlin

Official Berlin can take little credit for the city's intellectual achievements after 1890. William II himself had strong and decidedly unenlightened views on culture. He regarded himself the arbiter of taste, as he explained when he dedicated the Hohenzollern statues in the Siegesallee:

To us, the German people, ideals have become permanent possessions, whereas among other peoples they have been more or less lost. Only the German nation is left, and we are called upon to preserve, cultivate and continue these great ideals, and among those ideals is the duty to offer to the toiling classes the possibility of elevating themselves to the beautiful and of raising themselves above their ordinary thoughts. If art, as so frequently happens now, does nothing more than paint misery more ugly than it is, it sins against the German people.[5]

For that reason, when the judges wanted to bestow upon Gerhart Hauptmann the Schiller prize for his play *The Sunken Bell*, which unsparingly portrayed the misery of the working class, the Kaiser ordered instead that the award be given to the uncelebrated writer of a historical play. For him,

[5] Masur, *Imperial Berlin*, p. 211.

National Gallery, Berlin
Built in 1865–1876 in the form of a Corinthian temple to house the work of contemporary artists, the gallery suffered from the conservative taste of its directors. (Courtesy of the German Information Center)

historical plays were the great uplifter of the working class and could "inculcate respect for the highest traditions of the German Fatherland." He felt much the same about sculpture, as the Siegesallee showed. And in art he was an unabashed opponent of every modern tendency. The museum entrusted with the patronage of contemporary artists, the National Gallery, was so out of date that the more forward-looking artists seceded in 1898 and formed the *Sezession* group, whose Impressionist paintings were labeled by the Kaiser "art from the gutter." The break was thus official; artists and writers who refused the stultifying conservative standards of official art could expect no patronage from the court or the government.

Court interference was least effective in music because the break with tradition was led by the charismatic Richard Wagner. Wagner was certainly in harmony with the spirit of the Second Reich in his desire to bring the German people to a new spiritual and cultural rebirth based on a revival of its medieval legends and its folk spirit. But he remained the man who had taken part in the 1849 revolution in Dresden, a self-appointed prophet who felt that he had to tear down all the conventions of society. At the end of his greatest work, *The Ring of the Nibelungen*, he wrote lines, which he never set to music, that expressed his whole philosophy: "Not goods nor gold nor divine splendor; not house nor estate nor lordly pomp; not the treacherous covenant of gloomy treaties nor the hard law of hypocritical custom: blissful in lust and woe, love alone sets you free." The redeeming power of love that ignored all convention was to be celebrated again and again in his operas, most notably in *Tristan and Isolde*; but the anarchism implied was too strange a message for the Hohenzollern monarchy to accept.

In musical style, Wagner was even less conventional. He wrote first two operas (*Rienzi* and *The Flying Dutchman*) in the grand operatic tradition of Italy, followed by *Tannhaüser* in 1845 and *Lohengrin* in 1848, which took up the style of German Romantic opera. Then he invented a new art form, the *Gesamtkunstwerk* ("Total Work of Art"), which combined music, drama, poetry, and the visual arts in one overpowering experience intended to regenerate its audience. In the four operas that were to compose *The Ring* cycle, the characters of Germanic folk legend, Wotan, Siegfried, Brünnhilde, and the Walkyrie, became for him strange cosmic creatures protesting against his own age. In *The Ring* the gods have been mastered by chaos itself. "What I deeply loathe I give to thee as my heir, the futile splendor of the Divine: let thine envy greedily gnaw it up," Wotan howls to the Walkyrie. In technique, he explored new harmonies and rhythms, refusing to give his gift of melody full play but disciplining it to the demands of his musical drama. In 1864 Wagner found the fame and fortune that he considered his due, when the king of Bavaria became his patron and sponsored the building in Bayreuth of Wagner's own opera house, which was to be the shrine of the Wagner cult that soon spread over all Europe.

Wagner and Strauss

Richard Wagner (1813–1883) *Although Wagner never resided in Berlin, his operas were produced at the Royal Opera by the composer-conductors Giacomo Meyerbeer and Richard Strauss. (Courtesy of the German Information Center)*

The Prussian State Opera, Berlin

The opera was built in 1740–1743 as part of the monumental reconstruction on Unter den Linden begun by Frederick the Great in the early part of his reign. Although badly damaged during the Second World War, the structure has been renovated according to the original design of Frederick's architect, Knobelsdorff. (Courtesy of the German Information Center)

In Berlin, acceptance of Wagner was slow, however, in coming. Audiences jeered at his opera *The Mastersingers* in 1870. But in the battle between the followers of Brahms and Wagner that convulsed the Berlin music world in the 1870s, Wagner finally triumphed. His acceptance opened the way for Richard Strauss, in spite of the Kaiser's profound disapproval of his musical style and his operatic plots. As director of the Royal Opera orchestra, Strauss was able to modernize programs, bringing in the music of Mahler and Berlioz; and he was even able to present his own operas after they had been tried out in the more liberal atmosphere of Dresden. Even then, he had to make compromises to meet the demands of the Kaiser. To produce the sultry, erotic scenes of *Salome*, with its dance of the seven veils and the final aria of Salome to the severed head of John the Baptist, he had to permit the star of Bethlehem to illuminate the night sky as reassurance to the Kaiser's wife. Even then the Kaiser was heard to remark after the performance, "That's a nice snake I've reared in my bosom." And the charming *Rosenkavalier* had to be modified to make the buffoonery of Baron Ochs acceptable to the court.

Max Reinhardt and the Free Stage

In the drama Berlin was able to surge ahead more quickly because the Kaiser's interference was minimal. The middle classes, and especially the large Jewish population of Berlin, felt the need for the presentation of modern drama of the highest quality and saw the opportunity in the lightening of the censorship and licensing laws that followed unification. The result was the Free Stage movement, which built its own theater and presented a new form of Naturalist drama, of which the plays of Gerhart Hauptmann were the best examples. His play *The Weavers*, with its harsh representation of conditions of the Silesian poor, brought the Socialist laborers into the audience and so shocked the Kaiser that he had the imperial arms removed from the theater after it had the effrontery to present the play. The Free Stage's forward-looking impetus was further increased by the appointment of the great young director Max Reinhardt, who gave Berlin Wilde's *Salome*, Ibsen's *Ghosts*, and a host of other plays by such modern dramatists as Wedekind, Gogol, and Schnitzler. Reinhardt set the fashion, and by 1900 almost thirty theaters had been founded to meet the Berliners' thirst for serious drama. Even before 1914 Berlin had become one of the most creative theatrical centers of Europe, to which, after the four-year madness of the World War, Germany's brightest minds would instinctively gravitate. The Berlin of 1920 characterized by the playwright Carl Zuckmayer is recognizably the same Berlin as that of the last years of the Second Reich:

This city devoured talents and human energies with a ravenous appetite, grinding them small, digesting them or rapidly spitting them out again. It sucked into itself with hurricane force all the ambitious in Germany, the true and the false, the nonentities and the prize winners, and, after it had swallowed them, ignored them. . . .

We called her proud, snobbish, nouveau riche, uncultured, crude. But secretly everyone looked upon her as the goal of their desires. Some saw her as hefty, full-breasted, in lace underwear, others as a mere wisp of a thing, with boyish legs, in black silk stockings. The daring saw both aspects, and her very reputation for cruelty made them the more aggressive. All wanted to have her; she enticed all; and her first reaction was to slam the door in the face of every suitor. . . . [The best minds] encountered her scepticism, her skittishness and disdain; usually they were rudely rejected several times before they could make good their claim to her attentions.

But once they had done so, their triumph might be absolute. To conquer Berlin was to conquer the world. [6]

[6]Carl Zuckmayer, *A Part of Myself*, trans. Richard and Clara Winston (New York: Harcourt Brace Jovanovich, 1970), p. 217.

March of the Weavers, by Käthe Kollwitz (1867–1945) *Kollwitz used her deeply compassionate art to champion the poor and the oppressed. She first became known for her illustrations to Gerhardt Hauptmann's tragedy of life among the workers in Silesia, called* The Weavers. *(Collection of The Grunwald Center for the Graphic Arts, UCLA)*

Expressionism

For poets and painters, the imperial city exercised the same attraction. Their most memorable movement was Expressionism, a name applied to the form that tried to go beyond the surface explored by the Impressionists or Naturalists to a deeper psychological reality. In a sense, such great German poets as Stefan George and Rainer Maria Rilke were part of this movement, but they were only infrequent visitors in Berlin and preferred Paris or Munich. Others stayed, however, finding in the bleakness of the northern city a suitable setting for the anguish with contemporary society that they tried to express. The poem *The War*, for example, written by Georg Heym in 1912, saw in the cities of the West the prowling figure of the coming catastrophe:

> *Resurrected is he from ancient sleep,*
> *Risen once more from the vaulted deep,*
> *Tall and unknown in the twilight he stands*
> *And he pulps the moon in his two black hands.*
>
> *For through the cities, evening noises wade*
> *The stranger's dark presence and his frosty shade—*
> *And all the whirling markets stiffen to ice.*
> *All's quiet. Each looks around and no man knows....*
>
> *A city went under in that yellow smoke*
> *Jumped into the abyss and never spoke ...*
> *But giant-like above the glowing ruins*
> *He stands who thrice his bright torch turns*
>
> *Above the ragged clouds' storm-scattered light*
> *Towards the icy wilderness of the night*
> *And sets the darkness blazing like a witch*
> *Above Gomorrah's sea of burning pitch.*[7]

The painters, too, tried to express the alienation of the artist in the city, seeking new techniques to show the suffering of the city poor, the loneliness of the night streets, and the savagery of the new industrialism. Already by 1914, Berlin was viewing the first works of the leaders of the avant-garde in the interwar years, among others Oskar Kokoschka and Käthe Kollwitz, whose illustration *The Weavers* was denied the gold medal awarded it by the jury because her style displeased the Kaiser's court.

University of Berlin

Deeply traditional, hierarchical, and conservative, the University of Berlin nevertheless made a great contribution to Berlin's intellectual life. In physics in particular, with Planck and Einstein, it could lay claim to leadership of the new research. In economics it had Werner Sombart, an outspoken critic of modern capitalism whose social conscience had failed to keep up with its productive advances. In philosophy there was Wilhelm Dilthey, who taught that ideas had to be studied as the expression of a particular

[7]Cited in Mander, *Berlin: The Eagle and the Bear*, p. 113.

historical situation rather than in the abstract. It was, however, the historians who were most responsible for Germanophilism, enshrining the Germanic state as the highest fulfillment that could be achieved by the combined efforts of German individuals. The great historian Leopold von Ranke, professor of European history at Berlin from 1825, had already taught the importance of the state as "a living thing, an individual, a unique self" and politics as "the field of power and of foreign affairs." From here his many disciples had carried the emphasis on state power to imply a justification of the extension of the controls of the Prussian state, and had seen their duty as historians to attempt to influence the political process in that direction. Heinrich von Treitschke's annual course on politics proclaimed the need of the state for increasing its power, if necessary by military action. The ultimate expression of this view came during the World War, when Otto von Gierke, one of Berlin's leading legal historians, wrote in *The German Folk Spirit in the War*, "If we achieve our war aims, the triumph of our arms will bring about the triumph of the truth. For in world history success utters the decisive word. Even those formerly incapable of being taught this will now realize that success in war is not an accident, but rather the outcome of eternal laws, in which God's rule reveals itself." In this way the intellectuals gave an ideological justification, which the middle classes and, in 1914, even the working classes accepted, for the predominance in the new Germany of the Prussian military tradition and of its upholders, the Junkers.

Even in the vast new industrialized Berlin the military were ubiquitous. **The Barracks City** The Kaiser set the example, for nothing pleased him more than to wear a uniform from his large collection. He appeared at a dinner of the Berlin Motor Club wearing the uniform of a general of engineers, and rumor had it he dressed as an admiral for a performance of *The Flying Dutchman*. But his favorite was a cuirassier's outfit, with polished breastplate and helmet topped with a golden eagle. His language reflected the same preoccupation with military accouterments and frequently proved a diplomatic embarrassment to his country, as when he spoke of his mailed fist or of himself as a knight in shining armor. But at times his pronouncements had a more sinister ring: "In the present social confusion it may come about that I order you [army recruits] to shoot down your own relatives, brothers or parents, but even then you must follow my orders without a murmur." And again, "The only nations which have progressed and become great have been warring nations. Those which have not been ambitious and gone to war have been nothing." Army officers were compelled to appear always in uniform, except on those rare occasions when they might visit an art exhibit of which the Kaiser disapproved. Members of the bourgeoisie were encouraged to don uniforms themselves, since acceptance as an officer of the reserve smoothed their acceptance into society. The rest of the population was drafted into uniform by the conscription laws. With many exemptions, young men were drafted into the infantry

The Kaiser in Costume
(The Graphic, *September 21, 1907*)

for two years or the artillery for three, and then were kept in the first reserves until the age of thirty-nine and the second reserves until forty-five, during which time they were hammered into the military mold by career N.C.O.s, known as the *Feldwebel*.

"Berlin swarms with soldiers," wrote Henry Vizetelly. "Perhaps no other capital in Europe presents such a military aspect. Regiments sallying forth in spick and span brightness, or returning to barracks half-smothered in the dust or bespattered by the mud picked up during the morning's manoeuvres, orderlies mounted or on foot hurrying to and fro between the different ministries and public offices, squads in charge of waggons," all composed the permanent garrison of Berlin. In 1875 Vizetelly listed within the city limits two regiments of Grenadiers of the Guards, the First Foot Guards, the Fusiliers of the Guard, the Riflemen of the Guard, the Pioneers of the Guard, the railroad battalion, the Cuirassiers of the Guard, the First and Second Dragoons of the Guard, the Second Uhlans of the Guard, the Third Squadron of the Garde du Corps, and two regiments of field artillery. Their castellated barracks rose from the flat fields surrounding the city, giving substance to the saying that in northern Germany there were no cathedrals but only barracks and arsenals. But Berlin was also the central training point for the leaders of the German army. The Central Cadet School trained one-third of the officers in the Prussian service; specialized training was provided by the United Artillery and Engineer School; advanced scientific education was given to selected officers in the War Academy. But by far the most important of the army's buildings was the Red House, the group of red brick buildings on one side of the Königsplatz occupied since 1871 by the general staff. Behind the stone-dressed walls decorated with helmets, eagles, and mythological warriors, the strategy of the German army was planned, and the advice (and many critics would say the orders) of the army for the emperor prepared.

The power of the general staff derived from the German constitution, which gave the Reichstag control only over certain parts of financing and administration and made the commanders of the army and navy responsible directly to the emperor. William II was available for regular consultation more frequently to his military than to his civilian advisors, and the chief of the general staff saw him at least once a week. Not only was it the constitutional duty of the military representatives to explain their desired policies directly to the Kaiser, but his manner of work and his own need for constant flattery also made him receptive to all forms of backstairs influence. The military was influential in forcing the resignation of Chancellor Caprivi, who was a general himself; and during the chancellorship of Prince Hohenlohe, military intrigues led to the dismissal of a war minister, a foreign minister, and an interior minister. The army had become "a state within the state" and indeed seemed to be carrying on the long tradition summarized by an eighteenth-century historian that Prussia was not "a country that had an army, but an army that had a country which it used as a billeting area." Even Bismarck had great difficulties with the general staff, as when he attempted to force it to accept his doctrine of the political advantages of limited war; and after 1871 the assumption of the planners in the Red House was still that a short decisive war achieving total victory was the goal of military planning. From 1879, Moltke drew up annual plans for a double deployment against France and Russia; and as the French fortification lines along the frontier of Alsace-Lorraine grew stronger, the need to be ready for a decisive blow in the west became the general staff's preoccupation. At times they discussed the need of preventive war, of an attack on the French before they could gain strength for the war of revenge that the annexation of Alsace-Lorraine had made inevitable; and there was even talk of an attack on the Russians.

The general staff itself was expanded to meet the demands of its growing duties. From sixty-four officers in 1857, it grew to two hundred and thirty-nine when Moltke resigned in 1888. Its technical facilities multiplied. "In this vast factory," wrote a French observer, "war is prepared just like some chemical product; within these walls all the various directing

The German General Staff

strings that regulate the German army are made to meet in order to be under the control of one master-hand, so that the troops in fact scarcely march a step, explode a cartridge, or fire a cannon shot without orders from here, while not so much as a military gaiter button can be sewn on anywhere in Europe without a note being taken of it." Three geographical sections of the general staff studied the armies of possible enemies; a subsection studied foreign railroads; trigonometrical and topographical sections prepared detailed maps of areas of possible military operations; there was even a section for military history so that none of the lessons of past wars should be forgotten.

In 1899 Count Alfred von Schlieffen, a meticulous, proud, professional soldier of disastrously limited political vision, became chief of the general staff, and at once began to elaborate plans for the expected two-front war. Germany had the advantage, he wrote, "of lying between France and Russia and separating these allies. . . . Germany must strive, therefore, first, to strike down one of the allies while the other is kept occupied; but then, when the one antagonist is conquered, it must, by exploiting its railroads, bring a superiority of numbers to the other theater of war, which will also destroy the other enemy." He became convinced that Germany, to carry through this deceptively simple scheme, would have to deal with France first, and that this could only be achieved by invading it through neutral Belgium. The plan was complete by 1905. The war, according to Schlieffen, would begin with a two-pronged attack of German forces on France, the right wing that would pass across northern Belgium being seven times stronger than the left wing, which would engage the French in Alsace. In six weeks, in which every day's campaign was carefully orchestrated in advance, the French line would be broken and the major French armies encircled. The decisive victory would be followed by the transfer of the majority of German strength to the Russian front. Schlieffen assumed that the six Belgian divisions would not fight and that Britain would not enter the war to defend Belgium, dangerous miscalculations due to his lack of interest in political considerations. His successor at the general staff accepted the basic Schlieffen Plan but decided to modify it to strengthen the left flank at the expense of the right, a decision that may have prevented the German army in 1914 from achieving a decisive breakthrough.

By 1905, then, the role of the army in German politics had become a major threat to the peace of Europe. According to Gordon Craig, "Schlieffen and Moltke ["the younger," Schlieffen's successor and nephew of Field Marshall Helmuth von Moltke] devised, and imposed upon the German army, the most rigid operational plan which had ever been accepted by any modern army, and one, moreover, which had dangerous political implications which were never fully understood by the political leaders of the country or, for that matter, by the soldiers themselves."[8]

Count Alfred von Schlieffen (1833–1913)
As head of the general staff, Schlieffen prepared the plan for a lightning attack on France through neutral Belgium, which, with modifications, was used in 1914. (Courtesy of the German Information Center)

[8]Gordon Craig, *The Politics of the Prussian Army, 1640–1945* (New York: Oxford University Press, 1964), p. 256.

THE KAISER'S EBULLIENT RIDE TO ARMAGEDDON

After the defeat of France, Bismarck's somewhat unrealistic view of the European state system had envisaged Germany as a disinterested power, concentrating on safeguarding what it possessed and suppressing the tensions provoked by the quarrels of the other, less satisfied powers. The Triple Alliance of Germany, Austria-Hungary, and Italy, cemented in 1882 and backed by occasional renewals of the platonic friendship with Russia, had been the central strut of his diplomatic structure. But even before Bismarck had been forced from office, his basic assumption that Germany need not be a direct participant in the colonial disputes or in the struggle to profit from the weakness of the Turkish Empire had been jettisoned; and after 1890, Germany found itself centrally involved in almost all the major disputes in Europe and beyond.

Many internal forces were pushing the Berlin government to take a more active role in international affairs. The power of the army to influence policy, a direct result of the constitution, had been reinforced by the military predilections of the Kaiser himself, while the Reichstag's financial controls were exercised only once every seven years until 1893 and every five years thereafter. From 1898, when the Reichstag passed the first naval bill creating a war fleet, a new pressure group was created in Berlin. Under Navy Secretary Alfred von Tirpitz, the Ministry of the Navy, backed by such nationalist pressure groups as the Navy League, began to press for a more active role overseas. They found considerable public backing, especially as the middle classes considered the navy more democratic than the army; and this enthusiasm was fanned by an extensive program of public relations, in which Tirpitz sponsored lectures, organized public tours of the new ships, sent free pamphlets into the schools, and even paid for the writing of suitable novels about the navy. The program created prosperity for the shipbuilders of the great port cities like Hamburg and Bremen and was welcomed by the shipyard workers. In the Kaiser it had its greatest supporter. "Our future lies on the water," he declared. The program was of course a direct challenge to Great Britain—the second navy bill of 1900 envisaged a fleet of thirty-eight battleships, which according to Tirpitz's "risk theory" would be large enough to inflict such serious damage on the superior British fleet that it would never be attacked.

This fleet also seemed a necessary adjunct to the great merchant marine that was being constructed to enable Germany to find the export markets needed for its vast new industries. Between 1887 and 1912, German exports had risen 185 percent, German imports by 243 percent. Here was an unfavorable trade balance that had to be rectified. Moreover, the great German banks and the new trusts were vitally interested in expanding their opportunities overseas and in the developing regions of Europe. These economic forces formed a further pressure group in Berlin that sought more effective governmental foreign involvement. The close fusion of the aims of industrialists and politicians was achieved in the years after

1900. The construction of the Berlin-to-Baghdad railroad, begun in 1899 and supported with great enthusiasm by the Kaiser, led even more directly to tension with Britain and Russia, when the Germans used it to exercise strong political controls over the Turkish Empire.

The drive for colonies was even more effective in isolating Germany. Germany had seized parts of eastern and southwestern Africa in the 1880s. In the 1890s it had turned to the South Pacific and acquired some Samoan islands, and had even attempted to establish a base in the Philippines. When the Germans finally took a Chinese port for themselves in 1897, the Kaiser exalted the occasion with one of his most blustering speeches, since the "Yellow Peril" to Europe was one of his constant fears. "Thousands of German Christians will breathe again when they see the ships of the German navy in their vicinity," he said. "Hundreds of German merchants will shout with joy in the knowledge that the German Empire has at long last set foot firmly in Asia, hundreds of thousands of Chinese will shiver if they feel the iron fist of the German Empire lying firmly on their back."

There was thus in existence a tacit coalition of the Kaiser, army and navy officials, and great business firms and banks, supported to a large extent by the middle classes and even some sections of the working class, which felt that Germany's material interests were involved in a successful resolution of almost all the important international crises. This does not imply that Germany plotted the First World War, or was solely responsible for its outbreak. What it does suggest is that Germany would not exercise a restraining influence when crises broke out.

Political Difficulties of the Third French Republic

Bismarck's greatest fear had been of the consummation of a Franco-Russian alliance, which finally occurred in 1894. Yet the internal political problems of both France and Russia in the half-century before 1914 seemed to make the possibility of significant international action by either of those countries unlikely.

The Third French Republic, which was slowly given a constitution during the decade of the 1870s in a piecemeal series of laws, was very unstable. In March 1871, the authority of the new government was challenged by a revolt in Paris. The city was seized by a coalition of extreme radicals, socialists, and anarchists, who declared Paris to be governed by its municipal council or Commune. Most workers in the city and large numbers of refugees supported the new regime; but the republican government withdrew the army from the city, and prepared, after the flight of many middle-class residents, to reconquer Paris by force. In vicious fighting in May, after the perpetration of many atrocities by both sides, the city was recaptured. Perhaps 20,000 of the city's defenders were shot, and later 40,000 were arrested. Thus the Third Republic began ominously, with a military subjugation of the working class of its capital city by an army representing largely the bourgeois section of the population.

The republic was probably saved in the 1870s only by the inability of the monarchists to agree on a candidate for a restored throne. Continual disagreements between supporters of a Bourbon, an Orleanist, and a Bonaparte claimant paralyzed the monarchists, and left the republic in existence by default. The party system that developed after 1875 had many failings, however. On the extreme right there remained a group of conservatives still opposed to the very existence of the republic. In the 1880s, as their monarchical hopes faded for lack of a suitable pretender, they turned in some desperation to the ideal of a soldier-savior, a man on horseback; but their candidate for installation in power through a coup d'état, General Boulanger, turned out to be an adventurer without backbone. After a brief flurry of support for him had been fomented by the right-wing forces in 1887–1889, he fled the country for fear of government reprisal. Power devolved upon a coalition of center parties, known in the 1880s as the Opportunists and in the 1890s as the Moderates. These groups failed to achieve governmental stability; and the constant changes of personnel in the ministries and the frequent overthrow of governments prevented the establishment of long-term reforms. Indeed, the Opportunists and Moderates devoted an excessive effort to attacking the Catholic Church, which was disestablished in 1905, and too little to dealing with necessary social reform. Their reputation was tarnished by frequent revelations of financial improprieties on the part of high government officials. As a result, radical groups on the left increased in strength, and some social reform was finally enacted. In 1903 a law enforcing health standards in factories was finally passed; in 1906 employers were compelled to give workers a day of rest each week; and in 1911 old age pensions were enacted. This belated legislation was due in part to the successes of the French Socialist party at the polls, and to the lash of the oratory of its leader Jean Jaurès. Although the Socialists did not participate in a cabinet until 1936, their pressure was felt in a salutary way through the first third of the twentieth century.

The most disruptive scandal of the Third Republic was however the Dreyfus affair, which split the whole of French society into two irreconcilable factions for almost twenty years. Dreyfus, the only Jewish officer on the French general staff, was convicted of selling French military secrets to the Germans, and even though he protested his innocence, he was sent to Devil's Island. Leading intellectuals were finally convinced by evidence brought by Dreyfus's brother and a few officers that Dreyfus had been convicted on forged evidence, and that the army because of its anti-Semitism had hushed up the affair. Eventually a coalition of center and left forces in French politics forced a reconsideration of the case, and in 1906 Dreyfus was found innocent. But the damage had been done in every sphere of French society. The painters Monet and Degas quarreled and never spoke again. Writers like Barrès took public issue with Zola and Anatole France. A wave of anticlericalism broke against the Church for the part played by the Assumptionist fathers in accusing Dreyfus. Trust in the army was poisoned, as the full details of the case became known. For Proust, in whose novel the Dreyfus affair constantly recurs, the whole affair was irrational: "When we find systems of philosophy which contain the most truths dic-

Alfred Dreyfus (1859–1935)
In 1894 Dreyfus, a captain in the French army, was sentenced to life imprisonment on Devil's Island off the coast of French Guiana for allegedly releasing classified military information to the Germans. After years of fierce confrontation between pro- and anti-Dreyfus forces, whose numbers included some of France's most illustrious literary and political figures, Dreyfus was finally completely exonerated in 1906. (BBC Hulton Picture Library)

tated to their authors, in the last analysis, by reasons of sentiment, how are we to suppose that in a simple affair of politics, like the Dreyfus case, reasons of this order may not, unknown to the reasoner, have controlled his reason?"[9]

In view of this internal discord, it is hardly surprising that France failed to follow a consistent foreign policy in Europe. The one constant factor was the desire for the return of Alsace-Lorraine, but even that ceased to be worth a renewed war with Germany in the minds of most French people. Some politicians even suggested that France's best interests would be served by a reconciliation with Germany, while it embarked upon the expansion into Africa, Indochina, and the Pacific that marked its new imperialism in the 1870s and 1880s. Only in 1894 did the French conclude a military alliance with Russia; and for years it remained doubtful whether any serious commitment to support each other in time of war would be made by either power. Even the military understanding with Britain known as the Entente Cordiale of 1904 was of uncertain strategic value to France, since Britain's unwillingness to intervene militarily in continental Europe was widely recognized. Only after 1905, when the Germans thwarted the first French attempt to bring Morocco under France's control, did the French face up to the need for military preparedness that confrontation in Europe with the Triple Alliance would involve.

The Weakness of Imperial Russia

Russia's failure to match the rapid military modernization programs of the other European powers in the nineteenth century became obvious after its defeats in the Crimean War (1853–1856), which persuaded Tsar Alexander II (reigned 1855–1881) to embark on a broad program of reform within Russia. Elected local assemblies were set up. The law courts were modernized. The army was reorganized. And in 1861, in the Emancipation Proclamation, the Russian peasants were freed from serfdom to their landlords. Although they remained tied to their village community, they were given about half the land in communal ownership. They remained dissatisfied, however, with their lack of personal rights, the burden of payment for the land, and the denial to them of education and financial help. While some peasants rose to become prosperous, most were backward and occasionally on the edge of starvation, and often engaged in arson or murder against the rich landholders. Their condition led such populist groups as "Land and Freedom" in the 1870s to "go to the people," to help at the local level, while more impatient revolutionaries like the "People's Will" turned to assassination. After many attempts, they finally killed Alexander II in 1881. His successor Alexander III (reigned 1881–1894) returned to a policy of repression, with strict censorship, arrest and execution of revolutionaries, and reduction of the powers of the local assemblies. National and religious minorities such as the Catholic Poles and the Jews were persecuted. The one progressive step undertaken was the start of industrialization, through

[9]Proust, *Remembrance of Things Past*, V, 407.

Russian Peasants, 1901, from a Painting by D. K. Fendrikh
Before the Revolution, starving Russian peasants fled to the cities in search of a better way of life. (Novosti Press Agency [A. P. N.])

the aid of foreign capital, which, under the minister of finance Sergei Witte in 1892–1903, brought about a great expansion in Russian railroad construction and in coal and steel production. The effect of industrialization and of the urbanization that accompanied it, however, was to create yet another discontented group, the urban proletariat.

Opposition to the continuing policy of repression under Tsar Nicholas II (reigned 1894–1917) came to a climax when Russian defeats in a war with Japan in 1904–1905 demonstrated that Russian industrialization was far from being sufficiently advanced to enable Russia to overcome a much smaller country at the outer edges of its Asian territories. The constitutional freedoms grudgingly granted in 1905, in response to the pressures of workers, peasants, sailors, and the middle classes, were far from satisfactory for the masses of the people; and groups like the Social Revolutionaries, a new party of peasant populists dedicated to terrorism, and the two wings of the Social Democratic party, the Mensheviks and the Bolsheviks, continued to agitate for radical change. Russia was therefore a far from secure ally for the French in spite of the reinforcement in 1899 of their military pact of 1894; and Britain delayed until 1907 before entering into a tenuous agreement with the tsarist government. Nevertheless the Russians had drawn the French into their most important quarrel in Europe, their struggle to advance the interests of the independent Slavic states of the Balkans, especially Serbia, at the expense of the Turkish and of the Austro-Hungarian empires.

German ties to the disintegrating Austro-Hungarian Empire were eventually to turn a political crisis in the Balkans into a full-scale European war. The principal difficulties facing the government of the Austrian Empire after the repression of the revolutionary uprisings of 1848 were the continuing demands of liberals for greater self-government and the growing pressures from the non-German nationalities in the empire for greater autonomy. Both by inclination and education, Emperor Francis Joseph

The Breakdown of the Multinational Austro-Hungarian Empire

(reigned 1848–1917) was sharply opposed to compromises with either liberalism or nationalism. Throughout the 1850s he allowed the imperial cabinet dominated by the minister of the interior, Alexander Bach, to enforce a rigid policy of centralization. Bohemia and Hungary were punished for their revolutionary activity by being subjected to direct rule by the Viennese bureaucrats, who were known as "Bach's hussars"; both lost the right to self-government they had enjoyed before 1848. But this system of suppressing both liberalism and nationalism together was shaken by military defeat. In 1859 the Austrian army was defeated by the armies of France and Piedmont-Savoy in Lombardy, and the emperor was compelled to recognize the loss of Lombardy to Piedmont-Savoy. To win the support of the liberals, he then granted an imperial "Diploma," establishing an imperial parliament or *Reichsrat;* its members were chosen by provincial diets that were again permitted. As modified in 1861, however, the Diploma restricted power in the Reichsrat to the larger landlords and the richer urban classes. The Hungarians refused to cooperate with the system, demanding autonomy instead; and their example was soon followed by the Poles and Czechs. As a result the minimal power over legislation exercised by the Reichsrat (which had no control over the executive powers of the emperor) was wielded largely by the well-to-do German section of the population. In 1866, the empire suffered the shattering military defeat by Prussia and its allies at the Battle of Königgrätz and was compelled to acquiesce in Prussian absorption of most of northern and central Germany. In its weakened situation, the imperial government found it necessary to make a settlement with the largest national minority in the empire, the Magyars of Hungary.

By the *Ausgleich* or Compromise of 1867, the Austrian Empire was split into two parts and known henceforth as the Dual Monarchy of Austria-Hungary. Francis Joseph was to be emperor of Austria and king of Hungary, and through three imperial ministers, was to control the foreign affairs, armed forces, and finances of both sections of the empire. Vienna was to be the capital of the Austrian section of the empire, and Budapest of the Hungarian. In each city there was to be a bicameral parliament and a cabinet government, with control over internal affairs. In fact, the suffrage was so restricted that in Austria, the German one-third of the population ruled the other two-thirds, which was composed mainly of Poles, Czechs, Ruthenians, Italians, and Slovenes. In Hungary the Magyar half of the population ruled over increasingly turbulent minorities of South Slavs (Croats, Serbs, and Slovenes), Rumanians, and Ruthenians.

The Ausgleich did not succeed in either Hungary or Austria. In Hungary, many Magyars were still dissatisfied. The remaining followers of Louis Kossuth wanted complete independence under a republic. Both peasants and industrial workers of Magyar nationality felt that they were unrepresented by the Liberal party, which dominated the Hungarian parliament for the last thirty years of the nineteenth century. The non-Magyar groups were outraged at the manipulation of the suffrage, the Magyar domination of the civil service and the professions, and the Magyar influence in the elementary and secondary schools. The South Slavs in particular turned increasingly to their conationals outside the empire for support, seeing in the independent state of Serbia a potential ally.

In Austria the Ausgleich worked comparatively smoothly until 1879. Francis Joseph permitted the German liberals to introduce moderate constitutional reforms, confirming greater civil rights, restricting the power of the Catholic Church, and reforming the army. He even attempted a settlement of the Czech problem in 1871 by granting greater self-rule to Bohemia, but dropped the plans in face of German opposition. In 1879 he appointed Count Edward Taaffe as premier, after the liberals had opposed his foreign policy; and Taaffe proved extremely skillful in balancing concessions to the various national groups. In particular, he appeased the Czechs by increasing the use of the Czech language and by authorizing a Czech university in Prague. After the resignation of Taaffe in 1893, however, the system came under attack from German groups seeking closer ties with Germans outside Austria and greater power for themselves inside Austria; from the Young Czech movement demanding autonomy for Bohemia; and from the Social Democratic party, founded in 1888, that sought genuine social reform on behalf of the working classes. Parliamentary government broke down between 1893 and 1900, and Francis Joseph responded by legislating by decree and by nominating only civil servants to the cabinet. The adoption of universal suffrage in 1907 gave non-Germans a majority in the Reichsrat, split the chamber between conservative parties and the reforming Social Democrats, and merely increased the parliamentary confusion.

Thus, as Francis Joseph hung determinedly onto what he could save of the traditional powers and policies of the empire, the Dual Monarchy became an increasingly ramshackle construction that would simply collapse under the weight of the great European crises of 1905–1914.

The main breakdown in Bismarck's planning was the conclusion of the Franco-Russian alliance in 1894. Although the Kaiser had refused to renew the Reinsurance Treaty with Russia in 1890, he had warned his cousin Nicholas II of Russia of the dangers of allying with France: "Take my word for it, Nicky . . . the curse of God lies heavy on that nation. Heaven has imposed a sacred duty . . . on us Christian kings and emperors—to uphold the divine right of kings."

With the conclusion of the Entente Cordiale of 1904 between France and Britain and the pact of 1907 between Britain and Russia, Europe had been divided into two competing alliance systems. The German system seemed the weaker, since Italy had made it clear it would not fight against France; and the Austro-Hungarian Empire, if reliable as an ally, was more likely to be a source of provocation than an element in keeping peace. But the strength of the German army and economy seemed to the German government to outweigh these weaknesses; and in fact most statesmen in

International Crises and the Alliance Structures

Europe concluded that they had created a genuine balance of power that would be a guarantee of the peace on which continuance of the existing social structure depended. "Nations and Empires crowned with princes and potentates rose majestically on every side," wrote Winston Churchill, "lapped in the accumulated treasures of the long peace. All were fitted and fastened, it seemed securely, into an immense cantilever. The two mighty European systems faced each other glittering and clanking in their panoply, but with a tranquil gaze. A polite, discreet, pacific, and on the whole sincere diplomacy spread its web of connections over both. A sentence in a dispatch, an observation by an ambassador, a cryptic phrase in a parliament seemed sufficient to adjust from day to day the balance of the prodigious structure."[10] The balance made every crisis seem manageable, and thereby in itself contributed to the coming of war.

The system was tested in two important areas. The French, having followed Bismarck's invitation by moving eastward from Algeria into Tunisia in 1881, had begun in the 1900s to look westward as well, into Morocco. The British had agreed to give them a free hand; but in 1905, the Kaiser landed in Tangiers and emphasized that he recognized the Sultan as an "independent ruler," while the German government demanded that the French give up their plans for Morocco. German intervention forced the calling of an international conference at Algeciras in 1906, in which the Germans were supported only by Austria-Hungary and Morocco; and the French were given permission to take over the Moroccan police and to run the state bank, measures that were obviously preliminary to Morocco's becoming a French protectorate. The crisis had strengthened the Franco-British understanding without any corresponding gain to Germany. In 1911 the Germans precipitated a new crisis by sending their gunboat *Panther* to the Atlantic port of Agadir in protest against the French occupation of the Moroccan capital city of Fez. They were finally fobbed off with some small pieces of the Congo, and Morocco became a French protectorate. Throughout the crisis, however, the diplomats had been appalled that they all seemed to be threatening to wage a war that none of them wanted. To avoid such a situation again, all powers determined on greater armaments and on closer military coordination with their allies.

Meanwhile in the Balkans, Austria and Russia were moving closer to conflict. Since the Congress of Berlin in 1878, the Bulgarians had looked to the Russians to help them complete their national independence from the Turks; and the Serbs hoped for Russian aid in gaining control of Bosnia-Herzegovina, which the Austrians had just brought under their administration. Austria, on the other hand, feared all nationalist movements in that region, in part because it saw the area as the only region open to its territorial expansion but principally because it was afraid that the success of the South Slavs in creating a large nation-state under Serbia would sim-

---

[10] Winston S. Churchill, *The World Crisis* (New York: Scribners, 1924), p. 199.

ply encourage the subject nationalities within the Austro-Hungarian Empire to seek independence. Not only would Bosnia-Herzegovina and Slovenia join a South Slav state, but the Poles would pursue the recreation of Poland, and the Czechs and Ruthenians would seek one or more independent states; and the whole fragile structure of the Austro-Hungarian Empire would fall apart. Both Russia and Austria felt it essential to act quickly, since in 1908 a Young Turk revolution threatened them with the modernization and the reassertion of Turkish power. That year, the Russian foreign minister agreed to allow Austria to annex Bosnia-Herzegovina permanently in return for its agreement to Russian naval use of the straits through Turkey from the Black Sea to the Mediterranean. Austria annexed the provinces without warning, and the ensuing international protests were so great that the Russian foreign minister denied his agreement and dropped his demand for passage through the straits. The Serbs appealed to the Russians for help in an immediate war against Austria but were told to bide their time: "Your day of joy will come." But perhaps the deciding factor in the crisis had been the German decision to back up Austria, regardless of international opinion. The chancellor had even gone to the extent of dispatching an ultimatum to Russia demanding that it accept the annexation.

In 1912 a new Balkan crisis erupted when Serbia, Montenegro, Bulgaria, and Greece suddenly attacked Turkey in order to seize most of its remaining possessions in Europe; they were so successful that they had to be stopped from capturing Constantinople by intervention of the major powers. The victors then quarreled over the disposition of the spoils, and the greatest gainer, Bulgaria, was attacked in a second Balkan war by Serbia, Greece, Rumania, and Turkey. In August 1913, after Bulgaria had been thoroughly defeated, Serbia and Greece split Macedonia between them; Rumania expanded southward down the Black Sea coast; Albania was recognized as an independent state. The Balkan wars had caused further tension between Russia and Austria. The Germans had, however, persuaded Austria not to come to the aid of Bulgaria, while the English had pressed the Russians not to allow the Serbians to become too ambitious. But such restraint was achieved only with great difficulty, and from 1912 all the diplomats of the great powers became infected with a sense of the inevitability of war among them in the near future. The Kaiser was particularly gloomy about "the fight to the finish between the Slavs and the Germans," since the "Gauls" and the "Anglo-Saxons" would aid the Slavs. Foreboding over the possibility of war compelled the very powers that had urged restraint on their allies to make greater protestations of support lest the long-standing alliances fall apart on the very edge of the catastrophe. Thus, when the final crisis was precipitated in June 1914 by the murder of the heir to the Austrian throne at Serajevo in Bosnia by a terrorist trained in Serbia, the diplomats were more anxious to reassure their allies than to end the tension with their enemies.

Archduke Francis Ferdinand and His Wife Before Their Assassination, Serajevo, 1914

Francis Ferdinand, the heir to the Austrian throne, had married the Czech Sophie Chotek in 1900. Their assassination in Serajevo by a Bosnian terrorist trained in Serbia provoked the Austrian ultimatum to the Serbian government that precipitated the First World War. (H. Roger-Viollet)

The Serajevo Crisis

The murder provided an excuse for Austria to begin the preventive war it had long desired against Serbia, because it suspected, correctly as it turned out, that the murder had been planned at high levels of the Serbian government for fear that the reformer Francis Ferdinand would win the loyalty of the South Slavs inside the Austrian Empire. The military gained the upper hand in Vienna, persuading the government to issue so strong an ultimatum to the Serbian government that it could not accept it without losing its independence. When the ultimatum was rejected, the Austrian army bombarded Belgrade, secure in the knowledge that the Kaiser, with his chancellor's acquiescence, had agreed that war with Serbia was unavoidable and had promised German aid if Russia came to Serbia's aid.

During the next critical days, war between the great powers became inevitable because none of the governments, neither the monarchs nor the civilians, dared refuse the mobilization orders that their military staffs demanded. The Russian government ordered general mobilization on July 30, 1914, which in German eyes was tantamount to a declaration of war because it meant mobilization along the Russo-German border as well as along the Russo-Austrian frontier. The German government demanded that the Russians cancel their mobilization, and when no reply came declared war on Russia on August 1. The Germans also sent an ultimatum to France, demanding that France guarantee its neutrality in the coming fighting by handing over several border fortresses to Germany, which was refused. It was a greater surprise when the Belgian government refused to give German troops permission to pass across its territory. Nevertheless, on August 3, Germany declared war against France, and invaded Belgium according to the split-second timing of the Schlieffen Plan. The British, who had been hesitating, found the violation of Belgian neutrality sufficient reason for declaring war on Germany.

Thus Germany found itself involved in a war for which it would, when defeated, be held principally responsible by its victors. The debate over German responsibility has exercised historians since 1914; but several factors stand out. The international system, based on the maintenance of a balance of power among competing alliance systems, was far less stable than its creators believed. One reason for the instability was the misunderstanding of the nature of modern war, in which armies are supplied and transported by the products of industrialism; few diplomats or military planners conceived of a war lasting more than a few months. Hence all military planning assumed the need of short, strictly organized schedules of attack. But the decision to mobilize was virtually the equivalent of a declaration of full-scale war, and was regarded as such by a country's neighbors. There were even some leaders who argued that war was a social good that revived the creative spirits of jaundiced nations, as well as a necessary instrument in the struggle for existence among nations, which was the international equivalent of the Darwinian concept of evolution. Some diplomats, especially in England, may have lost control of events; but the most recent evidence seems to show that by 1914 most civilian diplomats had come to agree with their military leaders that their goals could only be achieved by war. In this respect, the blame for the war can be distributed rather impartially among all the belligerents.

It was perhaps out of a feeling of relief that the long-expected struggle had at last come that the war was greeted with jubilation in all the capital cities of the belligerent powers. The joyful reaction of the crowds in Berlin on July 31, when the Kaiser declared from the palace balcony that "the sword has been forced into our hand," was no different from that of the excited throngs in the streets of Paris and London. The mobilization order the next day filled Unter den Linden with cheering crowds and officers standing erect in their cars waving their handkerchiefs. The crowds sang "Now Thank We All Our God" in the Palace Square and roared for the Kaiser, who told them, "I know no parties any more. Only Germans." The Social Democrats, every one of whom the Kaiser had once declared to be "an enemy of the Empire and Fatherland," reciprocated by voting the war credits. Like clockwork, the men of military age in Berlin reported to their units, were issued uniforms and weapons, and within hours were sitting in railroad wagons moving westward. In the general staff building, the oiled machine hummed effectively, even though its chief, Moltke, had been in tears briefly when the Kaiser had cheerfully told him to abandon the attack on France and transfer the troops against Russia instead, only to rescind the order shortly after. The Kaiser himself, however, was far from optimistic. White, haggard, and exhausted, he saw that the encirclement of Germany had been achieved. "The world will be involved in the most terrible of wars," he lamented, "the ultimate aim of which is the ruin of

The Call to Arms, by Auguste Rodin (1840–1917) *(The Rodin Museum, Philadelphia)*

Germany." Two weeks later, he left Berlin for the army headquarters at Koblenz, to await the results of the Schlieffen Plan. "The Kaiser is never going to ride on a white horse with his paladins through the Brandenburg Gate as conqueror of the world," the industrialist Walther Rathenau remarked. "On the day he did so, history would have lost its meaning."

THE FIRST WORLD WAR

Failure of the Schlieffen Plan

In just over a month of fighting, two deeply disturbing features of the war were evident even to the generals who had unleashed the first campaigns: a quick victory was impossible, and the human and material losses incurred by industrializing the means of warfare were on a scale never before seen. The Schlieffen Plan had at first seemed to go according to schedule. Although the Belgians had declared war rather than allow the Germans passage across their borders, their great fortresses had not proved a major obstacle. The right wing had swung along the Channel coast to enter France on August 27 and at one time was within forty miles of Paris. But the British had supplied an unexpectedly large expeditionary force, which helped strengthen the French center; the Russians penetrated into East Prussia and thus compelled the Germans to detach part of their forces from the western to the eastern front; and the poor leadership of Moltke had allowed his two armies on the Belgian front to lose contact. The French commander Joffre seized his opportunity to counterattack, and threw in his reserve against the dangerously extended German line to the east of Paris. In the first Battle of the Marne, the Germans were forced to retreat to the line of the river Aisne, where they were able to establish a strong defense line. By November, when the winter rains began and operations literally bogged down, the war of rapid movement originally planned by the generals had turned into a slogging match between entrenched armies, disposed in double lines of ditches behind barbed wire barriers along a front that stretched all the way from the Channel coast to Switzerland. The lines would move but a few miles in the next four years.

This stalemate was the result of enormous losses on both sides. The British lost half of their professional soldiers in the defense of the city of Ypres. In only four days of fighting in the Battle of the Frontiers, the French army had suffered 140,000 casualties; in the first sixteen months, over 600,000 of their soldiers had been killed. German losses were on a similar scale, as army commanders threw in troops in senseless bayonet charges. At the fort of Liège, a Belgian officer related, the Germans "made no attempt at deploying but came on line after line, almost shoulder to shoulder, until as we shot them down, the fallen were heaped on top of each other in an awful barricade of dead and wounded that threatened to mask our guns." By the end of the Battle of the Marne, German casualties were 650,000. It was, however, in the trenches that the full horror of the

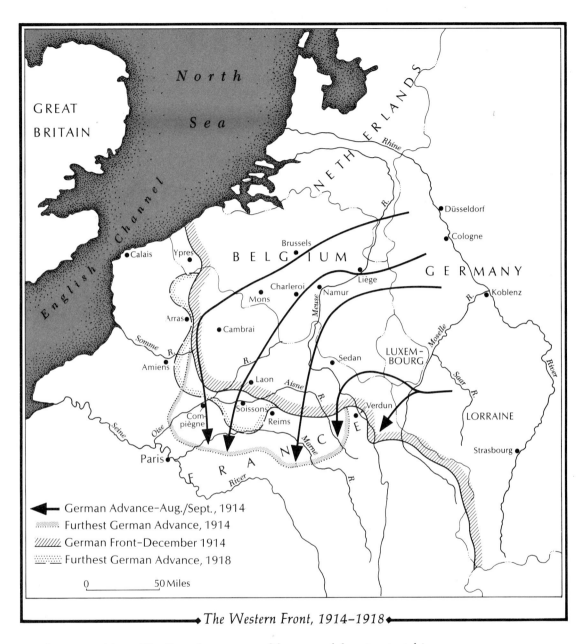

Map legend:

→ German Advance—Aug./Sept., 1914
▨ Furthest German Advance, 1914
▨ German Front—December 1914
▨ Furthest German Advance, 1918

0 ————— 50 Miles

◆ *The Western Front, 1914–1918* ◆

war became evident. The lines became steadily more elaborate, stretching miles back to the rear with communication trenches, dugouts, command posts, fortified bastions, machine gun nests, and camouflaged artillery. Normal military activity consisted of the exchange of rifle fire or the throwing of grenades, accompanied by planned artillery barrages. But at frequent intervals, the army commanders mounted massive assaults intended to drive back the enemy over a long salient, or less frequently, to establish a breakthrough in his line that would enable him to be attacked from the rear. Such attacks began at night with a long artillery barrage intended to blow away the enemy's barbed wire, flatten his front trenches, and destroy his morale. Then, at first light of dawn, the attacking army, usually carring heavy packs and fixed bayonets, would go "over the top" in long lines that walked slowly, in rapidly diminishing numbers, toward the enemy's trenches. Occasionally, poison gas would be hurled ahead of them, but it would often blow back into their own faces. No more vicious or militarily ineffective method of slaughter could have been imagined. Throughout 1915 the French mounted a "war of attrition," a series of attacks at different points of the German line that achieved nothing except punishing losses for both sides. In 1916 the Germans attempted to break the French line by capturing the pivotal fortress of Verdun; although they failed to capture it, they lost 336,000 men in the attempt. To the suffering of the fighting, the weather added a new element. As the bombardments destroyed the foliage and even the topsoil along the four-hundred-mile front, the rains turned the land surface into a kind of moonscape of muddy pools from which bodies protruded and in which men drowned. Disease was spread among the troops by rats and polluted food and drink. "We are not in fact leading the life of men at all," wrote one young soldier, "but that of animals living in holes in the ground and only showing our heads outside to fight and to feed."

Soldiers in Gas Masks
The horrors of trench warfare were compounded when the Germans used poison gas against the French in 1915. The French retaliated by using gas shells lobbed into German lines. Gas masks provided inadequate protection. (H. Roger-Viollet)

◆ *The Eastern Front, 1914–1918* ◆

The front in the East was more mobile, but the sufferings were no less great. The Kaiser had been appalled in 1914 when the Russian army had penetrated his "lovely Masurian lakes" in East Prussia, but a new team of generals, Hindenburg and Ludendorff, had driven the invaders back at the Battle of Tannenberg. The German armies had then been able to relieve

The War in the East

THE FIRST WORLD WAR

Field Marshal Paul von Hindenburg (1847–1934)
Hindenburg was made chief of the general staff in 1916, and assumed supreme command of the forces of Germany and its allies. (Courtesy of the German Information Center)

the Austrians at the southern end of the line by attacking in central Poland, and by the end of 1914 the front had been briefly stabilized on a long curving line from East Prussia to Lodz in central Poland and on to the Carpathian Mountains and the Black Sea. The next year, however, the Germans took command of the whole front and, mixing their divisions with Austria's far less reliable troops, hit the Russians in Galicia in May at a time when they were disorganized, hungry, and badly armed. Russian casualties by September, when the Russian army had been pushed back almost two hundred miles into Russia itself, were a million. Nevertheless, in 1916, even though the attempt by the British to seize the Dardanelles and Constantinople to open a direct route to Russia had failed, the Russians put together another vast army, with which they recouped many of their territorial losses. But the cost in lives and materiel of the 1916 campaign brought Russia to revolution the following March; and although Russia did not officially stop fighting until the Bolshevik revolution in November, its contribution to the Western allies during 1917 was not great. In March 1918, at the conclusion of the Treaty of Brest Litovsk with the new Bolshevik government of Russia, the Germans appeared to have won an enormous triumph by forcing Russia to give up Poland, the Baltic states, Finland, and the Ukraine, all of which became German satellite states.

Broadening of the War

The original combatants continually pressured other powers to join the war, as new means of breaking the balance of strength between them. Japan entered the war against Germany in 1914, simply to seize the German possessions in China and the Pacific. Turkey had entered the war on Germany's side at the end of 1914, as a consequence of the great economic influence Germany had come to exercise there before the war. Italy, which had denied that the Austrian attack on Serbia compelled it to enter the war under the obligations of the Triple Alliance, had succumbed to secret British offers of territorial compensation from Austria; in 1915, it entered the war on the side of the Entente, only to suffer dreadful losses in battles in the snows of the Italian Alps. The Bulgarians joined Germany and Austria in September 1915, to take a share in the disintegration of Serbia. The Rumanians joined the Entente in 1916 in the hopes of taking part of Hungary. But the most important new belligerent was the United States, which declared war on Germany in April 1917 after the Germans began unlimited submarine warfare against neutral ships entering the war zone around Britain. American supplies and in 1918 American soldiers were to be the decisive factors in blunting the last German offensives in the West.

The Last Campaigns

During the last months of the war in 1918, the stalemate in the West was broken and a war of movement again became possible. The introduction of the tank by the British finally rendered the trench lines penetrable. The use of the airplane not only made small-scale bombing possible but gave far more accurate reconnaissance information. Shock troops employed by the German high command were often able to break through the Western

Tanks on the Western Front, September 1918
The tank was first used by the British in 1916. Within a year, it had transformed the character of mechanized warfare by reintroducing mobility to the armies, whose approximate equality of firepower had led to the useless slaughter of trench fighting. (H. Roger-Viollet)

lines and cause havoc in selected areas in the rear. But the chief factor was Ludendorff's decision in the spring of 1918 to throw all Germany's remaining strength into one big effort to defeat France. For four months, from March to June 1918, Ludendorff struck without respite at different sections of the front, but one by one the blows were parried—by the French, the British, and the Americans. When in June the Germans tried once again to march down the Marne to Paris, they were thrown back; and all their fronts began to collapse at once, in Bulgaria, Turkey, Serbia, Italy, and along the whole Western front.

Berlin had seen little of the Kaiser during the years of war, since he had preferred to wander by royal train from one headquarters to another, rarely consulted by the military and largely protected from the realities of the front. Propaganda pictures of him were taken from time to time in a specially constructed trench in the park of his requisitioned villa at Spa; and he showed his continuing taste for bellicose rhetoric with such recommendations as "Take no prisoners" and "We know our goals, our rifles cocked and traitors to the wall." But he had become an increasingly unreal figure to Berliners, who were concerned with staying alive through the years of universal shortage. Such products as tea, coffee, and sugar slowly vanished. Ersatz, or substitute, supplies were made with great ingenuity—sausages from nuts, coffee from barley, soap from sand. In the harsh Turnip Winter of 1916, even potatoes were hard to obtain, and many people had to live on turnips. Clothes had to be constantly repaired because wool and cotton were unobtainable. From 1916, morale began to break, as the reports of the suffering at the front, of the apparently endless fighting, and of the incredible losses became widely known in spite of strict censorship. The reaction of the conservative groups, both military and business, was to demand national unity, which in fact became a method of avoiding democratization of power. In the Reichstag, the Socialist party had split in 1915 between the Majority Social Democrats, who favored continuance of the war but without annexationist goals, and the Independent Social Democrats, who opposed the war. In the summer of 1917, the Majority Social Democrats joined with moderate liberals from the Progressive and National-Liberal parties and with the Catholic Center in demanding a reconsideration of war aims and constitutional reform; and a majority of the Reichstag voted the Peace Resolution demanding a peace without annexations. These demands were ignored until the costly failure of the last great German offensive in France in 1918. The German military leaders recognized at that point that the war was lost. On October 3, Ludendorff informed the Kaiser that the German army could no longer go on fighting and that he should sue for peace. He also recommended that a new government should be formed that would represent the majority in the Reichstag. A liberal aristocrat, Prince Max of Baden, agreed to establish a new government that included the Progressive party, the Center party, and the Majority Social Democrats; and in the last weeks of October a number of constitutional changes increasing the power of the Reichstag were accepted. Negotiations were begun with the allies for an armistice, which was concluded on November 11.

On October 30, however, spontaneous uprisings began in the German navy and in the seaport towns. The immediate cause was the plan by insubordinate naval officers to sail the fleet, without central government instructions, for a probably suicidal attack on the British navy. Discontented crew members, already resentful of harsh discipline and poor living conditions, mutinied, and were joined by workers from the cities. Revolutionary committees of soldiers and workers were formed in Kiel and Wilhelmshaven, and their example was soon followed in many of the important cities of northern Germany. On November 8 Munich was seized by left-wing revolutionaries, and Bavaria was declared a separate republic. Within two weeks every one of the minor princes of Germany had been driven from his throne; and crowds of workers and soldiers began to fill the streets of Berlin itself. Officers were occasionally assaulted, and their epaulets removed. Red flags appeared on some buildings. On November 9, however, the Kaiser was forced to abdicate, and a new government formed by the Majority Social Democrats and the Independent Social Democrats. The abdication removed one important source of grievance of many of the workers, and the proclamation of a German republic under a Social Democratic chancellor, Friedrich Ebert, promised a new beginning. When a Communist revolt did break out in Berlin in January 1919, it was suppressed with considerable bloodshed by the Social Democratic minister of the army, Gustav Noske.

It was thus an ironic epilogue to the days of imperial Berlin that it was not the Kaiser but a Socialist who welcomed the return of the Berlin divisions on December 11 as they marched through the Brandenburg Gate to become a guarantee against social revolution. "I salute you," Chancellor Ebert shouted to the defeated army, "who return unvanquished from the field of battle." It was a remark worthy of the Kaiser himself.

Friedrich Ebert (1871–1925)
A trade union leader and Social Democratic deputy, Ebert became first President of the Weimar Republic in 1919. (Courtesy of the German Information Center)

SUGGESTED READING

Berlin is a city about which it is hard to be nostalgic, especially as so many of the imperial buildings were destroyed in the Second World War. But Gerhard Masur has painstakingly assembled the most salient information on the city's life under Bismarck and William II in *Imperial Berlin* (1971), while John Mander, *Berlin: The Eagle and the Bear* (1959) evokes the literary and artistic background. Observant visitors from abroad do much to give a feeling for Berlin society, especially the thorough, whimsical, and informative volumes of Henry Vizetelly, *Berlin Under the New Empire: Its Institutions, Inhabitants, Industry, Monuments, Museums, Social Life, Manners, and Amusements* (1879). Poulteney Bigelow, an American who lived much of his life in Prussia, has left *Prussian Memories, 1864–1914* (1915), and J. F. Dickie, pastor of the American Church, paints a sympathetic picture of the Kaiser in *In the Kaiser's Capital* (1912). For daily life, especially of the army, see Pierre Bertaux, *La Vie quotidienne en Allemagne au temps de Guillaume II en 1900* (1962). The musical life of the capital, seen through the career of Richard Strauss, is sardonically described by Barbara Tuchman in *The Proud Tower* (1962). Good novels that illustrate the life of Berlin include Theodor Fontane, *Effi Briest*, and Heinrich Mann, *Little Superman*. For memoirs of writers who spent part of their lives in Berlin, see Carl Zuckmayer, *A Part of Myself* (1970) and Stefan Zweig, *The World of Yesterday* (1943). A useful social analysis is provided in Ernest Bramsted, *Aristocracy and the Middle Classes in Germany: Social Types in German Literature, 1830–1900* (1964).

On the unification of Germany, the most reliable studies are Otto Pflanze, *Bismarck and the Development of Germany: The Period of Unification, 1815–1871* (1963); C. W. Clark, *Franz Josef and Bismarck: The Diplomacy of Austria Before the War of 1866* (1934); Eugene N. Anderson, *The Social and Political Conflict in Prussia, 1858–1864* (1954); and Erich Eyck, *Bismarck and the German Empire* (1958). Bismarck tells his own story, with considerable reliance on hindsight, in *Bismarck, the Man and Statesman* (1899), while Louis L. Snyder, *The Blood and Iron Chancellor: A Documentary-Biography of Otto von Bismarck* (1967) relies mostly on excerpts from primary accounts to create a biography. Finally, Werner Richter, *Bismarck* (1965) makes entertaining reading. J. Alden

Nichols, *Germany After Bismarck: The Caprivi Era, 1890–1894* (1958) shows the political struggles that followed the dismissal of Bismarck.

The best biography of William II is Michael Balfour's *The Kaiser and His Times* (1964). Virginia Cowles, *The Kaiser* (1963) concentrates largely on the man himself, thus permitting many of the Kaiser's outbursts to be compared with his later version of the events in *The Kaiser's Memoirs* (1922). The Kaiser is placed in the gallery of doomed monarchs in Edmond Taylor's well-documented *The Fall of the Dynasties: The Collapse of the Old Order, 1905–1922* (1963).

The role of the army in German politics is thoroughly elucidated in Gordon A. Craig, *The Politics of the Prussian Army, 1640–1945* (1964) and Walter Goerlitz, *History of the German General Staff, 1657–1945* (1953), while Hans Kohn, *The Mind of Germany: The Education of a Nation* (1958) demonstrates the power of Germanophilism as a support for militarism. The nationalism that arose from cultural crisis is studied by Fritz Stern, *The Politics of Cultural Despair: A Study in the Rise of the Germanic Ideology* (1965).

Good surveys of the Second Empire of Napoleon III are provided by J. P. T. Bury, *Napoleon III and the Second Empire* (1964) and J. M. Thompson, *Louis Napoleon and the Second Empire* (1954). The new political elite created by Napoleon III is analyzed in Theodore Zeldin, *The Political System of Napoleon III* (1958). The repression of opposition is detailed in Howard C. Payne, *The Police State of Louis Napoleon, 1851–1860* (1966). The contribution of the empire to French economic development is seen as part of a longer process in Tom Kemp, *Economic Forces in French History* (1971) and Charles P. Kindleberger, *Economic Growth in France and Britain, 1851–1950* (1964). The emperor's policies on behalf of the working class are weighed by David I. Kulstein, *Napoleon III and the Working Class* (1969). Delightful essays on aspects of life in Paris are centered on different figures in politics and culture in Roger L. Williams, *Gaslight and Shadow: The World of Napoleon III* (1957).

The best introduction to the politics of the Third Republic in France is David Thomson, *Democracy in France Since 1870* (1969), which can be supplemented with two surveys, D. W. Brogan's sparkling *France Under the Republic (1870–1939)* (1940) and Alfred Cobban, *A History of Modern France*, vol. 3 (1965). On right-wing groups, see René Rémond, *The Right Wing in France* (1966); on the Church, Adrien Dansette, *Religious History of Modern France* (1961) and John McManners, *Church and State in France, 1870–1914* (1972); on the army, Pierre de la Gorce, *The French Army: A Military–Political History* (1963). Recent evidence on the Dreyfus affair is presented in Douglas Johnson, *France and the Dreyfus Affair* (1967). Among many fine biographies are J. P. T. Bury, *Gambetta and the Making of the Third Republic* (1973) and Harvey Goldberg, *The Life of Jean Jaurès* (1962).

On the Austrian Empire in the reign of Francis Joseph, one could begin with the brief introduction by A. J. May, *The Habsburg Monarchy, 1867–1914* (1951). The problem of the minority nationalities is discussed at length and with great learning by R. A. Kann, *The Multinational Empire* (1950). J. Redlich, *Emperor Francis Joseph of Austria* (1929) is a pleasant but somewhat old-fashioned biography. For Vienna in the second half of the nineteenth century, one should turn again to Ilsa Barea, *Vienna* (1966).

The causes of World War I have been the subject of continual debates since 1914. A very full account of the principal events is given by Luigi Albertini, *The*

Origins of the War of 1914 (1952–1957), but Lawrence Lafore, *The Long Fuse: An Interpretation of the Origins of World War I* (1965) is more sparkling. The whole controversy over Germany's expansionist aims was reopened by Fritz Fischer, with *Germany's Aims in the First World War* (1967), which painstakingly shows that civilian as well as military leaders were obsessed with turning the war to the profit of Germany. The influence of the war on German society is discussed by Gerald D. Feldman, *Army Industry and Labor in Germany, 1914–1918* (1966), the front line graphically reconstructed by Barbara Tuchman, *The Guns of August* (1962) and Alistair Horne, *The Price of Glory: Verdun, 1916* (1963). Erich Maria Remarque's best novel, *All Quiet on the Western Front* (1970), first published in 1928, gains its authenticity from the author's own experiences, but one should contrast it with Ernst Jünger, *Storm of Steel* (1929) to understand the attraction some found in trench life. Paul Fusell shows how the First World War created a new sense of the reality of warfare, which had vitally important psychological consequences, in his *The Great War and Modern Memory* (1975).

28

THE MOSCOW OF LENIN AND STALIN

The incessant rumbling by day and night in the street outside our walls is as inseparable from the modern soul as the opening bars of an overture are inseparable from the curtain, as yet secret and dark, but already beginning to crimson in the glow of the footlights. The city [Moscow], incessantly moving and roaring outside our doors and windows, is an immense introduction to the life of each of us. It is in these terms that I should like to write about the city.—Posthumous notes of Yurii Andreievich Zhivago. From Boris Pasternak, Doctor Zhivago, *trans. Max Hayward and Manya Harari (New York: Pantheon, 1958), p. 489. Reprinted by permission of Pantheon Books, a Division of Random House, Inc., and William Collins Sons & Co., Ltd.*

On the night of March 9–10, 1918, Vladimir Ilyich Lenin, the chairman of the Council of People's Commissars, which had governed Russia since the successful Communist seizure of power the previous November, reversed Peter the Great's momentous decision to move the capital of Russia from Moscow to his new city of Saint Petersburg. Traveling secretly by train in fear of assassination attempts by political enemies from the Social Revolutionary party, the whole government was transferred back from the western outpost on the Neva to the heart of old Muscovy. Within a few weeks Lenin and his ministers were established in cramped, uncomfortable quarters in the old Court of Chancery Building in the Kremlin, where in symbolic austerity they planned the strategy of victory in the civil war then raging and the simultaneous transformation of Russian society.

There were many reasons for the move back to Moscow.

(Left Page) St. Basil's Cathedral *(Inge Morath/Magnum Photos)*; (Inset) Lenin and Stalin *(BBC Hulton Picture Library)*

Petrograd, as Saint Petersburg was renamed in 1914, was vulnerable to attack from Finland and Estonia.[1] The Communist leaders needed a central position from which to organize the defense of the territory they controlled against the White, or counterrevolutionary, forces. But Lenin was also aware that Moscow, for the great majority of Russians, had never ceased to be the true capital of a unified country. Saint Petersburg had represented the alien, Westernized veneer that differentiated the possessing classes from the masses. "We are good revolutionists," Lenin told them, "but I don't know why we should feel obligated to prove that we also stand on the heights of foreign culture."[2] The buildings of Moscow, and especially of the Kremlin, represented an older, truer Russia, "white and shining little mother Moscow"; and it was essential that Moscow should take the lead, and be the finest example, of the revolutionary change in Russian society that the new leaders were determined to bring about.

[1]Petrograd was renamed Leningrad on Lenin's death in 1924.
[2]David Shub, *Lenin* (Baltimore: Penguin, 1976), p. 377.

◆ The Moscow of Lenin and Stalin ◆

Period Surveyed	From the Revolution of March 1917 to the Second World War
Population	1.7 million (1917); 3.9 million (1935); 4.1 million (1939)
Area	30.8 square miles (1901); 88.0 square miles (1917); 337.7 square miles (1939)
Form of Government	Communism. Moscow capital of federal union (Union of Soviet Socialist Republics) and seat of Supreme Council of USSR and Presidium. Also capital of largest constituent republic. Policymaking by Communist party; Central Committee in Kremlin. Local government by Moscow City Council
Political Leaders	Lenin; Stalin; Trotsky; Kamenev; Zinoviev; Zhdanov
Economic Base	National bureaucracy. Textiles; light and heavy engineering; electrical industry; transportation
Intellectual Life	Theatrical productions (Meyerhold); cinema (Eisenstein); novel (Alexei Tolstoy, Ehrenburg, Pilnyak, Paustovsky, Sholokov); poetry (Pasternak, Mayakovsky)
Principal Buildings	Pre-1917: Kremlin; Monasteries (Novo-Devichy, Donskoi); St. Basil's Cathedral; Bolshoi Theater Post-1917: Moscow Cooperatives Building; Lenin Mausoleum; Subway; Council of Ministers Building; Lenin State Library
Public Entertainment	Theater (ballet, opera, symphony, drama, circus); Sports (swimming, skating, skiing, hiking, track, soccer)
Religion	Officially discouraged. Russian Orthodox, Jewish

In the brief isolation of his first-class compartment on the train journey to Moscow, Lenin wrote an essay, *The Principal Tasks of Our Time*, summarizing his views of the importance for humanity of the events of the previous weeks and of the changes he was about to introduce:

In our day the history of humanity has reached one of those immensely great and difficult turning points, of vast—and one may add without the least exaggeration of world-liberating—significance. . . . It has been given to Russia to have observed with clarity, and with extraordinary sharpness and anguish to have lived through, one of the most sudden turns of history, the turn which leads away from imperialism to the communist revolution. In a few days we utterly destroyed one of the most ancient, powerful, barbaric, and ferocious monarchies. . . . From one end of our immense country to the other we have seen the victorious and triumphal march of Bolshevism. We have raised up the lowest strata of the toiling masses, who were oppressed by Tsarism and the bourgeoisie, to freedom and independence. We have inaugurated and strengthened the Soviet Republic, a new

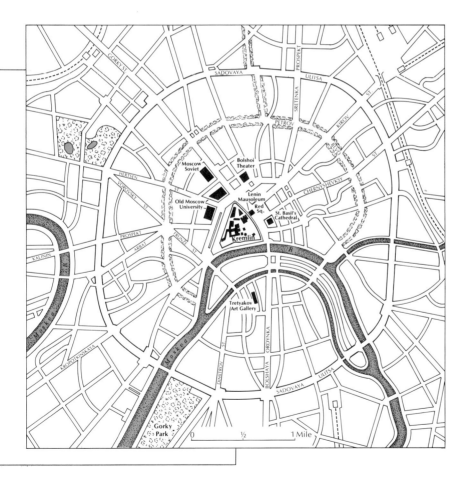

kind of stage, immeasurably superior and more democratic than the best of the bourgeois parliamentary republics.[3]

The fascination of Moscow's history during the twentieth century is thus not merely to see the rise of another world city, struggling with the problems of industrialism, mushrooming growth, and technological change, but also to see the experience of a great old city, steeped in a traditional culture, meeting the demands of a political and social experiment of unparalleled intensity. To study Moscow is to observe the Communist revolution at once from above and from below.

LENIN AND THE NOVEMBER REVOLUTION

Lenin and the Bolshevik Movement

The Russian Social Democratic Labor party had been founded in 1898 on strictly Marxist principles, largely because the political repression in Russia made the idea of a reforming Socialist party that would work within the existing political system ludicrous. Its leaders were compelled to live in exile in Switzerland, from which they smuggled their propaganda into Russia. When the party held its second congress in 1903, at first in a grubby flour mill in Brussels and later in stifling trade union halls in London, the expected harmony within the party was shattered by a long dispute over doctrine and tactics. A brilliant, self-confident young lawyer named Vladimir Ilyich Ulianov (1870–1924), who used the pseudonym Lenin, challenged the view of several older leaders of the party, that Russia would pass through a long capitalist phase in which the Socialists would collaborate with the bourgeois and that the Socialist party should broaden its membership as widely as possible in preparation for that phase. Lenin believed that the party must cut short the bourgeois phase of the revolution, and that to do so it must itself become an elite of disciplined, professional revolutionaries. On the crucial vote of whether the party should be limited, as Lenin proposed, to those who were active members of one of its organizations, or broadened to include those who gave "regular personal cooperation under the guidance of one of its organizations," Lenin won a two-vote majority. He immediately labeled his faction the Bolsheviks (or "majority") and his opponents the Mensheviks (or "minority"), politically useful labels even when they were no longer accurate. The congress thus left Lenin in undisputed control of one faction of a tiny party led by exiles; but from this position of political leverage he discovered the methods of gaining power. He wanted, Trotsky remarked later, not the "dictatorship of the proletariat" but "dictatorship over the proletariat." The future of the revolution in Russia would be the creation of one leader of political genius.

[3]Robert Payne, *The Life and Death of Lenin* (New York: Simon and Schuster, 1964), pp. 456–457.

Lenin and His Wife Nadezhda Krupskaya at Gorki, 1922
Krupskaya (1869–1939), an active revolutionary herself, married Lenin (1870–1924) in 1898. After his paralytic stroke in 1922, she acted on Lenin's behalf in party matters and quarreled with Stalin even before her husband died in 1924. She was especially influential in educational reform. (H. Roger-Viollet)

Lenin was the son of a school inspector from a town on the Volga. His elder brother was hanged for attempting to assassinate the tsar when Lenin was only sixteen; and embittered against the regime, Lenin himself joined a terrorist organization at the University of Kazan. He was expelled, but managed through independent study to get his law degree from the University of Saint Petersburg. He was, however, far more interested in theoretical Marxism than in law, and within four years he was arrested for trying to convert the workers of Russia to socialism. He spent three years in exile in Siberia and then in 1900 was permitted to go into exile in Switzerland. From his own experience with the Russian police, he was convinced that terrorist methods were useless; and from his attempts at propagandizing the masses, he had concluded that "by their own efforts the working class can only arrive at a trade union mentality." He was able to spread these views as editor of the party newspaper, *Iskra*, but in 1902 he poured his whole philosophy of revolution, in a bitter, sarcastic, visionary stream of ideas, into his finest book, *What Is to Be Done?* He dismissed democracy as the banner under which the workers are exploited and predatory wars fought. He lashed out at those who gave the revolutionary leaders advice without joining them, and he sketched his concept of the small revolutionary elite infiltrating all the levels of society from the postal services even to the police and the imperial court. But above all he proclaimed that the proletarian revolution would begin in Russia: "The destruction of the most powerful bulwark of European and (we may even say) of Asiatic reaction, would surely make the Russian proletariat the vanguard of the international proletarian revolution."

Such a prophecy seemed idle dreaming when Lenin wrote it. Russia was by far the most backward of all the big European countries. Peter's Westernization had not included any sharing of political responsibility; and at the end of the nineteenth century, political parties were still forbidden, and Russia possessed no central representative body. The only institutions

The Beginning of Russian Industrialization

where self-government was permitted were the *zemstvos*, or local government bodies, established in 1864, where the more liberal-minded among the aristocracy and the middle classes struggled to improve local economic conditions. Any attempt to move beyond such narrow tasks brought immediate intervention from the vast police force, whose informers were ubiquitous. The political immobility was reinforced by the resilience of the entrenched bureaucracy, a system of vested interests opposed to any change in the absolutist system and in particular to any form of popular accounting for its own actions. In spite of the fact that seventy-five percent of the population was still engaged in agriculture in 1914, operating under deplorable working and living conditions that the Emancipation Proclamation of 1861 had inadequately improved, the peasantry had failed to respond to either the idealism of the "Land and Freedom" movement or the terrorism of the "People's Will" in the 1880s or the Social Revolutionaries in the 1900s.

The beginning of industrialization in Russia in the 1890s vastly increased the need for, and made possible, political change. The building of railroads from the 1870s had provided a first stimulus to the iron industry, especially in the Donets basin; in the 1890s, concerned with the military need for rapid transportation to the west, the government had doubled railroad mileage. Textile production, which accounted for one-third of all Russian industrial output at the end of the century, was encouraged, as was the engineering industry, by the imposition of heavy tariffs on imports. Foreign capital and foreign industry were welcomed, especially in 1892–1903 when Count Witte was finance minister. Both the French government and private French investors poured money into Russia from the 1890s on, financing among other things the building of the Trans-Siberian railroad; and more than two hundred foreign companies began operations. The government also attempted to provide a labor force for the factories, two-fifths of which employed more than a thousand people, by making it easier for the peasant to leave his village community. Although many returned home for the harvest weeks, large numbers of peasants moved into the industrial cities, where they often lived in the factory itself or in barracks nearby. Their wages were so low that women and children were compelled to work also, and only in 1882 was the first law passed that restricted child labor. Russia, in short, was experiencing belatedly the rise of a proletariat and the largely unregulated expansion of its urban centers. It was among these groups that the Bolsheviks found their crucial support.

Capitalist Moscow

The main locations of Russian industry by 1900 were the coal and iron basin of the Donets, the oil region of Baku on the Caspian Sea, newer cities like Rostov-on-Don, and especially the suburbs of Saint Petersburg and Moscow. The rise of industry in Moscow compensated for its loss of political importance to Saint Petersburg, and throughout the second half of the nineteenth century Moscow's industrial growth paralleled that of its rival. Moscow had only 360,000 inhabitants in 1860, but this number had risen

Moscow Before the Reconstruction of the 1930s
In the middle distance the elaborate turrets of the Kremlin wall can be seen. Within are the bulbous domes of the Kremlin's four cathedrals. (National Archives)

to 1.7 million by 1917. While Saint Petersburg was the seaport and the heart of the shipbuilding industry, Moscow was the railroad hub and the main railroad engineering center. Saint Petersburg concentrated on foreign trade, Moscow on the home market. Saint Petersburg engaged in cotton spinning and making yarn, Moscow in the finishing of textiles. Moscow's central position in a region devoted largely to textile mills was somewhat similar to Manchester's; and Lenin himself pointed out that "if Russia is to be compared with west European industrial countries (as is often done here), then these countries should be compared with just this one area, for it alone has conditions approximately similar to those of the industrial capitalist countries."[4] The people of Moscow took pride in this expansion. In 1881, the playwright Ostrovsky noted that "Moscow's population is predominantly commercial and industrial. . . . Moscow is perpetually young, and is being continually rejuvenated; through it the great might of the people keeps surging into Russia. . . . Everyone who has brains and strength of character, everyone who has discarded the bast sandals and the homespun coat, strives to live in Moscow."[5]

There was, however, an important change in the social character of the city. The boyars, whose old ways Peter had determined to uproot, had been replaced by a new aristocracy of merchants, who bought up the old aristocratic homes or built new ones in wildly imaginative period revivals.

[4] Yuri Saushkin, *Moscow* (Moscow: Progress Publishers, 1966), p. 53.
[5] Ibid., pp. 53–54.

Winter in Moscow, 1912
The charm of prerevolutionary Moscow lay in the mingling of many different architectural styles, all softened by the winter sunshine and the falling snow. Scattered throughout the city, the monasteries were recognizable by their gently rounded domes and elaborate gateways. (H. Roger-Viollet)

Up to the 1850s Moscow had enjoyed a harmonious mixing of styles. For two centuries, from the building of the Kremlin in the late fifteenth century to the accession of Peter, it had been decorated with a wide variety of boyar homes and Orthodox churches, many of them colorful fantasies in a style called Moscow baroque, a whimsical composition of cupolas, octagonal steeples, false gables, and fantastic brickwork. In the eighteenth century this style gave way to a sober modification of the rococo palaces of contemporary France, and Russian rococo in its turn was superseded by a heavy Greek and Roman revival. But with the influx of the new capitalists from the surrounding cities, many of the older buildings in the city center were torn down to make way for new mansions in many different styles, such as neo-Byzantine, neo-Renaissance, and neo-Pskovian. The results are still startling, even after acquaintance with the oddities erected around London or Berlin; and the private mansions were far less exuberantly revivalist than the railroad stations, the polytechnical museums, the art galleries, or the hall for the city council. Moscow in short had adopted the appurtenances of all the great capitalist cities of the West, covering them with a thin veneer of motifs drawn from a conscientiously discovered past. The factories and the workers' barracks were relegated to the outer suburbs, well beyond the city's official boundary at the Kamer-Collegium Wall; and it was here, in October 1905, that some half a million workers began a strike that culminated in December in the seizure of Moscow's largest cotton mill.

The 1905 Revolution in Saint Petersburg and Moscow

The uprising of 1905 had begun in Saint Petersburg in January, when striking workers were shot down by the hundreds on the square in front of the Winter Palace as they tried to present notice of their grievances to the tsar. A general strike proclaimed by the workers of Saint Petersburg was soon respected by all the other large industrial cities of Russia including Moscow;

and it was followed by peasant uprisings in which many landlords were murdered. The crew of the battleship *Potemkin* mutinied in June; and many soldiers and sailors joined spontaneously with the workers in informal committees for political action, called *soviets*. The tsar's concessions were piecemeal and insincere: he first granted a consultative assembly, then election by restricted suffrage, then a broader franchise with a ministry responsible to the parliament, and finally secret universal male suffrage. With the grant of constitutional government, most middle-class reformers and peasants declared themselves satisfied; and thus, when the principal Bolshevik leaders reached Russia in November, it was to witness the final repression of the workers' revolt rather than to take command of a revolution. The Soviet of Workers' Deputies of Saint Petersburg, which had been formed in October, was suppressed after only fifty days, and its leaders arrested. The peasants were cowed by shootings and burnings. But the greatest repression took place in Moscow, where about eight thousand workers threw up barricades and maintained a sniping battle with the local troops until, after nine days, the tough Semionovsky Guards and artillery were sent from Saint Petersburg. The new troops bombarded the workers into submission, and killed over a thousand men, women, and children.

Boris Pasternak, in his novel *Doctor Zhivago*, described the Cossacks' scattering of a procession of workers just before the uprising:

When the dragoons charged, the marchers at the rear first knew nothing of it. A swelling noise rolled back to them as of great crowds shouting "Hurrah," and individual screams of "Help!" and "Murder!" were lost in the uproar. Almost at the same moment, and borne, as it were, on this wave of sound along the narrow corridor that formed as the crowd divided, the heads and manes of horses, and their saber-swinging riders, rode by swiftly and silently.

Half a platoon galloped through, turned, re-formed, and cut into the tail of the procession. The massacre began.

A few minutes later the avenue was almost deserted. People were scattering down the side streets. The snow was lighter. The afternoon was dry like a charcoal sketch. Then the sun, setting behind the houses, pointed as though with a finger at everything red in the street—the red tops of the dragoons' caps, a red flag trailing on the ground, and the red specks and threads of blood on the snow.[6]

The 1905 revolution left behind only a vague constitution, and as Lenin said, the "revolutionary education" of the Russian people. The tsar might have turned the constitutional changes to his own advantage by striking an alliance with the moderate elements within the new parliament, or Duma. But he was a weak, stubborn man, unable to conceive of the end of autocracy and deeply influenced by the irresponsible chidings of his in-

Collapse of the Tsarist System, 1906–1917

[6] Boris Pasternak, *Doctor Zhivago*, trans. Max Hayward and Manya Harari, translation revised by Bernard Guilbert Guerney (New York: Pantheon, 1958), pp. 36–37. Reprinted by permission of Pantheon Books, a Division of Random House, Inc., and William Collins Sons and Co., Ltd.

Tsar Nicholas II (Reigned 1904–1917) and His Family
(Brown Brothers)

sensitive wife, Alexandra. He turned more and more to right-wing reactionaries like the anti-Semitic Black Hundreds, and allowed the debauched monk Rasputin, who had won the tsarina's blind devotion by his power to stop the bleeding of her hemophiliac son, to nominate worthless ministers to his government. The powers of the first two Dumas were strictly circumscribed, the suffrage for the third sharply restricted. As a result, the parliament became a purely consultative body whose recommendations were largely ignored. The tsarist autocracy fell back on its old pillars of support—the bureaucracy, the aristocracy, the Church, and especially the army. It failed to realize that the industrialization of Russia, which continued at a frenzied pace in the last decade before the First World War, was increasing the strength of the middle classes, who sought parliamentary power, and of the industrial proletariat, who demanded a betterment of their conditions in some urgent manner that was still to be defined.

Russia's entry into war with Germany, Austria-Hungary, and Turkey in 1914 destroyed the basis of the power of the tsar. The government mobilized sixteen million men, whom it threw into battle against the efficient German forces without adequate weapons, ammunition, food, uniforms, medical supplies, transport, or leadership. When the tsar himself took personal command at the front in 1915, it increased the incompetence of the military command and cast the government in Petrograd into the purblind control of his wife and Rasputin. By 1916, the aristocracy itself was estranged from the tsar; two aristocrats even murdered Rasputin, and others spoke of overthrowing the tsar himself. The bureaucracy was demoralized by the incompetence and inconsistency of the changing ministries; and the tsar and his ministers refused to give greater powers to such local authorities as the zemstvos, who were sincerely trying to further the war effort. In 1915 they prorogued the Duma, which had supported the mobilization, because it demanded the institution of parliamentary responsibility as the sole method of winning the war. Above all, the tsar lost the support of the army, which for almost three years had fought with extraordinary bravery, suffering terrible losses against superior German forces. During 1916 the army slowly began to disintegrate, with over one and a half million deserting. For the peasants the war was an unmitigated disaster: they had provided the majority of the men slaughtered. Their farms were turning to waste for lack of workers, seeds, and fertilizer; their animals were taken to feed the armies. But it was among the workers of the cities that the suffering and the discontent were greatest.

Nicholas II in Captivity
The tsar was photographed in the captivity of Communist troops in December 1917, seven months before his murder. (National Archives)

Since the greater part of industry had been turned over to war production, the supply of consumer goods had almost ceased. Food was scarce because of the disorganization of the railroad system and breakdown of the farms. Fuel was almost impossible to obtain in the long winters. And the cities grew in size as workers were drafted into the munitions factories and new recruits for the armies swelled the barracks. The uprising in March 1917 was a spontaneous demonstration against conditions that had become intolerable in the cities, not a planned revolution; and from October 1916, when 150 mutinous soldiers had been executed for firing on the police instead of on demonstrating workers, Petrograd had been in constant tension.[7] In March, however, furious housewives attacked bakeries and foodshops in a "bread riot." Women textile workers went on strike and were joined by the men from the munitions factories; and within a short time all the factories were closed. On the third day of the rioting, some troops refused to support the police against the crowd. On the fifth day, March 12, the Volinski Guards regiment, ignoring its officers, marched to the neighboring barracks with its band playing the Marseillaise. Persuading the other troops to participate in the revolt, it was joined that same day by almost all the regiments in the capital. At the same time, the factory workers again formed a Soviet of Workers' Deputies, which established an office in one wing of the Tauride Palace, where the Duma parliamentarians were setting themselves up as an alternative government to the tsar's. The Duma executive committee collaborated with the Soviet long enough to bring Petrograd back to order the next day. Then on March 14 the Duma representatives declared themselves to be the provisional government of Russia; and at their demand, on March 15 the tsar abdicated. He was brought as a virtual prisoner first to his palace outside Petrograd and later to Ekaterinburg (now Sverdlovsk), where in July 1918 he and his whole family were killed by Communist guards.

[7]The Bolsheviks adopted the Gregorian calendar on February 14, 1918, which would have been February 1 on the old Julian calendar. Thus the March Revolution actually began on February 27, 1917 by the Julian calendar, and the November Revolution on October 25. The two revolutions are therefore often referred to as the February and the October revolutions.

From the March to the November Revolution, 1917

After the March Revolution, freedom in Russia was complete but chaotic. The legal power lay in the hands of the provisional government as the representative of the constitutionally elected Duma. But while granting such traditional rights of parliamentary democracies as freedom of speech and assembly, and suffrage to both men and women, the middle-class leaders who controlled the provisional government failed to meet the people's demands for peace and land. Although the government was headed after July by a fiery, charismatic leader, Alexander Kerensky, from the Social Revolutionary party, it remained procrastinating and unrealistic. Kerensky even believed that a great new offensive he launched against the Germans would solidify the country in his support, whereas it simply increased the number of desertions to over two million. A committee was formed to study the land question, but the impatient peasants began to seize the land themselves and to murder their landlords. While failing to gain the support of the soldiers and the peasants, the provisional government was even less likely to win the trust of the workers, who were forming their own committees throughout the country on the pattern of the Petrograd soviet. These soviets slowly became the real power in the cities, controlling local administration and constantly interfering with the enforcement of the orders of the provisional government. The chaos was compounded, however, by the fact that the leaders of the soviets, who were mostly Mensheviks and Social Revolutionaries, in the early weeks after the March Revolution did not wish to seize power. They collaborated with the provisional government and thus disgusted their own supporters, who in July rioted on the streets of Petrograd against them. The way to power was thus open to the Bolsheviks, the one faction that could offer self-confident leadership in bringing about revolutionary social change.

Lenin had lived in poverty in Switzerland during the first years of the war, supporting himself with literary jobs and fulminating against the working classes, who had allowed the capitalists to use them as cannon fodder in a war in which they had no class interest. When the news of the March Revolution reached him, Lenin tried frantically to find a way to get back to Russia. To his surprise he was given a comfortable passage in a sealed train across Germany by the German government, which saw correctly that the Bolsheviks would attempt to force Russia to withdraw from the war. When he arrived at the Finland station in Petrograd on April 16, a great crowd was waiting for him; and he at once placed himself at the head of the most radical elements of the revolution:

The people needs peace; the people needs bread; the people needs land. And they give you war, hunger, no bread—leave the landlords still on the land. . . . We must fight for the social revolution, fight to the end, till the complete victory of the proletariat. Long live the world social revolution!

Vladimir Ilyich Lenin
(H. Roger-Viollet)

Nevertheless, it took months of organization before the Bolsheviks were able to win over the city workers. Lenin, liberally supplied with funds by

Trotsky Addresses Red Army Soldiers in Moscow
As commissar of war in 1918, Trotsky was responsible for the creation of the Red Army. By combining soldiers from the tsarist army with new recruits, he was able to put together an effective fighting force that numbered three million by the end of the civil war. (Popperfoto)

the German government, was able to spread his views through the newspaper *Pravda* and in vast numbers of pamphlets, and to put together workers' armed forces, called Red Guards. His supporters were able to win controlling positions on factory committees and in the district soviets, as disgust with the moderate leadership grew. When the forces of a Cossack general, Kornilov, moved against Petrograd in the hope of destroying the provisional government, the Bolsheviks led the organization of the city's defense. At that point Lenin announced that the moment for the seizure of power had come. The execution of the coup was left to Trotsky, who was then the president of the Petrograd soviet. In a perfectly planned operation on the night of November 6, detachments of the Red Guards and the regular army seized the main government buildings. The only bloodshed occurred in the attack on the Winter Palace, where a few loyal troops tried to defend the provisional government. The next morning Lenin announced a new government, the Council of People's Commissars, with himself as chairman. The council's first decrees announced the state's expropriation of all land and its distribution to those who worked it, and demanded immediate peace without annexations. There was surprisingly little opposition at first to this seizure of power. Kerensky, who had escaped in disguise, was unable to rally any support in the army. Most of the big cities had recognized the new government within a month; and the other parties, like the Mensheviks and the Social Revolutionaries, tried to oppose the Bolsheviks by boycotting the meeting of the Congress of Soviets. Only in Moscow was there a dramatic clash.

The November Revolution in Moscow

Perhaps the most exciting and the most beautiful description of Moscow in 1917 is given by the writer Konstantin Paustovsky in his autobiography, *The Story of a Life*. As a young newspaper reporter on the eve of the March Revolution, he had found a dejected, rebellious city, isolated in the wilderness of the unchanging Russian countryside.

... Woods filled with bandits, unusable roads, decayed old settlements, ancient peeling churches, little horses with manure stuck to their skin, drunken fights, cemeteries with overturned gravestones, sheep living inside the peasants' huts, snotty children, straitlaced monasteries, God's fools clustered on church porches, markets filled with rubbish and the squeal of pigs and obscene cursing, decay, poverty, and thievery. And through all this wilderness around Moscow, where the wind whistled in the bare birch twigs, could be heard the repressed agonizing crying of women. They were crying for their soldiers—mothers and wives, sisters and sweethearts. [8]

The overthrow of the tsar brought elation, instant excitement, and disorderly change. Through a cold spring of hailstorms, the people of Moscow debated endlessly in the open air; and it seemed to Paustovsky that the debaters were slowly dividing into two camps, the "camp of the Bolsheviks and the workers, and the camp of the Provisional Government, of the intelligentsia, of men who seemed to have the highest sort of principles but who turned out to be boneless distraught people. . . . The state was falling to pieces like a handful of wet mud."

The idyllic aspect of the first days of the Revolution was disappearing. Whole worlds were shaking and falling to the ground. . . . On the walls of buildings the wind ruffled dozens of posters. The air was filled with the kerosenelike smell of printer's ink, and the smell of rye bread. The army brought this second village smell with it. The city was filled with soldiers pouring back from the front in spite of Kerensky's strident orders.

Moscow was transformed into a turbulent military camp. The soldiers settled in around the railroad stations. The squares in front of them were wreathed in smoke like the ruins of a conquered city. This was the smoke not of gunpowder but of cheap tobacco. . . . The whole city was on its feet. Apartments were empty. People spoke at meetings for nights on end, loafed sleepily around the streets, then sat down and argued in public squares on the sidewalks. . . . Four months had gone by since the Revolution, but the excitement had not died down. Anxiety still filled people's hearts. [9]

Fighting began in Moscow two days after the successful assault on the Winter Palace in Petrograd. At first the Bolsheviks held the Kremlin itself, where they had installed a Military Revolutionary Committee, but the city government and most of the army officers and cadets of the military colleges remained loyal to the provisional government. In a quick blow, the

[8] From *The Story of a Life*, by Konstantin Paustovsky, translated by Joseph Barnes. Copyright © 1964 by Random House, Inc. Reprinted by permission of Pantheon Books, a division of Random House, Inc., and William Collins Sons and Co., Ltd.

[9] Ibid., pp. 487, 489.

city government's Committee of Public Safety seized the Kremlin and shot the soldiers defending it. By the evening of November 9, the whole of the center of the city was in the hands of the Whites; but all the industrial suburbs were loyal to the Bolsheviks. Moreover, armed workers were pouring in from the surrounding towns, so that on November 13 the Reds were able to resume their offensive on the center of the city. After many hours of constant fighting with rifles, machine guns, and hand grenades, the Whites were driven back into the Kremlin itself. Paustovsky, who had been trapped for days in his lodgings in the middle of the fighting, emerged into the shattered streets.

Frozen blood lay in a ribbon on the stones around our gate. The buildings, riddled by machine-gun fire, were dropping sharp shards of glass out of their windows, and you could hear it breaking all round us. . . . It was all over. Through the cold dark there came from the Tverskoi the sounds of a band, and singing:

> *"Nobody gives us our salvation*
> *Not God, the Tsar, nor anyone.*
> *We will win our liberation*
> *With a power all our own."* [10]

Meanwhile, artillery had been called in to bombard the Kremlin, that holiest of all Russian shrines. According to John Reed, an American Communist journalist who had been following the revolution in Petrograd, the news shocked all Petrograd: "Thousands killed; the Tverskaya and the Kuznetsky Most in flames; the church of Vasili Blazheiny a smoking ruin; Usspensky Cathedral crumbling down; the Spasskaya Gate of the Kremlin tottering; the Duma burned to the ground. Nothing that the Bolsheviki had done could compare with this fearful blasphemy in the heart of Holy Russia." He found most of the rumors exaggerated, however, when he reached Moscow three days later. But the mass burial by the Kremlin wall of the five hundred workers killed in the fighting was for him an unforgettable experience:

Through all the streets to the Red Square the torrents of people poured, thousands upon thousands of them, all with the look of the poor and toiling. A military band came marching up, playing the Internationale, *and spontaneously the song caught and spread like wind-ripples on a sea, slow and solemn. . . . A bitter wind swept the square, lifting the banners. Now from the far quarters of the city the workers of the different factories were arriving, with their dead. They could be seen coming through the Gate, the blare of their banners, and the dull red—like blood—of the coffins they carried. . . . All day long the funeral procession passed, coming in by the Iberian Gate and leaving the Square by way of the Nikolskaya, a river of red banners, bearing words of hope and brotherhood and stupendous prophecies, against a background of fifty thousand people—under the eyes of the world's workers and their descendents forever.* [11]

[10]Ibid., p. 505.
[11]John Reed, *Ten Days That Shook the World* (New York: Modern Library, 1935), pp. 257–258.

LENIN'S MOSCOW

When Lenin transferred the government to Moscow in March 1918, the city had already experienced the startling pace with which the Bolsheviks were "cutting away whole layers of a way of life," as Paustovsky wrote, "throwing them away, and laying the basis for a new life. It was still hard to imagine what this new life might be. The change took place so unexpectedly that our very existence sometimes lost its reality and seemed as unstable as a mirage."[12]

The Land Decree had permitted the peasants to take over the land, and only in the summer of 1918 were they compelled to contribute part of their produce to feeding the cities. In the first weeks, even the members of the Council of People's Commissars lived on sour cabbage soup and black bread. All the banks were nationalized, although small withdrawals by private citizens were still permitted. The factories were handed over to the control of workers' committees, and an eight-hour day for workers instituted. A deliberate attempt was made to encourage the rise of a new type of Soviet woman, by the granting to women of equality before the law, legalized divorce and abortion, and equality of education. To enable women to enter the work force in greater numbers, maternity leaves and nursing breaks were provided, and equal pay for equal work was decreed; and a special Women's Department was set up under Alexandra Kollontai, the commissar for social welfare.

[12]Paustovsky, *Story of a Life*, p. 506.

Young Woman Addressing the Workers During the November Revolution, 1917
Women factory workers played an important part in the demonstrations in March 1917 that toppled the tsarist government and in the overthrow of the provisional government in November 1917. (H. Roger-Viollet)

Arrest of a Political Prisoner by the Secret Police (Cheka)
The Cheka was created in December 1917 to suppress the political opponents of the Revolution.   (National Archives)

All potential sources of rivalry to the Bolshevik leaders were destroyed. The popularly elected Constituent Assembly, chosen on November 25, was allowed to meet only once, since the Social Revolutionaries held a majority of the seats. The city dumas and the local zemstvos were both abolished. Opposition newspapers were banned. The only parties other than the Bolshevik party that were allowed to operate were the Social Revolutionaries and the Mensheviks. The Church was separated from the state, and its functions drastically reduced. Its lands had already been confiscated, and its other possessions soon passed into the hands of the state. Terror was accepted as an essential instrument of government. "Do you really think that we shall be victorious," Lenin asked, "without using the most cruel terror?" On December 20 the Cheka, the Extraordinary Commission for Combating Counterrevolution and Speculation, was established under Felix Dzerzhinsky. It was a secret political police, with power of immediate arrest and punishment. Finally, only six days before the move to Moscow, the Bolshevik representatives signed the Treaty of Brest Litovsk with Germany, by which they bought peace at a very high price— the loss of one-quarter of Russia's territory and over sixty million people. Lenin believed, however, that he had saved the revolution; Germany's gains, he predicted, would be ephemeral.

Once installed in the Kremlin, the Bolshevik government showed even in its living quarters that the confused improvisations of the early days in the Smolny Institute in Petrograd, where government ministries consisted of trestle tables in overcrowded halls and the state treasury was kept in a wardrobe in Lenin's room, were over. Lenin himself had a five-room apartment with a large reception room where the Council of People's Commissars could meet, and a private telephone system by which he could be in immediate contact with army or local Bolshevik leaders. The other commissars all had apartments nearby and ate together in a large Kremlin mess hall. It was close-knit, relatively efficient, and intentionally austere. The three hundred leaders who lived within the Kremlin permitted almost no one to penetrate the closely guarded walls because of the constant danger to which they felt exposed not only from aristocratic and bourgeois elements but even from within the revolutionary movement. The most dangerous of the attacks came in July 1918, when the left-wing Social Revolutionaries attempted to overthrow the government and murder Lenin. After September, when the head of the Cheka in Petrograd was assassinated, Lenin unleashed the secret police in a wave of terror intended to cow all opposition, even though he had restrained it somewhat after an attempt on his own life the previous month.

War Communism

The terror and the isolation seemed the necessary protection for leaders engaged in a gigantic social experiment in the midst of civil war. The most extensive changes were brought about by a policy known as war communism. By this policy, Lenin proposed to bring about total control over the economic life of every individual in Russia. After a few months of untrammeled enjoyment of their newly acquired lands, the peasants were forced to hand over a large portion of their produce to the state, which became the sole distributor and stockpiler of foodstuffs. The farms that they had expected to own were declared state property. The workers' committees

Streetside Market, Moscow
The sale of private possessions continued throughout the 1930s in open-air markets, in spite of state control of the retail trade.
(National Archives)

ceased to manage the factories, and the Communist party took over the nationalized companies under the instructions of a central economic committee within the Kremlin. All foreign and internal trade was brought under state control, and a system of regimentation of labor introduced. Workers had to possess a passport. If they did not work, they did not receive a ration book for food. Workers could be drafted to jobs where they were needed, although the most menial tasks were reserved for the bourgeoisie. Private wealth was severely restricted: the most obvious luxuries like paintings and furs were confiscated, and the inheritance of private property was banned. All apartment buildings were taken over, and "living space" assigned according to need.

The Civil War and the New Economic Policy

Realization of the full import of these measures by the possessing classes and the peasantry helped to produce the civil war. A base for counterrevolution had been provided by the intervention of the Western allies for the ostensible purpose of protecting the large quantities of supplies they had sent to Russia. In reality the allies stepped in to bring about the overthrow of the Communist regime and the reentry of Russia into the war with Germany. The British moved into the Arctic ports and Baku, the French into Odessa, the Japanese and later the Americans into Vladivostok. Anti-Bolshevik, or White, regimes were encouraged in these areas. But many other opposition groups were organized around the periphery of the great central region where Bolshevik control was firm. Minority nationalities like the Ukrainians joined the Whites in the South. In the Urals and Siberia, a second army was formed under Admiral Kolchak. In the Baltic states, White forces were supported after 1918 by demobilized German soldiers of the so-called Free Corps. The civil war seriously threatened Bolshevik control. At one time the armies of General Denikin, moving from the Ukraine, reached to within two hundred fifty miles of Moscow, and those of Yudenich from Estonia penetrated the outer suburbs of Petrograd. Conditions in the cities under Bolshevik control were fearsome. Famine, typhus, riots, and looting made life uncertain for all. Medical supplies ran short in the Kremlin polyclinic itself. In April 1918 Trotsky, as commissar for war, persuaded the government to institute universal military service for workers and peasants and to use tsarist officers under close political supervision to command them. From then on young party workers from Moscow were taken with Trotsky to the front, where they were used to stiffen the fighting resolve of the rank and file, and they were soon followed by thousands of workers from the industrial suburbs. Slowly the new army grew in size and efficiency, reaching 800,000 by the end of the year and three million before the end of 1920. The Whites quarreled among themselves and made their cause unpopular by restoring the land to its former landlords and by carrying out vicious executions. Trotsky profited from his central position, moved his armies by railroad with great logistic genius, and in two years had broken all three White armies. The last White and foreign forces were evacuated from Russian soil in 1922. By

Leon Trotsky (1879–1940)
This photograph was taken in 1920, when Trotsky was directing the organization and strategy of the Communist forces in the Russian civil war. (National Archives)

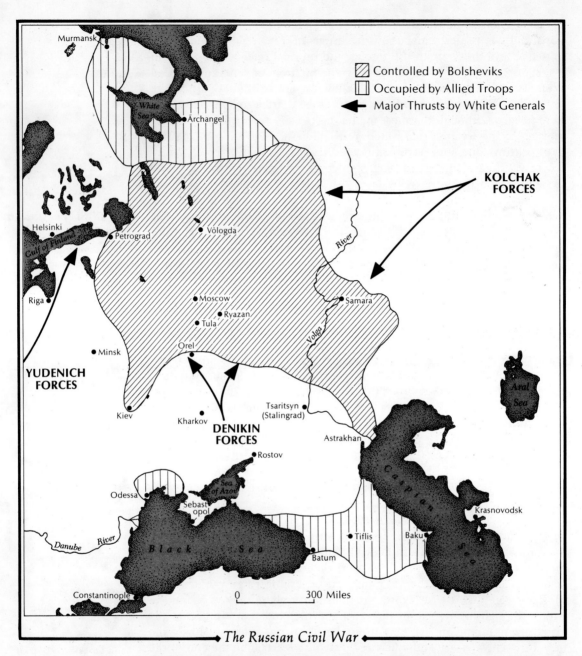

Controlled by Bolsheviks
Occupied by Allied Troops
Major Thrusts by White Generals

KOLCHAK FORCES

YUDENICH FORCES

DENIKIN FORCES

Murmansk
White Sea
Archangel
Helsinki
Gulf of Finland
Petrograd
Vologda
Riga
Moscow
Ryazan
Tula
Minsk
Orel
Kiev
Kharkov
Samara
Volga
Tsaritsyn (Stalingrad)
Astrakhan
Aral Sea
Caspian Sea
Krasnovodsk
Rostov
Odessa
Sea of Azov
Sebastopol
Danube River
Black Sea
Tiflis
Baku
Batum
Constantinople
River

0   300 Miles

◆ *The Russian Civil War* ◆

then the old order in Russia had capitulated to the new. Two million Russians had fled into exile. The political opposition was broken. But the economic chaos was complete. The true opposition remaining was the passive resistance of peasant and worker to the nationalizing state that demanded work with no reward. Half the workers of Moscow had moved back to the countryside, where they could find food. Industrial production for the country as a whole was down to fourteen percent of prewar figures. But the final blow was the revolt of the sailors at the Kronstadt naval base in March 1921, which convinced the realistic Lenin that he had to pull back from massive socialization for a while.

The New Economic Policy of 1921–1928 permitted the peasants to sell their produce for whatever price they could get, in order to make available some form of consumer goods that private traders, soon known as NEP men, could bring into the cities to sell. With goods for purchase, the worker was encouraged to put in longer hours in the factory, thereby restoring the productivity of industry. But the "controlling heights of industry" remained in the hands of the state; no industries were denationalized. The policy worked. The famine of 1920–1921, in which as many as five million died, was alleviated. Slowly agricultural and industrial production returned to prewar levels, and the popularity of the Communist government rose with it.

Lenin himself, however, had suffered in 1922 a paralytic stroke that for the last two years of his life left him able to understand but unable to command. He watched with frustration the rise to prominence in the party of a tough, maneuvering Georgian named Joseph Vissarionovich Dzugashvily, who had taken the name Stalin ("man of steel") on joining the revolutionary movement. Stalin was using his role as general secretary of the party to make himself rather than Trotsky the heir to Lenin's power. In an addition to the political testament he had written for the party's guidance after his death, Lenin tried to give warning against Stalin. On December 24, 1923, he cautioned that "Comrade Stalin, having become general secretary, has concentrated enormous power in his hands, and I am not sure that he always knows how to use that power with sufficient caution." On January 4, 1924, two weeks before his death, Lenin added a postscript: "Stalin is too rude, and this fault, entirely supportable in relation to us Communists, becomes insupportable in the office of General Secretary. Therefore I propose to the comrades to find a way to remove Stalin from that position and appoint to it another man who in all respects differs from Stalin in one characteristic—namely, more patient, more loyal, more polite, and more attentive to comrades, less capricious, etc." Having created a dictatorship, Lenin had at the last moment become aware of the abuses to which it could be put. After his death on January 21, 1924, his body was embalmed and placed in a wooden mausoleum in Red Square; in 1930, the present mausoleum of granite and porphyry was inaugurated. Lenin had become a figure of religious awe, his tomb visited by millions every year. The damaging testament was suppressed by the party Central Committee, however, and Stalin dominated even the burial ceremonies.

Within four years, Stalin had destroyed his opposition and was the unchallenged ruler of Russia. He had been a successful but not an outstanding revolutionary leader before 1917. After being educated in a seminary, he had become a professional Bolshevik organizer, working un-

Rise of Stalin

Lenin's Funeral
January 1924. Stalin (left front) and members of the Politburo lead Lenin's funeral cortege through Red Square. (Sovfoto/Eastfoto)

derground and being frequently arrested. He played only a minor part in the November Revolution, and was given the peripheral post of commissar of nationalities in the first Council of People's Commissars. But by his ability to handle multifarious details of administrative work, he slowly became indispensable in the party apparatus; and without Lenin's realizing his intention at first, he used the powers of general secretary to fill all the provincial and many central party offices with new men dependent entirely on him. While Lenin was dying, Stalin had forged an alliance with Zinoviev and Kamenev, the party chiefs of Petrograd and Moscow, to isolate Trotsky; and he was able to persuade the Central Committee to dismiss Trotsky from the post of war commissar in 1925, from the Central Committee in 1927, and from the party itself in 1929. Trotsky went into exile, where he fulminated against the Stalinist regime until, on Stalin's orders, he was brutally assassinated in 1940. With Trotsky defeated, Stalin turned against his allies. Kamenev and Zinoviev were expelled from the party in 1927, and all of the original associates of Lenin soon followed. By 1928 Stalin felt prepared to change the whole direction of the party policy; in the first Five-Year Plan, he would hurl Russia into the Iron Age.

Moscow in the 1920s

During the 1920s, at least after the inauguration of the New Economic Policy, life in Moscow had been materially adequate and socially exciting. Food and a minimum amount of consumer goods had percolated back, through the agency of the NEP men. The trade unions had been permitted to stand up for workers' rights, and could even bargain for higher wages. Many small workshops had been opened by artisans. Although few new houses were built, cramped quarters were available for most people by a sharing out of rooms in the larger buildings. Educational opportunities became available to all workers with the opening of a new nine-year polytechnic school for all children and free schooling through the age of seventeen. Women had entered the work force, accounting for just under a quarter of the Russian labor force by 1928. Furthermore, women composed almost one-third of the students in higher education and almost one-tenth of all party members.

In intellectual life, too, there was much exciting innovation. The nationalized theaters had been placed under the supervision of an experienced director, Vsevolod Meyerhold, who was determined to throw over the classical in favor of a proletarian theater. He did away with curtains, footlights, and even costumes; changed scenery in sight of the audience; and filled the stage with vast spectacles of workers in revolutionary action. The movie houses showed the masterpieces of directors like Sergei Eisenstein, who gave many younger Russians a lasting impression of the revolutionary days with his film *October*. The NEP permitted the private publishing of books, with the result that many imaginative novels of the revolutionary struggles and of the civil war were produced. Some writers who had gone into exile came back, such as Alexei Tolstoy and Ilya Ehrenburg. To Ehrenburg, life in Moscow during the time of the New Economic Policy was a strange mixture of idealism and materialism:

I was astonished when I saw Moscow again. I had gone abroad in the last weeks of War Communism. Everything looked different now. Ration cards had disappeared, people were no longer 'registered.' Administrative personnel was greatly reduced and no one was working out grandiose projects. . . . Old workers and engineers were painfully getting production on its feet. Consumption goods

Scene from *October*, by Sergei Eisenstein (1927)
In his silent movie October, *which recounts the events of the "Ten Days That Shook the World," the Communist Revolution, Eisenstein's most exciting scenes were of the capture of the Winter Palace in St. Petersburg, which was the seat of the provisional government. (Museum of Modern Art/ Film Stills Archive)*

had made their appearance. The peasants had begun to bring poultry to the markets. The Muscovites had grown fatter and were more cheerful. I was both pleased and saddened. . . . From the point of view of the politician or the production expert the new line was correct; we know now that it produced what it was intended to produce. But the heart has its reasons: NEP often seemed to me to have a sinister grimace.[13]

The NEP men, he found, were dancing to the phonograph records of Paris and London, wearing bright tight-fitting suits, eating huge meals in restaurants, and driving around town in smart drozhkys. The young, he thought, were an idealistic new generation, romantic in "the bold attempt to mass-produce tangible myths, in series," in the factories and schools. The party, he claimed, remained puritanical: members worked fourteen hours a day and "ate humble rissole in the canteen." By 1926, he felt "the stifling, brutal life of NEP's last years was being played out. Everybody traded in everything, wrangled, prayed, swilled vodka and, dead drunk, fell like corpses in the gateways. The yards were filthy. Vagrant children huddled in the cellars."[14] In 1928, Stalin brought a sharp surgical end to this epoch.

STALIN'S IRON AGE

First Five-Year Plan, 1928–1932

The first Five-Year Plan had been under discussion for three years, and when presented to the party congress it was elaborated to the minutest detail. Stalin returned to the original plans of 1917 for total socialization of the Russian economy, but he linked them to a newer and perhaps more important concept: the Communist state was to become a totalitarian machine for the forced industrialization of an underdeveloped country. Principal emphasis was placed on accelerated growth of heavy industry, especially coal and iron, engineering, and electrification. Vast new centers of industry were to be created, notably in the Urals and Siberia. Large numbers of workers were to be transferred to such new cities as Magnitogorsk in the Urals; others, including the inmates of labor camps run by the secret police, were to be employed in building roads, railroads, and canals. Detailed goals were laid down for every branch of production; and these had to be met if managers wanted to avoid demotion or even imprisonment, and if workers wanted to eat. Rewards, most often verbal, were given to those who exceeded their norms. The industrialization of agriculture was conceived as a necessary accompaniment to the growth of heavy industry. Tractors were to be produced to mechanize the countryside. The maze of inefficient individual peasant holdings was to be replaced by large consolidated farms called collectives, in which the peasants would be paid

---

[13]Ilya Ehrenburg, *Truce 1921–33* (London: MacGibbon and Kee, 1963), pp. 66, 69.
[14]Ibid., p. 139.

Socialist Realism in Art
During the 1930s, Stalin insisted that literature and art glorify the role of the worker in the economic reconstruction of Russia being undertaken in the Five Year Plans. Women workers are shown here giving their opinions to architects who are preparing plans for a new factory; a bust of Stalin looks benignly on. The return to Realism was intended to make art comprehensible to the working masses, and all forms of experimentation were banned. (Tass from Sovfoto)

laborers. Each collective farm would also be assigned a quota and would be allowed itself to consume only what it produced beyond that quota. Increased production in the countryside would enable the growing urban population of the industrial centers to be fed and would free many peasants to become industrial workers. Since almost no material incentives would be provided for the worker, consumer goods being kept at the absolute minimum, a vast propaganda effort would be needed to persuade the workers that they were building for the future. In subordinating their own immediate well-being to the needs of the state's industrialization, the Soviet citizens would not only be creating a new civilization but would be changing their own personalities as well. The Five-Year Plan would help create a new Soviet mentality.

Urban Growth During the Five-Year Plan

The Five-Year Plan vastly accelerated the urbanization of Russia. Moscow itself grew to a population of 3.9 million by 1935, and its industrial base changed from predominantly light industry concentrated on textiles to engineering industries, especially the manufacturing of automobile parts, tractors, machine tools, and precision instruments. Those who immigrated to Moscow were usually uprooted peasants, torn from their farms by the collectivization program. They were largely unskilled in industrial trades and unaccustomed to the tedious discipline of factory life. Even in the capital city they found living accommodations barbaric, with several families often crowded into a single room and kitchen; and they reacted with drunkenness, indiscipline on the job, and absenteeism. In the Urals and beyond rather than in Moscow, however, the most dramatic scenes of the great urbanization were played. There a great mixing occurred of the unwilling peasant population with an enthused idealistic aristocracy of labor, many of whom were young workers persuaded by the government's propaganda to build socialism in the wilderness. "Komsomols [young Communists], fired with enthusiasm, set off for Magnitogorsk or Kuznetsk," wrote Ehrenburg. "They believed it was enough to build huge factories to create an earthly paradise. In freezing January metal scorched the hands. People seemed to be frozen to the marrow; there were no songs, no flags, no speeches. The word 'enthusiasm,' as so many others, has been devalued by inflation, yet there is no other word to fit the days of the first Five-Year Plan; it was enthusiasm pure and simple that inspired the young people to daily and unspectacular feats."[15] There were of course the thousands of "specials," the former kulaks (well-to-do peasants) who were drafted into the factories and supervised by the secret police, but on the job there was little to choose between their conditions and those of the average worker. John Scott, a young American who went out to Magnitogorsk in 1931 to work as a welder and see the new state in action, described in *Behind the Urals* (1942) the creation of this vast city in the steppes of Siberia by workers who reported at six in the morning in a temperature of forty-five degrees below zero; he noted the ragged clothes and insufficient food, the constant political interference in technical plans, the huge waste of lives from inadequate safety precautions and poor materials. The enthusiasm ran thin, he reported; the "population was taught by a painful expensive process to work efficiently, to obey orders, to mind their own business, and to take it on the chin with a minimum of complaint." The town they created was far from beautiful. In 1933 Magnitogorsk was a harsh, grey, dusty maelstrom of half-finished blast furnaces and wooden barracks. By 1940 it was beginning to have pretensions to urban amenity, with broad paved streets, large five-story apartment buildings, fountains, children's playgrounds, orchestras and singing societies, and a system of schools ranging from nurseries to a teachers' college and a mining and metallurgical institute.

Magnitogorsk, while one of the largest new cities, was only one of many. Throughout the Urals and Siberia, new cities were created—Krivoy-Rog, Kursk, and Gornaia-Shorii for iron mining; Krasnoiarsk, Irkutsk, and Novosibirsk for steel and heavy engineering; Frunze, Pavlodar, and Omsk for agricultural machinery. Great new dams, like that at Dnieprostroy on the Dnieper River, not only provided hydroelectric power to wide areas but also served as nuclei around which steel, chemical, and aluminum factories were grouped. The second Five-Year Plan, for 1933–1937, carried on

[15]Ibid., p. 221.

the expansion of these new centers, especially the iron- and steel-producing cities, and also increased the emphasis on machine tools, nonferrous metals, and transportation. Not only were the railroad lines to be given a second track and many new lines constructed, but rivers were to be widened, new canals like the Moscow-Volga Canal built, and a highway network begun. A third plan in 1938 had similar goals but had to be shelved with the coming of World War II. The success of these plans in turning Russia into a highly industrialized state and in transferring the center of Russian industry from the west into the Urals and Siberia is undoubted, even though very few of the unrealistic goals of the plans were actually met. Steel production, for example, did reach 17 million tons by 1937, from only 4 million in 1928; coal production was 128 million tons compared with 31.

The Opening of a New Factory
During the Five-Year Plans factory openings were celebrated as national triumphs of the working class.

The Opening of the Dnieprostroy Dam, 1932
The food line in the foreground is testimony to the price Russian workers paid for great public works, such as this dam and power station on the Dnieper River. (National Archives)

Peasants on a Collective Farm in the 1930s

In spite of desperate opposition, almost all of Russia's agricultural population had been grouped on collective farms by 1938. (National Archives)

Collectivization of Agriculture

However, the collectivization of agriculture, which was regarded as the necessary accompaniment of these industrial changes, was carried through only at the cost of class war in the countryside, the death of between five and ten million peasants, and a widespread famine in 1930–1931. To force the peasantry to bring their livestock, machinery, and land into collective farms, Stalin turned the poorest peasants against the kulaks, who numbered just under a million. Then, to bring the mass of small proprietors into the collectives as well, he found that he had to use the Red Army against them. Recalcitrant peasants were machine-gunned into submission and sent by the millions into Siberia or forced labor camps. The peasants replied by burning down their own houses and killing (and eating) their livestock. Collectivization continued, however, and by 1930 over half the Russian landholdings had been collectivized. By 1938 the process was almost complete. But the economic consequences had been disastrous. Half of Russia's horses and cattle and two-thirds of its pigs and sheep had been slaughtered. This time it was not the urban workers but the peasantry that starved, since the government forced the compulsory delivery of quotas to the cities. The peasants began to flock into the cities, as the government desired, to provide the unskilled labor for the construction of the new industrial plants. In spite of its adverse results on food production, Stalin had therefore achieved his main goal for the countryside. He had brought under control the one sector of the economy and of the population that had resisted the direct controls of the state. Socialized cities and individualistic farming could not continue side by side.

MOSCOW DURING THE IRON AGE

The determination to encourage industrialization in the east of Russia and to restrict the growth of the cities of European Russia was confirmed in 1931, when the Party Central Committee defined Moscow's position in the new state. To avoid "creating huge cities with an agglomeration of a great number of enterprises in the existing urban centers," and especially to prevent the building of new industrial enterprises in Moscow itself, the city's population was not to grow beyond five million. To achieve this, not only were no new factories to be started in Moscow, but unsanitary old ones were to be moved fifty to one hundred kilometers away; special passports were required for residence in Moscow; and frequently, after slum clearance, the inhabitants of the cleared areas were moved out of Moscow. Within these limits, Moscow was to become a showplace of the new workers' society, especially as it would be the main center visited by delegations from foreign countries, tourists, and journalists. In Moscow the superiority of the Socialist society had to receive physical demonstration.

Various options were considered in dealing with the largely unplanned city. According to the detailed announcement of the Ten-Year Plan (1935):

Ten-Year Plan for Moscow

Moscow, which for many centuries had developed in chaotic fashion, reflected, even in the best years of its development, the barbaric character of Russian capitalism. The narrow and crooked streets, the districts intersected by a multitude of lanes and blind alleys, the uneven distribution of buildings between the center and the outskirts of the city, the center encumbered with warehouses and small enterprises, the low, decrepit houses huddled together, the haphazard distribution of the industrial enterprises, railroads and other branches of economy and public service, hinder the normal life of the rapidly developing city, particularly in respect of traffic, and make imperative a radical and planned reconstruction. . . .

The Central Committee of the Party and the Council of People's Commissars reject the projects of preserving the present city intact as a museum-city and of creating a new city outside the limits of the present one. The Central Committee of the Party and the Council of the People's Commissars also reject the proposals to demolish the existing city and to build a new city in its place according to a totally different plan. . . . It is necessary to retain the historical outlines of the city, but radically to replan it by coordinating the network of its streets and squares. . . . The hilly contours of the city, the Moscow river and the Yauza river, which intersect the city in different directions, the fine parks of Moscow—all these individual sections of the city in all their variety taken as a whole make it possible to create a truly socialist city. [16]

[16] E. D. Simon, *Moscow in the Making* (London: Longmans, Green, 1937), pp. 184–185.

The control by the state of all property rights made wide-scale planning possible on a hitherto unknown scale. By decree all suburban areas were to be annexed to the central city as "reserve city land," to which the city building codes would be applied. A green belt of forests and parks ten kilometers in width was to be preserved around the built-up area to "serve as a reservoir of fresh air for the city and a place of recreation for its inhabitants." The rivers were to be banked with granite-faced walls, and broad streets constructed along their length as the city's main throughways; and architecturally harmonious apartment buildings and public offices were to be constructed along them. A large new area beyond the Lenin hills was to be annexed and developed into apartments to relieve the city's congestion. Impressive public buildings were to be constructed on the main squares, in front of the railroad stations, at principal intersections, and at viewpoints above the Moscow River. A central heating system for the whole city was to use steam from turbines at the new electric power plants; an underground pipe and cable system was to combine telephone, telegraph, light and power cables, and gas and water mains, to give ease of access and to remove the visual annoyance of wires and pipes above ground. Finally, vast provisions were to be made for the improvement of the living conditions of the workers. Schools, outpatient clinics, dining rooms, kindergartens, nurseries, theaters, cinemas, clubs, hospitals, and stadiums were to be located at central points in groups of apartment buildings. Like all the other planning of the Iron Age, it was immensely ambitious and could only be achieved in part.

Socialist Realism in Moscow Architecture

Much of the reconstruction went according to plan. The streets were widened and covered with asphalt, and the river embankments built. Many of the new public buildings, built from the 1920s until the mid-1930s, were in the most advanced styles then being adopted only on a small scale in western Europe. Le Corbusier, for example, was consulted on the replanning of Moscow; he designed several buildings, including the airy, glass-fronted Centrosoyuz for the Moscow cooperatives. Soviet architects themselves drew inspiration from the ideas of the architect Gropius and his Bauhaus, an art and design institute in Weimar, Germany; and exciting new buildings in concrete and plate glass were designed for use as palaces of labor, the offices of the newspaper *Pravda*, the Moscow planetarium, and workers' apartments and clubs. In the planning of the suburban towns around Moscow, the urbanists engaged in a fruitful debate between those who favored concentration of population and those who wanted to scatter apartment houses among the forests, and for a while the adherents of the "Green City" concept were able to give free play to the idea of moving the workers and their automobiles (still to be constructed) into the fresh air of the green belt.

Between 1931 and 1935, however, these creative ideas for urban architecture were stifled. The official policy of the state in all the arts was declared to be "Socialist realism." The definition itself was somewhat misty:

Apartment Building, Kotelnicheskaya Embankment, Moscow (1949–1953)

Most of the Moscow skyscrapers in the so-called "wedding-cake" style, incorporating traditional decorative motifs to embellish stark concrete facades, were erected during the last eight years of Stalin's life, between 1945 and 1953. (H. Roger-Viollet)

"In architecture, Socialist realism means the intimate union of ideological expression with the truth of artistic expression, and the effort to adapt every building to the technical, cultural, or utilitarian demands which are its own." In practice, under the cultural controls of Stalin and his collaborator Zhdanov, architectural style was to return to a monumentalism based on a mingling of period revivals. At first the "realist" architects turned to safe and undemonstrative Italian Renaissance models, especially the airy villas of Palladio in northern Italy. Nonfunctional pilasters and heavy balconies and balustrades, inside and outside, were in some curious way supposed to express the artistic wishes of the Soviet worker. Palladio was followed by a vast medley of other styles, including Greek, Roman, Florentine, neo-Muscovite, and baroque, all characterized by high ceilings, sculptured fountains, inset columns, and vast, glistening candelabras. The victory of the realists over their opponents, who were condemned as "formalists" and thus politically as well as architecturally unreliable, came with the competition for a great central "Palace of the Soviets." The formalist Guinzburg designed an ascetic composition of sharp angles in plain white concrete, surmounted by a huge glass dome. The realists who won the competition projected a series of superimposed drums, placed upon a vast colonnade like the death temple of an Egyptian dynasty, topped with a gigantic statue of Lenin. Taller than the Empire State Building and the Eiffel Tower, it was intended to become the central point of the whole Moscow skyline. Its construction was interrupted by the Second World War, and its foundation later turned into the largest swimming pool in Moscow. But the victory of the realists was assured, and until Stalin's death in 1953, the architecture of Moscow turned to ever more grandiose variations on the "wedding-cake style" invented during the 1930s.

The Moscow Subway   The most notable examples of the new realist style were to be found in the main stations of the Moscow Metro, the subway begun in 1931 as the supreme demonstration of the Socialist state's urban preoccupation. The party had ordered completion of the first section of the Metro by November 1934 for the seventeenth anniversary of the Revolution, and no expense in money, labor, or risk was spared to achieve the goal. The first section was to cost half a billion rubles, at a time when the Five-Year Plan was appropriating less than that each year to the industries making consumer goods. The head of the work was Nikita Khrushchev, a former mine worker from the Ukraine.

"At the construction sites as everywhere," Khrushchev warned the workers who were falling behind in their efforts to drive the underground tunnels through dense brown mud under houses that frequently collapsed, "mere words are not enough. We need a Bolshevist organized system, clearness of purpose, knowledge of the matter, and ability to fulfill without fail the plan assigned by the party and Government. . . . Under the influence of self-seekers who have wormed themselves into our construction sites, some workers have begun to think along the following lines: why don't we try to get our norms revised downwards? Pernicious and disorganizing aspirations of this kind must be severely put down."[17] He himself plunged into the waterlogged shafts, inspecting the work, raising the norms, threatening and cajoling.

In spite of his efforts and those of thousands of Young Communists who were used for unskilled work, the first section was a year late in completion. But it immediately became the showplace of the new city, because never before had subway stations been decorated with porphyry, granite, bronze, marble, mosaics, statues, bas-reliefs, and crystal candelabras. It was ironic that the style of Socialist realism in architecture should have been outlawed two decades later by Khrushchev. In the Decree on Eliminating Waste in Building Design in 1955, Khrushchev noted:

Completely unjustified tower-like superstructures and numerous decorative colonnades, porticos, and other architectural excesses borrowed from the past have

[17]Cited in Lazar Pistrak, *The Grand Tactician: Khrushchev's Rise to Power* (New York: Praeger, 1961), pp. 82–83.

become characteristic of apartments and public buildings, as the result of which state funds have been overexpended on housing construction in the last few years to an extent that would have provided many million square meters of living space for the working people. . . .

An improper architectural trend is also evident in the design and construction of railroad stations, and manifests itself in the erection of palatial stations. In spite of their great cost, these stations do not provide the essential comforts for passengers. [18]

During the 1920s many Communist leaders had believed that writers should be permitted to move slowly toward the new society as, in Trotsky's famous phrase, "fellow travelers"; and without strict controls over their style, Soviet writers had succeeded in producing literature of considerable quality. Vladimir Mayakovsky had become the poet hero of the Revolution, declaiming to vast crowds such verses as "I love the hugeness of our plans, The boldness of our mile-long strides." Isaac Babel had recovered the style of the great nineteenth-century novelists in his *Red Cavalry* of 1926. Yevgeny Zamyatin was able to read aloud his satirical fantasy *We* and to publish his less pointed short stories. Boris Pilnyak had drawn upon the style of the Parisian Symbolists in his novel *The Naked Year* (1922). And the efforts of the militant Association of Proletarian Writers to force the more independent literary figures to proletarian themes had even been rebuked by the Central Committee!

In 1930, however, everything changed. Mayakovsky, finding himself under sharp criticism and despairing of the new political controls, committed suicide after writing one last poem:

> *I am also fed up*
> *With the agit-prop [Department for Agitation and Propaganda];*
> *I too could compose*
> *Ballads about you—*
> *It is pleasanter and pays more—*
> *But I forced myself*
> *By planting my foot on the throat of my own song.* [19]

The Central Committee turned on Pilnyak and Zamyatin with the accusation that they had published works abroad, and thus these two leading writers were made scapegoats as a warning to the rest. Stalin himself stepped into the literary debate with warnings to writers who had failed to strike a suitable propagandist note. On one occasion, he wrote a letter to a poet about the latter's critical verses, published in *Pravda*, on Ukraine miners. "You announce to the whole world that Russia in the past was a vessel of filth and indifference," Stalin raged, "and that present-day Russia is no

Socialist Realism in Art and Literature

---

[18] Ibid., p. 99.

[19] Cited in Marc L. Slonim, *Soviet Russian Literature: Writers and Problems, 1917–1967* (New York: Oxford University Press, 1967), pp. 27–28.

better, that laziness and the desire to 'sit on the stove' are to all intents and purposes national characteristics of the Russian people—and that means, of Russian workers—who after accomplishing the October revolution did not cease to be Russians. And you call that Bolshevik criticism! No, my honored Comrade Demyan, that is not Bolshevik criticism but a slander on our people. It is the degradation of the USSR, the degradation of the proletariat of the USSR, the degradation of the Russian proletariat. And after that you expect the Central Committee to be silent! Just who do you take us for?" [20]

All writers were grouped into one organization, the All-Union Organization of Associations of Proletarian Writers, whose head was brother-in-law of the chief of the secret police. There was to be a "draft of shock-workers into literature." Writers were to exalt the goals of the Five-Year plans. Many did, publishing such novels as *Cement, Energy, The Big Assembly Line*, and *Hydrocentral*. Occasionally a fine novel was created in these difficult conditions, such as Michael Sholokov's *Virgin Soil Upturned*. But almost all experimentalism was condemned, and in the late 1930s some of the best of the earlier Soviet writers, such as Isaac Babel and Boris Pilnyak, died during imprisonment. In painting and sculpture, Socialist realism wiped out all creativity, leaving behind only the gigantic monumentalism of exuberant muscular workers exultant in the completion of superhuman tasks in industry and agriculture.

All aspects of life had to be mobilized for the strengthening of the Russian economy. "No, Comrades, the pace must not be slackened," Stalin had declared in 1931.

To slacken the pace would mean to lag behind; and those who lag behind are beaten. We do not want to be beaten. No, we do not! Russia . . . was ceaselessly beaten for her backwardness. She was beaten by the Mongol Khans, she was beaten by the Turkish Beys, she was beaten by the Swedish feudal lords, she was beaten by the Anglo-French capitalists, she was beaten by the Japanese barons, she was beaten by all—for her backwardness. . . .

We are fifty or a hundred years behind the advanced countries. We must make good this lag in ten years. Either we do it or they crush us. [21]

THE GREAT PURGES

The disciplining of intellectuals was only the forerunner of a major search for disloyalty within the Communist party itself that began in 1934. The purge and punishment of disloyal elements took place in every section of the country, but the most dramatic events were enacted in

[20] Max Hayward and Leopold Labedz, eds., *Literature and Revolution in Soviet Russia, 1917–1962* (New York: Oxford University Press, 1963), p. 56.
[21] Cited in Edward Crankshaw, *Khrushchev: A Career* (New York: Viking, 1966), pp. 76–77.

Purge Trials in Moscow
The most dramatic of the carefully staged purge trials of 1936–1938 were those of the "old Bolshevik" leaders, such as Zinoviev and Kamenev, who had worked with Lenin to carry out the Russian Revolution. As a result of torture by the secret police, all confessed to crimes against the state and were executed. (BBC Hulton Picture Library)

Moscow, with the secret police as the producers of the drama and the purged as principal actors.

The purge was already a frequently used device within the Russian Communist party before 1934. There had been at least four large purges during the 1920s. A sweep of those held responsible for the shortcomings of the collectivization program was carried out in 1930, and yet another in 1933 to "achieve a higher ideological standard of party members." Following the assassination in Leningrad on December 1, 1934, of Stalin's presumed heir, Sergei Kirov, however, a purge unparalleled in its scope and savagery began. Khrushchev later suggested that Stalin was responsible for Kirov's murder and used it as an excuse to impose a new regime of terror against former critics and possible rivals. The murder of Kirov was held to be the work of supporters of Zinoviev and Kamenev, with whom Stalin had earlier allied to oust Trotsky; and they and thousands of their supposed accomplices were arrested in 1934–1935. In August 1936, the most important of the Old Bolsheviks suddenly emerged, briefly, from the prisons of the NKVD (the new designation of the secret police) for a show trial, in which most of them confessed to organizing terrorism against Stalin, to working for Trotsky, and to having murdered Kirov. They were immediately executed, but their confessions were held to have implicated even more of the original Bolsheviks who had been Lenin's collaborators. A second show trial was held in January 1937, in which all seventeen prisoners confessed that they were guilty of sabotage, collaboration with Germany and Japan, and plots to dismember the Soviet Union. Thirteen were executed; the others disappeared. That summer, when the purge was extended to the highest levels of the Red Army, the chief of general staff and civil war hero Marshall Tukachevsky and a large number of other commanders were found guilty of treason and executed. Finally, a fourth show trial in March 1938 of the remaining Old Bolsheviks led to the execution of eighteen more prominent leaders, including even a former head of the secret police.

The public trials caused a tremendous sensation. The spectacle of Lenin's most trusted collaborators, including all the members of his Politburo except Stalin and Trotsky, confessing to crimes they could not possibly have committed, implied that their minds had been broken. Khrushchev, in his denunciation of Stalin in his secret speech to the Twentieth Party Congress in 1956, charged that physical torture had been used. "Confessions of guilt of many arrested and charged with enemy activity were gained with the help of cruel and inhuman tortures," Khrushchev explained.

Facts prove that many abuses were made on Stalin's orders without reckoning with any norms of Party and Soviet legality. Stalin was a very distrustful man, sickly suspicious; we knew this from our work with him. He could look at a man and say: "Why are your eyes shifty today?" or "Why are you turning so much today and avoiding looking me directly in the eyes?" The sickly suspicion created in him a general distrust even toward eminent party workers whom he had known for years. Everywhere and in everything he saw "enemies," "two-facers" and "spies."

Possessing unlimited power he indulged in a great willfulness and choked a person morally and physically. A situation was created where one could not express one's own will.

When Stalin said that one or another should be arrested, it was necessary to accept on faith that he was an "enemy of the people." Meanwhile Beria's gang, which ran the organ of state security, outdid itself in proving the guilt of the arrested and the truth of materials which it falsified. And what proofs were offered? The confessions of the arrested, and the investigative judges accepted these "confessions." And how is it possible that a person confesses to crimes which he has not committed? Only in one way—because of application of physical methods of pressuring him, tortures, bringing him to a state of unconsciousness, deprivation of his judgment, taking away of his human dignity. [22]

[22] Cited in Basil Dmytryshyn, *USSR: A Concise History* (New York: Scribner's, 1965), p. 419.

The terror was not restricted to the upper levels of the Communist hierarchy or even to the party itself. It spread on a huge scale through all levels of society, with punishment varying from execution or deportation to a labor camp to ejection from the party or loss of a job. A balance sheet is impossible. But some of the prominent statistics speak for themselves. Of 1,966 delegates to the Seventeenth Party Congress of 1934, 1,108 were arrested. Of 139 members and candidates of the party's Central Committee in 1934, 98 were arrested and shot. Over one and a half million members and candidate members were dropped from the party. Half the officer corps of the army were arrested. Perhaps five percent of the entire population were arrested for some length of time, and over eight million sent to labor camps. No one could feel safe, no matter how loyal his past or even how blank his mind. John Scott found that in Magnitogorsk, thousands had been arrested, mostly at night, and "people were afraid of anyone and anything foreign." George Kennan, attached to the American embassy in Moscow, saw that a "terrible cloud of suspicion and violence, of sinister, unidentifiable terror and *sauve qui peut* denunciations, began to gather over Russia. . . . If in earlier stages of the development of Soviet power there had been vestiges of belief that society would be genuinely benefited by all the cruelty and suffering, here, in the Russia of the purges, was cynicism, shamelessness, contempt for humanity—all triumphantly enthroned." And Ilya Ehrenburg, returning to Moscow from the Spanish civil war in 1937, was amazed and disoriented at the ubiquitous fear and suspicion. The composer Prokofieff told him, "Today one must work. Work's the only thing, the only salvation." At the newspaper *Izvestia*, they had stopped putting nameplates on the doors: "Here today and gone tomorrow," a messenger girl explained. Meyerhold's theater had been closed, and he himself was soon arrested. Ehrenburg only got back to Spain after sending two personal letters to Stalin.

The most inexplicable suffering, however, was that of apolitical citizens, represented by the Leningrad typing-pool supervisor Olga Petrovna in Lydia Chukovskaya's heartbreaking little book *The Deserted House*. Olga's son, a loyal Komsomol worker, is implicated by a former schoolmate's confession in a plot he knows nothing of; Petrovna slowly breaks down in the misery of the faceless oppression. She has to line up for days on end to gain ten-second interviews with clerks in the prosecutor's office. She is denounced in the typing pool and compelled to resign her job. Friends cross the street to avoid her. Her neighbors plot to take her room. Finally, when a letter is smuggled to her from her son, begging her to intercede, she realizes that her action would only increase his troubles. In a gesture of ultimate despair, she burns the letter.

The effect of the purges went very deep. At the political level, they had removed all important critics of Stalin's policies and had reinforced his dictatorship at all stages of the party hierarchy. But it was in the armed forces that the most deleterious effects were observed, as the purges not only removed the most competent of the older generation but deprived their replacements of the willingness to take personal initiative. The poor performance against the Finns in the Winter War of 1939–1940 and the early defeats by the Germans during the invasion of 1941 were due, to an important degree, to the weakening of the officer corps.[23]

THE MEANING OF THE REVOLUTION

What then was the meaning of the Soviet experience two decades after the Revolution? Both Communist apologists and Western observers were in agreement that a vast social and political revolution had taken place and had made possible one of the most gigantic experiments in the remodeling of a society ever undertaken. But what had occurred?

There were many for whom the essence of the experiment was the reimposition of the tyranny of one man, now far greater in its mastery over the individual citizen because of the physical controls available to the twentieth-century state. To some Stalin was thus the reincarnation of Russia's historic tyrants, a new Ivan the Terrible; to others he was the inevitable product of the Communist insistence on the elite's leadership of the proletarian dictatorship that Lenin had made the key idea of Bolshevism— the pig who turns into an exploiting farmer himself, as in George Orwell's fable *Animal Farm*.

For many observers the foremost feature of the two decades was the industrialization of an underdeveloped country. Again, however, the industrialization could be interpreted in several ways. For the official apologists in Soviet Russia itself, the industrialization carried through in the Five-Year plans was a highly successful method of speeding up the transition that Marx had described, from capitalism to the ultimate stage of communism via an intermediate period of socialism. By 1936 it was held that Russia no longer needed the dictatorship of the proletariat, since class antagonism had vanished; and Russia was about to achieve the final Communist society. Both Soviet and Western observers, however, felt that this forced industrialization through the political control of the Communist party had lessons for other underdeveloped countries. The Soviet regime claimed that the success of its experiment proved that communism was not only the necessary instrument for the end of exploitation in industrialized societies like those of western Europe but a means by which the underdeveloped regions of the world, namely Asia, Africa, and South America, could achieve both a more just society and progress in economic development.

Finally there were others who looked primarily at the human impact of the Revolution. To some it was a gigantic tragedy in which human life

[23]Stalin's policies from 1939 to his death in 1953 are described in Chapter 26.

had been lost on a terrifying scale to satisfy the whims of an autocrat who cynically based his power on a pseudo-ideology. To others it was an exciting experiment in human brotherhood, in the creation of a new type of human being who would lack the economic greed, the self-interest, and the ruthlessness inculcated by the struggle for survival in a capitalist society. The very possibility that this might be occurring drew visitors to Moscow by the millions during the 1930s, and it gave the average Russian a tiny ray of hope throughout the darkest days of the purges that a better society was in the making. Without that hope—and the deep-rooted attachment to Russia itself—the Bolshevik experiment would have been swept away in the torrent of suffering that the Second World War was about to inflict on the Russians.

SUGGESTED READING

Nothing betters the superb vignettes of life in Moscow during the first three decades of the twentieth century in Boris Pasternak's *Doctor Zhivago* (1958), but Konstantin Paustovsky's memoirs, *The Story of a Life* (1964) is a close rival. Moscow is more effectively approached through the reminiscences and novels of Russian and foreign writers than through a more academic treatment. Ilya Ehrenburg, in *Men, Years—Life* (1963), not only gives short portraits of almost all Europe's leading literary figures but does so against a background of Europe's political upheavals, most of which he witnessed personally. Yevgeny Zamyatin's *We* (1924) is a fantasy about the world after the Revolution, in which everyone has become a number. It provided inspiration for George Orwell's *1984* (1949) and Aldous Huxley's *Brave New World* (1932), both of which are in part comments on the Russian Revolution. The American Communist reporter John Reed gives an exciting account of the November Revolution in Petrograd and a description of Moscow immediately after the Revolution in *Ten Days That Shook the World* (1919); Eugene Lyons was stationed as reporter in Moscow in 1928–1934, as he relates in *Assignment to Utopia* (1937); and George F. Kennan, *Memoirs, 1925–1950* (1967) summarizes the atmosphere of Moscow on the eve of the purges. The suffering of ordinary people during the 1930s is captured in Lydia Chukovskaya's *The Deserted House* (1967), while Stalin's daughter, Svetlana Alliluyeva, gives a view of life inside the Kremlin hierarchy in *Twenty Letters to a Friend* (1967).

Anatole Kopp, *Power and Revolution: Soviet Architecture and City Planning 1917–1935* (New York: A. Braziller, 1970), translated by Thomas E. Benton, is the best treatment of the exciting innovations in architecture and city planning in Moscow during the 1920s. E. D. Simon et al., *Moscow in the Making* (1937) describes the new city plan and comments on the nature of Moscow city government under the Communists. Michael F. Hamm, ed., *The City in Russian History* (1976) has good essays on urban planning before 1917 and on the ideas of the city planners in the 1920s. For the building of the subway, one should read the biographies of Nikita Khrushchev, such as Lazar Pistrak, *The Grand Tactician: Khrushchev's Rise to Power* (1961) or Edward Crankshaw's somewhat polemical *Khrushchev: A Career* (1966), or see Z. Troitskaya, *The L. M. Kaganovich Metropolitan Railway of Moscow* (1955). Valentin Gonzalez ("El Campesino") tells of his work on the later section of the subway in *Listen, Comrades: Life and Death in the So-*

viet Union (1952). For short summaries of Moscow's city growth, see the two sur-veys published in the Soviet Union, Yuri Saushkin, *Moscow* (1966) and the very fine *Moscow: Architecture and Monuments* (1968) of M. Ilyin. Peter Hall, *The World Cities* (1966) concentrates on city planning for the future. For a pictorial view of Moscow in 1928, see Alexys A. Sidorow, *Moskau* (1928).

For broad analyses of the causes of the Russian Revolution, see M. T. Florinsky, *The End of the Russian Empire* (1961), which emphasizes the role of war; Bernard Pares, *The Fall of the Russian Monarchy* (1939), in which he ex-plains from personal acquaintance the breakdown of all the social forces that sup-ported the tsardom; and Theodore von Laue, *Why Lenin? Why Stalin?* (1971), an admirably condensed attempt to "view the emergence of Russian communism as an integral part of European and global history." Pre-Soviet Russia comes alive in Henri Troyat, *Daily Life in Russia Under the Last Tsar* (1979). The detailed events of 1917 can be followed in N. N. Sukhanov, *The Russian Revolution, 1917: A Personal Record* (1955); Leon Trotsky, *The History of the Russian Revolution* (1932–1933); William H. Chamberlin, *The Russian Revolution, 1917–1921* (1935); Robert V. Daniels, *Red October* (1967); and Alexander Kerensky, *The Kerensky Memoirs* (1965). On the civil war, see David Footman, *Civil War in Russia* (1961).

Among the many biographies of Lenin, good narrative is provided by David Shub, *Lenin: A Biography* (1976) and Robert Payne, *The Life and Death of Lenin* (1964), both of which are rich in primary materials. H. C. Morgan, *Lenin* (1971) is highly appreciative of Lenin's constructive achievements and should be compared with Robert Conquest's *V. I. Lenin* (1972), which sets out to show where the Bol-shevik elite went wrong. Adam Ulam's *The Bolsheviks* (1965) is primarily about Lenin. Nikolai Valentinov's *Early Years of Lenin* (1969) and the shorter Rolf H. W. Theen, *Lenin: Genesis and Development of a Revolutionary* (1973) are useful on Lenin's formative experiences. Robert H. McNeal's excellent biography of Le-nin's wife, *Bride of the Revolution: Krupskaya and Lenin* (1972) is also good on the aftereffects of Lenin's influence following his death.

Isaac Deutscher has provided two indispensable studies, his two-volume life of Trotsky, *The Prophet Armed, 1879–1921* (1954) and *The Prophet Unarmed, 1921–1929* (1959), and *Stalin: A Political Biography* (1967). E. H. Carr's com-prehensive study of the first decade of Communist rule, which eschews narrative in favor of political and economic analysis, is composed of *The Bolshevik Revolu-tion* (1951–1953), *The Interregnum, 1923–1924* (1954), and *Socialism in One Country, 1924–1926* (1961). The capture during the Second World War of the documents from the Soviet archives in Smolensk made it possible to reconstruct in detail the process of Communist takeover of a big city, which is summarized in Merle Fainsod's excellent *Smolensk Under Soviet Rule* (1958).

On the Five-Year plans, see William H. Chamberlin, *Russia's Iron Age* (1934), by a perspicacious reporter; John Scott, *Behind the Urals: An American Worker in Russia's City of Steel* (1942), a very well-written account of Magnitogorsk dur-ing the 1930s; and Fedor Belov, *A History of a Soviet Collective Farm* (1955), a personal account of the collectivization of agriculture. Overall industrial results are collated in Naum Jasny, *Soviet Industrialization, 1928–1952* (1961).

Marc L. Slonim provides a short survey of the main figures of Soviet literature in *Soviet Russian Literature: Writers and Problems, 1917–1967* (1967), which can be compared with the Soviet view of the same writers in K. Zelinsky, *Soviet Literature: Problems and People* (1970). The papers of a fine symposium covering the whole development of Soviet literature are collected in Max Hayward and Leopold Labedz, eds., *Literature and Revolution in Soviet Russia, 1917–1962* (1963). Abram Tertz (Andrei Siniavsky) condemns the Stalinist influence on literature in *On Socialist Realism* (1960). For the methodology of the cultural movements of the 1930s, see C. Vaughan James, *Soviet Socialist Realism: Origins and Theory* (1973). For the innovations in painting during the early days of the Revolution, turn to Robert C. Williams, *Artists in Revolution: Portraits of the Russian Avant-Garde, 1905–1925* (1978).

For various verdicts on communization as a human experience, see the comments of the English Socialists Sidney and Beatrice Webb, *Soviet Communism: A New Civilization* (1944); Milorad Drachovitch, ed., *Fifty Years of Communism in Russia* (1968); and Klaus Mehnert, *Soviet Man and His World* (1962). A well-balanced collection of verdicts on politics, economics, society, and culture is brought together in Daniel R. Brower, ed., *The Soviet Experience: Success or Failure?* (1971).

29

EUROPE FROM WAR TO WAR,
1919–1945

During the 1920s, Paris once again exercised political and cultural hegemony in the West. Its intellectual preeminence was well deserved. Not only did its own artists and thinkers continue that great creative flowering that began during the Belle Epoque before the war, but it also became the haven for foreign intellectuals whose native urban centers could not compete with the City of Light as congenial environments for creative activity—for many of Russia's intelligentsia fleeing the Bolshevik revolution; for Viennese and Hungarians who found that Vienna and Budapest had turned provincial with the loss of their status as imperial capitals; for Italians escaping Mussolini's Fascism; and for Americans disillusioned with the materialism of the Roaring Twenties back home or merely unable to relinquish the city that had entranced them as soldiers during the war. But the political hegemony of Paris was essentially superficial. It was due to the temporary abasement of Germany and to the self-imposed isolation from the international system of the two major world powers—the United States, retreating in revulsion against further costly intervention in European affairs; and the Soviet Union, quarantining itself and concentrating on recovering from civil war and on building socialism.

The Great Depression of 1929–1933 exposed the unreality of French hegemony, however, by destroying the prosperity that had lulled the other powers into accepting France's pretensions. The depression persuaded France and its principal ally, Britain, of their own economic weakness and military incapacity, thereby attuning them to accept appeasement of military aggressors. Moreover, it further increased the unwillingness of the

Liberation of Paris, 1944   *(Robert Capa/Magnum Photos)*

United States to risk military commitments to the European powers. Finally, it brought to power in Germany the Nazi party, which under Adolf Hitler was to use the vast economic and military resources of Germany for premeditated aggression. Thus in the 1930s, the center of political dominance in the West passed from Paris to Berlin—from the capital of the Third Republic to the capital of the Third Reich. Berlin was a society in many ways the antithesis of everything that Western civilization had created in the previous two thousand years: a Nazi totalitarian state based on the perverted racist doctrines of a sadistic madman.

THE LAST HEGEMONY OF PARIS

Paris Peace Conference of 1919

When the armistice agreement of November 11, 1918, finally concluded the fighting of the First World War, citizens of the victorious nations responded with a mixture of relief and jubilation. Siegfried Sassoon expressed the general delight with a poem that began:

Everybody suddenly burst out singing
And I was filled with such delight
As prisoned birds must find in freedom. [1]

That night the crowds went wild in London's Trafalgar Square, on the Champs Elysées in Paris, and in Times Square in New York in celebration of the end of the bloodletting. Sixteen million people had died in the war, and another twenty million had been wounded. The French army had mobilized over eight million men, and three-quarters of them had been killed or wounded; one-twentieth of the French population had died. Britain had lost about 900,000 soldiers; Italy about 650,000; and the United States, in little more than a year of fighting, 126,000. The Allied victors had spent $156 billion, the defeated Central powers $63 billion. The sharp-tongued French premier Clemenceau, nicknamed "the tiger," who had lashed France to final victory, slowly came to dominate the proceedings of the peace conference, which began in Paris in January. In Lord Keynes's harsh but essentially truthful picture of him in *The Economic Consequences of the Peace* (1919), Clemenceau appears as the epitome of the cynical, Machiavellian, old world statesman; his primary preoccupation is to prevent the foolish, unrealistic scruples of American President Woodrow Wilson from stopping the permanent debilitation of Germany. In a classic passage, Keynes sums up Clemenceau and his vision of France:

He felt about France what Pericles felt of Athens—unique value in her, nothing else mattering; but his theory of politics was Bismarck's. He had one illusion—

Georges Clemenceau, by Auguste Rodin
Rodin's craggy bronze captured perfectly the ferocity of "the tiger," as Clemenceau was called. (Philadelphia Museum of Art: Given by Jules Mastbaum)

[1] From "Everyone Sang" in *Collected Poems* by Siegfried Sassoon. Copyright 1920 by E. P. Dutton, copyright renewed 1948 by Siegfried Sassoon. Reprinted by permission of Viking Penguin, Inc., and George Sassoon.

France; and one disillusion—mankind, including Frenchmen, and his colleagues not least. His principles for the peace can be expressed simply. In the first place, he was a foremost believer in the view of German psychology that the German understands and can understand nothing but intimidation, that he is without generosity or remorse in negotiation, that there is no advantage he will not take of you, and no extent to which he will not demean himself for profit, that he is without honor, pride, or mercy. Therefore you must never negotiate with a German or conciliate him; you must dictate to him. On no other terms will he respect you, or will you prevent him from cheating you. But it is doubtful how far he thought these characteristics peculiar to Germany, or whether his candid view of some other nations was fundamentally different.[2]

With that premise it was easy to justify territorial dismemberment and economic exactions from Germany. Alsace and Lorraine were returned to France, which also won control of the mining region of the Saar for fifteen years. The Polish state, which had been divided among Russia, Prussia, and Austria in the three partitions of 1772, 1793, and 1795 and reconstituted on November 9, 1918, was given the Polish Corridor, a broad strip of territory separating East Prussia from the main body of Germany. The German colonial empire was divided among the Allies, and its merchant fleet shared out as reparations. During the following two years, it was to pay $5 billion in reparations; the total amount to be paid was later settled at $31 billion. To ensure the military weakness of Germany, its army was to be reduced to 100,000 men; the left bank of the Rhine and a strip fifty kilometers wide on the right bank were to be permanently demilitarized; and occupation troops, mostly from France, were to be stationed in the Rhineland for fifteen years. The Germans were appalled by this dictated settlement, which they labeled the *Diktat*, but were compelled to accept it unchanged under the threat of Allied invasion. Their representatives appeared at the Palace of Versailles on June 28, 1919, to give ceremonial atonement to the French for Bismarck's choice of the same Hall of Mirrors for the declaration of the German Empire in January 1871. Harold Nicolson described the ceremony in his diary that evening:

Through the door at the end appear two huissiers [ushers] with silver chains. They march in single file. After them come four officers of France, Great Britain, America and Italy. And then, isolated and pitiable, come the two German delegates, Dr. Müller and Dr. Bell. The silence is terrifying. Their feet upon a strip of parquet between the savonnerie carpets echo hollow and duplicate. They keep their eyes fixed away from those two thousand staring eyes, fixed upon the ceiling. They are deathly pale. They do not appear as representatives of a brutal militarism. . . . Suddenly from outside comes the crash of guns thundering a salute. It announces to Paris that the second Treaty of Versailles [the first being the treaty of 1871 at the end of the Franco-Prussian War] had been signed by Dr. Müller and Dr. Bell. Through the few open windows comes the sound of distant crowds

[2]John Maynard Keynes, *The Economic Consequences of the Peace* (New York: Harper Torchbook, 1971), pp. 32–33.

Signature of the Treaty of Versailles in the Hall of Mirrors, June 28, 1919
(National Archives)

cheering hoarsely. . . . We kept our seats while the Germans were conducted like prisoners from the dock, their eyes still fixed upon some distant point of the horizon.[3]

Equally momentous changes were being ratified in other suburban palaces of Paris that spring. The peace conference had also sanctioned the dismemberment of the Austro-Hungarian and Turkish empires. It gave to the new state of Czechoslovakia not only the Czech provinces of Bohemia and Moravia, Slovakia, and the Ukrainian province of Sub-Carpathian Ruthenia, but also the border province of the Sudetenland, where almost three million Germans lived. Serbia expanded to become the South Slav state of Yugoslavia. The aggrieved Hungarians were left with a small state of only eight million inhabitants. In addition to the formerly German territories of the Polish Corridor, Poland was permitted, after four years of fighting with Soviet Russia, to annex a large strip of territory in White Russia; and following a plebiscite in 1921, it annexed a valuable industrial section of the German province of Silesia. The Turks lost the Arab provinces in the Middle East, Britain taking up mandates over Palestine, Iraq, and Jordan, and France over Lebanon and Syria. Finally, the independence of Finland, Estonia, Latvia, and Lithuania, granted at the Treaty of Brest Litovsk, was left undisturbed.

Thus a line of new or remodeled states stretched from the Arctic to the Mediterranean in place of the three great empires that had collapsed during the war. Although these states all possessed fine written constitutions, they were economically backward, socially divided, and politically unstable. Eastern Europe had become a political vacuum, inviting the intervention of Germany from the west and Russia from the east. Its social divisions gave the Fascist states allies in the landed aristocracy and the

[3]Harold Nicolson, *Peacemaking* (London: Constable, 1934), pp. 366–371.

Legend:
—·— German Empire, 1914
||| Russian Empire, 1914
•••• Austro-Hungarian Empire, 1914
∷ Territorial Losses of the Empires: 1918–1923

Central Europe Between the Wars

well-to-do bourgeoisie and gave to Communist Russia supporters among certain sections of the industrial proletariat and the farming population. Eastern Europe became the greatest threat to the maintenance of a workable balance-of-power system during the interwar years.

French Enforcement of the Treaty of Versailles	The French soon discovered that they would be the chief enforcers of the treaty from which they had the most to gain. The American Senate refused to ratify the Treaty of Versailles; the United States did not even join the League of Nations. The French therefore sought to build up an alliance system with Poland, Czechoslovakia, Rumania, and Yugoslavia. As long as Germany remained quiescent, these alliances with states whose military strength was grossly overestimated appeared to give France the ability to threaten Germany with a two-front war. The French therefore felt strong enough for several years to use military force to ensure that Germany kept the obligations imposed on it by the Treaty of Versailles.

In response to what they regarded as a deliberate default on reparations payments, the French took over the customs collection at the German border, moved into several Rhineland towns, and in 1923, occupied the vast industrial region of the Ruhr. The Germans replied with passive resistance. All industries closed down; transportation stopped; and government workers refused to collaborate. For months the French tried desperately to break the resistance by arresting leaders of the general strike, using soldiers to run essential services and confiscating industrial produce. The German currency collapsed; Communist coups were attempted in several industrial cities; Hitler made a first attempt to seize power in Munich; separatist movements attempted to gain autonomy for the Rhineland. But France found the occupation of the Ruhr too costly. Its own currency began to waver, owing to the burden of the occupation army and the total cessation of reparations payments. Finally in 1924 it accepted the Dawes Plan, which scaled down German reparations payments and guaranteed large American loans to back the currency and industrial recovery.

The Years of Hope, 1924–1929	After the crisis of 1923–1924, Europe enjoyed half a decade of economic prosperity, during which French hegemony was expressed in the organization of various schemes of international cooperation. Largely through the work of French Foreign Minister Aristide Briand, the Germans were persuaded to accept the permanence of their new border with France, at a dramatically harmonious meeting of the British, French, and German foreign ministers in the Swiss lakeside town of Locarno in 1925. The Germans were welcomed to the League of Nations; they joined with almost every nation in the world in signing the Kellogg-Briand peace pacts of 1928, by which the signatories renounced recourse to war for the settlement of international disputes; and they even for a time considered joining with France in a European federal union. The continuance of this "spirit of Locarno" was, however, dependent on the economic prosperity that in the late 1920s was making territorial losses seem far less significant than enjoyment of the material benefits of the new industrial productivity.

The prosperity of 1924–1929 was real. Throughout Europe there was a general stabilization of the currencies, which led many countries to revert to the gold standard. Technological advances, many of them the result of the war, were creating whole new industries, among them oil refining and the manufacture of automobiles, airplanes, artificial fibers, chemical fertilizers, and electrical appliances. Older industries were revitalized by new methods of organization. The number of cartels increased enormously, especially in Germany, where the new giants included the great chemical trust, I. G. Farben, and Europe's largest steel trust, Vereinigte Stahlwerke; and a number of conglomerates were formed. "Americanization" of production included the use of management consulting firms, the introduction of time-and-motion studies, and widespread attempts at standardization of parts and use of the conveyor belt for mass production. Spending on public works projects and on public housing gave a boost to the construction industry and stimulated the production of cement, timber, brick, and paintstuffs. The increase in real wages acted as a stimulus to the consumer industries; the manufacture of such items as cosmetics and processed foodstuffs grew in importance.

There were, however, many precarious features underlying this prosperity. Agriculture never knew the well-being of the cities. Even among the industrial population, unemployment remained high during the best years. In England, for example, it never sank below one million, roughly one-tenth of the working population. Many of the cartels were unstable structures that fell apart in times of economic recession, destroying smaller companies that might have been able to survive on their own initiative. The dependence of Europe on American loans, many of them short-term, and on the continuance of large American imports from Europe, was especially risky. The American economy was based on overextended credit, especially for stock exchange speculation; and the collapse of this credit structure would inevitably produce vast repercussions in Europe as short-term loans would be called in, new loans would diminish, and the market for European exports would be greatly restricted.

The depression was precipitated by the Wall Street crash of October 1929, which in a few weeks reduced the value of the American industrial stocks by half. Five thousand American banks failed; farm prices collapsed; industrial companies cut back on work forces, thereby further reducing the demand for goods. Within three years, American unemployment had reached twelve million. The industrial areas of Europe were the first to feel the effects of the American crash, especially those that had borrowed heavily from American banks. In May 1931 the greatest Austrian bank, the Credit-Anstalt, which held two-thirds of Austria's assets, collapsed. The panic immediately spread through parts of eastern Europe, for which the Credit-Anstalt had been banker. Panic-stricken depositors withdrew their savings, precipitating more bank failures. Industries reduced production and laid off workers; and desperate governments made matters worse by decreeing economy measures and higher taxes that increased the recession. The huge German bank, the Darmstädter National, failed shortly after the Credit-Anstalt, and a similar depression spiral soon affected Germany. Unemployment rose steadily until it hit six million in 1932. In Brit-

The Great Depression of 1929-1933

Crowds Outside the Stock Exchange on Wall Street After the Crash of October 1929

In a week of panic selling following the start of the Wall Street Crash on October 24, the major industrial shares fell in value to only two-fifths of the year's high. (National Archives)

ain, where the Bank of England was paying out over $12 million in gold each day, the Labour government resigned and was replaced by a National Government that took Britain off the gold standard. Economy measures failed to halt the recession, however, and England's unemployment rose to over 2.5 million. The effects of the depression upon millions of individual families in Europe and the United States were overwhelming, producing a kind of depression psychosis, a desperation in which people lost all hope for the future and all trust in their established institutions. It was this state of mind that both made it possible for Fascist governments to come into power in Germany and eastern Europe and prevented the democratic governments from rousing their citizens to take action against Fascism.

France at first escaped the worst effects of the depression. Its agriculture had absorbed many of the unemployed industrial workers who had gone home to the family farms; and it had reduced the impact of unemployment by sending home thousands of foreign workers. But in 1932, France, too, felt the depression's impact. Tourism, especially from the United States, was greatly reduced; export markets, particularly for French luxury goods, were closed; agricultural prices and income dropped. The customary budget surplus had been replaced by a deficit of 6 billion francs. Governments began to fall like ninepins; in 1932–1934 there were six different French governments. France slowly lost the belief in its own economic strength and military importance that had given it the self-confidence to attempt to dominate the European state system throughout the 1920s. It turned in on itself, occupied with the problems of economic recovery and political instability. And in 1930, almost as a symbol of their loss of confidence, the French began construction of the Maginot Line, a steel and concrete fortification along the whole border from southern Belgium to Switzerland, intended to halt a German invasion.

THE GOLDEN TWENTIES IN BERLIN AND PARIS

T he most scintillating centers of Europe's intellectual and artistic life during the prosperous years of the 1920s were Berlin and Paris. With the formation in Germany of the Weimar Republic (so called because the national assembly drawing up the new constitution had met in Goethe's home town of Weimar to symbolize the break with Prussian militarism), Berlin unleashed all the creative drives that had been restrained during the reign of William II. There was a new freedom of expression, especially in the sardonic wit for which the Berliner had been noted throughout Germany, and an unleashing of all kinds of social inhibitions, which found expression in jazz, gaudy night clubs, drugs, and drunkenness: "Berlin transformed itself into the Babel of the world," wrote Stefan Zweig. The multiplicity of political parties gave vigor to a political debate that had been sadly unrealistic during most of the Second Reich. The University of Berlin entered its most fecund period; its professors included Friedrich Meinecke in history and Einstein and Planck in physics. One of the main training schools in the new art of psychoanalysis was the Berlin Psychoanalytical Institute, which produced many of the decade's greatest psychologists. But it was in the arts that Berlin especially excelled. With forty theaters, two great orchestras, three operas, one hundred and twenty newspapers, and most of the great publishing houses, it centralized German culture without stifling it. Bertolt Brecht, the innovative left-wing playwright, moved to Berlin in 1925, to join in the collaboration with Kurt Weill that three years later produced *The Threepenny Opera*. Georg Grosz and Käthe Kollwitz revealed the sufferings of the poor in spare, heartbreaking sketches. The Expressionist painters, including the notable immigrants Wassily Kandinsky and Paul Klee, experimented with the use of color and abstract design to represent what was intuitively rather than intellectually understood. Cinema above all struck out in new directions, from the dark cruelty of *The Cabinet of Dr. Caligari* (1920) to the pacifist *All Quiet on the Western Front* (1930).

Beneath the surface in Weimar Germany, however, there was a sense of desperation that was alien to the spirit of Paris. The recurrent economic crises, especially the great inflation of 1923, had made everyone skeptical of the future and had left them with a deep distrust of the capacity of the

Berlin During the Weimar Republic

republican politicians. The atmosphere of the last years before Hitler was captured by the English novelist Christopher Isherwood, who eked out a mean existence among the worst Berlin slums during the collapse of the Weimar Republic, in *The Last of Mr. Norris* (1935) and *Goodbye to Berlin* (1939). Visiting Isherwood in his scrofulous neighborhood, the poet Stephen Spender found "there was a sensation of doom to be felt in the Berlin streets."

In this Berlin, the poverty, the agitation, the propaganda, witnessed by us in the streets and cafes, seemed more and more to represent the whole life of the town, as though there were almost no privacy behind doors. Berlin was the tension, the poverty, the anger, the prostitution, the hope and despair thrown out on to the streets. . . .

[We] became ever more aware that the carefree personal lives of our friends were facades in front of the immense social chaos. There was more and more a feeling that this life would be swept away. When we were on holiday at Insel Ruegen, where the naked bathers in their hundreds lay stretched on the beach under the drugging sun, sometimes we heard orders rapped out, and even shots, from the forest whose edges skirted the shore, where the [Nazi] Storm Troopers were training like executioners waiting to martyr the armed and self-disarmed.[4]

[4]Stephen Spender, *World Within World* (London: Hamish Hamilton, 1951), pp. 129–131.

Workers, by George Grosz (1893–1959), from Folio *Im Schatten*
In the 1920s, Grosz satirized German bourgeois society in a series of scathing pen and ink drawings, in which the capitalists turn into grotesque monsters while the workers are dehumanized. (Courtesy of the Fogg Art Museum, Harvard University. Purchase-Friends of Fogg Art Museum. Reproduced with permission of the estate of George Grosz, Princeton, New Jersey.)

In Paris there was little sense of the fragility of the exhilarating lifestyle that was drawing admirers from all over the world. For Paris, the twenties was a new and even more wonderful Belle Epoque. Intellectuals and artists found that many of the innovations that had been ignored or scorned when they were conceived in the last years before the World War were now accepted and admired by the members of the educated public. They followed Picasso as he moved from Cubism back to figurative painting and then on into Surrealism, in which the distorted images of the subconscious mind were depicted. They paid increasingly high prices for the more easily accepted works of Utrillo and Bonnard and showed a new appreciation of the experiments in Cubism that Braque and Léger continued to make. Even Dadaism, the cult of nonsense invented by the Rumanian expatriate Tristan Tzara, found its advocates. Dada called for the rejection of all established styles, the abandonment of reason, the overthrow of authority, the expression of the immediate impulse or thought or emotion.

A Second Belle Epoque in Paris

For literary innovation, too, there was a new receptivity. Although Proust had died in 1922, the remaining volumes of *Remembrance of Things Past* continued to appear until 1927, to constant acclaim. André Gide (1869–1951), praised by the Dadaist and Surrealist writers, was recognized as the master literary craftsman of the generation. In his *Journals* and especially in the novel *The Counterfeiters* (1926), he wrestled in a severely disciplined classical manner with the problem of reconciling one's hidden drives with the demands of society. For him, the individual consciousness had rights that were denied it by rigid social convention, rights that he justified by slowly revealing to the public his own inner deviations. Behind Gide followed a group of younger writers, all bent on experimentation. Among them were Surrealists like Paul Eluard and Louis Aragon, whose literary explorations finally took political form and brought them into the Communist party. In music, Stravinsky had conquered: the scandal of the first performance of *The Rite of Spring* was forgotten. He again worked with Diaghilev and the Ballets Russes, which, reassembled in postwar Paris, turned to ever more innovative styling, exploring the unconscious in dance forms and rejecting the conventionally pretty for stark, angular effects of lighting and choreography.

Paris became home to a group of young American expatriates who combined determination to enjoy Paris to the full with the discipline for producing fine writing. They formed almost a world of their own on the Left Bank, living in cold, uncomfortable flats six or eight floors up, making do on pickings from occasional journalism or sale of a short story, recreating the "Vie de Bohème" with a consciousness and a vivacity that exceeded even that of the fin de siècle. The shrill awareness of the precarious nature of their good fortune, of the still inexplicable brutality of the war that lay behind them, and of the uncertainty of the political future was captured by F. Scott Fitzgerald in books like *The Great Gatsby* and by Ernest Hemingway in *The Sun Also Rises*. It remained a constant in their daily lives, as Hemingway described it later in his superb little memoir *A Moveable Feast*. "Paris was a very old city and we were young and nothing was simple there," Hemingway wrote, "not even poverty, nor sudden money, nor the moonlight, nor right and wrong nor the breathing of someone who lay beside you in the moonlight." The wild cacophony of their lives comes through in all the writing of this Parisian generation of Americans—in the disconnected phrases of the poems of e e cummings, in the cinematic sequences of John Dos Passos, and especially in the myriad themes of *Ulysses*, the masterpiece by the Irishman James Joyce, who was recognized by the whole American colony as its commanding genius.

In Berlin this frenetic age of literary and artistic creation came to an abrupt end with the appointment of Adolf Hitler as chancellor in January 1933. In Paris economic depression combined in the 1930s with fear that the Nazi transformation of Germany was a direct threat to France itself. Politics became increasingly important, even to those literary and artistic figures who tried most vigorously to avoid its entanglement. During the

Ernest Hemingway (1898–1961)

In The Sun Also Rises *(1926), Hemingway portrayed the American writers and artists of "the lost generation" who had settled in Paris after the First World War to lead the Bohemian life of the Left Bank. (National Archives)*

1930s all groups in French society found that they had to come to terms with the phenomenon of Fascism, both in its internal manifestations as a right-wing threat to French democratic institutions and as an external danger embodied in Hitler's Third Reich. Between 1930 and 1933 most of the literary expatriates in Paris went home; and their departure symbolized the end of the second Belle Epoque.

FASCISM IN ITALY

In 1919 most western European leaders felt that the main threat to the stability of their political and social institutions was the Bolshevik regime in Russia. But by 1923 all Communist attempts to take power had failed. The Spartacus uprising of German Communists in January 1919 had been put down with bloody violence by the freelance bands of demobilized soldiers called the *Freikorps*. The Communist regime installed in Hungary under Béla Kun was ousted by a monarchist Rumanian army in November 1919 after only six months in power. And various sporadic Communist uprisings in the industrial cities of Germany between 1920 and 1923 were repressed by the regular army. By 1923 it was obvious that the hope of a continentwide proletarian revolution, which Lenin and Trotsky had believed might occur at the end of the war, had been shattered. Yet as Communism receded as an immediate threat to the democratic governments, it was replaced by the challenge of Fascism, a right-wing totalitarian movement that took power in Italy in 1922, and in 1933–1939 in one form or another seized control of most of the governments of central and eastern Europe.

Suppression of the Spartacus Uprising in Berlin, January 1919
German troops, using a tank borrowed from the British army, move through a working-class section of Berlin. (Courtesy of French Embassy Press and Information Division)

The Fascist Seizure of Power, 1922

Benito Mussolini (1883–1945) had been a Socialist agitator before the First World War; he had thrown his considerable talents as journalist and orator into organizing Italian migrant labor and into opposing Italy's war to seize Libya in 1911. During the First World War, however, he changed course completely, demanding intervention by Italy, serving in the army himself, and glorifying the moral benefits of war in raising the spiritual caliber of the nation. By 1922 Mussolini had laid down the propagandist slogans that were to bring him to power. Man exists for the state and is not fully alive unless he is part of the state. Man must sacrifice himself for the state; the highest form of sacrifice occurs in war. Democracy is a form of dictatorship of the majority and must be replaced by the rule of an elite guided by a leader, a *Duce*. The Duce embodies in himself the will of the nation, and thus can never be wrong in any of his actions: "Il Duce ha sempre ragione" ("The leader is always right") he later emblazoned on buildings throughout Italy. The nation is a body that exists permanently in time, binding together the generations of past and future; the present Italian generation must recreate the glories of the Roman Empire. The new Italy must transform the Adriatic into an Italian lake and the Mediterranean into "our sea"; and it must win "sun and earth" in the colonial territories of Africa.

The social turmoil of 1919–1922 in Italy gave Mussolini his opportunity. The parliamentary government lacked the ability to take firm action. The Social Democrats, who were the largest party in the Chamber, refused

Mussolini Speaking in Rome, 1934

Mussolini had favored pacifism at the outbreak of the First World War. As leader of the Fascist party, and, after 1922, as head of the Italian government, he struck increasingly militaristic poses and repeatedly declared that Italy's destiny was to restore the greatness of the Roman Empire. (United Press International, Inc.)

to collaborate with a bourgeois government. The new Catholic party, called the *Popolari*, although moderately reformist, could not cooperate with the anticlerical Socialists. The conservative parties, who together held a majority, lacked leadership and often quarreled among themselves. Prime ministers were usually extremely old men out of touch with the postwar realities. This unstable regime was faced with three major challenges. First, the workers of the northern factories, supported by vast numbers of demobilized soldiers who could not find work, were engaged in a bitter wage dispute with the factory owners; and in 1920 they began to seize control of their factories in a movement that spread to fifty-nine Italian cities. This labor unrest, strategy for which was taken from the workers' movement in Russia, was eventually fused by grants of higher wages; but the possessing classes remained fearful of future moves by the unions. Second, after the government had reneged on its wartime promises to redistribute land among the peasantry and returning soldiers, landless laborers throughout Italy began to seize unworked land. Third, extreme nationalists were outraged that Italy had gained so little at the peace conference, especially in the coastal areas of the Adriatic; and about 8,000 war veterans had followed the colorful poet Gabriele D'Annunzio in the takeover of the port of Fiume, which was claimed by the new Yugoslav state. When the Italian government decided to oust D'Annunzio, many nationalists began to seek a more extreme right-wing party that would reassert Italy's legitimate demands.

To capitalize on middle-class fear of social revolution and to enlist the nationalists in his movement, Mussolini posed as the defender of Italy against internal subversion and foreign betrayal. In March 1919, he formed armed bands of ex-soldiers called *fasci di combattimento* ("fighting bands"), whom he turned loose to beat up Socialists and leftist Catholics, to destroy their offices and printing presses, and to disrupt their meetings. He was joined by increasing numbers of right-wing activists, and by 1922 the Fascist movement had 300,000 members. Unemployment continued to rise. No politician could form a coherent majority in the Chamber. Hundreds of small towns were being seized by the Fascist strong-arm groups. Finally, in October 1922 Mussolini felt strong enough to proclaim a "March on Rome" by every Fascist in Italy. Only about 10,000 of his black-shirted followers finally made it to the capital, but the government resigned in terror. Mussolini was then invited by King Victor Emmanuel II to form a government, all the legal forms being scrupulously respected.

Fascist Internal Policy

During the next seven years, Mussolini painstakingly wiped out all opposition. Rival political parties found their offices destroyed, and their leaders were beaten up in the streets or arrested. One leading Socialist was brutally murdered and his body flung into the Tiber. A new election law gave a majority of the seats in parliament to the party that won the greatest number of votes. The resultant Fascist-controlled parliament abolished all other political parties. All judges were replaced with loyal Fascists; trade unions were turned into Fascist corporations; and all local government was made directly responsible to the central government. Recalcitrant opponents were exiled to prison islands off the coast of Italy or sent into remote villages in the southern mountains. Mussolini's greatest success was to make a concordat with the papacy, which from the time of Italian unification in 1871 had refused to have any dealings with the new Italian state. In return for large financial concessions, continuing Church influence on Italian education, and the recognition of the formal independence of the tiny Vatican City as a separate state, the pope agreed to establish diplomatic relations with the Fascist government.

During the 1920s Mussolini achieved considerable popularity at home without causing much opposition abroad. His public works policies, which included the draining of marshes, the building of new roads, and the construction of many public buildings, helped maintain employment. Big companies found the Fascist government willing to give them a free hand in industrial planning and to help them by keeping the labor force disciplined. The Fascist regime hoped to increase the population by initiating a drive to persuade Italian migrants to return from abroad; by glorifying motherhood through propaganda; and by limiting the educational and employment possibilities for women outside the home. (In fact, however, especially as the army was increased in size, women found jobs in the factories and enjoyed a greater public role than Fascist theory assigned to them.) Bombastic speeches restored national pride without exacting a high price. Mussolini seemed to have made dictatorship respectable; and to many conservative Europeans, his regime, and those of the military dictator Primo de Rivera in Spain from 1923 to 1930 and of the military-backed presidency of Antonio de Oliveira Salazar in Portugal established in 1926, were models of firm, anti-Communist government.

THE WEIMAR REPUBLIC AND THE RISE OF NAZISM

Adolf Hitler

The National-Socialist (Nazi) movement in Germany had a more brutal vigor and more sinister leadership than Italian fascism, although many of the tenets of its ideology were similar to those of Italian fascism; but the government of the Weimar Republic proved more resilient than that of the Italian state. Whereas Mussolini was able to take control of Italy only three years after creation of the Fascist movement, fourteen years of effort were needed before Hitler could take power in Germany.

The Nazi movement in Germany was the brainchild of a sallow, dark-eyed young Austrian with a fine command of emotive oratory and a bundle of neurotic hatreds. Adolf Hitler's most lasting obsession, his abhorrence of the Jews, was probably acquired during his early days in prewar Vienna. Here, he claimed, denied admission to the Academy of Fine Arts, he was forced to earn a meager living by manual labor and the sale of little picture postcards he painted of Viennese buildings. The Jews came to represent "the evil spirits leading our people astray," the inspiration for the modern art and music he despised, the cosmopolitan bourgeois elite that dominated Viennese life. By 1913, when he moved to Munich to avoid the Austrian draft, he considered the Jews poisonous dregs in the pure Aryan blood.

In 1914 he enrolled in a Bavarian regiment; and in four years of service on the western front, he acquired an admiration for war, in which "individual interest—the interest of one's own ego—could be subordinated to the common interest." When he returned to Munich, his aim was to create an ideology backed by ruthless physical force. In 1919 he joined a small group of anti-Semitic amateur politicians, renamed it the National-Socialist German Workers party, and made himself its leader, or *Führer*. By 1923 he had already gathered around himself many of the party's principal organizers, including scar-faced Ernst Röhm, who put together the brown-shirted storm troops of the Sturm-Abteilung (SA); Rudolf Hess; and Hermann Göring. At that time he judged that the succession of crises, both political and economic, to which the government of the Weimar Republic and its constituent states like Bavaria had been subjected since 1918, had brought Germany to the point where a determined movement like his own could seize power by force.

The Weimar regime was undoubtedly extremely unstable. The pressure of the Communists and left-wing Socialists, who had been temporarily beaten back by the demobilized soldiers of the Free Corps in January 1919 in the suppression of the Spartacus uprising in Berlin, had revived under the guidance of the Comintern; and in 1923 the army had to be used to eject the Communists from several important industrial cities they had seized in the Rhine valley. The opposition of the extreme right-wing forces to the new state was still strong. In 1920, the army had refused to take action when Berlin was seized by groups of the Free Corps in the "Kapp Putsch"; and Kapp (the nominal leader of the coup) and his supporters were ejected only by a general strike led by the Socialist trade unions. France's demands for acceptance of the Treaty of Versailles, surrender of war criminals, and payment of reparations brought about the resignation of several chancellors who lacked the courage to accept the responsibilities of the lost war. The inflation of the currency, which, it has been suggested, had been encouraged by the German governments as a method of reducing payments on the national debt and of easing payment of reparations, was brought to disastrous levels by the French invasion of the Ruhr and the German government's declaration of passive resistance. In November 1923, Hitler decided to use his storm troopers to take control of Bavaria. With a force of about three thousand men, he captured the Bavarian government leaders during a Munich beer hall rally but fled the next day when his troopers were routed by determined police action. Arrested and subsequently jailed for eight months, he used the time to write his memoirs, *Mein Kampf.*

When Hitler emerged from jail in 1924, Germany was feeling the first elation of returning prosperity, and the Nazis made little progress in winning support. The years 1924 to 1929 were the most successful of the Weimar Republic. It became clear that the new constitution, with its guarantees of civil rights, its careful balancing of the powers of the central government and of the states, and its encouragement of political participation through a modified form of proportional representation, was winning support. A working coalition of the Social Democratic, Center, Democratic, and People's parties held power. Gustav Stresemann, as foreign minister in 1924–1929, brought continuity to Germany's foreign policy, bringing the country back to full participation in international affairs through the Locarno conference, membership in the League of Nations, and signature of the Kellogg-Briand peace pacts. Yet there were many political weaknesses in the Weimar regime that became more evident when the prosperity failed. The coalition that extended from the workers' representatives in the Social Democratic party to the business representatives in the People's party lacked agreement on social and economic principles.

The Nationalist party on the extreme right, backed by important non-parliamentary pressure groups like the militaristic Stahlhelm, was growing in popularity, while even at the height of the prosperity in 1928 the Communist party on the extreme left received over three million votes in the Reichstag election. Moreover, the great powers given by the constitution to the president, who chose the chancellor, dissolved the Reichstag, and had power to authorize the chancellor to govern by decree in an emergency, could easily be misused. On the death of the first president, Ebert, in 1925, Field Marshal Hindenburg, then 78 years old, was elected president. Hindenburg's sympathy for the military and the aristocratic conservatives of eastern Germany, combined with his increasing senility, were to make him susceptible to the machinations of unscrupulous politicians in the crisis of 1930–1933 when the depression hit Germany.

During the 1920s, Hitler devoted himself to the careful grooming of his party for a semilegal conquest of power. He showed great skill in developing propaganda devices such as banners, the swastika, armbands, jackboots, disciplined hordes of marching men, and innumerable hate-provoking slogans. His ideology took form as a consistent political doctrine that could be easily grasped by the unsophisticated public. All nations were part of a racial hierarchy, he held, in which superiority was dependent on quality of blood. The Jews were an impurity in the German blood that would have to be removed; the Slavs were subhuman (*Untermenschen*), and their future was to act as laborers for the Germans. All Germans should live in the German fatherland, especially those who had been forcibly separated by the territorial annexations of the Treaty of Versailles. Germany itself, however, was too small for the German people, who needed living space (*Lebensraum*) that they would find by repossession of Germany's colonial empire and especially by expansion into the vast plains occupied by the Slavs of Poland and Russia. Germany should be gov-

Hindenburg as President of the Weimar Republic
Hindenburg's age and political inexperience made him incapable as president of preventing Hitler from becoming chancellor in 1933, even though Hindenburg personally detested the Nazi leader. (Hoover Institution)

erned by a new elite, the Nazi party, under a Führer; then it would recognize those qualities that were necessary for its own greatness. To be a National Socialist, his propaganda chief Josef Goebbels wrote, meant nothing less than *"Kampf, Glaube, Arbeit, Obfer"* ("struggle, belief, work, sacrifice"), ideal qualities for the service of a totalitarian state.

The depression of 1929–1933 gave the Nazis their opportunity to capitalize on the discontent of six million unemployed people, of white-collar workers who had lost their savings, of conservatives sick of the indecisiveness of the Weimar regime. Although Hindenburg permitted Heinrich Brüning, the Center party chancellor, to govern by decree in 1930–1932, the economic situation only continued to worsen. The National Socialists, who had received only 800,000 votes in the Reichstag election of 1928, obtained over six million in 1930. With increased financial support from business groups and the lower middle class, they mounted a massive campaign in the elections of July 1932 and received over thirteen million votes. With 230 members, they became the largest party in the Reichstag. Hitler, however, had failed to defeat Hindenburg in the presidential elections of April–May 1932; and it required several months of nerve-wracking plotting with Hindenburg's favored advisors before Hitler could be appointed chancellor. After Hindenburg fired Brüning in May 1932, he appointed the conservative aristocrat Franz von Papen as chancellor, with a government composed of the representatives of the landed and industrial classes. Disappointed in the elections of July 1932, Papen persuaded Hindenburg to dissolve the Reichstag and call new elections in November, in which the Nazi vote fell to eleven million. Even though the Nazis were still the largest party in the Reichstag, Hindenburg preferred to appoint another of his military favorites, General Kurt von Schleicher, as chancellor, but this action brought Hitler and Papen into

Reich Chancellor Adolf Hitler

In postcards on sale throughout Germany after his nomination as chancellor, Hitler wears his Nazi party uniform and the Iron Cross.
(Hoover Institution)

partnership. Papen, believing that he could manipulate Hitler from behind the scenes, was able to persuade Hindenburg to appoint Hitler as chancellor, with Papen as vice chancellor. Thus, as a result of a series of shady deals among the conservative politicians around Hindenburg, Hitler was able to take power legally.

That night, the Nazis gave Berlin a spectacle that dwarfed any demonstration of William II's day. The French ambassador, André François-Poncet, later described the scene:

In massive columns, flanked by bands that played martial airs, [the Nazi stormtroopers] emerged from the depth of the Tiergarten and passed under the triumphal arch of the Brandenburg Gate. The torches they brandished formed a river of fire, a river with hastening, unquenchable waves, a river in spate sweeping with a sovereign rush over the very heart of the city. From these brown-shirted, booted men, as they marched by in perfect discipline and alignment, their well-pitched voices bawling warlike songs, there arose an enthusiasm and dynamism that were extraordinary. The onlookers, drawn up on either side of the marching columns, burst into a vast clamor. The river of fire flowed past the French Embassy, whence, with heavy heart and filled with foreboding, I watched its luminous wake; it turned down the Wilhelmstrasse and rolled under the windows of the Marshal's palace.

The old man [President Hindenburg] stood there leaning upon his cane, struck by the power of the phenomenon which he had himself let loose. At the next window stood Hitler, the object of a very tempest of cheers, as wave upon wave kept surging up from the alleys of the Tiergarten.[5]

HITLER'S GERMANY, 1933–1939

Berlin Under the Nazis

The Nazis changed the atmosphere of Berlin in a few weeks. At first life went on as usual, with many people expecting the Nazis, once in power, to moderate their propagandist attacks on such groups as the Jews. In February, however, the Reichstag building was set on fire, possibly by a crazed Communist put up to the job by the Nazi storm troopers; and the incident was used as an excuse for suspending guarantees of individual liberty and for banning the Communist party. In March Hitler forced through the Reichstag the Enabling Act, which granted him authority to govern by decree for four years, a power he used shortly after to ban all political parties except the Nazis, to destroy the trade unions, and to bring the law courts under Nazi control. In June 1934 he purged his own party of possible opposition elements by murdering several hundred storm troop leaders in the "Night of Long Knives." Finally, when Hindenburg died in August 1934, Hitler himself took the offices of both president and chancellor. Within eighteen months he had exceeded the powers Mussolini had accumulated in twelve years.

[5] André François-Poncet, *The Fateful Years* (New York: Harcourt Brace, 1949), p. 48.

The Nazis made it evident to Berlin that they were serious, humorless renovators who intended to wipe out what they felt were Jewish cultural depravities of the Weimar period. During the next six years, there was an exodus of many of Germany's leading intellectual and artistic figures, including Heinrich and Thomas Mann, Gropius, Grosz, Kandinsky, Zweig, Zuckmayer, Einstein, and thousands of others. The Nazis welcomed the exodus and turned to the creation of a distinctively Nazi culture. Atonal music, abstract painting, and stream-of-consciousness literature were banned. Hitler's taste in music ran to Wagner and a few light operas, although Wilhelm Furtwängler and the Berlin Philharmonic continued to give superb performances of the most established classics. The approved taste in art, a robust naturalism similar to that of the contemporary Socialist Realism in Russia, was displayed in Munich in 1937 in an exhibition of German art that was run parallel to a show of decadent art, including works of Post-Impressionist and abstract painters. In architecture the steel and concrete structures of Gropius and his followers were replaced by a monstrous neobaroque style in which Hitler himself, the architect manqué, took constant interest.

Hitler had grandiose plans for making Berlin a worthy capital of the vast empire he proposed to win for Germany, even though the Nazis had never done well in elections in Berlin and though Munich always remained the "capital of the [National-Socialist] movement." He admired the remodeling of Vienna in the 1860s but thought the finest of all urban planners was Haussmann, who had remodeled Paris for Emperor Napoleon

Nazi Party Rally, Nuremburg
The annual rally of several hundred thousand party members was carefully planned to impress onlookers with the irresistible power of the Nazi movement. (National Archives)

III. At times he may have toyed with the idea of creating a great new capital city in an uninhabited part of Germany, to put himself on the level of Peter the Great; but he soon decided that Berlin was the only suitable setting for the monumental vistas he had in mind. Albert Speer, his architect during the 1930s, claimed that Hitler's desire to outdo all existing buildings—a larger Arc de Triomphe, a wider and longer Champs Elysées, a statue bigger than the Statue of Liberty, even a suspension bridge grander than San Francisco's Golden Gate—was not only egomania but a matter of policy. He wanted to "transmit his time and its spirit to posterity," because his buildings would represent the rebirth of national grandeur after a period of decline. He began with the theatrical settings for the huge party rallies in Nuremberg, moved on to a large remodeling of the chancellery, and kept Speer at work for almost a decade on models of the vastest city rebuilding ever undertaken. "Berlin is a big city," he told Speer, "but not a real metropolis. Look at Paris, the most beautiful city in the world. Or even Vienna. Those are cities with grand style. Berlin is nothing but an unregulated accumulation of buildings. We must surpass Paris and Vienna."[6] His plans called for a three-mile-long avenue, with a domed hall at one end several times larger than Saint Peter's Cathedral in Rome and an Arch of Triumph at the other end four hundred feet high. Beside the great dome, around a new Adolf Hitler Platz, were to be grouped the main buildings of the Third Reich: a new chancellery, the High Command of the Armed Forces, and the Reichstag.

National-Socialist Internal Policy

The majority of Germans found Hitler's first six years in office an exciting and gratifying time. Most of the six million unemployed were back at work within three years. The rearmament program; the public works projects, which included the famous freeways, or Autobahn network; the conscription of workers into labor battalions; the provision of inexpensive open-air vacations; the general sense of purpose and strength displayed by the new regime: these won Hitler widespread support. He had begun to court the women's vote in 1931–1932, largely by presenting himself as the defender of the home during the crisis of unemployment and inflation; and many lower-middle-class women, especially those of a conservative and religious background, rallied to him. Although like Mussolini he emphasized women's role in the home and in childbearing, by 1938 the shortage of labor had compelled the Nazis to introduce a "labor year" for women in some kind of national production. Although concentration camps had been set up and the secret police, the *Gestapo*, were active, most people were able to convince themselves that the Jews were in most cases being permitted to leave the country without molestation. The industrialists, pleased to be given a free hand in a program of concentration of ownership, were made prosperous by large-scale state contracts for armaments. But the Germans did not follow Hitler gladly into war; and as it be-

[6] Albert Speer, *Inside the Third Reich: Memoirs* (New York: Macmillan, 1970), p. 75.

came evident in 1938–1939 that he was bent on military adventures, his popularity dipped so greatly that Nazi officials had difficulty in assembling enthusiastic crowds when Hitler appeared in public. By then, however, all opposition inside Germany had been cowed, and the Germans could only follow him sullenly into war. Fortunately for them, the disarray among Germany's future conquerors was to make his early victories cheap.

THE COMING OF THE SECOND WORLD WAR

Hitler's first aim was to overthrow the Treaty of Versailles. This implied the withdrawal of Germany from the League of Nations and its disarmament conferences, the return of the Saar to Germany, large-scale rearmament, the remilitarization of the Rhineland, and the return to Germany of the territories incorporated in the new Polish state. The restoration of Germany's prewar position was only the preliminary, however, to the goal of achieving the reunification of German blood and German land (*Blut und Boden*) within the Third Reich. The immediate goal, apart from the restoration of the Germans of Poland and the Free City of Danzig, was the annexation to Germany of the Sudetenland of Czechoslovakia and the whole of Austria; but the "Germanness" of Alsace-Lorraine, Luxembourg, and Slovenia would eventually require their return to Germany also. Finally, Hitler considered that this Greater Germany would need *Lebensraum* ("space to live"), which it would find at the expense of the supposedly inferior races in the East of Europe, the Slavs of Poland and Russia. In *Mein Kampf*, he had announced:

We put an end to the perpetual Germanic march towards the south and west of Europe and turn our eyes towards the lands of the east. We finally put a stop to the colonial and commercial policy of prewar times and pass over to the territorial policy of the future. But when we speak of new territory in Europe today, we must principally think of Russia and the border states subject to her. Destiny itself seems to wish to point out the way for us here. . . . This colossal empire in the east is ripe for dissolution. [7]

Hitler's Foreign Policy

The Policy of Appeasement

Only strong concerted action by the Western democracies—Britain, France, and the United States—in coalition with the Soviet Union could have blocked Hitler's expansionist ambitions. The Western democracies, however, were in disarray. The United States alone possessed the economic resources and the population adequate to meet the German challenge; in 1919 its population was 105 million compared with 59 million in Germany. But the experience of the First World War had left Americans isolationist; and as late as 1937, President Franklin D. Roosevelt was unable to rouse any public support for measures that would quarantine military ag-

[7] Alan Bullock, *Hitler, A Study in Tyranny* (New York: Harper Torchbook, 1964), p. 318.

gressors in Europe. Britain and France were thus left as the sole bulwark against Hitler in the West. The British, however, struggling to overcome their economic problems at home, felt incapable of making any military effort in Europe. The First World War had cost them one-quarter of their national wealth; the general strike of 1926 had brought the country to the verge of civil war in the streets; and no government dared take action that would increase the level of unemployment. Britain's political leaders, vapid Socialists like Ramsay Macdonald and insensitive businessmen like Stanley Baldwin, were unable to provide the kind of inspiring direction that alone could have persuaded the British people of the need of new sacrifices to meet a renewed German danger in Europe. Moreover, the British were disturbed that the Treaty of Versailles had denied to Germany those rights of self-determination that they and the Americans had come to believe they were fighting for in the First World War; and a number of the members of the British upper classes were frankly sympathetic to the kind of leadership the Nazis were providing.

The French were facing great political disruption at home. Right-wing groups, some of them sympathetic to Nazi Germany, were attacking the failing democratic structure and its scandal-stained practitioners; on the left, the Communists had made great headway in gaining control of the trade unions and in winning electoral support. With a shaky political system, a depressed economy, and an atrociously anachronistic military leadership, France relied on the supposed impregnability of its Maginot Line.

Stalin was well aware of Hitler's ultimate intention of attacking Russia. Many of Russia's war industries were being transferred to the Urals and beyond, and high priority was given to the needs of the army. Russia joined the League of Nations in 1934 and attempted to negotiate a security pact for most of the eastern European countries. Both the British and French governments remained distrustful of Stalin's intentions; and the purge trials in Moscow, especially those of the top military leadership, seemed to them to be making a military alliance with Russia less valuable. No grand alliance therefore existed that could stop Hitler.

Aggression by Stages, 1933–1939

Hitler's first infringement of the Treaty of Versailles occurred in March 1935, when he announced that Germany was rearming. He picked the Heroes' Memorial Day, commemorating the two million soldiers killed in World War I, for the announcement; arranged a picturesque ceremony in the opera house, where Beethoven's Funeral March was played; and succeeded in creating in Berlin an atmosphere of euphoria. He was certain at that point, however, that no action would be taken against Germany. In 1931, when the Japanese had invaded the Chinese province of Manchuria, the only response of the League of Nations was to pass a vote of censure. Poland, the keystone of the French alliance system in eastern Europe, had signed a ten-year nonaggression pact with Hitler in 1934, and good relations were being established with the right-wing regimes in Rumania, Bulgaria, and Hungary.

Nazi Parade for Prince Paul of Yugoslavia in Berlin, June 2, 1939
Paul, the regent of Yugoslavia, sought close relations with Nazi Germany but was overthrown in 1941, when he attempted to link Yugoslavia to the Axis Alliance.
(National Archives)

The next year world attention shifted to Italy's aggression—the invasion of the poor, almost defenseless African state of Ethiopia in October 1935, during which Mussolini used tanks, dive-bombers, and poison gas. The League of Nations was shocked, not least by the impassioned appeal to it for aid by the Ethiopian emperor, Haile Selassie, and agreed to impose economic sanctions on Italy. Since no embargo was put on oil and since the Suez Canal remained open to Italian ships carrying troops and military supplies, the embargo proved to be a farce. Within eight months, Italy was in complete control of Ethiopia.

Just before the Ethiopian war ended, Hitler made a daring infringement of the Treaty of Versailles. On the night of March 7, 1936, with only the nucleus of Germany's new army yet created, he moved a division of troops into the demilitarized areas of the Rhineland against the advice of the General Staff. Three brigades were stationed close to the French border, in a direct challenge to France's will to resist him. The Poles demanded that the French act; together they could raise ninety divisions. Hitler himself admitted that "the forty-eight hours after the march into the Rhineland were the most nerve-wracking of my life. If the French had then marched into the Rhineland we would have had to withdraw with our tails between our legs."[8] The French, unable to persuade the British to move, contented themselves with a diplomatic protest.

In July, the opening of the Spanish civil war (1936–1939) gave Hitler's armed forces the opportunity to try out their new techniques. Spain had been tottering on the verge of military insurrection since it had become a republic in 1931 because the Republicans included not only moderate middle-class liberals but a wide array of extremists, including Communists, Trotskyites, and Anarchists, many of whom wanted to use the new government to attack the great landowners and the Church. When in February 1936 a Popular Front government of moderate Republicans, Socialists, Communists, and Anarchists won a small majority in the elections, the army in Spanish Morocco, under the leadership of General Francisco Franco, decided to revolt. In July, the armed forces seized most of the south and west of Spain; the Republicans were left with the industrialized triangle of the east, including the big cities of Madrid, Valencia, and Barcelona, and an army consisting mainly of workers. Mussolini intervened at once on the side of Franco, sending him large numbers of airplanes and trucks and seventy thousand men. Shortly after, Hitler too decided that Franco's political opinions were close enough to his own to justify the dispatch of aid, mostly in the form of planes, pilots, tanks, and technicians. In October Stalin decided to aid the Republican side, thereby transforming the civil war into an international ideological war. Russian military supplies, experts, and political commissars reached Spain in large numbers by the end of the year; volunteers pouring in from all over Europe and America were organized by the Communists as International Brigades. Once again the British and French stood aside helplessly. The Republicans were unable to hold out against the forces of Franco and his Italian and German allies. Madrid fell in March 1939 after a heroic defense. Franco at once set up a rigidly authoritarian regime, in which prominent positions were given to Spanish Fascists.

While the British and French were distracted by the Spanish war, Hitler had begun the second part of his program, the absorption into Germany of all people of German blood. In 1938 he summoned Austrian Chancellor Kurt von Schuschnigg to his mountain retreat in the Bavarian Alps and demanded that he remodel his government to include three Austrian Nazis. When Schuschnigg surprised him on returning to Vienna by ordering a plebiscite so that Austrians could demonstrate that they did not want to be

[8]Ibid., p. 345.

united to Germany, Hitler gave orders for the German army to invade Austria. Schuschnigg was forced to resign, an Austrian Nazi was made chancellor, and Hitler entered Vienna to a conqueror's welcome on March 14. For him, it was a personal revenge for all the humiliations of the years before the First World War to see the Ring filled with cheering crowds and to be received in the Hofburg Palace of the Habsburg dynasty. The plebiscite, then conducted by the Nazis in both Germany and Austria, gave ninety-nine percent approval of the union of Germany and Austria. Although the Treaty of Versailles expressly forbade such a fusion, Britain and France were again unable to interfere. The French were in the middle of a cabinet crisis; the British prime minister, Neville Chamberlain, told Parliament with amazing candor that "nothing could have arrested what actually has happened—unless this country and other countries had been prepared to use force." Chamberlain had accepted Hitler's claim that he wanted only to permit Germans to return to their fatherland; and in September, at the Munich conference, he and the French prime minister agreed to permit Hitler to take the Sudetenland of Czechoslovakia on the ground that a majority of its population was German, even though it contained most of the country's border fortresses. German troops moved in on October 1, 1938, meeting no resistance from the Czechs. Chamberlain told the British that he had won "peace in our time." His error was brought home to him the following March when the German army invaded the main body of Czechoslovakia. In April Mussolini followed Hitler's example by annexing Albania. Finally driven to action, the British and French guaranteed that they would come to the military aid of Poland if, as seemed likely, it should be attacked by Germany.

Chamberlain with Hitler in Munich, September 1938
On September 30, 1938, British Prime Minister Neville Chamberlain and French Premier Edouard Daladier agreed to permit Germany to annex from Czechoslovakia the largely German-speaking Sudetenland. Although Mussolini was present, the Czech government was not invited; and the Munich Pact came to be regarded as the most supine example of appeasement of the Nazi and Fascist dictators by the Western democracies. (BBC Hulton Picture Library)

THE COMING OF THE SECOND WORLD WAR

Nazi Troops in Czechoslovakia, 1939

In March 1939, Hitler forced the Czech government to agree to the dismemberment of its country. Slovakia was to become a puppet state under German control, while Bohemia and Moravia were to be German protectorates. German troops met no resistance when they entered Prague. (Eastfoto)

The spineless betrayal of Czechoslovakia by the British and French persuaded Stalin that he must safeguard Russia's interests at their expense if necessary; accordingly, he entered negotiations with the Germans that culminated, in August 1939, in the signature of the Nazi-Soviet Non-aggression Pact. To gain Russian neutrality during his attack on Poland, Hitler agreed to add to the pact a "secret, additional protocol," which, as amended in October, gave Russia the right to establish a "sphere of interest" that included the eastern third of Poland as well as Estonia, Latvia, Lithuania, Finland, and the Rumanian province of Bessarabia. Hitler then ordered the attack on Poland to begin on September 1; the British and French governments, somewhat to his surprise, declared war on Germany in defense of Poland on September 3.

The eruption of what everyone recognized to be the beginning of a new world war caused elation nowhere—not even in Berlin. The American journalist William Shirer, crossing Unter den Linden on his way to broadcast the news of the dawn attack on Poland to the United States, was struck by the apathy of the people on the streets. The men working on a new building for the chemical trust did not buy the extra newspaper editions that the newsboys were hawking, and even the handpicked Reichstag seemed dazed and unresponsive. In France there was a sense of dull despair at the inevitability of new destruction. The writer Simone de Beauvoir noted in her diary: "Unthinkable prospect: another day after this, and another, and another—much worse, too, for then we shall be fighting. Only stopped from crying by the feeling that there would be just as many tears left to shed afterwards."[9] In London, air raid sirens sounded within minutes of the declaration of war; and Winston Churchill was probably not alone in his reaction: "As I gazed from the doorway along the empty street and at the crowded room below, my imagination drew pictures of ruin and carnage and vast explosions shaking the ground; of buildings clattering down in dust and rubble, of fire brigades and ambulances scurrying through the smoke, beneath the drone of hostile airplanes."[10] As in no previous war, the cities of the West lay vulnerable; in 1939 it was hard to predict whether the scourge of air warfare would spare any, on either side. The destruction, as W. H. Auden envisaged it in *The Age of Anxiety*, was ubiquitous and impartial:

> Dull through the darkness, indifferent tongues
> From bombed buildings, from blacked-out towns,
> Camps and cockpits, from cold trenches,
> Submarines and cells, recite in unison
> A common creed, declaring their weak
> Faith in confusion. The floods are rising;
> Rain ruins on the routed fragments
> Of all the armies; indistinct
> Are friend and foe, one flux of bodies
> Miles from mother, marriage, or any
> Workable World[11]

THE SECOND WORLD WAR

The first city to suffer the destructive powers of aerial and artillery bombardment was Warsaw. The rapidity of the attack enabled the Germans to destroy most of Poland's five hundred planes before they could leave the ground. Stuka dive-bombers supported the tank columns in attacks on the immaculate but ineffective cavalry of the Polish army, strafed fleeing civilians, and struck at the central core of the Polish capital. Within a week the main body of the Polish army had been destroyed; Cracow, Poland's second city, fell on September 6; and Warsaw fought heroically until September 27, when it too surrendered. The Russians moved into Poland on September 17 and annexed the eastern third of the country. Poland had fallen before any British or French troops could come to its aid.

The German Onslaught, 1939–1941

[9]Simone de Beauvoir, *Prime of Life* (Harmondsworth, England: Penguin, 1965), p. 361.
[10]Winston S. Churchill, *The Second World War* (Boston: Houghton Mifflin, 1948), I, 408.
[11]Copyright 1947 by W. H. Auden and renewed 1975 by Monroe K. Spears and William Meredith, executors of the estate of W. H. Auden. Reprinted from *W. H. Auden: Collected Poems*, by permission of Random House, Inc., and Faber and Faber Ltd.

In the west, where a small British expeditionary force had been dispatched to France, there was inactivity along the whole front. That quiet winter, when the French played cards in the airy cellars of the Maginot Line fortresses, came to be called the "Phony War," the *drôle de guerre*; to the Germans, it was a *Sitzkrieg* ("a sitdown war"), very different from their *Blitzkrieg* attack on Poland.

When Britain and France failed to seek peace, Hitler ordered preparations for a major invasion of the West in the spring of 1940. As a preliminary to that attack, however, he decided to carry through a quick, inexpensive occupation of Denmark and Norway to safeguard his ore supplies from Sweden and to prevent the British from sealing the Baltic. German troops met no resistance in Denmark, whose flat lands and open cities were indefensible; Norwegian resistance was overcome within five weeks, and Hitler was ready to move the attack westward on May 10.

With an army of 136 divisions, Hitler launched simultaneous attacks on the neutral countries of Holland, Belgium, and Luxembourg. The Dutch, whose neutrality had not been broken since 1815, fought back savagely against superior forces; and the Nazis vowed, on May 14, to make an exemplary punishment of the city of Rotterdam. German bombers struck at the heart of the old city, killing eight hundred civilians, making 78,000 homeless, and destroying, among many other historical treasures, the home of the philosopher Erasmus. On the fifth day of fighting, the Dutch army surrendered. A second and larger German force entered Belgium and captured Brussels. After eighteen days of resistance, the Belgian king, Leopold, against the advice of his government, ordered his troops to stop fighting. The British and French armies, which had rushed to the aid of the Belgians, were trapped by the main German armored divisions. They withdrew to the beaches of the tiny French port of Dunkirk, where they were saved from annihilation by a strange armada of tiny sailboats, tugboats, and fishing vessels that sailed from England to evacuate them to the warships waiting offshore. About 300,000 soldiers were carried back to England, but one-third of the improvised evacuation fleet was destroyed. It was a great defeat, but Britain had at least saved its only trained soldiers.

The German attack resumed on June 5. The French were fatalistically accepting defeat. Army leaders in the cabinet demanded surrender. Nazi sympathizers welcomed the invaders. Paris, undefended and abandoned by the government, was occupied on June 14. On June 16 Marshal Pétain, a First World War hero and now the main proponent of defeatism, became premier and at once sought a cease-fire. For Hitler, the moment was one of his greatest triumphs. He forced the French to sign an armistice agreement—which left Pétain's government in control of the southern third of France only—in the same railroad car in the clearing at Compiègne where Marshal Foch had presented the armistice terms to the Germans on November 11, 1918. At the end of the month, Hitler visited Paris for the first time. He found a silent city, from which more than half the population had fled as refugees. Giant swastika flags flew from the Chamber of Depu-

"Abandoned Populations, Trust the German Soldier!"
In the early days of occupation after the defeat of France in 1940, German propagandists made vain efforts to win the support of the French people. (Hoover Institution)

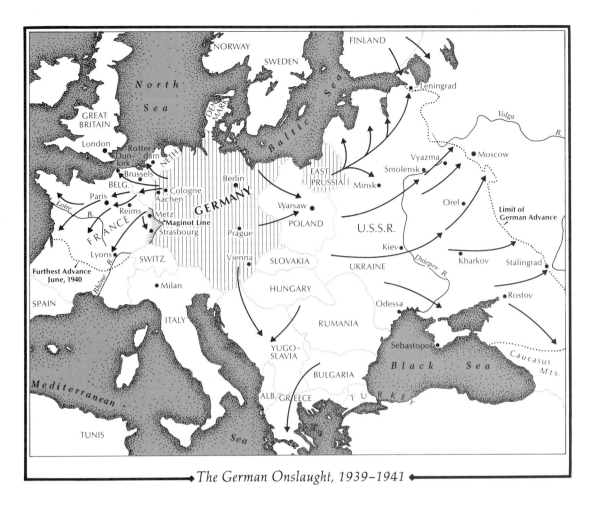

◆ *The German Onslaught, 1939–1941* ◆

Hitler at the Eiffel Tower, Paris, June 1940
Hitler was disappointed with the architecture of Paris, which he considered inferior to that of Vienna and the cities of Italy. (Brown Brothers)

ties. The Hotel Crillon on the Place de la Concorde had been turned into the German headquarters. German tanks were drawn up along the entry to the Champs Elysées. German soldiers with cameras were acting like excited tourists. Hitler followed their example, went up the Eiffel Tower, surveyed the city from the terrace of the Sacré Coeur church in Montmartre, and spent a long time gazing at Napoleon's tomb in the Invalides. "That was the greatest and finest moment of my life," he remarked later.

Hitler proved surprisingly reluctant to authorize a full-scale invasion of England after the fall of France. He feared that the cost of getting an army across the Channel would not be justified by the expected gains; and he wanted no delay in his coming attack on Russia. He therefore authorized an invasion only if a preliminary air assault proved effective. The British, however, were quite well prepared to throw back the German planes. They had several hundred fighter planes of superior quality to the German and were equipped with the newly invented radar, which gave them advance warning of where and in what strength the Germans were attacking. The Channel was a formidable barrier in view of British naval strength, and the British army was increasing in size daily. British morale had improved enormously since the appointment of Winston Churchill as prime minister in May. In his first important speech in that office, reporting the evacuation from Dunkirk, he had struck a note of proud defiance:

Even though large tracts of Europe and many old and famous states have fallen or may fall into the grip of the Gestapo and all the odious apparatus of Nazi rule, we shall not flag or fail. We shall go on to the end, we shall fight in France, we shall fight in the seas and oceans, we shall fight with growing determination and growing strength in the air, we shall defend our island, whatever the cost may be, we shall fight on the beaches, we shall fight on the landing-grounds, we shall fight in the fields and in the streets, we shall fight in the hills; we shall never surrender, and even if, which I do not for a moment believe, this island or a large part of it were subjugated and starving, then our Empire beyond the seas, armed and guarded by the British fleet, would carry on the struggle, until, in God's good time, the New World, with all its power and might, steps forth to the rescue and the liberation of the Old. [12]

Through late August and September, the German air force sustained heavy losses; but many of its planes got through, especially after Hitler ordered the bombing of England's large cities in retaliation for the bombing of Berlin. Deaths of civilians increased, and large parts of the slum dwellings of the East End, the docks of the Pool of London, and the old blocks around Saint Paul's Cathedral in London were destroyed. In the north, industrial cities were heavily damaged. But the attacks had failed. In October Hitler began to transfer his troops eastward. "Russia must be liquidated. Spring, 1941. The sooner Russia is smashed, the better," he ordered.

Unfortunately for Hitler, his invasion of Russia was delayed by the

[12]Churchill, *Second World War*, II, 118.

need to come to the aid of his ally Mussolini, whose troops had invaded Greece in October 1940. When the Yugoslavs then refused to allow German troops to cross their territory, he unwisely expanded his Balkan operation even further, to include "Operation Punishment" against the Yugoslavs. In April 1941, both Yugoslavia and Greece were defeated. German troops attacked Russia along its whole border from Finland to the Black Sea at dawn on June 22, 1941, a month behind schedule.

Stalin had made little preparation to meet this invasion. He had taken over Estonia, Latvia, Lithuania, and the Rumanian province of Bessarabia in 1940; and as a result of the Winter War against Finland (November 1939–March 1940), the Finnish threat to Leningrad had been lessened by the annexation of the Finnish province of Karelia. He had slightly increased the number of divisions on the Polish border. But he had gone to extraordinary lengths to avoid provoking the Germans, supplying them with food and raw materials and forbidding any of his military staff to prepare even defensive strategy for repelling a German attack. Russia's industry was not even put on war footing. Although Stalin later claimed he had gained two years to prepare for the invasion by making the Non-aggression Pact of 1939, his new territorial acquisitions were overrun by the Germans in a few days. By December German forces were moving into the suburbs of Leningrad and Moscow, and a third German army was driving across the Ukraine toward the oilfields of the Caucasus. But the coming of the Russian winter stalled the German troops just short of their objectives; the lost month in the Balkans had been crucial. Instead of permitting the Germans to install themselves until spring in fortified defense shelters, as they had hoped, Stalin mounted a massive counterattack of forces that had regrouped beyond Moscow and drove the Germans back two hundred miles. The possibility of German defeat was suddenly glimpsed, especially as that same month the United States, with its Pacific fleet heavily damaged by a surprise Japanese attack on Pearl Harbor in the Hawaiian Islands, had declared war on Japan; and Germany and Italy, in fulfillment of the Tripartite Pact they had signed with Japan in September 1940, had declared war on the United States.

In November 1942 the Americans and British launched a three-headed attack on French North Africa, which was ruled after the defeat of 1940 by the Pétain government from its new capital city of Vichy in central France. In many ways, however, the invasion worsened the French political situation. German troops occupied the southern third of France, which had been assigned to the Pétain government at the armistice, although the Vichy regime was permitted to go on functioning. French North Africa was without a legal government, and Roosevelt and Churchill were divided over possible candidates. Roosevelt favored General Giraud, a professional soldier with no political ambitions; Churchill supported General Charles de Gaulle, a brilliant, thorny, ambitious leader who had originally made

The Beginning of the Allied Counteroffensive, 1942–1943

General Charles de Gaulle in 1945

De Gaulle became known as "the man of June 18" after his appeal in 1940 on London radio for the creation under his leadership of a Free French fighting force to continue the war against Germany. (Hoover Institution)

his name as a theorist of tank warfare. In June 1940 de Gaulle had fled to London, where he had proclaimed himself the leader of continuing French resistance to the Germans through a movement called Free France. De Gaulle regarded himself as the sole claimant to rule French North Africa and eventually France itself. "I was France," he remarked later, by way of explanation. In spite of Roosevelt's intense dislike of this prickly genius, de Gaulle slowly emerged as one of the greatest and most farsighted political leaders of the twentieth century. Emmanuel d'Astier summed up the reasons for his magnetism:

In three days I have seen him make unequal use of his three weapons: prestige, secrecy, and cunning. His cunning is mediocre, but his secrecy, supported by a natural, icy prestige derives from: his height? . . . Or from his appearance, which is always so typical of himself, like a portrait of himself, a picture showing a lack of sensitivity to the warmth of life? Or from his inspired voice, its broken cadences emerging from an inanimate body lacking in all animal warmth, a voice issuing from a waxwork? Or from his aloofness from his fellow men? Or from his language, always too infallible even when his thought is not, approximating in certain of his utterances to the great sermons of the eighteenth century? Or from his remoteness, his expressionless body and his few gestures which, in the last analysis, are as solemn and inevitable as his adjectives? . . . I do not know. He remains a mystery, this man, motivated by one historical idea, the greatness of France, and whose single voice seems to replace all others, the voice of God, man, progress and all ideologies. [13]

At the Casablanca conference of January 1943, Roosevelt and Churchill agreed that Giraud and de Gaulle should be joint presidents of a committee controlling French North Africa and the French army; but de Gaulle soon took sole command. It was also agreed that the next Allied military operation should be an amphibious invasion of Sicily from North Africa; this began in July 1943.

The Germans withdrew to southern Italy, where they prepared a defense line north of Naples, using the monastery of Monte Cassino as the principal defense barrier across the route to Rome. The invasion of Italy drove the Fascist Grand Council to vote for Mussolini's deposition on July 25. The next day he was arrested and replaced as premier by an old, conservative soldier, Marshal Pietro Badoglio. In a few hours, Italian Fascism was dismantled. Badoglio, however, did not sign an armistice with the Allies until September. By then Hitler's troops had occupied the whole of northern Italy. Mussolini, rescued by German paratroops, was reinstalled in the north as puppet ruler of a German-dominated Italian Social Republic. The Allies did not break the line at Monte Cassino until May 1944, and they were blocked north of Florence until April 1945. Thus Italy suffered more heavily after the armistice than before. Italians in the north

[13]Emmanuel d'Astier, *Seven Times Seven Days* (London: MacGibbon and Kee, 1958), pp. 132–133.

were compelled to fight against the Italian army in the south; heavy reprisals were taken by the Germans against the Resistance movement, and vast destruction of roads, bridges, railroads, factories, homes, and art treasures occurred in the bombing and the northward advance of the Allies.

On the Russian front, Hitler had mounted new offensives in 1942 to capture the oil fields of the Caucasus, the Donets industrial basin, and the communications center of Stalingrad on the river Volga. Stalin, however, was determined for reasons of prestige not to abandon the city that carried his name, and for identical reasons, Hitler was determined to take it. Thus the Battle of Stalingrad (September 1942–February 1943) commanded the greatest resources both sides could muster, with hand-to-hand fighting taking place in every block of the city as the Germans drove in. Soviet forces succeeded in surrounding 200,000 German troops in the ruined city. After weeks of suffering from artillery bombardment, frostbite, starvation, and lack of medicine, the Germans—against Hitler's express orders—surrendered; they then numbered 91,000. The Russian victory was the turning point of the war. After Stalingrad, the Russian attack increased in momentum, bringing to bear upon the German armies what many historians deem the principal force responsible for Hitler's ultimate defeat. By July 1943 the Red Army had taken Kharkov and Kiev, and by January 1944 it moved into the Baltic states in the north and Odessa in the south. Hitler's ''Fortress Europe'' was collapsing.

Women Leaving Bomb Shelter, Stalingrad, 1942
A German army of half a million soldiers battled its way into Stalingrad in vicious house-to-house fighting but was met by a Soviet counterattack. When the last remnants of the German army surrendered in February 1943, the city was in total ruin. (Sovfoto/Eastfoto)

Attack on Hitler's "Fortress Europe," 1944

On June 6, 1944, D-Day, a vast sea and airborne force composed of American, British, Canadian, and French troops commanded by General Dwight D. Eisenhower struck at the beaches of Normandy and in spite of harsh resistance succeeded in putting 130,000 men ashore by nightfall. During the next week, the Allied armies took control of fifty miles of coast and landed over 300,000 men. In August a second invasion force landed in the south of France and moved rapidly northwards up the Rhône valley to establish a common front across France with the rapidly advancing armies from Normandy. The Resistance forces in Paris rose spontaneously on August 19, and in a week of street fighting took possession of large parts of the city, losing over 3,000 men. But on August 25, French and American armored detachments forced their way into the city; that afternoon, General de Gaulle, whose authority had been universally recognized as each section of France was liberated, strode down the whole length of the Champs Elysées acclaimed by a crowd of millions in triumphant apotheosis. By the end of September 1944, most of France was in Allied hands and the German border had been penetrated in several places.

Sniper Fire on the Place de la Concorde, Paris, August 26, 1944 *(Courtesy of French Embassy Press and Information Division)*

The Russians had also attacked in coordination with the D-Day invasions, and by July they had driven Finland from the war and were established in the heart of Poland. But Russian actions during the remainder of

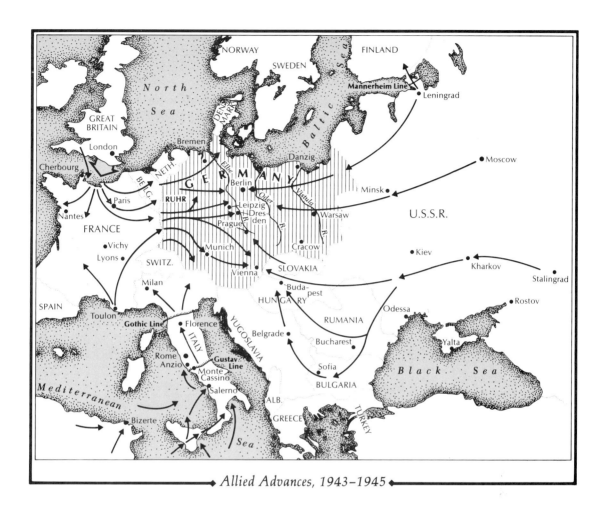

◆ *Allied Advances, 1943–1945* **◆**

1944 have been the subject of considerable controversy. On August 1, 1944, the underground forces in Warsaw, which were sympathetic to the anti-Communist government-in-exile in London, rose in rebellion against the Nazis in the hope of taking possession of the capital before the Red Army could install a pro-Communist regime. Within three days, the underground was in command of most of Warsaw; but the Germans counter-attacked, using dive-bombers and heavy artillery. The Russians refused aid to the Polish underground (which itself, ironically enough, had refused to aid the Jews of the Warsaw ghetto in their uprising against the Nazis in 1943). After sixty-three days of fighting, the poor remnant of the Warsaw underground surrendered to the Germans a city totally ruined. Only in January 1945 did the Red Army take Warsaw. Meanwhile, Stalin detached several large armies to conquer the Balkans. Rumania and Bulgaria were taken by September 9. Russian tanks then advanced into Yugoslavia to meet the Communist partisans of Marshal Tito, who had been fighting in the western mountains. By December 1944, the Red Army was in the suburbs of Budapest, which fell the following February.

Yalta Conference

When Churchill and Roosevelt met with Stalin at the Yalta conference in the Russian Crimea (February 1945), they found that there was almost nothing they could do to halt the communization of eastern Europe. Marshal Tito had enormous popular support in Yugoslavia for the imposition of a Communist regime through his partisan movement. Albania was already in the hands of Communist-dominated forces, which after driving out the Italians and Germans had set up a provisional government under the veteran Communist Enver Hoxha. Coalition governments in which the Communists held crucial ministries were in power in Rumania and Bulgaria, which were both occupied by the Red Army. Poland was ruled by a provisional government installed by the Red Army, which refused to have any relations with the Polish government in London. Only in Greece, where Churchill had used British troops in December to break the Communist underground armies, had a pro-Western government been put in power. Roosevelt, moreover, wanted two major concessions from Stalin— agreement to the final details of a United Nations Organization that was to be set up at war's end, and Russian participation in the final stages of the

The Big Three at Yalta, February 1945
President Franklin D. Roosevelt, seated between British Prime Minister Winston S. Churchill and Russian Premier Josef Stalin, returned exhausted from Yalta and died only two months later. (National Archives)

war against Japan, which, Roosevelt had been warned, might cost up to a million American casualties. Stalin agreed to both of Roosevelt's proposals and in return was promised the grant to Russia of the Japanese territories of southern Sakhalin Island and the Kurile Islands and a lease on the Chinese city of Port Arthur. In eastern Europe Stalin made no concessions of any significance, merely promising free elections and the representation of the London Poles in the Polish government.

Shortly after the conference, both western and eastern fronts sprang to life again. The Germans were fighting a last, desperate struggle under the goad of the SS and the ravings of Hitler, who had barely escaped assassination in July 1944 in the explosion of a time bomb set by a group of military and civilian conspirators seeking to overthrow the Nazi regime. By 1945 Hitler was a physical wreck, his strength holding up only through injections received from a quack doctor. He was prepared to sacrifice what little manpower and economic potential Germany still possessed to postpone the inevitable defeat for a few more weeks. Germany itself had been subject to continual pounding from the air since 1942, when the British air force had decided to break German morale by bombing the civilian population out of their homes. In 1943 they had dropped firebombs on Hamburg nightly for a week, destroying most of the city and causing a million inhabitants to flee. American planes dropped even heavier loads on oil supplies, railroads, and factories, but in the last months, their destruction became almost indiscriminate. Small baroque cities like Würzburg, which had little military value, were destroyed in a few minutes. In spite of this pounding, German morale remained largely unaffected. More important, the German economy continued to produce the materials of war. In 1945 Hitler still had armies of seven million men and was beginning to deploy long-range rockets against England. The force ranged against the Germans was, however, overwhelming. By April, Eisenhower had captured the great industrial area of the Ruhr, and his troops had reached the Elbe. He then drove southwestward to prevent the establishment of a Nazi redoubt in the Alps, leaving the final assault on Berlin to the Russians.

The Red Army, meanwhile, had finally captured Warsaw and Budapest in February. The northern armies broke through the defenses of Danzig and moved toward Berlin. Günter Grass, in *The Tin Drum*, described how his hero, the dwarf Oskar, saw the burning of Danzig's medieval streets:

After that we seldom emerged from our hole. The Russians were said to be in Zigankenberg, Pietzgendorf, and on the outskirts of Schidlitz. There was no doubt that they occupied the heights, for they were firing straight down into the city.

[14] *Götterdämmerung*, the "Twilight of the Gods," is the final holocaust destroying the gods and their palace Valhalla in the old Germanic legend of the Ring of Nibelungs. Wagner's opera *Götterdämmerung* was one of Hitler's favorite pieces of music.

> *Götterdämmerung in Germany, 1945* [14]

Danzig Before the Destruction of 1945
Danzig prospered in the Middle Ages as one of the principal German trading cities on the Baltic Sea and as a member of the Hanseatic League. Most of its 260,000 German inhabitants were expelled in 1945 when the city was made part of Poland. (Courtesy of the German Information Center)

Inner City and Outer City, Old City, New City, and Old New City, Lower City and Spice City—what had taken seven hundred years to build burned down in three days. Yet this was not the first fire to descend on the city of Danzig. For centuries Pomerelians, Brandenburgers, Teutonic Knights, Poles, Swedes, and a second time Swedes, Frenchmen, Prussians, and Russians, even Saxons, had made history by deciding every few years that the city of Danzig was worth burning. And now it was Russians, Poles, Germans, and Englishmen all at once who were burning the city's Gothic bricks for the hundredth time. Hook Street, Long Street, and Broad Street, Big Weaver Street, and Little Weaver Street were in flames; Tobias Street, Hound Street, Old City Ditch, Outer City Ditch, the ramparts and Long Bridge, all were in flames. Built of wood, Crane Gate made a particularly fine blaze. In Breechesmaker Street, the fire had itself measured for several pairs of extra-loud breeches. The Church of St. Mary was burning inside and outside, festive light effects could be seen through its ogival windows. What bells had not been evacuated from St. Catherine, St. John, St. Brigit, Saints Barbara, Elisabeth, Peter, and Paul, from Trinity and Corpus Christi, melted in their belfries and dripped away without pomp and ceremony. . . . Only the West Prussian Fire Insurance Building, for purely symbolic reasons, refused to burn down. [15]

[15] Günter Grass, *The Tin Drum* (Greenwich, Conn.: Fawcett, 1962), pp. 378–379.

The Bombing of Berlin, June 1944
This photo, taken by an American bombing crew, may be compared with the street plan of Berlin on page 319. Central Berlin, with Museum Island and Unter den Linden, can be distinguished in the bottom left corner. (National Archives)

The Russians mounted their final attack on Berlin on April 16; within nine days the city was surrounded; and Hitler, living his last days amid the remnants of his hierarchy in an underground concrete bunker beneath the bombed-out chancellery, prepared to take the remaining inhabitants of Berlin to their deaths with him. "If the war is to be lost, the nation also will perish," Hitler declared. "This fate is inevitable. There is no need to consider the basis even of a most primitive existence any longer. On the contrary, it is better to destroy even that, and to destroy it ourselves. The nation has proved itself weak, and the future belongs solely to the stronger eastern nation. Besides, those who remain after the battle are of little value; for the good have fallen."[16] Through incessant air raids and artillery bombardment, the Russian forces fought into the city block by block until they were close enough to shell the chancellery itself. Hitler dictated his last will and testament, married his mistress Eva Braun, and then on April 30, joined her in suicide. Their bodies were cremated in the chancellery garden. Goebbels poisoned his six children and shot his wife and himself.

[16]Bullock, *Hitler,* p. 775.

On May 2 the Russians took the chancellery, and at the opposite end of the Unter den Linden, raised the red flag over the Brandenburg Gate. The final German surrender was signed in ceremonies at Rheims on May 8 and in Berlin on May 9.

Defeat of Japan

At its greatest extent the Japanese empire comprised a million and a half square miles of territory. It included most of China, Hong Kong, Borneo, the Dutch East Indies, Malaya, Burma, Guam, Wake Island, and the Philippines. The American counterattack had begun in the summer of 1942. The campaigns were slow and expensive, involving bloody battles for small Pacific islands that Japanese suicide troops held with fanatical obstinacy. But the capture of the Mariana Islands in June 1944 brought the American bombers within reach of the home islands of Japan, and the Philippines were retaken in the spring of 1945. Nevertheless, savage Japanese resistance on the atoll of Iwo Jima, seven hundred fifty miles from Japan, inflicted 27,000 casualties on the American attackers and warned of the formidable losses that would be incurred in invading Japan itself. For this reason President Roosevelt felt the promise of Russian intervention against Japan that he had won at Yalta was crucial. In July 1945, however, Harry S Truman, who had become president at Roosevelt's death in April, was informed that the team of scientists who had been attempting for four years to develop an atomic bomb had finally succeeded. Although warned that the United States possessed a weapon of terrible destructive power, the Japanese government refused to surrender; and Truman ordered the dropping of the first atomic bomb, on the port city of Hiroshima on August 6, 1945. The explosion killed over 70,000 people immediately, and most of the city was laid waste. Two days later, the Soviet Union declared war and invaded Manchuria. Even then, the Japanese military refused to surrender, and a second atomic bomb was dropped on Nagasaki, killing 36,000 people. At that point, Emperor Hirohito finally intervened, ordering his government to seek an armistice, which was signed on a warship in Tokyo Bay on August 28, 1945. After almost six years of fighting, the guns finally fell silent.

Destruction of the Second World War

The destruction of the Second World War exceeded even that of the First. Seventeen million soldiers and at least as many civilians had been killed. Mass murder carried out in concentration camps like Dachau and Auschwitz, which the Nazis had set up throughout occupied Europe, had caused the loss of at least six million Jews and hundreds of thousands of other victims—members, or suspected members, of Resistance movements; many of the eastern European intelligentsia; gypsies; the chronically sick. Populations had been uprooted on a gigantic scale. Eleven million prisoners of war and forced laborers had been deported to Germany. Six million Germans had been driven from the Oder-Neisse territories Russia had handed to Poland, and up to two million more were being expelled from the other eastern European states. And these vast movements of populations were taking place across a continent in ruins. The bombing, the artillery bombardments, and the street fighting had inflicted damage equaled only by the Thirty Years' War. Some cities, like Warsaw, Budapest, and Berlin, had suffered destruction of ninety percent of their buildings; and many lovely smaller cities, especially in Germany, Poland, and Russia, had been totally wasted. Moreover, the economic structure was in a shambles. Canals were blocked, bridges blown up, and railroads unusable. A scorched-earth policy, adopted by both Germans and Russians, had ruined most of the Ukraine's industrial plants, many of the Caucasus oil installations, and huge agricultural areas. Even where factories had not been destroyed, they were working with worn, outdated equipment. Sewers were flooded, dams destroyed, electricity and telephone lines down. At the end of the war, one hundred million Europeans were on the edge of starvation; agricultural production had fallen by as much as two-thirds of prewar level and industrial production by at least half in many areas. Only the United States appeared to have emerged from the war with its resources enhanced and its vigor undiminished; and many Europeans began to ask, though reluctantly, if the future of Western civilization lay with the colossus across the Atlantic, the heir to a Europe that had gone to its own suicide.

The Freeing of Prisoners at the Wöbbelin Concentration Camp near Berlin *(National Archives)*

SUGGESTED READING

The atmosphere of the Paris peace conference of 1919 is admirably described in Harold Nicolson, *Peacemaking 1919* (1933); its conclusions are blasted with literary and economic genius by John Maynard Keynes, *The Economic Consequences of the Peace* (1920) and defended by Etienne Mantoux, *The Carthaginian Peace* (1946) and Paul Birdsall, *Versailles Twenty Years After* (1941). Arno Mayer's *Politics and Diplomacy of Peacemaking* (1967) is a challenging reappraisal from a New Left viewpoint, which seeks to cast Wilson primarily as an opponent of Bolshevism. C. A. Macartney and A. W. Palmer, *Independent Eastern Europe* (1962) surveys the results of the conference's work in the new states of eastern Europe; the political struggles of the Weimar Republic in Germany can be untangled in Erich Eyck, *A History of the Weimar Republic* (1962–63) and S. William Halperin, *Germany Tried Democracy* (1946); the chaos of French politics is made clear in René Rémond, *The Right in France* (1972) and Denis W. Brogan, *France Under the Republic* (1940).

Sean Glynn and John Oxborrow, *Interwar Britain: A Social and Economic History* (1976) give an interpretive analysis of such topics as economic growth and overseas commerce. Charles S. Maier, *Recasting Bourgeois Europe: Stabilization in France, Germany, and Italy in the Decade After World War I* (1975) argues that the middle classes retained power by creating interest groups that operated in industry, agriculture, and commerce.

The diplomacy of the 1920s is briefly surveyed in Sally Marks, *The Illusion of Peace: International Relations in Europe, 1918–1933* (1976). The results of Locarno are appraised in Jon Jacobsen, *Locarno Diplomacy: Germany and the West, 1925–1929* (1972). The coming of the Great Depression in America is dramatically described in John K. Galbraith, *The Great Crash, 1929* (1955); its effects in Europe are analyzed in W. Arthur Lewis, *Economic Survey, 1919–1939* (1949) and Charles P. Kindleberger, *The World in Depression, 1929–1939* (1973). For a broader view of what went wrong with the American and western European economies, see Joseph S. Davis, *The World Between the Wars, 1919–1939: An Economist's View* (1975).

The flavor of the American literary colony in Paris during the 1920s is caught by Ernest Hemingway, *A Moveable Feast* (1964) and John Dos Passos, *The Best Times* (1966). Simone de Beauvoir describes Jean Paul Sartre and his circle during their early days as little known writers in *Memoirs of a Dutiful Daughter* (1962) and *The Prime of Life* (1962). H. Stuart Hughes explores the social ideas of Paris intellectuals in *Consciousness and Society* (1958) and *The Obstructed Path* (1968).

On the phenomenon of Fascism, Ernst Nolte, *Three Faces of Fascism* (1966) provides a complex philosophical and sociological explanation; Hannah Arendt, *The Origins of Totalitarianism* (1966) traces the progression from anti-Semitism through imperialism to the totalitarian state in Russia and Germany. Mussolini's career is well documented in Sir Ivone Kirkpatrick, *Mussolini: A Study in Power* (1964), which lacks the ideological background that can be found to some degree in Herman Finer, *Mussolini's Italy* (1935). Adrian Lyttelton, *The Seizure of Power: Fascism in Italy, 1919–1929* (1973) is very good on Mussolini's exploitation of the weakness of the postwar Italian state. His economic policies are weighed in Edward R. Tannenbaum, *The Fascist Experience: Italian Society and Culture, 1922–1945* (1972).

For the political history of the Weimar Republic, see Erich Eyck, *A History of the Weimar Republic* (1962). The standard biography of Hitler is Alan Bullock's *Hitler: A Study in Tyranny* (1952). For the economic and social changes instituted by the Nazis, see David Schoenbaum, *Hitler's Social Revolution: Class and Status in Nazi Germany, 1933–1939* (1966) and Franz Neumann, *Behemoth: The Structure and Practice of National Socialism* (1944). On the reasons for Hitler's success in taking power, see the useful symposium of Maurice Baumont et al., *The Third Reich* (1955), and especially William S. Allen's account of the takeover of one town, *The Nazi Seizure of Power* (1955). Karl D. Bracher, *The German Dictatorship* (1970) is perhaps the finest synthesis of all aspects of Nazi rule. On the army, see J. W. Wheeler-Bennett, *The Nemesis of Power: The German Army in Politics, 1918–1945* (1953); on Himmler's SS, consult G. Reitlinger, *The S.S.: Alibi of a Nation, 1922–1945* (1957); on the concentration camps, see Eugen Kogon, *The Theory and Practice of Hell* (1950). Jill Stephenson, *Women in Nazi Society* (1976) demonstrates that Hitler envisaged little change in the traditional role of women in German society. The cultural aspirations of the Third Reich can be measured in Barbara M. Lane, *Architecture and Politics in Germany, 1918–1945* (1968), Robert R. Taylor, *The Word in Stone: The Role of Architecture in the Nationalist Socialist Ideology* (1974), and Albert Speer, *Inside the Third Reich: Memoirs* (1970); but they should be compared with the tense creativity of the Weimar period, as seen in Peter Gay, *Weimar Culture: The Outsider as Insider* (1968). A less admiring view of Weimar from the inside is found in Christopher Isherwood's novels, *The Last of Mr. Norris* (1935) and *Goodbye to Berlin* (1939) and in the memoirs of Stephen Spender, *World Within World* (1951).

The Italian conquest of Ethiopia is admirably analyzed in George W. Baer's two studies, *The Coming of the Italian-Ethiopian War* (1967) and *Test Case: Italy, Ethiopia, and the League of Nations* (1976). Italy's contribution to the Fascist victory in the Spanish civil war is systematically treated in John F. Coverdale, *Italian Intervention in the Spanish Civil War* (1976). The reasons for the failure of the Spanish Republic are explained in Gabriel Jackson, *The Spanish Republic and Civil War* (1965) and in Stanley Payne's two studies, *The Spanish Revolution* (1970) and *Politics and the Military in Modern Spain* (1967). The campaigns of the war can be followed in Hugh Thomas, *The Spanish Civil War* (1965).

The policy of appeasement is sharply criticized in A. L. Rowse, *Appeasement: A Study in Political Decline, 1933–1939* (1963) and Lewis Namier, *Diplomatic Prelude, 1938–1939* (1948), and explained in Arnold Wolfers, *Britain and France Between Two Wars* (1940). American policy is roundly condemned by William Appleman Williams, *The Tragedy of American Diplomacy* (1962) and calmly analyzed in Jean-Baptiste Duroselle, *From Wilson to Roosevelt: Foreign Policy of the United States, 1913–1945* (1963). Keith G. Feiling's *The Life of Neville Chamberlain* (1946) is informative but oversympathetic.

Winston Churchill and Charles de Gaulle have given classic accounts of the war from their personal vantage points, the former his six-volume *The Second World War* (1948–1953) and the latter his three-volume *War Memoirs* (1958–1960). The best short accounts are Cyril Falls, *The Second World War: A Short History* (1948) and Basil Liddell-Hart, *The Second World War* (1972). Nazi occupation policies are described in Arnold and Veronica M. Toynbee, eds., *Hitler's Europe* (1954), and the Russian takeover in eastern Europe is summarized in Hugh Seton-Watson, *The East European Revolution* (1956). Gordon Wright, *The Ordeal of Total War, 1939–1945* (1968) is particularly strong on the economic, psychological, and scientific dimensions of the struggle. Alan S. Milward, *War, Economy, and Society, 1939–1945* (1977) shows that differences in economic planning caused the belligerents to adopt different military strategies.

30

NEW YORK CITY: THE CRISIS OF THE METROPOLIS

Ah, what can ever be more stately and admirable to me than mast-
hemmed Manhattan?
River and sunset and scallop-edg'd waves of flood-tide?
The sea-gulls oscillating their bodies, the hay-boat in the twilight, and
the belated lighter?
What gods can exceed these that clasp me by the hand, and with voices I
love call me promptly and loudly by my nighest name as I approach?—
Walt Whitman, "Crossing Brooklyn Ferry." From Leaves of Grass *by Walt*
Whitman. Reprinted by permission of Doubleday & Company, Inc.

The most impressive characteristic of New York City throughout its history has been its intensity. In 1906, the English novelist H. G. Wells saw New York's material progress as "something inevitable and inhuman, as a blindly furious energy of growth that must go on. . . . New York's achievement is a threatening promise, growth going on under a pressure that increases, and amidst a hungry uproar of effort."[1] New York City epitomized many of the most characteristic features of the American experience—the mingling of ethnic groups, the escape of the immigrant from the imprisonment of economic or social deprivation, the encouragement of productivity in every field by the lure of vast material reward,

[1]Cited in Bayrd Still, ed., *Mirror for Gotham: New York as Seen by Contemporaries from Dutch Days to the Present* (New York: New York University Press, 1956), p. 278.

New York City *(Russell Thompson/Taurus Photos)*

the unrestricted freedom of capitalist enterprise, the abandonment of the old in favor of the excitement of the new. The result was a city endlessly renewing itself, in population, in talent, in physical appearance, and in character. To the great French architect Le Corbusier, New York was "a city in the process of becoming. Today it belongs to the world. Without anyone expecting it, it has become the jewel in the crown of universal cities. . . . Crown of noble cities, soft pearls, or glittering topazes, or radiant lapis, or melancholy amethysts! New York is a great diamond, hard and

◆ *Twentieth-Century New York City* ◆

Period Surveyed	From the American Revolution (1776–1783) to the present, with special emphasis on the interwar years (1918–1941) and the post-1945 period
Population	24,000 (1776); 33,000 (1790); 60,500 (1800); 1 million (1860); 5 million (1910); 7.4 million (1940); 7.7 million (1960); 7.5 million (1974); 7.1 million (1980)
Area	Manhattan, 22 square miles. New York City, including the five boroughs but excluding water area, 319 square miles
Form of Government	Municipal government of New York City by mayor, City Council, and Board of Estimate
Political Leaders	New York City mayors: James Walker (1926–1932); Fiorello LaGuardia (1934–1946); Robert F. Wagner (1954–1966); John V. Lindsay (1966–1974)
Economic Base	Banking and insurance; company administrative offices; stock exchange; printing and publishing; textiles and clothing; metal products; food processing; television and radio; entertainment (theater, ballet, opera, records); transportation (port, railroads, trucking, airlines)
Intellectual Life	Interwar years: drama (Eugene O'Neill); novel (Theodore Dreiser, Sinclair Lewis, John Dos Passos, F. Scott Fitzgerald); painting (George Bellows, John Sloan) Post-1945: architecture (Frank Lloyd Wright, Gordon Bunshaft, Mies van der Rohe, Walter Gropius, Eero Saarinen); Drama (Eugene O'Neill, Tennessee Williams, Edward Albee); novel (James Baldwin, Truman Capote, Norman Mailer, Mary McCarthy, John Updike); painting (Jackson Pollock, Mark Rothko, Andy Warhol, Claes Oldenburg); sculpture (George Segal, Robert Stankiewicz)
Principal Buildings	Pre-1914: Brooklyn Bridge, City Hall, Fifth Avenue mansions, Flatiron Building, Woolworth Building Interwar Years: Chrysler Building, Empire State Building, Rockefeller Center Post-1945: United Nations, Seagram Building, Lever House, Guggenheim Museum, World Trade Center
Public Entertainment	Baseball, football, basketball; theater (opera, symphony, musicals, drama, popular music); automobile touring; ocean bathing
Religion	Catholic (48 percent); Jewish (23 percent); Protestant (23 percent)

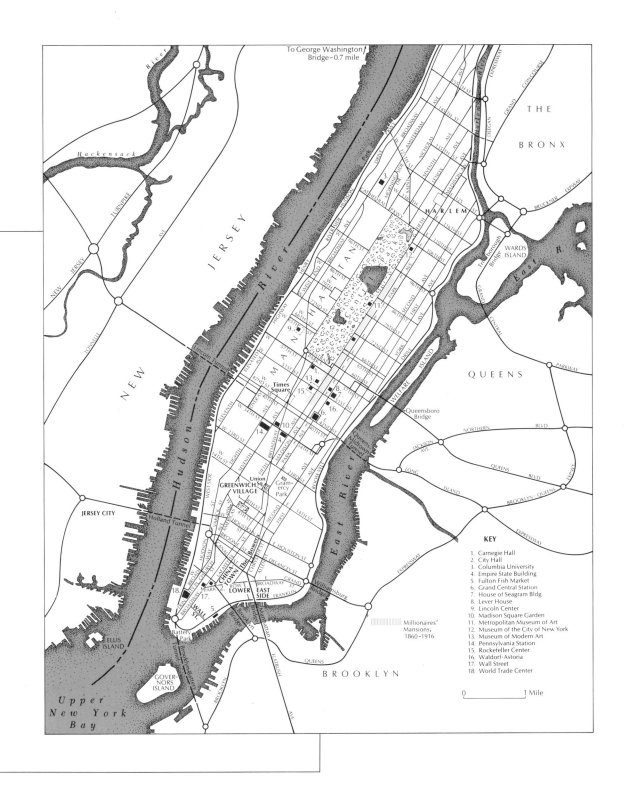

KEY

1. Carnegie Hall
2. City Hall
3. Columbia University
4. Empire State Building
5. Fulton Fish Market
6. Grand Central Station
7. House of Seagram Bldg.
8. Lever House
9. Lincoln Center
10. Madison Square Garden
11. Metropolitan Museum of Art
12. Museum of the City of New York
13. Museum of Modern Art
14. Pennsylvania Station
15. Rockefeller Center
16. Waldorf-Astoria
17. Wall Street
18. World Trade Center

Millionaires' Mansions, 1860–1916

0   1 Mile

NEW YORK CITY IN THE NINETEENTH CENTURY

dry, sparkling, triumphant."[2] Perhaps the height of confidence and delight in this creation was reached in the decade after the First World War. Then, the Soviet poet Mayakovsky could stand on Brooklyn Bridge, and see around him in microcosm the achievements of all America:

I clamber,
               with pride,
                              on to Brooklyn Bridge.
As a beauty-drunk artist
                              thrusts his eyes
into a museum-madonna
                              love-gazing sharp-edged
so I,
     enveloped
                    in star-studded skies,
look
     at New York
                         through Brooklyn Bridge.
New York,
               oppressive and stuffy
                                   by nightfall,
forgets
          its oppression
                              and straining heights,
and only a few
                    household ghosts shine sprightful
in the shimmer
                    of windows' transparent fires. . . .
If
   this world of ours
                         should come to an end,
and our planet
                    in chaos
                                   burst into bits,
and one thing
                    alone
                              remained of men
this spanning earth's ruins uprearing bridge—
then,
     as from a tiny
                    needle-thin bone
a museum
          restores
                         a giant brontosaurus,
a centuries-hence
                         geologist
                                   from this bridge alone

[2]Ibid., p. 335.

could
         recreate
                    the days now before us.
"This very
         paw of steel,"
                    he would say,
"oceans and prairies
                    united,
from here
         Europe swept
                    to the west-far-away,
putting
         Indian feathers
                    to windy flight. . . .
I know—
         by these lines of electric strands—

Brooklyn Bridge
(Courtesy of Trans World Airlines)

                    this
                          was the epoch
                                        that followed steam.
                    Here
                          people
                                  the skies
                                             in aeroplanes spanned,
                    here
                          people
                                  orated
                                         by radio-beam.
                    Here
                          life
                                for some
                                          was comfort unalloyed,
                    for others—
                                  a desperate
                                               drawn-out howl. . . ."
                    I stare,
                          as an Eskimo out-stares an express,
                    drinking it in,
                                    like a drowning man air.
                    Brooklyn Bridge—
                                      yes . . .
                    is something
                                 beyond compare![3]

    Yet from the crash of 1929 and especially during the quarter-century following the Second World War, New Yorkers recognized that the often predicted self-destruction of their city had begun. Political corruption had left a legacy of inefficiency in city government. The city's bankers had failed to provide leadership or resources in handling the breakdown of the city's infrastructure, the weakening of its economic base, and the worsening of its social tensions. Union power had imposed great financial burdens in labor costs upon inadequate city revenues. Large migrations had produced racial tension. The three million most recent immigrants to the city, the blacks and the Puerto Ricans, were unable to break out of their poverty. The intellectual life of the city was being stifled by the harshness of living conditions. The constant rebuilding seemed to have bereft the city of the charm of the old, replacing it with a new that was aesthetically sterile and humanly restrictive. The freedom of productive enterprise had led to the pollution of air and water and the strangling of the streets with traffic. And the violence of the city's life, which French novelist Paul Morand in the 1920s could describe as "New York's supreme beauty, its truly unique quality [which] gives it nobility, excuses it, makes its vulgarity for-

[3]"Brooklyn Bridge," from *Mayakovsky*, trans. and ed. Herbert Marshall (London: Dennis Dobson Publishers, 1965), pp. 336–340. Reprinted by permission of Dobson Books Ltd.

gettable,"[4] had become intolerable, driving the middle classes to the suburbs and turning the central core of the city into a residence only for the very poor and the very rich. "What oppresses New Yorkers today," a prominent New Yorker commented in 1971, "is a double sense of diminution: first, that the mundane problems of life in their city become daily more difficult; and second, that the unique element in New York that compensated for its hardships—the pride of cosmopolitan citizenship—is wasting away. Manhattan—the cosmopolis—the world city—has begun to lose its quality."[5]

In part, the change in the character of New York City has been the result of peculiarly American conditions of government, economic policy, and society. But its difficulties are, in an advanced form, those of any world city. For that reason New York raises some vital questions on the future of the city in the preservation and expansion of civilization. In the most elementary form, the question one must ask is whether the world city can maintain even a minimum of tolerable living conditions for its people—in housing, public services, employment, clean air and water, and individual safety. This problem is compounded by the fact that the individual city no longer stands isolated in the countryside but forms part of an urbanized region of increasing size. New York stands in a contiguous belt of cities and suburbs stretching from southern New Hampshire to northern Virginia that has been aptly labeled Megalopolis. In the second place, the question arises whether the world city is still the most effective unit for the production of wealth in present and future technological conditions. And finally, most apposite to our present inquiry, one must consider whether the world city can continue to be the center of intellectual creativity that cities have been throughout Western civilization.

NEW YORK CITY IN THE NINETEENTH CENTURY

When we get piled upon one another in large cities," Thomas Jefferson had warned in 1787, "we shall become as corrupt as in Europe, and go to eating one another as they do there." At that time, there seemed little threat of such cannibalism, since the line of tiny towns that had played so large a part in organizing the American Revolution were still countrified in appearance and character and were dependent for their expansion on trade in the agriculture of their hinterland. The first federal census of 1790, which classified as urban twenty-four towns of more than 2,500 inhabitants, found they contained only five percent of the country's population. New York, the second largest city, had only 24,000 inhabitants at the time of the Revolution. The choice in 1790 of an undeveloped meadowland on the banks of the Potomac River for Washington, the fed-

[4]Paul Morand, *New York* (New York: Henry Holt, 1930), p. 315.
[5]Roger Starr, "The Decline and Decline of New York," *New York Times Magazine*, Nov. 21, 1971.

eral capital, further ensured that, in contrast with the situation in European states, no large commercial city would be stimulated in its growth by the presence of the central government.

By 1860, however, one-fifth of the country's population lived in towns of more than 2,500 inhabitants. There were one hundred and one cities with more than 10,000 inhabitants; eight with more than 100,000; and one, New York, with more than a million. The stimulus to city growth was many-sided. Population, fed by a high birthrate and an open-door immigration policy, rose by one-third every decade to reach thirty-one million by 1860. The opening of the continent to settlement beyond the Allegheny Mountains had spurred the development of millions of farms that were purchasers of city goods from farm machinery to clothing, and sellers of produce to the commercial middlemen of the cities. Chicago, from which 5,000 miles of railroad track branched out in all directions, had become the railroad hub of the continent. Pittsburgh, ideally located at the junction of the Allegheny and Monongahela rivers, was manufacturing the goods bought by the westward migrant hordes. Cleveland, aided by lake and canal transportation, was building a large iron industry. In the South, the slave plantations, traditionally oriented to large-scale markets overseas, were shipping their cotton and sugar to booming cities like New Orleans. The coming of the techniques of England's industrial revolution to the northeastern states had led to the foundation of cotton and woolen mills in towns like Lowell in Massachusetts; and Boston had found new strength as the financial and marketing center for the textile industry. But in spite of this competition, New York had established a preeminence that appeared unassailable.

New York's Economic Preeminence, 1790–1860

New York's natural advantages were very great. Manhattan Island was situated on a large sheltered bay with channels forty-five feet deep at the piers, a rocky bottom that made dredging unnecessary, and freedom from ice and fog. The Hudson River and its tributary the Mohawk led directly into a vast hinterland, access to which was further improved with the construction in 1817–1825 of the Erie Canal linking the Hudson River directly with the Great Lakes. As New York's merchants were ambitious and skillful in profiting from these advantages, New York quickly became the nation's principal wholesaler and financial center. Commercial banks sprang up to finance the shipment of southern cotton and the purchase of imports and manufactured goods by western suppliers. Maritime coverage was supplied by insurance companies. Securities specialists set up the New York Stock and Exchange Board in 1817. The presence of the markets and of a large work force made manufacturing profitable. Shipbuilding was carried out on the East River. Heavy engineering factories supplied steam engines and locomotives. The raw materials passing through New York harbor began to be processed in the city. Raw sugar was turned into molasses and rum, hides into boots and saddles. Meat was packed, textiles turned into ready-made clothes. Finally, employment opportunities encouraged a good proportion of the immigrants, most of whom reached America through New York, to stay in the city.

This vast growth inevitably changed the character of New York. In 1821, one English visitor could report that there were "no dark alleys, whose confined and noisome atmosphere marks the presence of a dense and suffering population, no hovels, in whose ruined garrets, or dank and gloomy cellars, crowd the wretched victims of vice and leisure, whose penury drives to despair, ere she opens them to the grave." By 1860 this pleasant picture was no longer accurate, if it ever had been. The physical separation of rich and poor had accelerated the decay of many poorer areas. As Lower Manhattan was turned over almost exclusively to business,

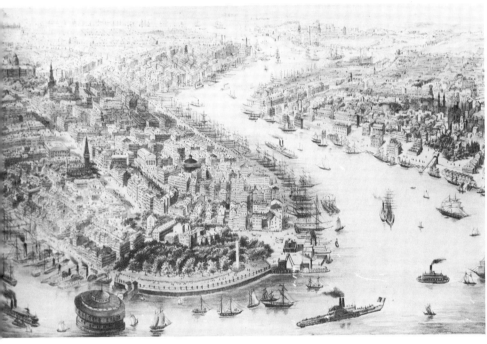

View of New York in 1852 and in the 1960s

In 1852, Manhattan still resembled a European city. By the late 1960s, half a century of skyscraper building had given it a unique profile among world cities. (Above, the Edward W. C. Arnold Collection, lent by the Metropolitan Museum of Art, photo courtesy of the Museum of the City of New York. Below, photo courtesy of the New York Convention and Visitors Bureau.)

Hammerstein's Roof Garden, by William James Glackens (1870–1938)

Hammerstein was the most exuberant theatrical impresario in early twentieth-century New York. (Collection of Whitney Museum of American Art, New York)

the well-to-do moved northward, the wealthiest constructing fine brownstone mansions on Fifth Avenue north of Washington Square. The middle classes were scattering, many of them commuting by steam ferry to Brooklyn or New Jersey or by horse-drawn streetcar to the new blocks just south of Forty-second Street. The working classes—mostly immigrants, since the foreign-born composed almost half the city's population—tended to group in the most run-down sections, especially on the East Side, though the poorest of all lived in shanties just north of the built-up area on Forty-second Street. The death rate, which rose from one death per 46.5 persons in 1810 to one in 27 in 1859, was an indicator of the overcrowding, the lack of sanitation, and the inadequate medical care in a large section of the population. Many died of typhoid, typhus, cholera, consumption, yellow fever, and even plague. Thus, for most immigrants to New York, the New World failed to offer the bright prospects they had expected; and the presence of pauperized immigrants huddled in city slums was to become one of the outrages most widely advertised by the city reformers of the next thirty years.

There was as yet little cultural vitality to the city. Columbia University had less than two hundred students; there were only three theaters; the favorite museum was Barnum's collection of oddities. The city's character was unabashedly shaped by the hurried creation of material prosperity. Even then, however, the city's energy found admirers among the literati, including the poet Walt Whitman, who loved the "tall masts of Manhattan":

City of hurried and sparkling waters! city of spires and masts!
City nested in bays! my city![6]

In 1870, Whitman still found New York and Brooklyn irresistible:

The splendor, picturesqueness, and oceanic amplitude and rush of these great cities, the ... lofty new buildings, facades of marble and iron, of original grandeur and elegance of masses, with the masses of gay color, the preponderance of white and blue, the flags flying, the endless ships, the tumultuous streets, Broadway, the heavy, low musical roar, hardly ever interrupted, even at night; the jobbers' houses, the rich shops, the wharves, the great Central Park and the Brooklyn Park of hills. ... these, I say, and the like of these completely satisfy my senses of power, fulness, motion, &c and give me, through such senses ... a continued exaltation and absolute fulfilment. Always, more and more ... I realize ... that not Nature alone is great in her fields of freedom and the open air, in her storms, the shows of night and day, the mountains, forests, seas—but in the artificial, the work of man too is equally great—in this profusion of teeming humanity—in these ingenuities, streets, goods, houses, ships—these hurrying, feverish, electric crowds of men, their complicated business genius (not least among the geniuses), and all this mighty, many-threaded wealth and industry concentrated here.[7]

In the half-century following the outbreak of the Civil War (1861–1865), America's urbanization continued at an ever faster pace. By 1910, over forty-five percent of the population lived in towns of over 2,500 inhabitants; and for the first time, the census bureau classified as metropolitan twenty-five cities with a central-city population of over 200,000. New York, in spite of its five million population had become one metropolis among many, although still by far the largest.

After 1865, New York could not maintain its hegemony. Industry diversified and spread to distant regions of the country; fresh sources of finance became available in metropolitan centers; and a number of new and

New York's Changing Economic Function

[6]"Manahatta," from Walt Whitman, *Leaves of Grass* (Garden City, N.Y.: Doubleday, 1948), p. 395.
[7]Cited in Still, *Mirror for Gotham*, pp. 200–201.

more efficient ports were created, not only on the Pacific and Gulf coasts but on the East Coast as well. The port of New York slowly lost its predominant importance in the city's economy. The railroads replaced coastal shipping; the growing manufacturing capacity at home reduced the share of imports in the nation's consumption; shipbuilding could not be carried out economically in the overcrowded city. After the 1880s New York's share of the nation's manufacturers also began to decline. For many industries it was hampered by distance from raw materials. The very efficiency of the railroad networks made it possible for producers in the Midwest or West to undercut New York producers. The great new automobile industry found it profitable to locate in the Midwest, near both the sources of raw materials and the big markets; and this industry drew to it other subsidiary industries like rubber manufacturing and glass making.

New York proved its continuing vitality, however, by concentrating on those manufacturing industries for which transportation costs were relatively unimportant. Above all it became the nation's chief producer of ready-made clothing, aided in this expansion by the shift from homemade

A Sweatshop on Ludlow Street, by Jacob Riis (1849–1914)
In the "sweating" system widely used in New York, an employer supplied materials to workers in their homes and paid extremely low prices by the piece for their work. (Photograph by Jacob A. Riis. The Jacob A. Riis Collection, Museum of the City of New York.)

to ready-to-wear clothing and by the arrival in New York of several million immigrants from eastern and southern Europe willing to work for little wages in the city's sweatshops. By 1910, the apparel industry was employing 236,000 New Yorkers. A second form of adaptation was the concentration in New York of the book and periodical publishing industry, which had previously been located primarily in Boston; this was aided particularly by the migration to the city of many European intellectuals, especially Jews who were driven out by the persecutions that began in the 1880s and continued through most of the twentieth century.

Still more important than manufacturing, however, was New York's primacy as the financial and service center of the expanding national economy. Life insurance companies were almost always located in downtown Manhattan, near Wall Street, from the Civil War on. Banks continued to maintain their central offices in the same area and thus exerted an attraction on large companies that needed constant contact with the money market. The change in the capitalist system from industrial to financial capitalism was directly beneficial to New York. Many of the great trusts that controlled huge industrial empires throughout the country were dominated in whole or in part by large New York banks, and thus of necessity they also located their central offices in New York. The need for direct communication with customers, bankers, or even rivals persuaded many other industrial companies to establish themselves in New York, and they in turn were followed by other organizations depending on them, such as trade unions or research institutes. This proliferating industrial and financial bureaucracy in turn created new satellite companies in New York such as real estate firms, architectural and construction companies, advertising agencies, and engineering consultants. Finally, New York expanded its retail sales outlets, remaining the nation's largest shopkeeper. Great department stores were constructed just to the north of the financial district, the most impressive being the neighboring Macy's and Gimbel's. Luxury shops proliferated from Thirty-fourth Street northward.

A New City Profile

New York's appearance changed rapidly as it sought to meet the demands of its new economic functions. The skyscraper was the answer to the demand of the financial and industrial organizations for the proximity that was essential to their efficient conduct of business. In New York, brick and mortar construction provided a massive base for buildings as high as eleven stories in the 1870s; but with the adoption of steel frame construction, there began a competition for height that can only be compared with the rivalry of the cathedral builders of thirteenth-century France. By the 1890s, New York had a skyline with six buildings over 300 feet high and one, the Park Row Business Building, 392 feet high. The assembling and dispersal of the hundreds of thousands of people who worked in the skyscraper canyons required miracles of urban transportation. From 1867 the elevated railroads began to carry the clanking, filthy steam-powered trains between the houses on the city's poorer streets, providing an efficient alter-

View of New York in 1870
Unlike modern designers, the architects who planned the Brooklyn Bridge (center left) took a minimum of city land for the construction of points of access. (Harper's Weekly, *November 19, 1870)*

native to the five main street railways whose carriages were drawn by horses. Only in 1904, with the improvement of the electric railroad, was the first New York subway constructed, which ran from City Hall to 145th Street. To New Yorkers the most exciting improvement in their transportation network was the linking of Manhattan to Brooklyn provided by the Brooklyn Bridge, a mile-long suspension bridge that carried two railroad lines, four lanes of traffic, and a footpath.

The housing to which the trains and trolleys carried New York's workers was more varied than even that of prerevolutionary Paris. The existence of an aristocracy of wealth, consisting of the tycoons of railroads, banks, steel works, and real estate, was blatantly evident in the new homes going up along Fifth Avenue from Forty-sixth Street to Seventy-second. Here were palaces in every style from French Renaissance to debased Byzantine, belonging to the Vanderbilts (New York Central Railroad), the Astors (real estate, after an early fortune in fur trade), Jay Gould (finance), Collis P. Huntington (Southern Pacific Railroad), and many others of the inner group called the Four Hundred, a title invented in 1892 after Mrs. Astor sent out exactly four hundred invitations to a ball at her home. This social elite indulged in conspicuous spending on an almost unparalleled scale, supporting the great hotels (or even running them, in the case of the Astors' Waldorf-Astoria), dining at Delmonico's or the Brunswick Restaurant, attending the Metropolitan Opera House. Most middle-class New Yorkers sought to live in the long terraces of brownstone houses but often had to settle for less commodious wooden-frame structures that speculative builders were erecting beyond Central Park or in Brooklyn.

In sharp contrast, over one and a half million poor people lived in tenements, barracks-like buildings invented in the 1850s, lacking plumbing and heat, each designed to house some five hundred people. From the 1870s, a law requiring bedrooms to have a window led to the construction of tenements shaped like dumbbells, with small, foul-smelling passages five feet wide supplying fresh air and light to all inside rooms. The plight of tenement dwellers was exposed in 1888 in Jacob Riis's *How the Other Half*

Sixth Avenue Elevated at Third Street, by John Sloan (1871–1951)
(Collection of Whitney Museum of American Art, New York)

Battery Court, by Jacob Riis

As a newspaper reporter, Riis was familiar with conditions of the New York poor and tried to stir the public conscience with his books and photographs. (Photograph by Jacob A. Riis. The Jacob A. Riis Collection, Museum of the City of New York.)

Lives, in which the photographs were an even more scalding testimony than the bitterly denunciatory text.

Almost as shocking as the city-condoned wretchedness of the tenements was the governmental neglect of normal city functions. Indeed, New York had become the prototype of crooked city government in the late nineteenth century. Mayor William M. Tweed, the "Boss," and his Tammany Hall ring of crooked cronies, created an organized political empire based on disciplined control of the immigrant groups, which was able to bilk the city of over $100 million. Almost no controls were placed on any form of real estate development, whether for factories, stores, or residences. The creation of Central Park was a fine exception to the neglect of provision of open space. Pollution of the waterways was unrestricted. Streets were paved poorly, if at all. Lighting was inadequate, as were garbage collection and sewage disposal. "No one as yet has approached the management of New York in a proper spirit," Rudyard Kipling commented in 1892, "that is to say, regarding it as the shiftless outcome of squalid barbarism and reckless extravagance." New York's streets, he went on, were "first cousins to a Zanzibar foreshore, or kin to the approaches of a Zulu kraal."

The situation worsened between 1900 and 1914, during the last great migratory wave, which brought to the United States more than nine million people from the poorer regions of Europe, mostly Italy, Russia, the Balkans, and the Austro-Hungarian Empire. Yet at the same time the reformers of the Progressive movement found widespread support for their demand that the most blatant injustices in American society, of which the "Shame of the Cities" was notorious, should be remedied. New York was of necessity in the eye of the Progressive hurricane. Its skyline and mansions were the product of many of the most significant economic achievements of the last half-century—the opening of the continent, the creation of the world's most productive industrial system, the mobilization of vast capital resources for the multiplication of wealth, the provision of work for the fastest-growing population on earth. But New York also represented the price America had paid—the perversion of democracy into boss rule through entrenched political machines, the widening of the gulf of rich and poor, the abuse of natural resources for private profit, the failure to protect the individual citizen against the power of the large private company.

So although the Progressive movement demanded reform at the national level also, one of its most effective campaigns was for municipal reform. It is now recognized that in part the Progressives were fighting for a restoration of the political power of the older migrant groups of northern European stock represented by the professional middle classes; but some social progress was achieved. The power of Tammany Hall had been broken by the end of the century, especially because of the efforts of the "muckraking" journalists to expose city corruption. Some improvement in tenement housing was forced by creation of a tenement house department. A few more parks were provided. And New York was even given its first city plan in 1912 and its first zoning regulation in 1916. The achievements were minor, but they were at least a start that seemed to many reformers to promise that New York too might become a "City Beautiful."

THE REWARDS OF INTENSITY: NEW YORK
BETWEEN THE WARS

From the First World War to shortly after the end of the second, New York was appreciated not only as the center of the wealth-creating segment of American society but as a genuine cosmopolis as well. At last it had become one of the world's great centers of civilization.

By the time the hundred-and-second story of the Empire State Building had been completed in 1931, New York was recognized as having created for itself in about thirty years an architectural character as distinct as that

The Skyscraper City

The Vertical City
The Empire State Building, completed in 1931, dominates the skyline of midtown Manhattan. To the right is the Pan Am Building, constructed over Grand Central Station on Park Avenue. (Courtesy of the New York Convention and Visitors Bureau)

which Pericles gave Athens or Ivan the Great gave the Moscow Kremlin. Moreover, its appearance was totally representative of the culture that created it. The buildings represented the enormous financial power of the great corporations, the two hundred or so giant companies that dominated the American economy. The tallest of the buildings followed the pattern of the Gothic-topped shaft of the Woolworth Building (1913). Other great towers ended in the skies in Roman temples, or Strozzi palaces, or even Mayan pyramids, the efflorescence of period detail due principally to the architect's need to give the skyscraper of the American Telephone and Telegraph Company (1924) or of the McGraw-Hill Publishing Company (1931) or of the Chrysler Automobile Company (1929) a distinctive, recognizable outline. Next to the pillars of the skyscrapers, New York developed the setback silhouette or "ziggurat," in which, in the architect's pursuit of light and air, the upper stories of the cube-shaped buildings were narrowed. Only occasionally, however, were skyscrapers grouped in balanced

Office Girls, by Raphael Soyer (1899–)
(Collection of Whitney Museum of American Art, New York)

New York City by Night
As one looks south from central Manhattan, the Empire State Building dominates the view. In the distance are the illuminated arches of the Verrazano-Narrows Bridge, constructed across the entrance to New York Bay. (Courtesy of Trans World Airlines)

relationships with space left at their bases where pedestrians could enjoy malls, gardens, or even ice rinks, as in Rockefeller Center (1931–1940).

Yet the two clusters of skyscrapers—the older grouping on the tip of Manhattan that struck the imagination of the visitor arriving by ocean liner, and the uptown grouping between Thirty-second Street and Central Park—were immensely exciting. They had created a sharp, rectangular city whose verticality was enhanced by the dry sparkle of a sky that was still clear to view, a city that to the English poet Rupert Brooke "gave a kind of classical feeling, classical, and yet not of Europe. . . . that characteristic of the great buildings of the world, an existence and meaning of their own." The skyscrapers had finally achieved the scale required by the physical grandeur of Manhattan's setting, the long southward sweep of the Hudson River, the "bright, breezy bay" that Henry James admired, and the granite outcroppings that were still impressive along Riverside Drive or across the river in the Palisades of New Jersey. Throughout the 1920s amazed European writers, artists, and architects swelled the bookstores of Paris and London with their accounts of Western civilization's new metropolis. The best qualified commentator of all was perhaps the town planner Le Corbusier, who deliberately shocked New Yorkers by telling them that their skyscrapers were too small. They had indeed conceived the solution to urban congestion, he said, the "Cartesian skyscraper" in which three to four thousand people could be concentrated on two and a half acres, using only eight to twelve percent of the ground and leaving the rest free for parkland

and people. But they had not built it. In New York, Le Corbusier charged, skyscrapers were put up as "acrobatic feats, a banner in the sky, a fireworks rocket, an aigrette in the coiffure of a name henceforth listed in the financial Almanach de Gotha." Even so, he had to admit that New York was a "beautiful catastrophe," especially at night:

The night was dark, the air dry and cold. The whole city was lighted up. If you have not seen it, you cannot know or imagine what it is like. You must have had it sweep over you. Then you begin to understand why Americans have become proud of themselves in the last twenty years and why they raise their voices in the world and why they are impatient when they come to our country. The sky is decked out. It is a Milky Way come down to earth; you are in it. Each window, each person, is a light in the sky. At the same time a perspective is established by the arrangement of the thousand lights in each skyscraper; it forms itself more in your mind than in the darkness perforated by illimitable fires. The stars are part of it also—the real stars—but sparkling quietly in the distance. Splendor, scintillation, promise, proof, act of faith, etc. Feeling comes into play; the action of the heart is released; crescendo, allegro, fortissimo. We are charged with feeling, we are intoxicated; legs strengthened, chests expanded, eager for action, we are filled with confidence. That is the Manhattan of vehement silhouettes. Those are the varieties of technique, which is the springboard of lyricism. The fields of water, the railroads, the planes, the stars, and the vertical city with its unimaginable diamonds. Everything is there, and it is real. [8]

The New Bohemia

The New Yorkers who responded most enthusiastically to the excitement of the upward-thrusting city preferred, however, to live in the oases where the older, horizontal city had not yet been torn down. In the years immediately preceding the First World War and in the interwar years, gathered in a Bohemian world whose center was the walk-up flats of Greenwich Village to the south of Washington Square, New York's literary figures pushed into the forefront of revolution in literature.

New York had attracted America's literary giants before. In the 1840s Melville, Irving, and Poe had moved there; in the 1880s, it had drawn Edith Wharton, Walt Whitman, Mark Twain and, fleetingly, Henry James. Artists and sculptors had found occasional patronage from the society leaders for portraits or house decoration. But unlike the patriciate of Florence or the aristocracy of Paris, the Four Hundred of New York had done little to foster the cultural life of their city. They had bought their paintings in Europe, usually old masters that were secure investments. Only at the very end of the century did any of the vast wealth of Fifth and Madison avenues spill over to the cultural benefit of other New Yorkers. In 1895 the New York Public Library was formed in the consolidation of three privately endowed libraries, including the Astor collection. The Metropolitan Museum of Art, limping along since 1870, blossomed only after the com-

[8] Cited in Alexander Klein, ed., *The Empire City*, trans. Francis E. Hyslop, Jr. (New York: Rinehart, 1955), p. 448.

pletion of its new home on Fifth Avenue in Central Park in 1902. The Metropolitan Opera House did not become a financial and artistic success until a great showman, Maurice Grau, attracted the wealthy to the Diamond Horseshoe of his rebuilt theater, giving them for the opening performance in 1903 the young Enrico Caruso in *Rigoletto*. But it was the advent of the mass audience for books, newspapers, theater, and radio that changed the character of literary New York. For perhaps the first time it became easy for an author at a relatively young age to make a living from writing; a single best seller, like Sinclair Lewis's *Main Street*, published when he was thirty-five, could set up a writer for years. Journalism provided alternative employment in lean times, and the theater offered new sources of riches and instant success.

The objective of the "lost generation" of writers, as Gertrude Stein had labeled them, was to express the American scene in contemporary language. They strove to break with the European models that had still lingered on in the classical writers of the nineteenth century. The effort had begun with several older writers who had come to New York before the First World War. Theodore Dreiser's first novel, *Sister Carrie* (1900), had shocked its publisher into stopping its distribution, but Dreiser had gone on to explore such facets of New York life as *The Financier* (1912) and *The Titan* (1914). Dreiser set the pattern of lashing out at the city he loved in spite of its shortcomings in *The Color of a Great City* (1923); he pinpointed the city's attraction to the novelist:

The thing that interested me then as now about New York—as indeed about any great city, but more definitely New York because it was and is so preponderantly large—was the sharp, and at the same time immense, contrast it showed between the dull and the shrewd, the strong and the weak, the rich and the poor, the wise and the ignorant. . . . the number from which to choose was so great here that the strong, or those who ultimately dominated, were so very strong, and the weak so very, very weak—and so very, very many.

To F. Scott Fitzgerald, writing in the 1920s, the gaudiness and the underlying tragedy of the carnival atmosphere permeating New York offered the theme suited to his style and his character; and he became the exponent of the Jazz Age, of such people as he created in *The Beautiful and the Damned* (1922). John Dos Passos picked up the Dreiser indictment of America, especially in his trilogy *U.S.A.* (1930–1936). After the success of *Tortilla Flat*, John Steinbeck settled for a time, writing on about California, since he found the atmosphere of the city more conducive to hard literary work than that of any other place.

Of all the writers who capitalized on the separation from a rural background that New York forced, the most vociferous was Thomas Wolfe. Beginning with *Look Homeward, Angel* in 1929 and ending with *You Can't Go Home Again* (1940), Wolfe told the story of his own flight from the poverty of the North Carolina hills, and of his battle with New York:

F. Scott and Zelda Fitzgerald and Their Daughter Scottie in Paris in the 1920s
After two years of riotous living in New York City, in 1922 Fitzgerald and his wife Zelda, the daughter of an Alabama judge, left to join the group of American expatriates living in Paris. (Brown Brothers)

For the first time his vision phrased it as it had never done before. It was a cruel city, but it was a lively one, a savage city, yet it had such tenderness; a bitter, harsh and violent catacomb of stone and steel and tunneled rock, slashed savagely with light, and roaring, fighting a constant ceaseless warfare of men and of machinery; and yet it was so sweetly and so delicately pulsed, as full of warmth, of passion and of love as it was full of hate.[9]

The artists, too, were gathering in Greenwich Village, where one millionaire at least had set out to help contemporary painters. Gertrude Vanderbilt Whitney established her studio and in 1908 displayed such innovative painters as George Bellows and John Sloan, who in 1913 had

[9]Cited in V. S. Pritchett, *New York Proclaimed* (New York: Harcourt Brace & World, 1965), p. 5.

shocked the conservative art patrons with the Armory Show's post-Impressionist, Cubist, and abstract art. During the interwar years, American art came to be accepted by wealthy collectors. The Museum of Modern Art opened in 1929 under Rockefeller patronage. The Whitney studio was replaced by the Whitney Museum of American Art in 1931.

Finally, in communications and popular entertainment, New York reigned supreme. The one exception was movie-making, whose capital was established in the warmer climate of Hollywood. New York's newspapers ranged from the world's finest reporting in the *New York Times* to the most yellow. Broadway, illuminated by the new electric lights, had become the Great White Way, with shows ranging from Eugene O'Neill's *Mourning Becomes Electra* (1931) to the Ziegfeld Follies. Tin Pan Alley songsters were turning out jingles for the new radio stations; soap opera was being manufactured on a mass-production basis; jazz and ragtime bands were proliferating as rapidly as the speakeasies that legal prohibition of the sale of alcoholic drinks had fostered.

White Way, by John Sloan
The section of Broadway above Times Square was known as the Great White Way because of the profusion of flashing electric signs from advertisements and theaters. (Philadelphia Museum of Art: Given by Mrs. Cyrus McCormick)

THE CRISIS OF THE WORLD CITY

Dreiser in the early 1920s described a "poor, half-demented, and very much shriveled little seamstress" who told him she preferred poverty in New York to a fifteen-room mansion in the country: "The color and noise and splendor of the city as a spectacle was sufficient to pay her for all her ills." Slowly in the decade following the Wall Street crash in 1929 and with growing speed following the Second World War, the rewards of New York life ceased for many to compensate for the difficulties of living there; and New York faced, in an aggravated form, the universal problems of a mid-twentieth-century metropolis, complicated by specifically American social difficulties.

At the heart of the problems of the great urban agglomerations of the West has been population growth. Although the populations of the industrialized Western countries, as compared with those of the underdeveloped regions of the world, grew less quickly in the post-1945 period, they did not level off as many demographers had confidently predicted they would. Instead, after the expected "baby boom" that followed the Second World War, the birthrates settled at far higher levels than before the war. For Europe as a whole, the population rose from 393 million in 1950 to 427 million in 1960 and 462 million in 1970; the population of the United States rose from 150 million in 1950 to 176 million in 1960 and 204 million in 1970. This growth was accompanied by a large-scale exodus from farming, caused in part by the inability of small farmers to compete with mechanized well-capitalized farms and by the reduced number of laborers required on those farms. To those who left the land unwillingly, the city provided alternative employment or, at worst, welfare payments; to the majority, however, it offered better pay and a more interesting life. Hence there was an increase in not only the absolute size of the urban population, but also the percentage of the population living in urban areas. In the United States, the urban percentage of the population rose from fifty-one percent in 1920 to seventy percent in 1960.

For New York, as for most American cities, the fast-paced influx of population precipitated a worsening of racial tensions. New York had always been a city of immigrants, but it had never been a melting pot. The pattern had been one of attempted social and economic discrimination against new immigrant ethnic groups, and of eventual breakthrough by the groups to higher positions of employment and better living conditions. The "old stock" of British ancestry had dominated the city until the 1840s; and assimilating the Dutch and the French, it had been able to control the city's business world until the 1970s. The Germans and the Irish had arrived in large numbers after the 1840s and were able from the 1870s in their turn to take over the city's political life. After the 1880s Italians and southern and eastern European Jews poured into the city in a wave halted only by the immigration restrictions of 1924; and after years of hardship, both groups fought their way upward into political and eco-

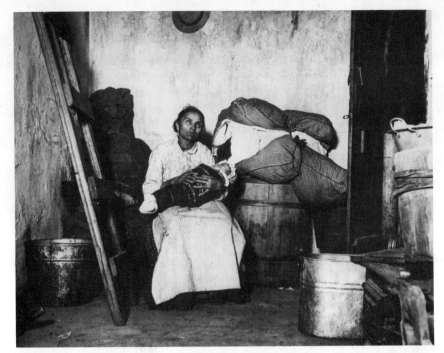

Italian Ragpicker and Her Child in a New York Tenement, by Jacob Riis

Some of the poorest New Yorkers survived by selling torn-up scraps of cloth from old clothes or the cuttings of garment factories to paper mills for the manufacture of fine stationery or cigarette papers. (Photograph by Jacob A. Riis. The Jacob Riis Collection, Museum of the City of New York.)

nomic significance. But the vast black and Puerto Rican immigration after 1945 elicited even greater discrimination than the earlier arrivals. New York's black population expanded from 300,000 in 1930 to 1.7 million in 1970, gathering primarily in Harlem but also in ghettoes in other sections of the city. The Puerto Ricans, who constituted eleven percent of the New York City population in 1970, experienced difficulties similar to those of the blacks, both in finding housing and in securing jobs.

Thus New York came to display in all its complexity the racial crisis gnawing at the vitality of all American city life. Large sections of the central core of the city had become ghettoes for racial minorities. Previously successful channels of upward social mobility, such as schooling, small-scale enterprise, and even political involvement, had failed to raise the economic level of those minorities. A worsening crime rate among the deprived or alienated inhabitants of the ghetto had increased the flight of other city residents from the central city. The financial plight of a city government grappling with the problems of its poor had been exacerbated by the difficulty of drawing on the financial resources of the suburbs to which many whites had fled, by inadequate financial backing from a rurally dominated state government, and by ineffective federal intervention in the city's difficulties.

Not only were the poor and underprivileged attracted to the growing cities like New York. The great cities remained the natural points of concentration of government, administrative offices of business and finance, the vast pool of white-collar labor, educational and entertainment resources, communications industries, and the service industries supplying the needs of an urban agglomeration. Occasionally the process could be modified by deliberate governmental intervention, as when the Soviet government attempted to discourage the growth of Moscow, or the British government founded new satellite cities to siphon off the growth of London. But a far more common characteristic was the spatial expansion from a central city or group of cities to produce a vast semiurbanized hinterland, such as that stretching around the cities of the Ruhr basin in western Germany and especially that of the eastern seaboard of the United States, from Boston to Washington, D.C.: a form of expansion that posed new types of problems in urban existence.

The most immediate result was pollution of the environment. The air above the West's cities had been blackened with coal smoke throughout the nineteenth century, but by the mid-twentieth, there were additional sources of air pollution: the automobile; the burning of fuel oil for electricity, which produced sulfur dioxide in the atmosphere; and the effluents from industrial plants, especially from metallurgical and chemical factories. To make matters worse, weather conditions sometimes compounded the chemical problem—as when sunshine photochemically changed hydrocarbons into other toxic substances, or inversion layers prevented the polluted air from escaping. All western cities were experiencing smog alerts by the 1950s. In London four hundred deaths were attributed to the smog of 1962. Water pollution also became a health hazard. In the 1960s many American cities were flushing raw sewage into their neighboring rivers and lakes, and even more dangerous compounds were being jettisoned by industrial companies. A further problem was that the noise levels of industrial cities were in some cases shown to be at least three and a half times greater than those of the countryside. And there was insufficient provision of green space within the city itself to counter the effects of overcrowding. Too often, in the rapid expansion of the nineteenth and twentieth centuries, the development of amenities of a particular location—the views of and access to rivers, the use of the waters for swimming and fishing, even the architectural grandeur of the juxtaposition of fine buildings and broad waterways as in Constantinople and Saint Petersburg—was lost.

The great expansion of city suburbs in the period since 1945, facilitated by the automobile and the truck, also presented problems for the cities. Retail and service industries followed the middle classes to the suburbs, and eventually even the administrative offices of the large companies left the congested city centers. The dispersion of economic activity led to even greater dispersion of housing. The process of spatial expansion, which most urban planners felt was only in its infancy in the early 1970s, was already beginning to link previously separated metropolitan centers. The Greek city planner Constantinos Doxiadis has predicted that by the end of the twenty-first century all the great metropolitan centers of the world will have coalesced to form a continuous urbanized band across all the economically viable portions of the globe, a territory that he calls Ecumenopolis.

The French geographer Jean Gottmann has labeled the "almost continuous stretch of urban and suburban areas from southern New Hampshire to northern Virginia and from the Atlantic shore to the Appalachian foothills" Megalopolis. Although he exaggerates the extent to which farmland and open space has disappeared in this area, Gottmann draws several valid conclusions about the nature of contemporary urban growth. In Megalopolis, he points out, "we must abandon the idea of the city as a tightly settled and organized unit in which people, activities, and riches are crowded into a very small area clearly separated from its nonurban surroundings. Every city in this region spreads out far and wide around its original nucleus; it grows amidst an irregularly colloidal mixture of rural and suburban landscapes; it melts on broad fronts with other mixtures, of somewhat similar though different texture, belonging to the suburban neighborhoods of other cities. . . . So great are the consequences of the general evolution heralded by the present rise and complexity of Megalopolis that an analysis of this region's problems often gives one the feeling of looking at the dawn of a new stage in human civilization." [10]

Gottmann found the future of New York and of its megalopolitan region bright, in part because of the very coalescence of the society along the five-hundred-mile seaboard. He recognized that it had already achieved "*on the average*, the richest, best educated, best housed, and best serviced group of similar size (i.e., in the 25-to-40-million-people range) in the world"; the greatest concentration of universities and cultural facilities in the United States; administrative predominance in economics and politics; and the most important position on earth as a crossroads where people, ideas, and goods must pass. But he also noted that this region was pioneering in a totally new urban process, as novel as that which affected England during the industrial revolution. He isolated in particular a revolution in land use, which included the abolition of the distinction between the city and the country, the movement of goods and people on a hitherto unknown scale, and the dispersal of population; "new patterns of intense living," represented not by density of population but by density of activity; and an integration of personal contacts throughout the region, indicated by the scale of such "flows" as telephone calls, highway and air traffic, and movement of goods. Megalopolis, Gottmann felt, possessed the ability to deal with the problems arising from its novel form of society. New forms of regional government, conceived on a scale that would relate to the density of contact within Megalopolis, were needed. A massive attack on environmental pollution with the highest technology available should be combined with renewed emphasis on spatial planning, to preserve the amenities of the rural landscape and to promote the most ef-

---

[10] Jean Gottmann, *Megalopolis: The Urbanized Northeastern Seaboard of the United States* (New York: Twentieth Century Fund, 1961), pp. 3, 5, 9.

La Chiffonnière ("the Rag Lady"), by Jean Dubuffet (1901–)
In the postwar years in New York City, outdoor sculpture has often been used in Central Park and in the plazas of the new skyscrapers to make contemporary art a part of daily living, an approach to art similar to that of the citizens of Renaissance Florence. (Courtesy of the New York Convention and Visitors Bureau)

ficient use of land for productive or residential purposes. The taxation structure within the area would have to be renovated, and state and federal resources committed to the cities on a greater scale. Major programs for breaking the cycle of poverty within the inner city should be implemented. And most difficult and important of all, a beginning would have to be made, by whatever means were available, to reduce racial tension and improve the conditions of racial minorities. There were few New Yorkers, however, who shared Gottmann's optimism.

THE CONTINUING VITALITY OF THE TROUBLED CITY

In spite of the overwhelming pessimism of those who had experienced New York's growing problems in the years after 1945, the city's vitality remained undeniable. Its port was the second largest in the world, exceeded only by Rotterdam and carrying twice the freight handled by London. A large number of corporations chose to move into the city, especially in the boom years of the late 1950s. Another boom that began in 1969 proved excessively speculative, but the decline in the cost of office space that resulted from overbuilding did at least have the advantage of making New York City competitive with other urban centers. Until 1969 the city increased the number and size of companies settling there—not only banks, insurance companies, and stock-brokerage houses, but also such related companies as advertising firms, corporate law offices, management and engineering consultation firms, and branches of large foreign companies. In particular, the central position of New York finance in world trade, at least until the revival of western Europe in the late 1950s, was responsible for a further increase in the expansion of employment in the downtown region.

Interior of the Guggenheim Museum, New York, by Frank Lloyd Wright (1869–1959)
Wright's design, inspired by a nautilus shell and executed in concrete, is an outstanding example of his ability to use natural forms and contemporary materials. (Courtesy of the New York Convention and Visitors Bureau)

United Nations Secretariat Building, New York

Le Corbusier's influence is reflected in the first of the city's glass-walled sky-scrapers. (*Courtesy of Trans World Airlines*)

The great building boom, at least in office construction, brought into the city the finest architects who had ever worked there. The emphasis was no longer on maximum height as a source of corporate individuality. Now designers experimented with the new use of materials, bringing out the surface quality in stone and concrete or the reflections of light or other buildings in glass; with variety through grouping, clustering several build-ings or parts of one building; and with the use of curtain walls that could be machine-made and assembled in panels. Frank Lloyd Wright's Guggen-heim Museum (begun in 1956) was an exercise in the combination of nat-ural form, blending the smooth swirl of a nautilus shell with the rough surface texture of cream-colored concrete. Totally different were the glass-walled skyscrapers, beginning with the unbroken thirty-nine stories of the United Nations Secretariat building (1950) and progressing to Gordon

Bunshaft's Lever House (1951), which seems to float upon its supporting pillars. However, the most beautiful of all the curtain-wall skyscrapers was the Seagram Building, erected in 1958 by Mies van der Rohe. Not only was half the site given to a garden patio with fountain pools and green marble benches, but the curtain wall, made of bronze with amber glass, achieved the architect's goal of creating a sensation of free-flowing space within the building. Although other buildings erected on Park Avenue failed to meet the standards of Lever House or the Seagram Building, nevertheless the harmony of their glass walls had created a new focus of architectural excitement in the city.

The other arts also continued to flourish. The Broadway theater produced not only a long series of glamorous musicals, but also the penetrating drama of Eugene O'Neill, Tennessee Williams, and Edward Albee. In painting in particular, New York artists struck out in a multitude of personal ways. Until the mid-1950s the prevailing style was abstract Expressionism, or "action painting," a kind of imageless energetic expression of personal intuition. Jackson Pollock led the way with shimmering, agitated

Grayed Rainbow, 1953, by Jackson Pollock (1912–1956) *In Pollock's "action" paintings, swirling lines and color are used to create a sense of driving energy. (Courtesy of the Art Institute of Chicago)*

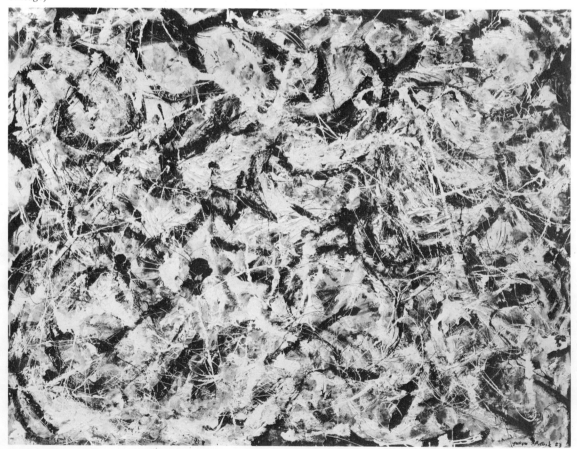

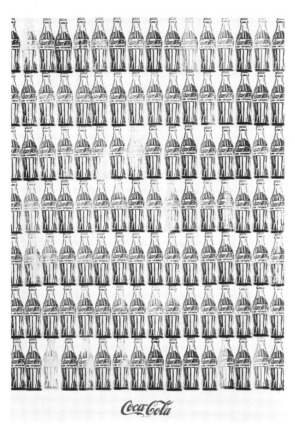

Green Coca-Cola Bottles, by Andy Warhol (1930?–   )
(Collection of the Whitney Museum of American Art, New York)

fields of color; Willem de Kooning combined mastery of savage color with a Surrealistic imagery; Mark Rothko set out to purify painting of the organic forms visible even in Surrealism and from 1947 created brilliantly colored compositions of parallel masses of varying density. By 1955 the abstract Expressionists had become popular and even well paid. In reaction to them, younger artists sought new forms of expression and brought back the exploration of human and material reality. Perhaps the most shocking to the public were pop artists like Andy Warhol and Claes Oldenburg, who used such means as comic strips, newspaper pages, multiple images like movie film, and banal subject matter like soup cans and hamburgers to comment on everyday reality. George Segal forced a new perception of human beings in relation to their surroundings by modeling people in plaster casts. Other artists became preoccupied with the machine, presenting machinery with human character and human beings as mechanical objects; Robert Stankiewicz's sculpture is an example. Artistically, New York had rarely been as creative; but there was a disturbing sense of violent protest about some artists and of delight in chaos about others that seemed to many to be a true mirror of the state of the city. The postwar artist had no message of comfort.

SUGGESTED READING

Two collections of engravings and historical photographs form the best introduction to the development of New York. John A. Kouwenhoven's *The Columbia Historical Portrait of New York* (1953) covers the whole sweep of the city's history; Grace M. Mayer, *Once Upon a City* (1958) is impressionistically organized, but draws on the superb photographs of the Byron family, made in 1890 to 1910. No good synthesis of the city's history exists, but there are some useful studies of different periods. They include Sidney I. Pomerantz, *New York: An American City, 1783–1803* (1965); Robert G. Albion, *The Rise of the New York Port* (1939); Seymour J. Mandelbaum, *Boss Tweed's New York* (1965), which sees Tweed as a "symbol of a society with a primitive communications network"; Allan Nevins and John A. Krout, eds., *The Greater City, New York, 1898–1948* (1948). The economic and social character of the city was thoroughly analyzed, and predictions made on its future growth, in the New York Metropolitan Region Study undertaken by the Graduate School of Public Administration of Harvard University. Among the nine volumes of its findings are Edgar M. Hoover and Raymond Vernon, *Anatomy of a Metropolis* (1959); Oscar Handlin, *The Newcomers* (1959); Robert M. Lichtenberg, *One-Tenth of a Nation* (1960), a particularly interesting examination of the relationship of the city's to the nation's economy; and Raymond Vernon, *Metropolis 1985* (1960). New York necessarily figures prominently in all the urban histories of the United States, including Charles N. Glaab and A. Theodore Brown, *A History of Urban America* (1967); Blake McKelvey, *The Urbanization of America: 1860–1915* (1963) and *The Emergence of Metropolitan America, 1915–1966* (1968); Bayrd Still, *Urban America: A History with Documents* (1974); Alexander B. Callow, Jr., ed., *American Urban History* (1973); Howard Chudacoff, *Evolution of American Urban Society* (1975); and Zane Miller, *Urbanization of America* (1973).

Good collections of contemporary comments on the city provide invaluable insights into the city's human character. Bayrd Still, *Mirror for Gotham: New York as Seen by Contemporaries from Dutch Days to the Present* (1956) makes good use of the comments of European visitors; Alexander Klein, ed., *The Empire City: A Treasury of New York* (1955) concentrates on the perceptions of recent American literary figures.

Among the rich variety of memoirs and novels dealing with New York life, for the late nineteenth century there is Edith Wharton, *The Age of Innocence* (1920); Rudyard Kipling, *Letters of Travel (1892–1913)* (1920); and Walt Whitman, *New York Dissected* (1936). For the Jazz Age of the interwar years, Le Corbusier described a "voyage to the land of timid people" in *When the Cathedrals Were White* (1947); Federico García-Lorca expressed views in both prose and poetry in *Poet in New York* (1955); the French writer Paul Morand composed a novelistic guidebook in *New York* (1930); Ford Madox Ford characterized its intellectual life in *New York Is Not America* (1927). E. B. White, *Here Is New York* (1949) was absorbed by the city's mysterious quality, as was V. S. Pritchett, *New York Proclaimed* (1965), in which Evelyn Hofer's photographs find beauty in the Bowery and elegance in coffeeshop plastic.

The racial problem in New York is described by Nathan Glazer and Daniel Patrick Moynihan in *Beyond the Melting Pot: The Negroes, Puerto Ricans, Jews, Italians, and Irish of New York City* (1970). The early history of Harlem is portrayed by Gilbert Osofsky, *Harlem: The Making of a Ghetto* (1966) and by James

Weldon Johnson, *Black Manhattan* (1930). The plight of the black in the ghetto is explained in Robert Weaver, *The Negro Ghetto* (1948) and made palpable in such books as James Baldwin, *Nobody Knows My Name* (1961) and Malcolm X, *Autobiography* (1965). The classic of Spanish Harlem is Piri Thomas, *Down These Mean Streets* (1971).

One of the best surveys of the changing position of women in American society is Mary Ryan, *Womanhood in America: From Colonial Times to the Present* (1975; rev. ed., 1979). The concentration is on women in the work force in Barbara Wertheimer, *We Were There: The Story of Working Women in America* (1976).

A very large number of good studies of other American cities are available for comparative study. Best served of all, perhaps, is Boston, with Samuel Bass Warner, *Streetcar Suburbs* (1969); Stephan Thernstrom, *The Other Bostonians: Poverty and Progress in the American Metropolis, 1880–1970* (1973); Peter R. Knights, *The Plain People of Boston, 1830–1860: A Study in City Growth* (1973). On Chicago, see Carl W. Condit, *Chicago, 1910–1929: Building, Planning, and Urban Technology* (1973) and *Chicago, 1930–1970: Building, Planning, and Urban Technology* (1974). The founding of Chicago's great cultural institutions, such as its orchestra, is detailed in Helen Lefkowitz Horowitz, *Culture and The City: Cultural Philanthropy in Chicago from the 1880s to 1917* (1976). For views of some western cities, see Gunther Barth, *Instant Cities: Urbanization and the Rise of San Francisco and Denver* (1975); Roger W. Lotchin, *San Francisco, 1846–1856: From Hamlet to City* (1979); Roger Sale, *Seattle: Past to Present* (1976); and John and Laree Caughey, eds., *Los Angeles: Biography of a City* (1976).

On the growth of suburbia, see Leo F. Schnore, *The Urban Scene: Human Ecology and Demography* (1965); on the suburbanite, see C. Wright Mills, *White Collar: The American Middle Classes* (1951) and Auguste C. Spectorsky, *The Exurbanites* (1955). Herbert J. Gans takes a positive view of suburban living in *The Levittowners* (1967); Jane Jacobs makes a plea for the central city in *The Death and Life of Great American Cities* (1961) and *The Economy of Cities* (1969). The geographer Jean Gottmann presents his view of the new form of social organization appearing in America in *Megalopolis: The Urbanized Northeastern Seaboard of the United States* (1961). The general urban crisis is discussed in Nathan Glazer, ed., *Cities in Trouble* (1970) and Irwin Isenberg, *The City in Crisis* (1968); the particular plight of New York is blasted in Richard J. Whalen, *A City Destroying Itself: An Angry View of New York* (1965). Yet perhaps New York's artists provide the most telling comment upon the impacts of mechanization, standardization, and meaningless violence, which have been three of their favorite themes. See Andy Warhol's montages of automobile accidents in John Coplans, *Andy Warhol* (1970); Rauschenberg's distorted cityscapes in Andrew Forge, *Rauschenberg* (1966); or Oldenburg's giant hamburgers in Barbara Rose, *Claes Oldenburg* (1970).

31

THE REVIVAL OF THE NON-WESTERN WORLD, 1914–PRESENT

To the peoples of the world beyond the West, for whom the nineteenth century had been an age of Western dominance, the twentieth century brought new hope that they could again take control of their own destinies. In the two great wars of 1914–1918 and 1939–1945, the European powers destroyed their own preeminence in the world. The dynamic economic system that had swept their merchants and soldiers into the remotest parts of Asia and Africa was in shambles. The political system of liberal democracy, which had been slowly advancing in even the most resolutely autocratic states of Europe, was challenged by the victory of Communism in Russia and the subsequent spread of Communist doctrines among revolutionary groups in many non-Western countries. The military superiority of the West in Asia was brought to an ignominious end by the advance of the Japanese armies in 1941–1942, and the restoration of colonial rule after the Second World War did not revive the myth of Western invincibility. Finally, in the Western countries themselves the very notion of a moral mission to take up the so-called white man's burden was being abandoned by the colonial rulers. The retention of colonies would be justified henceforth either in terms of material gain or in the name of a new moral mission to hold back the spread of Communism, which provided a final justification for the tragic struggles to prevent decolonization after 1945.

For most of the non-Western world the period between the First and Second World Wars was a time of slow preparation for the restoration of national autonomy, either—as in the case of China—by internal social and

Brasília, Brazil   *(Russell A. Thompson/Taurus Photos)*

political conflict for primacy or—as in the case of the colonies of the Western powers—by the rise of national independence movements. After 1945 the battles were joined, often becoming linked to the wider struggle of the Cold War between the Western and Communist blocs. Although by the 1970s the colonial struggles had ended with the independence of most, but not all, of the former colonies, the Third World (as the countries that were not members of either the Western or the Soviet bloc had come to be called) faced two continuing challenges—to find their own place in the ideological battle between the blocs and to meet the problems of underdevelopment at a time of massive population growth.

CHINA FROM THE 1911 REVOLUTION TO THE PEOPLE'S REPUBLIC

The Presidency of Yüan Shih-k'ai, 1912–1916

Sun Yat-sen's decision to step down as president of the new Chinese republic in 1912 in favor of Yüan Shih-k'ai, the commander-in-chief and prime minister named by the Manchu dynasty, in order to preserve Chinese unity under an an experienced leader with a national following, proved to be a mistake. Yüan did succeed in gaining recognition for the new republic from the Western powers in October 1913, and he did receive their financial support for a Reorganization Loan in April 1913. But the conditions they imposed were so exorbitant that many of his former supporters, believing he was mortgaging Chinese revenues to support the armed forced on which his personal power depended, decided to carry out a "second revolution"—against him. Several provincial governors who revolted were easily suppressed, however, and Sun and the other leaders fled to Japan. Yüan then banned their political party, the Kuomintang (National People's Party, or Nationalists) and suspended both the parliament in Peking and the assemblies in the provinces. He soon issued the Constitutional Compact in place of the republican constitution and made himself military dictator. Having destroyed the infant democracy, Yüan attempted in 1915–1916 to restore the empire, with himself as "Son of Heaven." The Japanese, who were taking advantage of the preoccupation of the European powers during the First World War to consolidate their own political and economic psition in China, strenuously objected; and the military governors of the provinces began to take up arms against Yüan's troops, forcing him to drop his ambition. After his death in June 1916, the only power capable of maintaining territorial control was in the hands of separatist military commanders—the "warlords" of the many regional armies.

Rule of the Warlords and Kuomintang Victory, 1916–1928

Warlordism was militarism in disintegration. The warlords, who varied from well-trained generals of the former dynasty to upstart adventurers, did not succeed in creating a political base for their power, although they often tried. Their urgent financial needs led to relentless exploitation of

◆ 20th-Century China ◆

their territorial bases, both in the cities and in the countryside, against which the nominal central government of the republic in Peking, which continued to enjoy the recognition of the major powers, could offer no protection. However, two factors did mitigate the sufferings of the Chinese people at the hands of the armies of the warlords. Since these armies had no nationalistic motive or ideological commitment, they were careful not to indulge in reckless campaigns that might endanger their own lives unnecessarily, or even interfere with their own enjoyment of the resources they controlled. They were also careful not to reduce the peasantry of the regions they ruled to penury, since they wished them to go on producing the food that could be expropriated.

After 1918, as a result of industrial development and cultural ferment in the cities, new groups of Chinese leaders emerged who offered appealing alternatives to warlord dominance. Idealistic students in the increasing number of schools and colleges were highly receptive to new periodicals, championing a wide variety of causes, that were published by Western-oriented intellectuals. The widely read magazine *New Youth*, with its slogan "Down with Confucius and Sons," sought to open the way for "Mr.

Sun Yat-sen (1867–1925)
Sun was revered by both the Communists and his own party, the Kuomintang, for his leadership during the revolution of 1911 and for his subsequent opposition to President Yüan Shih-k'ai. After Sun's death in 1925, both groups claimed to be his natural successors. (United Press International, Inc.)

Democracy and Mr. Science''; and the attack on the conservative traditions of Chinese society was advanced by the substitution of vernacular Chinese for the archaic classical style of writing. Western theories such as the pragmatism of John Dewey won many adherents; and the plays of Henrik Ibsen, with their call for the liberation of the individual, were discussed enthusiastically.

The students, who had begun by seeking freedom of the individual, turned to political activism when the diplomats at the Paris Peace Conference in 1919 failed to return to China Shantung Province, which Japan had seized from Germany (which had held it as a sphere of influence). To prevent the Chinese government from signing the Treaty of Versailles and to compel them to release students it had imprisoned, student leaders founded a great popular movement on May 4, 1919. The "May the Fourth Movement" rapidly won adherents throughout the country, not only among students but also among urban merchants and workers, and was able to compel the government to accede to its demands. Two political groups in particular profited from this nationalistic ferment: the revived Kuomintang of Sun Yat-sen and the Chinese Communist party.

In 1917 Sun returned to China from his Japanese refuge with a number of Kuomintang supporters and succeeded in getting the support of the local warlord at Canton for the creation of a semiautonomous state with its own parliament, bureaucracy, and taxation. Canton became the center from which the Kuomintang would take control of the whole of China by 1928. Three factors helped them to victory. First, the Soviet Union under Lenin's leadership decided to help all parties in Asia that were battling imperialism and capitalism—even those parties with bourgeois leaders—and to help the Kuomintang in particular, although as a disguised step toward an ultimate Communist triumph. In 1923 a clever Soviet organizer, Michael Borodin, was sent to Canton to help Sun reorganize the Kuomintang as a mass party with effective propaganda and efficient links between party leadership and local cells. Other Soviet advisers, including a thousand military officers, arrived at Canton, as did shipments of Soviet weapons. The infant Chinese Communist party was pressured by Stalin to collaborate with the Kuomintang at all levels.

Second, Sun developed an ideology for the Kuomintang, elaborating and modifying the Three Principles of the People, which he had originally enunciated in 1905. The first principle, *nationalism*, now called for the abolition of the unequal treaties and the reunion of the country by overthrow of the warlords. The second, *democracy*, affirmed the need for administrative experts as well as popular sovereignty through elections and such American devices as popular initiative of propositions and recall of elected officials. The third, *people's livelihood*, called for social reform and hinted at redistribution of farmland and regulation of private industry. Despite the vagueness of his programs, Sun won the support of many political activists and intellectuals, including some members of the May the Fourth Movement.

Third, the Kuomintang developed a powerful military force. Its leaders were trained in the military academy of Whampoa, which was directed from 1925 by a young officer named Chiang Kai-shek with the aid of a number of Soviet experts.

Chiang Kai-shek and His Wife Soong Mei-ling
In 1928, one year after his marriage to the sister-in-law of Sun Yat-sen, Chiang was made head of the Nationalist government and generalissimo of the Chinese armed forces. Soong Mei-ling proved a persuasive propagandist for the Kuomintang during the Second World War and the civil war.
(L'Illustration, *December 18, 1937*)

Chiang, who had been trained in a Japanese military academy and had visited the Soviet Union, was an astute politician as well as Sun's principal military commander. After Sun's death in 1925, Chiang was the natural successor, and he strengthened his position by marrying the sister of Sun's widow in 1927. However, he had to fight off not only the claims of rivals from the right, but also the more serious ambitions of those within the Kuomintang who were sympathetic to the Communists.

The Chinese Communist party, founded in 1921 at a secret meeting in Shanghai, had at first appealed to a small minority of Chinese intellectuals and students who had seen in Lenin's modification of the theories of Marxism a valid solution to China's problems. In particular, these intellectuals had felt that Lenin's views on feudalism, capitalism, and imperialism were an explanation of China's experience of warlords and landlords in the countryside, industrialists in the cities, and European financial power in the foreign concessions. The Chinese Communist party had won a wider following in 1925–1926 by organizing a series of popular anti-imperialist strikes of urban laborers, railway workers, and seamen. The Soviet Union nevertheless continued to support Chiang, who in 1926 embarked on a campaign to bring the north of China under his control. During this ten-month campaign, Chiang took the lead of the anti-Communist wing of the Kuomintang. When he took Shanghai in 1927, he destroyed the Communist labor movement and slaughtered Communists who revolted against his troops. The Kuomintang banned the Communist party and expelled the Soviet advisers from China.

When a young Communist, Mao Tse-tung, attempted to apply his new theories of a rural approach to Communist revolution by staging an "Autumn Harvest" uprising among the peasants of his native Hunan Province, it was quickly suppressed. Communist insurrections in several large cities, one of them led by a group that included Chou En-lai, also failed. In 1928 Chiang completed his so-called "Northern Expedition" by taking Peking, which was renamed Peiping ("Northern Peace"); but the Nationalist capital was to remain at Nanking. A number of warlords still in control of their provinces acknowledged Chiang's authority, which was also recognized by the foreign powers.

Nationalist Government in Nanking, 1928–1937

The Nanking government's greatest success was in reducing the power of the foreign governments in China. It recovered control over tariffs in 1929, as well as over administrative bodies like the Maritime Customs, which had been run by foreigners. A number of the treaty ports were returned to Chinese control, and Chinese were given a greater share in the government of Shanghai and other treaty ports.

During a decade of comparative stability, at least in urban areas, Westernization was pressed with great vigor by many groups, including educators, scientists, doctors, merchants, industrial managers, and bankers. Just as an earlier generation of Chinese leaders had sought to learn from Japan, so the Chinese of the 1930s regarded the United States as the model for economic development. Chiang's wife was a graduate of Wellesley College, and he took as his principal financial advisers her Harvard-educated brother and Oberlin-educated brother-in-law. Many Chinese students attended American universities with funds from the Boxer Indemnity that President Theodore Roosevelt had ordered remitted for that purpose. In China itself colleges and hospitals established by American missionaries and philanthropic foundations were among the best of such institutions in China. For his military forces, however, Chiang preferred the German model. General Hans von Seeckt, commander of the German army after the First World War, became Chiang's military adviser and helped plan the officer corps and command system and to build up Chiang's elite forces to 300,000 men.

With the technical cooperation of the League of Nations, Chiang established a National Economic Council for national reconstruction. Unfortunately, economic planning remained largely a matter of urban development, with industry and banking facilities largely confined to port cities and provincial capitals. Production of textiles and other consumer goods increased, and the infrastructure of highways, railroads, and telegraphs was strengthened. The peasants, however, who had been promised land reform by Sun Yat-sen, waited in vain for the Kuomintang to embark on its rural social program in more than a few "experimental" counties. In many parts of the country the rural people remained prey to warlords, whom Chiang had conciliated rather than crushed.

For the Communists peasant discontent was the key to future power. In 1927 Mao Tse-tung had disputed the prevailing Soviet line of analysis, which placed major emphasis on the urban workers, by asserting, in a report on the peasant situation in Hunan, that revolution in China must come through the poor peasantry. Although the party leadership, hiding in Shanghai's foreign settlement, continued to argue for urban revolution, Mao and his supporters established in 1931 a rural Soviet Republic in Kiangsi Province, near the border of Hunan, and expropriated the property of the landlords by force. Chiang undertook five extermination campaigns against the Communists encircled in that area.

In October 1934 the Communists broke out of the blockade and started the famous Long March, which in the next twelve months brought twenty thousand survivors over a six-thousand-mile trek to the northwestern city of Yenan. Here, under the inspiration of Mao—who was recognized as the top party leader midway during the Long March—and isolated from the controls of the Soviet Union, the Communists formed a new political base for their conflict with the Kuomintang.

As European influence in China declined, the Japanese had moved to replace it. They had entered the First World War for the primary purpose of taking Germany's possessions in China and the Pacific; in 1919, at the peace conference in Paris, the Japanese had insisted on retaining the German leasehold in Shantung, which they had seized in 1914. Although they

War with Japan, 1937-1945

relinquished Shantung in 1922, through an alliance with the local warlord the Japanese dominated the three provinces of Manchuria, with their largely Chinese population of 34 million, from Korea, which they had annexed in 1910.

In 1931, however, the Japanese forces in Manchuria, usually called the Kwantung Army, seized complete control of the three provinces. Manchuria was made into a puppet state of Japan called Manchukuo, under the nominal rule of the last Manchu emperor, P'u-yi. Although expelled from the League of Nations for this action, the Japanese refused to leave Manchuria, which they began to industrialize rapidly. In spite of widespread demonstrations in China, Chiang was unwilling to attack the Japanese before rebuilding his armed forces, although he did find the military strength to attack the Communist strongholds in Hunan.

In 1937 a minor incident provoked by local Japanese commanders near Peking expanded into a full-scale war in northern China, and soon fighting extended as far south as Shanghai. The Nationalist armies fought back, withdrawing slowly up the Yangtze Valley, until in 1938 they eventually settled at the remote western city of Chungking, the capital of the Nationalist government for the rest of the war. The Japanese, after gaining control of the coastal cities as far south as Canton, created two puppet governments, in Peking for northern China and in Nanking for central China,

Japanese Troops Attack near Shanghai, 1937
Chiang Kai-shek used his best troops to hold off the Japanese attack on Shanghai that was launched in August 1937. The city fell after three months of savage fighting. (National Archives)

in addition to the regime in Manchukuo. Playing on the theme of substitution of Asian for European control, the Japanese called on the Chinese to collaborate with them in creation of a "New Order" in East Asia. After 1938 there was only intermittent large-scale fighting between the Japanese and the Nationalist armies. Chiang, who had formed a second united front with the Communists in 1938, soon decided to use his armies to isolate Mao's forces in their Yenan stronghold. However, Chiang could not prevent the Chinese Communist forces from moving down into the North China Plain, where, with the help of thousands of idealistic recruits from urban schools and colleges, they organized guerrillas who operated away from Japanese-controlled cities and communication lines.

Meanwhile, Mao strengthened party organization and discipline and continued to enunciate his distinctive view of a Chinese Leninist party with a peasant base. Riding the tide of anti-Japanese nationalism and temporarily accepting cooperation with non-Communist elements of the population, by 1945 the Chinese Communists had succeeded in taking control of much of the North China countryside and had begun to create a number of "liberated areas" under their own administration. Mao also perfected his techniques for the creation of a totally devoted body of party workers, employing such devices as group criticism and confession of personal shortcomings in public meetings. Peasants were brought into the revolution under Communist leadership, and the regular forces of the party grew in size. When in 1945 the Nationalist armies returned to take control of the eastern cities, the rural bases of Communist control were secure for most of northern and central China.

For the Chinese people the war had been a time of great suffering. In the area of Nationalist control, hundreds of thousands of refugees had suffered malnutrition and disease, despite the $1.5 billion in aid that Chiang had received, mainly from the United States. Losses in the fighting with the Japanese had reached more than $3 million. Industry had suffered both during the retreat of Chiang's armies, which had destroyed factories to prevent them from falling into Japanese hands, and from the Soviet removal of the industrial plant of Manchuria to Russia in 1945. Agricultural production was low because of lack of livestock, seed, and fertilizer. Rampant inflation had wiped out the savings of most city dwellers. Thanks to U.S. loans, however, the government's foreign reserves were high; coastal cities that were lost early to the Japanese had been spared from aerial bombing; and the Japanese had even increased production of coal, iron, and electricity. Thus a new economic start was difficult, but not impossible, in 1945. In 1946, however, despite American efforts at mediation, the Kuomintang and the Communists ended all pretense of collaboration and began the savagely destructive civil war (1946–1949).

Chiang began the civil war overconfident in his own strength, since his troops outnumbered the regular army of the Communists by two or even three to one. However, he was defeated by his own strategic mistakes, by

The Civil War, 1946–1949

Mao Tse-tung with Communist Troops in Shansi Province, 1947
In the early months of the war, when the Nationalists appeared to have the upper hand, Mao used his control of the countryside to demonstrate the incorruptibility of his army by strict discipline and immediate social reform. (*Collection J.A.F./Paris/ Magnum Photos, Inc.*)

the venality of his deteriorating army and civil bureaucracy, and by the Communists' skill at both military and political warfare. In the military campaigns, which for most of the three years were fought primarily in Manchuria and North China, the Nationalists allowed themselves to become overextended as Mao pursued a policy of withdrawing from contested points to economize on combat losses. Moreover, the Nationalists were confined to holding cities, whereas Mao's forces retained control—and usually also the loyalty—of the countryside. Nationalist officers, many of them retained despite their incompetence because of their early training in Chiang's military academies, were no match for Mao's commanders, who had succeeded in organizing a new Communist army. The strictly enforced puritanical attitude of the Communist soldiers contrasted with the looting and cruelty of many of the ill-disciplined Nationalist troops. The Nationalist leaders were their own worst enemies, however. Chiang's relatives, especially the long-time finance minister H. H. Kung, were notoriously corrupt. Other Nationalist officials had grown rich from the seizure of Japanese properties as war booty; lower bureaucrats had followed their example, looting even hospital equipment and workshop tools. Peculation was almost a necessity for Kuomintang officials, who found it impossible to live on their pay in a time of hyperinflation resulting from government printing of currency and from the scarcity of produce moving into the cities—a result of Communist effectiveness in disrupting transport lines.

Politically, Chiang's regime became daily more dictatorial and the secret police ubiquitous. By contrast, Mao's ideology of peasant revolution, dramatized when the Communist troops shared in the agricultural work of the villages and when the properties of the landlords were expropriated, appealed to the masses in the countryside as well as to thousands of Nationalist troops who deserted to the Communists. Although the Kuomintang received considerable American aid and weapons, many rifles and artillery pieces were either surrendered to or captured by the Communists.

In late 1948 extremely costly battles were fought in Manchuria, and Chiang himself directed from a distance a campaign to the north of the Yangtze River in eastern China. In 1949 the Nationalist forces collapsed. In January Communist troops took Peking, in April Nanking, in May Shanghai, and in October Canton. As Chiang withdrew to Taiwan with the remnant of the Nationalist armies, Mao proclaimed the establishment of the People's Republic of China on October 1, 1949.

Mao declared in 1949 that it would take three years to recover from the destruction caused by the almost continuous fighting that had engulfed China since 1937. Besides seeking recovery, the new Communist government devoted its first three years to political and economic consolidation. The power of the Communist party was carried down to the lowest village level and was emphasized by mobilization of the people through mass meetings and political indoctrination. Land was redistributed among the peasants, and landlords accused of misdeeds were often executed after impromptu village trials. Land owned by temples, churches, and schools was also requisitioned. Other social reforms included equality for women in political rights, divorce, and property ownership. A serious attempt was made to weaken the age-old Chinese reliance on the family, often by urging children to denounce their parents for political shortcomings. Party discipline was maintained and a "three-anti" campaign was proclaimed—against waste, corruption, and bureaucratism. To build up the economy, Mao accepted Soviet economic aid, welcomed hundreds of Soviet advisers, and set up joint Sino-Soviet companies for exploitation of China's natural resources. Meanwhile, the last remnants of the imperialist era were removed with the takeover of all foreign enterprises. Britain alone lost investments valued at $800 million.

Consolidation of Communist Rule, 1949–1952

In 1953 the Communists introduced the First Five-Year Plan. Farm property was now collectivized, as in the Soviet Union in 1929. Peasants, only newly given land, were compelled to assign it to the cooperatives, in which they received a share of produce according to the size of their holdings. After 1955 a new stage of rural socialism was reached when the cooperatives were consolidated into collective farms, in which the peasants became in effect wage laborers. Some peasants resisted, killing their animals and de-

First Five-Year Plan, 1953–1957

Workers in the Anshan Steel Mill, Manchuria
Although constructed originally by the Japanese during their occupation of Manchuria, the Anshan steel mill was completely rebuilt during the First Five Year Plan (1953–1957). It is now one of the ten largest iron and steel complexes in the world. (Henri Cartier-Bresson/Magnum Photos, Inc.)

stroying their equipment; but such protest was not vigorous in comparison with that in the Soviet Union after 1929.

The collective farm became the center of peasant hopes for a better material and even cultural life. Rapid industrialization was pressed with the development of three major steel complexes, the opening of oil deposits in Sinkiang, and the building of railroads to the western parts of the country where settlement was encouraged. By extracting the produce of agriculture and by utilizing confiscated private capital as well as Soviet aid, the Five-Year Plan showed results. Trained personnel of the pre-1949 era were mobilized. Industrial production probably rose thirteen to fourteen percent annually, although agriculture lagged behind the needs of a population expanding by fifteen million a year. Material symbols of the new regime's ability to transform the country were evident in new dams, roads, railroads, irrigation and afforestation projects, and factories.

To ensure that the party would not become too rigid as modernization increased its controls, in February 1957 Mao invited the people to criticize the party and bureaucracy: "Let a hundred flowers bloom, and let a hundred schools of thought contend." But the vast outpouring of discontent quickly went beyond permissible limits, and within a few weeks Mao was compelled to clamp down on the critics, many of whom were severely punished.

The reasons for discontent were clear despite the First Five-Year Plan's success—rationing, food shortages, lack of fuel, the peasants' loss of private land, the intellectuals' loss of liberty. To meet the problem head on, Mao decided on a radical change of policy, which involved the abandonment of the Soviet Union as a model and which, within a few years, was to lead to an open break with the Soviet leadership internationally.

The Great Leap Forward, 1958–1960

In 1958 Mao announced the Great Leap Forward, a program that called for the maximum use of China's abundant rural labor by a regrouping of the peasantry in people's communes. The communes were to be an amalgamation of a number of the collective farms and were to undertake a vast range of tasks, from local government and mobilization for public works projects to steel production in tiny "backyard furnaces." Virtually all of China's rural population was grouped in these communes; a commune of moderate size would contain four or five thousand families. For Mao the communes were the Chinese answer to the problem of creating a Communist society in the underdeveloped rural societies of Asia, for which the Soviet model had proved inadequate.

Within a year, however, the insufficiently prepared program was failing, and party officials were being warned against "behaving like Utopians." Food supply had fallen so much that China purchased large amounts of cereals from Canada in 1961–1962. As early as December 1958, decisionmaking was transferred from the commune down to the production brigade, the basic unit for the distribution of produce and for taxation. Between 1960 and 1966 the communes were broken up into smaller units. The drive to force peasants to eat in mess halls was ended. Less emphasis was now placed on small-scale industrial production, and the exorbitant demands on the peasant for unpaid labor were reduced.

Between 1960 and 1966, as China slowly recovered from the excesses of the Great Leap Forward, Mao broke ties with the Soviet Union. He had already criticized the Soviet doctrine of coexistence with the West in 1957, when he declared: "I think the characteristic of the situation today is the East wind prevailing over the West wind. That is to say, the socialist forces are overwhelmingly superior to the imperialist forces"; and the Great Leap Forward had been explicitly presented as a model for the Third World in place of the Soviet example. In 1960 the Chinese supported the tiny European Communist state of Albania in its quarrel with the Soviet Union, which in return blasted Mao as an "ultra Leftist, an ultra dogmatist, indeed, a left revisionist!" More significantly, Soviet advisers were recalled, taking with them the plans of half-finished factories. The Soviet government began to woo the leaders of North Korea, North Vietnam, and India to emphasize to Mao that China was encircled by Soviet friends. By the mid-1960s China's rift with the Soviet Union was virtually complete.

The Great Proletarian Cultural Revolution, 1966–1969

By 1966 Mao had become dissatisfied with the decline in China itself of the revolutionary fervor that accompanied the economic reconstruction. He saw in the Soviet Union the dangerous elitism of an entrenched party apparatus, and he was determined to destroy in China tendencies he considered inimical to the proletarian culture his revolution was to nurture. Through a new movement of revolution from within the people themselves, most notably from within the young Red Guards, Mao intended to smash all the layers of past culture that hampered the proletarian culture—traditional Chinese culture, Western culture, and Soviet culture.

Mao saw evil principally in the cities and in the bureaucracy, including the party officials. For these reasons the Red Guards were loosed against such varied objects as Chinese traditional opera, Beethoven's symphonies, American-trained professors and their decadent writings and personal libraries, and party officials profiting from their superior status or secretly sympathetic to the Soviet Union.

The result of the Cultural Revolution, which involved mass demonstrations, violence against party officials at all levels, arrest of intellectuals, transfer of suspect groups to work in the remote countryside, and the closing of schools and universities, was a deep split in the party leadership. Mao was backed by the defense minister, Lin Piao, who put together a selection of Mao's quotations to form the "little red book" carried by all the Red Guards. More important, Mao had the backing of the thoroughly indoctrinated People's Liberation Army. Mao's wife Chiang Ch'ing took control of the arts, literature, and scholarship. She and three colleagues she brought to power, forming what later came to be known as the Gang of Four, plotted in the party central committee to shake up the top leadership. Prime Minister Chou En-lai, who also was foreign minister, was less supportive of the politics of violence but managed to preserve his own post. The principal victim was Liu Shao-ch'i, the head of state, who was expelled from the party in 1968 and persecuted to death. Liu's friend Teng Hsiao-p'ing, secretary-general of the party, was dismissed from office.

The chaos of the Cultural Revolution paralyzed industrial production and created an upheaval in the state and party machinery. The People's Liberation Army stood to gain, however, for Red Guard excesses had as early as 1966 led to participation by the army in administrative functions.

Cartoon of the Gang of Four on Trial
Although blame for the excesses of the Cultural Revolution was placed on the so-called Gang of Four, headed by Chiang Ch'ing, the widow of Mao Tse-tung, their condemnation was seen as implicating Mao himself in the responsibility for China's economic and political problems. (Henri Bureau/ SYGMA)

Army representatives sat in committees managing factories or universities, and military leaders were elected to many party posts. A split in the top army leadership was probably behind the fall of Lin Piao, the defense minister who had been designated Mao's "closest comrade in arms" and successor. Lin was reported to have been killed in a plane crash in September 1971 in the Mongolian People's Republic, on his way to the Soviet Union. Chou En-lai managed to maintain the essential machinery for diplomacy, foreign trade, and missile research. However, not until Mao's death in September 1976—which was followed almost immediately by the arrest of the Gang of Four and the restoration to power of the former party secretary-general, Teng Hsiao-p'ing—could the damage done by the Cultural Revolution be repaired. Gradually, thousands were released from prison, and schools and universities were reopened. One by one, the purged leaders were rehabilitated. The years after Mao's death in 1976 were years of normalization and reconstruction, with the Chinese population becoming increasingly aware of the extraordinary damage to their economy and society that the Cultural Revolution had inflicted for a decade.

In the early 1970s Premier Chou En-lai probably helped influence Mao in spearheading the two main trends of Chinese policy in the 1970s: reconciliation with the Western powers and pronounced emphasis on the country's economic development. Relations with the Soviet Union had continued to worsen in the late 1960s. The Chinese had regarded the Soviet invasion of Czechoslovakia in 1968 as proof of Soviet willingness to use force against Communist countries that rejected the Soviet Union as a model; and in the following years there had been border clashes between Chinese and Soviet forces. The Chinese therefore began to seek better relations with the Western countries and Japan, planning in particular to find in the United States a counterbalance to the threat of the Soviet Union. President Richard Nixon proved willing to reciprocate; and diplomatic contacts, strengthened by Nixon's visit to Mao Tse-tung in February 1972, culminated in full diplomatic relations between the United States and the People's Republic in 1979.

China's New Foreign Policy and Modernization Program

Chou had visualized the party's return to the goals of economic revival in his report to the party congress in 1975, which called for the "comprehensive modernization of agriculture, industry, national defense and science and technology before the end of the century, so that our national economy will be advancing in the front ranks of the world." After Mao's death in September 1976, this preoccupation was paramount in the goals of China's new leaders. Chou himself had died a few months before Mao. His successor as premier, Hua Kuo-feng, was named chairman of the party after Mao's death.

Hua, however, was soon overshadowed by Teng Hsiao-p'ing, the spokesman of pragmatists in the party who placed economic revival before political revolution. Reappointed vice-premier in 1977, Teng pressed for a program of Four Modernizations—of industry, agriculture, defense, and science and technology. Loans were sought from the Western powers. New trade treaties were negotiated with Japan, the United States, and Western Europe. Several thousand students were sent abroad to learn Western technology and science. To encourage output, industrial planning was decentralized, and factories were permitted to sell at a profit goods produced above their quotas. Peasants were allowed to cultivate more land in private plots. Finally, Mao Tse-tung's economic policies were denounced as erroneous; and a further attempt was made to discredit him by the condemnation for treason, after a public trial in 1980, of Mao's widow and the other members of the Gang of Four.

Mao's legacy was not entirely disowned, however. His contribution to the success of the Chinese Communist revolution would continue to be recognized, and elements in "The Thought of Mao Tse-tung" would remain as part of the ideological basis of the Chinese state and society. The Soviet Union could de-Stalinize more easily than China could discard Mao's heritage. China needed its own Lenin, and the bureaucratic nature of China's society as well as economic strategy pointed to the necessity for some basis of morality and idealism beyond the material incentive offered by the Four Modernizations.

Achievements of the Chinese Revolution

In spite of the disruption to Chinese economic development of the Great Leap Forward and the Cultural Revolution, the achievements of the new regime since 1949 have been outstanding. China's population rose from 583 million in 1953 to about 950 million in 1980; as far as is known, a minimum standard of food and shelter was provided for virtually everyone in China, something no previous regime had ever succeeded in doing. Although the estimated per capita income in 1980 was only about $460, there

Contemporary Sian
The ancient capital Ch'ang-an is now a thriving industrial city with a population of more than two million. Its most prominent monument is the inner city wall, built during the Ming dynasty, with the soaring bell tower visible at the end of the bicycle-filled street.
(© Gwendolyn Stewart, 1981)

seemed to be a far greater equality in distribution of the nation's wealth than in the Soviet Union. A new industrial base had been created, using China's natural resources in oil and mineral wealth. Foreign trade had risen to over $20 billion a year, and China had succeeded in acquiring foreign reserves that could be used for grain purchases in times of agricultural difficulties. Educational programs had expanded the minimum literacy to perhaps as high as ninety percent of the population, and efforts had been made to provide universal health care. A powerful army had been created, which, although it lacked the most modern conventional weapons, possessed the atomic bomb and intercontinental ballistic missiles.

Many difficult problems remained, however. Factional politics had by no means subsided. The new policy of emphasis on economic development through modernization had only just begun. Democratic rights were severely limited. A legacy of inertia remained as a result of the fluctuations between repression and encouragement of initiative. Population growth was only inadequately slowed by measures enforcing birth control, including penalties in wage payments for couples having more than two children; and excess of population over resources was bound to continue to threaten the economic gains. The demographic reality, as well as the requirements of economic modernization and international self-reassertion, would continue to impose enormous demands on the Chinese system.

JAPAN SINCE 1914: TO CATASTROPHE AND BACK

For Japan, the years between the First and Second World Wars were a time of choice—between the possibility of democratic transformation represented by the growing effectiveness of the political parties and the drive toward authoritarian rule dominated by the increasingly uncontrolled military. At the end of the First World War, Japan had been permitted by the Paris Peace Conference to retain the former German holdings in China and the German colonies of the Marshall, Caroline, and Mariana islands, which, along with its control over Taiwan and Korea and its indirect economic influence in Manchuria, made it one of the major imperial powers. At the Washington Disarmament Conference of 1921–1922, it was recognized as one of the world's greatest naval powers by agreement that its navy should be three-fifths the size of that assigned to Britain and to the United States—considerably larger than the navies permitted to France and Italy. Japan in return displayed a desire for conciliation by agreeing to respect the Open Door policy in China, promising (like the other powers) no further extension of its sphere of interest. At the end of the year, after private negotiations with the Chinese, the Japanese withdrew their troops from Shantung. These actions seemed to open for Japan a period of internal democracy and external restraint in which the primary goal of the successive governments was the economic development of Japan itself and of its empire.

Japan's Experiment with Democracy, 1918-1932

During the 1920s, democracy seemed to be taking root in Japan. In 1925 the vote was extended to all males over twenty-five, thus increasing the electorate from three to thirteen million and bringing into existence some lower-middle-class and working-class parties. These parties remained small, however, and power alternated, in a relatively efficient two-party system, between the older Seiyukai and the Kenseikai parties. A party with a majority in the Diet did not automatically form a government. Instead, a party leader formed a government and then sought a majority in the Diet from his own and other parties. Hence the personalities of the political leaders were the key to political stability.

A number of powerful leaders took office during the 1920s. The Seiyukei leader, Hara Kei, proved brilliant at creating strong political coalitions backed by supporters he had placed in the civil service; but his assassination by a right-wing fanatic in 1921 broke the carefully constructed alliances within his party. The Kenseikai prime minister, Kato Komei, during his term in office in 1924–1926, not only broadened the franchise but also introduced some social reforms that improved conditions for workers and decriminalized union activity.

Between 1927 and 1929 the Seiyukai returned to power under General Tanaka Giichi, primarily for the purpose of taking a strong line in foreign policy, as when they again threw the army into the Shantung Peninsula to block the advance there of the Kuomintang armies. The Kenseikai fought back, allying with dissidents from Tanaka's party to form a more broadly based party called the Minseito, which came to power in 1929 committed to a more moderate policy in China and further social reform at home.

This period of alternating rule by the two major parties through governments headed by their party presidents came to an end in May 1932 with the appointment as prime minister of Admiral Seito. From then until Japanese entry into the Second World War in 1941, almost all the cabinets were to be controlled by representatives of the military forces, and both political parties became increasingly vociferous in their opposition to the government.

Even during the 1920s, however, Japan's political parties were weakened by their ties to the great business trusts, known as *zaibatsu*, that dominated the Japanese economy. The zaibatsu had been formed in the late nineteenth century as vast family empires extending into banking, commerce, and industry. They had achieved a semimonopoly position by wiping out their smaller competitors in ruthless competition, and had then diversified. Besides controlling a wide variety of companies in horizontal combination, they also, like German companies such as I. G. Farben in the 1920s, extended their ownership of production of individual products from mines through manufacturing to sales outlets in a vertical combination. The largest of these zaibatsu was the Mitsui, which employed a million workers in Japan and another million abroad, in an interlocking conglomerate comprising almost four hundred companies and affiliates. The Mitsui family owned ninety percent of the shares of the trust. It exercised direct political power through the Seiyukai party. The Kenseikai-Minseito party was supported by the Mitsubishi trust, which poured money into its political campaigns and was accused of controlling the party's governmental policies.

The parliamentary regime might have survived if the country's economic growth had not been interrupted by the sufferings of the depression of 1930–1935. Between 1885 and 1910 Japanese gross national product had doubled, by 1920 it had tripled, and by 1930 it had quadrupled. Although primary emphasis was placed on the export of raw silk, exports in metallurgy, chemicals, and electronics had also been expanded; and the European countries and the United States were already beginning to complain about unfair competition from low-paid Japanese factory workers and to demand limits on Japanese exports. The industrial labor force grew rapidly, reaching six million in the 1930s, with a concurrent rise in urbanization. Even though Tokyo was half destroyed in the earthquake of 1923, which killed 130,000 people, it was immediately rebuilt, and by 1940, with over six million inhabitants, had become one of the world's largest cities. Rapid growth was also occurring in Osaka, Kyoto, and the port cities of Yokohama, Kobe, and Nagasaki. By the Second World War Japan had been transformed in less than half a century from a rural to an urban country in which almost half the population lived in cities of more than ten thousand people.

Industrialization made Japan more dependent on the outside world, not only as a market for its exports but also as the source of its raw materials. Japan imported eighty-five percent of its iron and steel, seventy-nine percent of its oil, and all of its rubber, as well as growing amounts of its food. At the same time, with population increasing by one million a year, a need was felt for outlets for Japanese emigration, which was blocked to the United States, Australia, and New Zealand by discriminatory laws against Asians. The onset of depression dramatized this fragile dependence on the outer world, and especially on the United States. Within two years the value of Japanese exports had been almost halved. The peasants in particular suffered from a drop in the price of raw silk and foodstuffs, and factory workers suffered from high levels of unemployment. Acquisition of an overseas empire in Manchuria offered the prospect of access to raw materials, control of a new market, employment as administrators for unemployed university graduates, and army control of a strategically vital area.

Divisions within the army postponed a military takeover of Japan's government until 1941. The most extreme groups were ultrarightists linked with civilian patriotic societies, who embarked on a campaign of assassinations that culminated in the brief seizure of parts of central Tokyo in 1936. This faction was crushed by a more extensive faction within the army, led by General Tojo Hideki, which was then able to press the succeeding governments for increased expenditures on the military and for the further shift of the economy toward war preparation.

Military Dominance and Preparation for War, 1932–1941

General Tojo Hideki (1884–1948)
Tojo, Japanese premier from October 1941 to July 1944, was held responsible for the surprise attack on the American fleet at Pearl Harbor in December 1941. After failing in a suicide attempt after Japan's defeat, he was tried as a war criminal and was executed in 1948.   (United Press International, Inc.)

The beginning of the war with China in 1937 gave the military almost a free hand in economic and military planning, despite the appointment of Prince Konoe Fumimaro as prime minister in 1937 to appease the political parties and business groups. The successes of Germany in 1939–1941, coming at a time when the United States was posing as the defender of China against Japanese aggression, persuaded Japanese supporters of military expansion that their best interests lay in alliance with the Nazis. In September 1940 Japan signed a defensive Tripartite Pact with Germany and Italy.

It has been suggested that American provocation of Japan at this time may have caused its decision both to expand its empire into Southeast Asia and into the Pacific and to attack the U.S. fleet at its base in Pearl Harbor in Hawaii. The American government had renounced its trade pact with Japan in July 1939, and in July 1940 had begun using licensing procedures to restrict the export of iron and oil to Japan. After the Japanese seizure of southern Indochina, the American government had joined with the British and Dutch in placing a total oil embargo on Japan. It is thus possible that the oil embargo made it imperative for the Japanese to seize new sources of oil in the Dutch East Indies (Indonesia), in an attack that could be broadened to include acquisition of the rubber, tin, and iron of the other European and American colonies in Asia. General Tojo became prime minister in October 1941; and in December 1941 the Japanese air force destroyed most of the Pacific fleet of the United States at Pearl Harbor, as a method of ending any threat from the United States while Japanese forces took Southeast Asia and the Pacific islands. By 1942 the Japanese were in control of Indochina, Singapore, Malaya, Burma, Indonesia, Hong Kong, the Philippines, and most of the Pacific islands.

Japan's empire in East Asia in 1942 covered a million and a half square miles and had a population of 140 million people. Its four years of rule had far-reaching consequences. In the first place, control of the empire gave Japan sources of foodstuffs desperately needed by the home islands, although raw materials were poorly exploited for lack of administrators and shipping.

Japan's Wartime Empire

Second, the Japanese made some effort to perpetuate their rule by persuading the peoples of the European colonial territories that they had come, as an Asian people, to liberate those regions by incorporating them in a Greater East Asia Co-Prosperity Sphere. Japanese destruction of the European armies had certainly destroyed the prestige of whites on which colonial rule had been partly based; and some collaborators were found among the colonial peoples, especially in Dutch Indonesia and in British Burma. The reality of Japanese exploitation was quickly felt, however; and in many parts of the empire resistance movements were formed, the most challenging being those in the Philippines and Malaya. These resistance groups, however, showed in 1945 that they had not fought the Japanese to welcome back the Europeans; in Indonesia, Burma, and Vietnam the guerrilla forces led the demand for independence from the Dutch, British, and French, respectively.

Third, the reconquest of the territories taken by Japan caused enormous physical damage, especially in the Pacific islands, where General Douglas MacArthur adopted, perhaps unnecessarily, a strategy of "island-hopping" in order to advance in stages toward the Japanese home islands. From 1944, however, the greatest damage was inflicted on Japan itself with the beginning of the firebombings that turned the wooden houses of its cities into infernos. Even before the dropping of the atomic bombs on Hiroshima and Nagasaki, the American air force had, in one raid on Tokyo on March 10, 1945, killed 100,000 people and burned most of the city.

Although General Tojo had been forced to resign in 1944, his successors as prime minister were unable to persuade the military to accept American demands for unconditional surrender. Only following the dropping of the atomic bombs did the emperor Hirohito (reigned 1926–   ) decide to do so. Defeat, followed by an American military occupation that lasted for the next seven years, drastically changed the character of Japanese society. If as supreme commander MacArthur behaved autocratically, his goal was the democratization of Japan. War criminals were brought to trial, al-

Japan Under Military Occupation, 1945-1952

though in a manner many observers felt infringed the basic principles of Western justice; and a number, including Tojo, were hanged. A large number of military and civilian officials were banned from holding office. The army was disbanded and all the paramilitary and patriotic societies banned. The power of the police was restricted. The Shinto religion was separated from the state.

A new constitution was introduced in 1947 that totally remodeled the prewar system, introducing party government similar to that in the British Parliament, with a cabinet chosen by the majority party. The many groups of civil servants and imperial officers who had influenced policymaking before the war were severely limited in their functions. Such rights as freedom of speech and assembly were guaranteed, as was the right to a minimum standard of living. The vote was given to all men and women aged twenty or over; in a further effort to enhance the position of women by weakening the patriarchal character of the Japanese family, the constitution stated: "Marriage shall be based upon the mutual consent of both sexes, and it shall be maintained through mutual cooperation, with equal rights of husband and wife as a basis." The emperor, though retained as a symbolic head of state, was given almost no political powers; and Hirohito himself declared in 1946 that the emperor was not divine.

Economic reforms included an effort to share out the farmland more fairly in small peasant plots, and an attempt was made to break up the zaibatsu. Only twenty-eight companies were split up, however; and the old giants of business very quickly reemerged with strong support from the Japanese people. Nevertheless, the American authorities felt that the occupation had succeeded quite quickly. In 1951 a peace treaty was signed by Japan and forty-eight countries with which it had been officially at war; but the Soviet Union and China were not among the forty-eight. The occupation ended on April 28, 1952.

Post-Occupation Japan The political system worked relatively smoothly after 1952, principally because the conservative parties enjoyed strong public support as a result of the success of their economic policies. At first, the two prewar parties, the Seiyukai (renamed the Liberal party) and the Minseito (renamed the Democratic party) competed, with the Liberals generally predominant because of the strong leadership of Yoshida Shigeru (prime minister 1946–1947 and 1948–1954).

Faced with strong Socialist opposition, however, the two parties recognized their common conservative philosophy and united in 1955 as the Liberal-Democratic party. The basis of support for the Liberal-Democrats was a coalition of business and banking interests, civil servants, and farmers, who often formed their own factions within the party and fought for representation in the cabinet. Economic policy favored freedom of action for business, with the government adopting a type of predictive planning similar to that introduced in France after 1945 and encouraging growth by liberal policies toward savings and capital investment, while the farmers were aided by financial subsidies.

In the late 1950s more conservative prime ministers threw out many of the restrictions on the police and on the powers of the central government that had been imposed during the occupation, and sought to build up the Japanese armed forces. After 1960, however, a number of skillful compromisers took power. Their primary goal was to foster the economic miracle that was transforming the Japanese standard of living. One prime minister, for example, promised to double the Japanese income in ten years and saw his promise fulfilled in seven.

In 1972 the choice of Tanaka Kakuei (prime minister, 1972–1974) seemed to begin a new era with the appointment of a self-made businessman who had not even attended the university; but Tanaka's resignation and subsequent arrest with a number of other party officials for financial misconduct tarnished the Liberal-Democratic party's reputation. The party recovered fairly quickly under new leadership, however. In the elections of 1980 it won forty-five percent of the vote and appointed yet another compromiser, Suzuki Zenko, as prime minister.

The opposition parties remained fragmented, and none were able to challenge the Liberal-Democrats. In 1960 the Socialist party itself split between a moderate wing and a more radical wing bitterly opposed to the continuance of the military concessions to the United States embodied in the security treaty signed that year. The Japanese Communist party, by maintaining a moderate stance and by disassociating itself from both the Soviet Union and China, slowly grew in strength to about ten percent of the electorate. Finally the Komeito, a "clean government" party based largely on a Buddhist group called the Soka Gakkai, gained a foothold in 1967 on a platform of international peace, internal morality, and improved living standards.

Throughout the postwar years the Japanese economy continued to boom. By 1979 the gross national product was over $1,000 billion. After the

The Ginza, Tokyo
Japan's postwar prosperity is glaringly obvious along the Ginza, one of Tokyo's principal streets, where large department stores attract shoppers by day and restaurants and cabarets are crowded with revelers by night. (Jacques Daune/SYGMA)

postwar reconstruction had been completed, the Japanese economy grew during the 1950s at the rapid rate of nine percent annually. This rate rose in the 1960s to eleven percent and by 1970 was more than thirteen percent. These rates could not be sustained in the 1970s, partly because they would have been excessive for an advanced economy, but also because Japan's lack of raw materials and especially of oil was beginning to put a brake on its expansion. Nevertheless, growth remained impressive, especially in comparison with the performance of the United States and western Europe in the 1970s. In 1981 a real growth rate of six percent was achieved.

There were many reasons for Japan's economic success. Agricultural production was modernized, freeing many workers to leave the farms for industry even as food production was increasing. New plant and technology were introduced, not only for new fields such as electronics and computer production, but also in older industries like shipbuilding and steel, with the result that Japan outstripped even the most advanced countries of western Europe. Japanese labor, often employed in hierarchical companies that guaranteed job stability in return for total loyalty, were hardworking, highly skilled, and well paid; managers proved even more dynamic than in the more strictly family-controlled prewar enterprises.

The great zaibatsu regained much of their prominence, especially the giant trusts of Mitsui, Mitsubishi, and Sumitomo, without, however, freezing out brilliant new entrepreneurs like the founders of Sony and Honda. The expansion of the Japanese home market acted as the principal stimulant to production, especially as Japanese consumers poured their wages into purchase of domestic appliances and automobiles, thus enabling the companies to make the economies of mass production that allowed them to undercut their competitors in the world market. By the 1970s the Japanese had the third largest share of the world's trade, even though that trade made up only about ten percent of Japan's gross national product.

The economic boom produced great changes in Japanese society. Perhaps the most notable was the continuing urbanization of the country. Half of Japan's population was crowded into three metropolitan areas: Tokyo, Osaka-Kyoto, and Nagoya. Tokyo alone had a population of almost nine million people. Density was three times the average for cities in the United States, with resulting problems of congestion and overburdening of city facilities and infrastructure even greater than those of New York City. In many ways the government's laissez-faire policies had made matters worse. Air pollution was universal, although air quality improved by 1980. Waterways were often polluted by industrial waste. Hospitals were inadequate, and housing within the expanding cities was insufficient and overpriced. Public transportation, especially the high-speed long-distance train system, remained excellent; and a dense commuter network made possible a dispersal of the urban population into widely spread suburbs around the old central districts.

Discontent expressed itself in various ways. University students, feeling neglected in the universities by faculty and administration and opposing the business orientation of the government, frequently rioted. Others sought a release in a new religious sect called the Soka Gakkai, which preached a return to Buddhism through highly organized community groups of worshippers. For most Japanese, however, the postwar years had brought such prosperity that the country's problems seemed minimal by comparison.

INDIA FROM THE BRITISH RAJ TO INDEPENDENCE

In almost every part of the colonial world, discontent with Western rule led to the formation of movements for independence and at times to armed revolt in the years between the First and Second world wars. In British India, as we saw in Chapter 25, opposition to British rule had already been expressed through the Indian National Congress and in such movements as the *swadeshi*, or boycott, campaigns. In 1919, however, the Indians felt outraged. They had expected to receive much greater autonomy as the reward for their loyal cooperation during the First World War, but they were given only minor concessions in the Government of India Act, which extended the franchise to only three million Indians. Moreover, in April, British troops commanded by Brigadier-General Dyer had attempted to give a salutary example of the government's intention of suppressing public disturbances by shooting down an unarmed crowd trapped in a walled field at Amritsar in the Punjab. This massacre, in which, according to the Congress's investigators, 1,400 were killed and 3,600 wounded, caused enormous indignation in India, especially when Dyer, having been punished solely by loss of his commission, was welcomed home by British conservatives as a hero. Rabindranath Tagore sent back his knighthood to the viceroy with a note that "badges of honour make our shame glaring in the incongruous context of humiliation." Millions began a policy of noncooperation, called *satyagraha* ("holding to the truth"), proclaimed by Mohandas Karamchand Gandhi (1869–1948). Gandhi was swept into the leadership of the independence movement, and his technique of passive resistance was made the instrument by which the British would eventually be ousted.

Unique among the great leaders of revolutions in the twentieth century, Gandhi was more a spiritual than a political leader, and his means to revolution were intended to be moral rather than material. Gandhi in fact came to be called Mahatma, or Great Soul, a name given to him by his friend Rabindranath Tagore. The son of a middle-class family in western India, Gandhi had studied law in London and then taken a legal post in South Africa. There, between 1893 and 1914, he had learned to organize the Indian workers against what he felt was the oppression and discrimination of the white community. In this work he himself had used the tradi-

The Indian Independence Movement, 1918–1939

Jawaharlal Nehru and Mahatma Gandhi, 1946
In their leadership of the Indian independence struggle against the British, Nehru (left) and Gandhi (right) complemented each other's contribution. While Gandhi brought spiritual drive to the movement of nonviolent resistance, Nehru proved to be a brilliant political organizer. (United Press International, Inc.)

tional Hindu practices of meditation, fasting, and nonviolence *(ahimsa)* as weapons against the forces of oppression.

Back in India in 1914, Gandhi established an *ashram*, or hermitage, from which he made contact with the Indian poor, including the untouchables, for whom he demanded the abolition of untouchability. In 1921–1922 so many Indians of all classes were ready to follow his first call for *satyagraha* that Gandhi himself had to intervene to prevent its deterioration into uncontrolled bloodshed. In 1930 he called a second *satyagraha* campaign in support of the Congress's demand for complete independence *(purna swaraj)* made at its session the previous year.

By then Gandhi had become the political ally of Jawaharlal Nehru (1889–1964), a brilliant young politician from a prominent Brahman family who had returned from an education at Harrow School and Cambridge University in England only to reject the influential role the British wished to give him. While Nehru was denouncing British misgovernment in the Congress, Gandhi dramatized his disobedience by a "march to the sea," leading thousands of his followers from his ashram to the Indian Ocean, where they used the natural salt in defiance of the government's salt tax.

Gandhi was jailed with thousands of his followers, including Nehru, but was released the following year when the British government decided on a policy of conciliation. However, the Government of India Act of 1935, the outcome of many years of negotiation, was still a disappointment to the Indians, even though it extended the franchise to thirty million voters. The provincial assemblies created to govern the eleven provinces administered by the British were restricted in their powers, and voting was to be by the divisive system of communal electorates for the different communities of Hindus, Moslems, Sikhs, and so on. Moreover, the elections in 1937 emphasized the split that had emerged between the largely Hindu Congress and the Moslem League.

Founded in 1905 to protect Moslem interests in the event of the formation of a Hindu government, the League had languished until its leadership was taken in 1934 by Mohammed Ali Jinnah (1876–1948). Jinnah, a secular-minded lawyer who had originally been a member of the Congress, now converted the League into a mass movement of India's seventy million Moslems demanding the grant of separate statehood for a Moslem-controlled community to be called Pakistan, a name formed from the Urdu for "land of the pure," but also an acronym: P (Punjab), A (Afghanistan), K (Kashmir), S (Sind), and -istan ("land of"). While Congress ran the provincial assemblies in 1937–1939, communal rioting between Hindus and Moslems gave forewarning of even worse troubles ahead.

The decision of the British to enter the Second World War without consulting India and to postpone until the war's end the grant of self-government, even though two million Indians fought for Britain in the war, drove the Congress into resistance. Gandhi embarked upon a new campaign of noncooperation in 1940, and thousands were again arrested. When the British, perturbed at the Japanese conquest of Burma and Malaya, again opened negotiations with the Indians in 1942, the offers made by their envoy, Sir Stafford Cripps, were found unsatisfactory. Congress called on its supporters to demonstrate under the slogan "Quit India." As many as sixty thousand, including Gandhi himself, were arrested by the British.

Independence Achieved, 1939–1947

The Moslems had continued to demonstrate for the division of India, and Gandhi and Jinnah failed to reach any compromise. Thus, when the British Labour government of Clement Attlee, elected in 1945 on a platform that included the promise of independence to India, sought to give the subcontinent the *swaraj* it had demanded for half a century, the principal stumbling block was the relationship between the Hindu and Moslem communities.

The cabinet mission sent by Attlee in 1946 failed to bring the Congress and the Moslem League into agreement on maintenance of a united India under a federal constitution. Jinnah called for direct action by the Moslems, provoking rioting that in Calcutta alone left five thousand dead and one hundred thousand homeless. The intensification of the slaughter by both Moslems and Hindus led Attlee to declare that Britain would leave in June 1948 whether a solution had been found or not; and the last British viceroy, Lord Mountbatten, chose a speedier solution by granting independence in August 1947 to a largely Moslem state of Pakistan and a mainly Hindu state of India.

Three provinces—Bengal, Punjab, and Assam—were divided to avoid leaving large minorities of Hindus under Moslem rule. Between ten and twelve million refugees fled, however—Hindus and Sikhs leaving Pakistan and Moslems leaving India. The refugees were frequently robbed as they traveled, and as many as a million were killed.

To put an end to the communal slaughter, Gandhi went on a final fast in January 1948, which he ended only when the Congress leaders promised at his bedside to protect Moslem lives and property in India. Fanatical Hindus, however, murdered Gandhi at his prayer meeting in Delhi, plunging both Hindus and Moslems throughout the subcontinent into a mourning that briefly calmed the animosity between the religions.

India Under Nehru, 1947–1964

Jawaharlal Nehru, affectionately known as Panditji, became India's first prime minister; the Congress party established its control not only of the House of the People, the lower chamber of parliament, where it won seventy-five percent of the seats, but also of most national and local administrative offices. Enormous problems faced the new state, which, with a population of 380 million, was the second largest and one of the poorest countries in the world.

The first problem was to settle the future of the princely states, which had been authorized to choose whether to join Pakistan or India. Two hundred and forty princes chose to join India immediately; and, after a brief period when many were used as governors, they were pensioned off and new administrators appointed. The Nizam of Hyderabad, a Moslem ruler of a largely Hindu state, was compelled to join India by an invasion of the Indian army in September 1948. In the northern state of Kashmir, however, where a Hindu prince governed mainly Moslem subjects, fighting broke out between the Indian and Pakistan armies, which was halted in 1949 when the United Nations supervised a cease-fire that left the state divided between India and Pakistan. New outbreaks of fighting in 1955, 1965, and 1971 led to some minor changes of boundaries.

The second problem was to organize the country's economic development, which Nehru tackled by bringing in a series of five-year plans whose purpose was the gradual socialization of the economy. The First Five-Year Plan (1951–1956) was a modest attempt to modernize agricultural production, especially through irrigation projects, and to rebuild the transportation network. The Second Five-Year Plan (1956–1961) developed the country's industrial base, exploiting its vast iron ore deposits and its coal and expanding its textile production. By 1961 Indian factories were producing for export heavy and light engineering goods in addition to more traditional cotton fabrics. However, food production, though increasing, failed to keep up with the growth of population, despite adoption of some family-planning measures in 1959. India remained a food importer. The Third Five-Year Plan (1961–1966) saw even greater advances in steel and chemical production and in electricity generation, with economic aid provided by both Western and Communist powers.

Slum Street, Bombay
India's economic progress has been hampered by the increase in population from 380 million in 1947 to 676 million in 1980. The homeless poor have crowded the slums of cities like Bombay and Calcutta, where thousands sleep on makeshift beds in the streets. (Poly-Press/Katherine Young)

The third problem, to establish a role for India in a world dominated by the conflict between the Western and Communist blocs, was solved by Nehru's policy of nonalignment. Accepted as one of the principal leaders of the Third World countries of Asia and Africa, Nehru attempted to maintain good relations with all groups. He persuaded the British to rename the British Commonwealth the Commonwealth of Nations, so that India could remain a member after becoming a republic in 1950. He sought friendship with the Communist government of China until frontier disputes in the Himalayas led to a brief border war in 1962. He accepted Soviet financial and technical aid for the economic plans but also received $5 billion from a group of six Western nations in the so-called Aid-to-India Club.

The Dominance of Indira Gandhi

Nehru's death in 1964 left a void in Indian leadership, not least because he himself had dispatched a number of the Congress leaders back to the countryside to work like Gandhi with the masses. For five years India was governed by a coalition of national and regional Congress party leaders, at first under the mild-mannered Lal Bahadur Shastri (prime minister 1964–1966) and then under Nehru's daughter, Indira Gandhi, who became prime minister on Shastri's death in 1966.*

Although chosen for the luster conferred on her by her father's popularity and because she was believed tractable, Indira Gandhi found herself

* Her husband, Feroze Gandhi, who died in 1960, was no relative of the Mahatma.

Indira Gandhi Receiving Congratulations on Her Election Victory (1980)
Although forced to resign in 1977 after eleven years as premier, Gandhi displayed her political charisma by winning a stunning victory in the parliamentary elections of January 1980. *(Laurent Maous/Gamma/ Liaison)*

hampered by the power of the old guard within the Congress party during her first years in office. Regional strife was growing, especially in the state of Kerala, where an elected Communist government had been ousted by the central government in 1959, and throughout the south, where the Congress party had been attempting to impose use of the northern language of Hindi on Tamil speakers.

Gandhi chose to split the party, forming in 1969 her own group—known as the New Congress party—and proclaiming a more rapid program of socialization. From that moment her supremacy in the Indian political arena was almost as great as her father's had been, especially since the 1971 elections gave her party an absolute majority in the House of the People. As her popularity with the masses grew, she became more autocratic. After Gandhi imposed emergency powers in 1975–1977 and arrested opposition leaders, a reaction set in against her; and she was compelled to resign after losing the elections in 1977. In spite of charges of corruption against her, however, she regained power with a landslide victory in the elections of January 1980.

Gandhi's foreign policy was marked by a continuance of the quarrels with Pakistan, as a result of which she turned to the Soviet Union for support. In 1971 Indian troops engaged the Pakistan army in Kashmir and in East Pakistan, where an independence movement led by Mujibur Rahman (1920–1975) was attempting to turn that oppressed, poverty-stricken province into the independent state of Bangladesh. The decision of China and the United States to support Pakistan further strengthened India's alignment with the Soviet Union, with which it had signed a treaty of peace, friendship, and cooperation in August 1971. Indian troops were quickly successful, compelling the Pakistan troops in Bangladesh to surrender within two weeks. Ten million refugees who had fled to India, many of them to the streets of Calcutta, returned to their newly independent state, which had clearly been born under India's protection.

Three years later India exploded an atomic bomb, thus becoming the world's sixth nuclear power. Gandhi's critics charged that a country in India's difficult economic position could not support the expense of war and nuclear armaments. It was true that despite attempts to increase agricultural production further through the introduction of highly productive new strains of wheat and rice (the "green revolution"), India's food problems remained grave. Population had expanded to 475 million in 1965 and to 676 million in 1980, when the annual gross national product per capita was barely $150. Industrialization, pressed in the Fourth (1970–1974) and Fifth (1974–1978) Five-Year Plans, had slowed down under the impact of the increase in oil prices by the oil-producing countries in 1974. The Sixth Five-Year Plan was not launched until 1980. Thus India, which had offered the world the example of the experiment of democracy in a vast and partly illiterate country, had failed to provide the economic underpinning on which the future of that political system depended.

While India was clinging to the forms of democratic government, Pakistan abandoned such hopes to search for efficient government through authoritarian rule. Jinnah himself, appointed the first governor-general, died in 1948; and the Moslem League became an instrument of powerful landlords. Pakistan's first prime minister, the popular Liaquat Ali Khan, was murdered by an Afghan fanatic in 1951; and his successor was dismissed two years later for economic incompetence. Meanwhile, the politicians took until 1956 to draft a constitution, when Pakistan became a republic with General Iskander Mirza as president. The country's situation remained precarious, however. The quarrels with India over Kashmir forced the expenditure of a large part of the meager revenues on the army, and the population could be kept from starvation only with large gifts of grain from the United States.

Pakistan Since 1947

To put an end to the bickering among the political factions and to handle the growing discontent in East Pakistan in 1958, General Mohammed Ayub Khan was appointed by Mirza to run the country through the army. Ayub Khan made himself head of state, declared martial law, and ran the country by decree. A few modest reforms were enacted, notably a redistribution of some farmland and the beginning of a program of industrialization. Considerable Western aid was received as a reward for Pakistan's membership in the Southeast Asia Treaty Organization, an American-sponsored military alliance formed in 1954 to block future Communist advances, from which Pakistan withdrew in 1972. However, Ayub

President Zia ul-Haq, 1979
After seizing power in Pakistan in July 1977, Zia imposed an increasingly authoritarian regime, in which all political parties were dissolved and the power of the army was extended over many areas of civilian life.
(Patrick Chauvel/SYGMA)

Khan's regime made no effort to reduce the stranglehold on Pakistan's industrial and financial resources of a small number of landed families; and the exploitation of East Pakistan continued.

A new capital city was built in Islamabad; and a National Assembly, elected under a new constitution written in 1962, met there in 1965. The appearance of democracy was a sham, however, and violent demonstrations broke out against Ayub Khan, who, losing the support of the army, was compelled to resign in 1969, only to be replaced by another army general, Yahya Khan. Although Yahya Khan used martial law to attack the corruption that had spread under Ayub Khan's regime, and then permitted national elections to be held in 1970, he canceled the results when Mujibur Rahman's independence movement won the majority of the seats in East Pakistan. The troops he sent into East Pakistan engaged in wholesale atrocities, thus provoking the Indian intervention; and, with the ignominious surrender of his army, Yahya himself resigned in December 1971.

His successor was the charismatic Ali Bhutto, the vice-premier and foreign minister, who recognized the independence of Bangladesh and settled outstanding grievances with India. The sad progression toward authoritarianism continued, however, even though Bhutto at first ended martial law and called new elections. Within four years Bhutto was outlawing opposition parties and jailing university students. In 1977, in a desperate attempt to hold onto power, he reintroduced martial law in several cities. But rioting was widespread, and hundreds were killed.

In July 1977 the army, under General Zia ul-Haq, seized power. Bhutto was arrested, tried for the murder of his political opponents, and executed in 1979. Martial law was imposed throughout the country, and elections were postponed. It soon became clear that Zia's proclaimed policy of Islamization was part of a religious reaction against secularization that was affecting many Moslem countries of the region—notably Turkey, Afghanistan, and Iran—in addition to Pakistan, and that was to culminate in the overthrow of the shah of Iran in 1979. Like Iran, Pakistan had experienced the weakening of the power of the Islamic clerics, a lessening of the social seclusion of women, and an emphasis on material values that many conservatives felt threatened the religious concerns of the society. For Pakistan, the religious revival created new problems by generating violent confrontations between Shi'ite and Sunni Moslems. It also sparked the opposition of many who saw the progress of Islamization as threatening to both the economic and the political gains of the past decade, at a time when Pakistan was severely strained by the entry of thousands of refugees from Afghanistan after the Soviet invasion in December 1979.

Independent Bangladesh

Independence did not solve the deep-rooted problems of Bangladesh. Mujibur Rahman, the "Father of Bangladesh," had followed the pattern of his Pakistani predecessors by declaring a national emergency in 1974 and taking the power to govern by decree. The army overthrew and killed him in

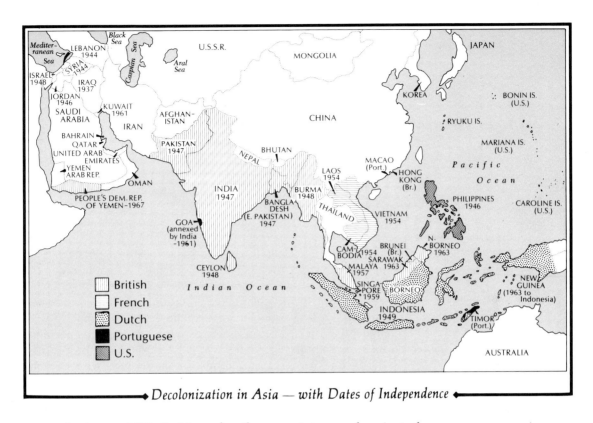

→ Decolonization in Asia — with Dates of Independence ←

a coup in August 1975. In November the army intervened again to force the resignation of his successor. Power was taken by Major-General Ziaur Rahman, who became president in 1977. Although governing with authoritarian controls, in 1979 Ziaur did permit relatively free elections, which were won by his own party. Nevertheless, unrest was endemic. Guerrillas operated among the hill tribes of the north. Strikes were frequent in the cities. And the high birth rate—forty-six per thousand—brought the population to ninety million by 1980, justifying Ziaur's enthusiastic if ineffective campaign for birth control.

THE DECOLONIZATION OF SOUTHEAST ASIA

Throughout the colonies of Southeast Asia, between 1919 and 1939, demands were voiced by nationalist groups for greater autonomy and, at times, for ultimate independence. Whereas the Americans and the British recognized that their colonies would have to be prepared for the tasks of self-government, the French and Dutch continued their autocratic rule and economic exploitation and thereby worsened the outbursts that would overthrow their rule after the Second World War.

The Philippines　　　　The first Asian colony to receive its independence was the Philippines, to which the United States ceded full sovereignty on July 4, 1946. Although the handing over of power by the United States was conducted amicably on both sides, the new country faced great problems. Fighting on its territory during the Second World War had caused enormous loss of life and destruction of property. Communist-dominated guerrillas known as Huks, who had been fighting against the Japanese, now turned their weapons against the new government and, with the aid of the debt-ridden peasantry of central Luzon, against the great landlords. On Mindanao in the south, the Moslems remained violently anti-Christian and frequently resorted to force to attempt to oust both Christian settlers and the Philippine authorities themselves.

The concessions the United States received at independence were also subject to great popular criticism within the Philippines. The United States retained the right to free trade for eight years after independence, in return paying large sums for the rehabilitation of the Philippine economy. Although the agreement was modified in 1954, after criticism had been leveled at it as a form of neocolonial exploitation, the United States retained preferential trading rights until 1974. The defense agreements were even more harshly criticized because they gave the United States a ninety-nine-year lease on military, air, and naval bases throughout the country. Although the United States recognized full Philippine sovereignty over the bases in 1956 and dismantled several of them shortly afterward, it was compelled to agree to a reduction of the length of the lease to twenty-five years (from 1967).

From the start, the democratic constitution did not work smoothly. The election of Manuel Roxas as president in 1946 was marked by corruption, and the new president found himself unable to throw off the power of the wealthy groups who had supported his election. His successor Elpidio Quirino (president 1948–1953) was equally unable to control the widespread graft and political violence, and the lack of genuine land reform strengthened the support received by the Huks. Stability was assured for a time by Ramón Magsaysay (president 1953–1957), who had brought the Huk insurrection under control not only by using the army effectively against the Huks, but also by promising pardons and the grant of land on islands other than Luzon to those who would surrender. By the time of his death, economic progress was under way, land reform was taking hold, and administrative corruption had been lessened.

In the early 1970s it became clear that the brief respite from troubles was over. Communist guerrilla forces were active in Luzon, especially because of the demands of the rapidly growing population for land. The Moslems were again in arms. The student population in the large cities had become radicalized. And violence seemed to have become an everyday occurrence. Pope Paul VI was attacked during a visit in 1970. The United States Embassy was stormed by rioters. An attempt was even made to take the presidential palace.

In these circumstances, Ferdinand Marcos, who had been elected president in 1965 and reelected to an unprecedented second term in 1969, decided in 1972 to declare martial law. A new constitution in 1973 gave him the right to extend his authoritarian government. Marcos's personal rule, which was increasingly criticized for human rights violations, abuses by the military, and corruption, failed to end the two main insurrections—by the Communists of the New People's Army and by the Moslems of the Moro Liberation Front—nor could it stop urban terrorism. In 1980 bombs were placed in a number of government buildings and at a large convention of American travel agents. Nevertheless, the economy showed some improvement, although per capita income was barely $600 in 1980. Future gains, moreover, were threatened by the rapid growth of the population, which had risen from twenty-seven million in 1960 to over forty-seven million twenty years later.

Of the British colonies, Burma and Ceylon developed the strongest nationalist movements. The Burmese elite, represented in the Young Men's Buddhist Association and in the broader General Council of Burmese Associations, was largely appeased by the grant of a partially elected legislature in 1923 and by the establishment of a fully elected assembly and responsible government in 1937, when Burma was separated from India. Local villagers remained discontented, however, and started countrywide riots that were suppressed by force. Finally, a new opposition group developed within the universities.

Burma

During the Japanese occupation local collaborators were permitted by the occupation authorities to establish a Burmese government, but it was so obviously under the control of the Japanese that part of its forces broke away under Aung San to form a resistance movement called the Anti-Fascist People's Freedom League (AFPFL). After 1945 the British Labour government saw in this organization the opportunity for a relatively smooth transition of power; and, even though Aung San was murdered by rivals in 1947, the British handed over power to the AFPFL in January 1948.

There was greater fighting after independence than before, as rival Communist guerrillas, known as the Red Flags and the White Flags, fought against the government and each other, and as the Karen people struggled for an independent state of its own. By 1950, however, Aung San's successor, U Nu, had brought the country back under control, suppressing the Communists and granting autonomy to the Karens. Nevertheless, other minorities remained discontented; the remaining Communist insurgents received aid from the Chinese. U Nu, who had temporarily handed power to the army under General Ne Win in 1958–1960, was overthrown in 1962 by Ne Win, who held power first as military ruler and then, from March 1974, as civilian president. Although insurgency among the minorities continued in the 1980s, the Burmese economy slowly revived in the 1970s. By 1980 the national income was increasing at a healthy 5.6 percent a year.

Ceylon (Sri Lanka)

Premier Sirivamo Bandaranaike During the Election Campaign, 1977
After her electoral defeat in 1977, Bandaranaike was accused of abusing her powers during her long rule as premier in 1960–1965 and 1970–1977. She was expelled from parliament in 1980. (Bruno Barbey/Magnum Photos, Inc.)

Malaysia and Singapore

The British had bowed to the demands of Ceylon's* independence movement, which was founded during the First World War, by granting universal suffrage in 1931. In February 1948 they granted full independence. Ceylon's greatest threat of violence lay in fighting among the Sinhalese majority and the Tamil minority who had migrated to the island from southern India. At first Ceylon clung closely to the British alliance, not least because of the aid extended by Britain and other Commonwealth countries through the Colombo Plan of 1950.

With the 1960 election victory of Sirivamo Bandaranaike, the widow of the prime minister assassinated the previous year, the socialization of the economy was pushed. After nationalization of British and American companies, relations with the Western powers worsened, at a time when the Tamils were again rioting against the banning of their political parties. Although Bandaranaike was ousted from power in 1965, she returned in triumph in 1970 to push her program of social reforms even more rapidly after declaration of a national emergency. She was defeated in 1977 after a violent election campaign, and in 1980 she was expelled from parliament for abuses of power by the new government of Junius Jayewardene, who had himself been forced to resort to emergency powers only two days earlier. For Ceylon, therefore, the years of independence had been uneasy, disturbed by communal violence and by problems of high inflation and unemployment.

By contrast, the grant of independence to the British colonies of the Malay Peninsula and the nearby islands was something of a success story. There had been little pressure for immediate independence in the Malay states, largely because of the distrust between Malays, Chinese, and Indians there. Resistance to the Japanese came primarily from Communist guerrillas from the Chinese community, who, disappointed after 1945 that the British government intended to hold on to Malaya for its tin and rubber, took to the jungles to oust the British.

The British sent large army and air forces against the insurgents but at the same time granted increased power to an alliance of Malays (under Tunku Abdul Rahman) and conservative Chinese. The Malayan Federation became independent within the Commonwealth in 1957. The British colonies of North Borneo and Sarawak were joined to the Malayan Federation and Singapore in 1963 to form the state of Malaysia; because of its overwhelmingly Chinese population, however, Singapore withdrew two years later.

Despite ongoing tension between the different ethnic groups, Malaysia prospered from its earnings from oil, tin, rubber, and palm oil. The party that had won independence, the United Malays National Organization, remained in power. By 1980 Malaysia was one of the most economically ad-

*Ceylon was renamed Sri Lanka in 1972.

vanced states of Asia, with a gross national product of over $15 billion and a population of only fourteen million.

Singapore's economy surged after independence. Its population of 2.4 million proved highly skillful in creating export industries, especially in textiles and electronics as well as the more traditional processed rubber. Its foreign trade was valued at $31 billion. Its location made it the transportation hub of Southeast Asia. Politically, it offered an example of stable rule under the leadership of Lee Kuan Yew, who headed the government from 1959 on.

An Indonesian Nationalist party under Sukarno had been founded in 1927 to agitate for independence. After collaborating with the Japanese during the occupation, Sukarno declared Indonesia independent in 1945. The Dutch, however, with a quarter of their national capital invested in the islands and over a quarter of a million Dutch citizens living there, fought back savagely for four years to suppress Sukarno's forces. Sukarno also faced a powerful Indonesian Communist movement, which he suppressed with considerable bloodshed while fighting a final successful campaign against the Dutch in 1948–1949.

The Dutch Ouster from Indonesia

In December 1949 Indonesian independence was recognized. Most of the Dutch were forced to return home, and most of the Dutch investments were expropriated. The powerful new state, which had a population of seventy-three million in 1953, opposed the United States and sought friendship with Communist China and the other Third World countries; but Sukarno's military adventurism, which included a war with Malaysia, proved disruptive to the economy, and his personal popularity plummeted.

The Communists again became powerful and in 1965 began a concerted move to take over the country, which was foiled by the army under General Suharto in 1966. The army reversed the direction of Indonesia's foreign policy, seeking closer ties with the West and breaking the Communist movement by force. As president from 1968, Suharto placed major emphasis on economic restoration, developing oil production, chemicals, textiles, rice, rubber, and copper production. However, with an increase in population to 144 million by 1980, the peasantry remained poor, per capita income reaching only $360 a year.

The French proved even less willing than the Dutch to give up their colonial holdings in Indochina. To protect their vast economic stake in industry, banking, and plantations, they moved large forces into the south of Vietnam in 1945, although they began negotiations with the Communist leader Ho Chi Minh, who had declared Vietnam independent in September.

The Tragic Independence Struggle in Indochina

Full-scale war broke out in 1946 after Ho's forces, known as the Viet Minh, had attacked the French in Hanoi. Led by the brilliant general Vo Nguyen Giap, the Viet Minh embarked on what it called revolutionary warfare, using terrorism, propaganda, and political indoctrination to win control of the peasantry. Receiving help from both the Soviet Union and Communist China, Ho Chi Minh's forces were able to make French losses intolerable.

Finally, when Giap's forces overwhelmed the French garrison of the important border fortress of Dien Bien Phu, the French political parties in desperation named Pierre Mendès-France premier, giving him the task of making immediate peace in Indochina. He did so with great skill, leaving North Vietnam in Ho Chi Minh's hands and giving independence at the same time to the states of South Vietnam, Laos, and Cambodia.

When Communist guerrilla forces continued to operate throughout Indochina, however, the American government decided that it would have to take over the anti-Communist military action in Vietnam from which the French had extricated themselves. The United States had already intervened in Asia in 1950–1953, when Communist forces from North Korea had invaded the non-Communist South, and had finally won an armistice that reestablished the border between North and South Korea at approximately its prewar position. Hoping to achieve a similar success in Vietnam, the United States began pouring increasing amounts of money and forces into South Vietnam in the 1960s. It supported one nationalist and anti-Communist leader after another, regardless of their corruption or the political repression they imposed, and thus found itself losing the political battle with the Communist guerrillas for the support of the peasantry. President Richard Nixon, finally recognizing the unpopularity of the war in the United States, withdrew U.S. troops under the pretext of creating a South Vietnamese army of genuine fighting power; in 1973 a cease-fire was agreed on. Two years later the South Vietnamese army collapsed, and the North Vietnamese forces and the guerrillas reunited the country. In the futile attempt to halt the communization of Vietnam, the French had lost almost 100,000 soldiers and the United States almost 50,000; Vietnamese military and civilian deaths numbered at least 1.5 million.

Cambodia, after five years of civil war in which the United States financed the anti-Communist government and supported its campaigns with bombing flights, was taken over by the Communist Khmer Rouge forces in 1975 as Democratic Kampuchea. Laos, after years of fighting between right-wing, centrist, and Communist factions, fell to the Communists in 1975 and was renamed the Democratic People's Republic of Laos.

The communization of Vietnam, Cambodia, and Laos followed somewhat different patterns. Although the Vietnamese government imprisoned 800,000 anti-Communists for "reeducation," it did not embark on the massive executions that had been feared. Socialization of the economy of South Vietnam was pushed slowly but firmly; and many people who had fled to the cities for safety during the fighting were relocated in the countryside. The political domination of the north over the south was symbolized by the renaming of Saigon as Ho Chi Minh City. Though aid was sought from both China and the Soviet Union, the Vietnamese also made

Vietnamese Refugee Boats in the Government Dockyard, Hong Kong
By 1980, more than a million refugees had fled from Indochina, many traveling in overcrowded boats to neighboring countries in Southeast Asia and to Hong Kong. About three-quarters of them eventually resettled in various Western countries and in China. (Keystone Press Agency, Inc.)

some effort to restore relations with the non-Communist powers. Vietnam joined the International Monetary Fund and the World Bank and opened ties with the non-Communist Association of Southeast Asian Nations.

Economic conditions remained poor, however, especially from 1979, when border disputes led to a brief war with China and when the Vietnamese intervened in Cambodia. Thousands of refugees began to flee from Vietnam. At least 250,000 ethnic Chinese moved to China, and as many more fled by boat to neighboring Asian countries.

The brutality of the regime of Pol Pot in Cambodia set a new standard of inhumanity as the inhabitants of the cities were driven into the jungle to open up new farmlands. Between two and three million of Cambodia's population of eight million were executed or died of overwork or starvation between 1975 and 1979. The Vietnamese-installed government that replaced Pol Pot's regime in 1979 was at first welcomed, but its harshness led to disillusionment. In 1981 fighting was still continuing between Vietnamese and Khmer Rouge guerrillas.

In comparison with that of Cambodia, the Communist regime in Laos proved less repressive. Although the monarchy was abolished, agricultural collectivization was pushed slowly, and the government attempted to keep out of the disputes between Vietnam and its neighbors. Nevertheless, economic conditions deteriorated, and over 170,000 Laotian refugees had fled to Thailand by 1980.

NEW NATIONS IN AFRICA

***The Last Years
of Colonialism***

For the European colonies in Africa, the interwar years brought only an intensification of the policies of economic exploitation and political tutelage that had been shaped between 1890 and 1914. Although Germany was stripped of its colonial possessions, these were redistributed among the victorious European powers as "mandates" of the League of Nations, which was supposed to exercise a vague supervision on behalf of the local inhabitants of those regions. Britain took German East Africa (Tanganyika) and shared with France the Cameroons and Togoland in West Africa. Belgium was given Ruanda and Burundi. South Africa took German South-West Africa (Namibia).

Since conditions improved slightly for the Africans under the mandates, in comparison with German rule, these territories remained fairly quiescent. In many other parts of the continent, however, discontent with European rule led to violent manifestations and at times to rebellion. Rif tribesmen in the interior of Morocco, under their brilliant Western-educated leader, Abd-el-Krim, held down an army of 280,000 French and Spanish troops until 1926, when Abd-el-Krim was finally captured. Rioting against British rule in Kenya in 1922 was led by the East Africa Native Association, but resistance was broken by force and the association's leader exiled. Resistance in the Belgian Congo took the form of a violent religious movement led by a carpenter who preached apocalyptic visions; again, however, the leader's arrest brought the movement under control.

Thus sporadic resistance was not sufficient to secure African independence. Nevertheless, after 1918 a number of forces began to work together for the eventual end of European rule. First, international movements, created largely by American blacks and West Indians, began to agitate for black rule in Africa. The Black Zionist Movement, founded in New York in the 1920s by Marcus Garvey, a charismatic Jamaican, inspired millions of black Americans with his call for a black empire in Africa. The movement was little known in Africa, however, and it collapsed in the late 1930s. More lasting in its influence was the movement of Pan-Africanism, whose leading exponents were the American black leader W. E. B. Dubois and the Senegalese Blaise Diagne. Through Pan-African Congresses summoned five times between 1919 and 1945, the leaders won a large following of young Africans to their detailed programs for political and social reform and the eventual end of European rule in Africa.

Second, a new generation of African leaders was being trained in the schools and universities of the colonial powers in Africa and in Europe as well as in the United States. Among the products of French universities was the brilliant poet and politician Léopold Senghor, who was to lead Senegal to independence in 1960 and become its first president, and Félix Houphouët-Boigny, who served in the French parliament and became the first president of the Ivory Coast on its independence in 1960. In the British colonies the most influential of the new leaders were Jomo Kenyatta in

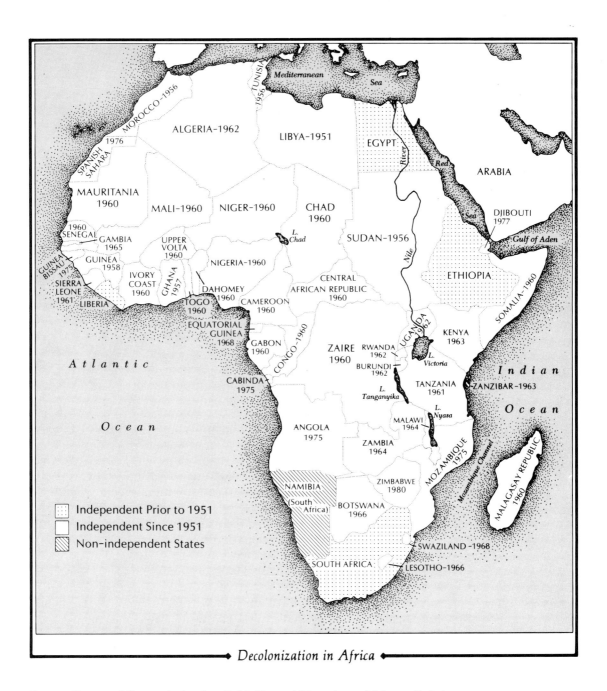

Independent Prior to 1951
Independent Since 1951
Non-independent States

◆ *Decolonization in Africa* ◆

Kenya, Kwame Nkrumah in the Gold Coast (Ghana), and Nnamdi Azikiwe in Nigeria. Although Kenyatta was educated mainly in London, Nkrumah and Azikiwe both attended Lincoln University in the United States. Even in the British and French colonies, however, the number of educated Africans was kept small; and almost no attempt was made to

Dar-es-Salaam, Tanzania
Tanzania's capital and largest port, Dar-es-Salaam, has attracted countless workers to its manufacturing and food-processing plants. Founded in 1866 by the Sultan of Zanzibar, the city is a mixture of the Arab, German, British, and African architecture of its successive rulers. (Keystone Press Agency, Inc.)

educate Africans for governmental responsibility in the Belgian, Spanish, and Portuguese colonies.

Third, the impact of economic development, even if largely directed toward foreign trade, was creating a new stratum of urbanized Africans. These included manual workers as well as a privileged group of educated administrators of the warehouses, factories, and even government offices. It was from these growing cities that the main drive for independence was to be organized. In West Africa the most important were Dakar in Senegal, Lagos and Ibadan in Nigeria, Accra in the Gold Coast, and Conakry in Guinea; in East Africa cities like Nairobi in Kenya and Dar-es-Salaam in Tanganyika were magnets for workers seeking to enter the cash economy.

Fourth, the Second World War made Africans aware of the feasibility of independence. In Asia the Japanese had easily driven the colonial powers from their possessions; in Europe the Africans saw Britain, France, and Belgium rescued by the intervention of the United States and the Soviet Union. Moreover, at a time when they perceived the weakness of the European powers, the Africans were conscious of the contribution they themselves had made with raw materials, money, and soldiers to the victory of the powers that occupied their country. They had even begun, through strikes in the ports and railroads, to make the colonial powers realize their dependence on the collaboration of the inhabitants of the colonial territories. Yet the independence movements in Africa after 1945 lagged behind those in Asia, which were largely successful in the 1940s and 1950s in forcing the withdrawal of the colonial powers. In Africa the Western-educated elites were small in number. Few Africans had been given political or administrative experience by the colonial authorities. Further, no organized resistance movement had come into being during the Second World War that could have forced concessions. As a result, independence came ten to twenty years later to the colonies in Africa than to the colonies in Asia.

Independence in the British Colonies

The British were more amenable to granting independence to the colonies in West Africa, where there were very few white settlers, than to those in East Africa. By 1950 the British were prepared to allow the Gold Coast a large degree of self-government. Nkrumah, however, called for a general strike and boycott to demand immediate independence. Jailed by the British, he was regarded as a martyr and had to be released to become prime minister in 1952. From that position he was able to negotiate the full independence of the new state, renamed Ghana, in 1957.

Although Nkrumah became increasingly autocratic as the ruler of a one-party state and was overthrown in an army coup in 1966, his example of leading Ghana to independence opened the floodgates in West Africa. The vast state of Nigeria attained independence in 1960, despite great difficulties in reconciling the ethnic rivalries between the three great regions into which the country was divided: the northern region, where the Moslem emirs had maintained a semifeudal control over the Hausa and Fulani peoples during the British system of indirect rule; the western region,

Kwame Nkrumah on Ghana's Independence Day, March 6, 1957
Nkrumah's popularity as the leader of Ghana's independence movement declined in the early 1960s, when his policies became increasingly repressive. He was ousted from power by an army and police coup in 1966. (United Press International, Inc.)

where the Yoruba predominated; and the eastern region, where the Ibo were the majority. The establishment of a federal state appeared to solve these problems. Offices in the central government were shared, with Abubakar Tafewa Balewa of the north becoming prime minister and Nnamdi Azikiwe of the east becoming first governor-general and then president.

Inefficiency, corruption, and ethnic rivalries continued, however; in January 1966 Ibo officers seized power in a military coup in which Balewa was murdered. Six months later, Hausa officers carried out another coup and made Lieutenant-Colonel Yakubu Gowon head of a military government. The Ibos then attempted to secede from Nigeria as the independent state of Biafra, only to be subdued in 1970 after three years of fierce resistance to the superior numbers and wealth of the Nigerians. Only then was Nigeria able to begin the economic recovery that its rich resources of cotton, groundnuts, palm oil, timber, cocoa, and petroleum made possible.

In East Africa the process toward independence was smoothest in Tanganyika, where Julius Nyerere, the leader of the Tanganyika African National Union, became the country's first prime minister when independence was granted in 1961. A year later he became president. In 1964 Tanganyika united with Zanzibar, which had been independent since 1963, to form the state of Tanzania. Nyerere followed a skillful program of nonalignment. He accepted aid from the West, the Soviet Union, and China, while establishing a form of village socialism and nationalizing banks and major industries. Northern Rhodesia (Zambia), rich in copper but in little else, followed a somewhat similar pattern under Kenneth Kaunda and his United National Independence Party, which from independence in 1964 sought to reduce European controls and to diversify the country's economic base.

In Kenya and in Southern Rhodesia, however, where substantial numbers of white settlers opposed independence because it would bring majority black rule, the struggle was longer and more bloody. In Kenya the Kikuyu tribe, who had been dispossessed of their tribal lands by white settlers in the early twentieth century, engaged in campaigns against the farmers in the "white highlands" between 1952 and 1956. The British replied with force, imprisoning such leaders as Jomo Kenyatta. With restoration of internal peace, however, the British rapidly increased black governmental responsibilities and in 1963 turned power over to Kenyatta and his Kenya African National Union. Serving as president until his death in 1978, Kenyatta sought closer relations with the United States and Britain, maintaining a form of democratic socialism at home that nevertheless welcomed large infusions of Western capital investment.

Resistance of the whites of Southern Rhodesia was more effective because they were five times larger in number than Kenya's fifty thousand whites. Nevertheless, with a black population of five million, their position was fragile in the long run, especially when the neighboring black African states permitted guerrilla forces to operate against the whites of Rhodesia

Jomo Kenyatta, 1893?-1978
Kenyatta was one of the most revered leaders of the independence movements in Africa. His personal prestige was vital, after the establishment of independence in 1963, in enabling Kenya to curb internal ethnic disputes and to forge an amicable relationship with Britain and other Western powers. (Ian Berry/Magnum Photos, Inc.)

after the latter unilaterally declared their independence from Britain in 1965. Fighting dragged on until 1980, when the whites of Rhodesia, the guerrillas and other groups of the country's blacks, and the British agreed on a formula for independence. The new country, renamed Zimbabwe, became independent in March 1980 with Robert Mugabe, a self-proclaimed Marxist, as prime minister, and a second guerrilla leader, Joshua Nkomo, as minister of home affairs. To the surprise of many Western observers, Mugabe embarked on a moderate program of reforms rather than outright socialization, seeking to reconcile the remaining whites and to maintain good relations with the Western powers as well as with the Communist bloc. The challenge of resettling the guerrillas and of calming the country's tribal conflicts remained extremely difficult, however.

South Africa

The long struggle of Rhodesia's whites against majority rule was possible only because of support from neighboring South Africa. In the aftermath of the Boer War (1899–1902), the British had sought a reconciliation between British and Boer settlers, giving the Union of South Africa self-government in 1909. However, the constitution disfranchised the black majority of the population, as well as the colored (or mixed-blood) and the Indian immigrants. It also favored the rural Boers over the urban British.

Thus in 1924–1939 the Afrikaner Nationalist Party of General James B. M. Hertzog was able to hold power and to enforce greater restrictions on blacks, including the setting aside of "reserved" areas for their residence in the interior. Much South African industry grew dependent on migrant laborers from the reserves, who could be paid lower wages and benefits than if they had been viewed as permanent residents where they worked.

After 1948 the strength of the Nationalist party grew continually, and a policy of *apartheid* (separation of the races) was imposed. Autonomous homelands for black Africans were planned. Strict controls on movement and employment of blacks in white-controlled regions were imposed, especially a hated passbook system that led to protest riots in Sharpeville in 1960, in which the police killed almost fifty black protesters. The postwar boom of the South African economy, based on gold, diamonds, engineering, textiles, and agricultural products, made South Africa the continent's richest country as well as its most powerful militarily. These successes merely enhanced the resentment of South African blacks against political disfranchisement, economic discrimination, and the innumerable social grievances implied by apartheid.

The independence of Zimbabwe, following the victory of Communist-dominated independence movements in the Portuguese colonies of Angola and Mozambique in 1975–1976, completed the isolation of South Africa as the single remaining white-dominated state on the continent, but further increased South Africa's unwillingness to hand over South-West Africa (Namibia) to any potentially unfriendly government.

Successful Transition in the French Colonies

In 1946 the French had attempted to assuage discontent with their rule by creating a French Union of their colonial territories. Increased autonomy at home was granted, along with representation in a colonial parliament in Paris. Nevertheless, the progress of the British colonies to independence led to similar demands in France's West African colonies; and the inability of the French army to crush the independence movements in Vietnam or Algeria also promised an early end to French imperialism. De Gaulle, however, once returned to power in 1958, carried out a brilliant transition of rule from the French to the native African leaders, which left almost every former colony firmly linked to France after independence. In 1958 every colony except Algeria was permitted to opt for independence by rejecting his new constitution. Only Guinea, under the leftist leader Sékou Touré, voted for independence in this way; and it was punished by severance of all financial and technical aid. The other African colonies were immediately granted internal autonomy and in 1959–1960 were allowed to negotiate their full independence, with continuing economic and military aid from France.

By the end of 1960, sixteen new states had been created from the former French empire in Africa. Many of these new states were headed by charismatic leaders such as Senghor in Senegal and Houphouët-Boigny in the Ivory Coast, whose personal popularity helped ensure political stability. In other states, such as Chad and Cameroon, tribal and occasionally religious rivalries caused internal conflicts; on several occasions the French intervened with military force to support presidents threatened with overthrow by rival forces.

At times the newly independent states became embroiled in the broader Cold War conflict. Sékou Touré in particular found it difficult to maintain his political independence while calling on Communist-bloc powers for economic support. The Central African Republic suffered most of all, however, from the dictatorial rule of Jean-Bedel Bokassa, a colonel who seized power in 1966 and stripped the country (renamed the Central African Empire) for his own benefit before finally being ousted by the French in 1979.

The French also attempted in the 1970s to become the principal patron of the Congo—the former Belgian Congo, which won its independence in 1960. The Belgians had pulled out of the Congo with great haste, leaving a well-developed mining industry, several modern cities, and almost no university graduates or trained administrators in the African population. The government had collapsed within two weeks, faced by the exodus of most Belgian administrators, a revolt in the army, and the attempted secession of the rich copper-mining province of Katanga. Although temporary peace was restored by 1963 with the intervention of a United Nations peacekeeping force, the Congolese army seized power in 1965 and made General Sese Seko Mobutu head of state. After several years of stability under Mobutu's rule, the country's economy was shaken by fluctuations in world copper prices and by a new attempt of Katanga (renamed Shaba) to secede in 1977–1978. Mobutu turned to the West, and especially to France, for aid. The French not only responded with large financial grants but also sent troops to help end the Shaba secession.

Independence did not prove a panacea for all the problems of Africa. First, many of the new states found themselves unwillingly embroiled in the Cold War conflict between the Western and Communist blocs. Although at times the countries could play off the blocs by inviting competition in aid giving between them, they also found themselves battlefields between competing armies aided, and at times even manned, by rival blocs. Angola in particular saw an outright civil war between factions supported by the United States and the Soviet bloc, in which victory was secured by the Communist forces only after Cuba had dispatched 21,000 troops in support.

Problems of Independent Africa

Second, the new states, whose boundaries were often artificial legacies of the colonial period that failed to correspond to historical or ethnic divisions, often engaged in war with each other. Togo, for example, was in constant dispute with Ghana over the future of British Togoland, which had opted to join Ghana. The Moroccans fought the Polisario liberation movement and their Algerian allies for control of the former Spanish Sahara, which had been divided in 1976 at independence between Morocco and

Mauritania. Territorial disputes between Ethiopia and Somalia—the former British Somaliland, which became independent in 1960—had by 1981 created one of the most serious refugee problems in the world, with over a million people, mostly women and children, on the edge of starvation.

Third, the new governments frequently felt a commitment to intervene economically or militarily in the internal affairs of other African states. Most of the African states insisted on a boycott of South Africa to attempt to compel it to hand over power to its black majority. For many years the states bordering on Zimbabwe aided the guerrillas operating against that country's white-controlled regime, and often sustained direct attack themselves. Tanzania plunged its economy into trouble through the expense of sending its army into neighboring Uganda to overthrow the brutal regime of Idi Amin (ruled 1971–1979). Libya's quixotic president Muammar al-Qaddafi not only fought brief skirmishes with the neighboring states of Tunisia and Egypt, but also intervened in the civil war in Chad in 1980–1981.

Fourth, and most significant in the long run, the new states faced deep-seated problems of underdevelopment. At independence, average per capita income in the new states was usually less than $100 a year. Even as late as 1980, per capita income was $110 in Mali and Upper Volta, $130 in Chad, and little more in most of the sub-Saharan countries, except those endowed with oil deposits. Capital remained scarce, leaving most countries dependent on the Western powers and, to a much smaller degree, on the Communist bloc for investments. The increase in oil prices after 1973 imposed great burdens. Food supply was low, barely reaching 2,000 calories and usually consisting of cereals; pricing policies that held down the prices paid the rural population for agricultural produce in order to feed the large numbers of urban poor only exacerbated the situation. Illiteracy remained high. Improved medical care, which did reduce the scourges of malaria and cholera, also allowed population to increase.

THE RESURGENCE OF ISLAM

**The Rise of
Arab Nationalism**

In 1914 almost all Arabs lived under foreign rule. Morocco, which had been an independent kingdom since the eleventh century, was made a French protectorate in 1912. Algeria, whose *deys* had enjoyed virtual autonomy under the Ottoman empire, had been conquered by the French in 1830–1837; Tunisia, whose *beys* enjoyed a similar autonomy, was forced to become a French protectorate in 1881. Egypt, which had experienced real independence—although nominally an Ottoman province—since the reign of Mohammed Ali (pasha, 1805–1849), was occupied by Britain in 1882. The remaining Arabs, except those living as ethnic minorities in the colonies in sub-Saharan Africa, lived in the Ottoman Empire, where at least until the mid-nineteenth century they had been reconciled to Ottoman domination by their common Moslem religion and their traditions of theocratic government. During the late nineteenth century, however, the Arabs within the Ottoman Empire were stimulated by new nationalist leaders to the realization that they were as exploited by the Moslem Ottomans as were Arabs outside the Ottoman Empire by infidel Europeans.

Many forces united to stimulate the cause of Arab nationalism. Western ideas of national independence and of the economic advances such independence made possible were popular among intellectuals educated in Europe or in Western schools and universities such as those established by missionaries in Syria and Lebanon. Fundamentalist Moslem opposition to the secularization of Turkish rule was kindled in Arabia by the Wahabi reform movement, whose principal supporter was the emir of the southern Arabian state of Nejd. Although driven back on several occasions, under Ibn Saud (king, 1925–1953) the Wahabi forces were able to establish control of almost all the Arabian Peninsula in a kingdom they named Saudi Arabia in 1932. Other tribal rulers, like those of the Hashemite family in the Hejaz in northern Arabia, were determined to use the nationalist movement to create powerful family kingdoms. Finally, to poorer Arabs, whether in the cities or in the countryside, the Turks had come to represent a corrupt, oppressive regime whose primary purpose was self-enrichment.

The Allies capitalized on all these sources of resentment to enlist the Arabs against the Turks during the First World War. In 1916 the Hashemite Sherif Hussein, king of the Hejaz (which included the holy cities of Medina and Mecca) rose in revolt after receiving vague promises from the British of Arab independence, and played an important part in driving the Turks from the Arabian Peninsula. The British, however, had made other, conflicting promises. In May 1916 they had made the secret Sykes-Picot Agreement with the French, to divide up the Arab countries of the Near East between them in spheres of influence; and in November 1917 the British foreign secretary, Lord Balfour, had promised "the establishment in Palestine of a national home for the Jewish people." The Paris Peace Congress (1919) deeply disappointed the Arabs. Hussein remained ruler of the Hejaz Kingdom, which, however, was conquered in 1924–1925 by Ibn Saud. Hussein's sons were made kings of newly created Arab states—Faisal of Iraq and Abdullah of Transjordan; but Iraq and Transjordan, as well as Palestine, were placed under British mandate. Syria and Lebanon were made mandates of France. Egypt remained a British protectorate, and the Sudan was an Anglo-Egyptian condominium dominated in fact by the British. British control was equally strong on the princely states like Oman and Kuwait that lined the Arabian Peninsula's southern and eastern coasts.

Arab national feeling was therefore directed largely against the British and French during the interwar years. The French made few concessions. They joined with the Spanish to defeat the Moroccan tribal leader Abd-el-Krim, and made only minor efforts to associate the Algerian and Tunisian

The Swearing-In of Dr. Chaim Weizmann as President of Israel, 1949
Since 1920, Weizmann had been leader of world Zionism, the movement to create a Jewish national state in Palestine. He served as president of the new state of Israel until his death in 1952. (Popperfoto)

political leaders in government. In Lebanon they favored the Christian Arabs over the Moslems, although the two communities were almost equal in size; and in Syria they suppressed a rebellion by the People's Party. The French believed that education and economic development would assuage Arab discontent. The British were soon compelled to give up open control in the more rebellious Arab states. The Nationalist Wafd party in Egypt organized violent opposition and forced Britain to give up its protectorate in 1922 and to relinquish its remaining controls over internal security and foreign policy in 1936. Thousands of lives were lost in a popular revolt against the British in Iraq in 1920; but in 1930, after promising them the use of military bases and transportation facilities, Faisal was finally able to persuade the British to grant independence. Abdullah was rewarded for his cooperation by the grant of independence to Transjordan in 1927. In Palestine, however, the British found themselves caught between the demands of the native Arabs and those of the Jews, whose Zionist organization, under the leadership of Chaim Weizmann, was pressing for greater opportunities for immigration to Palestine. Although the British imposed strict controls, the Jewish population of Palestine rose from 65,000 in 1919 to 445,000 in 1939. Arabs, who had outnumbered the Jews by ten to one in 1919, thus were less than two to one by 1939. Violence between the two communities and of both against the British increased rapidly.

Oil in the Postwar Years

After the Second World War the character of the Arab states was transformed dramatically by three factors—their position as the world's major oil producers; Pan-Arab nationalism, stimulated especially by the creation of the Jewish state of Israel; and social revolution.

The first oil deposits to be found in the Middle East were discovered in Iran before the First World War and exploited by the Anglo-Iranian Oil

Company. In the interwar years a partnership of British, Dutch, French, and American capital opened up the fields of Iraq, which were linked by pipeline to Palestine and Lebanon. The most significant development, however, was the opening of the deposits of Saudi Arabia in the 1930s by the Arabian-American Oil Company (Aramco).

After 1945 the exploitation of Arab oil vastly increased. Saudi Arabian production alone was boosted from 165,000 barrels daily in 1945 to 500,000 in 1950 and a million in 1955. Vast new fields were discovered in Kuwait, Qatar, and Bahrein, and were worked by British and American companies. Discontent with the low prices charged by the oil companies and the inadequate share of profits paid to the oil-producing countries first led to violence in 1951, when the Iranian government of Dr. Mohammed Mossadeq nationalized the Anglo-Iranian Oil Company. In 1953 the shah, Mohammed Reza Pahlavi (reigned 1941–1979), dismissed Mossadeq, fled the country when rioting broke out, but returned with army support only a few days later. A temporary compromise was reached on the oil question by forming a new National Iranian Oil Company, in which the international companies were permitted to share. Until the 1960s, most of the oil-producing countries seemed satisfied to share profits equally with the oil companies.

A renewed movement of nationalization of oil production began in the 1970s. In 1971 Libya nationalized its industry, which was largely owned by the British, and Algeria took a fifty-one percent share in the French companies controlling its production. The following year, Iraq took over all the oil companies operating there. Even more important in increasing revenues, however, was the decision in 1971 of the Organization of Petroleum Exporting Countries (OPEC) to increase its members' share of profits and to post higher prices on a regular basis. In 1974, following an embargo by the Arab states on supply of oil to the United States and other allies of Israel during the Arab-Israeli war of October 1973, OPEC quadrupled prices, increasing its revenues that one year by up to $65 billion. By 1980, after many other rises, the price of oil was more than ten times higher than in 1972; and the balance of economic power in the world had been slanted toward the oil producers. Saudi Arabia, the largest producer of all, was expected to receive $90 billion in 1980 alone.

The Arab countries were not immune to the problems caused by the rise in oil prices. Arab countries with insufficient deposits of their own, like Egypt and Morocco, faced balance-of-payments problems. Conservative countries, faced with the expenditure of vast revenues, feared that modernization would destroy their authoritarian governments and their social values. Divisions occurred between radical states seeking rapid economic development from oil revenues and conservative regimes, often with smaller populations and larger oil reserves, aiming at more moderate price rises. Inflation in the oil-consuming countries fed by the oil price increases raised the cost to the oil producers of the goods on which they spent their revenues. Recession in the United States and the western European nations reduced their ability to purchase the oil offered, contributing in part to a glut in world oil supplies by 1981. Finally, the vast pool of petrodollars, shifting unpredictably in search of higher short-term returns, threatened chaos to the whole structure of Western trade and finance, from which the oil producers would be major sufferers.

<table>
<tr><td>

Arab Nationalism After the Second World War

</td><td>

During the Second World War and in the immediate postwar years, Arab nationalists posed three demands—the end of foreign domination, the prevention of a Jewish state in Palestine, and the eventual union of the Arab world. During the war the British had reassumed control of Iraq and Egypt, had shared with the French the occupation of Syria and Lebanon, and had joined with the Soviet Union in taking over Iran. However, contrary to their policy after the First World War, in 1945 they tried conciliation. They pressured the French to recognize the independence of Syria and Lebanon in 1946. In Iraq they relied on the friendship of the pro-Western premier, Nuri es-Said, who dominated the Iraqi government from 1943 to 1958. The government of Transjordan received military and financial aid. In Palestine, after first trying to find a plan that would satisfy both Jews and Arabs, the British turned the problem over to the United Nations and, as in India, hurriedly withdrew their troops in May 1948. The Jewish leader David Ben-Gurion immediately proclaimed the foundation of the state of Israel.

</td></tr>
</table>

It appeared in 1948 that the emergence of a common enemy, Israel, would bring about the Pan-Arab unity that had been preached since the 1930s by the followers of Chekib Arslan, the author of a highly influential tract called *The Arab Nation*. The member countries of the Arab League— formed in 1945 by Iraq, Syria, Lebanon, Transjordan, Saudi Arabia, and Egypt—struck into Palestine on several fronts but, disunited and poorly armed, were rapidly defeated by the Israelis. All signed armistice agreements between February and April 1949. The new Israeli state survived the Arab economic boycott that followed with the help of contributions from Jews throughout the world, German reparations payments, and intense efforts at economic reconstruction.

To maintain the intense hatred of Israel, the neighboring Arab states refused to seek a solution to the problem of the Palestinian Arabs. The 900,000 who had fled from Israel during the fighting were housed in refugee camps around the borders of Israel. Transjordan annexed the territory of Palestine on the west bank of the Jordan, and Egypt annexed the Gaza Strip on the southern coast of Palestine, thus making it impossible to create a Palestinian Arab state as called for in the partition plan approved by the United Nations.

<table>
<tr><td>

Nasser and the Nationalization of the Suez Canal

</td><td>

Defeat in the war with Israel brought about political revolution in the Arab world. Syria experienced the first of a series of coup d'états in 1949, when the army overthrew the civilian government. It did not recover political stability until 1970, when the more pragmatic wing of the leading Ba'ath party, led by General Hafez al-Assad, drove out the more radical

</td></tr>
</table>

Egyptian President Gamal Nasser and Algerian Premier Ahmed Ben Bella, 1962
As president (1956–1970), Nasser supported left-wing and anticolonial forces throughout the Arab world. His aid to the Algerian forces fighting for independence from France was a significant factor in their victory in 1962. (United Press International, Inc.)

wing. In Egypt resentment turned against corrupt King Farouk, who in 1952 was ousted in an army plot that placed in power first General Mohammed Naguib and then, two years later, Colonel Gamal Abdel Nasser. The governments of both Naguib and Nasser attempted massive social reform in Egypt, redistributing the land to the peasants and seeking rapid economic development through industrialization and especially the building of a high dam at Aswan on the Upper Nile.

Nasser, however, had wider ambitions—to make himself the leader of the Arab world. To strengthen Egypt militarily, he accepted arms from Czechoslovakia and the Soviet Union, thereby infuriating the United States. He took the lead in the struggle with Israel by fomenting border clashes and denying use of the Suez Canal to Israeli shipping. He annoyed the French by supporting with money and propaganda the independence movements that were rapidly increasing in size in Tunisia and Morocco, and thus was partly responsible for forcing the French to grant those two countries their independence in 1956. It was Nasser's decision to give military training in Egypt to the guerrillas of the Algerian National Liberation Front that persuaded the French that it was necessary to overthrow him.

The British reached the same decision in 1956 when Nasser, who had suddenly been refused financial backing by the U.S. government for construction of the Aswan Dam, nationalized the British- and French-owned Suez Canal. In November 1956 Israeli forces invaded the Sinai Peninsula, and immediately afterwards British and French forces seized the Suez Canal against fierce Egyptian opposition. They were forced to withdraw ignominiously, however, under pressure from both the Soviet Union and the United States.

Nasser's prestige in the Arab world was further strengthened by the temporary fusion of Egypt and Syria in the United Arab Republic in 1958. This agreement was followed by the brutal murder by a Baghdad mob of Nasser's principal rival, the pro-British Iraqi premier Nuri es-Said, as well as of King Faisal II (reigned 1939–1958) and the crown prince. General Kassim, who had carried out the Iraqi coup, disappointed Nasser by challenging his leadership, but he was executed in a 1963 coup that brought a pro-Nasser government to power.

Although Syria withdrew from the United Arab Republic in 1961, Nasser continued to press for closer Arab unity. He revived the Arab League and intensified the quarrels with Israel. In 1967, after Nasser had requested the end of a United Nations peacekeeping force in Sinai and had closed the Gulf of Aqaba to Israeli shipping, the Israelis suddenly carried out a preemptive war and in six days (June 5–10) defeated the forces of Egypt, Jordan, and Syria. At the war's end Israel retained control of the Golan Heights in Syria, the west bank of the Jordan and the old city of Jerusalem, the Gaza Strip, and the Sinai Peninsula. In the three years before his death in 1970, Nasser became even more dependent on the Soviet Union, which replaced his lost military equipment and sent some 20,000 advisers to Egypt.

Growing Divisions of Radical and Conservative Governments

During the 1960s and 1970s only the common hatred of Israel and a common interest in increased oil revenues seemed to hold together the increasingly divergent radical and conservative regimes in the Arab world. During the 1960s the leader of the radical Arab states was Algeria, which won its independence from France in 1962 after seven years of fighting in which 10,000 French and 100,000 Arabs were killed. Under Ben Bella in 1962–1965 and Houari Boumedienne in 1965–1978, attempts were made to carry out an internal social revolution. Most of the French settlers fled for fear of violence, and their property was expropriated. Banks, mines, and other industrial sectors were nationalized in the 1960s, and in 1971 French-owned oil and natural gas companies were taken over. Other Arab states moved more rapidly leftward in their internal policies and alliances.

Libya, the former Italian colony that became independent in 1951, was taken over in 1969 in a coup by a group of young army officers led by Colonel Muammar al-Qaddafi. The conservative monarchy was abolished; and Qaddafi, using his vast oil revenues to compensate for the small size of his country's population (three million in 1980), attempted to make Libya a major world power. The Soviet Union sold Libya large quantities of sophisticated military equipment and supplied advisers and technical experts. Qaddafi supplied financial aid to terrorist groups operating in many countries and gave direct support to guerrillas attempting to overthrow the moderate regime of President Habib Bourguiba in Tunisia. In 1980 Libyan forces intervened in the civil war in neighboring Chad.

A similar desire to create a revolutionary Moslem state inspired the overthrow of the shah of Iran in 1979. Iran, though not an ethnically Arab state, was comparable in many ways to its Arab neighbors. Its autocratic ruler, Reza Pahlevi, had attempted to use vast oil revenues in a rapid modernization program. Highways, ports, and factories had been constructed. Land was distributed to the peasants. A semblance of parliamentary government had been introduced. But the shah had remained autocratic, employing a savage secret police to cow opposition and pouring revenues into a vast army and air force that was intended to maintain his power both at home and abroad. Corruption was endemic, with the shah and his family setting the example by amassing huge private fortunes. The pent-up resentment exploded when the fundamentalist Moslem leader, the Ayatollah Khomeini, launched crowds of students and workers against the shah's regime, which collapsed within days.

Ayatollah Khomeini, Iran, 1979

The revolution in Iran in 1979, led by Khomeini, was not only a rejection of the corruption and repression of the Shah's regime but also an attempt to recreate a fundamentalist Islamic society in which the mullahs, or clergy, would exercise a predominant role. (Abbas/Gamma/Liaison)

THE RESURGENCE OF ISLAM

1439

In some respects the new regime was clearly radical. Banks, insurance companies, and some industries were nationalized; foreign debts were repudiated. Hundreds were executed, and revolutionary guards controlled the streets. The year-long imprisonment of U.S. embassy employees by terrorists was supported by the new government. But the regime was also backward looking. Islamic purity was demanded. Women were expected to give up Western dress, and many lost their jobs. Leftist opposition groups were forced to go underground, and military force was used against ethnic minorities demanding greater autonomy.

Iraq became perhaps the most radical of the Arab states after a take-over of power in 1968. Public executions of accused spies for Israel were held. The Communist party was legalized and a treaty of friendship and alliance signed with the Soviet Union. Foreign oil companies were nationalized and the revenues plowed back into social programs at home. Iraq too rebuilt its military forces with purchases from the Soviet Union and France, partly to enforce its demands on neighboring Iran, with which it went to war in 1980.

In contrast with the radical states were the semifeudal regimes of Saudi Arabia and the states on the Persian Gulf. Dominated by members of the Saud royal family and run as a theocratic Islamic state, Saudi Arabia nevertheless embarked on large-scale modernization programs made possible by its possession of the world's largest oil reserves. Under its first king, Ibn Saud (reigned 1925–1953), it had begun to build schools, roads, railroads, and ports. Under Faisal, who ran the government first for his brother Saud (reigned 1953–1964) and then, after deposing Saud, in his own name from 1964 to 1975, the modernization program was speeded up. Large contracts were awarded to American and West European companies for industrial projects and for armaments, and rapid urbanization programs led to the growth of such cities as Riyadh and Ad-Dammam.

Similar programs were undertaken in the Gulf States in a comparable attempt to create economic modernization without affecting the conservative basis of their societies. Of the few Arab leaders who attempted to maintain a road between the conservatives and the radicals, perhaps the most important was Egypt's Anwar Sadat (president, 1970–1981). Sadat, who had been a military cadet with Nasser in the 1930s and had succeeded him as president, gave the first indication of a change in policy when in 1972 he expelled Egypt's Soviet advisers; but he reverted to Nasser's policies the following year, during the Yom Kippur War, by launching the Egyptian army against Israeli troops occupying Sinai, while Syrian troops attacked in the Golan Heights. After initial defeats the Israelis succeeded in reestablishing control in the southern section of the Suez Canal before international intervention led to a cease-fire.

Sadat then reversed his policies again. In 1975 he promised less militancy against Israel to gain return of part of the Sinai. In 1977 he made a dramatic and courageous visit to Israel to open new relations that might end the Arab-Israeli conflict peacefully. Finally, in 1978 he signed the

Signing of the Camp David Agreement, 1978

Egyptian President Anwar Sadat's willingness to negotiate directly with Israeli Premier Menachem Begin, under the sponsorship of U.S. President Jimmy Carter, provoked great animosity toward Sadat in the Arab world and was one reason for his assassination in 1981. (SYGMA)

Camp David accords with Israeli Premier Menachem Begin and U.S. President Jimmy Carter. These agreements promised Israeli withdrawal from Sinai and the future negotiation of autonomy for Palestinians in the Israeli-occupied territories of the West Bank and the Gaza Strip. Sadat thus completed the transition from friendship with the Soviet Union to reliance on the United States and the other Western powers for military and financial support. After his assassination in 1981 by Moslem fundamentalists, the prospects for a lasting peace in the Middle East appeared far less promising.

SOLUTIONS NEW AND OLD IN LATIN AMERICA

In many ways Latin America's problems have worsened in the twentieth century. First, underlying all other difficulties, is the growth of population, which improved medical care and food supply brought to calamitously high rates. Population had grown from 70 million in 1900 to 158 million by 1950, 200 million in 1960, and 320 million by 1975. Growing at a rate of almost three percent annually, it was expected to exceed 600 million by 2000. Hence every increase in production was almost immediately offset by increased population.

Second, except in a few countries such as Mexico and Cuba, where land reform has been carried out with some success, the share of the land owned by the peasantry has actually decreased, especially as modernization of productive techniques has made the great estates more efficient and less dependent on manual labor.

Third, the city slums have expanded at a frightening rate as a result of the influx of the excess population from the countryside, posing not only almost insoluble problems of public health, housing, and schooling, but also even more intractable difficulties in providing employment. Mexico City, for example, was thought to have a population of 1.5 million shanty dwellers in 1964.

Fourth, the trends of the world economy in the twentieth century turned against the monoculture that had been developed in the late nineteenth century. During the First and Second world wars Latin America could neither export its raw materials and minerals, except within the Western Hemisphere, nor obtain the manufactured goods on which it depended. Perhaps even more disastrous was the Great Depression, which drove down world prices for almost everything exported by Latin America, from copper and tin to rubber and sugar.

Fifth, foreign economic and military intervention continued, with the United States displacing the European countries as the principal source of outside capital and as the dominant force in laying down the direction of economic development. In Central America in particular, the system of monoculture was maintained, but United States companies also began to penetrate by investing in manufacturing plants where low-cost labor permitted cheaper production than in the United States. Unfortunately, President John F. Kennedy's Alliance for Progress of 1961, the major effort by a United States government to support economic development and social reform, made only minor gains. United States military intervention also continued, from the dispatching of marines to Nicaragua in 1912 to intervention in the Dominican Republic in 1965.

Faced with these problems, Latin American countries attempted three types of solutions. The most widespread was a return to authoritarian rule, usually by the military, in reinforcement of the social and economic privileges of the old elites, though often with the self-justification that order and economic progress went in tandem. The most repressive of these regimes were the dictatorships in the Central American and Caribbean countries, such as those of the Somoza family in Nicaragua, of Rafael Trujillo in the Dominican Republic, and of Fulgencio Batista in Cuba. More important, however, was the takeover of the largest and wealthiest states of Latin America by right-wing military regimes in the 1960s. Brazil was seized by the military in 1964 and was thrust into a rapid program of industrialization with the aid of foreign capital. For a number of years the economy boomed, led by such manufacturing industries as automobiles and textiles. The sparkling new capital city of Brasília was completed. The income per capita reached $1,570 by 1978. But the gains were purchased at the price of brutal police controls and of the worsening of the inequitable division of the country's income and wealth.

Labor discontent and disputed elections gave the military the excuse to take power in Bolivia, Paraguay, and Uruguay. In Chile the army alleged that the economic chaos created by the far-reaching economic reform program of the government of the Marxist president Salvador Allende (president 1970–1973) justified their imposition in 1973 of a viciously repressive regime. Similarly, the Argentine army claimed in 1976 that the country's chaotic descent into terrorism of both left and right made it necessary for it to overthrow the government of Isabel Perón and seize power itself.

A second solution was a reforming government, based on a fairly wide spectrum of popular support, that could embark on a more or less ambitious renovation of the economic and social structure—without, however, undertaking a full program of socialization. The Mexican revolution, despite a swing to the right in the 1950s, when once again the growth of large capitalist industries and great estates was encouraged, achieved a great deal during its first forty years. The constitution of 1917 guaranteed economic as well as political rights, including the right to strike, the eight-hour working day, and the restoration of communal lands taken since 1856. Many new schools and universities were constructed. Millions of acres were taken from the great estates and given to the peasants, especially under President Lázaro Cárdenas, who redistributed forty-five million acres. In 1938 the oil industry was nationalized, giving Mexico control of what proved in the 1970s to be some of the greatest reserves in the world.

Drastic social reform was also attempted by a few military regimes. After seizing power in 1968, the military in Peru nationalized the basic industries, redistributed much of the farmland among the peasants, and then restored civilian rule in 1980. The military regime that took over Panama in 1968 was successful in persuading the United States to relinquish control of the Panama Canal. The military in Ecuador, after seizing power in 1972, also attempted some land reform and controls over the foreign oil companies, but gave up power in 1979 with little achieved.

In Costa Rica and Venezuela reforms were carried out by stable democratic governments. Costa Rica was unusual in Latin America in conducting regular elections in which parties alternated in power, and was unique in abolishing its army in 1948. Venezuela, which had been governed by a military dictatorship since 1948, restored civilian rule in 1958 and provided a further example of moderate reform, which was made possible by its rapid increase in revenues from oil in the 1970s.

The third solution, a Marxist or Communist regime, was first attempted in Cuba when Fidel Castro, after fighting a two-year guerrilla war against the Batista dictatorship, took power in 1959. The large sugar estates became state farms. Foreign-owned industry, hotels, and other holdings were nationalized. A party dictatorship was created, using imprisonment, "schools of revolutionary instruction," and surveillance of suspected dissidents. For the masses, however, better schooling, health care, and working conditions won genuine loyalty and enabled the Castro regime to pose

Cuban Premier Fidel Castro at the United Nations, 1979
Since taking power in 1959, Castro has acted as spokesman for the revolutionary aspirations of Third World peoples and has aided insurgent forces in Africa and Latin America with soldiers and military supplies. (Michael Evans/Gamma/Liaison)

as a model for liberation movements throughout the Third World, such as the Sandinista movement, which overthrew the Somoza regime in Nicaragua in 1979.

Thus for Latin America, as for the other countries of the Third World, the problems of underdevelopment and overpopulation promised continuing involvement in the Cold War confrontation between the Western and Soviet blocs, since the choice of a solution to those problems was seen to imply commitment to the ideology of one bloc or the other.

SUGGESTED READING

Mary C. Wright has edited articles dealing with various aspects of the 1911 revolution in *China in Revolution: The First Phase, 1900–1913* (1968); but it is more revealing to follow the personalities in Ernest P. Young, *The Presidency of Yüan Shih-k'ai: Liberalism and Dictatorship in Early Republican China* (1977) and in two good biographies of Sun Yat-sen: Harold Z. Schiffrin, *Sun Yat-sen and the Origins of the Chinese Revolution* (1968) and C. Martin Wilbur, *Sun Yat-sen: Frustrated Patriot* (1976). The warlords become more than monster figures when approached individually through the scholarly biographies of James E. Sheridan, *Chinese Warlord: The Career of Feng Yu-hsiang* (1966) and Donald G. Gillin, *Warlord: Yen Hsi-shan in Shansi Province, 1911–1949* (1967). The basic work on the cultural and popular political movements in China around the time of the First World War is Chow Tse-tsung, *The May Fourth Movement: Intellectual Revolution in Modern China* (1960). The Kuomintang is studied in Hung-mao

Tien, *Government and Politics in Kuomintang China, 1927–1937* (1972) and in Lloyd E. Eastman, *The Abortive Revolution: China Under Nationalist Rule, 1927–1937* (1974).

Mao Tse-tung and his followers were made known in the West with publication of Edgar Snow, *Red Star over China* (1938). Stuart Schramm, *Mao Tse-tung* (1967) and Jerome Ch'en, *Mao and the Chinese Revolution* (1967) are reliable biographies of the great helmsman. For specialized articles on the Chinese city in the early twentieth century, see Mark Elvin and G. William Skinner, eds., *The Chinese City Between Two Worlds* (1974).

Wang Gungwu, *China and the World Since 1949: The Impact of Independence, Modernity, and Revolution* (1977) effectively relates the internal struggles of the Communist party to shifts in economic and international policy; Jean Chesneaux, *China: The People's Republic, 1949–1976* (1979) illustrates the political narrative with telling citations from both the summit and the base of Communist Chinese society. Firsthand observations of the Cultural Revolution may be found in Maria Antonietta Macciocchi, *Daily Life in Revolutionary China* (1972). The American playwright Arthur Miller was successful in persuading many of those who suffered in the Cultural Revolution to reveal their experiences. See Arthur Miller and Inge Morath, *Chinese Encounters* (1979). For change within the large southern city of Canton, see Ezra Vogel, *Canton Under Communism: Programs and Politics in a Provincial Capital, 1949–1968* (1969); John Wilson Lewis, ed., *The City in Communist China* (1971) explores the themes of order and modernization. David Bonavia and the Editors of Time-Life Books, *Peking* (1978) describes the details of daily life in the Chinese capital.

Edwin O. Reischauer, *The Japanese* (1977) is a highly informed introduction to twentieth-century Japan. The political struggles of the period from 1912 to 1926, during the reign of the Taisho emperor, are discussed in Peter Duus, *Party Rivalry and Political Change in Taisho Japan* (1968). The influence of the military in politics can be followed through the career of Tojo in Robert Butow, *Tojo and the Coming of the War* (1961). The politics of the years since the U.S. occupation are explained in Nathaniel Thayer, *How the Conservatives Rule Japan* (1969) and Nobutake Ike, *Japanese Politics: Patron-Client Democracy* (1972). For Japan's economic achievements in the twentieth century, see William W. Lockwood, *The Economic Development of Japan: Growth and Structural Change* (1954) and Byron K. Marshall, *Capitalism and Nationalism in Prewar Japan: The Ideology of the Business Elite, 1868–1941* (1967). David Kornhauser, *Urban Japan: Its Foundation and Growth* (1976) is an excellent short introduction but should be supplemented by a more detailed case study such as Gary D. Allinson, *Japanese Urbanism: Industry and Politics in Kariya, 1872–1972* (1975), which describes the city dominated by the Toyota automobile company, or, also by Allinson, *Suburban Tokyo: A Comparative Study in Politics and Social Change* (1979). Conditions in the 1950s are described in the fine study by Ronald P. Dore, *City Life in Japan* (1967).

The Indian independence movement should be approached through the words of its two principal leaders. See Mohandas K. Gandhi, *Gandhi—An Autobiography—The Story of My Experiments with Truth* (1970), as well as the more detailed descriptions in his *Young India, 1919–1922* (1924) and *Hind Swaraj* (Indian Home Rule), rev. ed. (1946). Jawaharlal Nehru described his role in the early struggles in *Toward Freedom* (1941) and his later activities in *An Autobiography* (1962). Biographical studies of the two include Krishna Kripalani, *Gandhi—A Life*

(1969); Dorothy Nomran, ed., *Nehru: The First Sixty Years*, 2 vols. (1965); and Michael Brecher, *Nehru: A Political Biography* (1970). Clement Attlee discusses briefly the attitude of the British Labour party toward Indian independence in *Twilight of Empire* (1962). On the end of the British Raj, see Michael Edwards, *The Last Years of British India* (1963) and T. W. Wellbank, ed., *The Partition of India* (1966). Problems of the Nehru period following independence are analyzed in W. Norman Brown, *The United States and India, Pakistan, Bangladesh* (1972) and P. J. Griffiths, *Modern India* (1965). The years of collective leadership and the personal rule of Indira Gandhi that followed are excellently surveyed in Stanley Wolpert, *A New History of India* (1977). More personal details can be found in Anand Mohan, *Indira Gandhi: A Personal and Political Biography* (1967) and M. K. Alexander, *Madame Gandhi: A Political Biography* (1969). On Pakistan, see K. B. Sayeed, *Pakistan: The Formative Phase, 1857–1948*, 2nd ed. (1968) and Herbert Feldman, *From Crisis to Crisis: Pakistan, 1962–1969* (1972). The creation of Bangladesh is explained in Subrata Roy Chowdhury, *The Genesis of Bangladesh* (1972).

The transition from British rule in Southeast Asia is masterfully analyzed by Nicholas Mansergh in *Survey of British Commonwealth Affairs: Problems of War-Time Co-operation and Post-War Change* (1958). On individual countries, see Frank N. Trager, *Burma's Independence* (1966); Willard A. Hanna, *The Formation of Malaysia* (1964); Wang Gungwu, ed., *Malaysia: A Survey* (1964); and Richard Butwell, *Southeast Asia Today and Tomorrow*, 2nd ed. (1964). Arend Lijphart, *The Trauma of Decolonization: The Dutch and West New Guinea* (1966) traces the evolution of Dutch thinking on decolonization. On Indonesian independence, see L. H. Palmier, *Indonesia and the Dutch* (1962) and J. D. Legge, *Indonesia* (1964).

A good historical survey of Indochina is John F. Cady, *Southeast Asia: Its Historical Development* (1964). French defeat in Vietnam is described in Ellen J. Hammer, *The Struggle for Indo-China* (1954); Donald Lancaster, *The Emancipation of French Indochina* (1961) and Bernard Fall, *The Two Viet Nams*, 2nd ed. (1967). On U.S. involvement in Vietnam, see David Halberstam, *The Best and the Brightest* (1972) and Frances FitzGerald, *Fire in the Lake: The Vietnamese and the Americans in Vietnam* (1972).

There is now an enormous literature on twentieth-century Africa. The origins of national independence movements and of the very concept of African nationalism are treated in Thomas Hodgkin, *Nationalism in Colonial Africa* (1957) and Guy Hunter, *The New Societies of Tropical Africa* (1962). A comparison of the movement in the colonies of different European nations may be made by studying reaction to British rule in Nigeria and Ghana in J. S. Coleman, *Nigeria: Background to Nationalism* (1958) and David Apter, *Ghana in Transition*, rev. ed. (1963); to French rule, in Michael Crowder, *Senegal: A Study of French Assimilation Policy*, rev. ed. (1967); and to Belgian rule, in Roger Anstey, *King Leopold's Legacy* (1966) and Crawford Young, *Politics in the Congo: Decolonization and Independence* (1965). On the struggles against regimes dominated by white settlers, see G. Bennett, *Kenya: A Political History* (1963); James Barber, *Rhodesia: The Road to Rebellion* (1967); Patrick O'Meara, *Rhodesia: Racial Conflict or Coexistence* (1975); and Gwendolen M. Carter and Patrick O'Meara, *Southern Africa in Crisis* (1977). To keep up with the rapidly changing situation in Africa, see the annual publication *Africa Contemporary Report*.

For historical perspective on Islam, see the massive three-volume work by

Marshall G. S. Hodgson, *The Venture of Islam: Conscience and History in a World Civilization* (1974) and the more accessible Bernard Lewis, *The Arabs in History*, 3rd ed. (1956), as well as his *Islam and the Arab World* (1976). British withdrawal from the Middle East is described in Elizabeth Monroe, *Britain's Moment in the Middle East, 1914–1956* (1963) and in George Kirk's volume, written for the Royal Institute of International Affairs, *Survey of International Affairs: The Middle East, 1945–1950* (1954). On the problems of relations of Israel and the Palestinian Arabs, see John N. Moore, *The Arab-Israeli Conflict: Readings and Documents* (1977) and William R. Polk, David M. Stamler, and Edmund Asfour, *Backdrop to Tragedy: The Struggle for Palestine* (1957). On Nasser's Egypt, see Jean and Simon Lecouture, *Egypt in Transition* (1958); and, on the British and French attempt to overthrow him by their invasion of Suez in 1956, see Guy Wint and Peter Calvocoressi, *Middle East Crisis* (1957) and Hugh Thomas, *The Suez Affair* (1967). Soviet penetration of the Islamic world is the subject of two reliable books by Walter B. Laqueur, *Communism and Nationalism in the Middle East* (1956) and *The Soviet Union and the Middle East* (1959). The finances of Middle Eastern oil before the price rises of the 1970s are discussed in Zuhayr Mkdashi, *A Financial Analysis of Middle Eastern Oil Concessions, 1901–1965* (1966); the finances of the oil companies are critically surveyed in Anthony Sampson, *The Seven Sisters* (1975).

Celso Furtado, *The Economic Development of Latin America* (1970) analyzes the enormous problems of Latin America in the twentieth century. It can be supplemented with the annual *Economic Survey of Latin America* published since 1948 by the Economic Commission for Latin America. The growth of population, which underlies all the economic problems, is described in Nicolás Sánchez-Albornoz, *The Population of Latin America* (1974). The suffering of the poor is described in E. R. Wolf and E. C. Hansen, eds., *The Human Condition in Latin America* (1972) and John Gerassi, *The Great Fear in Latin America* (1965). The cities, as the recipient of the excess population of the countryside, have mushroomed, as can be seen in W. D. Harris, *The Growth of Latin American Cities* (1971) and Jorge Hardoy, ed., *Urbanization in Latin America: Approaches and Issues* (1975). On the first of the twentieth-century revolutions in Latin America, see Frank Tannenbaum, *Mexico: The Struggle for Peace and Bread* (1950) and Howard Cline, *Mexico: Revolution to Evolution, 1940–1960* (1963). Useful studies of the Andean states include H. S. Klein, *Parties and Political Change in Bolivia, 1880–1952* (1969); James Malloy, *Bolivia: The Uncompleted Revolution* (1970); F. B. Pike, *The Modern History of Peru* (1967); and, for the Peruvian military regime's left-wing economic policies after 1968, E.V.K. Fitzgerald, *The State and Economic Development: Peru Since 1968* (1976). The Allende reform program in Chile is analyzed in Stefan de Vylder, *Allende's Chile* (1976) and P. E. Sigmund, *The Overthrow of Allende and the Politics of Chile, 1964–1976* (1977). Argentine politics are described in a good collection of essays edited by David Rock, *Argentina in the Twentieth Century* (1975). Contemporary Brazil is well surveyed in Rollie Poppino, *Brazil: The Land and the People*, 2nd ed. (1973) and Peter Flynn, *Brazil: A Political Analysis* (1978). On the military regime, see also G. A. Fiechter, *Brazil Since 1964—Modernization Under a Military Regime* (1975). Cuba's revolution under Fidel Castro is set in a historical background in Hugh Thomas, *Cuba: The Pursuit of Freedom* (1971). Carmelo Mesa Lago attempts an objective assessment of Castro's achievements in *Revolutionary Change in Cuba* (1971) and *Cuba in the 1970s*, rev. ed. (1978).

32

THE CONTEMPORARY AGE IN THE WEST

T hey fought the enemy," wrote the American poet Marianne Moore of the soldiers in the Second World War. "We fight/fat living and self-pity. Shine, O shine/unfalsifying sun, on this sick scene."[1]

The desolation left by the Second World War seemed to many in the West to be spiritual as well as material. Not only had there been immense destruction of the productive capacity so painfully built up in a century of industrialization, and of an even older cultural heritage. Indeed the malaise sank deeper into the Western consciousness, marked above all by a sense of personal involvement in the vast inhumanity of the preceding decade. The Soviet poet Yevtushenko expressed this feeling in his meditation "Babiy Yar," which concerns a hillside near Kiev where thousands of Jews had been massacred:

> *Over Babiy Yar*
> *there are no memorials.*
> *The steep hillside like a rough inscription.*
> *I am frightened.*
> *Today I am as old as the Jewish race.*
> *I seem to myself a Jew at this moment.*
> *I, wandering in Egypt.*
> *I, crucified. I perishing. . . .*

[1] Reprinted with permission of the Macmillan Company and Faber and Faber Ltd. from *The Complete Poems of Marianne Moore* by Marianne Moore. Copyright 1951 by Marianne Moore.

Georges Pompidou National Center of Art and Culture, Paris *(H. Roger-Viollet)*

Over Babiy Yar
rustle of the wild grass.
The trees look threatening, look like judges.
And everything is one silent cry.
Taking my hat off
I feel myself slowly going grey.
And I am one silent cry
over the many thousands of the buried;
am every old man killed here,
every child killed here. [2]

The problem of reconstruction was therefore of many dimensions. The physical damage had to be repaired, and the economy modernized. The traditional forms of society had to be changed, either by democratic modification or by revolutionary overthrow, to meet the demands of dissatisfied segments of the populace. But there had also to be spiritual stock-

Brandenburg Gate, East Berlin

The boundary between the Soviet zone and West Berlin cut across Unter den Linden behind the gate, leaving the historic center of Berlin in Communist control. (Courtesy of the German Information Center)

[2]Reprinted from Yevtushenko, *Selected Poems*, trans. Robin Milner-Gulland and Peter Levi (Penguin Modern European Poets, 1962), p. 83. Copyright Robin Milner-Gulland and Peter Levi, 1962. Reprinted by permission of Penguin Books Ltd.

taking, the coming to terms with the past and the formulation of a new sense of cultural identity. And this challenging task had to be undertaken in a time of unparalleled tension. Even before the Second World War had ended, the Soviet Union and the United States had confronted each other in an ideological conflict that soon divided Europe once again into two armed camps, both possessing continually growing mastery of the destructive power of nuclear energy. The economic and social reconstruction of Europe had to be undertaken under the direct influence of this clash of opposing ideologies. Eastern Europe was compelled to create a new form of society on the pattern of the Soviet Union; Western Europe revived its prewar political and economic structure, with some modifications, through the aid of the United States. The predominance of Europe and North America in the international state system was challenged by the reemergence of China as a world power and by the winning of independence by most of the European colonial territories in Asia and Africa; and when the United States attempted in the former French territories of Southeast Asia to repel the combined forces of Communism and nationalism, it suffered its most shattering reverse of the postwar years. The West's precarious reliance on the Middle Eastern states for the major part of its oil supplies was underlined by staggering price rises imposed by the producing countries, by left-wing and fundamentalist Islamic revolutions, and by the military advance of the Soviet Union into Afghanistan in 1979. Both Communist and non-Communist powers in the industrialized West and the oil-producing nations elsewhere, faced by the extreme poverty of the overpopulated and underdeveloped countries of the rest of the world, found themselves cast as the "haves" in a world of "have-nots." It was not surprising, therefore, that in spite of the restoration of its economic well-being, the spiritual unease of the West seemed only to intensify. In the 1980s Western civilization was increasingly uncertain of its course, or indeed of its very survival.

CULTURE IN AN AGE OF UNREST

In the immediate aftermath of the Second World War, many writers tried to come to terms with the enormity of suffering the war had inflicted and especially with the problem of human guilt and atonement. At first it was necessary to express what had been done, as when the Resistance writer Vercors described in *The Arms of Night* (1946) how the concentration camps in Germany had been used to destroy not only men's bodies but their ability to function as human beings. But it was also necessary to deal with the underlying causes of the inhumanity. For some the corruption of society had to be blamed; coming back to East Berlin in 1945, Bertolt Brecht summed up his condemnation in his play *Mother Courage*. Jean Anouilh demonstrated the corruption of power at all times and in all places in his new version of *Antigone*; Carlo Levi, pondering on his expe-

Albert Camus (1913–1960)
(Courtesy of French Embassy Press and Information Division)

rience of exile in a remote village of southern Italy in *Christ Stopped at Eboli* (1947), found much human suffering in the sheer inertia of an underdeveloped society. But some of the most telling commentaries sought moral or religious judgments on the wartime experience.

Albert Camus's *The Plague* (1947) presents a gruesome picture of the town of Oran in French Algeria during an outbreak of plague brought by infected rats. The town is isolated from the outer world, to live out, in a kind of allegory, the variegated human reactions to an intensity of suffering. At first, Camus describes the sense of exile of those imprisoned in the plague-ridden town, "that sensation of a void within which never left us, that irrational longing to hark back to the past or else to speed up the march of time, and those keen shafts of memory that stung like fire." Then follows a sense of panic as realization of the full danger and horror of the disease sinks in; then an interlude of complete lethargy, followed by an attempt to fight back against the disease; and at last a feeling that all individual destinies have been replaced by a "collective destiny, made up of plague and the emotions shared by all." And, when the gates of the city are opened at the end of the plague, Camus sees in microcosm the experience of all Europe at war's end:

Among the heaps of corpses, the clanging bells of ambulances, the warnings of what goes by the name of fate, among unremitting waves of fear and agonized revolt, the horror that such things could be, always a great voice had been ringing in the ears of these forlorn, panicked people, a voice calling them back to the land of their desire, a homeland. It lay outside the walls of the stifled, strangled town, in the fragrant brushwood of the hills, in the waves of the sea, under free skies, and in the custody of love. And it was to this, their lost home, toward happiness, they longed to return, turning their backs disgustedly on all else. . . .

None the less, he knew that the tale he had to tell could not be one of final victory. It could be only the record of what had had to be done, and what assuredly would have to be done again in the never ending fight against terror and its relentless onslaught. [He knew] that the plague bacillus never dies or disappears for good; that it can lie dormant for years and years in furniture and linen-chests; that it bides its time in bedrooms, cellars, trunks, and bookshelves; and that perhaps the day would come when, for the bane and the enlightenment of men, it would rouse up its rats again and send them forth to die in a happy city. [3]

The most popular answer to the question of personal responsibility was given by the existentialist philosophers, of whom Jean Paul Sartre was the most influential. For several years Sartre held court in the cafes of the Left Bank in Paris, teaching his large group of young disciples that everyone has complete freedom of choice in action and that by actions one not only gives value to his life but creates his own being. In a world that was absurd, meaningless, and incomprehensible, action in even the most baffling circumstances was essential. Sartre's ideas had a great vogue until the

[3] Albert Camus, *The Plague*, trans. Stuart Gilbert (New York: Knopf, 1962), pp. 65, 270, 278.

mid-1950s, when his retreat into a dogmatic defense of Communism lost him many followers. His demand for choice even rings mutedly, with religious overtones, in T. S. Eliot's play *The Cocktail Party*, in which the brittle chatter of an inconsequential party at the Chamberlaynes', whose marriage is breaking apart, culminates in acceptance of hard personal choices by each of the guests. One of them goes off to Africa and is crucified, whereupon the psychiatrist, who represents the wisdom of God, remarks:

> *. . . it was obvious*
> *That here was a woman under sentence of death.*
> *That was her destiny. The only question*
> *Then was, what sort of death? I could not know;*
> *Because it was for her to choose the way of life*
> *To lead to death, and without knowing the end*
> *Yet choose the form of death. . . .*

> Julia: *Everyone makes a choice, of one kind or another,*
> *And then must take the consequences. Celia chose*
> *A way of which the consequence was crucifixion;*
> *And now the consequence of the Chamberlaynes' choice*
> *Is a cocktail party.*[4]

The very inconsequence of the Chamberlaynes' choice gave it significance befitting their lives.

In the 1950s and 1960s the sense of disquiet remained, though its expression was directed at new targets. In England, for example, the protests of the "angry young men" represented outrage at continuing social discrimination. In France the rejection of the middle classes and especially of the wealthy upper crust, which had been stridently demanded by Sartre, took on forms of deliberately outrageous absurdity, in the plays of Jean Genet or the semi-monologues of Samuel Becket. In Germany, with Günter Grass and Heinrich Böll, the criticism was often brilliantly satirical. In the Soviet bloc, protest against the inhumanity of political intolerance achieved great psychological insight, as in Alexander Solzhenitsyn's *Cancer Ward*, or the Hungarian Tibor Dery's *Niki: The Portrait of a Dog*. In the United States, some of the finest writing expressed the suffering and the hopes of minority groups. The black search for identity, which had been cogently dramatized as early as 1940 in Richard Wright's *Native Son*, took on new dimensions in Ralph Ellison's *Invisible Man* (1952), which shows that even in personal contact the black remains invisible to the white, and James Baldwin's *Go Tell It on the Mountain* (1953), which concerns the author's own upbringing in the black community. The problems of the Jew in America gave Saul Bellow the opportunity to create a low-key folk hero in *The Adventures of Augie March* (1953); the eternal

Hero Construction, by Richard Hunt (1935– *(Courtesy of The Art Institute of Chicago)*

[4]From *The Cocktail Party*, by T.S. Eliot, copyright 1950 by T.S. Eliot, renewed 1978 by Esme Valerie Eliot. Reprinted by permission of Harcourt Brace Jovanovich, Inc., and Faber and Faber Ltd.

and universal difficulty of survival for the Jew was the theme of Bernard Malamud's *The Fixer* (1966). And women's demands for their liberation produced a call to action not only in such nonfiction as Betty Friedan's *The Feminine Mystique* (1963) but also in novels like Sylvia Plath's *The Bell-Jar* (1965) and Sue Kaufmann's *Diary of a Mad Housewife* (1967).

In art, too, there was a prevailing mood of disquiet and revolt. At its most extreme, it rejected all the material achievements of twentieth-century civilization, as in the pop art of Andy Warhol and Claes Oldenburg; and it saw a complete dehumanization of the individual, as in Richard Hunt's metal figures. But many artists set out in subtler ways to portray the uncertainty of the present—the uncertainty even of man's position in space, as in the hollowed-out figures of Henry Moore; the nightmare quality of his body reduced to its essential outlines, as in some of the sculptures of Alberto Giacometti; and the monstrous fear that informs William de Kooning's *Woman I.*

Thus, by the 1980s, it was clear that the postwar anxiety had not been mastered, but had even intensified. The age of tension had been reflected, as so often in the history of civilization, in its art and literature.

THE OPENING OF THE COLD WAR

The Age of the Continent State

T he uneasiness expressed by the writers and artists of this period was due in part to the continual threat of worldwide devastation posed by the confrontation of the Communist and non-Communist power blocs.

A totally new balance of forces characterized the West after 1945. In the interwar years, the chief states of Europe had been able to maintain an illusory predominance in world politics because the two most powerful states in the world, the United States of America and the Soviet Union, had withdrawn into isolationism—the one to avoid military involvement like that of the First World War, the other to carry through its social revolution. But from the moment those two continent states entered the Second World War, their overwhelming military and economic power dwarfed that of the other combatants. Only Germany was able to compare with them because it had already gained control of the resources of a large part of Europe. Stalin had summarized the situation with his usual succinctness at the Yalta conference when he remarked that great powers put an army of 5 million men into battle.

Both the Soviet Union and the United States derived predominance from their control over vast continental landmasses containing rich natural resources and inhabited by large populations. Both nations had seemingly unlimited supplies of coal, iron ore, oil, natural gas, lead, copper, zinc, sulphur, and potash. Both had huge forests and agricultural lands in climatic zones ranging from the Arctic to the subtropical. Both had invested heavily in the most advanced technologies for their industries and in the scientific education of their managers and engineers. Both had economies that were internally integrated; no barriers to the free movement of goods, capital, or labor existed in either nation. Both had populations three times the size of the largest European state, Germany, which had a population of about sixty million. The European continent was divided into twenty-nine states, whose boundary lines cut across natural economic units such as coal fields and even cities and slashed natural lines of communication. Thus the European powers gravitated inevitably into the orbit of one or the other of the two superpowers in the immediate postwar years.

Responsibility for the antagonism between the two power blocs has been disputed among historians. Writers of the so-called "New Left" have argued that the United States government, especially under the presidency of Harry S Truman in 1945–1953, attempted to push back Russian influence in both Europe and Asia. They suggest that one motive for the dropping of the atomic bombs on Japan was to prevent Russia from taking a share in the occupation of Japan; that American refusal to continue sending reparations from western Germany to Russia, as well as the cutoff in 1945 of Lend-Lease supplies, was an attempt to exert economic blackmail; and that the offer to give assistance to all European states through Marshall aid in 1947 was formulated in such a way that Russia could not accept it. Above all they argue that the Western powers acted before the Russians to form a military bloc: their creation in 1949 of the North Atlantic Treaty Organization occurred six years before the formation of the Warsaw Pact by the Communist powers.

Origins of the Cold War

Other historians have emphasized Stalin's actions in Russia and in eastern Europe as the primary cause for the American assumption of military and economic leadership of the Western powers. In Russia, Stalin reimposed strict Party controls at the end of the war to enforce his program for recreating Russia's war-damaged heavy industry and modernizing its military machine. Soldiers who might have been infected with Western ideas during the campaigns in Europe were transferred to Siberia. Several minority nationalities inside the Soviet Union who were suspected of having shown sympathy to the Germans were moved from their homes to newly colonized areas of the east. Intellectuals were once again forced into subservience by Andrei Zhdanov, Stalin's leading aide, whose *Zhdanovschina* punished any guilty of betraying the ideals of Socialist Realism, of expressing admiration for the West, or of failing to emphasize Russia's overwhelming superiority in all cultural and technical achievement. Behind this whole program of isolation of the Russian people from outside influences was the growing tyranny of Stalin, who once again, as at the time of the purge trials of the 1930s, was lashing out at his closest collaborators. As Khrushchev pointed out in his secret speech to the Party Congress in 1956, "After the war . . . Stalin became even more capricious, irritable and brutal; in particular his suspicion grew. His persecution mania reached unbelievable dimensions. Many workers were becoming enemies before his very eyes. After the war, Stalin separated himself from the collective even more. Everything was decided by him alone without any consideration for anyone or anything."[5] The secret police, renamed the MVD, engaged in widespread arrests, deportations, and executions under its sinister head, Lavrenti Beria. Up to five million people may have been sent to labor camps in the Arctic and in Siberia, to suffer the purgatory that Alexander Solzhenitsyn described in *One Day in the Life of Ivan Denisovich* (1962). At enormous cost to the Russian people, Stalin was thus able to act in foreign affairs from a position of strength.

The Communization of Eastern Europe

The political allegiance of eastern Europe was determined by the advance of the Red Army. By 1944 Russia had already reannexed Estonia, Latvia, Lithuania, and the Rumanian province of Bessarabia; and in 1945 it had taken the northern section of East Prussia and the Czech province of Sub-Carpathian Ruthenia. These areas were to remain integral parts of the Soviet Union. Beyond this boundary, however, the Soviet government was determined to create a line of friendly governments, both to safeguard its own security and to extend the Communist revolution; the interests of Russia went hand in hand with the extension of communization to eastern Europe.

In Yugoslavia and Albania, the native Communist leaders, Tito and Hoxha, were able to organize genuinely popular revolutionary movements that combined resistance to the German and Italian invaders with attacks on the representatives of the former possessing classes. The Russian army had swept briefly through eastern Yugoslavia but had established no form of Russian political controls, since communization was already assured. In the other states of eastern Europe, however, the Communists were a minority whose hold on the poorer classes was strongly challenged both by the Social Democrats and by various peasant or small-holder parties. In these countries, occupation by the Red Army made possible direct Russian interference.

In its occupation zone in Germany, the Soviet Union had moved rapidly to ensure Communist dominance. The pillars of the old society, the great landowners and the industrialists, had been dispossessed immediately. The non-Communist parties were sharply curtailed in their political activities. The provincial governments and, after 1949, the new central government were placed in the hands of the Communist-dominated Socialist Unity party; and compliance was ensured by the activities of the Soviet secret police and East Germany's own state security service. In Poland, the anti-Communist resistance forces had attempted to seize control of Warsaw in August 1944 but had been destroyed by the Germans in two months of savage street fighting. Thus, there was little organized opposition to the Communist-controlled provisional government, which was in-

[5]Cited in Basil Dmytryshyn, *USSR: A Concise History* (New York: Scribner's, 1965), p. 429.

Stalinallee, East Berlin
Built in the style of Soviet Socialist Realism in 1952–1964, the Stalinallee (now the Karl-Marx-Allee) was intended to be a show-place of Communist urban planning. (Courtesy of the German Information Center)

stalled in power after the Russian capture of Warsaw at the beginning of 1945. By 1948 Poland was firmly under the control of a coalition of Communists and left-wing Socialists; its industry was almost totally nationalized; its large estates had been annexed though not yet collectivized. In Rumania and Bulgaria, coalition governments were first established in 1944; but under the powerful leadership of Gheorghe Gheorghiu-Dej in Rumania and of Gheorghi Dimitrov in Bulgaria, the Communist parties were soon able to take complete control. The opposition of the peasant parties and of the Social Democrats was broken, and massive collectivization programs adopted. Dimitrov, who came to be considered a Bulgarian Lenin, on his death in 1949 was buried in a mausoleum on Sofia's main square similar to Lenin's. Hungary and Czechoslovakia at first appeared to resist the pattern of communization of the other eastern European states because of the strength of their non-Communist political parties. In Hungary, however, the Communists used the ministry of the interior to gain control of the police and the bureaucracy, and by 1949 their candidates were able to win ninety-five percent of the vote in national elections.

It was, however, the communization of Czechoslovakia that caused the greatest sensation in western Europe and the United States. President Eduard Beneš, whom the Red Army had restored to power in 1945, was a confirmed democrat who had nevertheless displayed sympathy throughout his career for the Soviet Union. Moreover, he had formed a genuine coalition government, in which the communist leader Klement Gottwald had become prime minister but in which the foreign ministry was in the hands of Jan Masaryk, the son of the country's founder. The Communist party, however, had gained control of most of the local police, the trade unions, and units of the army; and thus in February 1948, it was able to force Beneš to accept a Communist-controlled government by using the workers' militia to seize government offices and to occupy the headquarters of non-Communist political parties. Masaryk, who had stayed on as foreign minister, was found in the courtyard of his ministry a month later with a broken spine. Beneš resigned in June and died shortly thereafter. Following elections that gave them an eighty-nine percent majority, the Communists established a monolithic regime, purged up to half their own party, hanged several of its former leaders, and clamped down police-state controls.

The most dramatic demonstration of the resentment aroused in eastern Europe by the Soviet Union's control of the process of communization occurred in 1948, when Yugoslavia broke its ties with Russia. Tito had apparently been the most convinced of the Soviet satellites up to that time. But resentment had been building up against Russian interference with Yugoslavian internal affairs. In 1948, Yugoslavian and Soviet leaders engaged in a doctrinal battle, in which Tito was eventually blasted as a heretic. Stalin wrote:

The leaders of the Communist Party of Yugoslavia have taken a stand unworthy of Communists, and have begun to identify the foreign policy of the Soviet Union with the foreign policy of the imperialist powers. . . . Instead of honestly accepting this [Soviet] criticism and taking the ·Bolshevik path of correcting these mistakes, the leaders of the Communist Party of Yugoslavia, suffering from boundless ambition, arrogance and conceit, met this criticism with belligerence and hostility.

As a result, Yugoslavia was expelled from the newly founded international Communist Information Bureau (Cominform), and attempts were made to persuade dissident Yugoslavian Communists to overthrow Tito. Soviet pressure failed, because Tito's internal popularity and firm controls were unassailable, while his military forces would have made direct intervention against him very costly. Moreover, the Western powers came at once to his aid, with loans and surplus food supplies, thus creating an isolated example of an alternative road to Communism outside that of the Soviet Union.

Formation of the Western Bloc

The United States assumed, with considerable reluctance, the leadership of a Western bloc dedicated to the containment of further Communist expansion. In 1945–1946, it had tried to give up responsibilities in Europe by demobilizing most of its forces and cutting off programs of direct aid. In 1946, however, the American military government in Germany stopped sending dismantled factories to Russia as reparations, and an attempt was made to win over the West Germans to membership in a Western bloc by promising them self-government. In March 1947 Truman offered American financial and technical aid to Greece and Turkey under a new doctrine that guaranteed American willingness to "help free peoples to maintain their institutions and their national integrity against aggressive movements that seek to impose upon them totalitarian regimes." Three months later, Secretary of State Marshall offered large-scale financial aid to all of the European countries for their reconstruction; his offer was accepted only by the non-Communist countries. In 1949 the American government took the lead in the establishment of a military alliance, the North Atlantic Treaty Organization, composed of Canada and ten European countries, in which all members promised to act together to repel any armed attack on them in the North Atlantic area. The formation of NATO brought a stalemate in the confrontation of Russia and the United States in Europe. Only West Berlin, a Western outpost more than a hundred miles inside East Germany, provoked major disagreements between the blocs—primarily because it offered a route of escape for refugees from East Germany. Once that route had been closed with the erection of the Berlin Wall in 1961, West Berlin ceased to be a principal source of tension between the two blocs. In 1972 it was even possible for West Germany and the Soviet Union to recognize that the political changes brought about by the Second World War were unalterable in the immediate future. The Treaty of Moscow of 1972 between West Germany and the Soviet Union, which recognized the German loss of the Oder-Neisse territories and East Prussia, was almost the equivalent of a peace treaty ending the Second World War; and it promised a relaxation of tension of the Cold War in Europe.

The Helsinki Security Conference of 1975 even appeared to some observers to signal the end of the Cold War. Attended by thirty-five nations from Europe and North America, the conference concluded with agreements to recognize the inviolability of European frontiers, and thus all the boundary changes in eastern Europe at the end of the Second World War. In return, the Communist powers assented to increased contacts between the blocs, including eased travel and cultural exchanges and emigration.

Berlin Wall

The Berlin Wall was erected in 1961 and has been continually reinforced since. Its construction almost completely stopped the flow of refugees into West Berlin.

THE SOVIET BLOC AFTER STALIN

Collective Leadership
in Russia: The Thaw

In January 1953, the arrest of the leading doctors in the Kremlin was regarded as the opening of a new purge of the Soviet hierarchy; but Stalin suffered a fatal stroke two months later, and on March 9 his embalmed body was entombed next to Lenin's in the mausoleum on Red Square. Only then could the long-delayed political reconstruction take place within Russia.

Power in Russia was assumed by the "collective leadership" of representatives of the elites of Soviet society—the Party, the army, and the industrial bureaucracy. Together they ousted Beria from control of the secret police and had him secretly executed. Thousands who had been arrested in the last years of Stalin's life were released. Greater legal safeguards for Soviet citizens were guaranteed, and a relaxation of international tension promised. Within the Soviet satellites in eastern Europe, there was to be a relaxation of police powers, more freedom for national diversity, and a rehabilitation of survivors of previous purges. Thus Stalin's death was welcomed throughout Europe as the harbinger of a "thaw" in Stalinist autocracy.

Eastern Europe
After Stalin

The first reaction in eastern Europe to the lightening of controls was sporadic outbursts of violent protest against the harshness of living and working conditions. The raising of work norms provoked a general strike in East Berlin in 1953 that spread to most of the other cities of East Germany. Government buildings were set on fire, and Russian troops attacked. The uprising was checked only when the Russians sent three armored divisions into East Berlin.

Except in East Germany, the other Communist regimes all adopted some form of collective leadership and reduced the powers of the secret police. In Poland and Hungary in particular, this leniency encouraged great political ferment within the Communist parties and workers' organizations and among intellectuals. In Poland, factory workers rioted in the town of Poznan in June 1956, and perhaps a hundred were killed and hundreds were arrested by the police; but shortly after, control of the Polish Communist party was taken by a group headed by Wladislaw Gomulka, which was demanding greater internal liberalization. The Soviet government at first considered military intervention but eventually acquiesced in the appointment of Gomulka as head of a new Polish government. This solution, which effected a slight relaxing of domestic controls, prevented Polish unrest from turning into armed revolt.

In Hungary, however, discontent boiled over in October 1956, when workers and students united in Budapest in an armed uprising. Using rifles and Molotov cocktails, they murdered party officials and the secret police and attacked Russian tanks that patrolled the streets. The revolt spread to the rest of Hungary, and the Hungarian army joined the rebels. In the face of a Communist revolution led by the popular Communist leader Imre

East Berlin Uprising, 1953
In June 1953, resentment due to increased workloads and widespread repression by the East German government boiled over into a general strike with numerous attacks on the occupying Soviet troops. Only by bringing in three tank divisions were the Russians able to subdue the rioters. (Courtesy of the German Information Center)

Nagy, the Russians withdrew their troops from Hungary and appeared willing to acquiesce in the premiership of Nagy. For ten days there was self-congratulation throughout the country. Non-Communist political leaders were admitted to the government; freedom of speech and of the press was permitted; the security police were disbanded. Nagy, however, made the mistake of announcing Hungary's withdrawal from the Warsaw Pact, the military alliance of Russia and the Eastern European countries organized in 1955. On November 2, Soviet troops moved back into Hungary in great strength; and two days later, in spite of desperate resistance from every element of the population, their tanks seized control of the main government buildings in Budapest. The Soviet troops installed János Kádár as premier in place of Nagy, who, after being guaranteed a safe conduct out of the country, was arrested and later executed. Mass arrests and deportations followed, although about 200,000 Hungarians were able to flee to the West.

In Russia the collective leadership survived only two years, and by 1955 power was being exercised largely by one man, First Party Secretary Nikita Khrushchev. Khrushchev had been bitterly criticized by Party opponents in 1956 for provoking the revolt in Hungary by his policy of de-Stalinization; but he was able to fight off the attack and for the following seven years to maintain personal control of both Party and government. He also continued his policy of de-Stalinization of some aspects of Soviet life. Membership in the Party was broadened to include many more representatives of workers and peasants. The bureaucratic elite, the educated and well-paid Soviet bourgeoisie, whom Yugoslav writer Milovan Djilas called the "New Class," was compelled to achieve closer contact with the workers by enactment of a law requiring two years of manual labor before entry to schools of higher education. A new criminal code abolished categories such as "enemy of the people." Literary controls varied according to Khrushchev's whims, but literature continued to show considerable freedom and versatility—if not in the sanctioned publications at least in the underground press and in manuscripts sent abroad, such as Boris Pasternak's *Dr. Zhivago*. The most effective commentaries on the relative liberalization of Khrushchev's regime were both the ease with which he was overthrown during his vacation in 1964, by a vote of the Presidium led by Leonid Brezhnev and Alexei Kosygin, and the permission granted him to retire unmolested to his country home outside Moscow. Although at first a genuine form of collective rule was established, it became clear by the mid-1970s that Secretary General Brezhnev had achieved undisputed primacy within the Soviet government.

The evolution of government in Eastern Europe during this period of stabilization was quite varied. At one extreme was the regime of party secretary Walter Ulbricht in East Germany, which refused all except the most superficial forms of de-Stalinization. Gomulka in Poland, to the great surprise of those who had hailed his triumph in 1956 as proof of Poland's right to seek its own road to Communism, soon embarked on a "retreat from October," a reimposition of harsh political controls through a strictly purged Communist hierarchy. He did not, however, force collectivization of agriculture, and Poland remained the Eastern European country with the highest proportion of independent farmers. Gomulka's greatest failure, however, was in industrial policy; and, in December 1970, after nationwide rioting by Polish workers protesting poor living standards, he was compelled to resign. His successor, Edward Gierek, was no more successful in solving Poland's underlying economic problems; and, in 1980, after widespread strikes had compelled his government to recognize the right of workers to form independent trade unions, he too was forced to resign.

Hungary and Bulgaria managed to maintain a central position. Kádár, after an initial period of repression following his elevation to power by the Russians, cautiously began to relax his regime. With the rise in living standards that was achieved in the late 1960s, Hungarians who had origi-

Leonid Brezhnev Speaking in the Kremlin Great Palace, Moscow, 1977
After ousting Nikita Khrushchev from power in October 1964, Brezhnev slowly won preeminence among the Soviet leaders. In 1977 he became head of state in addition to remaining secretary general of the Communist Party. (Tass from Sovfoto)

nally regarded Kádár a traitor were beginning to consider him an acceptable leader within the limits imposed by Russia. In Bulgaria, economic conditions improved greatly under Vulko Zhivkov, a cautious, moderate man who sought better economic relations with the West, welcomed hundreds of thousands of tourists to the Bulgarian beaches along the Black Sea, and allowed a modified form of profit-and-loss accounting to be used as stimulus to industrial production.

Finally, Rumania attempted successfully and Czechoslovakia unsuccessfully to set off on independent roads to Communism. The Rumanian leader Gheorghiu-Dej refused to accept the economic role assigned to Rumania by the Council for Mutual Economic Assistance (Comecon), an economic union of the Eastern European Communist countries and Russia, whose purpose was to harmonize the region's economic planning. Instead of agreeing to concentrate on agricultural and oil production, he ordered "rapid and all-round industrialization" and sought aid from the West in planning new factories and in investment loans. Little by little he threw off Russian influences. Russian troops left the country in 1958; compulsory study of the Russian language was dropped in the schools; and the subordinate nature of the Rumanian party to the Soviet in international Communism, the much-vaunted Father-Party and Son-Party relationship, was denied. Gheorghiu-Dej's successor Nicolae Ceausescu was an even more convinced nationalist, daring to attack the necessity of the Warsaw Pact and the wisdom of dividing Europe into two opposed military blocs.

The Czechoslovak experiment in liberalized Communism, introduced in 1968 by the new Party secretary, Alexander Dubček, was a far more direct challenge to the supremacy of the Soviet model of Communism. It permitted widespread decentralization of industrial decisionmaking, introduced considerable freedom of the internal market, almost completely ended controls over freedom of expression, and permitted open criticism of the Soviet Union. To Russian leaders, Dubček's attitude was doubly dangerous—Czechoslovakia was renewing its traditional Western ties and moving to a position of neutrality in the Cold War; and it was permitting such internal political liberalism and encouraging such capitalistic industrial experiments that its society was ceasing to be genuinely Communist. In August 1968 Soviet armored columns, supported by troops from East Germany, Poland, and Hungary, invaded Czechoslovakia and occupied the whole country. The liberalization was immediately halted, and the control of the party's hard-liners reimposed. Dubček was kept as Party leader as a concession to Czech sentiments until April 1969, when he was replaced by Gustav Husák, a Slovak Communist willing to carry through the repression demanded by the Russians.

Russian Tanks in Prague, 1968
Although the Czech armed forces offered no resistance to the invasion of their country by the forces of the Soviet Union and other Warsaw pact nations, the Prague crowds often tried to convince the tank drivers that they had been sent on an aggressive mission against a friendly people. (United Press International, Inc.)

In 1961 tiny Albania proved that defection from the Soviet was also possible with the help of a powerful ally—in this case, China. By 1960 both the Albanians and the Chinese were outraged at the Russian leaders: the Albanians because of their courtship of Tito and their insistence on de-Stalinization in Albania, the Chinese because of Russian insistence on the superiority of their own version of Communism. In 1960–1961, when Albania openly sided with China, Russian aid was cut off, and the Russian submarine base in Albania closed down. The Albanians, ousted from Comecon, turned to the Chinese for technical and financial aid, which was at once dispatched. Within a few months, Albania was ostentatiously posing as China's principal ally in Europe. The split between the Chinese and the Russians intensified as the Chinese sought allies among non-aligned countries within the Eastern European bloc; among the Western European Communist parties; and especially in the United States, with whom China in the 1970s established diplomatic relations. In 1980, with the condemnation in the United Nations of the Soviet Union's invasion of Afghanistan by the United States, China, and many Western and non-aligned countries, it was clear that the "bipolar" world once dominated by the United States and Russia had been transformed into a "polycentric" system with several centers of power. While the Cold War had not ceased, its character had been profoundly altered.

POLITICAL RECONSTRUCTION OF WESTERN EUROPE

The Resistance movements in western Europe during the German occupation had envisaged a political renovation on a vast scale that the members would undertake at the end of the war. For the Communist parties, the ideal was the remodeling of society on the Soviet model; but in spite of their popularity in 1945, due to their exploits in the underground fighting, the Communist parties remained a minority in all the western European countries. The non-Communist groups, mostly Socialist or Christian Democratic in orientation, laid the blame for the Second World War on not only the Nazi regime but also the ineffectiveness of their own ruling classes and the anachronistic constitutional machinery they manipulated. Some went further and claimed that the political sickness of Europe, which had inflicted upon it two major wars in only a quarter of a century, was due to the existence of the nation-state itself; and they proposed that Europe seek the unification of its peoples in one federal state. All of these ideas were disappointed. As western Europe was liberated country by country, largely by American and British armies, old constitutions were restored, or new ones so similar to the old as to be indistinguishable were written. Most of the prewar leaders who had not been compromised by collaboration with the Germans reappeared and resumed their accustomed

Foiled Idealism of the Resistance Movements

places in the governments of the individual nation-states. Above all, no attempt was made to form any kind of federation, on the ground that such planning was too utopian in the face of the urgent need for economic reconstruction.

Weaknesses of Constitutional Renovation

The failure to modernize the political structure had baleful consequences that were felt for most of the postwar period. In France and Italy in particular, new constitutions were written that perpetuated the multiparty system of government. Constant juggling of ministerial positions among a small inner group of party bosses caused public disenchantment with the whole political process. The disenchantment increased the appeal of parties on the extreme left and on the right that denied the validity of the constitutional process itself and hence were never included within the process of alternation of power. Attempts to avoid the chaos of multiparty rule by entrusting strong powers to one person had a similar effect of estranging the public from the political process. In West Germany, which adopted in 1949 a new constitution drafted by brilliant constitutional lawyers determined to overcome the weaknesses of the Weimar constitution, power was monopolized by the seventy-three-year-old Konrad Adenauer, who emulated Bismarck by running a *Kanzlerdemokratie* ("chancellor democracy") until being forced out of office in 1963. When Charles de Gaulle

French Student Riots in Paris, May 1968
When they seized control of the university buildings and part of the surrounding area of the Left Bank, French students, to oppose the attacks of the police and the army, reverted to the traditional technique of Parisian revolutionaries of building street barricades. (Henri Cartier-Bresson/Magnum Photos)

became president of France in 1958, under a new constitution that had been tailor-made to meet his objections to multiparty democracy, his own presidential powers proved to be so grandly conceived that he eventually lost the support of many who had originally turned to him for discipline in government. The disillusionment became so great, especially among students and workers, that it provoked near-revolution in Paris in May 1968.

Student demonstrations, which began on a new campus on the edge of Paris with complaints against the outdated and overcrowded French university system, rapidly spread to the Sorbonne on the Left Bank. There, complaints of every kind, from criticism of the Gaullist regime and of the capitalist system to protest against American intervention in Vietnam, were voiced by a multitude of student groups. Violence erupted when the police intervened; the students succeeded in seizing the university buildings and battled the police with barricades in the streets. The three French trade unions then joined in revolt with a general strike, in part to support the students but primarily for higher wages. De Gaulle only succeeded in bringing peace to Paris by dismissing the parliament and calling new elections, in which his own supporters rallied to his defense. With this electoral mandate, de Gaulle ordered the police to clear the university of its occupiers. A year later, however, when the public took its revenge on him by voting down a referendum he had demanded, he resigned the presidency, to the regret of very few of the French people, who had once idolized him. In short, both the multiparty system and the system of strong rule by a president or a chancellor proved unsatisfactory—the one for its incoherence, the other for its lack of responsiveness to public opinion.

One area in which the restored governments of western Europe achieved a great popular success was the provision of a vast range of social services. From the end of the nineteenth century, the state had taken responsibility for various insurance programs for industrial workers; and in the interwar years the Scandinavian countries had begun to apply a moderate program of socialization that included public ownership of utilities, operation of hospitals, and insurance coverage for sickness, accidents, and old age. But after 1945 almost every European country, regardless of its constitutional system, adopted important programs for state provision of health care, housing, increased educational opportunities, and various forms of direct financial aid.

Creation of the Welfare State

Britain's Labour government embarked on the broadest of these programs in 1945. Basing its program on recommendations for the elimination of "want, ignorance, squalor, and disease" drawn up during the war, it determined that every citizen should receive a national minimum standard of living. Monetary assistance was given to large families, and numerous other payments were made by the state for maternity costs, sickness, pensions, and educational expenses. Against great opposition from the medical profession, the Labour government created the National Health Service, which was to provide everyone in the country with medical, dental, surgical, and hospital care without limit of cost, in return for the payment of a small weekly fee. Within three years, ninety-five percent of the population and ninety percent of the doctors had enrolled in the program. Public housing was constructed on a very large scale, so that eventually one in four of the population lived in buildings erected by one of the public authorities. Educational opportunity was opened to all, by the provision of free primary and secondary education and of scholarships to all needy students in higher educational institutions. For the first time in British history, entrance to the universities became dependent largely on ability.

Similar programs were instituted in most of the continental European countries. In the two to three years following the war, the Communists usually cooperated with Socialist and Christian Democrat parties in setting up social security systems. In France and Italy, insurance programs were usually preferred to outright socialization of medicine; the system of payments was unified under the state and gradually extended to include all segments of the population. Family allowances were paid to aid dependent children. Schools and public housing were constructed, and there was continual monitoring of work hours, paid vacations, and factory conditions. In Sweden, social security expenses absorbed one-third of the national budget, while in France and Italy employers contributed as much as one-third of a worker's wage toward social security benefits.

This increase in the powers of the state over the life of the individual citizen was usually welcomed. Many right-wing politicians even claimed that the true predecessor of the welfare state had been the Fascist or the National Socialist state, which had set out to provide similar benefits. Most Europeans recognized that the welfare program was simply a necessary extension of state services that implied no specific ideological commitment.

ECONOMIC RESURGENCE AND SOCIAL CHANGE

Throughout Europe, the first months after the end of the Second World War were spent in tackling the most immediate tasks of economic reconstruction. The transportation network had to be repaired. Electrical and telegraph wires had to be restrung. Reservoirs, water pipes, and sewer mains had to be brought into working order. War-damaged factories had to be reconstructed, housing repaired, and fuel provided for power and heating. Seed and fertilizer had to be provided to enable the farmers to bring their land back into cultivation. Over eleven million prisoners of war, forced laborers, and deportees had to be returned to their homes or to new countries willing to receive them. With considerable help from the United Nations Relief and Rehabilitation Agency (UNRRA), funded primarily by the United States, these jobs were carried out within two years by the individual national governments. Europe by the spring of 1947 was beginning to wear a deceptive air of successful convalescence.

At that point, it became clear that the reconstruction program had met the most immediate problems but had ignored the deeper economic problems, especially the lack of investment capital, that were preventing the European economy from embarking on a self-sustaining process of growth. On June 5, 1947, the American secretary of state, George C. Marshall, offered large-scale American aid to all the countries of Europe on the condition that they draw up a joint plan of economic reconstruction. The Russian government, meeting immediately with the British and French to discuss the plan, rejected the conditions for aid as unwarranted American interference in the internal affairs of other countries. It also compelled the other Eastern European countries to refuse to participate, and hence the plan was restricted to sixteen non-Communist countries. By 1952 these nations had received over $13 billion, mostly in the form of grants rather than loans. Although very little coordination of national planning took place, the plan was enormously successful. During the four years of its operation, the gross national product of the participating countries rose by one-quarter in real value; industrial production was thirty-five percent above prewar levels, and agricultural production ten percent higher.

The Marshall Plan

In the growing prosperity that followed Marshall aid, West Germany took the lead. Its currency had been stabilized by a harsh devaluation in 1948. Economics Minister Ludwig Erhard had allowed considerable freedom of planning and concentration to the major companies and banks, and they had engaged in vast programs of modernization. Workers had accepted long working hours and low wages; and there had been relatively few strikes. By 1953 production was fifty-three percent higher than before the war. Within three years, in spite of the annual flight to West Germany of over 200,000 East Germans, unemployment had been wiped out.

Western European Economic Miracles

By the middle of the 1950s it was clear that almost all of western Europe was enjoying a great economic boom, which was to continue with only minor setbacks until the 1970s. In France, for example, Marshall aid had been used in several "propulsive" sectors of the economy, such as steel and agricultural machinery, which led the recovery. Technological improvement was encouraged, new managerial techniques imported from the United States, and the distribution system modernized. For the first time in French history, the mass of the population began to receive a more equitable share of the national wealth; and by the 1960s, one-half of French homes had a refrigerator and almost as many an automobile. Italy, too, achieved a real growth rate of over five percent throughout the 1950s and 1960s, largely by concentrating on those areas of light industry in which its shortage of natural resources could be compensated for by skill in design and marketing. The Italian boom focused on such products as plastics, typewriters, washing machines, refrigerators, shoes, and textiles, in all of

Solar Furnace in the French Pyrenees
The French pioneered in the use of solar energy with the construction in 1969 of this giant solar furnace, which measures fifty-four meters in diameter and is composed of sixty-two pivoting mirrors. (Peter Menzel)

The Supersonic Airliner Concorde over Paris
(Courtesy of French Embassy Press and Information Division)

which it seized a large part of the European market. Britain was the main exception to the pattern of generalized prosperity. Many of its traditional markets overseas had been lost during the war. Its industrial facilities were outdated, its natural resources depleted. Labor unions permitted strikes to endanger productivity. Management, lacking imagination, failed to respond to the challenge of the continental countries. The most costly examples of shortsightedness occurred in 1950 when the Labour government refused to join the European Coal and Steel Community, and in 1958 when the Conservative government refused membership in the Common Market; for economic integration was to prove an important stimulus to the progress of the continental countries.

When in May 1950 French Foreign Minister Robert Schuman proposed the pooling of the coal and steel industries of France and Germany with those of any other European countries that would join them, he did so for political rather than economic reasons. He hoped to create a nucleus around which a genuine political union, a United States of Europe, would eventually be formed. His plan called for the free circulation within the European Coal and Steel Community (ECSC) of goods, workers, and capital in the coal and steel industries. The economic success of the plan, he believed, would be so great that it would lead the members of the Community to seek further ties that would eventually culminate in the creation of a European government. His proposal was accepted by Germany, Belgium, the Netherlands, Luxembourg, and Italy, and put into force in 1952. The economic results were even better than forecast. Political results, however, were disappointing. Even before the Community was in operation, the governments of the six member nations had attempted to create a similar organization called the European Defense Community (EDC) to run their armies on an integrated basis, and they had furthermore drawn up plans for a European Political Community, which would act as a European government. The French parliament, however, had refused to ratify the EDC Treaty in 1954, and the two plans had died as a result of that vote. In 1955, however, the six member nations agreed to study plans for the integration of all sectors of their economy in a European Economic Community (EEC), or Common Market, and for the fusion of their atomic energy industries in a European Atomic Energy Community (Euratom). After two difficult years, the completed treaties were signed on the Capitol Hill in Rome, a suitably symbolic setting for the recreation of a Europe that had not been united since the Roman Empire.

Economic Integration in Western Europe

Euratom was a failure almost from the start, since all its members individually pressed on with their own national atomic energy programs. The Common Market, on the other hand, was an extraordinary success. By 1968 all customs barriers among the six members had been abolished. An extremely complicated system of commodity markets had been created to integrate agricultural production at the same time as industrial produc-

Euratom and the Common Market

tion; and through this rather controversial machinery Community preference was extended to the farmers whose products received guaranteed prices or export subsidies. Favored treatment within the Common Market was given to migrant laborers of the member countries. An attempt was made to increase the free flow of capital in the Community; and in the 1970s a start was made on such delayed projects as regional planning, a common currency, and creation of Europeanwide companies. These measures opened to the industries and farms of the Community a market of over 200 million consumers and thus stimulated specialization and the rapid expansion of the most efficient companies. The Common Market played an important part in fostering the great economic boom that Europe enjoyed in the 1960s. The first decade of the Common Market's operation was the most prosperous Europe had ever known.

In 1961 the British recognized their mistake in not joining the Community, but their application for admission was vetoed two years later by French President de Gaulle. De Gaulle thus destroyed the expansive impetus of the Community at its most crucial point; and he continued to oppose all efforts to make the Community officials an independent supranational government. As a result the Common Market did not become more than an economic union, and even the entry in 1973 of Britain, Denmark, and Ireland offered little chance of stimulating future progress toward a political union. The Common Market was a great economic success, but at least up to the early 1970s, it had achieved few of the political goals of Robert Schuman's original proposal.

Nothing illustrated more effectively the inherent disunity among the nine members of the Common Market than their reaction to the energy crisis of 1973–1974. In November 1973, in the aftermath of the new Arab-Israeli war, the Arab oil producers placed an embargo on all oil supplies to the Netherlands and the United States as reprisal for their pro-Israeli stand, and raised the price of oil by four hundred percent. The price rise placed a great strain on the balance of payments of the Western countries, which incurred a deficit of $60 billion to the oil-producing countries by the end of 1974 alone. The Common Market countries, however, refused to take a common stand with the United States, gave only indirect help to the Netherlands, and engaged in bilateral bargaining with the oil producers. Summit meetings of the heads of government of the Common Market made no progress toward further solidarity, and in 1975 it was recognized that plans to achieve full economic and monetary unity by 1980 would have to be scrapped.

During the late 1970s, the economic situation in most western European countries worsened. Both inflation and unemployment rates rose as oil prices continued to increase. Only the exploitation of newly discovered oil wells in the North Sea promised relief from the economic crisis precipitated by the high cost of energy. Yet the Common Market remained a great hope for the southern states of Europe; it appeared likely that Portugal, Spain, and Greece, all of which had substituted democratic governments

Oil Rig in North Sea, Built in 1976
The exploitation of oil deposits beneath the North Sea during the 1970s proved a great asset to the economies of countries like Norway and Great Britain, which had been dependent on imports for a large part of their petroleum supplies. As the cost of oil from the Middle East rose, it became more economically feasible to construct the rigs that, though enormously expensive, were necessary for successful drilling in the savage northern waters. (Sygma)

for previously right-wing regimes, would be admitted as full members in the early 1980s. Finally, the first election of the Community's European Parliament by universal suffrage in 1979 promised a revival of public interest and support for the activities of the Community.

The economic revival of eastern Europe lagged far behind that of western Europe. Wartime destruction of lives and property, especially in the Soviet Union, had been very heavy. The refusal of Marshall aid implied that the Communist countries would have to rebuild their economies through their own hard work and self-denial. In Russia, Stalin imposed very high

The Slow Economic Revival of Eastern Europe

goals of heavy industrialization in the Reconstruction Plan of 1946, which was largely successful. In the 1950s greater flexibility was allowed to management, and greater incentives given to workers by provision of consumer goods. By 1960 industrial production had probably doubled. Agricultural production advanced much more slowly, in spite of various ambitious plans, like the Virgin Lands scheme, for bringing large new areas under cultivation; and the Russian peasantry remained unenthusiastic participants in collectivized farming.

In eastern Europe, after a slow recovery up to 1950, large-scale plans of industrialization were undertaken, especially in East Germany and Czechoslovakia. Concentrating largely on markets in eastern Europe and Russia, East Germany created a large iron and steel industry, restored chemical production, and rebuilt its optical and machine tool industries. After the flight of refugees to the West had been halted by the construction of the Berlin Wall in 1961, its economy boomed: its industrial production rose to the tenth highest in the world and the sixth highest in Europe. Rumania, too, strove to create a broad-based industrial economy, using its rich deposits of oil, natural gas, and metals; and during the 1960s, it quadrupled its industrial production. Agricultural collectivization, which was pushed with varying degrees throughout Eastern Europe, was not successful in creating large increases in production; and several countries, especially Poland and Hungary, allowed a considerable degree of private farming to continue to ensure adequate agricultural supplies for the cities.

By comparison with western Europe, eastern European development was slow. Relative to their own achievements during the interwar years, however, it was rapid, especially in the Balkan countries, which were converted from backward agricultural lands into modern industrialized states.

New Societies of Eastern and Western Europe

Social change was most dramatic in Eastern Europe, which underwent a social revolution similar to that of Russia after 1917. The old landed classes were rapidly dispossessed, and thus some of the most long-lived social aristocracies of Europe disappeared—the Junkers of East Germany, the aristocrats of Poland, the landed magnates of Hungary. But the peasants too, who had hoped as the result of the annexation of the lands of the aristocracy and the Church to become landholders themselves, were swept into the collective farms, and thus had to adapt to an entirely new way of life. The state took possession of the factories and housing of the old capitalist classes; and as a result, the class structure of Eastern Europe came to resemble that of the Soviet Union. Differences in salaries and personal wealth were much smaller than in the West, in part because of the lack of any investment opportunity. There was also far less differentiation in living conditions, both in housing and consumption. Equalization was furthered by state provision of most forms of recreation, from vacations to inexpensive theater; by the socialization of medical care; and by state provision of mass education. Yet in spite of these conditions, a new privileged class was created, consisting of party bureaucrats, military officers, and a

Supermarket, Nice, France
Although European countries were considerably slower than the United States to modernize their retail marketing facilities, chains of supermarkets serving a motorized clientele were operating on the edge of most large European cities by the 1970s. (Peter Menzel)

The New City of La Grande Motte, France
In 1961, the French government decided to open up the Mediterranean coast between Marseilles and the Spanish border to tourist development, and built six new resorts. The most dramatic of the new cities was La Grande Motte near Montpellier, which was composed almost entirely of gleaming pyramids of white concrete. (H. Roger-Viollet)

technological, artistic, and managerial elite, who enjoyed higher salaries, better educational opportunities, and access to rare consumer goods.

In Western Europe, the affluence produced unexpected social tensions. The class structure changed remarkably little. An upper class of the extremely wealthy, merging with the older aristocracy of birth, succeeded, in spite of many attempts by the state to achieve a redistribution of wealth, in holding on to its high salaries and its accumulated capital. It also retained a disproportionate share of places in higher education, upper managerial positions, and diplomatic and high-level civil service appointments. In Britain for example, one percent of the population owned two-fifths of the country's wealth. The middle classes were greatly benefited both by the economic boom and the welfare state. The boom created not only higher salaries but also more white-collar jobs in lower levels of industrial management and in the service sector. The welfare state removed the financial crisis of accident or sickness and made available to the children of middle-class parents the best educational opportunities. Preserves of privilege, like Oxford and Cambridge universities in England, or the Ecole Normale Supérieure in France, were opened to all; and many who profited from the educational openings were able to move without difficulty into the upper levels of business and government. Others, however, who lacked suitable family background ran into the invisible barriers to social upward mobility erected by the established upper class. In Britain this exclusion produced the phenomenon of the "angry young man," graphically portrayed in novels like Kingsley Amis's *Lucky Jim* and John Brain's *Room at the Top*, and in the plays of John Osborne. In France and Italy the protest often took political form, with many highly educated young men joining the Communist party in protest against the petrified social structure of their country. The riots in 1968 were essentially a protest by students against a society from which they felt isolated.

In the 1970s, especially in West Germany and Italy, small numbers of extreme radicals embarked on a widespread campaign of terrorism, directed particularly against business leaders and politicians, with the intention of paralyzing the normal workings of the capitalist system and political democracy.

The industrial working class enjoyed higher living standards and greater security from unemployment than ever before. Workers were able to engage in spending sprees on holidays, sports, household appliances, clothes, and even cars; but for many their affluence was insufficient compensation for the frustrations of their dull, repetitive work on the assembly line. Unable to change the nature of their work, they expressed their annoyance by frequent strikes for higher wages, regardless of increases in their own productivity. They wanted better educational opportunities for their children to enable them to avoid the drudgery of the factory but were rarely able to provide educational stimuli in their homes; and the children of workers rarely succeeded in gaining higher education and even more rarely high-ranking positions in business or government. In France, for example, only twelve percent of university students were children of workers; even in Britain, the proportion was only thirty percent.

Perhaps the greatest social changes occurred in rural areas. Peasants were leaving the countryside in droves, as the mechanization of agriculture reduced the number of unskilled workers needed, and as far greater opportunities for employment occurred in the cities. In Italy, for example, up to 300,000 were leaving agriculture each year; and the same phenomenon was observed in eastern Europe and Russia and even, in the 1960s, in Spain and Portugal. The peasants who did remain on the land in western Europe were compelled to change their way of life, consolidating their holdings, joining in cooperatives for marketing, and seeking greater technical education. Once the changes were accepted, the standard of life of the farmer rose rapidly, though not as rapidly as that of the industrial workers. Peasants became less isolated because they now possessed a car or motorcycle, a radio, and often a television set.

For women in the West, the postwar period brought great changes. The life expectancy of women had been growing throughout the twentieth century; and a woman in the 1970s could expect to live twenty-five to thirty years longer than her counterpart in the 1900s. Moreover, she could expect to live on average between four and seven years longer than a man. In countries that had suffered a great loss of males during the Second World War, the disparity in numbers between men and women was especially great. In Russia in 1967, for example, there were fifteen million more women than men. The effect was to increase the numbers of spinsters and especially of widows. On the other hand, women were marrying younger, having fewer pregnancies, and completing their families at earlier ages. About half had had their last child by the age of twenty-six and thus were able to reenter the work force if they had retired to bring up their children, with the expectation of being able to work for over thirty years more.

As women were becoming increasingly able and determined to work, more opportunities for them became available, especially in the service sector of the economy. In both the Communist and the non-Communist countries, women represented an increasing proportion of the work force; in the 1960s, they composed forty-eight percent of the Russian work force and between thirty-four and thirty-six percent of the work force of the United States and the countries of the Common Market. Whereas at the beginning of the century, the female work force had been predominantly young and single, by the 1970s it was primarily made up of women married and over thirty-five years of age. Education, both secondary and higher, was becoming more available; and there were signs that such traditional male preserves as the professions were opening to women. There were considerable differences by nationality, however. Whereas, for example, women constituted twenty-five percent of the medical profession in Britain, they composed only six percent in the United States.

As their participation in the labor force increased, however, women became increasingly aware of the persistence of discrimination against

Simone Veil, President of the European Parliament
Veil was chosen president of the first popularly elected parliament of the European Community in 1979. She had made her reputation as a lawyer after her return from German concentration camps, to which she, as a Jew, had been deported. Additionally, as minister of health, she had fought for liberal abortion and contraception laws. (R. Darolle/Sygma)

Women at Work in the Soviet Union
Although a greater percentage of women have jobs in the Soviet Union than in any other industrialized country, and the principle of equal pay for equal work is recognized, many women work at low-paying manual tasks, such as street cleaning, wall painting, and snow removal. (James Andamson/Sygma)

them. Average pay for women in almost every branch of employment remained lower than that of male workers. In France, for example, women in higher management received only sixty-three percent of the average salary of men. Access to higher education remained unequal, and women were still directed toward the arts rather than the sciences or the professions. Entry into the political sphere, although easing in some countries, remained difficult in spite of the occasional appointment of a female premier or cabinet minister. Thus it was not surprising that many Western European women in the 1970s followed the lead of the American women's movements and began to organize pressure groups for more rapid change in their statuses.

The flight from the land increased the urbanization of the European population. By 1970, eighty percent of Britain's population, seventy percent of West Germany's, and fifty-four percent of Russia's population lived in cities. In the Soviet Union and Eastern Europe, further attempts were made to regulate this urbanization with the foundation of new cities, through the establishment of either totally new communities in undeveloped regions or satellite towns on the edges of older cities. In western Europe, in

The New Urbanization

The Humanization of the Central City
In many West German cities, part of the shopping center has been closed to traffic, and pedestrian malls with fountains, benches, and open-air cafés abound. (German Center for Tourism, Munich)

ECONOMIC RESURGENCE AND SOCIAL CHANGE

New Skyscrapers of La Defense, Paris

French planners have attempted to alleviate the overcrowding of central Paris by creating a vast new center of government offices about five miles from the historical heart of the city. (Courtesy of the French Government Tourist Office)

spite of the foundation of a few new cities like the "new towns" around London, most of the population poured into the biggest cities. West Germany and Italy were fortunate that their delayed unification had left them with a large number of former capitals, like Stuttgart and Milan, where the urban amenities were still attractive to immigrants. But in most of the other countries, the choice of the migrants remained the capital city. In Europe, congestion of the large city was on a scale unknown even in the United States. Each of the European cities, as we have seen, possessed a small medieval heart of narrow, winding streets, in which most of the functions of government, economy, culture, and religion were centered. Around it had grown up in the nineteenth century a circle of residential and industrial suburbs. In the postwar period, spreading in a vast swathe around the cities, huge new housing settlements of unparalleled dullness were built. The employment of the new suburban dwellers in the heart of the old city caused overcrowding on the railroads and buses and especially on the roads leading into the city. Thus European cities came to know the problems that burdened New York City—pollution of air and water, breakdown of municipal transportation systems, increased crime, overcrowded housing, and even occasionally racial, ethnic, or religious confrontations.

THE HUMAN SCALE

Underlying much of this tension was a sense that the human being, the individual, had been lost sight of—by government, by industry, by educational institutions, by technology and science, by urban planners, by social morality, even by individuals themselves. And here we return, at the very end of this long journey through the cities of the past, to a central concept that underlies this whole book—the civilized city. In the great cities of world civilization, the individual was not forgotten. For the maximum number of human beings possible within the city's productive capacity, the truly civilized city enhanced the quality of life for the individual. It gave variety and meaning to work, and it enabled the efforts of individuals to be harmonized to create a more productive economic system. By competition, by interaction, and by reward, it encouraged creativity of mind; and the creativity of some enriched the lives of many others with an understanding of religion, society, science, and beauty. The very urban setting was a source of individual satisfaction because it was on a human scale, in its buildings and in the daily contact of widely varied human beings. These benefits were not enjoyed by all the inhabitants of the cities we have studied, and indeed often only by a minority. But for sufficiently large numbers of people the city provided so great an enhancement of individual life that it was the stimulus behind the most worthwhile—and unfortunately the least worthwhile—features of civilization. The present crisis of the city is one major facet of the crisis of civilization. As Lewis Mumford asks, "Can the needs and desires that have impelled men to live in cities recover, at a still higher level, all that Jerusalem, Athens, or Florence once seemed to promise?" His own answer is to call for a return to the values respected in those great cities:

The recovery of the essential activities and values that first were incorporated in the ancient cities, above all those of Greece, is accordingly a primary condition for the further development of the city in our time. Our elaborate rituals of mechanization cannot take the place of the human dialogue, the drama, the living circle of mates and associates, the society of friends. . . . When cities were first founded, an old Egyptian scribe tells us, the mission of the founder was to "put the gods in their shrines." The task of the coming city is not essentially different, its mission is to put the highest concerns of man at the center of all his activities: to unite the scattered fragments of the human personality, turning artificially dismembered men—bureaucrats, specialists, "experts," depersonalized agents—into complete human beings.[6]

In this way, the cities of the future can emulate the most significant achievement of the civilized cities of the past—to enhance the quality of human life.

[6]Lewis Mumford, *The City in History* (New York: Harcourt, Brace and World, 1961), pp. 569–570, 573.

The Human Scale: Amsterdam
(Consulate General of the Netherlands)

The Human Scale Forgotten: New York City
(Courtesy of Trans World Airlines)

SUGGESTED READING

All study of the postwar period becomes rapidly outdated, especially if the writer attempts to impose sweeping interpretations upon the overwhelming mass of his materials. One can choose therefore between unvarnished narrative, such as Wilfrid F. Knapp, *A History of War and Peace, 1939–1965* (1967), Peter Calvocoressi, *World Politics Since 1945* (1968), and Walter Laqueur's *Europe Since Hitler* (1970); and suggestive hypotheses such as Raymond Aron, *The Century of Total War* (1954), J. Ellul, *The Technological Society* (1965), and C. P. Snow, *The Two Cultures and a Second Look* (1964).

The Cold War can be approached from several directions. The motives of the American government are appraised approvingly by John Lukacs, *A New History of the Cold War* (1966) and Louis J. Halle, *The Cold War as History* (1967). For a balanced, almost impartial European viewpoint, see André Fontaine, *A History of the Cold War* (1969). For biting, "revisionist" reappraisals of American responsibility for the confrontation with Russia, see William A. Williams, *The Tragedy of American Diplomacy* (1962), Gabriel Kolko, *The Politics of War* (1968), and Gar Alperovitz, *Atomic Diplomacy* (1965). The revisionist controversy is analyzed in Robert James Maddox, *The New Left and the Origins of the Cold War* (1974), while John Lewis Gaddis draws on newly opened archives in *The United States and the Origins of the Cold War, 1941–1947* (1972). The best study of American motives in offering Marshall aid is John Gimbel, *The Origins of the Marshall Plan* (1976). Russian goals are analyzed in Adam B. Ulam, *Expansion and Coexistence* (1968) and Marshall D. Shulman, *Stalin's Foreign Policy Reappraised* (1963).

The most reliable account of the communization of Eastern Europe is Hugh Seton-Watson, *The East European Revolution* (1965), which should be supplemented with Zbigniew K. Brzezinski, *The Soviet Bloc: Unity and Conflict* (1961). For individual East European countries, see Richard Hiscock, *Poland: Bridge for the Abyss?* (1963); Ernst C. Helmreich, ed., *Hungary* (1957); Edward Taborsky, *Communism in Czechoslovakia, 1948–1960* (1961); and Stephen Fischer-Galati, ed., *Rumania* (1957). For East European events after the death of Stalin, see Paul E. Zinner, *Revolution in Hungary* (1962); J. F. Brown, *The New Eastern Europe: The Khrushchev Era and After* (1966); David Childs, *East Germany* (1969); and William E. Griffith, ed., *Communism in Europe: Continuity, Change, and the Sino-Soviet Dispute* (1964–1966). On the failure of the Dubček experiment in Czechoslovakia, see R. R. James, ed., *The Czechoslovak Crisis, 1968* (1968) and William Shawcross, *Dubček* (1970). An overview of relations among the Communist powers is given in A. Bromke and T. Rakowska-Harmstone, eds., *The Communist States in Disarray, 1965–1971* (1972).

For an analysis of the attempts of the Communist parties of Italy and Spain and, to a much lesser extent, France to follow policies at variance with those of the Soviet Union, consult Neil McInnes, *Euro-Communism* (1976).

Russia since Stalin can be approached through the career of Khrushchev, in Edward Crankshaw's overly polemical *Khrushchev: A Career* (1964) or Konrad Kellen, *Khrushchev: A Political Portrait* (1961); but more institutional studies can be revealing of the realities of Soviet life, as in Merle Fainsod, *How Russia Is Ruled* (1963); R. Kolkowicz, *The Soviet Military and the Communist Party* (1967); and David Granick, *The Red Executive* (1960). The origins of the dispute with China are surveyed in Klaus Mehnert, *Peking and Moscow* (1963) and Donald S. Zagoria, *The Sino-Soviet Conflict, 1956–1961* (1962). For an understanding of dissidence within the Soviet Union, see the harshly critical work by Andrei Amalrik, *Will the Soviet Union Survive Until 1984?* (1970) and the scholarly survey of Abraham Rothberg, *The Heirs of Stalin: Dissidence and the Soviet Regime, 1953–1970* (1972).

General surveys of postwar western Europe include Jacques Freymond, *Western Europe Since the War* (1964) and Stephen R. Graubard, *A New Europe?* (1968), a suggestive series of essays concentrating on European integration. The economic principles of European integration are boldly simplified in Dennis Swann, *The Economics of the Common Market* (1972), and the political attraction of the process subtly portrayed in Uwe Kitzinger, *The Politics and Economics of European Integration* (1964). F. Roy Willis discusses the troubled relationship of the two major Community partners in *France, Germany and the New Europe, 1945–1967* (1968) and shows the influence of integration on the social and economic structure of Italy in *Italy Chooses Europe* (1971). De Gaulle's attitude toward the Common Market is sharply criticized in Nora Beloff, *The General Says No* (1963) and sympathetically presented in Charles de Gaulle, *Memoirs of Hope: Renewal and Endeavor* (1971). The success of the Common Market in creating a new form of state in Europe is assessed in Carl Friedrich, *Europe an Emergent Nation?* (1969) and in Leon N. Lindberg and Stuart A. Scheingold, *Europe's Would-Be Polity* (1970).

The economic and political realities of the 1970s are assessed with depressing candor by Walter Laqueur, *A Continent Astray: Europe, 1970–1978* (1979), while Laqueur seeks the causes of one of the most disturbing phenomena of contemporary Europe in *Terrorism* (1977).

Among the many excellent studies of individual European nations, one of the most suggestive is John Ardagh, *The New France: A Society in Transition, 1945–1977* (1977). The presidency of Georges Pompidou is the principal theme of R. C. Macridis, *French Politics in Transition* (1975). Political developments in Italy are surveyed in Giuseppe Mammarella, *Italy After Fascism: A Political History, 1945–1963* (1964) and Norman Kogan, *A Political History of Postwar Italy* (1966). Social change in West Germany is analyzed in Ralf Dahrendorf, *Society and Democracy in Germany* (1968). British politics are soundly narrated in Francis Boyd, *British Politics in Transition, 1945–1963* (1964); British politicians are sharply criticized in Max Nicolson, *The System: The Misgovernment of Modern Britain* (1967) and viewed with bemused tolerance in Anthony Sampson, *Anatomy of Britain* (1962) and *The New Anatomy of Britain* (1972). Many useful statistical materials are gathered in A. H. Halsey, ed., *Trends in British Society Since 1900: A Guide to the Changing Social Structure of Britain* (1972). The rise of regional nationalism in Great Britain, with special emphasis on the Celts, is the theme of Tom Nairn, *The Break-up of Britain* (1977).

On the development of Socialism in Scandinavia, see Marquis Childs, *Sweden: The Middle Way* (1961) and William L. Shirer, *The Challenge of Scandinavia: Norway, Sweden, Denmark and Finland in Our Time* (1955), but a more negative judgment is pronounced by Roland Huntford, *The New Totalitarians* (1971). For Norway, see T. K. Derry, *A History of Modern Norway, 1814–1972* (1973). Franklin D. Scott, *Scandinavia* (1975) is the best short survey.

For the authoritarian leaders of Spain and Portugal, there are a number of good biographies. For Franco, see J. W. D. Trythall, *El Caudillo: A Political Biography of Franco* (1970) and Brian Crozier, *Franco* (1967). On his country, see Stanley Payne, *Franco's Spain* (1967) and George Hills, *Spain* (1970). On Portugal, see

Hugh Kay, *Salazar and Modern Portugal* (1970). Background for the transition to democratic government in Spain and Portugal, one of the few encouraging features of the 1970s, is given in M. Harsgor, *Portugal in Revolution* (1976) and Paul Preston, ed., *Spain in Crisis: The Evolution and Decline of the Franco Regime* (1976).

Andrew Shonfield, *Modern Capitalism* (1967) is an extremely optimistic view of Europe's supposed mastery of economic planning; M. M. Postan, *An Economic History of Western Europe, 1945–1965* (1967) explains the postwar economic miracles. On contemporary social change, see Gordon Wright, *Rural Revolution in France* (1964) and Laurence Wylie, *Village in the Vaucluse* (1957); David Granick, *The European Executive* (1962); F. Zweig, *The British Worker* (1952); and Anthony Sampson, *The New Europeans* (1968).

For reliable introductions to the literary and artistic movements of the postwar period, see Herbert Read, *A Concise History of Modern Painting* (1968) and his *Concise History of Modern Sculpture* (1964); Penelope Houston, *The Contemporary Cinema* (1963); Harry T. Moore, *Twentieth-Century German Literature* (1967); C. Mauriac, *The New Literature* (1959); and Maurice Nadeau, *The French Novel Since the War* (1967). A good introductory bibliography to postwar intellectual history will be found in Roland N. Stromberg, *After Everything: Western Intellectual History Since 1945* (1975).

For informed views on the city of the future, see Le Corbusier, *Toward a New Architecture* (1970), a reprinting of his farsighted work of 1924; Richard Eells and Clarence Walton, eds., *Man in the City of the Future* (1968), a collection of predictions by architects and urban theorists; Peter Cook, *Architecture: Action and Place* (1967); and William H. Whyte, *The Last Landscape* (1968). The vision of the coming urbanization of the planet is described in C. A. Doxiadis, *Ecumenopolis: Towards the Universal City* (1961). Finally, for a brave effort to look into the future for Europe itself, see Peter Hall, ed., *Europe 2000* (1977).

INDEX

Common Market, 1472; exploits North Sea oil deposits, 1473. *See also* London
Brooklyn Bridge, 1352-1354; *illus.* 1353
Bruckner, Anton, 969, 1190
Brüning, Heinrich, 1321
Buchan, John, 1175
Buenos Aires, 958, 1152; *illus.* 1152
Buffon, Comte de, 886; *illus.* 887
Bulgaria, 1247, 1254, 1326, 1339, 1457, 1462, 1463
Burma, 1107-1109, 1419
Burton, Richard Francis, 1081

Calcutta, founded, 1093, 1097-1100; districts of, 1100-1102; Tagore family in, 1103-1105; significance of, 1106-1107; riots in, 1411; *illus.* 1090-1091, 1100
Calonne, Charles Alexandre de, 928
Calvinism, and Henry IV, 844; and Louis XIV, 849-850; and Stuart kings, 858; in English civil wars, 859-860
Cambodia, 1422-1423
Camus, Albert, 1452; *illus.* 1452
Canton, 1132, 1140, 1389
Capetown, 1127
Caracas, 956, 957, 958
Carlsbad Decrees (1819), 983
Carlyle, Thomas, 1019, 1058
Carnegie, Andrew, 1173, 1174
Cartwright, Edmund, 1020
Casablanca conference, 1336
Castlereagh, Robert Stewart, 979, 980
Castro, Fidel (President, Cuba), 1443-1444; *illus.* 1444
Catherine II (Tsarina, Russia; the Great), 876, 894, 895
Catherine de Médicis, 827, 843; *illus.* 843
Catholic Church, and Galileo, 885; and French Revolution, 936; in Germany, 1226; and French Third Republic, 1241
Cavour, Camillo, 1214
Cayla, Comtesse du, *illus.* 901
Ceausescu, Nicolae, 1464
Cendrars, 1196
Ceylon (Sri Lanka), 1420
Cézanne, Paul, 1198-1200
Chadwick, Edwin, 1061
Chamberlain, Joseph, 1083

Chamberlain, Neville, 1329; *illus.* 1329
Chardin, Jean Baptiste Simeon, 876; *illus.* 909
Charles I (King, England), 858; *illus.* 859-860
Charles II (King, England), 860-861, 862-863
Charles IX (King, France), 843
Charles Albert (King, Piedmont-Savoy), 1005
Chartists, 1038-1039
Chekhov, Anton, 1180
Chemistry, development of, 883, 887; industrial advances in, 1172
Cheng Ho, 760
Chesterfield, Lord, 876, 910-911
Chiang Ch'ing, 1398, 1400; *illus.* 1400
Chiang Kai-shek (President, China), 1389-1390, 1393; *illus.* 1394
Chicago, 1169, 1346
Ch'ien-lung (Emperor, China), 764, 765
China, Ming, 753-762; Manchu, 762-765; Canton system in, 1132-1133; treaty system in, 1133-1134; Manchu decline, 1134; Taiping rebellion, 1135-1136; Shanghai, 1137-1139; spheres of influence in, 1139-1140; failure of reform, 1140-1142; Boxer uprising, 1142-1143; 1911 revolution, 1143-1144, 1386; warlords, 1386-1387; Kuomintang rise, 1388-1390; Nationalist rule, 1390-1391; Japanese war, 1391-1393; civil war, 1393-1395; Communist rule, 1395-1401
Chotek, Sophie, *illus.* 1248
Chou En-lai, 1390, 1398-1399
Chu Hsi, 754, 760
Chukovskaya, Lydia, 1297
Churchill, Winston, 1246, 1331, 1334, 1335, 1340; *illus.* 1340
Cid, Le (Corneille), 852
Cities, Ottoman, 737-739; Mogul, 748-753; Japanese, 771-774, 1408; Dutch, 788-789; baroque, 823-827; eighteenth-century French, 897-898, 906-911; and American Revolution, 924-926; Italian, and French Revolution, 949-951, 954; in Austrian Empire, 1002-1003; and Industrial Revolution, 1013-1014, 1024-1030; "world," 1051-1054; in late nineteenth century, 1157-1164, 1212-1214; improved amenities of, 1164-1167; techno-

logical change and, 1168-1171; in German Empire, 1220-1225; in nineteenth-century Russia, 1265-1268; Soviet, 1289-1293; American, 1349-1356; contemporary problems of, 1373-1377; in late twentieth century, 1479-1480. *See also* urban planning
Clark, Adam, 1169
Clemenceau, Georges, 1304-1305; *illus.* 1304
Clive, Robert, 1093
Cobbett, William, 1038
Code Napoléon, 946, 954-955
Colbert, Jean Baptiste, 827, 850, 851, 853, 886
Communist Information Bureau (Cominform), 1458
Communist Manifesto, The (Marx), 1027, 1043, 1045, 1177
Comte, Auguste, 1179
Condillac, Etienne, 899
Condorcet, Marquis de, 927, 937
Congo Free State, 1129-1130
Constantinople, 732, 736-737, 738-739
Constitution, Ottoman, 736-737; Dutch, 807-809; seventeenth-century French, 847-849; seventeenth-century English, 854-860; of U.S.A., 926; of French Revolution, 934-937, 942, 946; French, during Restoration, 984; of Austrian Empire, 987-989, 1243-1245; during 1848 revolutions, 1009-1010; of Second Reich, 1225, 1227; French, in Third Republic, 1240-1241; Japanese, 1402-1403, 1406-1407; Indian, 1412
Continental Congress, 912, 926
Continental System, 960, 961
Cook, James, 1114, 1117
Copernicus, Nicolaus, 884-885
Corneille, Pierre, 852
Corn Laws, British, 1055, 1056, 1071
Courbet, Gustave, 1196
Couthon, Georges, 939
Coysevox, Antoine, *illus.* 848
Crèvecoeur, Hector St. John de, 927, 928
Crimean War, 1216
Crompton, Samuel, 1019
Cromwell, Oliver, 860; *illus.* 860
Crozat, Antoine, 874
Cruikshank, George, *illus.* 1053, 1061
Crystal Palace, London, 1073-1074,

movement in, 1000-1002; of fin de siècle Vienna, 1190-1192; atonal, 1191; Wagner and Strauss, 1231-1232; Stravinsky, 1314; under Hitler, 1323. *See also* individual composers

Mussolini, Benito, 1316-1318, 1322, 1324, 1327, 1329; and Spanish Civil War, 1328; invades Greece, 1355; deposition of, 1336; *illus.* 1316

Mutsuhito (Emperor, Japan; "Meiji"), 1147; *illus.* 1147

Nagasaki, 769-770, 1145, 1344
Nagy, Imre, 1460-1461
Nanking, 754, 1136, 1390-1391
Nantes, Edict of, 844, 852
Napier, John, 884
Naples, 916, 1166
Napoleon I (Emperor, France), 929, 944, 945, 1165; Consulate of, 946; and Germany, 951-952; Italian rule of, 954; nationalist revolt against, 957-960; exile of, 962; defeat of, 1054; *illus.* 947, 952
Napoleon III (Emperor, France), 1042; and 1848 revolution, 1006, 1009; as emperor, 1212-1214; and Italian unification, 1214; and German unification, 1216-1219; *illus.* 1212
Naseby, Battle of (1645), 860
Nash, John, 1058; *illus.* 1059
Nasser, Gamal Abdel (President, Egypt), 1437-1438; *illus.* 1437
Nationalism, 912; and French Revolution, 948; Prussian, 953-954; Italian, 954-955; in Austrian Empire, 985-988; in music, 1001-1002
Naturalist school, of literature, 1180
Nazism, rise of, 1318-1322; in power, 1322-1324; Nuremberg rally, *illus.* 1323; internal policy, 1324-1325; foreign policy, 1325-1331. *See also* Hitler, Adolph
Necker, Jacques, 932
Nehru, Jawaharlal, 1410-1413; *illus.* 1413
Nelson, Admiral Horatio, 946, 960
Netherlands, under Charles V, 788-789; revolt of, 789-793; commerce of, 793-802; decline of, 816-820; annexes Indonesia, 1111-1112; settles South Africa, 1127;

and Second World War, 1332; decolonization by, 1421
Neumann, Balthasar, 881; *illus.* 828
New Economic Policy, in Russia, 1281, 1282-1284
Newman, John Henry (Cardinal), 1058, 1060, 1070
New Orleans, La., 1356
Newton, Isaac, 882, 884, 885-886, 1184, 1189; *illus.* 885
New York City, character of, 1349-1355; economic preeminence of, 1356-1359; changing economic function of, 1359-1360; skyscrapers in, 1361-1362, 1365-1369; tenements of, 1363-1364; immigrant population of, 1365; intellectual life of, 1369-1372; European migrants in, 1373-1374; blacks in, 1374; Puerto Ricans in, 1374; *illus.* 1348-1349, 1353, 1357, 1362, 1366, 1368; *map* 1351
New Zealand, 1113, 1115-1116
Nicholas I (Tsar, Russia), 1176
Nicholas II (Tsar, Russia), 1243; and 1905 Revolution, 1269; in captivity, *illus.* 1271; *illus.* 1270
Nicolson, Harold, 1305
Nigeria, 1427-1428
Night Watch, The (Rembrandt), 793, 813-814; *illus.* 814
Nixon, Richard (President, U.S.A.), 1399, 1422
Nkrumah, Kwame (President, Ghana), 1427; *illus.* 1427
Nobel, Alfred, 1173
Nobunaga (Oda), 765-766, 769, 770
North Atlantic Treaty Organization (NATO), 1455, 1459
Norton, Lady Caroline, 1039
Noske, Gustav, 1257
Novel, early development of, 1065; of Dickens, 1065-1067; Realist school of, 1179; Naturalist school of, 1179-1180; of Proust, 1181-1182; of Socialist Realism, 1294; twentieth-century, 1370-1371, 1453-1454
Nur Jahan (Mogul Empress), 746
Nyerere, Julius (President, Tanzania), 1428

O'Connor, John, *illus.* 1065
Oldenburg, Claes, 1381, 1454
O'Neill, Eugene, 1372, 1380

Oppenord, 873
Origin of Species, On the (Darwin), 1186, 1187, 1188
Orwell, George, 1298
Osaka, 767, 772
Ottoman Empire, 732-738. *See also* Turkey
Owen, Robert, 1040-1041, 1123
Oxford Movement, 1067-1070
Oyo, 770, 1123

Pacific Ocean, exploration, 1114; Australia, 1113-1115; New Zealand, 1115-1116; Tahiti, 1116-1117; Hawaii, 1117-1119; Philippines, 1119-1122; and Second World War, 1344
Paganini, Niccolò, 1001
Paine, Thomas, 1039
Painting, Ming, 760; *illus.* 761; Japanese, 774-775; Dutch, 809-816; *illus.* 785, 787, 792, 795, 796-797, 798, 805, 808, 811, 812, 813, 814, 816, 817; baroque, 835-836, 853; *illus.* 846, 847; rococo, 877-879; *illus.* 868, 872, 878, 890; Biedermeier, 989, 991; *illus.* 990, 991; Pre-Raphaelite, 1060; and Freudian psychology, 1184; in late-nineteenth-century Paris, 1194-1201; Impressionism and post-Impressionism, 1195, 1196-1199; *illus.* 1197; Fauvism, 1200; Cubism, 1200-1203, 1313; *illus.* 1201, 1313; Expressionism, 1234; *illus.* 1233; c. 1920, 1313, 1371, 1372; since 1945, 1380-1381; *illus.* 1380, 1381
Pakistan, 1411, 1415-1416
Pankhurst, Emmeline, 1076-1077
Papen, Franz von, 1321-1322
Paradise Lost (Milton), 863
Paris, baroque period, 823-824; *plan* 826; housing for nobility in, 829; and Henry IV's renovation of, 844-845; eighteenth-century, 870; *plan* 871; relationship to Versailles, 872-873; as cultural patron, 873-875; rococo style in, 875, 877-879; salons of, 875-877; *illus.* 876; revolution in, 916, 929; and taking of the Bastille, 932-933; *illus.* 933; Jacobins of, 937-938; reign of terror in, 942-944; and Napoleon, 945; as center of radicalism, 1039;

1 2 3 4 5 6 7 8 9 0